ASPECTS OF WORLD CIVILIZATION

Problems and Sources in History

Volume II

Edited by

PERRY M. ROGERS

Prentice Hall

Upper Saddle River, New Jersey 07458

Library of Congress Cataloging-in-Publication Data

Aspects of World civilization: problems and sources in history /
    edited by Perry M. Rogers.
        p.   cm.
    ISBN 0–13–080833–4
    1. World History—Sources. 2. Religions—History—Sources.
    3. History—Philosophy   I. Rogers, Perry McAdow.
    D20 .A87 2003
    909—dc21   202007628

Editorial director: Charlyce Jones-Owen
Senior acquisition editor: Charles Cavaliere
Associate editor: Emsal Hasan
Editorial assistant: Adrienne Paul
Senior managing editor: Jan Stephan
Production liaison: Fran Russello
Editorial/production supervision: Russell Jones (Pine
    Tree Composition)
Prepress and manufacturing buyer: Sherry Lewis
Cover director: Jayne Conte
Cover Image Specialist: Karen Sanatar

Cover designer: Kiwi Design
Cover art: Kitagawa Utamaro, Japanese, 1753–1806,
    Woodblock print; ink and color on paper, 37.2 × 26
    cm (14⅝ × 10¼"). Gift of Captain John C. Phillips.
    Courtesy, Museum of Fine Arts, Boston. Reproduced
    with permission © about 1797. All Rights Reserved.
Director, Image Resource Center: Melinda Lee Reo
Manager, rights & permissions: Zina Arabia
Interior image specialist: Beth Boyd
Photo researcher: Teri Stratford
Marketing manager: Sheryl Adams

For Ann
Elisa, Kit, and Tyler

This book was set in 10/11½ Baskerville by Pine Tree Composition, Inc.,
and was printed and bound by R.R. Donnelley & Sons, Inc.
The cover was printed by Phoenix Color Corp.

 © 2003 by Pearson Education, Inc.
Upper Saddle River, New Jersey 07458

Printed in the United States of America

10 9 8 7 6 5 4 3 2 1

ISBN 0-13-080833-4

Pearson Education Ltd., *London*
Pearson Education Australia Pty, Limited, *Sydney*
Pearson Education Singapore, Pte. Ltd.
Pearson Education North Asia Ltd. *Hong Kong*
Pearson Education Canada, Ltd., *Toronto*
Pearson Educación de Mexico, S.A. de C.V.
Pearson Education—Japan, *Tokyo*
Pearson Education Malaysia, Pte. Ltd.
Pearson Education, *Upper Saddle River, New Jersey*

Brief Contents

HISTORICAL INTERSECTIONS

HISTORICAL INTERSECTIONS

Contents

The Historical Intersection   BEIJING: 1966   *398*

China's Second Revolution (1976–2000)   403

Geographical Contents

Volume II

Africa and the Middle East

Asia

The Development of Fascism

The World Wars

The Americas

North American Civilizations

Latin American Civilizations

Preface

The Roman orator Cicero once remarked that "History is the witness of the times, the torch of truth, the life of memory, the teacher of life, the messenger of antiquity." In spite of these noble words, historians have often labored under the burden of justifying the value of studying events that are over and done. Humankind is practical, more concerned with its present and future than with its past. And yet the study of history provides us with unique opportunities for human self-knowledge. It teaches us what we have done and therefore helps define what we are. On a less abstract level, the study of history enables us to judge present circumstance by drawing on the laboratory of the past. Those who have lived and died, through their recorded attitudes, actions and ideas, have left a legacy of experience.

One of the best ways to travel through time and space and perceive the very "humanness" that lies at the root of history is through the study of primary sources. These are the documents, coins, letters, inscriptions and monuments of past ages. The task of historians is to evaluate this evidence with a critical eye and then construct a narrative that is consistent with the "facts" as they have established them. Such interpretations are inherently subjective and are therefore open to dispute. History is thus filled with controversy as historians argue their way toward the "truth." The only way to work toward an understanding of the past is through personal examination of the primary sources.

Yet, for the beginning student, this poses some difficulties. Such inquiry casts the student adrift from the security of accepting the "truth" as revealed in a textbook. In fact, history is too often presented in a deceptively objective manner; one learns "facts and dates" in an effort to obtain the "right answers" for multiple-choice tests. But the student who has wrestled with primary sources and has experienced voices from the past on a more intimate level accepts the responsibility of evaluation and judgment. He or she understands that history does not easily lend itself to "right answers," but demands reflection on the problems that have confronted past societies and are at play even in our contemporary world. Cicero was right in viewing history as the "life of memory." But human memory is fragile and the records of the past can be destroyed or distorted. Without the past, people have nothing with which to judge what they are told in the present. Truth then becomes the preserve of the ruler or government, no longer relative, but absolute. The study of history, and primary sources in particular, goes far in making people aware of the continuity of humankind and the progress of civilization.

Aspects of World Civilization offers the student an opportunity to evaluate the primary sources of the past and to do so in a structured and organized format. The documents provided are diverse in nature and include state papers, secret dispatches, letters, diary accounts, poems, newspaper articles, papal encyclicals, and propaganda flyers. Occasionally, the assessments of modern historians are included to lend perspective. All give testimony to human endeavor in world societies. Yet, this two-volume book has been conceived as more than a simple compilation of primary sources. The subtitle of the work, *Problems and Sources in History,* gives true indication of the nature of its premise. It is meant to provide the student with thoughtful and engaging material, that is focused around individual units that encompass time periods, specific events, and historical questions. Students learn from the past most effectively when posed with problems that have meaning for their own lives. In evaluating the material from *Aspects of World Civilization,* the student will discover that issues are not nearly as simple as they may appear at first glance. Historical sources often contradict each other and truth then depends on logic and one's own experience and outlook on life. Throughout these volumes, the student is confronted with basic questions regarding historical development, human nature, moral action, and practical necessity. The text is therefore broad in its scope and incorporates a wide variety of political, social, economic, religious, intellectual, and scientific issues. It is internally organized around *eight major themes* that provide direction and cohesion to the text while allowing for originality of thought in both written and oral analysis:

1. *Imperialism.* How has imperialism been justified throughout world history and what are the moral implications of gaining and maintaining empire? Is defensive imperialism a practical foreign policy option? This theme is often juxtaposed with subtopics of nationalism, war, altruism, and human nature.

2. *Church/State Relationships.* Is there a natural competition between these two controlling units in society? Which is more influential, which legacy more enduring? How has religion been used as a means of securing political power or of instituting social change?

3. *Beliefs and Spirituality.* The diverse religious heritage of world civilization forms the basis of this theme. In particular, the text covers the primary tenets and historical development of Judaism, Christianity, Islam, Hinduism, and Buddhism. It also focuses on the impact of ideas and philosophical movements on society. How have religious values and moral attitudes affected the course of world history? To what extent have spiritual reform movements resulted in a change of political or social policy? Are ideas more powerful than any army? Why have so many people died fighting for religions that abhor violence? Does every society need a spiritual foundation?

4. *Systems of Government.* This theme seeks to introduce the student to the various systems of rule that have shaped world civilization: classical democracy, representative democracy (republican government), oligarchy, constitutional monarchy, divine-right monarchy, theocracy, and dictatorship (especially fascism and totalitarian rule). What are the advantages and drawbacks to each? This rubric also includes the concepts of balance of power and containment, principles of succession, geopolitics, and social and economic theories such as capitalism, communism, and socialism.

5. *Revolution.* This theme seeks to define and examine the varieties of revolution: political, intellectual, economic, and social. What were the underlying and precipitating causes of political revolution? How essential is the intellectual foundation? Are social demands and spontaneity more important elements in radical action?

6. *Propaganda.* What is the role of propaganda in history? Many sections examine the use and abuse of information, often in connection with absolute government, revolution, imperialism, or genocide. How are art and architecture, as well as written material, used in the "creation of belief"? This theme emphasizes the relativity of truth and stresses the responsibility of the individual in assessing the validity of evidence.

7. *Women in History.* The text intends to help remedy the widespread omission of women from history and to develop an appreciation of their contributions to the intellectual and political framework of world civilization. At issue is how women have been viewed—or rendered invisible—throughout history and how individually and collectively their presence is inextricably linked with the development and progress of civilization. This inclusive approach stresses the importance of achieving a perspective that lends value and practical application to history.

8. *Historical Change and Transition.* What are the main determinants of change in history? How important is the individual in effecting change, or is society regulated by unseen social and economic forces? What role does chance play? What are the components of civilization and how do we assess progress or decline? Are civilizations biological in nature? Is a crisis/response theory of change valid? This theme works toward providing the student with a philosophy of history and against the tendency to divide history into strict periods. It stresses the close connection between the past and the present.

The *overriding theme* that provides a foundation and overall unity to the text is that of *cultural interaction.* How have the diverse cultures of the world been linked by political systems, economic contact, social and religious movements, philosophy, art, literature, and such variables as disease and war? In what ways have world civilizations over the centuries struggled with similar challenges and contributed to the progress or destruction of humanity? How has the world community become increasingly dependent on cooperation and international understanding in achieving domestic stability, security, and prosperity?

STRUCTURE OF THE BOOK

Each chapter begins with a *timeline chronology* so that students may visualize the historical parameters of the chapter. This is generally followed by a *series of quotations* from various historians, diplomats, philosophers, literary figures, or religious spokespersons who offer insight on the subject matter of the chapter. These quotations may well be used in conjunction with the study questions at the end of the unit. After the quotations, *chapter themes* are listed and framed by several questions that direct the reader to broader issues and comparative perspectives with ideas and events in other chapters. This feature acknowledges the changing perspectives of different eras while linking historical problems that emphasize the continuity of history. A *general introduction* then provides a brief historical background and focuses the themes or questions to be discussed in the chapter.

Following this general introduction, the primary sources are presented with extensive direction for the student. A *headnote* explains in more detail the historical or biographical background for each primary source and focuses attention on themes or interrelationships with other sources. Each chapter concludes with a *chronology* designed to orient the student to the broader context of history, and a series of *study questions* that can form the basis of oral discussion or written analysis. The questions do not seek mere regurgitation of information, but demand a more thoughtful response based on reflective analysis of the primary sources.

This analysis is even more specifically focused by the inclusion of *TimeLink* chapters throughout the sectional divisions. These chapters function as assessments of particular eras or historical problems that are connected intimately to the subject matter in the section and provide a direct comparison between societies. *TimeLink* chapters frame the readings with initial questions to consider and followup questions that provide links to visual and written sources in previous chapters. Each volume also contains eight to ten comparative sources in a feature called *The Historical Intersection*. These readings provide the student with an immediate opportunity to compare two documents, which, although from different eras and societies, are linked through one of the historical themes mentioned above. This interactive feature will help students analyze the continuity of the past and appreciate the relevancy of historical inquiry.

USE OF THE BOOK

Aspects of World Civilization offers the instructor a wide variety of didactic applications. The chapters fit into a more or less standard lecture format and are ordered chronologically. An entire chapter may be assigned for oral discussion, or sections from each chapter may satisfy particular interests or requirements. Some of the chapters provide extensive treatment of a broad historical topic ("Medieval Civilization in the West: The Sword of Faith"; "A Wealth of Riches, A Sea of Sorrows: The Linking of Transatlantic Economies"). In order to make them manageable and effective, some have been grouped them into topical sections (with correspondingly labeled study questions) that can be utilized separately, if so desired.

The chapters may also be assigned for written analysis. One of the most important concerns of both instructor and student in an introductory class is the written assignment. *Aspects of World Civilization* has been designed to provide self-contained topics that are problem-oriented, promote reflection and analysis, and encourage responsible citation of particular primary sources. The study questions for each chapter should generally produce an eight- to ten-page paper.

ACKNOWLEDGMENTS

This book has evolved over the years through contact with many colleagues and friends, who offered their insight and analysis of history, poetry, literature, and art. I would like to recognize in particular the influence of Susan Altan, Marsha Ryan, Jack Guy, Frank O'Grady, Thomas Tappan, Dan Hall, Mary Ann Leonard, and Diane Abel, whose frequent conversations stimulated my interest and whose perception often opened new avenues of thought. Linda Swarlis paved the way by investing me with new research skills and by connecting me with obscure sources at crucial times. Thanks to my colleagues who took the time to review both volumes: Thomas Saylor and Paul Hillmer, Concordia University, St. Paul; Robert Bucholz, Loyola University, Chicago; and Elaine Spencer and Nancy M. Wingfield, Northern Illinois University. Thanks also to the students of Columbus School for Girls, who continue to "test" the chapters in this book with their typical diligence and hard work; the final product has benefitted greatly from their suggestions and ideas. Finally, I owe the largest debt to my wife, Ann, whose strength and gentle confirmation of what is most valuable in life offers the greatest perspective of all, and to my children, who always help me laugh.

Perry M. Rogers
Westerville, Ohio

Part I

FOUNDATIONS OF THE MODERN WORLD (1600–1850)

1

"A Wealth of Riches, A Sea of Sorrows": The Linking of Transatlantic Economies

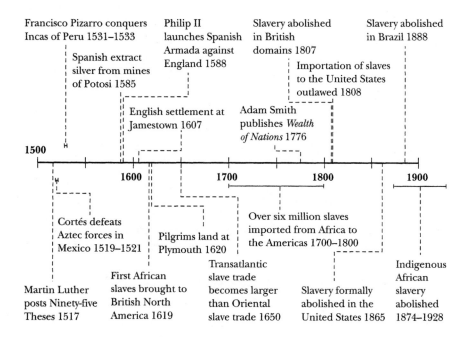

Francisco Pizarro conquers
Incas of Peru 1531–1533

Spanish extract
silver from mines
of Potosi 1585

Philip II
launches Spanish
Armada against
England 1588

Slavery abolished
in British
domains 1807

Slavery abolished
in Brazil 1888

Importation of slaves
to the United States
outlawed 1808

English settlement at
Jamestown 1607

Adam Smith
publishes *Wealth
of Nations* 1776

1500

1600   **1700**   **1800**   **1900**

Cortés defeats
Aztec forces in
Mexico 1519–1521

Pilgrims land at
Plymouth 1620

Over six million slaves
imported from Africa to
the Americas 1700–1800

Indigenous
African
slavery
abolished
1874–1928

Transatlantic
slave trade
becomes larger
than Oriental
slave trade 1650

Martin Luther
posts Ninety-five
Theses 1517

First African
slaves brought to
British North
America 1619

Slavery formally
abolished in the
United States 1865

The destiny of nations depends on how they nourish themselves.

—*Jean Anthelme Brillat-Savarin*

It should be noted that when he seizes a state, the new ruler ought to determine the injuries that he will need to inflict. He should then inflict them all at once, and not have to renew them every day.

—*Niccolò Machiavelli*

3

> The use of force is but temporary. It may subdue for a moment; but it does not remove the necessity of subduing again—and a nation is not governed, which is perpetually to be conquered.
>
> —*Edmund Burke*

CHAPTER THEMES

- *Systems of Government:* How did political and economic rivalry among European powers provide motives for exploration and conquest? How did the centralization of absolute monarchies and mercantile economies contribute to the maintenance of empire and the development of a restrictive colonial policy?

- *Imperialism:* Why did Europeans conquer and settle lands in the new worlds of America, Africa, and Asia? Why were they particularly successful in suppressing natives? How important is technology as a factor in progress and destruction? Is imperialism a process that inherently carries the seeds of genocide?

- *Propaganda:* How did Europeans justify their exploitation of the Americas? In order to justify conquest or genocide, must the conquered be methodically dehumanized? How has this process been repeated throughout history?

- *Church/State Relationships:* What role did the Catholic Church and Protestant religious exiles play in the settlement of the Americas? Are missionary motives simply another justification for conquest? Or did religious representatives work for accommodation and coexistence? Were they a positive force in the settlement of the Americas?

- *Historical Change and Transition:* What impact did the European exploration and conquest of the Americas have on the cultures of both regions? What are some of the "seeds of change" that ultimately linked these continents? Is the interaction between cultures both a beneficial and dangerous process? In our modern world, can a culture be truly homogeneous? What are the challenges of cultural integration and diversity?

- *The Big Picture:* Must exploration always result in exploitation? How have the European and American worlds been changed through "first contact" over five hundred years ago?

"In 1492, Columbus sailed the ocean blue." Often our childhood education is linked to simple, expressive phrases like this that encapsulate important events or ideas adults think are worth remembering. This rhyme does little beyond connecting an event with a date, but the ramifications of Columbus' voyages are vast indeed, for they changed the course of world history. The cultures of Europe and America each existed in old worlds with established societies, religions, and political organizations. Columbus' first contact with Native Americans in the Bahamas began a process of interaction and development that transformed each hemisphere and created a New World where cultures were blended, products exchanged, and societies redefined. This is a story of the transfer of plants and animals that affected the nutrition and movement of peoples, and it is a tragic saga of the decimation of whole Indian populations, the enslavement of African peoples, and the destruction of natural ecosystems. It is difficult to simplify in a phrase what was a complex human drama.

Since the Renaissance, European contact with the world has gone through distinct phases. The first phase, which ended by the seventeenth century, was one of exploration, conquest, and consolidation of territory in recently discovered lands. The second phase, during the seventeenth and eighteenth centuries, was characterized by colonial trade rivalry between England, France, Spain, and the Netherlands. The third phase of European contact with the world occurred in the nineteenth century and saw the establishment of European empires in Africa, India, and Asia. These empires disintegrated in the final stage after 1945 as Britain, France, and Germany, reduced by the destruction of World War II, retreated from control of their empires and acknowledged the sovereign legitimacy of indigenous governments. This chapter will focus on the first two phases.

There is perhaps no more important or tragic example of the debilitative effects of imperialism than the European domination of the Americas. We often regard the concept of exploration as a positive venture: Europeans took a courageous and imaginative step when Columbus, following the thirteenth century accounts of Marco Polo, set out to find Chipangu, an outer island of Japan. But exploration was only a means to an end as Portuguese and Spanish explorers were motivated by the lure of wealth, the spice trade in India, the gold and silver in the Americas, and the slaves of Africa. After Hernando Cortés and Francisco Pizarro conquered respectively the Aztecs in 1519 and the Incas in 1531, the door lay open for the European domination of a continent. Spanish conquistadores, French trappers, Dutch traders, and English religious refugees all sought to establish themselves on territory that was already occupied by indigenous peoples. Europeans ravaged their land, mocked their gods, banished their languages, decimated their populations through disease, and subjugated their children to a subservient and dependent status that is still in evidence today.

This dominance was certainly disproportionate to the geographic size or population of Europe. Although European apologists would concoct theories that explained and justified the domination of "inferior races," their conquest was not the result of racial superiority, but of technological supremacy. Gunpowder and naval power proved to be the decisive forces in the eradication of Native American cultures.

The contact between Europeans and American natives also changed the nature of both cultures. Europeans introduced horses, cows, pigs, wheat, barley, and sugar cane to the Americas. Horses alone proved instrumental in extending the horizons and altering the way of life for Indian tribes on the North American plains. Sugar cane has often been seen as the most detrimental contribution of the European world, since the human craving for sweetness resulted in the defoliation of the tropical environment for the establishment of cane plantations and the methodical integration of slavery into the economies and societies of Africa and the Americas.

American crops such as maize took root in Africa and contributed to better nutrition and higher population that perhaps promoted the slave trade itself. Likewise, the American potato was introduced to Europe and became the dominant food staple in Ireland. When the potato blight hit that country in 1854, the result was starvation and a new migration of Irish to America.

This interactive relationship might best be noted in the specter of disease. Although there is continuing controversy about what diseases were introduced by outsiders into the Americas, it is generally held that smallpox, cholera, measles, diphtheria, typhoid fever, some strains of influenza, and the plague came from Europe and Africa. The affect of these diseases on American populations without previous exposure or immunity was devastating. Indian populations may have declined by 75 percent.

The influx of spices into Europe from the Malabar coasts of India and the precious metals delivered by the Spanish treasure fleets from the Americas proved to be a mixed blessing for the economy of Europe and highlights the importance of interdisciplinary study. The increase in gold and silver bullion certainly paid for innovations in printing, shipping, mining, textile manufacturing, and weapons development. The influx of bullion alone allowed Spain to launch the Spanish Armada against England in 1588, France to develop its silk industry, and all of Europe to gorge on the bloody seventeenth century wars of religion. But it also contributed to serious inflation that saw prices doubling in Spain by 1600, and the cost of food and clothing increasing by 100 percent in Germany by 1540.

By the eighteenth century, European trade rivalries for the products and labor of the Americas intensified. European empires existed to enrich the coffers of government and the pockets of the commercial elite. The Americas also provided new opportunities for Europe's disaffected and dispossessed and acted as a "pressure valve" for the mother countries, draining excess population from competitive domestic economies.

The competition between the French and British in Canada, on the North Atlantic seaboard, and along the Saint Lawrence and Mississippi rivers was particularly vicious as Indians and colonists alike fought in bitter rivalry. Although its supremacy on the west coast of North America and in much of South America was secure during the eighteenth century, Spain competed with both France and England for the lucrative sugar trade in the Carribean. The lesson was clear: National prosperity was directly linked to the protection of foreign trade and the efficient management of overseas empire.

The regulation of these empires in the seventeenth and eighteenth centuries was managed through an informal economic system called *mercantilism*. Mercantilist businessmen believed that the world contained a very limited amount of natural resources and that each country was in dire competition with the other. A country could only call itself wealthy if it could amass more bullion, grow more crops, and manufacture more goods than any other. The economic well-being of a country was therefore directly tied to the vitality of its colonies and the ability of each nation to control its colonial markets. There were laws that regulated just what goods colonists could produce and in what quantity. Colonists had to purchase certain raw materials from Europe and all colonial goods had to be transported by ships from the mother country. National monopoly was the prime directive.

But mercantilism was an inherently awkward economic system. Ultimately, the home and colonial markets did not mesh and the colonial governments, especially in America, chafed at the restrictions and grew restive. And there were new economic theories on the horizon. In 1776, Adam Smith in his treatise, *The Wealth of Nations*, envisioned a world of limitless resources, where the only restrictions were tied to ability and ambition—capitalism was born.

This chapter will explore the political, social, economic, and cultural interactions between different worlds in conflict during the sixteenth through eighteenth centuries. This is not a simple story to be summed up in a cute phrase. History is a reflection of the complexity of human environments and as such is necessarily interactive. This is a bloody tale of the European encounter with the new worlds of Africa, Asia, and America. It is a story of greed, destruction, and ultimately of cultural awareness that affords perspective and presents new possibilities for the progress of world civilization.

ABSOLUTE POWER: THE CENTRALIZED STATE AND THE ADVANTAGES OF EMPIRE

"I Am the State": The Theory and Practice of Absolute Rule

"The Mortal God": Leviathan (1651)

THOMAS HOBBES

Thomas Hobbes was one of the great political philosophers of the seventeenth century. His major work, entitled Leviathan, *was published in 1651 and reflects the insecurity and fear of the English Revolution that had resulted in civil war (1642–1646) and had just seen the decapitation of a sovereign monarch in 1649. Hobbes himself, because of his aristocratic associations, had been forced to flee England. Not surprisingly,* Leviathan *is a treatise that advocates political absolutism. Its theme is power, and it justifies absolute rule as necessary in order to subdue man's violent nature and promote a reasonable existence. For Hobbes, the authority of the absolute monarch did not lie in hereditary right or in divine sanction, but only in his ability to achieve power and maintain it. In this sense, Hobbes borrowed much from the Renaissance political philosopher Niccolò Machiavelli. But Hobbes went much further by providing an integrated social and political philosophy of government.*

Nature has made men so equal, in the faculties of the body and mind; as that though there be found one man sometimes manifestly stronger in body, or of quicker mind than another; yet when all is reckoned together, the differences between man and man, is not so considerable.... For as to the strength of body, the weakest has strength enough to kill the strongest, either by secret machination, or by confederacy with others, that are in the same danger with himself. And as to the faculties of the mind.... I find yet a greater equality among men, than that of strength.... Such is the nature of men, that howsoever they may acknowledge many others to be more witty, or more eloquent, or more learned; yet they will hardly believe there are many so wise as themselves; for

they see their own wit at hand, and other men's at a distance....

From this equality of ability, arises equality of hope in the attaining of our ends. And therefore if any two men desire the same thing, which nevertheless they cannot both enjoy, they become enemies; and in the way to their end, which is principally their own conservation ... endeavour to destroy, or subdue one another. And from hence it comes to pass, that ... an invader has no more to fear than another man's single power; if one plants, sows, builds, and possesses a convenient seat, others may probably be expected to come prepared with forces united, to dispossess, and deprive him, not only of the fruit of his labour, but also of his life, or liberty. And the invader again is in the like danger of

"The Mortal God: Leviathan" is from W. Molesworth, ed., *The English Works of Thomas Hobbes*, vol. 3 (London: John Bohn, 1839), from chapters 13 and 17, pp. 110–113, 153, 157–158. Text modernized by the editor.

another.... [Thus], men have no pleasure, but on the contrary a great deal of grief, in keeping company, where there is no power able to over-awe them all....

So that in the nature of man, we find three principal causes of quarrel. First, competition; secondly, insecurity; thirdly, glory.

The first, makes men invade for gain; the second, for safety; and the third, for reputation. The first use violence, to make themselves master of other men's persons, wives, children, and cattle; the second, to defend them; the third, for trifles, as a word, a smile, a different opinion, and any other sign of undervalue, either direct in their persons, or by reflection in their kindred, their friends, their nation, their profession, or their name.

[Therefore, it is clear] that during the time men live without a common power to keep them all in awe, they are in that condition which is called war; and such a war is of every man, against every man.... In such condition, there is no place for industry; because the fruit thereof is uncertain: and consequently no culture of the earth; no navigation, nor use of the commodities that may be imported by sea; no commodious building; no instruments of moving, and removing, such things as require much force; no knowledge of the face of the earth; no account of time; no arts; no letters; no society; and which is worst of all, continual fear, and danger of violent death; and the life of man, solitary, poor, nasty, brutish, and short....

The final cause, end, or design of men, who naturally love liberty, and dominion over others, [is] the introduction of that restraint upon themselves, [by] which we see them live in commonwealths.... The only way to erect such a common power, as may be able to defend them from the invasion of foreigners, and the injuries of one another, and thereby to secure them in such sort, as that by their own industry, and by the fruits of the earth, they may nourish themselves and live contentedly; is, to confer all their

This illustration from the title page to *Leviathan* captures the essence of Thomas Hobbes's philosophy: The ruler is embodied by individuals who consent to his dominance for the general welfare. All look to him and in the process lose their individual authority, but gain stability and security. The Latin quotation reads, "Upon the earth, there is not his like." *(Bettmann)*

power and strength upon one man, or upon one assembly of men, that may reduce all their wills, by plurality of voices, unto one will. ... [All men shall] submit their wills ... to his will, and their judgments, to his judgment. This is more than consent, or concord; it is a real unity of them all, in one and the same person, made by covenant of every man with every man, in such manner, as if every man should say to every man, I authorize and give up my right of governing myself, to this man, or to this assembly of men, on this condition, that you give up your right to him, and authorize all his actions in like manner. This done, the multitude so united in one person, is called a COMMON-WEALTH.... This is the generation of that great LEVIATHAN, or rather, to speak more reverently, of that mortal god, to which we own

under the immortal God, our peace and defence. For by this authority, given him by every particular man in the commonwealth, he hath the use of so much power and strength conferred on him, that by terror thereof, he is enabled to perform the wills of them all, to peace at home, and mutual aid against their enemies abroad. And in him consists the essence of the commonwealth; which, to define it, is one person of whose acts a great multitude, by mutual covenants one with another, have made themselves every one the author, to the end he may use the strength and means of them all, as he shall think expedient, for their peace and common defence.

And ... this person, is called SOVEREIGN, and said to have sovereign power; and every one besides, his SUBJECT.

The Ideal Absolute State (1697)

JEAN DOMAT

The stable monarchy that Louis XIV inherited was largely the product of two master political craftsmen, cardinals Richelieu and Mazarin. These statesmen actually ran the day-to-day affairs of the French state under Louis XIII and during Louis XIV's minority, respectively. Under their strict control, the French nobility was subdued and made to realize that the king was absolute in his authority and would tolerate no defiance. It was under their direction, from 1610 to 1661, that absolutism was advanced out of the realm of theory and made a part of the political life of France. The practical rule of any government must be justified through some doctrine, whether it be a devotion to the principles of democracy or to the more blatant dictum "might makes right." Louis XIV justified his absolutism through the belief that God so willed it. Such a "divine-right" monarch ruled with the authority of God and was beholden to no power except that of God. For his part, the king was accountable to God and was expected to rule with the best interests of his people at heart.

The following selection explains the theoretical basis of Louis's absolutism. Jean Domat (1624–1696), one of the most renowned jurists and legal scholars of his age, was responsible for a codification of French law that was sponsored by the king himself. This document is from his treatment of French public law and may be regarded as the official statement of divine-right absolutism.

All men being equal by nature because of the humanity that is their essence, nature does not cause some to be inferior to others. But in this

natural equality, they are separated by other principles that render their conditions unequal and give rise to relationships and dependencies that determine their varying duties toward others and render government necessary. . . .

The first distinction that subjects some persons to others is that which birth introduces between parents and children. . . . The second distinction among persons is that which requires different employments in society and unites all in the body of which each is a member. . . . And it is these varying occupations and dependencies that create the ties that form society among men, as those of its members form a body. This renders it necessary that a head coerce and rule the body of society and maintain order among those who should give the public the benefit of the different contributions that their stations require of them. . . .

Since government is necessary for the common good and God himself established it, it follows that those who are its subjects must be submissive and obedient. For otherwise they would resist God, and the government which should be the source of the peace and unity that make possible the public good would suffer from dissension and trouble that would destroy it. . . .

As obedience is necessary to preserve the order and peace that unite the head and members of the body of the state, it is the universal obligation of all subjects in all cases to obey the ruler's orders without assuming the liberty of judging them. For otherwise each man would be master because of his right to examine what might be just or unjust, and this liberty would favor sedition. Thus every man owes obedience even to unjust laws and orders, provided that he may execute and obey them without injustice. And the only exception that may exempt him from this obligation is limited to cases in which he may not obey without violating divine law. . . .

According to these principles, which are the natural foundations of the authority of those who govern, their power should have two essential attributes: first, to cause justice to rule without exception and, second, to be as absolute as the rule of justice, that is, as absolute as the rule of God Himself who is justice, rules according to its principles, and desires rulers to do likewise. . . .

Since the power of princes comes to them from God and is placed in their hands as an instrument of his providence and his guidance of the states that He commits to their rule, it is clear that princes should use their power in proportion to the objectives that providence and divine guidance seek . . . and that power is confided to them to this end. This is without doubt the foundation and first principle of all the duties of sovereigns that consist of causing God Himself to rule, that is, regulating all things according to His will, which is nothing more than justice. The rule of justice should be the glory of the rule of princes. . . .

The power of sovereigns includes the authority to exercise the functions of government and to use the force that is necessary to their ministry. For authority without force would be despised and almost useless, while force without legitimate authority would be mere tyranny. . . .

There are two uses of sovereign power that are necessary to the public tranquillity. One consists of constraining the subjects to obey and repressing violence and injustice, the other of defending the state against the aggressions of its enemies. Power should be accompanied by the force that is required for these two functions.

The use of force for the maintenance of public tranquillity within the state includes all that is required to protect the sovereign himself from rebellions that would be frequent if authority and force were not united, and all that is required to keep order among the subjects, repress violence against individuals and the general public, execute the orders of the sovereign, and effect all that is required for the administration of justice. Since the use of force and the occasions that require it are never-ending, the government of the sovereign must maintain the force that is needed for the rule of justice. This requires officials and ministers in various functions and the use of arms whenever necessary. . . .

One should include among the rights that the law gives the sovereign that of acquiring all the evidences of grandeur and majesty that are needed to bring renown to the authority and dignity of such great power and to instill awe in the minds of the subjects. For although the latter should view royal power as from God and submit to it regardless of tangible indications of grandeur, God accompanies his own power with a visible majesty that extends over land and sea. . . . When He wishes to exercise his August power as lawgiver, He proclaims his laws with prodigies that inspire reverence and unspeakable terror. He is therefore willing that sovereigns enhance the dignity of their power . . . in such manner as to win the respect of the people. . . .

The general duties . . . of those who have sovereign authority include all that concern the administration of justice, the general polity of the state, public order, tranquillity of the subjects, security of families, attention to all that may contribute to the general good, the choice of skillful ministers who love justice and truth . . . discrimination between justice and clemency whenever justice might suffer from relaxation of its rigor, wise distribution of benefits, rewards, exemptions, privileges and other concessions, wise administration of the public funds, prudence regarding foreigners, and all that may render government agreeable to the good, terrible to the wicked, and entirely worthy of the divine function of ruling men by wielding power that comes only from God and is a participation in his own.

As the final duty of the sovereign, one may add the following which stems from the administration of justice and includes all others. Although his power seems to place him above the law, since no man has the right to call him to account for his conduct, he should observe the laws that concern himself not only because he should be an example to his subjects and render their duty pleasant but because he is not dispensed from his own duty by his sovereign power. On the contrary, his rank obliges him to subordinate his personal interests to the general good of the state, which it is his glory to regard as his own.

The Sighs of Enslaved France (1690)

PIERRE JURIEU

On October 22, 1685, Louis XIV annulled the Edict of Nantes, which had provided political and religious freedom for the French Protestants, or Huguenots, since 1598. Louis was determined to control a nation that was unified politically under his rule and religiously under his faith; Catholicism was to be the only accepted religion for the French people. As a result of the revocation of the Edict of Nantes, the persecution of Huguenots began in earnest. The author of the following memoirs cannot be positively identified, but they are probably from the pen of Pierre Jurieu, a Calvinist pastor who had fled to Holland. Louis endured much criticism from such dissidents in exile. Jurieu's memoirs are among the most provocative because they characterize Louis's absolutism as oppressive and responsible for many of the ills of France.

The oppression of the people is caused primarily by the prodigious number of taxes and excessive levies of money that are everywhere taken in France. Taxes and finance are a science today, and one must be skilled to speak knowledgeably of them, but it suffices for us to relate what we all feel and what the people know of the matter. There are the personal and [land taxes]. There are taxes on salt, wine, merchandise, principal, and revenue. This miserable century has produced a flood of names [of taxes], most of which were unknown to our ancestors or, if some were known, they were not odious because of the moderation with which they were imposed and levied. . . . It does not serve my purpose to acquaint you with the details of these taxes so that you may feel their weight and injustice. It will suffice to enable you to understand the horrible oppression of these taxes by showing (1) the immense sums that are collected, (2) the violence and abuses that are committed in levying them, (3) the bad use that is made of them, and (4) the misery to which the people are reduced.

First, dear unfortunate compatriots, you should realize that the taxes that are taken from you comprise a sum perhaps greater than that which all the other princes of Europe together draw from their states. One thing is certain, that France pays two hundred million in taxes of which about three-fourths go into the coffers of the king and the rest to expenses of collection, tax-farmers, officials, keepers, receivers, the profits of financiers, and new fortunes that are created in almost a single day. For the collection of the salt tax alone, there is a great army of officers and constables. . . .

If tyranny is clear and evident in the immense sums that are levied in France, it is not less so in the manner of collecting them. Kings were established by the people to preserve their persons, lives, liberty, and properties. But the government of France has risen to such excessive tyranny that the prince today regards everything as belonging to him alone. He imposes taxes at will without consulting the people, the nobles, the Estates, or the Parlements. I shall tell you something that is true and that thousands know but most Frenchmen do not. During Colbert's ministry [supervisor of the royal finances] it was discussed whether the king should take immediate possession of all real and personal property in France and reduce it to royal domain, to be used and assigned to whomever the court judged appropriate without regard for former possession, heredity, or other rights. . . .

How much abuse and violence is committed in the collection of taxes? The meanest agent is a sacred person who has absolute power over gentlemen, the judiciary, and all the people. A single blow is capable of ruining the most powerful subject. They confiscate houses, furnishings, cattle, money, grain, wine, and everything in sight. The prisons are full of wretches who are responsible for sums that they impose upon other wretches who cannot pay what is demanded of them. Is

there anything more harsh and cruel than the salt tax? They make you buy for ten or twelve sous per pound something that nature, the sun, and the sea provide for nothing and may be had for two farthings. Under pretext of exercising this royal right, the realm is flooded with a great army of scoundrels called constables of the gabelle [salt tax] who enter houses, penetrate the most secret places with impunity, and do not fail to find unauthorized salt wherever they think there is money. They condemn wretches to pay huge fines, cause them to rot in prison, and ruin families. They force salt upon people everywhere and give each family more than three times as much as they can consume. In the provinces by the sea, they will not permit a poor peasant to bring home salt water; they break jugs, beat people, and imprison them. In a word, every abuse is committed in levying this and other taxes which is done with horrible expense, seizures, imprisonments, and legal cases before the collectors and courts with costs far above the sums involved. . . .

This is how all of France is reduced to the greatest poverty. In earlier reigns, that is, during the ministries of Cardinal Richelieu and Cardinal Mazarin, France was already burdened with heavy taxes. But the manner of collecting them, although not entirely just, nevertheless exhausted the realm much less than the way in which they are collected today. . . . The government of today has changed all of this. M. de Colbert made a plan to reform the finances and applied it to the letter. But what was this reformation? It was not the diminution of taxes in order to relieve the people. . . . He increased the king's revenue by one half. . . .

After this, if we examine the use that is made of these immense sums that are collected with such abuses and extortion, we shall find all the characteristics of oppression and tyranny. It sometimes happens that princes and sovereigns exact levies that appear excessive and greatly inconvenience individuals, but are required by what are called the needs and necessities of the state. In France there is no such thing. There are neither needs nor state. As for the state, earlier it entered into everything; one spoke only of the interests of the state, the needs of the state, the preservation of the state, and the service of the state. To speak this way today would literally be a crime of lese majesty [treason]. The king has taken the place of the state. It is the service of the king, the interest of the king, the preservation of the provinces and wealth of the king. Therefore the king is all and the state nothing. And these are no mere figures of speech but realities. At the French court, no interest is considered but the personal interest of the king, that is, his grandeur and glory. He is the idol to which are sacrificed princes, great men and small, families, provinces, cities, finances and generally everything. Therefore, it is not for the good of the state that these horrible exactions are made, since there is no more state. . . .

This money is used solely to nourish and serve the greatest self-pride and arrogance that ever existed. It is so deep an abyss that it would have swallowed not only the wealth of the whole realm but that of all other states if the king had been able to take possession of it as he attempted to do. The king has caused himself to receive more false flattery than all the pagan demi-gods did with true flattery. Never before was flattery pushed to this point. Never has man loved praise and vainglory to the extent that this prince has sought them. In his court and around himself he supports a multitude of flatterers who constantly seek to outdo each other. He not only permits the erection of statues to himself, on which are inscribed blasphemies in his honor and below which all the nations of the earth are shown in chains; he causes himself to be represented in gold, silver, bronze, copper, marble, silk, in paintings, arches of triumph, and inscriptions. He fills all Paris, all his palaces, and the whole realm with his name and his exploits, as though he far surpasses the Alexanders, the Caesars, and all the heroes of antiquity.

The Colonization and Settlement of the New World

Although the Portuguese and the Spanish took the lead in exploring and methodically exploiting new worlds for economic gain in the fifteenth and sixteenth centuries, other European nations did not stand idly by. England, France, and the Netherlands often staked their competitive claims to the same regions in North America. A race of sorts was on to occupy and explore the forests and waterways of Canada and the east coast of North America. Early explorers such as Jacques Cartier, Samuel de Champlain, and Henry Hudson would establish bases for economic gain and religious freedom that would become important in the "planting" of colonists in the New World.

Although most governments gave their sanction and even economic support to these activities, the English proved hesitant. Religious freedom became a primary inspiration for English colonization. The following selection is William Bradford's account of the Pilgrim landing at Plymouth in 1620. Note Bradford's concerns as the colonists faced the dangerous unknown.

The Landing at Plymouth (1620)

WILLIAM BRADFORD

Being thus arrived in a good harbor and brought safe to land, [the colonists] fell upon their knees and blessed the God of Heaven, who

"The Landing at Plymouth" is from William Bradford, *History of the Plymouth Plantation,* contained in James Harvey Robinson and Charles A. Beard, *Readings in Modern European History* (Boston: Ginn and Company, 1908), vol. 1, pp. 123–125. Text modernized by the editor.

had brought them over the vast and furious ocean, and delivered them from all the perils and miseries thereof, again to set their feet on the firm and stable earth, their proper element. And no marvel if they were thus joyful. . . .

But here I cannot but stay and make a pause, and stand half amazed at this poor people's present condition; and so I think the reader will too, when he well considers the same. Being thus passed the vast ocean, and a sea of troubles before in their preparation . . . , they had now no friends to welcome them, nor inns to entertain or refresh their weatherbeaten bodies, no houses or much less towns to [inhabit], to seek for aid. . . . And since the season was winter, and they that know the winters of [their own] countries know them to be sharp and violent, and subject to cruel and fierce storms, dangerous to travel to known places, much more to search an unknown coast. Besides, what could they see but a hideous and desolate wilderness, full of wild beasts and wild men? . . . [Because summer was over], all things stood upon them with a weatherbeaten face; and the whole country, full of woods and thickets, represented a wild and savage [terrain]. If they looked behind them, there was the mighty ocean which they had passed, and was now a [primary] bar and gulf to separate them from all the civilized parts of the world. . . .

What could now sustain them but the spirit of God and his grace? May not and ought not the children of these fathers rightly say: Our fathers were Englishmen who came over this great ocean, and were ready to perish in this wilderness; but they cried unto the Lord, and he heard their voice, and looked on the adversity. Let them therefore praise the Lord, because He is good and His mercies endure forever. Yea, let they who have been redeemed of the Lord, show how He has delivered them from the hand of the oppressor. When they wandered in the desert wilderness, and found no city to dwell in, both hungry and thirsty, their soul was overwhelmed in them. Let them confess before the Lord His loving kindness, and His wonderful works before the sons of men.

"Murdered in Cold Blood" (1643)

DAVID PIETERZEN DE VRIES

The early Dutch colonists settled primarily in New York along the banks of the Hudson River. New Netherland, as it was called by its founder Henry Hudson in 1609, was settled through large grants of land to wealthy Dutchmen called patroons, who in turn agreed to settle fifty tenants within four years. David Pieterzen de Vries was a landowner in the Netherlands who settled in New Amsterdam (New York City) as a patroon in the 1640s. Relations with the Algonquin and Raritan Indian tribes had generally been cordial until the arrival of Governor Willem Kieft in 1642. When Kieft tried to tax the natives and force them off their land, the relationship degenerated as de Vries relates in his account of a vicious massacre.

The 24th of February, sitting at a table with the Governor, he began to state his intentions, that he had a mind to *wipe the mouths* of the savages; . . . Moreover, as I was the first to come from Holland or Zeeland to plant a colony, [I requested] that he should consider what profit he could derive from this business, as he well knew that on account of trifling with the Indians we had lost our colony in the South River at Swanendael, in the Hoere-kil, with thirty-two men, who were murdered in the year 1630; and that in the year 1640, the cause of my people being murdered on

Staten Island was a difficulty which he had brought on with the Raritan Indians, where his soldiers had for some trifling thing killed some savages. . . . But it appeared that my speaking was of no avail. He had, with his co-murderers, determined to commit the murder, deeming it a [glorious] deed, and to do it without warning the inhabitants in the open lands that each one might take care of himself against the retaliation of the savages, for he could not kill all the Indians.

When I had expressed all these things in full, sitting at the table, and the meal was over, he

"Murdered in Cold Blood" is from David Pieterzen de Vries, *Voyages from Holland to America* (New York: Billin and Brothers, 1853), pp. 114–117.

told me he wished me to go to the large hall, which he had been lately adding to his house. Coming to it, there stood all his soldiers ready to cross the river to Pavonia to commit the murder. Then spoke I again to Governor Willem Kieft: "Let this work alone; you wish to break the mouths of the Indians, but you will also murder our own nation, for there are none of the settlers in the open country who are aware of it. My own dwelling, my people, cattle, corn, and tobacco will be lost." He answered me, assuring me that there would be no danger; that some soldiers should go to my house to protect it. But that was not done. So was this business begun between the 25th and 26th of February in the year 1643.

I remained that night at the Governor's, sitting up. I went and sat by the kitchen fire, when about midnight I heard a great shrieking, and I ran to the ramparts of the fort, and looked over to Pavonia. I saw nothing but firing, and heard the shrieks of the savages murdered in their sleep. I returned again to the house by the fire. Having sat there awhile, there came an Indian with his squaw, whom I knew well, and who lived about an hour's walk from my house, and told me that they two had fled in a small skiff, which they had taken from the shore at Pavonia; that the Indians from Fort Orange had surprised them; and that they had come to conceal themselves; that they who had killed their people at Pavonia were not Indians, but the Swannekens, as they call the Dutch, had done it. They then asked me how they should get out of the fort. I took them to the door, and there was no sentry there, and so they betook themselves to the woods. When it was day the soldiers returned to the fort, having massacred or murdered eighty Indians, and considering they had done a deed of [glorious] valor, in murdering so many in their sleep; where infants were torn from their mother's breasts, and hacked to pieces in the presence of the parents, and the pieces thrown into the fire and in the water, and other sucklings, being bound to small boards, were cut, stuck, and pierced, and miserably massacred in a manner to move a heart of stone.

Some were thrown into the river, and when the fathers and mothers endeavored to save them, the soldiers would not let them come on land but made both parents and children drown—children from five to six years of age, and also some old and decrepit persons. Those who fled from this onslaught, and concealed themselves in the neighboring sedge, and when it was morning, came out to beg a piece of bread, and to be permitted to warm themselves, were murdered in cold blood and tossed into the fire or the water. Some came to our people in the country with their hands, some with their legs cut off, and some holding their entrails in their arms, and others had such horrible cuts and gashes, that worse than they were could never happen. And these poor simple creatures, as also many of our own people, did not know any better than that they had been attacked by a party of other Indians—the Maquas. After this exploit, the soldiers were rewarded for their services, and Director Kieft thanked them by taking them by the hand and congratulating them. . . .

This is indeed a disgrace to our nation, who have so generous a governor in our Fatherland as the Prince of Orange [Frederick Henry], who has always endeavored in his wars to spill as little blood as possible.

As soon as the savages understood that the Swannekens had so treated them, all the men whom they could surprise on the farmlands, they killed; but we have never heard that they have ever permitted women or children to be killed. They burned all the houses, farms, barns, grain, haystacks, and destroyed everything they could get hold of. So there was an open destructive war begun. They also burnt my farm, cattle, corn, barn, tobacco-house, and all the tobacco. . . . While my people were in alarm, the savage whom I had aided to escape from the fort in the night came there, and told the other Indians that I was a good chief, that I had helped him out of the fort, and that that killing of the Indians took place contrary to my wish. Then they all cried out together to my people that they would not shoot them; that if they had not destroyed my cattle they would not do it, nor burn my house; . . . but hearing now that it had been done contrary to my wish, they all went away, and left my house unbesieged. When now the Indians had destroyed so many farms and men in revenge for their people, I went to Governor Willem Kieft, and asked him if it was not as I had said it would be, that he would only effect the spilling of Christian blood. Who would now compensate us for our losses? But he gave me no answer. He said he wondered that no Indians came to the fort. I told him that I did not wonder at it: "why should the Indians come here where you have so treated them?"

ECONOMIES OF EXPLOITATION

The Mercantile Economy and the Birth of Capitalism

Since the Renaissance, Europeans had sought new economic horizons. The commercial revolution of the sixteenth century and the exploration of the Americas had resulted in the establishment of colonies that engendered competition among imperial powers. Dominance and success in this commercial rivalry required that nations such as Spain, France, Great Britain, and the Netherlands become efficient producers and resourceful traders. To this end, governments focused their domestic economies and strictly regulated their foreign colonies in order to produce profit at each turn. This was especially important because these powers were constantly at war with each other in the eighteenth century, often squandering the precious wealth that they had accumulated.

To the extent that there was any formal economic theory behind this process of accumulating wealth, it was called mercantilism. Mercantilism gradually became a structured economic system based on the notion that the world was an arena of scarce resources. Since gold, silver, and other products were limited, governments had to regulate trade with protective tariffs, navigation laws that restricted trade with rivals, and domestic monopolies on salt and gunpowder. Mercantilist statesmen believed that their economies could grow only at the expense of others.

Although this economic system developed in the seventeenth century, it became more pronounced in the eighteenth as the wars in Europe and North America forced each country to become even more heavy-handed. The following selection by Sir William Keith, English Governor of Pennsylvania from 1712–1726, encapsulates the tenets of mercantilism and the "Old Colonial System" that drew every ounce of profit from the colonies. But there were also critics and the reaction to this economic regulation reached a climax in the late eighteenth century with the ideas of Adam Smith.

Economic Regulation: "The Maxim of All Polite Nations"

SIR WILLIAM KEITH

When either by conquest or increase of people, foreign provinces are possessed, and colonies planted abroad, it is convenient, and often necessary, to substitute little dependant provincial governments, whose people being enfranchised, and made partakers of the liberties and privileges belonging to the original Mother State, are justly bound by its laws, and become subservient to its interests, as the true end of their incorporation.

Every act of a dependant provincial government therefore ought to terminate in the advantage of the Mother State, unto whom it owes its being, and by whom it is protected in all its valuable privileges: hence it follows, that all advantageous projects or commercial gains in any colony, which are truly prejudicial to, and inconsistent

"Economic Regulation" is from Sir William Keith, *A Collection of Papers and Other Tracts, Written Occasionally on Various Subjects* (London: J. Mechell, 1740), pp. 169–170, 173–175.

with the interest of the Mother State, must be understood to be illegal, and the practice of them unwarrantable, because they contradict the end for which the colony had a being, and are incompatible with the terms on which the people claim both privilege and protection. . . .

It has ever been the maxim of all polite nations, to regulate their government to the best advantage of their trading interest. . . . By this short view of trade in general we may plainly understand that those colonies can be very beneficially employed both for Great Britain and themselves, without interfering with any of the staple manufactures in England.

But in order to set this point yet in a clearer light, we will proceed to consider some of the obvious regulations on the American trade, for rendering the colonies truly serviceable to Great Britain.

1. That all the product of the colonies, for which the manufacture and trade of Britain has a constant demand, be enumerated among the goods which by law must be first transported to Britain, before they can be carried to any other market.
2. That all kinds of woollen manufactures for which the colonies have a demand, shall continue to be brought from Britain only, and linens from Great Britain and Ireland.
3. All other European commodities to be carried to the colonies, (salt excepted) entry thereof to be first made in Britain, before they can be transported to any of the English colonies.
4. The colonies to be absolutely restrained in their several governments from laying any manner of duties on shipping or trade from Europe, or upon European goods transported from one colony to another.

Supposing these things to be done, it will evidently follow that the more extensive the trade of the colonies is, the greater will be the advantages accruing to Great Britain therefrom; and consequently, that the enlargement of the colonies, and the increase of their people, would still be an addition to the national strength. . . .

From what has been said of the nature of colonies, and the restriction that ought to be laid on their trade, it is plain that none of the English plantations in America can with any reason or good sense pretend to claim an absolute legislative power with themselves; so that let their several Constitutions be founded by Charters, Royal Patents, . . . or what other legal authority you please; yet still they cannot be possessed of any rightful capacity to contradict, or evade the true intent and force of any Act of Parliament, wherewith the wisdom of Great Britain may think fit to affect them from time to time.

The Wealth of Nations (1776)

ADAM SMITH

Adam Smith can rightly be considered one of the most influential thinkers of the Enlightenment. He studied moral philosophy at Oxford and in his mid-twenties conceived of an economic philosophy of "the obvious and simple system of natural liberty," which the world would come to know as capitalism. In response to the restrictive emphasis of mercantilism, Smith conceived of an expansive universe, full of opportunity for the individual or nation to exercise initiative, accumulate wealth, and serve others in the process.

The following selection is an excerpt from his major work, The Wealth of Nations. *It focuses on Smith's view of human nature and the "invisible hand" of competition as guide to*

"The Wealth of Nations" is from Adam Smith, *An Inquiry into the Nature and Causes of the Wealth of Nations*, ed. Edwin A. Seligman (London: J. M. Dent, 1901), pp. 12–15, 400–401, 436–437.

an economic system based on individual self-interest. If one views the Industrial Revolution of the early nineteenth century and the birth of Marxism in 1848 as being directly influenced by Smith's theories, then his impact on the history of the twentieth century is immeasurable.

Human Nature and the Division of Labor

This division of labour, from which so many advantages are derived, is not originally the effect of any human wisdom, which foresees and intends that general opulence to which it gives occasion. It is the necessary, though very slow and gradual, consequence of a certain propensity in human nature which has in view no such extensive utility; the propensity to truck, barter, and exchange one thing for another.

Whether this propensity be one of those original principles in human nature, of which no further account can be given; or whether, as seems more probable, it be the necessary consequence of the faculties of reason and speech, it belongs not to our present subject to enquire. It is common to all men, and to be found in no other race of animals, which seem to know neither this nor any other species of contracts. . . . In civilized society, [man] stands at all times in need of the cooperation and assistance of great multitudes, while his whole life is scarce sufficient to gain the friendship of a few persons. In almost every other race of animals each individual, when it is grown up to maturity, is entirely independent, and in its natural state has occasion for the assistance of no other living creature. But man has almost constant occasion for the help of his brethren, and it is in vain for him to expect it from their benevolence only. He will be more likely to prevail if he can interest their self-love in his favour, and show them that it is for their own advantage to do for him what he requires of them. Whoever offers to another a bargain of any kind, proposes to do this. Give me that which I want, and you shall have this which you want, is the meaning of every such offer; and it is in this manner that we obtain from one another the far greater part of those good offices which we stand in need of. It is not from the benevolence of the butcher, the brewer, or the baker, that we expect our dinner, but from their regard to their own interest. We address our-

selves, not to their humanity but to their self-love, and never talk to them of our own necessities but of their advantages. . . .

The difference of natural talents in different men is, in reality, much less than we are aware of; and the very different genius which appears to distinguish men of different professions, when grown up to maturity, is not upon many occasions so much the cause, as the effect of the division of labour. The difference between the most dissimilar characters, between a philosopher and a common street porter, for example, seems to arise not so much from nature, as from habit, custom, and education. When they came into the world, and for the first six or eight years of their existence, they were, perhaps, very much alike, and neither their parents nor playfellows could perceive any remarkable difference. About that age, or soon after, they come to be employed in very different occupations. The difference of talents comes then to be taken notice of, and widens by degrees, till at last the vanity of the philosopher is willing to acknowledge scarce any resemblance. . . . By nature a philosopher is not in genius and disposition half so different from a street porter, as a mastiff is from a greyhound, or a greyhound from a spaniel, or this last from a shepherd's dog. . . . Among men, on the contrary, the most dissimilar geniuses are of use to one another; the different produces of their respective talents, by the general disposition to truck, barter, and exchange, being brought, as it were, into a common stock, where every man may purchase whatever part of the produce of other men's talents he has occasion for. . . .

The Invisible Hand

As every individual, therefore, endeavors as much as he can both to employ his capital in the support of domestic industry, and so to direct that industry that its produce may be of the greatest value; every individual necessarily labours to render the annual revenue of the society as great as he can. He generally, indeed, neither intends to promote the public interest, nor knows how much he is promoting it. . . . He intends only his own security; and by directing that industry in such a manner as its produce may be of the greatest value, he intends only his own gain, and he is in this, as in many other cases, led by an invisible hand to promote an end which was no part of his intention. Nor is it always the worse for the society that it was no part of it. By pursuing his own interest he frequently promotes that of the society more effectually than when he really intends to promote it. I have never known much good done by those who affected to trade for the public good. . . . The statesman, who should attempt to direct private people in what manner they ought to employ their capitals, would not only load himself with a most unnecessary attention, but assume an authority which could safely be trusted, not only to no single person, but to no council or senate whatever, and which would nowhere be so dangerous as in the hands of a man who had folly and presumption enough to fancy himself fit to exercise it.

Unreasonableness of Restraints

Each nation has been made to look with an invidious eye upon the prosperity of all nations with which it trades, and to consider their gain as its own loss. Commerce, which ought naturally to be, among nations, as among individuals, a bond of union and friendship, has become the most fertile source of discord and animosity. . . . The violence and injustice of the rulers of mankind is an ancient evil, for which, I am afraid, the nature of human affairs can scarce admit of a remedy. But the mean rapacity, the monopolising spirit of merchants and manufacturers, who neither are, nor ought to be, the rulers of mankind, though it cannot perhaps be corrected, may very easily be prevented from disturbing the tranquility of anybody but themselves.

That it was the spirit of monopoly which originally both invented and propagated this doctrine cannot be doubted; and they who first taught it were by no means such fools as they who believed it. In every country it always is and must be the interest of the great body of the people to buy whatever they want of those who sell it cheapest. The proposition is so very manifest that it seems ridiculous to take any pains to prove it; nor could it have ever been called in question had not the interested sophistry of merchants and manufacturers confounded the common sense of mankind. Their interest is, in this respect, directly opposite to that of the great body of the people. As it is the interest of the freemen of a [guild] to hinder the rest of the inhabitants from employing any workmen but themselves, so it is the interest of the merchants and manufacturers of every country to secure to themselves the monopoly of the home market. Hence in Great Britain, and in most other European countries, the extraordinary duties upon almost all goods imported by alien merchants. Hence the high duties and prohibitions upon all those foreign manufactures which can come into competition with our own. Hence, too, the extraordinary restraints upon the importation of almost all sorts of goods from those countries . . . whom national animosity happens to be most violently inflamed. . . . This very competition, however, is advantageous to the great body of the people, who profit greatly besides by the good market which the great expense of such a nation affords them in every other way. . . .

The African Slave Trade

Twenty-two people were sleeping; I herded them as if they had been cattle towards the boats.

—*Diogo Gomes (ca. 1460 on the Gambia River)*

Whether it was my ship or any other ship, the whole of the officers and crew were employed altogether in endeavouring to keep the slaves in a healthy state and in good spirits.

—*Captain Thomas Tobin*

Sharks are the invariable outriders of all slave ships crossing the Atlantic, systematically trotting alongside, to be handy in case a dead slave is to be decently buried.

—Herman Melville

How is it that we hear the loudest yelps for liberty among the drivers of Negroes?

—Dr. Samuel Johnson

Only the poor speak ill of the slave trade.

—Domingo del Monte

In the sixteenth and seventeenth centuries, as European states such as Portugal, Spain, France, and England became more politically centralized under the direction of powerful monarchs, the competition to explore, develop, and control new economic markets grew ever more intense. The lifeline of each country, its future success or failure, depended on the cultivation and exploitation of the world's resources—especially those of the Americas. Spanish mining operations in Central and South America were intended systematically to extract and export the wealth of the continent. The Spanish treasure fleets that carried the gold and silver of the New World to the coffers of the Old were defended by Caribbean forts and citadels, as well as by an attitude of superiority that dehumanized native workers and justified their exploitation. But as the numbers of Native American workers declined due to disease and the harsh working conditions, the Spanish and Portuguese sought other sources of cheap labor; they increasingly turned to Africa and its plentiful supply of slaves.

Slavery was certainly not new to the sixteenth and seventeenth centuries. Slaves and the slave trade had existed since antiquity in the societies of the Near East, Greece and Rome, the Arab world, and the eastern Chinese empires. Virtually every premodern state depended on slavery to some extent. Prior to about 1650, Africa had suffered no greater exploitation than other areas. But with the development of the plantation systems of Brazil, the West Indies, and the United States, where the cultivation of sugar cane, cotton, tobacco, and indigo demanded a huge supply of labor, the business of supplying slaves became a lucrative and dominant economic force. It has often been noted that the world's demand and near addiction to the "sweet taste" produced the brutal sugar cane plantations that led to some of the greatest agonies and social repercussions in world history.

Although the Portuguese pioneered the occidental slave trade in the fifteenth and sixteenth centuries, and held a virtual monopoly until the incursions of the Dutch about 1650, they in turn depended on the efforts of the internal slave trade throughout the African continent. For centuries, tribal kings had sold their captured enemies. But the increasing demand for slaves created more opportunities for the development of this trade. Since Europeans were vulnerable to the tropical diseases of Africa, native middlemen and Arab raiders haunted the forests and savannas of deepest Africa and forcibly extracted whole families, separating them and marching them to the Gold Coast of West Africa for sale to the slavers. They then loaded their human cargos onto ships bound for the far reaches of Brazil, the West Indies, and the United States. The horrors of this "middle passage" reverberate in the journals of slave captains and in the oral and written traditions of the slaves themselves. Packed into the holds of ships, thousands of slaves died from disease, malnourishment, and the violent acts of the slavers who regarded their cargo as a perishable economic investment and nothing more. The slaves were then sold at auction to a life of servitude, often brutal, always dehumanizing.

It is difficult to estimate the numbers of slaves extracted from Africa beginning in the mid-fifteenth century to the decline of the slave trade after 1870. Recent scholarship indicates that at a minimum, Africa lost about thirteen million people to the Atlantic slave trade and another five million to the oriental trade. The social and political consequences of this phenomenon are equally difficult to ascertain. Certainly the western and eastern slave trades took many of the strongest young men and women. This dramatic reduction of population likely led to Africa's inability to compete with the industrial world in the twentieth century. Some have even postulated that the social dislocation of slavery affected the ratio of males to females, impacting birth rates, workforce balance, family stability, and the institution of marriage itself.

The following sources trace the development of slavery from capture and transport to the Gold Coast, to the transatlantic passage and the auction block. Though the voices of abolition were heard especially throughout the nineteenth century, indigenous slavery in Africa was ended over a long period from 1874 on the Gold Coast to 1928 in Sierra Leone. The Atlantic slave trade, which was such a complex part of the ongoing economic interaction between Europe and the civilizations of the East and West, remains one of the great tragedies of world history.

Capture: "Farewell, Place of My Birth"

SAMUEL AJAYI CROWTHER

Samuel Ajayi Crowther was a boy of 13 when he was taken captive in Oyo, a region of modern-day Nigeria. This area was caught up in the Yoruba Wars between competing local tribes and a large Islamic population. We know little of the conflict, but Crowther was sold and resold several times on his way down the coast to Lagos. In 1822, he was shipped to Brazil, but was captured at sea by two vessels of the British antislavery squadron and sent to Freetown, Sierra Leone, where he learned to read and write. After further schooling in London and West Africa, he married, was ordained a deacon and priest in the Anglican church, became a missionary in Sierra Leone, and later in the Yoruba country of his birth. His most important work was the Niger Mission he founded in 1857, which led to his consecration as bishop in 1864. In all, he played an important role in the establishment of Christianity and British enterprise in Nigeria before his death in 1891. The following excerpt from Samuel Crowther's account of his life describes his capture and the beginning of his journey to the coast.

For some years, war had been carried on in my Oyo country, which was always attended with much devastation and bloodshed; the women, such men as had surrendered or were caught, with the children, were taken captives. The enemies who carried on these wars were principally the Oyo Muslims, with whom my country abounds—with the Fulbe, and such foreign slaves as had escaped from their owners, joined together, making a formidable force of about 20,000, who annoyed the whole country. They had no other employment but selling slaves to the Spaniards and Portuguese on the coast.

The morning in which my town, Osgun, shared the same fate which many others had experienced, was fair and delightful; and most of the inhabitants were engaged in their respective occupations. We were preparing breakfast without any apprehension; when, about 9 o'clock a.m., a rumor was spread in the town, that the enemies had approached with intentions of hostility. It was not long after when they had almost

---

"Capture" is from *Journals of the Reverand James Frederick Schön and Mr. Samuel Crowther* (London, 1842), pp. 371–376.

surrounded the town, to prevent any escape of the inhabitants; . . .

Here a most sorrowful scene imaginable was to be witnessed!—women, some with three, four, or six children clinging to their arms, with the infants on their backs, and such baggage as they could carry on their heads, running as fast as they could through prickly shrubs. . . . While they found it impossible to go along with their loads, they endeavored only to save themselves and their children: even this was impracticable with those who had many children to care for. While they were endeavoring to disentangle themselves from the ropy shrubs, they were overtaken and caught by the enemies with a noose of rope thrown over the neck of every individual, to be led in the manner of goats tied together, under the drove of one man. In many cases a family was violently divided between three or four enemies, who each led his away, to see one another no more. Your humble servant was thus caught— with his mother, two sisters (one an infant about ten months old), and a cousin—while endeavoring to escape in the manner above described. My load consisted in nothing else than my bow, and five arrows in the quiver; the bow I had lost in the shrub, while I was extricating myself, before I could think of making any use of it against my enemies. The last view I had of my father was when he came from the fight, to give us the signal to flee: he entered into our house, which was burned some time back for some offence given by my father's adopted son. Hence, I never saw him more. Here I must take thy leave, unhappy comfortless father! I learned, some time afterward, that he was killed in another battle.

Our conquerors were Oyo Muslims, who led us away through the town. On our way, we met a man sadly wounded on the head, struggling between life and death. Before we got half way through the town, some Fulbe, among the enemies themselves, hostilely separated my cousin from our number. . . .

The flames [from the burning village were] very high. We were led by my grandfather's house, already desolate; and in a few minutes after, we left the town to the mercy of the flame, never to enter or see it any more. Farewell, place of my birth, the playground of my childhood, and the place which I thought would be the repository of my mortal body in its old age!

We were now out of Osgun, going into a town called Iseyin, the rendezvous of the enemies, about twenty miles from our town. On the way, we saw our grandmother at a distance, with about three or four of my other cousins taken with her, for a few minutes: she was missed through the crowd, to see her no more. Several other captives were held in the same manner as we were: grandmothers, mothers, children, and cousins, were all led captives. O sorrowful prospect! The aged women were to be greatly pitied, not being able to walk so fast as their children and grandchildren: they were often threatened with being put to death upon the spot, to get rid of them, if they would not go as fast as others; and they were often as wicked in their practice as in their words. O pitiful sight! Whose heart would not bleed to have seen this? Yes, such is the state of barbarity in the heathen land.

The Slave System (1797)

MUNGO PARK

Mungo Park (1771–1806?) was a Scottish physician who led two expeditions to explore the Gambia and Niger rivers. Along the way, he recorded scientific information in his journals and commented on West African society and slavery. Opposed to the slave trade, Park hoped that his explorations might help develop economic alternatives for European investment. In

"The Slave System" is from Mungo Park, *Travels in the Interior District of Africa* (London, 1799), pp. 287–288; 296.

his second expedition to Africa, he tragically drowned in the Niger River while escaping from hostile natives. Mungo Park was a man of great tenacity who, through his personal courage and curiosity, inspired others to penetrate the interior of Africa. His observations in the next two sources reveal much about the internal slave trade of West Africa.

The slaves in Africa, I suppose, are nearly in the proportion of three to one to the freemen. They claim no reward for their services except food and clothing, and are treated with kindness or severity according to the good or bad disposition of their masters. . . . [Prisoners of war or slaves purchased with money] are considered as strangers and foreigners, who have no right to the protection of the law, and may be treated with severity or sold to a stranger according to the pleasure of their owners. There are, indeed, regular markets where slaves of this description are bought and sold, and the value of a slave in the eye of an African purchaser increases in proportion to his distance from his native kingdom; for when slaves are only a few days' journey from the place of their birth, they frequently effect their escape; but when one or more kingdoms intervene, escape being more difficult, they are more readily reconciled to their situation. On this account the unhappy slave is frequently transferred from one dealer to another, until he has lost all hopes of returning to his native kingdom. The slaves which are purchased by the Europeans on the Coast are chiefly of this description; a few of them are collected in the petty wars, . . . which take place near the Coast, but by far the greater number are brought down in large caravans from the inland countries, of which many are unknown even by name to the Europeans. The slaves which are thus brought from the interior may be divided into two distinct classes; *first,* such as were slaves from their birth, having been born of enslaved mothers; *secondly,* such as were born free, but who afterward, by whatever means, became slaves. Those of the first description are by far the most numerous; for prisoners taken in war (at least such as are taken in open and declared war, when one kingdom avows hostilities against another) are generally of this description. . . .

War is, of all others, the most productive source, and was probably the origin of slavery; for when one nation had taken from another a greater number of captives than could be exchanged on equal terms, it is natural to suppose that the conquerors, finding it inconvenient to maintain their prisoners, would compel them to labor; at first perhaps only their own support, but afterward to support their masters. Be this as it may, it is a known fact that prisoners of war in Africa are the slaves of the conquerors; and when the weak or unsuccessful warrior begs for mercy beneath the uplifted spear of his opponent, he gives up at the same time his claim to liberty; and purchases his life at the expense of his freedom. . . .

It is evident from its nature and extent, that [slavery] is a system of no modern date. It probably had its origin in the remote ages of antiquity, before the Muslims explored a path across the Desert. How far it is maintained and supported by the slave traffic, which, for two hundred years, the nations of Europe have carried on with the natives of the Coast, it is neither within my province nor in my power to explain. If my sentiments should be required concerning the effect which a discontinuance of that commerce would produce on the manners of the natives, I should have no hesitation in observing that, in the present unenlightened state of their minds, my opinion is that the effect would neither be so extensive or beneficial, as many wise and worthy persons fondly expect.

Slave Transport
MUNGO PARK

My clothes were had by this time become so very ragged, that I was almost ashamed to appear out of doors; but Karfa, on the day after his arrival, generously presented me with such a garment and trousers as are commonly worn in the country.

"Slave Transport" is from Mungo Park, *Travels in the Interior District of Africa* (London, 1799), p. 299.

The slaves which Karfa had brought with him were all of them prisoners of war; they had been taken by the Bambarran army in the kingdoms of Wassela and Kaarta, and carried to Segu, where some of them had remained three years in irons. From Segu they were sent, in company with a number of other captives, up the Niger in two large canoes, and offered for sale at Tamina, Bammakoo, and Kancaba, at which places the greater number of the captives were bartered for gold dust, and the remainder sent forward to Kankaree.

Eleven of them confessed to me that they had been slaves from their infancy; but the other two refused to give any account of their former condition. They were all very inquisitive; but they viewed me at first with looks of horror, and repeatedly asked if my countrymen were cannibals. They were very desirous to know what became of the slaves after they had crossed the salt water. I told them that they were employed in cultivating the land, but they would not believe me; and one of them, putting his hand upon the ground, said, with great simplicity, "Have you really got such ground as this to set you feet upon?" A deeply rooted idea that the whites purchase Negroes for the purpose of devouring them, or of selling them to others, that they may be devoured hereafter, naturally makes the slaves contemplate a journey towards the coast with great terror, insomuch that the Slatees [overseers] are forced to keep them constantly in irons, and watch them very closely to prevent their escape. They are commonly secured by putting the right leg of one and the left of another into the same pair of fetters. By supporting the fetters with a string, they can walk, though very slowly. Every four slaves are likewise fastened together by the necks with a strong rope or twisted thongs; and in the night an additional pair of fetters is put on their hands, and sometimes a light iron chain passed round their necks.

Such of them as evince marks of discontent, are secured in a different manner. A thick billlet of wood is cut about three feet long, and a smooth notch being made upon one side of it, the ankle of the slave is bolted to the smooth part by means of a strong iron staple, one prong of which passes on each side of the ankle. All these fetters and bolts are made from native iron; in the present case they were put on by the blacksmith as soon as the slaves arrived from Kancabe, and were not taken off until the morning on which the coffle departed for Gambia.

African middlemen transport captured slaves to the coast in this eighteenth century print. *(North Wind Picture Archives)*

The Atlantic Passage to the New World

The Slavers: "We Take So Much Pain to So Little Purpose" (1694)

CAPTAIN THOMAS PHILLIPS

Once slaves had been delivered to the coast by middlemen or tribal kings themselves, negotiations began in earnest. At first, payment consisted of baubles and beads, but quickly became more sophisticated. Some later exchanges were even made in gold. Slave captains worked out arrangements with their financial backers to outfit the ship and then realize their gains at auction in the Americas. This excerpt from the journal of a successful slave captain named Thomas Phillips, concentrates on the business of slavery, its pitfalls and the uncertainties for profit. His ship, Hannibal, *set sail in 1694 with 650 slaves from the Gold Coast of Africa destined for Barbados. It was a difficult voyage and a dirty business.*

Having bought my complement of 700 slaves, 480 men and 220 women, and finished all my business at Whidaw [on the Gold Coast], I took my leave of the old king. . . and parted, with many affectionate expressions on both sides, being forced to promise him that I would return again the next year, with several things he desired me to bring from England. . . . I set sail on the 27th of July in the morning, accompanied with the East-India Merchant, who had bought 650 slaves, for the Island of St. Thomas . . . from which we took our departure on August 25th and set sail for Barbados.

We spent in our passage from St. Thomas to Barbados two months eleven days, from the 25th of August to the 4th of November following: in which time there happened such sickness and mortality among my poor men and Negroes. Of the first we buried 14, and of the last 320, which was a great detriment to our voyage, the royal African Company losing ten pounds to every slave that died, and the owners of the ship ten pounds ten shillings, being the freight agreed on to be paid by the charter-party for every Negro delivered alive ashore to the African Company's agents at Barbados. . . . The loss in all amounted to near 6500 pounds sterling.

The distemper which my men as well as the black mostly died of was the white flux, which was so violent and inveterate that no medicine would in the least check it, so that when any of our men were seized with, we esteemed him a dead man, as he generally proved. . . .

The Negroes are so incident to the small-pox that few ships that carry them escape without it, and sometimes it makes vast havoc and destruction among them. But although we had 100 at a time sick of it, and that it went through the ship, yet we lost not above a dozen by it. All the assistance we gave the diseased was only as much water as they desired to drink, and some palm-oil to anoint their sores, and they would generally recover without any other helps but what kind nature gave them. . . .

But what the small-pox spared, the flux swept off, to our great regret, after all our pains and care to give them their messes in due order and season, keeping their lodgings as clean and sweet as possible, and enduring so much misery and stench so long among a parcel of creatures nastier than swine, and after all our expectations to be defeated by their mortality. . . .

No gold-finders can endure so much noisome slavery as they do who carry Negroes; for

"The Slavers" is from Awnsham and John Churchill, eds., *A Collection of Voyages and Travels,* vol. 6 (London, 1746). Account modernized by the editor.

those have some respite and satisfaction, but we endure twice the misery; and yet by their mortal-ity our voyages are ruined, and take so much pains to so little purpose.

The Middle Passage and Auction (1756)

OLAUDAH EQUIANO

Olaudah Equiano (1745?–1797) was captured at age 11 from his home in the southern Benin region of Nigeria. He was taken to Barbados in 1756 and sold to a British naval offi-cer in Virginia who took him to England as his servant. In his remarkable life, Equiano was sold again to West Indies slavers and finally bought by Robert King, a Quaker merchant from Philadelphia, who allowed Equiano to engage in petty trade while he served as an assistant to one of his captains in the Carribean. Equiano finally purchased his freedom in 1766.

In these memoirs written in 1789, Equiano describes the brutal "middle passage" across the Atlantic and the auction itself in Barbados. Equiano was actively engaged in the antislavery movement in England and petitioned Queen Victoria to bring the slave trade to an end.

The first object which saluted my eyes when I ar-rived on the coast was the sea, and a slave ship, which was then riding at anchor, and waiting for its cargo. These filled me with astonishment, which was soon converted into terror, which I am yet at a loss to describe, not the then feelings of my mind. When I was carried on board, I was immediately handled, and tossed up, to see if I were sound, by some of the crew; and I was not persuaded that I had got into a world of bad spirits, and that they were going to kill me. Their complexions too differing so much from ours, their long hair, and the language they spoke, which was very different from any I had ever heard, united to confirm me in this belief. Indeed, such were the horrors of my views and fears at the moment, that, if ten thousand worlds had been my own, I would have freely parted with them all to have exchanged my con-dition with that of the meanest slave in my own country. When I looked round the ship too, and saw a large furnace or copper boiling, and a multitude of black people of every description chained together, every one of their counte-nances expressing dejection and sorrow, I no longer doubted of my fate; and, quite overpow-ered with horror and anguish, I fell motionless on the deck and fainted. When I recovered a lit-tle, I found some black people about me, who I believed were some of those who brought me on board, and had been receiving their pay; they talked to me in order to cheer me, but all in vain. I asked them if we were not to be eaten by those white men with horrible looks, red faces, and long hair. They told me I was not. . . .

Soon after this, the blacks who brought me on board went off, and left me abandoned to despair. I now saw myself deprived of all chance of returning to my native country, or even the least glimpse of hope of gaining the shore, which I now considered as friendly; and I even wished for my former slavery, in preference to my present situation, which was filled with hor-rors of every kind, still heightened by my igno-rance of what I was to undergo. I was not long suffered to indulge my grief; I was soon put down under the decks, and there I received such a salutation in my nostrils as I had never experienced in my life; so that, with the loath-someness of the stench, and crying together, I became so sick and low that I was not able to eat, nor had I the least desire to taste anything. I now wished for the last friend, death, to relieve me. . . .

"The Middle Passage and Auction" is from Olaudah Equiano, *The Interesting Narrative of Olaudah Equiano, or Gustavus Vasa, the African,* 2 volumes (London, 1789), pp. 50–57.

In a little time after, amongst the poor chained men, I found some of my own nation, which in a small degree gave ease to my mind. I inquired of them what was to be done with us? They gave me to understand we were to be carried to these white people's country to work for them. I then was a little revived, and thought, if it were no worse than working, my situation was not so desperate: but still I feared I should be put to death, the white people looked and acted, as I thought, in so savage a manner; for I had never seen among any people such instances of brutal cruelty; and this not only shown towards us blacks, but also to some of the whites themselves. One white man in particular I saw, when we were permitted to be on deck, flogged so unmercifully with a large rope near the foremast, that he died in consequence of it; and they tossed him over the side as they would have done a brute. This made me fear these people the more; and I expected nothing less than to be treated in the same manner. . . .

The stench of the hold while we were on the coast was so intolerably loathsome that it was dangerous to remain there for any time, and some of us had been permitted to stay on the deck for the fresh air; but now that the whole ship's cargo were confined together, it became absolutely pestilential. The closeness of the place, and the heat of the climate, added to the number in the ship, which was so crowded that each had scarcely room to turn himself, almost suffocated us. This produced copious perspiration, so that the air soon became unfit for respiration, from a variety of loathsome smells, and brought on a sickness among the slaves, of which many died, thus falling victims to the improvident avarice, as I may call it, of their purchasers. This wretched situation was again aggravated by the galling of the chains, now become insupportable; and the filth of the necessary tubs, into which the children often fell, and were almost suffocated. The shrieks of the women, and the groans of the dying, rendered the whole a scene of horror almost inconceivable. . . .

One day, when we had a smooth sea, and moderate wind, two of my wearied countrymen, who were chained together (I was near them at the time), preferring death to such a life of misery, somehow made through the nets, and jumped into the sea; immediately another quite dejected fellow, who, on account of his illness, was suffered to be out of irons, also followed their example; two of the wretches were drowned, but they got the other, and afterwards flogged him unmercifully, for thus attempting to prefer death to slavery. In this manner, we continued to undergo more hardships than I can now relate; hardships which are inseparable from this accursed trade. Many a time we were near suffocation, from the want of fresh air, which we were often without for whole days together. This, and the stench of the necessary tubs, carried off many. . . .

At last, we came in sight of the island of Barbados, at which the whites on board gave a great shout, and made many signs of joy to us. We did not know what to think of this; but, as the vessel drew nearer, we plainly saw the harbor, and other ships of different kinds and sizes: and we soon anchored among them off Bridgetown. . . . We were conducted immediately to a merchant's yard, where we were all penned up together like so many sheep in a fold, without regard to sex or age. As every object was new to me, everything I saw filled me with surprise. What struck me first was, that the houses were built with bricks, in stories, and in every other respect different from those I have seen in Africa: but I was still more astonished on seeing people on horseback. I did not know what this could mean; and indeed I thought these people were full of nothing but magical arts. . . .

We were not many days in the merchant's custody, before we were sold after their usual manner, which is this: on a signal given (as the beat of a drum), the buyers rush at once into the yard where the slaves are confined, and make choice of the parcel they like best. . . . In this manner, without scruple, are relations and friends separated, most of them never to see each other again. . . .

O, ye nominal Christians! Might not an African ask you, learned you this from your God who says unto you, do unto all men as you

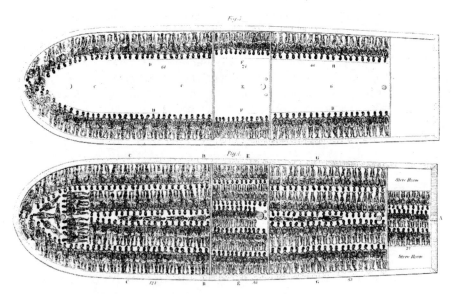

The Atlantic passage to the Americas aboard slave ships resulted in the deaths of thousands of slaves crammed as they were into the putrid holds. This diagram of the loading plan for the slave ship, *The Brookes*, testifies to the nightmare of the "middle passage." *(Photographs and Prints Division, Schomburg Center for Research in Black Culture, the New York Public Library, Astor, Lennox, and Tilder Foundations)*

would men should do unto you? Is it not enough that we are torn from our country and friends to toil for your luxury and lust of gain? Must every tender feeling be likewise sacrificed to your avarice? Are the dearest friends and relations, now rendered more dear by their separation from their kindred, still to be parted from each other, and thus preventing from cheering the gloom of slavery with the small comfort of being together, and mingling their sufferings and sorrows? Why are parents to love their children, brothers their sisters, or husbands their wives? Surely this is a new refinement in cruelty, which, while it has no advantage to atone for it, thus aggravates distress, and adds fresh horrors even to the wretchedness of slavery.

Abolition and Africa:
"One Universal Den of Desolation, Misery, and Crime"
THOMAS BUXTON

The antislavery movement gathered momentum in eighteenth century Britain, France, and the United States, as religious organizations and some political leaders demanded the abolition of what was regarded as a colonial evil. In 1807, Britain finally took the step of outlawing the trade and ending slavery within its colonies. The United States followed suit by 1808 with a ban against the further importation of slaves. For many abolitionists, it was not enough to argue simply that the slave trade was immoral. They employed other economic justifications as well.

In the following selection, Thomas Buxton (1786–1845), a brewer and leading abolitionist, sought to convince his British countrymen that Africa represented a great investment

"Abolition and Africa" is from Thomas Fowell Buxton, *The African Slave Trade and Its Remedy* (London, 1840), pp. 264–269.

opportunity. He reasoned that if Britain developed the substantial natural resources of Africa, then the slave trade would die on its own accord. Buxton argued that businessmen would "gain by selling the productive labor of the people rather than the people themselves."

But what is the true remedy? It cannot be too deeply engraved upon the minds of British statesmen, that it is beyond our power to rescue Africa, if the burden is to fall wholly and permanently on ourselves. It is not the partial aid, lent by a distant nation, but the natural and healthy exercise of her own energies, which will ensure success. We cannot *create* a remedy; but, if it be true that this remedy already exists, and that nothing is wanting but its right application—if Africa possesses within herself vast, though as yet undeveloped resources—we may be competent to achieve the much less onerous task of calling forth her powers, and enabling her to stand alone. . . .

Our system hitherto has been to obtain the cooperation of European powers, while we have paid very little attention to what might be done in Africa itself, for the suppression of the Slave Trade. Our efforts in that direction have been few, faint, and limited to isolated spots, and those by no means well chosen. . . . If, instead of our expensive and fruitless negotiations with Portugal, we had been, during the last twenty years, engaged in extending our intercourse with the nations of Africa, unfolding to them the capabilities of her soil, and the inexhaustible store of wealth which human labor might derive from its cultivation, and convincing them that the Slave Trade alone debars them from enjoying a vastly more affluent supply of our valuable commodities, and if we had leagued ourselves with them to suppress that baneful traffic, which is their enemy even more than it is ours, there is reason to believe that Africa would not have been what Africa is, in spite of all our exertions—one universal den of desolation, misery, and crime.

Why do I despair of winning the hearty cooperation of those European powers who now encourage or connive at the Slave Trade? I answer, because we have no sufficient bribe to offer. The secret of their resistance is the 180 per cent profit which attaches to the Slave Trade. This is a temptation which we cannot outbid. It has

been, and it will be, the source of their persevering disregard of the claims of humanity, and of their contempt for the engagements, however solemn, which they have contracted with us.

But why do I entertain a confident persuasion that we may obtain the cordial concurrence of the African powers? Because the Slave Trade is not their gain, but their loss. It is their ruin, because it is capable of demonstration, that, but for the Slave Trade, the other trade of Africa would be increased fifty or a hundred-fold. . . .

If it be true that Africa would be enriched, and that her population would enjoy in multiplied abundance, those commodities, for the acquisition of which we now incur such intense misery, the one needful thing, in order to induce them to unite with us in repressing the Slave Trade, is to convince them that they will gain by selling the productive labor of the people, instead of the people themselves. . . .

Legitimate commerce would put down the Slave Trade, by demonstrating the superior value of man as a laborer on the soil, to man as an object of merchandise; and if conducted on wise and equitable principles, might be the precursor, or rather the attendant, of civilization, peace, and Christianity, to the unenlightened, warlike, and heathen tribes who now so fearfully prey on each other, to supply the slave-markets of the New World. In this view of the subject, the merchant, the philanthropist, the patriot, and the Christian, may unite; and should the government of this country lend its powerful influence in organizing a commercial system of just, liberal, and comprehensive principles—guarding the rights of the native on the one hand, and securing protection to the honest trader on the other—a blow would be struck at the nefarious traffic in human beings, from which it could not recover; and the richest blessings would be conferred on Africa, so long desolated and degraded by its intercourse with the basest and most iniquitous part of mankind.

CHRONOLOGY: The Linking of Transatlantic Economies

1394–1468	Reign of Portuguese Prince Henry the Navigator, who organized and sanctioned Portuguese exploration on the coasts of Africa and India.
1478–1492	Florence ruled by Lorenzo d'Medici, called "The Magnificent." Florence at height of political and artistic influence.
1487	Bartholomew Dias opens spice routes to the East.
1492	Columbus' first voyage to the eastern Bahamas in search of a route to India.
1498	Vasco da Gama trades on Malabar coast of India.
1500	The Portuguese arrive in Brazil.
1517	Protestant reformer Martin Luther posts Ninety-five Theses on Wittenberg church door in hopes of engaging clerical authorities in debate.
1519–1521	Hernando Cortés lands on the coast of Mexico and brutally defeats Aztec forces.
1526	Afonso I, King of Kongo, writes to Portuguese King Joao III requesting him to condemn slavery.
1531–1533	Francisco Pizarro conquers Incas in Peru.
1558–1603	Reign of Queen Elizabeth of England, last Tudor monarch.
1584	Colonization of North America proposed to Elizabeth I by Richard Hakluyt and Sir Walter Raleigh.
1585	Silver mines of Potosi, Bolivia, bring extraordinary wealth to Spain.
1588	King Philip II launches Spanish Armada against England.
1607	English settlement of Jamestown.
1608	Samuel de Champlain founds Quebec.
1619	First African slaves brought to British North America.
1620	Pilgrims land at Plymouth.
1624	Dutch colony New Netherland founded.
1628–1630	Puritans establish Massachusetts Bay Colony near Boston.
1643–1715	Reign of French King Louis XIV.
1650	Transatlantic slave trade surpasses in volume the older oriental slave trade.
1673	Exploration of the Mississippi River by Jacques Marquette and Louis Joliet.
1700–1800	Over six million slaves imported from Africa to the Americas.
1754–1763	French and Indian War in America.
1769	Father Junipero Serra begins establishment of California missions.

1776	Adam Smith publishes *The Wealth of Nations*.
1807	Slavery abolished in British domains.
1808	Importation of slaves to the United States outlawed.
1865	Slavery abolished in the United States (13th Amendment to the Constitution).
1874–1928	Indigenous African slavery abolished.
1888	Slavery abolished in Brazil.

STUDY QUESTIONS

1. Discuss the ideas of Thomas Hobbes contained in the excerpt entitled *Leviathan*. What is his view of human nature, and how does he justify absolute monarchy? Be specific in your assessment. How does Hobbes's *Leviathan* reflect the uncertainty of the time?
2. Louis XIV was a divine-right monarch. What does this mean, and how did Louis use religion to strengthen his political position in the state? How compelling in support of absolutism are the arguments of Jean Domat on "The Ideal Absolute State"? What are the responsibilities of the king and the political advantages of absolute rule? Do the criticisms of Pierre Jurieu in "The Sighs of Enslaved France" seem valid to you? Why should a historian be somewhat careful in the judgments drawn from this evidence?
3. How does William Bradford's account of the Pilgrim landing at Plymouth reflect the dangers of colonization? What were his primary concerns and how did religious faith sustain these early settlers?
4. Carefully read the account of David Pieterzen de Vries entitled "Murdered in Cold Blood." What were the motives for slaughter and what did the perpetrators hope to gain? Why was it more important for the Europeans to dominate the Native Americans than to coexist with them?
5. What are the primary tenets of mercantilism as noted by Sir William Keith in the selection entitled "The Maxim of All Polite Nations"? As the ruler of a state, would you find his arguments compelling? Why might mercantilism develop naturally in response to the European competition for empire in the Americas and in the East? How do the mercantilist arguments differ from those of Adam Smith as expounded in the selection entitled "The Wealth of Nations"? Do you find his view of human nature and self-interest to be persuasive? According to Smith, what are the primary ingredients of success in the world? How do you define the principle of the "invisible hand"?
6. What are the most memorable sections of Samuel Crowther's account of his capture? Who enslaved him and why? How does Crowther's experience compare with that of others described in the 1797 selection on the slave system by Mungo Park?
7. Compare Mungo Park's account of the transport of slaves from the interior of Africa to the Gold Coast with Olaudah Equiano's account of the transatlantic passage from Africa to Barbados. What were some of the common fears of slaves?
8. What was the attitude of Captain Thomas Phillips, the slave ship master, toward his cargo? He was frustrated that those who ran the slave trade "endured twice the misery" as other seekers of gold. Why was that?

9. According to Olaudah Equiano, how was the slave auction conducted? Analyze the last paragraph of this selection. What were some of the tragedies and hypocrisies concerning the slave trade that Equiano emphasized?
10. What is the argument of abolitionist Thomas Buxton? Do you see his point? Which is the more effective argument for the abolition of slavery: It is a regressive system of labor that stifles other economic possibilities; or, it is a moral affront to humanity? Why did the slave trade die? Why did it take so long to end slavery in parts of Africa itself?

2

Enlightenment and Revolution: "Man Is Born Free and Everywhere He Is in Chains"

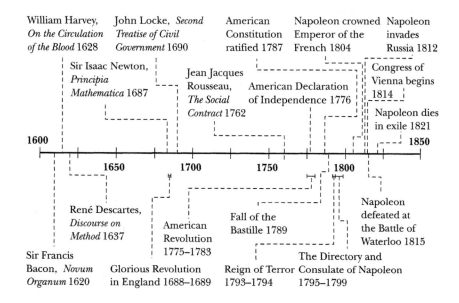

William Harvey, *On the Circulation of the Blood* 1628

John Locke, *Second Treatise of Civil Government* 1690

American Constitution ratified 1787

Napoleon crowned Emperor of the French 1804

Napoleon invades Russia 1812

Sir Isaac Newton, *Principia Mathematica* 1687

Jean Jacques Rousseau, *The Social Contract* 1762

American Declaration of Independence 1776

Congress of Vienna begins 1814

Napoleon dies in exile 1821

1600

1650

1700

1750

1800

1850

René Descartes, *Discourse on Method* 1637

American Revolution 1775–1783

Fall of the Bastille 1789

Napoleon defeated at the Battle of Waterloo 1815

Sir Francis Bacon, *Novum Organum* 1620

Glorious Revolution in England 1688–1689

Reign of Terror 1793–1794

The Directory and Consulate of Napoleon 1795–1799

CHAPTER THEMES

- *Systems of Government:* Did the French Revolution result in a democratic system of government for France or in the tyranny of Napoleon? How easily can the process of democracy degenerate into extremism? Most importantly, is freedom just a state of mind?

- **Revolution:**   To what extent does revolution depend on a fortuitous blend of popular anger and resentment, philosophical ideas, and fanatical leadership? Without the ideas of Locke, Rousseau, and other thinkers of the Enlightenment, would the American or French Revolutions have succeeded? Are the political, social, and economic elements of all revolutions interchangeable? Can one predict when a revolution will occur?

- **Imperialism:**   Many eighteenth-century French statesmen believed that it was important to export the ideals of the French Revolution through war and imperialism. Is this a valid goal? Can one impose the ideals of democracy on other people? How important is foreign war to the success of a domestic revolution?

- **Church/State Relationships:**   How did the leaders of the French Revolution suppress the Catholic Church and then use religion to their advantage? Does a revolution produce its own pantheon of gods that is syncretized with the political leadership, thus rendering a church/state relationship unnecessary? To what extent were Napoleon and George Washington spiritual leaders?

- **Propaganda:**   Was Napoleon's rise from soldier to emperor primarily the result of his military ability, his luck, or the cultivation of his image? Does one gain power through military or political ability and maintain power through creation of belief? Did the painter Jacques-Louis David actually create the image of Napoleon for posterity? Was it real?

- **Beliefs and Spirituality:**   The advancements of Scientific Revolution were the result of a spirit of rational inquiry and confidence in the ability of human beings to understand and improve their world. Do the demands of science necessarily preclude the validity of religion? Can science and religion coexist with mutual respect and even admiration?

- **Historical Change and Transition:**   Why do certain eras of history seem to explode with creativity and intellectual risk while others stagnate? What do the Scientific Revolution and the Enlightenment have in common with the spirit of fifth-century Athens or the Renaissance era? How important is the "hero" in history? Did Robespierre and Napoleon "create" and control the French Revolution? Or was it created by social and economic forces? Must every revolution go through a violent phase that devours its leaders before another "hero" arrives to create stability? Is history thus a contest between the forces of revolution and reaction?

- **The Big Picture:**   Why must one "dare to know"? Does intellectual inquiry require risk and even courage, or are these matters confined to political and military concerns? Is human progress more dependent on the mind than on the sword?

SECTION I: THE INTELLECTUAL FRAMEWORK

When the great eighteenth-century thinker Immanuel Kant challenged his contemporaries to "Dare to Know!" he was also voicing a classic intellectual defiance of authority. The origin of the phrase can be traced to the Roman poet Horace, but nearly every era has possessed those individuals who are not satisfied with maintaining adherence to the "established doctrine" as defined by those in positions of authority. One must be bold in seeking knowledge, for there are many impediments to its attainment. Ideas have power. If successfully transmitted and accepted by the general population, they threaten the status quo, whatever its nature. This makes the pursuit of ideas a risky business that requires an intangible confidence, a willingness to gamble on the potential of an uncertain future. Curiosity and determination, therefore, coupled with a measure of defiance, are the essential components of progress.

Just as the individual in our modern society struggles to define and seek personal knowledge in order to make rational judgments independent of advertisers, politicians, and television preachers, so too did individuals in the seventeenth and eighteenth centuries struggle against similar constraints imposed on them by secular and spiritual institutions. Despite the condemnation of the Catholic Church and the intimidation of the Inquisition, people gradually changed the way they viewed the world around them. The long religious wars between Catholics and Protestants had ended by 1648, leaving people disillusioned and repulsed. Their belief had been shaken by the mindless fighting of the Thirty Years' War. Instead, many invested their confidence in a new association between Protestantism and monarchy. The compatibility between the Calvinists and commerce allowed the developing middle class to seek godly profit and at the same time build the economic foundations of a strong, centralized state. Contemporary with these political and economic developments was the rising influence of philosophers and writers whose primary concern lay within the realm of science and letters. With the aid of hindsight that only history can afford, we can now ascertain that most of the intellectual, political, economic, and social characteristics associated with the modern world came into being during the seventeenth and eighteenth centuries.

The human experience in Europe was indeed transformed. In the salons of Paris, in the coffee houses of London, the talk was of machines and the heavens, of natural laws and moral responsibility, of education and the purpose of religion. The ideals of reform captured the imagination and directed the energy of many writers, who exported great advancements in science and political thought throughout the world.

In the interest of understanding more fully the broad dimensions of this complex period, this section has been divided into two parts: the Scientific Revolution of the sixteenth and seventeenth centuries, and the Enlightenment of the eighteenth century. Although the study of ideas does not so easily lend itself to chronological arrangement as does political history, it is still possible to see intellectual development over time. The Enlightenment movement drew confidence from the scientific worldview that had developed as a result of the efforts and sacrifices of the pioneers of modern science.

Juxtaposed with the chaos of religious warfare and its attendant human destruction during the seventeenth century was an intellectual attempt to foster progress in the realm of science. Sweeping changes took place in humanity's conception of the universe and of one's place in it. Although the movement has been called the Scientific Revolution, the changes were not rapid, nor did they involve large numbers of people. On the contrary, the revolution evolved slowly, through experimentation, often in makeshift laboratories. Yet great thinkers such as Sir Isaac Newton, René Descartes, and Francis Bacon attempted to discover the physical and natural laws of the universe and to organize and criticize that diverse body of knowledge. Thus did Descartes champion the principles of deduction and invent analytical geometry; so too did Newton seek to explain motion in the universe through observation, experimentation, and induction. Others, like John Locke, even endeavored to explain human relationships through such rational thought.

The eighteenth century has been called the Age of Reason, or the Enlightenment. The writers and thinkers of this time, following precedents set in the preceding century, were convinced that natural laws governed the universe and that a human, being essentially a rational creature, could further discover and apply those laws in the world. These intellectuals, called *philosophes,* examined and challenged the economic theories and political and religious assumptions of the day. The *philosophes* were diverse in their thought and often contended among themselves, but they were united by the conviction that one had natural rights (defined by political philosopher John Locke as life, liberty, and property) and that one must control one's own destiny for the sole purpose of a better life on earth. Thus the political divine-right absolutism of King Louis XIV (1643–1715), although providing security, could not be tolerated by many *philosophes* because it curtailed individual liberty. Similarly, the *philosophes* were generally opposed to the accepted economic theory of mercantilism, which sought complete government control of the national economy and especially promoted the establishment of foreign trading monopolies. The production and distribution of goods in colonial markets were therefore regulated for the benefit of the mother country. The theory of capitalism was born as a reaction to this strict economic regulation by the state. Adam Smith, in his treatise *The Wealth of Nations* (1776), argued that such a rigid monopolistic policy restricted individual initiative and the natural pursuit of profit. In spiritual matters as well, the *philosophes* regarded religion, especially Christianity, as fantasy that drew humanity away from the rational world into a realm of hope and belief in a nonexistent life beyond. The spiritual world was not subject to reason or proof and therefore drew scorn from the *philosophes.* Indeed, they contended that organized religion sought to control thought and was therefore anathema to true intellectual freedom.

But the rationalists of the Enlightenment were also adamant that knowledge must have practical purpose and inquiry must yield useful knowledge. Perhaps the best-known and most influential *philosophe* of them all, Voltaire, exclaimed: "What light has burst over Europe within the last few years! It is the light of common sense." Reason was synonymous with common sense. To the intellectuals of the time, anyone who could rid the mind of the chains of thought and social constraints established by the political and religious institutions of the day could possess reason. Yet there is a certain naïveté in this relationship between reason and common sense that also characterized the *philosophes.* This naïveté appears most clearly in their conception of "progress." They professed a profound faith in the future, and some even predicted a united era of peace and prosperity by the dawn of the twenty-first century. When one compares George Orwell's dire predictions in his novel *1984,* the contrast between the cockiness of the Age of Reason and the brutal realities of the twentieth century is staggering. The *philosophes* had none of the fear and distrust of human nature and technology that has been reflected in our experience with poisonous gas and nuclear destruction. For the enlightened thinker, education in the simple laws of nature, technological progress, and increased production could only bring increased happiness. And for the eighteenth century, that was enough. Humankind was breaking its medieval chains, discarding archaic attitudes, and taking the risks requisite of a new era where religion was but a personal choice, and monarchs seemingly embodied Plato's ideal of philosopher- kings. It was therefore reasonable to think that happiness was in the offing.

This section introduces some of the most important personalities, ideas, and attitudes of this remarkable period. In so many ways, by "daring to know," the scientists and philosophers of the seventeenth and eighteenth centuries picked up the gauntlet laid down by the thinkers of the Renaissance and provided the intellectual challenge for future generations.

The Scientific Revolution

He who desires to have understanding must be free in mind.

—*Alcinous*

All nature and nature's law lay hid in night / God said let Newton be and all was light.

—*Alexander Pope*

The real and legitimate goal of the sciences, is the endowment of human life with new inventions and riches.

—*Francis Bacon*

Science has done more for the development of western civilization in one hundred years than Christianity has done in eighteen hundred years.

—*John Burroughs*

Science and the Church

One of the most important and fundamental areas of investigation during the Scientific Revolution was astronomy. For centuries, humans had subscribed to a geocentric theory that placed earth at the center of the universe with all the planets orbiting around it. This theory, ascribed to the Egyptian astronomer Ptolemy (fl. 150 C.E.) and supported by Aristotelian physics, maintained that the earth had to be the center of the universe because of its heaviness and that the stars and other planets existed in surrounding crystalline spheres. Beyond these crystalline spheres lay the realm of God and the angels. This view was supported by the Catholic Church, which saw humanity as the central focus of God's creation and therefore at the epicenter of all existence. Biblical support for the geocentric theory included Psalm 104: "Thou didst set the earth on its foundation, so that it should never be shaken." Still, there were mathematical problems associated with this theory. For one, it was difficult to explain the motion of the planets, which seemed to be moving in noncircular patterns around the earth. At times the planets actually appeared to be going backward. This was explained by epicycles. Ptolemy maintained that planets make a second revolution in an orbit tangent to the first. It was therefore difficult to predict the location of a planet at any given time. A Polish astronomer named Nicolaus Copernicus (1473–1543) attempted to eliminate many of the mathematical inconsistencies by proposing that the sun, not the earth, was the center of the universe. In most other ways, including the acceptance of epicycles and the circular orbit of planets, Copernicus' system was still Ptolemaic. Yet Copernicus freed scientists from a rigid conception of cosmic structure and in essence proposed the empirical evidence of mathematics as the cornerstone of scientific thought.

The first selection is the simple statement by Copernicus proposing the heliocentric theory; it is excerpted from a letter entitled Commentariolus, *written sometime after 1520. In 1543, Copernicus published* On the Revolutions of the Heavenly Spheres. *The second excerpt is from the preface of that work and was addressed to Pope Paul III. In it, Copernicus explains why he questioned the geocentric theory.*

The Heliocentric Statement (ca. 1520)

NICOLAUS COPERNICUS

What appears to us as motions of the sun arise not from its motion but from the motion of the earth and our sphere, with which we revolve about the sun like any other planet. The earth has, then, more than one motion.

On the Movement of the Earth (1543)

NICOLAUS COPERNICUS

I may well presume, most Holy Father, that certain people, as soon as they hear that in this book about the Revolutions of the Spheres of the Universe I ascribe movement to the earthly globe, will cry out that, holding such views, I should at once be hissed off the stage. . . .

So I should like your Holiness to know that I was induced to think of a method of computing the motions of the spheres by nothing else than the knowledge that the mathematicians [who had previously considered the problem] are inconsistent in these investigations.

For, first, the mathematicians are so unsure of the movements of the Sun and Moon that

From *Three Copernican Treatises* by Edward Rosen, translator, copyright © 1939 Columbia University Press, p. 58. Reprinted with the permission of the publisher.

"On the Movement of the Earth" is from Copernicus, *De Revolutionibus Orbium Caelestium* (1543), trans. John F. Dobson and Selig Brodetsky, published in *Occasional Notes of the Royal Astronomical Society*, vol. 2, no. 1 (London: Royal Astronomical Society, 1947), excerpts from the preface and Book I.

they cannot even explain or observe the constant length of the seasonal year. Secondly, in determining the motions of these and of the other five planets, they use neither the same principles and hypotheses nor the same demonstrations of the apparent motions and revolutions. . . . Nor have they been able thereby to discern or deduce the principal thing—namely the shape of the Universe and the unchangeable symmetry of its parts. . . .

I pondered long upon this uncertainty of mathematical tradition in establishing the motions of the system of the spheres. At last I began to chafe that philosophers could by no means agree on any one certain theory of the mechanism of the Universe, wrought for us by a supremely good and orderly Creator. . . . I therefore took pains to read again the works of all the philosophers on whom I could lay hand to seek out whether any of them had even supposed that the motions of the spheres were other than those demanded by the [Ptolemaic] mathematical schools. I found first in Cicero that Hicetas [of Syracuse, fifth century B.C.E.] had realized that the Earth moved. Afterwards I found in Plutarch that certain others had held the like opinion. . . .

Thus assuming motions, which in my work I ascribe to the Earth, by long and frequent observations I have at last discovered that, if the motions of the rest of the planets be brought into relation with the circulation of the Earth and be reckoned in proportion to the circles of each planet, . . . the orders and magnitudes of all stars and spheres, nay the heavens themselves, become so bound together that nothing in any part thereof could be moved from its place without producing confusion of all the other parts of the Universe as a whole.

Science and the Bible:
Letter to the Grand Duchess of Tuscany (1615)

GALILEO GALILEI

After Copernicus, the quest for rational truth was continued by Tycho Brahe, who compiled accurate tables of astronomical observations, and Johannes Kepler, who analyzed these tables and posited the elliptical orbits of planets. And yet this progress in scientific thought was to encounter various roadblocks beyond the difficulties of gathering and interpreting data. For the Catholic Church, the question was not one of empirical evidence and rational inquiry but rather of faith and authority.

During the sixteenth century, the church established an organization that was designed to maintain purity of doctrine and authority over the faithful. The Inquisition, as it came to be called, was administered by Dominican friars, whose responsibilities had always involved the explanation of doctrine to those who had strayed from the path. Now they were actively to seek out those whose deeds and ideas seemed to contradict established Catholic doctrine. The Inquisition became a vehicle for reform through coercion, with allegiance being obtained through argument, intimidation, and torture, if necessary.

During the seventeenth century, the church found itself embroiled in events that again threatened its established authority. The attack was now centered on the new scientific theories that challenged Catholic doctrine and were being pursued and advocated independently of church control. At the forefront of the controversy was one of the most influential scientists in history—Galileo Galilei.

Galileo was born in Pisa, Italy, in the year of Shakespeare's birth and Michelangelo's death (1564). He had much in common with these great men since he played the lute, painted, wrote poetry, and enjoyed polemics and satire. In 1592, Galileo was appointed professor of mathematics at the University of Padua, and he remained in this position for eighteen years, supporting a mistress, two daughters, a son, and a widowed mother on a small income supplemented by tutoring. During this time, Galileo came to doubt the teachings of Aristotle and other ancient philosophers and scientists, which were accepted by the church as being consistent with Catholic doctrine. Galileo had admired the mathematical aesthetics of the Copernican theory and became even more confirmed in his support of this thesis after viewing the heavens through a new instrument that he had recently improved—the telescope. Galileo considered himself a devout and obedient son of the church, but he believed that the Bible conveyed truth figuratively as well as literally. He argued that scientific facts must first be discovered, then interpreted according to observation. As Galileo noted, "The Bible shows the way to go to Heaven, not the way the heavens go." No one, not even the pope, could alter the facts.

Galileo's response to charges that the ideas of Copernicus contradicted the Bible is contained in the following letter to the Grand Duchess of Tuscany in 1615. Nevertheless, the next year the heliocentric theory was condemned as formally heretical. For his impertinence and continuing adherence to the Copernican theory, Galileo was twice ordered to appear before the Inquisition, though he was a frail man of 70. Under threat of torture, he finally recanted his position. Only in 1992 was Galileo formally absolved from his sin by Pope John Paul II.

From *Discoveries and Opinions of Galileo* by Galileo Galilei, translated by Stillman Drake, copyright © 1957 by Stillman Drake, pp. 175, 177–179, 181–184, 189–190, 194–195. Used by permission of Doubleday, a division of Random House, Inc.

Some years ago, as Your Serene Highness well knows, I discovered in the heavens many things that had not been seen before our own age. The novelty of these things, as well as some consequences which followed from them in contradiction to the physical notions commonly held among academic philosophers, stirred up against me no small number of professors—as if I had placed these things in the sky with my own hands in order to upset nature and overturn the sciences. . . .

Showing a greater fondness for their own opinions than for truth, they sought to deny and disprove the new things which, if they had cared to look for themselves, their own senses would have demonstrated to them. To this end they hurled various charges and published numerous writings filled with vain arguments, and they made the grave mistake of sprinkling these with passages taken from places in the Bible which they had failed to understand properly, and which were ill suited to their purposes. . . .

Persisting in their original resolve to destroy me and everything mine by any means they can think of, these men . . . know that as to the arrangement of the parts of the universe, I hold the sun to be situated motionless in the center of the revolution of the celestial orbs while the earth rotates on its axis and revolves about the sun. They know also that I support this position not only by refuting the arguments of Ptolemy and Aristotle, but by producing many counter-arguments; in particular, some which relate to physical effects whose causes can perhaps be assigned in no other way. In addition there are astronomical arguments derived from many things in my new celestial discoveries that plainly confute the Ptolemaic system while admirably agreeing with and confirming the contrary hypothesis. . . . These men have resolved to fabricate a shield for their fallacies out of the mantle of pretended religion and the authority of the Bible. These they apply, with little judgment, to the refutation of arguments that they do not understand and have not even listened to.

First they have endeavored to spread the opinion that such propositions in general are contrary to the Bible and are consequently damnable and heretical. . . . Next, becoming bolder, and hoping (though vainly) that this seed which first took root in their hypocritical minds would send out branches and ascend to heaven, they began scattering rumors among the people that before long this doctrine would be condemned by the supreme authority. . . .

They go about invoking the Bible, which they would have minister to their deceitful purposes. Contrary to the sense of the Bible and the intention of the holy Fathers, if I am not mistaken, they would extend such authorities until even in purely physical matters—where faith is not involved—they would have us altogether abandon reason and the evidence of our senses in favor of some biblical passage, though under the surface meaning of its words this passage may contain a different sense. . . .

I think in the first place that it is very pious to say and prudent to affirm that the holy Bible can never speak untruth—whenever its true meaning is understood. But I believe nobody will deny that it is often very abstruse, and may say things which are quite different from what its bare words signify. . . .

This being granted, I think that in discussion of physical problems we ought to begin not from the authority of scriptural passages, but from sense-experiences and necessary demonstrations; for the holy Bible and the phenomena of nature proceed alike from the divine Word, the former as the dictate of the Holy Ghost and the latter as the observant executrix of God's commands. It is necessary for the Bible, in order to be accommodated to the understanding of every man, to speak many things which appear to differ from the absolute truth so far as the bare meaning of the words is concerned. But Nature, on the other hand, is inexorable and immutable; she never transgresses the laws imposed upon her, or cares a whit whether her abstruse reasons and methods of operation are understandable to men. For that reason it appears that nothing physical which sense-experience sets before our eyes, or which necessary demonstrations prove to us, ought to be called in question (much less condemned) upon the testimony of biblical passages which may have some different meaning beneath their words. For the Bible is not chained in every expression to conditions as strict as those which govern all physical effects; nor is God any less excellently revealed in Nature's actions than in the sacred statements of the Bible. . . .

From this I do not mean to infer that we need not have an extraordinary esteem for the passages of holy Scripture. On the contrary, having arrived at any certainties in physics, we ought to utilize these as the most appropriate aids in the true exposition of the Bible and in the investigation of those meanings which are necessarily contained therein for these must be concordant with demonstrated truths. I should judge the authority of the Bible was designed to persuade men of those articles and propositions which, surpassing all human reasoning, could not be made credible by science, or by any other means than through the very mouth of the Holy Spirit. . . .

But I do not feel obliged to believe that the same God who had endowed us with senses, reason, and intellect has intended to forgo their use and by some other means to give us knowledge which we can attain by them.

The New Scientific Method

"I Think, Therefore I Am": Discourse on Method (1637)

RENÉ DESCARTES

René Descartes was born in 1596 in western France but lived primarily in Holland for the last twenty years of his life. He attended Jesuit schools and graduated in law from the university in Poitiers. He was not attracted to a legal career, however, and became a soldier in the German wars of the time. It was while he was billeted in a German town that he had an intellectual revelation akin, as he later maintained, to a religious conversion. He had a vision of the great potential for progress, if mathematical method were to be applied to all fields of knowledge. He thus pursued a career devoted to the propagation of a strict method, best exemplified by his invention of analytical geometry. Descartes believed that human beings were endowed by God with the ability to reason and that God served as the guarantor of the correctness of clear ideas. The material world could thus be understood through adherence to mathematical laws and methods of inquiry. Descartes championed the process of deductive reasoning whereby specific information could be logically deduced from general information. His method was influential well into the eighteenth century, when it was supplanted by the method of scientific induction, whereby generalizations could be drawn from the observation of specific data.

The following selection is drawn from Descartes' most famous work, Discourse on the Method of Rightly Conducting the Reason *(1636).*

As a multitude of laws often furnishes excuses for vice, so that a state is much better governed when it has but few, and those few strictly observed, so in place of the great number of precepts of which logic is composed, I believed that I should find the following four sufficient, provided that I made a firm and constant resolve not once to omit to observe them.

The first was, never to accept anything as true when I did not recognize it clearly to be so, that is to say, to carefully avoid precipitation and prejudice, and to include in my opinions nothing beyond that which should present itself so clearly and so distinctly to my mind that I might have no occasion to doubt it.

"'I Think, Therefore I Am'" is from René Descartes, T*he Discourse on Method and Metaphysical Meditations,* trans. G. B. Rawlings (London: Walter Scott, 1901), pp. 32–35, 60–61, 75–76.

The second was, to divide each of the difficulties which I should examine into as many parts as were possible, and as should be required for its better solution.

The third was, to conduct my thoughts in order, by beginning with the simplest objects, and those most easy to know, so as to mount little by little, as if by steps, to the most complex knowledge, and even assuming an order among those which do not naturally precede one another.

And the last was, to make everywhere enumerations so complete, and reviews so wide, that I should be sure of omitting nothing. . . .

I had long remarked that, in conduct, it is sometimes necessary to follow opinions known to be very uncertain, just as if they were indisputable, as has been said above; but then, because I desired to devote myself only to the research of truth, I thought it necessary to do exactly the contrary, and reject as absolutely false all in which I could conceive the least doubt, in order to see if afterwards there did not remain in my belief something which was entirely indisputable. Thus, because our senses sometimes deceive us, I wanted to suppose that nothing is such as they make us imagine it; and because some men err in reasoning . . . and judging that I was as liable to fail as any other, I rejected as false all the reasons which I had formerly accepted as [true]; . . . I resolved that everything which had ever entered into my mind was no more true than the illusions of my dreams. But immediately afterwards I observed that while I thus desired everything to be false, I, who thought, must of necessity [exist]; and remarking that this truth, I think, therefore I am, was so firm and so assured that all the most extravagant suppositions of the skeptics were unable to shake it, I judged that I could unhesitatingly accept it as the first principle of the philosophy I was seeking. . . .

After this, and reflecting upon the fact that I doubted, and that in consequence my being was not quite perfect (for I saw clearly that to know was a greater perfection than to doubt), I [wondered where] I had learned to think of something more perfect than I; and I knew for certain that it must be from some nature which was in reality more perfect. [And I clearly recognized that] this idea . . . had been put in me by a nature truly more perfect than I, which had in itself all perfections of which I could have any idea; that is, to explain myself in one word, God. . . .

Finally, whether awake or asleep, we ought never to allow ourselves to be persuaded of the truth of anything unless on the evidence of our Reason. And it must be noted that I say of our Reason, and not of our imagination or of our senses: thus, for example, although we very clearly see the sun, we ought not therefore to determine that it is only of the size which our sense of sight presents; and we may very distinctly imagine the head of a lion joined to the body of a goat, without being therefore shut up to the conclusion that a chimaera exists; for it is not a dictate of Reason that what we thus see or imagine is in reality existent; but it plainly tells us that all our ideas or notions contain in them some truth; for otherwise it could not be that God, who is wholly perfect and veracious, should have placed them in us.

"I Learn and Teach from the Fabric of Nature": On the Circulation of the Blood (1628)

WILLIAM HARVEY

William Harvey has been termed the father of modern physiology. He was heir to a legacy of interest in the internal workings of the human body that had been most recently in evidence among artists during the Renaissance. But whereas Michelangelo studied the body to better represent the human form, Harvey sought to discover the internal workings on their own scientific merit. In

"'I Learn and Teach from the Fabric of Nature'" is from R. Willis, trans., *The Works of William Harvey* (London: Sydenham Society, 1847), pp. 5–7, 31–32, 45–47.

this, he was more closely akin to the earlier scientific studies of Leonardo da Vinci. Harvey built upon the work of the Greek physician Galen (fl. 150 C.E.), who demonstrated that the arteries carried blood instead of air. Harvey's exacting methods set the pattern of scientific research for generations. In the following selection, which was an address to the Royal College of Physicians in 1628, he gave the results of his methodical dissections and experiments.

As this book alone declares the blood to course and revolve by a new route, very different from the ancient and beaten pathway trodden for so many ages, and illustrated by such a host of learned and distinguished men, I was greatly afraid lest I might be charged with presumption did I lay my work before the public at home, or send it beyond seas for impression, unless I had first proposed its subject to you, had confirmed its conclusions by ocular demonstrations in your presence, had replied to your doubts and objections, and secured the assent and support of our distinguished President. For I was most intimately persuaded, that if I could make good my proposition before you and our College, . . . I had less to fear from others. . . . For true philosophers, who are only eager for truth and knowledge, never regard themselves as already so thoroughly informed, but that they welcome further information from whomsoever and from whencesoever it may come; nor are they so narrow-minded as to imagine any of the arts or sciences transmitted to us by the ancients, in such a state of forwardness or completeness, that nothing is left for the ingenuity and industry of others. . . . Neither do they swear such fealty to their mistress Antiquity, that they openly, and in sight of all, deny and desert their friend Truth. . . .

My dear colleagues . . . I profess both to learn and to teach anatomy, not from books, but from dissections; not from the positions of philosophers, but from the fabric of nature. . . .

From these and other observations of the like kind, I am persuaded it will be found that the motion of the heart is as follows:

First of all, the auricle contracts, and in the course of its contraction throws the blood, (which it contains in ample quantity as the head of the veins, the store-house and cistern of the blood,) into the ventricle, which being filled, the heart raises itself straightway, makes all its fibers tense, contracts the ventricles, and per-

forms a beat, by which beat it immediately sends the blood supplied to it by the auricle into the arteries; the right ventricle sending its charge into the lungs by the vessel which is called *vena arteriosi,* but which, in structure and function, and all things else, is an artery; the left ventricle sending its charge into the aorta, and through this by the arteries to the body at large. . . .

Thus far I have spoken of the passage of the blood from the veins into the arteries, and of the manner in which it is transmitted and distributed by the action of the heart. . . . But what remains to be said upon the quantity and source of the blood which thus passes, is of so novel and unheard-of character, that I not only fear injury to myself from the envy of a few, but I tremble lest I have mankind at large for my enemies. . . . Still, the die is cast, and my trust is in my love of truth, and the candor that inheres in cultivated minds. And when I surveyed my mass of evidence, . . . I revolved in my mind, what might be the quantity of blood which was transmitted, in how short a time its passage might be effected, and the like; . . . I began to think whether there might not be A MOTION, AS IT WERE, IN A CIRCLE. Now this I afterwards found to be true; and I finally saw that the blood, forced by the action of the left ventricle into the arteries, was distributed to the body at large . . . impelled by the right ventricle . . . through the veins, and so round to the left ventricle in the manner already indicated. . . .

The heart, consequently, is the beginning of life; the sun of the microcosm, even as the sun in his turn might well be designated the heart of the world; for it is the heart by whose virtue and pulse the blood is moved, perfected, made apt to nourish, and is preserved from corruption and coagulation; it is the household divinity which, discharging its function, nourishes, cherishes, quickens the whole body, and is indeed the foundation of life, the source of all action.

THE ENLIGHTENMENT

Intellect does not attain its full force unless it attacks power.

—Madame de Staël

Reason is the greatest enemy that faith has. It never comes to the aid of spiritual things,
but . . . struggles against the divine Word, treating with contempt all that emanates from God.

—Martin Luther

I respect faith, but doubt is what gets you an education.

—Wilson Mizner

Thoughts on the Human Condition

The Blank Slate of the Mind:
An Essay Concerning Human Understanding (1690)

JOHN LOCKE

John Locke was one of the most important figures of this period of scientific discovery and reason. He initiated the Age of Enlightenment in England and France, was an inspirer of the U.S. Constitution, and remains a powerful influence on the life and thought of Western civilization. Locke was educated at Oxford, where he was fascinated with experimental science. He became a physician but was particularly attracted to human relationships concerning how people learn, and how they are best governed. Well known in the academic circles of England and France, his political philosophy was to provide a confirmation of the Glorious Revolution of 1688 and a framework for the American and French revolutions of 1776 and 1789.

The following selection from one of his primary works investigates a seminal question debated in the Enlightenment: Are children born with any innate ideas that have been inherited from parents, or are all ideas products of associations within society? This work extended empirical investigation into the realm of the human mind and reveals Locke's inquiring nature and intellectual depth.

It is established opinion among some men, that there are in the understanding certain innate principles; some primary notions, characters, as it were stamped upon the mind of man, which the soul receives in its very first being, and brings into the world with it. It would be sufficient to convince unprejudiced readers of the falseness of this supposition, if I should only show . . . how men, barely by the use of their natural faculties, may attain to all the knowledge they have, without the help of any innate impressions; and may arrive at certainty, without any such original notions or principles. . . .

Let us then suppose the mind to be, as we say, white paper, void of all characters, without any ideas:—How comes it to be furnished? Whence comes it by that vast store which the busy and boundless fancy of man has painted on it with an almost endless variety? Whence has it all the materials of reason and knowledge? To this I answer, in one word, EXPERIENCE. In that all our knowledge is founded; and from that it ultimately

"The Blank Slate of the Mind" is from John Locke, *An Essay Concerning Human Understanding*, ed. A. D. Fraser (Oxford: Clarendon Press, 1894), vol. 1, pp. 37–38, 121–124.

derives itself. Our observation employed either, about external sensible objects, or about the internal operations of our minds perceived and reflected on by ourselves, is that which supplies our understandings with all the materials of thinking. These two are the fountains of knowledge, from whence all the ideas we have, or can naturally have, do spring. . . .

The understanding seems to me not to have the least glimmering of any ideas which it does not receive from [sensation or reflection]. External objects furnish the mind with the ideas of sensible qualities, which are all those different perceptions they produce in us; and the mind furnishes the understanding with ideas of its own operations.

He that attentively considers the state of a child at his first coming into the world, will have little reason to think him stored with plenty of ideas that are to be the matter of his future knowledge. It is by degrees [that] he comes to be furnished with them. . . . But all that are born into the world being surrounded with bodies that perpetually and diversely affect them, variety of ideas, whether care be taken about it or not, are imprinted on the minds of children. Light and colors are busy at hand everywhere when the eye is but open; sounds and some tangible qualities fail not to solicit their proper senses; but yet I think it will be granted easily, that if a child were kept in a place where he never saw any other but black and white till he were a man, he would have no more ideas of scarlet or green than he that from his childhood never tasted an oyster or a pineapple has of those particular relishes. . . .

"The Greatest Happiness of the Greatest Number": On Crimes and Punishments (1764)

CESARE BECCARIA

Cesare Beccaria was the son of a Milanese aristocrat of modest means. He was educated initially at a Jesuit school, an experience that he later described as "fanatical" and stifling to "the development of human feelings." At the age of 26, he became an international celebrity with the publication of his work on criminal law in 1764. Translated into several languages, it enjoyed a remarkable success in France, where it went through seven editions in six months. In it, Beccaria lashed out against the barbarities of the day, including the torture of prisoners in order to induce confession, the corruption of judges, and degrading and brutal punishments. Penalties, he concluded, should be scaled to the offense. Beccaria was the first modern writer to advocate the complete abolition of capital punishment, and his treatise remains the most important and influential volume written on criminal justice.

If we look into history, we shall find that laws, which are, or ought to be, conventions between men in a state of freedom, have been, for the most part the work of the passions of a few, or the consequences of a fortuitous or temporary necessity; not dictated by a cool examiner of human nature, who knew how to collect in one point the actions of a multitude, and had only this end in view, the greatest happiness of the greatest number. . . .

Observe that by justice I understand nothing more than that bond which is necessary to keep the interest of individuals united, without which men would return to their original state of barbarity. All punishments which exceed the necessity of preserving this bond are in their nature unjust. . . .

The end of punishment, therefore, is no other than to prevent the criminal from doing further injury to society, and to prevent others

"'The Greatest Happiness of the Greatest Number'" is from Cesare Beccaria, *An Essay on Crimes and Punishments*, trans. E. D. Ingraham (Philadelphia: H. Nicklin, 1819), pp. xii, 18–19, 47, 59–60, 93–94, 104–105, 148–149.

from committing the like offence. Such punishments, therefore, and such a mode of inflicting them ought to be chosen, as will make the strongest and most lasting impressions on the minds of others, with the least torment to the body of the criminal.

The torture of a criminal during the course of his trial is a cruelty consecrated by custom in most nations. It is used with an intent either to make him confess his crime, or to explain some contradiction into which he had been led during his examination, or discover his accomplices, or for some kind of metaphysical and incomprehensible purgation of infamy, or, finally, in order to discover other crimes of which he is not accused, but of which he may be guilty.

No man can be judged a criminal until he be found guilty; nor can society take from him the public protection until it has been proved that he has violated the conditions on which it was granted. What right, then, but that of power, can authorise the punishment of a citizen so long as there remains any doubt of his guilt? This dilemma is frequent. Either he is guilty, or not guilty. If guilty, he should only suffer the punishment ordained by the laws, and torture becomes useless, as his confession is unnecessary. If he be not guilty, you torture the innocent; for in the eye of the law, every man is innocent whose crime has not been proved. . . .

Crimes are more effectually prevented by the certainty than by the severity of punishment. . . . In proportion as punishments become more cruel, the minds of men, as a fluid rises to the same height with that which surrounds it, grow hardened and insensible; and

the force of the passions still continuing, in the space of an hundred years the wheel [torture device] terrifies no more than formerly the prison. That a punishment may produce the effect required, it is sufficient that the evil it occasions should exceed the good expected from the crime, including in the calculation the certainty of the punishment, and the privation of the expected advantage. All severity beyond this is superfluous, and therefore tyrannical.

The punishment of death is pernicious to society, from the example of barbarity it affords. If the passions, or the necessity of war, have taught men to shed the blood of their fellow creatures, the laws, which are intended to moderate the ferocity of mankind, should not increase it by examples of barbarity, them more horrible as this punishment is usually attended with formal pageantry. Is it not absurd, that the laws, which detest and punish homicide, should, in order to prevent murder, publicly commit murder themselves? . . .

It is better to prevent crimes than to punish them. This is the fundamental principle of good legislation, which is the art of conducting men to the maximum of happiness, and to the minimum of misery, if we may apply this mathematical expression to the good and evil of life. . . .

Would you prevent crimes? Let the laws be clear and simple, let the entire force of the nation be united in their defence, let them be intended rather to favour every individual than any particular classes of men; let the laws be feared, and the laws only. The fear of the laws is salutary, but the fear of men is a fruitful and fatal source of crimes.

What Is Enlightenment? (1784)

IMMANUEL KANT

Immanuel Kant was a German philosopher whose comprehensive and systematic work in the theory of knowledge, ethics, and aesthetics greatly influenced subsequent philosophy. Kant's entire life was spent in Königsberg, where he was educated and served as a popular teacher

Foundations of the Metaphysics of Morals, 2/E, by Kant, (trans. L. W. Beck), © 1990, pp. 83–85, 88. Reprinted by permission of Pearson Education, Inc., Upper Saddle River, NJ.

and lecturer at the local university. In his writings, he hoped to avoid the confusion of earlier thinkers by examining the possibilities and limitations of applied reason. He sought to accept the rationalism of the Enlightenment while still preserving a belief in human freedom, immortality, and the existence of God. In fact, Kant found the world open to pure reason to be quite limited and postulated a sphere of moral reality known only by "practical reason and conscience." Although he hoped to raise philosophy to the level of a science, he believed that all things could not be proved by discursive reasoning—God and eternal life among them.

In the following selection, Kant seeks to define the Enlightenment by empowering the individual to break away from a somnolent dependence toward an active intellectual existence. Only through such personal initiative could one attain true enlightenment.

Enlightenment is man's release from his self-incurred tutelage. Tutelage is man's inability to make use of his understanding without direction from another. Self-incurred is this tutelage when its cause lies not in lack of reason but in lack of resolution and courage to use it without direction from another. Dare to Know! Have courage to use your own reason!—that is the motto of enlightenment.

Laziness and cowardice are the reasons why so great a portion of mankind, after nature has long since discharged them from external direction, nevertheless remains under lifelong tutelage, and why it is so easy for others to set themselves up as their guardians. It is so easy not to be of age. If I have a book which understands for me, a pastor who has a conscience for me, a physician who decides my diet, and so forth, I need not trouble myself. I need not think, if I can only pay—others will readily undertake the irksome work for me.

That the step to competence is held to be very dangerous by the far greater portion of mankind (and by the entire fair sex)—quite apart from its being arduous—is seen to by those guardians who have so kindly assumed superintendence over them. After the guardians have first made their domestic cattle dumb and have made sure that these placid creatures will not dare take a single step without the harness of the cart to which they are confined, the guardians then show them the danger which threatens if they try to go alone. Actually, however, this danger is not so great, for by falling a few times they would finally learn to walk alone. But an example of this failure makes them timid and ordinarily frightens them away from all further trials.

For any single individual to work himself out of the life under tutelage which has become almost his nature is very difficult. He has come to be fond of this state, and he is for the present really incapable of making use of his reason, for no one has ever let him try it out. Statutes and formulas, those mechanical tools of the rational employment or rather misemployment of his natural gifts, are the fetters of an everlasting tutelage. Whoever throws them off makes only an uncertain leap over the narrowest ditch because he is not accustomed to that kind of free motion. Therefore, there are only few who have succeeded by their own exercise of mind both in freeing themselves from incompetence and in achieving a steady pace.

But that the public should enlighten itself is more possible; indeed, if only freedom is granted, enlightenment is almost sure to follow. For there will always be some independent thinkers, even among the established guardians of the great masses, who, after throwing off the yoke of tutelage from their own shoulders, will disseminate the spirit of the rational appreciation of both their own worth and every man's vocation for thinking for himself. . . .

For this enlightenment, however, nothing is required but freedom, and indeed the most harmless among all the things to which this term can properly be applied. It is the freedom to make public use of one's reason at every point. But I hear on all sides, "Do not argue!" The officer says: "Do not argue but drill!" The tax collector: "Do not argue but pay!" The cleric: "Do not argue but believe!" Only one prince in the world [Frederick the Great of Prussia] says, "Argue as much as you will, and about what you will, but obey!" Everywhere there is restriction on freedom...

On Universal Toleration

VOLTAIRE

The Enlightenment is often characterized as an era of empirical reasoning and critical thought, of doubt and skepticism, of individual assertion at the expense of formal control by the state or church. For the most part, this is a fair assessment. God, if he existed, was prone to be antiseptic, the "great clock-winder," who created the universe and then sat back, uninvolved in the lives of his creations. This philosophy, called deism, *generally prevailed among the* philosophes. *It did not deny the existence of God, but it gave virtually no support to organized religion. The deists particularly denounced the mysteries of the Christian religion such as the Trinity and miracles like the Virgin Birth and the Eucharist. Since God was disinterested in the affairs of the world, formal prayers were useless. Deism enabled many of the* philosophes *to effect a reconciliation between a perfect God and an imperfect world.*

Voltaire was the quintessential personality of the Enlightenment. An author of dramas, histories, and scathing satires, his wit and intellectual power dominated the age. Voltaire was an adamant opponent of organized religion, but one of the most enthusiastic advocates of religious toleration and the deist viewpoint. The first selection is from his famous Treatise on Toleration. *In the letter that follows, Voltaire argues for the logic and necessity of a supreme deity. His ideas are generally representative of the enlightened thinkers of the age.*

It does not require any great art or studied elocution to prove that Christians ought to tolerate one another. Nay, I shall go still farther and say that we ought to look upon all men as our brethren. How! Call a Turk, a Jew, and a Siamese, my brother? Yes, doubtless; for are we not all children of the same parent, and the creatures of the same Creator?

But these people hold us in contempt, and call us idolaters! Well, then, I should tell them that they were to blame. And I fancy that I could stagger the headstrong pride of an imam, or a talapoin [religious leaders], were I to address them in the following manner:

"This little globe, which is no more than a point, rolls, together with many other globes, in that immensity of space in which we are all alike confounded. Man, who is an animal, about five feet high, is certainly a very inconsiderable part of the creation; but one of those hardly visible beings says to others of the same kind inhabiting another spot of the globe: Hearken to me, for the God of all these worlds has enlightened me. There are about nine hundred millions of us little insects who inhabit the earth, but my ant-hill is alone cherished by God, who holds all the rest in horror and detestation; those who live with me upon my spot will alone be happy, and all the rest eternally wretched."

They would here stop me short and ask, "What madman could have made so ridiculous a speech?" I should then be obliged to answer them, "It is yourselves."...

O you different worshippers of a God of mercy! If you have cruel hearts, if, while you adore that Deity who has placed the whole of His law in these few words, "Love God and your neighbor," you have loaded that pure and holy law with sophistical and unintelligible disputes, if you have lighted the flames of discord sometimes

"On Universal Toleration," is from Tobias Smollett, ed., *The Works of Voltaire* (London: E. R. DuMont, 1901), vol. 4, pp. 272–273, 275–276, 278. Text modernized by the editor.

for a new word, and at others for a single letter only; if you have annexed eternal punishment to the omission of some few words, or of certain ceremonies which other people cannot comprehend, I must say to you with tears of compassion for mankind: "Transport yourselves with me to that great instant in which all men are to receive judgment from the hand of God, who will then do unto every one according to their works, and with me behold all the dead of past ages appearing in His presence. Are you very sure that our heavenly Father and Creator will say to the wise and virtuous Confucius, to the great legislator Solon, to Pythagoras, Socrates, Plato, the divine Antoninus, the good Trajan, to Titus, the delight of humankind, and to many others who have been the models of humankind: 'Depart from me, wretches! into torments that know neither alleviation nor end; but are, like Himself, everlasting.'"

I think I see you start with horror at these words. . . .

May all men remember that they are brethren! May they alike abhor that tyranny which seeks to subject the freedom of the will, as they do the rapine which tears from the arms of industry the fruits of its peaceful labors! And if the scourge of war is not to be avoided, let us not mutually hate and destroy each other in the midst of peace; but rather make use of the few moments of our existence to join in praising, in a thousand different languages, from one extremity of the world to the other, Thy goodness, O all-merciful Creator, to whom we are indebted for that existence!

"If God Did Not Exist, He Would Have to Be Invented"

VOLTAIRE

To Frederick William, Prince of Prussia:

Monseigneur, the royal family of Prussia has excellent reasons for not wishing the annihilation

"'If God Did Not Exist, He Would Have to Be Invented,'" is from S. G. Tallentyre, trans., *Voltaire in His Letters* (New York: G. P. Putnam's Sons, 1919).

of the soul. It has more right than anyone to immortality.

It is very true that we do not know any too well what the soul is: no one has ever seen it. All that we do know is that the eternal Lord of nature has given us the power of thinking, and of distinguishing virtue. It is not proved that this faculty survives our death: but the contrary is not proved either. It is possible, doubtless, that God has given thought to a particle to which, after we are no more, He will still give the power of thought: there is no inconsistency in this idea.

In the midst of all the doubts which we have discussed for four thousand years in four thousand ways, the safest course is to do nothing against one's conscience. With this secret, we can enjoy life and have nothing to fear from death.

There are some charlatans who admit no doubts. We know nothing of first principles. It is surely very presumptuous to define God, the angels, spirits, and to pretend to know precisely why God made the world, when we do not know why we can move our arms at our pleasure. Doubt is not a pleasant condition, but certainty is an absurd one.

What is most repellent in the System of Nature [by the Baron d'Holbach] . . . is the audacity with which it decides that there is no God, without even having tried to prove the impossibility. There is some eloquence in the book: but much more rant, and no sort of proof. It is a pernicious work, alike for princes and people: "Si Dieu n'existait pas, il faudrait l'inventer." [If God did not exist, he would have to be invented].

But all nature cries aloud that He does exist: that there is a supreme intelligence, an immense power, an admirable order, and everything teaches us our own dependence on it.

From the depth of our profound ignorance, let us do our best: this is what I think, and what I have always thought, amid all the misery and follies inseparable from seventy-seven years of life. . . . I am, with deep respect, Voltaire

Thoughts on Government: The Political Framework

The following selections present a theoretical foundation for the political structure of human society and present justification for the elimination of absolute monarchy. John Locke (1632–1704) was an English political philosopher whose Second Treatise of Civil Government *(1690) later influenced both the French and American revolutions. It is also the first philosophical statement of liberalism, a doctrine that sought the limitation of the arbitrary power of government and the establishment of legal equality, religious toleration, and freedom of the press. The second selection is from* The Social Contract *(1762) by Jean-Jacques Rousseau (1712–1778). Although Rousseau spent much of his life in intimate contact with the* philosophes, *he rejected their attitude that the human being is a rational creature whose confidence in reason would result in liberty and equality. Rousseau advocated the elimination of political despotism and the introduction of a new social order in which only the authority of the "general will" of the governed placed limits on individual freedom. His ideas provided the most inspirational justification for revolutionary action during the eighteenth century.*

Second Treatise of Civil Government (1690)

JOHN LOCKE

Political power, then, I take to be a right of making laws with penalties of death, and consequently all less penalties, for the regulating and preserving of property, and of employing the force of the community, in the execution of such laws, and in the defence of the commonwealth from foreign injury; and all this only for the public good. . . .

Chapter II: Of the State of Nature

To understand political power right, and derive it from its original, we must consider what state all men are naturally in, and that is, a state of perfect freedom to order their actions and dispose of their possessions and persons, as they think fit, within the bounds of the law of nature; without asking leave, or depending upon the will of any other man.

"Second Treatise of Civil Government" is from John Locke, *The Treatises of Government* (London, 1694).

A state also of equality, wherein all the power and jurisdiction is reciprocal, no one having more than another; there being nothing more evident, than that creatures of the same species and rank, promiscuously born to all the same advantages of nature, and the use of the same faculties, should also be equal one amongst another without subordination or subjection; unless the lord and master of them all should, by any manifest declaration of his will, set one above another, and confer on him, by an evident and clear appointment, an undoubted right to dominion and sovereignty. . . .

But though this be a state of liberty, yet it is not a state of license: though man in that state has an uncontrollable liberty to dispose of his person or possessions, yet he has not liberty to destroy himself, or so much as any creature in his possession, but where some nobler use than its bare preservation call for it. The state of nature has a law of nature to govern it, which obliges every one: and reason, which is that law, teaches all mankind, who will but consult it, that being equal and independent, no one ought to harm another in his life, health, liberty, or possessions. . . . Every one, as he is bound to preserve himself, . . . ought he, as much as he can, to preserve the rest of mankind, and may not, unless it be to do justice to an offender, take away or impair the life, or what tends to the preservation of life, the liberty, health, limb, or goods of another.

And that all men may be restrained from invading others' rights, and from doing hurt to one another, and the law of nature be observed, which willeth the peace and preservation of all mankind, the execution of the law of nature is, in that state, put into every man's hands, whereby every one has a right to punish the transgressors of that law to such a degree as may hinder its violation: for the law of nature would, as all other laws that concern men in this world, be in vain, if there were nobody that in the state of nature had a power to execute the law, and thereby preserve the innocent and restrain offenders. . . .

And thus, in the state of nature, "one man comes by a power over another"; but yet this is not an absolute or arbitrary power.

Chapter III: Of the State of War

[It is reasonable and just that . . .] I should have a right to destroy that which threatens me with destruction; for, by the fundamental law of nature, man being to be preserved as much as possible, when all cannot be preserved, the safety of the innocent is to be preferred: and one may destroy a man who makes war upon him, or has discovered an enmity to his being, for the same reason that he may kill a wolf or a lion; because such men are not under the ties of the common law of reason, have no other rule, than that of force and violence, and so may be treated as beasts of prey, those dangerous and noxious creatures, that will be sure to destroy him whenever he falls into their power.

And hence it is, that he who attempts to get another man into his absolute power, does thereby put himself into a state of war with him; it being to be understood as a declaration of a design upon his life: for I have reason to conclude, that he who would get me into his power without my consent, would use me as he pleased when he got me there, and destroy me too when

he had a fancy to it; for nobody can desire to have me in his absolute power, unless it be to compel me by force to that which is against the right of my freedom, i.e., make me a slave. To be free from such force is the only security of my preservation; and reason bids me look on him, as an enemy to my preservation, who would take away that freedom which is the fence to it; so that he who makes an attempt to enslave me, thereby puts himself into a state of war with me. He that, in the state of nature, would take away the freedom that belongs to any one in that state, must necessarily be supposed to have a design to take away everything else, that freedom being the foundation of all the rest; as he that, in the state of society, would take away the freedom belonging to those of that society or commonwealth, must be supposed to design to take away from them every thing else, and so be looked on as in a state of war.

Chapter IV: Of Slavery

The natural liberty of man is to be free from any superior power on earth, and not to be under the will or legislative authority of man, but to have only the law of nature for his rule. . . . Freedom of men under government is, to have a standing rule to live by, common to every one of that society, and made by the legislative power erected in it; a liberty to follow my own will in all things, where the rule prescribes not; and not to be subject to the inconstant, uncertain, unknown, arbitrary will of another man: as freedom of nature is, to be under any other restraint but the law of nature.

This freedom from absolute, arbitrary power, is so necessary to, and closely joined with a man's preservation, that he cannot part with it, but by what forfeits his preservation and life together. . . .

Chapter VIII: Of the Beginning of Political Societies

Men being, as has been said by nature, all free, equal, and independent, no one can be put out of this estate, and subjected to the political power of another, without his own consent. The only way, whereby any one divests himself of his natural liberty, and puts on the bonds of civil society, is by agreeing with other men to join and unite into a community, for their comfortable, safe, and peaceable living one amongst another, in a secure enjoyment of their properties, and a greater security against any, that are not of it. This any number of men may do, because it injures not the freedom of the rest; they are left as they were in the liberty of the state of nature. When any number of men have so consented to make one community or government they are thereby presently incorporated, and make one body politic, wherein the majority have a right to act and conclude the rest. . . . And thus every man, by consenting with others to make one body politic under one government, puts himself under an obligation, to every one of that society, to submit to the determination of the majority, and to be concluded by it; or else this original compact, whereby he with others incorporate into one society, would signify nothing, and be no compact, if he be left free, and under no other ties than he was in before in the state of nature.

Chapter XV: Of Despotical Power

Despotical power is an absolute, arbitrary power one man has over another, to take away his life whenever he pleases; and this is a power which neither Nature gives, for it has made no such distinction between one man and another, nor compact can convey. . . . For having quitted reason, which God has given to be the rule betwixt man and man, and the peaceable ways which that teaches, and made use of force to compass his unjust ends upon another where he has no right, he renders himself liable to be destroyed by his adversary whenever he can, as any other noxious and brutish creature that is destructive to his being. . . .

Chapter XIX: Of the Dissolution of Government

The reason why men enter into society, is the preservation of their property; and the end why they choose and authorize a legislative, is, that there may be laws made, and rules set, as guards and fences to the properties of all the members of the society: to limit the power, and moderate the dominion, of every part and member of the society: for since it can never be supposed to be the will of the society, that the legislative should have a power to destroy that which every one designs to secure by entering into society, and for which the people submitted themselves to legislators of their own making; whenever the legislators endeavour to take away and destroy the property of the people, or to reduce them to slavery under arbitrary power, they put themselves into a state of war with the people, who are thereupon absolved from any farther obedience, and are left to the common refuge, which God hath provided for all men, against force and violence. Whensoever therefore the legislative shall transgress this fundamental rule of society; and either by ambition, fear, folly or corruption, endeavour to grasp themselves, or put into the hands of any other, an absolute power over the lives, liberties, and estates of the people, by this breach of trust they forfeit the power the people had put into their hands for quite contrary ends, and it devolves to the people, who have a right to resume their original liberty, and, by the establishment of a new legislative, (such as they shall think fit) provide for their own safety and security, which is the end for which they are in society. What I have said here, concerning the legislative in general holds true also concerning the supreme executor, who having a double trust put in him, both to have a part in the legislative, and the supreme execution of the law, acts against both, when he goes about to set up his own arbitrary will as the law of the society. . . .

Whosoever uses force without right, as every one does in society, who does it without law, puts himself into a state of war with those against whom he so used it; and in that state all former ties are cancelled, all other rights cease, and every one has a right to defend himself, and to resist the aggressor.

The Social Contract (1762)

JEAN-JACQUES ROUSSEAU

Of the Social Compact

We will suppose that men in a state of nature are arrived at that crisis when the strength of each individual is insufficient to defend him from the attacks he is subject to. This primitive state can therefore subsist no longer; and the human race must perish, unless they change their manner of life.

As men cannot create for themselves new forces, but merely unite and direct those which already exist, the only means they can employ for the preservation is to form by aggregation an assemblage of forces that may be able to resist all assaults, be put in motion as one body, and act in concert upon all occasions.

This assemblage of forces must be produced by the concurrence of many: as the force and the liberty of a man are the chief instruments of his preservation, how can he engage them without danger, and without neglecting the care which is due to himself? This doubt, which leads directly to my subject, may be expressed in these words:

Where shall we find a form of association which will defend and protect with the whole aggregate force the person and the property of each individual; and by which every person, while united with ALL, shall obey only HIM-SELF, and remain as free as before the union? Such is the fundamental problem, of which the Social Contract gives the solution.

The articles of this contract are so unalterably fixed by the nature of the act, that the least modification renders them vain and of no effect. They are the same everywhere, and are everywhere understood and admitted, even though they may never have been formally announced: so that, when once the social pact is violated in any instance, all obligations it created

cease; and each individual is restored to his original rights, and resumes native liberty, as the consequence of losing that conventional liberty for which he exchanged them.

All the articles of the social contract will, when clearly understood, be found reducible to this single point—THE TOTAL ALIENATION OF EACH ASSOCIATE, AND ALL HIS RIGHTS, TO THE WHOLE COMMUNITY. For every individual gives himself up entirely—the condition of every person is alike; and being so, it would not be the interest of anyone to render himself offensive to others.

Moreover, the alienation is made without any reserve; the union is as complete as it can be, and no associate has a claim to anything; for if any individual was to retain rights not enjoyed in general by all, as there would be no common superior to decide between him and the public, each person being in some points his own

Jean-Jacques Rousseau brilliantly challenged the established thought of his day and even alienated several *philosophes.* He outlined a political structure that he hoped would nurture human virtue. *(Library of Congress)*

"The Social Contract" is from Jean-Jacques Rousseau, *An Inquiry into the Nature of the Social Contract* (London, 1791), pp. 33–49.

proper judge, would soon pretend to be so in everything; and thus would the state of nature be revived, and the association become tyrannical or be annihilated.

Finally, each person gives himself to ALL, but not to any INDIVIDUAL: and as there is no one associate over whom the same right is not acquired which is ceded to him by others, each gains an equivalent for what he loses, and finds his force increased for preserving that which he possesses.

If, therefore, we exclude from the social compact all that is not essentially necessary, we shall find it reduced to the following terms:

"We each of us place, in common, his person, and all his power, under the supreme direction of the general will; and we receive into the body each member as an indivisible part of the whole."

From that moment, instead of so many separate persons as there are contractors, this act of association produces a moral collective body, composed of as many members as there are voices in the assembly; which from this act receives its unity, its common self, its life, and its will. This public person, which is thus formed by the union of all the private persons, took formerly the name of city, and now takes that of republic or body politic. It is called by its members state when it is passive, and sovereign when in activity: and whenever it is spoken of with other bodies of a similar kind, it is denominated power. The associates take collectively the name of people, and separately that of citizens, as participating in the sovereign authority: they are also styled subjects, because they are subjected to the laws. But these terms are frequently confounded, and used one for the other; and a man must understand them well to distinguish when they are properly employed.

Of the Sovereign Power

The sovereign power being formed only of the individuals which compose it, neither has, or can have, any interest contrary to theirs; consequently the sovereign power requires no guarantee towards its subjects, because it is impossible that the body should seek to injure all its members: and shall see presently that it can do no injury to any individual. The sovereign power by its nature must, while it exists, be everything it ought to be: it is not so with subjects towards the sovereign power; to which, notwithstanding the common interest subsisting between them, there is nothing to answer for the performance of their engagements, if some means is not found of ensuring their fidelity.

In fact, each individual may, as a man, have a private will, dissimilar contrary to the general will which he has as a citizen. His own particular interest may dictate to him very differently from the common interest; his mind, naturally and absolutely independent, may regard what he owes to the common cause as a gratuitous contribution, the omission of which would be less injurious to others than the payment would be burdensome to himself; and considering the moral person which constitutes the state as a creature of the imagination, because it is not a man, he may wish to enjoy the rights of a citizen, without being disposed to fulfill the duties of a subject: an injustice which would in its progress cause the ruin of the body politic.

In order therefore to prevent the social compact from becoming an empty formula, it tacitly includes this premise, which alone can give effect to the others—That whoever refuses to obey the general will, shall be compelled to it by the whole body, which is in fact only forcing him to be free; for this is the condition which guarantees his absolute personal independence to every citizen of the country: a condition which gives motion and effect to the political machine; which alone renders all civil engagements legal; and without which they would be absurd, tyrannical, and subject to the most enormous abuses.

Of the State

The passing from a state of nature to a civil state, produces in man a very remarkable change, by substituting justice for instinct, and giving to his actions a moral character which they wanted before.

It is at the moment of that transition that the voice of duty succeeds to physical impulse; and a sense of what is right, to the incitements of appetite. The man who had till then regarded none but himself, perceives that he must act on other principles, and learns to consult his reason before he listens to his propensities.

SECTION II: THE ERA OF REVOLUTION

One of the most exciting periods of change and development in world civilization occurred in Europe during the seventeenth and eighteenth centuries. The attitudes and ideas that flourished during this time have formed the intellectual and political bases of our modern Western world.

Although the writers and thinkers of this period generally advocated intellectual freedom and political equality, it should be added that the eighteenth-century Enlightenment was not initially a concerted effort, but took shape in individual minds over several generations; it did not become a conscious movement until about 1750. Yet the ideas of such important figures as John Locke, the Baron de Montesquieu, Voltaire, Denis Diderot, Jean-Jacques Rousseau, and Thomas Jefferson were to be influential apart from the theoretical and abstract world of thought. They were to give philosophical justification to the notion that it was proper and desirable to remove a monarch who was incompetent or inattentive to the needs of the people. Revolution often requires philosophical inspiration in order to succeed; without the underlying attitude that revolution can be a proper and progressive act, perhaps the American and French middle classes would not have been motivated to lead revolts against the established order.

And yet the American and French Revolutions in 1775 and 1789 respectively did not simply happen as a result of intellectual commitment to abstract principles. In fact, there existed more tangible evidence that revolution could succeed and produce desired results. The precedents were clear. In 1649, the English executed their monarch, Charles I, for his autocratic behavior, and in 1688, Parliament established itself as the supreme depository of law and the "popular will" by restricting monarchical authority. It should be remembered, however, that the English had a long tradition of representative government and monarchical limitation dating back most importantly to the Magna Carta in 1215. The French lacked this tradition, and their representative institution, the Estates-General, had not met in 175 years. More recent precedent for French revolutionary action existed in the American example. In 1776, the American colonies declared their independence from Britain and were supported in this venture by the French government itself. It was one of the most momentous acts of political will in world civilization.

The second section of this chapter will explore some of the ideological, economic, and social origins of the American and French revolutions, as well as some of their most important events. Revolutions generally go through conservative and radical phases. Differences among revolutionaries often result in violence. The path toward freedom or despotism is littered with bodies and bloodshed. And in the power vacuum created by such chaos, the door is left open for a transfer of power. This potential for political chaos was a dominant fear in the new American Republic. And during the French Revolution, an individual seized the initiative, filled the power vacuum, and altered its course. His name was Napoleon Bonaparte.

The American Revolution (1775–1800)

By 1763, when the French and Indian war ended, the American colonies had grown to be a strong and thriving part of the British Empire. Although linked to Great Britain through a common heritage, Americans had honed characteristics that allowed them to survive and prosper in the New World. Fiercely independent and resourceful, Americans often exchanged traditional European social and political mores for an expedient philosophy based on adaptation to the circumstances of the moment. And although there were certainly British "loyalists" within the colonies, a new prosperous, educated middle class of lawyers and businessmen took leadership in the promotion of their own self-interest. Before the French and Indian War, British authorities had been rather lax in their political and economic regulation of the colonies. But the growing economic demands of the British empire required that Britain look to stricter policies of taxation.

Therefore, in 1764 Parliament passed the Sugar Act, which was intended to stop illegal colonial smuggling and to raise revenue. But with the French expulsion from North America, the colonists were no longer threatened and forced to seek British protection. Americans began to see themselves in a new light as a separate people with special needs and opportunities. They were willing to risk the displeasure of Great Britain.

For a decade from 1765 to 1775, disputes between Parliament and the American colonists flared unabated. The British continued to impose revenue bills that fueled American resistence and a tirade of legal objections. "Taxation without representation" became the main issue that united colonists in their rejection of British authority. In April 1775, armed conflict between the British army and the colonists broke out in Massachusetts at Lexington and Concord. The "shot heard 'round the world" had been fired and the American army tentatively began besieging British troops in Boston. In May 1775, the Second Continental Congress convened and made the fateful decision to resist hard-line British control, as noted in the following excerpt from the "Declaration of the Causes and Necessity of Taking up Arms," written chiefly by Thomas Jefferson and John Dickinson.

"Resolved to Die Free Men, Rather Than to Live Slaves"

THOMAS JEFFERSON AND JOHN DICKINSON

If it was possible for men, who exercise their reason to believe, that the Divine Author of our existence intended a part of the human race to hold an absolute property in, and an unbounded power over others, marked out by his infinite goodness and wisdom, as the objects of a legal domination never rightfully resistible, however severe and oppressive, the Inhabitants of these Colonies might at least require from

"Resolved to Die Free Men" is from W.C. Ford, ed., *Journals of the Continental Congress*, Volume II (Washington DC: U.S. Government Printing Office, 1904), pp. 63ff.

the parliament of Great Britain some evidence, that this dreadful authority over them, has been granted to that body. But a reverence for our great Creator, principles of humanity, and the dictates of common sense, must convince all those who reflect upon the subject, that government was instituted to promote the welfare of mankind, and ought to be administered for the attainment of that end. The legislature of Great Britain, however, stimulated by an inordinate passion for a power, not only unjustifiable, but which they know to be peculiarly reprobated by the very constitution of that kingdom, and desperate of success in any mode of contest, where regard should be had to truth, law, or right, have at length, deserting those, attempted to effect their cruel and impolitic purpose of enslaving these Colonies by violence, and have thereby rendered it necessary for us to close with their last appeal from Reason to Arms. Yet, however blinded that assembly may be by their intemperate rage for unlimited domination, so to slight justice and the opinion of mankind, we esteem ourselves bound, by obligations of respect to the rest of the world, to make known the justice of our cause. . . .

But why should we enumerate our injuries in detail? By one statute it is declared, that parliament can "of right make laws to bind us IN ALL CASES WHATSOEVER." What is to defend us against so enormous, so unlimited a power? Not a single man of those who assume it, is chosen by us; or is subject to our control or influence; but, on the contrary, they are all of them exempt from the operation of such laws. . . . We saw the misery to which such despotism would reduce us. We for ten years incessantly and ineffectually besieged the Throne as supplicants; we reasoned, we remonstrated with parliament, in the most mild and decent language. But Administration, sensible that we should regard these oppressive measures as freemen ought to do, sent over fleets and armies to enforce them. The indignation of the Americans was roused, it is true; but it was the indignation of a virtuous, loyal, and affectionate people. A Congress of Delegates from the United colonies was assembled at Philadelphia, on the fifth day of last September. We resolved again to offer an humble and dutiful petition to the King, and also addressed our fellow-subjects of Great Britain. We have pursued every temperate, every respectful measure: we have even proceeded to break off our commercial intercourse with our fellow-subjects, as the last peaceable admonition, that

our attachment to no nation upon earth should supplant our attachment to liberty. This, we flattered ourselves, was the ultimate step of the controversy. But subsequent events have shown, how vain was this hope of finding moderation in our enemies. . . .

Our cause is just. Our union is perfect. Our internal resources are great, and, if necessary, foreign assistance is undoubtedly attainable. We gratefully acknowledge, as signal instances of the Divine favor towards us, that his Providence would not permit us to be called into this severe controversy, until we were grown up to our present strength, had been previously exercised in warlike operation, and possessed of the means of defending ourselves. With hearts fortified with these animating reflections, we most solemnly, before God and the world, declare, that, exerting the utmost energy of those powers, which our beneficent Creator has graciously bestowed upon us, the arms we have been compelled by our enemies to assume, we will, in defiance of every hazard, with unabating firmness and perseverance, employ for the preservation of our liberties; being with our one mind resolved to die freemen rather than to live Slaves. . . .

With an humble confidence in the mercies of the supreme and impartial Judge and ruler of the universe, we most devoutly implore his divine goodness to protect us happily through this great conflict, to dispose our adversaries to reconciliation on reasonable terms, and thereby to relieve the empire from the calamities of civil war.

By order of Congress
JOHN HANCOCK
President

The Declaration of Independence (1776)

On June 7, 1776, Richard Henry Lee of Virginia introduced into Congress a resolution that "these united colonies are, and of right ought to be, free and independent states." While this resolution was hotly debated, a committee consisting of John Adams, Benjamin Franklin, Thomas Jefferson, and others was appointed to draft a Declaration of Independence. Al-

"The Declaration of Independence" is from *Revised Statutes of the United States,* 2nd edition (Washington DC: Government Printing Office, 1878), pp. 3-6.

though a passage indicting the slave trade was removed in deference to the interests of the southern colonies, the declaration stands as "an expression of the American mind." The document served to unite the new nation during the grueling struggle ahead.

When in the course of human events, it becomes necessary for one people to dissolve the political bands which have connected them with another, and to assume among the Powers of the earth, the separate and equal station to which the Laws of Nature and of Nature's God entitle them, a decent respect to the opinions of mankind requires that they should declare the causes which impel them to the separation.

We hold these truths to be self-evident, that all men are created equal, that they are endowed by their Creator with certain unalienable Rights, that among these are Life, Liberty and the pursuit of Happiness. That to secure these rights, Governments are instituted among Men, deriving their just powers from the consent of the governed. That whenever any form of Government becomes destructive of these ends, it is the right of the People to alter or to abolish it, and to institute new government, laying its foundation on such principles and organizing its powers in such form, as to them shall seem most likely to effect their Safety and Happiness. Prudence, indeed, will dictate that governments long established should not be changed for light and transient causes; and accordingly all experience hath shown, that mankind are more disposed to suffer, while evils are sufferable, than to right themselves by abolishing the forms to which they are accustomed. But when a long train of abuses and usurpations, pursuing invariably the same Object evinces a design to reduce them under absolute

Despotism, it is their right, it is their duty, to throw off such government, and to provide new guards for their future security. Such has been the patient sufferance of these Colonies; and such is now the necessity which constrains them to alter their former Systems of Government. The history of the present King of Great Britain is a history of repeated injuries and usurpations, all having in direct object the establishment of an absolute Tyranny over these States. To prove this, let Facts be submitted to a candid world. . . .
[There follows a detailed list of abuses]

We, therefore, the Representatives of the united States of America, in General Congress, Assembled, appealing to the Supreme Judge of the world for the rectitude of our intentions, do, in the Name, and by the Authority of the good People of these Colonies, solemnly publish and declare, That these United colonies are, and of Right ought to be Free and Independent States; that they are Absolved from all Allegiance to the British Crown, and that all political connection between them and the State of Great Britain, is and ought to be totally dissolved; and that as Free and Independent States, they have full Power to levy War, conclude Peace, contract Alliances, establish Commerce, and to do all other Acts and Things which Independent States may of right do. And for the support of this Declaration, with a firm reliance on the Protection of Divine Providence, we mutually pledge to each other our Lives, our Fortunes and our sacred Honor.

"The Fundamental Maxims of True Liberty": Farewell Address (1796)

PRESIDENT GEORGE WASHINGTON

From 1775 to 1783, Americans waged a successful war against British imperial forces. With the aid of France, the American colonies successfully declared and defended their independence and in the process founded a new nation. But its success as an independent, sovereign state was certainly not guaranteed. The gravest danger threatening the new American nation

"The Farewell Address" is from J.D. Richardson, ed., *Messages and Papers of the Presidents* (Washington, DC: Government Printing Office, 1898), pp. 210ff.

was that its union, inspired by the Enlightenment ideals of the Declaration of Independence in 1776 and shaped by the delicate balances within the Constitution by 1791, might dissolve amidst the conflicting interests of political factions. The United States was a fragile patchwork of personal self-interest, regional identity, and federal accord. Although a governmental structure had been embraced, no one knew how the Constitution would stand up to the challenges presented by developing political parties.

So great was the fear of factional dispute and political chaos that George Washington in his Presidential Farewell Address of 1796 decided to warn against disruptive sectional spirit and involvement with foreign nations. Such concerns proved pivotal, as within the next half-century the United States would be engaged in a disastrous civil war.

In contemplating the causes which may disturb our union it occurs as matter of serious concern that any ground should have been furnished for characterizing parties by geographical discriminations—*Northern* and *Southern, Atlantic,* and *Western*—whence designing men may endeavor to excite a belief that there is a real difference of local interests and views. One of the expedients of party to acquire influence within particular districts is to misrepresent the opinions and aims of other districts. You can not shield yourselves too much against the jealousies and heart-burnings which spring from these misrepresentations; they tend to render alien to each other those who ought to be bound together by fraternal affection. . . .

To the efficacy and permanency of your union a government for the whole is indispensable. . . . This Government, the offspring of our own choice, uninfluenced and unawed, adopted upon full investigation and mature deliberation, completely free in its principles, in the distribution of its powers, uniting security with energy, and containing within itself a provision for its own amendment, has a just claim to your confidence and your support. Respect for its authority, compliance with its laws, acquiescence in its measure, are duties enjoined by the fundamental maxims of true liberty. The basis of our political systems is the right of the people to make and to alter their constitutions of government. But the constitution which at any time exists till changed by an explicit and authentic act of the whole people is sacredly obligatory upon all. The very idea of the power and the right of the people to establish government presupposes the duty of every individual to obey the established government. . . .

[The spirit of party], unfortunately, is inseparable from our nature, having its root in the strongest passions of the human mind. It exists under different shapes in all governments, more or less stifled, controlled, or repressed; but in those of the popular form it is seen in its greatest rankness and is truly their worst enemy. . . .

It serves always to distract the public councils and enfeeble the public administration. It agitates the community with ill-founded jealousies and false alarms; kindles the animosity of one part against another; foments occasionally riot and insurrection. It opens the door to foreign influence and corruption, which find a facilitated access to the government itself through the channels of party passion. Thus the policy and the will of one country are subjected to the policy and will of another. . . .

Nothing is more essential than that permanent, inveterate antipathies against particular nations and passionate attachments for others should be excluded, and that in place of them just and amicable feelings toward all should be cultivated. The nation which indulges toward another an habitual hatred or an habitual fondness is in some degree a slave. It is a slave to its animosity or to its affection, either of which is sufficient to lead it astray from its duty and its interest. Antipathy in one nation against another disposes each more readily to offer insult and injury, to lay hold of slight causes of umbrage, and to be haughty and intractable when accidental or trifling occasions of dispute occur. . . .

The great rule of conduct for us in regard to foreign nations is, in extending our commercial relations to have with them as little *political* connection as possible. So far as we have already formed engagements let them be fulfilled with perfect good faith. Here let us stop. . . .

Taking care always to keep ourselves by suitable establishments on a respectable defensive posture, we may safely trust to temporary alliances for extraordinary emergencies. . . .

"LIBERTY, EQUALITY, FRATERNITY!": THE FRENCH REVOLUTION (1789–1815)

A time of revolution is not the season of true liberty. Alas! the obstinacy and perversion of men is such that she is too often obliged to borrow the very arms of despotism to overthrow him, and in order to reign in peace must establish herself by violence.

—*William Wordsworth*

The greatest dangers to liberty lurk in insidious encroachment by men of zeal—well-meaning, but without understanding.

—*Justice Louis D. Brandeis*

Extremism in the defense of liberty is no vice. And . . . moderation in the pursuit of justice is no virtue.

—*Barry Goldwater*

True tragedy arises when the idea of "justice" appears to be leading to the destruction of higher values.

—*Max Scheler*

The Outbreak of Revolution (1789–1791)

The wars and extravagance of King Louis XIV had sent France to the brink of bankruptcy by 1715—and Louis was a competent and diligent administrator. His heirs, on the other hand, were not particularly dedicated to the governance of France. Louis XV (1715–1774) was poorly educated and preferred to allow his mistresses (one of whom had been a Parisian prostitute) to control the politics of state. Louis XVI (1774–1792) was well educated but more interested in hunting than in administration. From 1715 to 1789, the French economy spiraled into chaos. With the nobility and church exempt from taxation, the burden fell upon the Third Estate.

The French Revolution drew much of its support from the Third Estate, a conglomeration of middle-class professionals, artisans, and peasants. As a group, the middle class or bourgeoisie *was ambitious, educated, and competent. Could they be expected to sit idly by while the nobility held offices that should have been theirs? Inspired by philosophical ideals as well as by potential economic and social advantages, they provided the leadership for the revolution. Lower members of the Third Estate, the artisans and peasants, generally could not read and were not concerned with philosophical justifications. It was the peasantry that labored under intolerable taxes, rents, and* corvées *(feudal services), which they were forced to undertake by the nobility without payment. What were their demands? Did their needs justify revolution?*

By August 1788, Louis XVI had decided to summon the Estates-General, a convocation of the three estates, which had not met since 1614, in order to solve the government's financial problems. Louis was in debt, and he wanted the Estates-General to raise new taxes. This pamphlet by the Abbé Sieyès (1748–1836) was issued in January 1789, before the Estates-General met. It was intended to unite the various interests within the Third Estate toward a common cause: reform of the unequal voting procedure that gave advantage to the first two estates.

"What Is the Third Estate?" (January 1789)

THE ABBÉ SIEYÈS

What Does the Third Estate Demand? To Become Something

The true petitions of this order may be appreciated only through the authentic claims directed to the government by the large municipalities of the kingdom. What is indicated therein? That the people wishes to be something, and, in truth, the very least that is possible. It wishes to have real representatives in the Estates General, that is to say, deputies drawn from its order, who are competent to be interpreters of its will and defenders of its interests. But what will it avail it to be present at the Estates General if the predominating interest there is contrary to its own! Its presence would only consecrate the oppression of which it would be the external victim. Thus, it is indeed certain that it cannot come to vote at the Estates General unless it is to have in that body an influence at least equal to that of the privileged classes; and it demands a number of representatives equal to that of the first two orders together. Finally, this equality of representation would become completely illusory if every chamber voted separately. The third estate demands, then, that votes be taken by head and not by order. This is the essence of those claims so alarming to the privileged classes, because they believed that thereby the reform of abuses would become inevitable. The real intention of the third estate is to have an influence in the Estates General equal to that of the privileged classes. I repeat, can it ask less?

Documentary Survey of the French Revolution by Stewart, John Hall, © 1951, pp. 46, 51–52. Reprinted by permission of Pearson Education, Inc., Upper Saddle River, NJ.

What Remains to Be Done: Development of Some Principles

The time is past when the three orders, thinking only of defending them-selves from ministerial despotism, were ready to unite against the common enemy. . . .

•••

The third estate awaits, to no purpose, the meeting of all classes, the restitution of its political rights, and the plenitude of its civil rights; the fear of seeing abuses reformed alarms the first two orders far more than the desire for liberty inspires them. Between liberty and some odious privileges, they have chosen the latter. Their soul is identified with the favors of servitude. Today they dread this Estates General which but lately they invoked so ardently. All is well with them; they no longer complain, except of the spirit of innovation. They no longer lack anything; fear has given them a constitution.

The third estate must perceive in the trend of opinions and circumstances that it can hope for nothing except from its own enlightenment and courage. Reason and justice are in its favor; . . . there is no longer time to work for the conciliation of parties. What accord can be anticipated between the energy of the oppressed and the rage of the oppressors?

They have dared pronounce the word secession. They have menaced the King and the people. Well! Good God! How fortunate for the nation if this desirable secession might be made permanently! How easy it would be to dispense with the privileged classes! How difficult to induce them to be citizens!

•••

In vain would they close their eyes to the revolution which time and force of circumstances have effected; it is none the less real. Formerly the third estate was serf, the noble order everything. Today the third estate is everything, the nobility but a word. . . .

In such a state of affairs, what must the third estate do if it wishes to gain possession of its political rights in a manner beneficial to the nation? There are two ways of attaining this objective. In following the first, the third estate must assemble apart: it will not meet with the nobility and the clergy at all; it will not remain with them,

either by order or by head. I pray that they will keep in mind the enormous difference between the assembly of the third estate and that of the other two orders. The first represents 25,000,000 men, and deliberates concerning the interests of the nation. The two others, were they to unite, have the powers of only about 200,000 individuals, and think only of their privileges. The third estate alone, they say, cannot constitute the Estates General. Well! So much the better! It will form a National Assembly.

The Tennis Court Oath (June 20, 1789)

From the outset, the Estates-General was hampered by organizational disputes. After several weeks of frustration, the Third Estate invited the clergy and nobility to join them in organizing a new legislative body. Only a few of the lower clergy accepted, but the National Assembly was thus formed on June 17, 1789. Three days later they were accidentally locked out of their usual meeting place, and they marched to a nearby tennis court, where they took an oath to draft a new constitution for France. This is one of the most important documents of the revolution. The oath was taken orally and individually with but one vote in dissension. The president of the National Assembly was barely able to save the dissenter from bodily harm.

The Oath of the Tennis Court by Jacques-Louis David. Having pledged their cooperation in the establishment of the National Assembly, members from the different estates took the famous oath to write a new constitution for France. *(Giraudon/Art Resource, New York)*

"The Tennis Court Oath" is reprinted with permission of Macmillan Publishing Company from *A Documentary Survey of the French Revolution*, edited by John Hall Stewart, p. 88. Copyright 1951 by Macmillan Publishing Company, renewed 1979 by John Hall Stewart.

The National Assembly, considering that it has been summoned to establish the constitution of the kingdom, to effect the regeneration of public order, and to maintain the true principles of monarchy; that nothing can prevent it from continuing its deliberations in whatever place it may be forced to establish itself; and, finally, that wheresoever its members are assembled, there is the National Assembly;

Decrees that all members of this Assembly shall immediately take a solemn oath not to separate, and to reassemble wherever circumstances require, until the constitution of the kingdom is established and consolidated upon firm foundations; and that, the said oath taken, all members and each one of them individually shall ratify this steadfast resolution by signature.

The Fall of the Bastille (July 14, 1789)

The Bastille was a fortress built to protect the eastern gates of Paris. It had also been used as a prison for political offenders of the Old Regime. Hence, it served as a symbol of monarchical despotism. On July 14, 1789, a mob, irritated at the dismissal of a popular minister of the king, paraded through the streets of Paris, searching for arms and clashing with the military. They stormed the Bastille and slaughtered many of its small garrison. Although this act yielded few political prisoners of the king, the event would provide a catalyst to the revolution and is commemorated today in France with special reverence. Louis XVI, however, did not view it with such import. The entry in his diary for July 14, 1789, was "rien" (nothing), signifying that he failed to kill any game in his hunt that day. The following accounts of the fall of the Bastille are drawn from various witnesses and contemporaries of the event.

The fortress of the Bastille. When King Louis XVI was informed that the Bastille had been stormed by a Parisian crowd on July 14, 1789, he said, "It is then a revolt." "No, Sire," replied the duke. "It is a revolution." *(Robert, Hubert "Demolition of the Bastille." 1789. Musee de la Ville de Paris, Musee Carnavalet, Paris, France, Giraudon/Art Resource)*

E.L. Higgins, *The French Revolution as Told By Contemporaries.* Copyright © 1966 by Houghton Mifflin Company, pp. 98–100. Reprinted with permission.

The Surrender

It was then that M. de Launay [commander of the forces of the Bastille] asked the garrison what course should be followed, that he saw no other than to blow himself up rather than to expose himself to having his throat cut by the people, from the fury of which they could not escape; that they must remount the towers, continue to fight, and blow themselves up rather than surrender.

The soldiers replied that it was impossible to fight any longer, that they would resign themselves to everything rather than destroy such a great number of citizens, that it was best to put the drummer on the towers to beat the recall, hoist a white flag, and capitulate. The governor, having no flag, gave them a white handkerchief. An officer wrote out the capitulation and passed it through the hole, saying that they desired to render themselves and lay down their arms, on condition of a promise not to massacre the troop; there was a cry of, "Lower your bridge; nothing will happen to you!"

•••

The little drawbridge of the fort being first opened, Elie [one of the leaders of the attacking force] entered with his companions, all brave and honorable men, and fully determined to keep his word. On seeing him the governor went up to him, embraced him, and presented him with his sword, with the keys of the Bastille.

"I refused his sword," said Elie to me, "and took only the keys." His companions received the staff and the officers of the garrison with the same cordiality, swearing to serve them as guard and defense; but they swore in vain.

As soon as the great bridge was let down (and it is not known by what hand that was done) the people rushed into the court of the castle and,

full of fury, seized on the troop of Invalides. Elie and the honest men who had entered with him exerted all their efforts to tear from the hands of the people the victims which they themselves had delivered to it. Ferocity held obstinately attached to its prey. Several of these soldiers, whose lives had been promised them, were assassinated; others were dragged like slaves through the streets of Paris. Twenty-two were brought to the Grève, and, after humiliations and inhuman treatment, they had the affliction of seeing two of their comrades hanged. When they were presented at the Hotel de Ville, a furious madman said to them: "You deserve to be hanged; and you shall be so presently." De Launay, torn from the arms of those who wished to save him, had his head cut off under the walls of the Hotel de Ville. In the midst of his assassins, he defended his life with the courage of despair; but he fell under their number. De Losme-Salbray, his major, was murdered in the same manner. The adjutant, Mirai, had been so, near the Bastille. Pernon, an old lieutenant of the Invalides, was assassinated on the wharf Saint-Paul, as he was going to the hall. Another lieutenant, Caron, was covered with wounds. The head of the Marquis de Launay was carried about Paris by this same populace that he would have crushed had he not been moved to pity. Such were the exploits of those who have since been called the heroes and conquerors of the Bastille.

The King Informed of the Fall of the Bastille

When M. de Liancourt had made known to the king the total defection of his guards, the taking of the Bastille, the massacres that had taken place, the rising of two hundred thousand men, after a few moments' silence the king said, "It is then a revolt." "No, Sire," replied the duke. "It is a revolution."

Declaration of the Rights of Man (August 27, 1789)

The Declaration of the Rights of Man, issued by the National Assembly on August 27, 1789, served as a preamble to the French constitution, which was as yet unwritten. Its articles detail abuses of the Old Regime and were imitative of American bills of rights that had been at-

"Declaration of the Rights of Man" is from James H. Robinson and Charles A. Beard, eds., *Readings in Modern European History*, vol. 1 (Boston: Ginn and Company, 1908), pp. 260–262.

tached to state constitutions. The declaration in turn influenced several European constitutions in the nineteenth century.

The representatives of the French people, organized as a National Assembly, believing that the ignorance, neglect, or contempt of the rights of man are the sole causes of public calamities and of the corruption of governments, have determined to set forth in a solemn declaration the natural, inalienable, and sacred rights of man, in order that this declaration, being constantly before all the members of the social body, shall remind them continually of their rights and duties; in order that the acts of the legislative power, as well as those of the executive power, may be compared at any moment with the objects and purposes of all political institutions and may thus be more respected; and, lastly, in order that the grievances of the citizens, based hereafter upon simple and incontestable principles, shall tend to the maintenance of the constitution and redound to the happiness of all. Therefore the National Assembly recognizes and proclaims, in the presence and under the auspices of the Supreme Being, the following rights of man and of the citizen:

Article

1. Men are born and remain free and equal in rights. Social distinctions may be founded only upon the general good.
2. The aim of all political association is the preservation of the natural and imprescriptible rights of man. These rights are liberty, property, security, and resistance to oppression.
3. The principle of all sovereignty resides essentially in the nation. No body nor individual may exercise any authority which does not proceed directly from the nation.
4. Liberty consists in the freedom to do everything which injures no one else; hence the exercise of the natural rights of each man has no limits except those which assure to the other members of the society the enjoyment of the same rights. These limits can only be determined by law.
5. Law can only prohibit such actions as are hurtful to society. Nothing may be prevented which is not forbidden by law, and no one may be forced to do anything not provided for by law.
6. Law is the expression of the general will. Every citizen has a right to participate personally, or through his representative, in its formation. It must be the same for all, whether it protects or punishes. All citizens, being equal in the eyes of the law, are equally eligible to all dignities and to all public positions and occupations, according to their abilities, and without distinction except that of their virtues and talents.
7. No person shall be accused, arrested, or imprisoned, except in the cases and according to the forms prescribed by law. Any one soliciting, transmitting, executing, or causing to be executed, any arbitrary order, shall be punished. But any citizen summoned or arrested in virtue of the law shall submit without delay, as resistance constitutes an offense.
8. The law shall provide for such punishments only as are strictly and obviously necessary, and no one shall suffer punishment except it be legally inflicted in virtue of a law passed and promulgated before the commission of the offense.
9. As all persons are held innocent until they shall have been declared guilty, if arrest shall be deemed indispensable, all harshness not essential to the securing of the prisoner's person shall be severely repressed by law.
10. No one shall be disquieted on account of his opinions, including his religious views, provided their manifestation does not disturb the public order established by law.
11. The free communication of ideas and opinions is one of the most precious of the rights of man. Every citizen may, accordingly, speak, write, and print with freedom, but shall be responsible for such abuses of this freedom as shall be defined by law.
12. The security of the rights of man and of the citizen requires public military forces. These forces are, therefore, established for the good

of all and not for the personal advantage of those to whom they shall be entrusted.

13. A common contribution is essential for the maintenance of the public forces and for the cost of administration. This should be equitably distributed among all the citizens in proportion to their means.

14. All the citizens have a right to decide, either personally or by their representatives, as to the necessity of the public contribution; to grant this freely; to know to what uses it is put; and to fix the proportion, the mode of assessment and of collection and the duration of the taxes.

15. Society has the right to require of every public agent an account of his administration.

16. A society in which the observance of the law is not assured, nor the separation of powers defined, has no constitution at all.

17. Since property is an inviolable and sacred right, no one shall be deprived thereof except where public necessity, legally determined, shall clearly demand it, and then only on condition that the owner shall have been previously and equitably indemnified.

The Radicalization of the Revolution (1792–1794)

On June 20, 1791, the royal family managed to get out of Paris. Traveling in disguise with false passports, they were detained and arrested in Varennes, about one hundred fifty miles from Paris. The king was disgraced and the monarchy suffered a humiliating blow. The months following the king's flight from Paris were tense and saw the eventual erosion of royalist support and the abolition of the monarchy in September 1792. Louis was indicted for treason on December 11, 1792. The king denied most of the charges and blamed the rest on others. Nevertheless, a narrow majority of votes in the Assembly sent him to the guillotine. The following excerpt is an eyewitness account of the execution by Henry Edgeworth de Firmont, the king's confessor, who accompanied Louis to the scaffold. Justification for regicide came two days later by way of a proclamation of the government to the French people.

The Execution of Louis XVI (January 21, 1793)

HENRY EDGEWORTH DE FIRMONT

The carriage arrived . . . in the greatest silence, at the Place Louis XV, and came to a halt in the middle of a large empty space that had been left around the scaffold. This space was bordered with cannon; and beyond, as far as the eye could reach, was a multitude in arms. . . .

As soon as the king descended from the carriage, three executioners surrounded him and wished to take off his coat. He repulsed them with dignity and took it off himself. The executioners, whom the proud bearing of the king had momentarily disconcerted, seemed then to

resume their audacity and, surrounding him again, attempted to tie his hands. "What are you trying to do?" asked the king, withdrawing his hands abruptly.

"Tie you," replied one of the executioners.

"Tie me!" returned the king in an indignant tone. "No, I will never consent; do what you are ordered to do, but I will not be tied; renounce that idea." The executioners insisted, they lifted their voices, and seemed about to call for help in order to use force. . . .

"Sire," I said to him with tears, "in this new outrage I see only a final resemblance between Your Majesty and the Saviour who is to reward you."

At these words he lifted his eyes to heaven with a sorrowing look that I cannot describe . . . and, turning to the executioners, said: "Do what you wish; I will drain the cup to the dregs."

The steps that led to the scaffold were extremely steep in ascent. The king was obliged to

E.L. Higgins, *The French Revolution as Told By Contemporaries.* Copyright © 1966 by Houghton Mifflin Company, pp. 272–273. Reprinted with permission.

"The executioners seized [Louis XVI's head] by the hair, and showed it to the multitude, whose cries of 'Long live the Republic!' resounded to the very bosom of the Convention."—Henry Edgeworth de Firmont. *(New York Public Library Picture Collection)*

hold to my arm, and by the pains he seemed to take, feared that his courage had begun to weaken; but what was my astonishment when, upon arriving at the last step, I saw him escape, so to speak, from my hands, cross the length of the scaffold with firm step to impose silence, by a single glance, upon ten or fifteen drummers who were in front of him, and with a voice so strong that it could be heard at the Pont-Tournant, distinctly pronounce these words forever memorable: "I die innocent of all the crimes imputed to me. I pardon the authors of my death, and pray God that the blood you are about to shed will never fall upon France."

The executioners seized him, the knife struck him, his head fell at fifteen minutes after ten. The executioners seized it by the hair, and showed it to the multitude, whose cries of "Long live the Republic!" resounded to the very bosom of the Convention, whose place of meeting was only a few steps from the place of execution.

Thus died, at the age of thirty-eight years, four months, and twenty-eight days, Louis, sixteenth

of his name, whose ancestors had reigned in France for more than eight hundred years. . . .

Immediately after the execution, the body of Louis was transported to the cemetery of the ancient Church of the Madeleine. It was placed in a pit six feet square, close to the wall of the Rue d'Anjou, and dissolved instantly by a great quantity of quicklime with which they took the precaution to cover it.

Proclamation of the Convention to the French People (January 23, 1793)

Citizens, the tyrant is no more. For a long time the cries of the victims, whom war and domestic dissensions have spread over France and Eu-

E.L. Higgins, *The French Revolution as Told By Contemporaries.* Copyright © 1966 by Houghton Mifflin Company, p. 392. Reprinted with permission.

rope, loudly protested his existence. He has paid his penalty, and only acclamations for the Republic and for liberty have been heard from the people. We have had to combat inveterate prejudices, and the superstition of centuries concerning monarchy. Involuntary uncertainties and inevitable disturbances always accompany great changes and revolutions as profound as ours. This political crisis has suddenly surrounded us with contradictions and tumults.

But the cause has ceased, and the motives have disappeared; respect for liberty of opinion must cause these tumultuous scenes to be forgotten; only the good which they have produced through the death of the tyrant and of tyranny now remains, and this judgment belongs in its entirety to each of us, just as it belongs to the entire nation. The National Convention and the French people are now to have only one mind, only one sentiment, that of liberty and civic fraternity.

Now, above all, we need peace in the interior of the Republic, and the most active surveillance of the domestic enemies of liberty. Never did circumstances more urgently require of all citizens the sacrifice of their passions and their personal opinions concerning the act of national justice which has just been effected. Today the French people can have no other passion than that for liberty.

"Virtue and Terror": Speech to the Convention (February 5, 1794)
MAXIMILIEN ROBESPIERRE

One of the most dramatic personalities of the French Revolution was Maximilien Robespierre (1758–1794), who dominated the principal policy-making body in the state, the Committee of Public Safety. An ardent democrat, Robespierre believed in a republic of virtue that demanded selfless adherence to republican ideals. Those who supported the monarchy or were more moderate in their republican zeal became threats to the success of the revolution and had to be eliminated. Terror, according to Robespierre, was "swift, inflexible justice" and therefore virtuous. The Reign of Terror, which lasted from 1793 to 1794, saw the execution by the guillotine of more than 25,000 people, from both the political left and right, many without proper trials.

The aims of the revolution are presented in the following selection by Robespierre. The next document is a law that transferred the administration of the Terror from the Convention to the Committee of Public Safety. This enactment provided a general definition of an "enemy of the Republic" and increased the number of victims sacrificed to the purity of the revolution. Historians generally agree that this law not only damaged the ideals of the French Revolution, but also was the ultimate cause of Robespierre's downfall. He fell victim to colleagues who feared his menacing power and was himself executed a month and a half after the law was ratified. With Robespierre's death, the Terror came to an end. The revolution continued, but without the bloodshed that had devoured its own children.

What is the aim we want to achieve? The peaceful enjoyment of liberty and equality, the reign of that eternal justice whose laws have been engraved, not in stone and marble, but in the hearts of all men, even in the heart of the slave who forgets them or of the tyrant who denies them.

We want a state of affairs where all despicable and cruel passions are unknown and all kind and generous passions are aroused by the laws; where ambition is the desire to deserve glory and to serve the fatherland; where distinctions arise only from equality itself; where the citizen submits to the magistrate, the magistrate to the people and

"'Virtue and Terror'" is from Richard W. Lyman and Lewis W. Spitz, eds., *Major Crises in Western Civilization*, vol. 2 (New York: Harcourt, Brace & World, 1965), pp. 71–72.

the people to justice; where the fatherland guarantees the well-being of each individual, and where each individual enjoys with pride the prosperity and the glory of the fatherland; where all souls elevate themselves through constant communication of republican sentiments and through the need to deserve the esteem of a great people; where the arts are the decorations of liberty that ennobles them, where commerce is the source of public wealth and not only of the monstrous opulence of a few houses.

In our country we want to substitute morality for egoism, honesty for honor, principles for customs, duties for decorum, the rule of reason for the tyranny of custom, the contempt of vice for the contempt of misfortune, pride for insolence, magnanimity for vanity, love of glory for love of money, good people for well-bred people, merit for intrigue, genius for wit, truth for pompous action, warmth of happiness for boredom of sensuality, greatness of man for pettiness of the great; a magnanimous, powerful, happy people for a polite, frivolous, despicable people—that is to say, all the virtues and all the miracles of the Republic for all the vices and all the absurdities of the monarchy.

In one word, we want to fulfill the wishes of nature, accomplish the destiny of humanity, keep the promises of philosophy, absolve Providence from the long reign of crime and tyranny. What kind of government can realize these marvels? Only a democratic or republican government. But what is the fundamental principle of the democratic or popular government, that is to say, the essential strength that sustains it and makes it move? It is virtue: I am speaking of the public virtue which brought about so many marvels in Greece and Rome and which must bring about much more astonishing ones yet in republican France; of that virtue which is nothing more than love of the fatherland and of its laws.

If the strength of popular government in peacetime is virtue, the strength of popular government in revolution is both virtue and terror; terror without virtue is disastrous, virtue without terror is powerless. Terror is nothing but prompt, severe, and inflexible justice; it is thus an emanation of virtue; it is less a particular principle than a

consequence of the general principle of democracy applied to the most urgent needs of the fatherland. It is said that terror is the strength of despotic government. Does ours then resemble despotism? Yes, as the sword that shines in the hands of the heroes of liberty resemble the one with which the satellites of tyranny are armed. Let the despot govern his brutalized subjects through terror; he is right as a despot. Subdue the enemies of liberty through terror and you will be right as founders of the Republic. The government of revolution is the despotism of liberty against tyranny.

The Administration of Terror (June 10, 1794)

1. In the Revolutionary Tribunal there shall be a president and four vice-presidents, one public prosecutor, four substitutes for the public prosecutor, and twelve judges.
2. The jurors shall be fifty in number. . . .
4. The Revolutionary Tribunal is instituted to punish the enemies of the people.
5. The enemies of the people are those who seek to destroy public liberty, either by force or by cunning.
6. The following are deemed enemies of the people: those who have
   - instigated the re-establishment of monarchy, or have sought to disparage or dissolve the National Convention and the revolutionary and republican government of which it is the center;
   - betrayed the Republic in the command of places and armies, or in any other military function, carried on correspondence with the enemies of the Republic, labored to disrupt the provisioning or the service of the armies;
   - supported the designs of the enemies of France, either by countenancing the sheltering and the impunity of conspirators

"The Administration of Terror" is reprinted with permission of Macmillan Publishing Company from *A Documentary Survey of the French Revolution*, edited by John Hall Stewart, pp. 528–529. Copyright 1951 by Macmillan Publishing Company, renewed 1979 by John Hall Stewart.

and aristocracy, by persecuting and calumniating patriotism, by corrupting the mandataries of the people, or by abusing the principles of the Revolution or the laws or measures of the government by false and perfidious applications;

- deceived the people or the representatives of the people, in order to lead them into undertakings contrary to the interests of liberty;
- sought to inspire discouragement, in order to favor the enterprises of the tyrants leagued against the Republic;
- disseminated false news in order to divide or disturb the people;
- sought to mislead opinion and to prevent the instruction of the people, to deprave morals and to corrupt the public conscience, to impair the energy and the purity of revolutionary and republican principles, or to impede the progress thereof, either by counter-revolutionary or insidious writings, or by any other machination;. . .
- Finally, all who are designated in previous laws relative to the punishment of conspirators and counter-revolutionaries, and who, by whatever means or by whatever appearances they assume, have made an attempt against the liberty, unity, and security of the Republic, or labored to prevent the strengthening thereof.

7. The penalty provided for all offences under the jurisdiction of the Revolutionary Tribunal is death.

8. The proof necessary to convict enemies of the people comprises every kind of evidence, whether material or moral, oral or written, which can naturally secure the approval of every just and reasonable mind; the rule of judgments is the conscience of the jurors, enlightened by love of the Patrie; their aim, the triumph of the Republic and the ruin of its enemies; the procedure, the simple means which good sense dictates in order to arrive at a knowledge of the truth, in the forms determined by law.

9. Every citizen has the right to seize conspirators and counter-revolutionaries, and to arraign them before the magistrates. He is required to denounce them as soon as he knows of them.

The Execution of Robespierre (July 28, 1794)

DURAND DE MAILLANE

Robespierre's turn had come at last. By fawning upon the people he had become their idol, and this will happen to any man who declaims against the rich, causing the people to hope for a division of the spoils. Through the populace, he ruled the Jacobin Club; through the Jacobin Club, the Convention and through the Convention, France. He dictated decrees and directed the administration. Nothing was done except by his orders or with his approval. His caprices were flattered, and his very manias were praised. The tribunal beheaded those he designated without investigation. His power seemed too terrible to his accomplices as it did to his victims. A number had been sacrificed already and others feared the same fate. They banded together to pull down the idol they themselves had set up.

•••

[The committee of general security] ordered that he [Robespierre] be taken to the prison of the Conciergerie. His trial was short. On the following day he was guillotined, together with Saint-Just, Couthon, and his other accomplices. It was quite a distance from the Palais de Justice to the scaffold, and the immensity of the long Rue Saint-Honore had to be traversed. Along the whole course, the people pursued Robespierre with hoots and maledictions. He had been given a conspicuous place in the tumbril, his face half covered by a dirty, bloodstained cloth which enveloped his jaw. It may be said that this man, who had brought so much anguish to others, suffered during these twenty-four hours all the pain and agony that a mortal can experience.

The Napoleonic Era (1796–1815)

What is the throne?—a bit of wood gilded and covered with velvet. I am the state—I alone am the representative of the people....France has more need of me than I of France.

—Napoleon Bonaparte (1814)

Do you know what astounds me most about the world? It is the impotence of force to establish anything. In the end, the sword is always conquered by the mind.

—Napoleon Bonaparte (1808)

Men of genius are meteors destined to be consumed in lighting up their century.

—Napoleon Bonaparte (1791)

The mere name of Napoleon (1769–1821) evokes a wide array of emotions. As is the case with most influential individuals, he inspires controversy. Some historians have described him as a force for good, a lawgiver and reformer who spread revolutionary ideals throughout Europe. Others have viewed him as an egomaniac whose lust for conquest overshadowed any other secondary achievements. Whatever final judgment one may make, it is clear that Napoleon Bonaparte had a brilliant mind, equally at home in the context of law and military strategy.

Napoleon was born in 1769 to a poor family of lesser nobility on the island of Corsica. The "little Corporal," as he was called, went to French schools and obtained a commission as a French artillery officer. He was enthusiastic about the revolution of 1789 and was rewarded for his military service against the British with a promotion to brigadier general. After the fall of Robespierre in 1794, Napoleon's radical political associations threatened his career, but he was able to convince the new government of his loyalty. This government was called the Directory, and it was composed of people who had benefitted from the recent revolution and whose major goal was to perpetuate their own rule. Their chief opposition came from royalists, who supported a monarch as head of France and who had won a majority of the seats in the legislature in 1797. With the aid of Napoleon, the Directory succeeded in overthrowing the elected officials and placed their own supporters in the legislature. Napoleon then received a command against the Austrians and Sardinians that resulted in a swift victory for the French and eventual annexation of Italy. Napoleon was hailed as a hero and decided to sail to Egypt, there to fight the British fleet and, it was hoped, cut off British contact and trade with her colonies in the East. However, the invasion of Egypt (1798) was a failure for the French; Napoleon abandoned his troops and returned to Paris, where he overthrew the Directory that he had once championed (November 10, 1799). Establishing a new government called the Consulate, he then issued the Constitution for the Year VIII (December 1799), which promoted liberal ideas such as universal manhood suffrage and a system of governmental checks and balances, but in reality granted Napoleon virtual dictatorial power as first consul. His position was confirmed by a plebiscite that approved the new constitution by a vote of 3,011,077 to 1,567. Both the middle and lower classes seemed satisfied to accept the security that Napoleon offered.

Napoleon then quickly consolidated his rule by achieving peace with Austria and Britain and by restoring order at home. In 1801, he concluded a concordat with the Catholic Church, which in fact resulted in the subordination of the church to the state; there would be no controversy between secular and religious authority in Napoleonic France. So satisfied were French citizens that in 1802 they voted Napoleon consul for life. In 1804, there was simply no one with enough authority to grant him the final accolade, so Napoleon crowned himself

Napoleon I, Emperor of the French. The pope sat nearby, watching the ceremony. Napoleon had achieved the ultimate authority, which had escaped even Charlemagne.

In his decade as emperor, Napoleon conquered most of Europe, spreading France's revolutionary ideals. It was at this time, too, that he paid great attention to domestic concerns and soon instituted reforms and programs, including a codification of laws known as the Napoleonic Code. His glory came to an end in 1814 when he was finally defeated by a coalition of European powers. Napoleon's brief return from exile was unsuccessful and resulted in his defeat by Lord Wellington at Waterloo. The victors agreed at the Congress of Vienna in 1815 that no single state should dominate Europe—power must be balanced. Another Napoleon would not be tolerated. The great general was ingloriously exiled to St. Helena, an isolated and inaccessible rock in the Atlantic. He died there in 1821 of stomach cancer or, as some modern researchers advocate, the victim of gradual poisoning. Even in death, Napoleon remains a controversial figure.

In this section, we will look at Napoleon's rise to power and especially his reforms and attempts to consolidate his position. Napoleon was certainly a military leader of genius, but his achievements often inspire philosophical rather than military analysis. His career raises questions about the nature of power and the ability of the individual to change the course of history. Is history motivated by social and economic forces over which individuals have no control? Or does the "hero" actually change history by force of personality and ability? Did Napoleon make France a great nation through his reforms and conquests? If so, does progress come about because of the imposition of reforms upon a people? Was Napoleon, who overthrew the legitimate, elected government of France and installed a dictatorship, necessary for the progress of a revolution dedicated to liberty and equality?

The Realities of Power (1796)

NAPOLEON BONAPARTE

After the Reign of Terror in 1794, the French Revolution entered a moderate period known as Thermidor that retreated from the violent radicalism of Robespierre. A new government called the Directory was formed, and it governed the French Republic rather ineffectively until 1799. In that year, Napoleon Bonaparte, who had supported the Directory and had earned fame as the military protector of the Republic, returned to Paris from his Egyptian campaign and promptly overthrew the government. In its place he established the Consulate. Napoleon, as first consul, was given significant power over his other two colleagues. On December 15, 1799, the Consulate proclaimed the end of the French Revolution. The ideals that founded the Republic ostensibly had not changed, but the leadership certainly had. The following excerpt is from a conversation Napoleon had with one of his confidants in 1796, three years before coming into power. It reveals much about Napoleon's ambition.

What I have done so far is nothing. I am but at the opening of the career I am to run. Do you suppose that I have gained my victories in Italy in order to advance the lawyers of the Directory? Do you think, either, that my object is to establish a Republic? What a notion! A republic of thirty million people, with our morals and vices! How could that ever be? It is a chimera with which the French are infatuated but which will pass away in time like all others. What they want is glory and

"On the Realities of Power" is from *Memoires of Miot de Melito*, in James H. Robinson, ed., *Translations and Reprints from the Original Sources of European History*, rev. ed., vol. 2, pt. 2 (Philadelphia: University of Pennsylvania Press, 1900), pp. 2–3.

the gratification of their vanity; as for liberty, of that they have no conception. Look at the army! The victories which we have just gained have given the French soldier his true character. I am everything to him. Let the Directory attempt to deprive me of my command and they will see who is master. The nation must have a head, a head rendered illustrious by glory and not by theories of government, fine phrases, or the talk of idealists, of which the French understand not a whit. Let them have their toys and they will be satisfied. They will amuse themselves and allow themselves to be led, provided the goal is cleverly disguised.

Theme: Historical Change and Transition

The Historical Intersection

FLORENCE: 1512

How a Prince Should Keep His Word

NICCOLÒ MACHIAVELLI

Over the centuries, the name of Machiavelli has become synonymous with evil. The adjective "Machiavellian" still evokes images of deceit and political backstabbing. Machiavelli's ideas were condemned by the church as immoral and inspired by Satan himself. In reality, Niccolò Machiavelli (1469–1527) was a loyal citizen of Florence who had been schooled in the classics and had chosen a career in public service. He disliked the rule of the Medici family and was a great advocate of republicanism. The Florentine republic was successful until 1512, when a Spanish mercenary army defeated Machiavelli's personally trained Florentine militia. They reinstalled Medici rule, and Machiavelli was tortured on the rack and thrown into prison for a time. He retired to the country and wrote a little book entitled The Prince. *In it, Machiavelli gives the wisdom of his experience in politics. It is a manual of power: how to obtain it, maintain it, and lose it. In his analysis, Machiavelli is brutally realistic about the nature of human beings and the world of power politics: Learn the rules and you may survive and prosper. In the political chaos of Renaissance Italy, where alliances shifted frequently and distrust prevailed, such a guide proved useful and popular. Some of Machiavelli's most important ideas from* The Prince *are excerpted below. Napoleon Bonaparte learned his lessons well.*

(contd)

Compare and Contrast:

- Compare Napoleon's political vision carefully with Machiavelli's ideas from *The Prince*. Must the goals of power always be "cleverly disguised?" How important is deceit in gaining and maintaining power?

How praiseworthy it is for a prince to keep his word and to live by integrity and not by deceit everyone knows; nevertheless, one sees from the experience of our times that the princes who have accomplished great deeds are those who have cared little for keeping their promises and who have known how to manipulate the minds of men by shrewdness; and in the end they have surpassed those who laid their foundations upon honesty.

You must, therefore, know that there are two means of fighting: one according to the laws, the other with force; the first way is proper to man, the second to beasts; but because the first, in many cases, is not sufficient, it becomes necessary to have recourse to the second. Therefore, a prince must know how to use wisely the natures of the beast and the man. . . .

Since, then, a prince must know how to make good use of the nature of the beast, he should choose from among the beasts the fox and the lion; for the lion cannot defend itself from traps and the fox cannot protect itself from wolves. It is therefore necessary to be a fox in order to recognize the traps and a lion in order to frighten the wolves. Those who play only the part of the lion do not understand matters. A wise ruler, therefore, cannot and should not keep his word when such an observance of faith would be to his disadvantage and when the reasons which made him promise are removed. And if men were all good, this rule would not be good; but since men are a sorry lot and will not keep their promises to you, you likewise need not keep yours to them. A prince never lacks legitimate reasons to break his promises. Of this one could cite an endless number of modern examples to show how many pacts, how many promises have been made null and void because of the infidelity of princes; and he who has known best how to use the fox has come to a better end. But it is necessary to know how to disguise this nature well and to be a great hypocrite and a liar: and men are so simpleminded and so controlled by their present necessities that one who deceives will always find another who will allow himself to be deceived. . . .

A prince, therefore, must be very careful never to let anything slip from his lips which is not full of the five qualities mentioned above: he should appear, upon seeing and hearing him, to be all mercy, all faithfulness, all integrity, all kindness, all religion. And there is nothing more necessary than to seem to possess this last quality. And men in general judge more by their eyes than their hands; for everyone can see but few can feel. Everyone sees what you seem to be, few perceive what you are, and those few do not dare to contradict the opinion

(contd)

of the many who have the majesty of the state to defend them; and in the actions of all men, and especially of princes, where there is no impartial arbiter, one must consider the final result. Let a prince therefore act to seize and to maintain the state; his methods will always be judged honorable and will be praised by all; for ordinary people are always deceived by appearances and by the outcome of a thing; and in the world there is nothing but ordinary people. . . .

Consider This:

- What does the excerpt on Napoleon's political goals reveal about his commitment to the democratic ideals of the French Revolution? Was Machiavelli correct? Must any ideal in the political world remain of secondary importance to the necessity of gaining and maintaining power?
- Has the nature of political power changed in our contemporary world or has technology simplified the "creation of belief" and thus made personal freedom even more difficult to maintain?

The Prince by Niccolò di Bernardo Machiavelli, translated by Mark Musa and Peter Bondanella, from *The Portable Machiavelli*, edited by Peter Bondanella, copyright © 1979 by Viking Penguin, Inc., pp. 135–136. Used by permission of Viking Penguin, a division of Penguin Putnam Inc.

Suppression of the Newspapers (1800)

In order to consolidate the new regime, Napoleon sought to control the flow of information in the state. In the first document, note the reasons given for suppression of the newspapers. Between July 1801 and April 1802, Napoleon went on to reorganize the religious institutions of France by redefining and controlling the position of the Roman Catholic Church.

The consuls of the Republic, considering that a part of the newspapers which are printed in the department of the Seine are instruments in the hands of the enemies of the Republic; that the government is particularly charged by the French people to look after their security, orders as follows:

1. The minister of police shall permit to be printed, published, and circulated during the whole course of the war only the following newspapers: . . . [Here follows the names of thirteen newspapers], and newspapers devoted exclusively to science, arts, literature, commerce, announcements and notices.

2. The minister of the general police shall immediately make a report upon all the newspapers that are printed in the other departments.

3. The minister of the general police shall see that no new newspaper be printed in the department of the Seine, as well as in all the other departments of the Republic.

"Suppression of the Newspapers" is from Frank M. Anderson, ed., *The Constitutions and Other Illustrative Documents of the History of France*, 2nd ed., revised (New York: Russell and Russell, 1908), p. 282.

4. The proprietors and editors of the newspapers preserved by the present order shall present themselves to the minister of the police in order to attest their character as French citizens, their residences and signatures, and they shall promise fidelity to the constitution.

5. All newspapers which shall insert articles opposed to the respect that is due to the social compact, to the sovereignty of the people and the glory of the armies, or which shall publish invectives against the governments and nations who are the friends or allies of the Republic, even when these articles may be extracts from foreign periodicals, shall be immediately suppressed.

6. The minister of the general police is charged with the execution of the present order, which shall be inserted in the Bulletin of the Laws.

Articles for the Catholic Church (1802)

1. No bull, brief, rescript, decree, injunction, provision, signature serving as a provision, nor other documents from the court of Rome, even concerning individuals only, can be received, published, printed, or otherwise put into effect, without the authorization of the government.

4. No national or metropolitan council, no diocesan synod, no deliberative assembly, shall take place without the express permission of the government.

6. There shall be recourse to the Council of State in every case of abuse on the part of the Superiors and other ecclesiastical persons.

The cases of abuse are usurpation or excess of power, contravention of the laws and regulations of the Republic, infraction of the rules sanctioned by the canons received in France, attack upon the liberties, privileges and customs of the Gallican church, and every undertaking or any proceeding which in the exercise of worship can compromise the honor of the citizens, disturb arbitrarily their consciences, or degenerate into oppression or injury against them or into public scandal.

"Articles for the Catholic Church" is from Frank M. Anderson, ed., *The Constitutions and Other Illustrative Documents of the History of France*, 2nd ed., revised (New York: Russell and Russell, 1908), p. 299.

Why the French Submitted to Napoleon's Rule (1804)
COMTESSE DE RÉMUSAT

Five years after Napoleon became head of the French government as First Consul (1799), then as Consul for Life (1802), he moved to expand his power. On May 18, 1804, the Senate decreed that he should be made Emperor of the French. The people of France overwhelmingly approved of this measure through a plebiscite. Napoleon now had complete control of France's government and fate.

But why did the French people willingly submit to the despotism of Napoleon? In the next selection, the Comtesse de Rémusat (1780–1821), lady-in-waiting to Napoleon's wife, Josephine, and the author of some lively memoirs, gives her assessment. Appropriately, Napoleon found divine sanction for his power. The second offering recounts a catechism written during the reign of Louis XIV and modified to meet Napoleon's particular needs. Its questions and answers address the duties of French citizens toward their emperor.

"Why the French Submitted to Napoleon's Rule" is from James H. Robinson and Charles A. Beard, eds., *Readings in Modern European History*, vol. 1 (Boston: Ginn and Company, 1908), pp. 333–334.

I can understand how it was that men worn out by the turmoil of the Revolution, and afraid of that liberty which had long been associated with death, looked for repose under the dominion of an able ruler on who Fortune was seemingly resolved to smile. I can conceive that they regarded his elevation as a decree of destiny and fondly believed that in the irrevocable they should find peace. I may confidently assert that those persons believed quite sincerely that Bonaparte, whether as Consul or Emperor, would exert his authority to oppose the intrigues of faction and would save us from the perils of anarchy.

None dared to utter the word "republic," so deeply had the Terror stained that name; and the government of the Directory had perished in the contempt with which its chiefs were regarded. The return of the Bourbons could only be brought about by the aid of a revolution; and the slightest disturbance terrified the French people, in whom enthusiasm of every kind seemed dead. Besides, the men in whom they had trusted had one after the other deceived them; and as, this time, they were yielding to force, they were at least certain they were not deceiving themselves.

The belief, or rather the error, that only despotism could at that epoch maintain order in France was very widespread. It became the mainstay of Bonaparte; and it is due to him to say that he also believed it. The factions played into his hands by imprudent attempts which he turned to his own advantage. He had some grounds for his belief that he was necessary; France believed it, too; and he even succeeded in persuading foreign sovereigns that he constituted a barrier against republican influences, which, but for him, might spread widely. At the moment when Bonaparte placed the imperial crown upon his head there was not a king in Europe who did not believe that he wore his own crown more securely because of that event. Had the new emperor granted a liberal constitution, the peace of nations and of kings might really have been forever secured.

The Imperial Catechism (April 1806)

Question: What are the duties of Christians toward those who govern them, and what in particular are our duties towards Napoleon I, our emperor?

Answer: Christians owe to the princes who govern them, and we in particular owe to Napoleon I, our emperor, love, respect, obedience, fidelity, military service, and the taxes levied for the preservation and defense of the empire and of his throne. We also owe him fervent prayers for his safety and for the spiritual and temporal prosperity of the state.

Question: Why are we subject to all these duties toward our emperor?

Answer: First, because God, who has created empires and distributes them according to his will, has, by loading our emperor with gifts both in peace and in war, established him as our sovereign and made him the agent of his power and his image on earth. To honor and serve our emperor is therefore to honor and serve God himself. Secondly, because our Lord Jesus Christ himself, both by his teaching and his example, has taught us what we owe to our sovereign. Even at his very birth he obeyed the edict of Caesar Augustus; he paid the established tax; and while he commanded us to render to God those things which belong to God, he also commanded us to render unto Caesar those things which are Caesar's.

Question: Are there not special motives which should attach us more closely to Napoleon I, our emperor?

Answer: Yes, for it is he whom God has raised up in trying times to reestablish the public worship of the holy religion of our fathers and to be its protector; he has reestablished and preserved public order by his profound and active wisdom; he defends the state by his mighty arm; he has become the anointed of the Lord by the

"The Imperial Catechism" is from James H. Robinson and Charles A. Beard, eds., *Readings in Modern European History*, vol. 1 (Boston: Ginn and Company, 1908), pp. 351–352.

consecration which he has received from the sovereign pontiff, head of the Church universal.

Question: What must we think of those who are neglecting their duties toward our emperor?

Answer: According to the apostle Paul, they are resisting the order established by God himself, and render themselves worthy of eternal damnation.

Theme: Church/State Relationships

The Historical Intersection

SWITZERLAND: 1541

The Genevan Catechism

JOHN CALVIN

Although Lutheranism formed the basis of the Protestant Reformation, by the mid-sixteenth century, it had lost much of its energy and was confined to Germany and Scandinavia. The movement was spread throughout Europe by other reformers, the most influential of whom was John Calvin (1509–1564). Calvinism became popular in the Netherlands and Scotland and it formed the core of the Puritan belief that was to be so influential in the colonization of America. The following catechism reveals Calvin's strict regulation of lives and beliefs in Geneva.

Compare and Contrast:

- Compare the structure of John Calvin's Genevan Catechism with that of Napoleon's Imperial Catechism. What do they demand respectively of the citizens of Geneva and the populace of France?

The minister: Have we in the supper simply a signification of the things above mentioned, or are they given to us in reality?

The child: Since Jesus Christ is truth itself there can be no doubt that the promises he has made regarding the supper are accomplished, and that what is

(contd)

figured there is verified there also. Wherefore according as he promises and represents I have no doubt that he makes us partakers of his own substance, in order that he may unite us with him in one life.

The minister: But how may this be, when the Body of Jesus Christ is in heaven, and we are on this earthly pilgrimage?

The child: It comes about through the incomprehensible power of his spirit, which may indeed unite things widely separated in space.

The minister: You do not understand then that the body is enclosed in the bread, or the blood in the cup?

The child: No. On the contrary, in order that the reality of the sacrament be achieved our hearts must be raised to heaven, where Jesus Christ dwells in the glory of the Father, whence we await him for our redemption; and we are not to seek him in these corruptible elements.

The minister: You understand then that there are two things in this sacrament: the natural bread and wine, which we see with the eye, touch with the hand and perceive with the taste; and Jesus Christ, through whom our souls are inwardly nourished?

The child: I do. In such a way moreover that we have there the very witness and so say a pledge of the resurrection of our bodies; since they are made partakers in the symbol of life.

Consider This:

- Should we characterize Calvin as a spiritual leader and Napoleon as a political leader? How do these documents blur the boundaries of such designations? In order to obtain effective control over people, must spiritual leaders grant themselves political power and must political leaders claim spiritual authority?

"The Genevan Catechism" is from James H. Robinson, ed., *Translations and Reprints from the Original Sources of European History*, vol. 3 (Philadelphia: University of Pennsylvania, 1902), pp. 8–9.

Napoleon's Defeat and Exile:
"We Stand as Martyrs to an Immortal Cause!" (1815)
NAPOLEON BONAPARTE

Beginning in 1792 and continuing throughout much of the revolution, France was at war against various coalitions of European nations. Revolutionary ideology was exportable and threatened the very foundation of enlightened despotism. As the French revolutionaries attacked

"Napoleon's Defeat and Exile" is from R. M. Johnston, ed., *The Corsican: A Diary of Napoleon's Life in His Own Words* (Boston: Houghton Mifflin, 1910), pp. 468–469.

the church, monarchy, and aristocracy, most of Europe, including Great Britain, reacted by re-pressing liberal reform movements. These wars at once threatened the revolution and also granted it purpose and unity. Napoleon, a military commander of genius and overreaching am-bition, capitalized on this French "spirit of the times" and sought first to link himself with the revolutionary forces within the state and then, as Consul and Emperor, to dominate Europe both militarily and culturally from 1803 to his final defeat at Waterloo in 1815. In the process, he inspired France and certainly changed the course of history. Napoleon believed that his actions were directed toward a destiny that he was compelled to achieve by fate.

The image of Napoleon and his glorious reputation as a military genius was cultivated through the paintings of Jacques Louis David and the memoirs of Napoleon's commanders. Without doubt, Napoleon demonstrated organizational ability and strategic brilliance. This, coupled with a nearly limitless supply of well-trained French soldiers, allowed him to domi-nate and expand his control over the European continent.

Napoleon's grand ambitions, however, proved his undoing during his famous invasion of Russia through Poland in June 1812. After the victory of the Duke of Wellington over the French forces at Waterloo in 1815, Napoleon was sentenced to permanent exile on the South Atlantic is-land of St. Helena. The following selection from his diary gives indication of his dominant per-sonality and spirit. However, he remained on this isolated rock until his death in 1821.

What infamous treatment they have held in store for us! This is the agony of death! To injus-tice, to violence, they add insult and slow tor-ture! If I was so dangerous, why didn't they get rid of me? A few bullets in my heart or in my head would have settled it; there would have been some courage at least in such a crime! How can the Sovereigns of Europe permit the sacred nature of sovereignty to be attainted in me? Can't they see that they are killing them-selves at St. Helena? I have entered their capitals as a conqueror; had I been moved by such mo-tives, what would have become of them? They all called me their brother, and I had become so by the will of the people, the sanction of victory, the character of religion, the alliances of policy and of family. . . . Apart from that, who has

there been in history with more partisans, more friends? Who has been more popular, more beloved? Who ever left behind more ardent re-grets? Look at France: might not one say that from this rock of mine I still reign over her? . . .

Our situation may even have good points! The Universe watches us! We stand as martyrs to an immortal cause! Millions of men weep with us, our country sighs, and glory has put on mourning! We struggle here against the tyranny of the gods, and the hopes of humanity are with us! Misfortune itself knows heroism, and glory! Only adversity was wanting to complete my ca-reer! Had I died on the throne, in the clouds of my almightiness, I would have remained a prob-lem for many; as it is, thanks to my misfortunes, I can be judged naked.

The Role of Great Men in History

G. W. F. HEGEL

Napoleon's career has inspired many questions: What is the role of the "great man" or "hero" in history? Can the course of history be changed by a dynamic individual of ability and resolve? Or does history progress by uncontrollable economic and social "forces"? The last selection is by

"The Role of Great Men in History" is from G. W. F. Hegel, *The Philosophy of History*, trans. J. Sibree (New York: Dover, 1956), pp. 30–31. Reprinted by permission of the publisher.

G. W. F. Hegel, a German philosopher who believed that "heroes" such as Caesar, Alexander, and Napoleon were unconscious instruments of a "world spirit" (Zeitgeist) that lay behind the development of human history. The chosen passage reveals Hegel's thoughts about how heroes could change the course of history. Hegel is representative of the romantic belief, current in the early nineteenth century, that human history was connected with much larger spiritual forces.

Such are all great historical men—whose own particular aims involve those large issues which are the will of the World-Spirit. They may be called Heroes, inasmuch as they have derived their purposes and their vocation, not from the calm, regular course of things, sanctioned by the existing order: but from a concealed fount—one which has not attained to phenomenal, pre-sent existence—from that inner Spirit, still hidden beneath the surface, which, impinging on the outer world as on a shell, bursts it in pieces, because it is another kernel than that which belonged to the shell in question. They are men, therefore, who appear to draw the impulse of their life from themselves; and whose deeds have produced a condition of things and a complex of historical relations which appear to be only their interest, and their work.

Such individuals had no consciousness of the general idea they were unfolding, while prosecuting those aims of theirs; on the contrary, they were practical, political men. But at the same time they were thinking men, who had an insight into the requirements of the time—what was ripe for development. This was the very Truth for their age, for their world: the species next in order, so to speak, and which was already formed in the womb of time. It was theirs to know this nascent principle; the necessary, directly sequent step in progress, which their world was to take; to make this their aim, and to expend their energy in promoting it. World-historical men—the Heroes of an epoch—must, therefore, be recognized as its clear-sighted ones: their deed, their words are the best of that time.

CHRONOLOGY: Enlightenment and Revolution

Section I: The Intellectual Framework

1543	Nicolaus Copernicus: *On the Revolutions of the Heavenly Spheres.*
1605	Sir Francis Bacon: *The Advancement of Learning.*
1609	Johannes Kepler: *On the Motion of Mars.*
1620	Sir Francis Bacon: *Novum Organum.*
1628	William Harvey: *On the Circulation of the Blood.*
1632	Galileo Galilei: *Dialogues on the Two Chief Systems of the World.*
1637	René Descartes: *Discourse on Method.*
1682–1725	Reign of Peter the Great of Russia. In 1697, the Tsar visits western Europe to study the skills necessary to build Russia into a strong, modern state.
1687	Sir Isaac Newton: *Principia Mathematica.*
1688–1689	Glorious Revolution in England.
1690	John Locke: *Essay Concerning Human Understanding; Second Treatise of Civil Government.*

1693	John Locke: *Some Thoughts Concerning Education.*
1713–1740	Frederick William I builds up the military power of Prussia.
1740–1748	Maria Theresa succeeds to the Austrian throne. War of the Austrian Succession: Frederick II of Prussia invades Austrian province of Silesia in violation of Pragmatic Sanction; Maria Theresa fights Frederick to a stalemate, but loses Silesia in the Treaty of Aix-la-Chapelle.
1748	The Baron de Montesquieu: *The Spirit of the Laws;* David Hume: *Inquiry into Human Nature.*
1751	Denis Diderot: First volume of the *Encyclopedia* appears.
1756–1763	Seven Years War: France, Austria, Sweden, and Russia vs. Prussia (supported financially by Great Britain).
1762	Jean-Jacques Rousseau: *The Social Contract;* and *Emile.*
1763	Voltaire: *Treatise on Toleration.*
1764	Voltaire: *Philosophical Dictionary.*
1764	Cesare Beccaria: *On Crimes and Punishments.*

Section II: The Era of Revolution

1765	Stamp Act Congress.
1775–1783	American Revolution.
1776	The American Declaration of Independence.
1776	Edward Gibbon: *The Decline and Fall of the Roman Empire.*
1776	Adam Smith: *The Wealth of Nations.*
1787	Ratification of the Constitution of the United States.
May 1789–June 1789	ESTATES-GENERAL: Monarchy still in control of the government. War is the expected foreign policy of the ancien régime.
1789–1791	NATIONAL ASSEMBLY: Nominal absolute monarchy. State church exists with priests paid by the state.
June 20, 1789:	Tennis Court Oath.
July 14, 1789:	Fall of Bastille.
August 27, 1789:	Declaration of the Rights of Man.
July 12, 1790:	Civil Constitution of the Clergy adopted.
1791	Adoption of the American Bill of Rights.
June 24, 1791:	Louis XVI and family are caught trying to flee France.
1791–1792	LEGISLATIVE ASSEMBLY: Constitutional monarchy. War is promoted to solve domestic problems. State church.

October 1, 1791:	Legislative Assembly convenes.
September 2, 1792:	The September Massacres.
1792–1794	THE CONVENTION: Committee of Public Safety administers government. Universal manhood suffrage. Cult of Reason promoted. Reign of Terror (1793–1794).
September 21, 1792:	The Convention meets and the monarchy is abolished.
January 21, 1793:	Louis XVI is executed.
July, 1793:	Robespierre enters the Committee of Public Safety.
October 16, 1793:	Queen Marie-Antoinette is executed.
November 10, 1793:	The Cult of Reason is proclaimed.
April 6, 1794:	Execution of Danton and Desmoulins.
May 7, 1794:	Cult of the Supreme Being proclaimed.
June 10, 1794:	Law of 22 Prairial is adopted (Administration of Terror).
July 28, 1794:	Execution of Robespierre.
1795–1799	THE DIRECTORY AND CONSULATE: Thermidorian Reaction. Restricted franchise. Separation of church and state promoted.
August 22, 1795:	Directory established.
November 10, 1799:	Consulate established with Napoleon as first consul.
December 15, 1799:	Consulate proclaims end of French Revolution.
1802	Napoleon concludes a concordat with Pope Pius VII: Clergy must swear loyalty oath to the state.
1802	Napoleon proclaimed consul for life.
1804	Napoleon crowned emperor of the French; Civil Code issued.
1805	Nelson defeats French fleet at Trafalgar; Napoleon's victory at Austerlitz.
1806	Napoleon's victory at Jena.
1812	Invasion of Russia and French defeat at Borodino.
1813	French defeat at Leipzig (Battle of Nations).
1814	Congress of Vienna convenes in September.
1815	Napoleon escapes from Elba and returns to Paris. The Duke of Wellington commands coalition forces in victory over Napoleon at Waterloo.
1821	Napoleon dies in exile on South Atlantic island of St. Helena.

STUDY QUESTIONS

Section I: The Intellectual Framework

1. How do some of Descartes' ideas on scientific method show the influence of Sir Francis Bacon? What did Descartes mean by the phrase "I think, therefore I am"? Why was this so fundamental to his method? Reconstruct his logic for the existence of God. Do you find it compelling?

2. Read Copernicus' statement on the movement of the sun and earth. What reasons does he give for supporting the heliocentric theory? Is he convincing? Why is it significant that Copernicus refers to ancient authors like Cicero and Plutarch?

3. What were Galileo's specific ideas regarding the relationship between science and the Bible? Be particular in your analysis. Why were Galileo's ideas considered dangerous by the Inquisition? Did the Inquisition do the church more harm than good?

4. Consider the words of Martin Luther quoted at the beginning of this chapter: "Reason is the greatest enemy that faith has. It never comes to the aid of spiritual things, but . . . struggles against the divine Word, treating with contempt all that emanates from God." Does it surprise you that this statement comes from the leader of the Protestant Reformation? Discuss the compatibility of science and religion in light of this quotation.

5. What are some of the current areas of tension between science and religion? In our quest for knowledge and understanding about the world around us and our place in it, must one choose between the mind and the spirit?

6. Why did William Harvey want to present his findings in an address before the Royal College of Physicians? What was he afraid of? Why were his discoveries about the heart and circulation of blood so important and perhaps so threatening?

7. Do you find Locke's assertion that the mind is a blank slate at birth and that there are no innate ideas to be a compelling argument? This still remains a disputed issue in modern psychology—can you solve it? What notions and actions are instinctive to human beings and what is learned through experience?

8. What mathematical equation did Cesare Beccaria apply to "the good and evil of life"? How do you think he might have reacted to our modern concern over capital punishment? Ultimately, how does a society prevent crime?

9. How does Immanuel Kant answer the question "What is Enlightenment?" In what ways do you see his views on freedom and risk in evidence throughout this chapter?

10. Why was toleration so important to Voltaire? Do you regard him as a religious individual? Why is deism a comfortable philosophy?

11. What are the arguments used by Locke and Rousseau to justify revolution? Who or what is the "sovereign power" Rousseau mentions? Comment in particular on Rousseau's belief that "whoever refuses to obey the general will shall be compelled to it by the whole body." Isn't this a form of tyranny?

12. Note the excerpts under the section "The Political Framework." In order to be enduring, must revolutions have precedents for action (like the Glorious Revolution or the American Revolution)? Must they have some philosophical justification?

Section II: The Era of Revolution

13. In the document entitled "Resolved to Die Free Men Rather Than to Live Slaves," Thomas Jefferson and John Dickinson argued that the British Crown was a despotism that was

"blinded . . . by [its] intemperate rage for unlimited domination." What are the arguments that the authors present for the necessity of taking up arms against Great Britain? Compare these with the justifications noted in the Declaration of Independence. How are these two documents illustrative of Enlightenment political ideals as argued by John Locke and others earlier in the chapter?

14. James Madison, the primary architect of the Constitution, warned about the "violence of faction" that threatened to destroy the new nation. What were George Washington's ideas on the subject in his *Farewell Address* of 1796? What warnings did he give to the nation in hopes of maintaining political unity?

15. What is a revolution? How do you distinguish it from a riot or a rebellion? What political, social, or economic conditions existed in eighteenth-century France that contributed to the French Revolution? In a general sense, do you think that difficult conditions precede any successful revolution?

16. What were the specific demands made by the Third Estate? Do they seem reasonable to you?

17. Read the Tennis Court Oath carefully. Does it call for radical action? Why is it considered to be one of the most important documents of the French Revolution?

18. Why was the fall of the Bastille such an important event? After reading the pertinent selections, discuss how important violence is in a revolution. Do most successful revolutions promote violence to some degree?

19. What are the most important ideas contained in the Declaration of the Rights of Man? Compare them with those contained in the American Declaration of Independence. Why were these documents essential to the American and French Revolutions? What do they tell you about the Old Regime of Louis XVI and the British Crown? Do you believe (as did most of the *philosophes*) that there are "natural rights" for all human beings and that a government should protect these rights? How is this "natural rights" argument reflected in the various documents of the French revolution?

20. Analyze the speech of Robespierre. How did he justify the use of terror in the promotion of revolution? Note, in particular, the juxtaposition of virtue and terror. In an ethical sense, can virtue ever be promoted by terror?

21. How did Napoleon come to power in 1799? Carefully read the statement he made "On the Realities of Power." What does this say about Napoleon's commitment to democratic ideals? At the time, though, to progress as a nation did France need less ideal and more practical inspiration and leadership? Was Napoleon a hypocrite who saved France from chaos? If so, do you condemn him for his hypocrisy?

22. On becoming first consul, Napoleon consolidated his position by suppressing the newspapers and reorganizing the state's religious institutions. Read these selections. Are these actions consistent with democratic government? From Napoleon's perspective, why were these actions essential to the stability of the state? Why is it essential in time of revolution for the state to control religious organization?

23. Was Napoleon an absolute monarch in the tradition of Louis XIV? Was he a democrat, or the first of the "modern dictators" in the fascist mold of Mussolini and Hitler? Does the distinction between a democrat and a dictator blur when one is trying to achieve and consolidate power?

24. Note Napoleon's comments in exile on St. Helena. Was he a progressive or destructive force in French history? Did he embody Hegel's conception of the term "hero"? How? Was the philosophy of Jean-Jacques Rousseau every bit as much a force for the promotion of historical change as were the actions of Napoleon Bonaparte?

3

The Varieties of Freedom: Revolution in Latin America

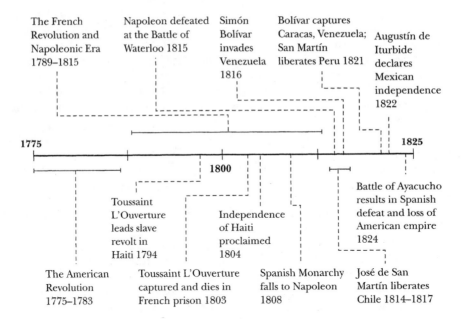

The French Revolution and Napoleonic Era 1789–1815

Napoleon defeated at the Battle of Waterloo 1815

Simón Bolívar invades Venezuela 1816

Bolívar captures Caracas, Venezuela; San Martín liberates Peru 1821

Augustín de Iturbide declares Mexican independence 1822

1775

1800

1825

Toussaint L'Ouverture leads slave revolt in Haiti 1794

Independence of Haiti proclaimed 1804

Battle of Ayacucho results in Spanish defeat and loss of American empire 1824

The American Revolution 1775–1783

Toussaint L'Ouverture captured and dies in French prison 1803

Spanish Monarchy falls to Napoleon 1808

José de San Martín liberates Chile 1814–1817

The success of the American and French revolutions of the late eighteenth century shattered the illusion of invincible royal authority and replaced it with a new political assumption: Human beings were endowed by God with natural rights to life, liberty and property. People had a right to freedom and could govern themselves through democratic institutions. Political authority was no longer completely invested in a monarch, but rather in representatives elected to fulfill the "popular will." In establishing constitutions, these new republics struggled to define the relationship between executive and legislative authority. The United States maintained a precarious balance between political factions, while France opted for military glory and the dominant authority of the Emperor Napoleon.

Revolution is an inherently unstable process, but it is attractive, and the spark that was ignited in the English colonies of America and in France inspired independence movements throughout Latin America. Between 1804 and 1824, France withdrew from Haiti, Portugal abandoned Brazil, and Spain was driven from all of its American empire except for Cuba and Puerto Rico. These independence movements were led by individuals educated in Enlightenment thought, who engaged the social and economic forces of the time, risking everything in order to establish a new political order.

It is a curious paradox that revolution often is inspired by leaders who seek to embody the "will of the people" for the greater "liberty of the people" and in so doing, fashion their own dictatorships within a "free nation." By appealing to the concerns of specific social and economic interest groups and to the larger unity of all, leaders can identify their own success with the "destiny of the nation." This emphasis on national identity and unity in the face of foreign threat is a prerequisite to freedom. It is also the seed of dictatorship. For once the foreign enemy is repelled, then national unity must be maintained amidst developing political factions. The ensuing domestic chaos presents opportunities for the military leadership to purge competing ideologies for the benefit of domestic peace. This recurring political dilemma of granting "natural freedoms" and then controlling the "excesses of freedom" is perhaps the most dangerous threat to the democratic process. Until a democratic tradition is established wherein people accept a chronic, but benign and low-grade political instability, and an unyielding, but respectful pattern of initiative, compromise, and balance, the success of new democracies faces perpetual threat.

This dilemma has been of particular concern in Latin America. The independence movements from about 1800 to 1825 were generally led by a Creole elite—merchants, landowners, and professionals—who were born in Latin America, and wanted to throw off the political yoke of Spain, Portugal, and France. At the same time, they sought to preserve and enhance their own social and economic status within the new nations. Few Indians, Blacks, Mestizos, Mulattos, or slaves benefitted from the end of European rule.

Thus, the motives of Latin American independence leaders have sometimes been called into question. The names of Toussaint L'Ouverture (1744–1803), José de San Martín (1778–1850), Bernardo O'Higgins (1778–1842), Simón Bolívar (1783–1830), and Augustín de Iturbide (1783–1824) all ring as political liberators. But their demonstrative actions in establishing their own positions through small dominant political and military factions called *juntas* saddled Latin America with a political tradition of "paternalism," wherein the leader provided for his countryman as a father would for his children: enough freedom to prevent all-out revolution, but not enough freedom to become dangerous to the stability of the leader's control. The development of "strongman rule" by *El Caudillo*, the dictator, has consigned many Latin American countries to that democratic dilemma of freedom and repression. Right-wing dictatorships have played a prominent role in nineteenth and twentieth century Latin America. In Argentina alone, the imprint of military rule is dominant from Juan Manuel de Rojas (1793–1877) to Juan Perón (1895–1974), and Leopoldo Galitieri (b. 1926), who led Argentina into the disastrous

Falkland Islands conflict with Great Britain in 1982. The repressive control of General Augusto Pinochet (b. 1915) over the government of Chile from 1973 to 1998 is undeniable, as was that of Porfirio Diaz in Mexico from 1876 to 1911, General Manuel Noriega in Panama from 1983 to 1989, the Somoza regime in Nicaragua from 1936 to 1989, the Stroessner regime in Paraguay from 1954 to 1989, and the Duvalier dictatorship in Haiti from 1957 to 1986.

Many of the countries of Latin America—such as Brazil, Costa Rica, Mexico, Panama, and Argentina—now enjoy relatively stable civilian democracies. Problems such as inflation, overpopulation, poverty, and education continue to threaten stability, but the road to independence that was forged in the early nineteenth century remains one of the crucial steps to political freedom in world history. This chapter emphasizes the issues and problems associated with the very different revolutions in Haiti and in Venezuela, led by two of the most dominant personalities of the age: Toussaint L'Ouverture and Simón Bolívar.

THE "BLACK JACOBIN": TOUSSAINT L'OUVERTURE

To consider oneself different from ordinary men is wrong, but it is right to hope that one will not remain like ordinary men.

—Yoshida Shōin

On November 29, 1803, the French colony of Saint Domingue, composed overwhelmingly of former slaves, who worked the notorious plantations on the island, announced to the world a revolutionary event:

> *"The independence of Saint Domingue is proclaimed; returned to our primitive dignity, we have claimed our rights; we swear never to yield them to any power on earth. The frightful veil of prejudice is torn to pieces. Be it so forever! Woe be to whomsoever would dare again to put together the bloody tatters!"*

This was only the second independent nation in the Western hemisphere and the first that was dedicated to the liberty of black people. The creation of what is known today as Haiti, a "Black Republic," threatened the extensive plantations of the Caribbean and indeed, the entire colonial system that depended on a cheap supply of slave labor. More ominous perhaps was the threat that Blacks could share in the Enlightenment conception of natural rights that had propelled the political revolutions in the United States and France. The assumptions upon which the rule of European and American slave holders rested—that Blacks were naturally docile, stupid, and inferior—could no longer be held. This was a new nation of independent, autonomous individuals, a republic forged from the sacrifices of thousands, but especially from the efforts of one man—Toussaint L'Ouverture.

Toussaint was born on a Caribbean plantation around 1744. He was the alleged son of an African (Arada) chief who had learned to read and write. A devout Roman Catholic, he was somewhat detached from African culture and especially distrusted the voodoo worship that had become common on the plantations. By all accounts he was a model slave who served his generous master with loyalty and acted as a Headman, or steward, organizing the plantation and acting as an intermediary between the master and his slaves. This position allowed him a perspective to fulfill his leadership potential. He understood the degradation of slavery and the desire for freedom, but he also feared the potential for rage and self-destruction that would accompany any revolt.

Colonial society on the island of Saint Domingue was composed of three castes. The Whites, who numbered about 35,000 consisted of two groups: the grand blancs *(the Creole plantation elite and local merchants) and the* petits blancs *(overseers, artisans, small planters, shopkeepers, and soldiers). They were united primarily by color. The second caste consisted of free people of color (called the* affranchis*). They shared some freedoms with the Whites, but were denied full equality and restricted to certain dress and occupations. Some were very poor and most were dependent on Whites in some way. They generally supported the cultural hegemony of White Creole society, accepted the slave system and refused to see common cause with Black slaves. The last caste was that of slaves. There were about 450,000 on Saint Domingue at the time. The plantation system was based on dehumanization and terror, inspired by vicious and arbitrary punishments. Small revolts were frequent and there were permanent communities of runaway slaves called Maroons that existed in the hills. Though there were several conspiracies to unite the Maroons with slaves and drive the Whites from the island by 1760, there was no general rebellion. This was soon to change.*

The Call to Arms

In the last decades of the eighteenth century, the French ruled Saint Domingue with a Governor (for military affairs) and an agent or Intendant *for the administration of the bureaucracy. There were many grievances against French colonial policy, especially by the White caste, since the cost of imported slaves was high and most of the profits from exports were returned to France. This was a fluid political environment where each of the social castes could be played against another for short-term gain.*

In August 1791, there was a slave rebellion for independence that drove the White factions together and closer to the French while the Spanish (hoping to undermine the French economy) supported the slaves. The rebellion quickly failed, but the new revolutionary government in France granted full citizenship to the affranchis *(people of color). This frightened the Whites, who actually withdrew their support from France and gained the support of Great Britain by 1793.*

This was a crucial time and the instability provided an opportunity for new leadership. Toussaint L'Ouverture made his move to rally the slaves and unite them with the affranchis.

Keep in Mind . . .

- What was Toussaint's cause?

- Note the messianic emphasis of Toussaint's leadership.

"Join Me, Brothers!"
TOUSSAINT L'OUVERTURE

August 25, 1793

Having been the first to champion your cause, it is my duty to continue to labor for it. I cannot

"Join Me, Brothers!" is from John R. Beard, *Toussaint L'Ouverture: A Biography and Autobiography* (Boston, 1863), p. 85.

permit another to rob me of the initiative. Since I have begun, I will know how to conclude. Join me and you will enjoy the rights of freemen sooner than any other way. Neither whites nor mulattoes have formulated by plans; it is to the Supreme Being alone that I owe my inspiration. We have begun, we have carried on, we will know how to reach the goal.

August 29, 1793

Brothers and Friends:

I am Toussaint L'Ouverture. My name is perhaps known to you. I have undertaken to avenge you. I want liberty and equality to reign throughout Saint Domingue. I am working towards that end. Come and join me, brothers, and combat by our side for the same cause.

Loyalty to the French Republic (1799)
TOUSSAINT L'OUVERTURE

In 1792, the revolution in France fell under the control of radical leaders called the Jacobins who eliminated their rivals during the Terror of 1793–1794. Toussaint L'Ouverture derived support from this faction when they officially liberated the slaves of Saint Domingue on February 4, 1794. Toussaint's Black nationalist movement had been defused in 1794 by this emancipation decree. Called the "Black Jacobin" by some, Toussaint L'Ouverture continued to support the unstable French government until 1797 when he decided to made a bid for independence.

Toussaint neutralized the British by promising not to expand his revolution to their plantations in Jamaica. In 1798, Toussaint expelled the French, but in the process of consolidating his gains and thus avoiding French retaliation, he downplayed any thought of independence and avowed his loyalty to the French Republic as the following source indicates.

Strong in my conscience, I shall not remind you, Citizen-directors, of all I have done for the triumph of liberty, the prosperity of Saint Domingue, the glory of the French Republic; nor will I protest to you my attachment to our mother country, to my duties; my respect to the constitution, to the laws of the Republic, and my submission to the government. I swear to you I

am faithful, and my future conduct, more than all oaths, will prove to you that I shall always be faithful.

If the defense of my cause, that of the freedom of my brethren, needed cunning and intrigue and manly eloquence, in order to triumph over my enemies, I would give it up and weep over France; but, as I am persuaded that it is

"Loyalty to the French Republic" is from John R. Beard, *Toussaint L'Ouverture: A Biography and Autobiography* (Boston, 1863), pp. 100–101.

sufficient to present the truth for it to be apprehended by the republican government, I am satisfied with setting before you an exposition of my conduct . . . and repose on you justice for the verdict which is to result.

As soon as I had reestablished the public tranquillity, I sent to the Commissioner Roume—your delegate in what was formerly the Spanish part of this island—to entreat him in the name of the public safety to come and take the reins of government . . . ; persuaded that his determination will be conformed to the wishes of all good Frenchmen, I impatiently await his arrival, in order to aid him with all my power in the important functions of his new position.

Consider This:

- How did Toussaint present himself to the slaves in "Join Me, Brothers!" and to the French in his loyalty declaration? Was he consistent?

Power, Betrayal, and Death (1800–1803)

Forced Labor Decree (1800)

TOUSSAINT L'OUVERTURE

From 1797 to 1800, Toussaint maintained the unity of his various factions and focused them against the forces of his opponents. His emphasis on "no reprisals" won him respect and a number of towns surrendered to him.

By 1801, at the head of a 20,000 man army, Toussaint controlled all. He retained the loyalty of his commanders through a combination of charisma, coercion, and reward. In 1801, Toussaint offered a new constitution to Saint Domingue that officially concentrated all power in his hands, with authority to appoint his successor. The next document is a Forced Labor Decree that displayed his dominance and militarized the entire state. In a sense, everyone was placed under a strict organization that committed them to a designated economic and social status. Former slaves, in contrast, had expected complete freedom of movement and association. It was at this point that Toussaint began to lose the support of his most important faction. There was no longer any advantage in supporting him.

Keep in Mind . . .

- Note how Toussaint likens all inhabitants of Saint Domingue to soldiers in the army.

- What seems of greatest importance to Toussaint in this decree?

Citizens,

After putting an end to the war in the South, our first duty has been to return thanks to the Almighty; which we have done with a zeal becoming so great a blessing: Now, Citizens, it is necessary to consecrate all our moments to the prosperity of Saint Domingue, to the public tranquillity, and consequently, to the welfare to our fellow citizens.

But to attain this end in an effectual manner, all the civil and military officers must make it their business, every one in their respective department, to perform the duties of their offices with devotion and attachment to the public welfare.

You will easily conceive, Citizens, that Agriculture is the support of Government; since it is the foundation of Commerce and Wealth, the source

"Forced Labor Decree" is from John R. Beard, *Toussaint L'Ouverture: A Biography and Autobiography* (Boston, 1863), pp. 122–123.

of Arts and Industry, it keeps everybody employed, as being the mechanism of all Trades. And, from the moment that every individual becomes useful, it creates public tranquillity; disturbances disappear together with idleness, by which they are commonly generated, and everyone peaceably enjoys the fruits of his industry. . . .

In order to secure our liberties, which are indispensable to our happiness, every individual must be usefully employed, so as to contribute to the public good, and the general tranquillity.

Considering that the soldier, who has sacred duties to perform, as being the safeguard of the people, and in perpetual activity, to execute the orders of his Chief, either for maintaining interior tranquillity, or for fighting abroad the enemies of the country, is strictly subordinate to his superior officers; and as it is of great importance that overseers, drivers and field-Negroes, who in like manner have their superiors, should conduct themselves as officers, subalterns, and soldiers in whatever may concern them.

Considering that when an officer, a subaltern, or a soldier deviates from his duty he is delivered over to a court-martial to be tried and punished according to the laws of the Republic, for in military service no rank is to be favored when guilty: the overseers, drivers and field-Negroes, as subject to constant labor, and equally subordinate to their superiors, shall be punished in like manner, in case of failure in their respective duties.

Whereas a soldier cannot leave his company, his battalion, or half-brigade, and enter into another, without the severest punishment, unless provided with a permission in due form from his Chief, field-Negroes are forbidden to quit their respective plantations without a lawful permission. This is by no means attended to, since they change their place of labor as they please, go to and fro, and pay not the least attention to agriculture, though it is his only means of furnishing sustenance to the military, their protectors. They even conceal themselves in towns, in villages, and mountains, where, allured by the enemies of good order, they live by plunder, and in a state of open hostility to society.

Whereas, since the revolution, laborers of both sexes, then too young to be employed in the field, refuse to go to it now under pretext of freedom, spend their time in wandering about, and give a bad example to the other cultivators; while, on the other hand, the generals, officers, and soldier, are in a state of constant activity to maintain the sacred rights of the people. . . .

I do most peremptorily order as follows:

Article 1: All overseers, drivers, and field-Negroes are bound to observe, with exactness, submission, and obedience, their duty in the same manner as soldiers. . . .

Article 2: All overseers, drivers, and field-laborers, who will not perform the duties required

This image of a determined Toussaint L'Ouverture, who began the revolt that led to Haitian independence in 1804, emphasizes his role as military leader. *(Historical Pictures/Stock Montage, Inc.)*

of them, shall be arrested and punished as severely as soldiers deviating from their duty. After which punishment, if the offender be an overseer, he shall be enlisted in of the regiments of the army in Saint Domingue. If a driver, he shall be dismissed from his employment and placed among the field-Negroes, without ever being permitted to act as a driver again. And, if a common-laborer, he shall be punished with the same severity as a private soldier, according to his guilt. . . .

Article 5: Parents are earnestly entreated to attend to their duty towards their children, which is, to make them good citizens; for that purpose they must instruct them in good morals, in the Christian religion, and the fear of God. Above all, exclusive of this education, they must be brought up in some specific business or profession to enable them not only to earn their living, but also to contribute to the expenses of the Government. . . .

Article 7: The overseers and drivers of every plantation shall make it their business to inform the commanding officer of the district in regard to the conduct of the laborers under their management, as well as of those who shall absent themselves from their plantations without a pass; and of those who, residing on the estates, shall refuse to work. They shall be forced to go to the labor of the field, and if they prove obstinate, they shall be arrested and carried before the military commandant, in order to suffer the punishment above prescribed, according to the expediency of the case. . . .

Article 13: I command all the Generals of department, Generals, and other principal Officers in the districts to attend to the execution of this regulation, for which they shall be personally responsible. And I flatter myself that their zeal in assisting me to restore the public prosperity will not be momentary, convinced as they must be, that liberty cannot exist without industry. . . .

Consider This:

- Why did Toussaint address the inhabitants of Saint Domingue as "Citizens"?

- Toussaint mentioned the need to maintain the "sacred rights of the people," but did not define them. Why?

- How does the Forced Labor Decree explain why Toussaint lost the support of former slaves? What was he trying to do?

The Memoirs of Toussaint (1803)
TOUSSAINT L'OUVERTURE

In 1802, the government of France was controlled by the First Consul, Napoleon Bonaparte. In addition to all of his conquests in Europe, Napoleon envisioned an American empire. France's relationship with Toussaint L'Ouverture became an increasingly important concern. Was Toussaint loyal to France? Or was he truly an independence leader who sought to establish a new Haitian republic? Napoleon wanted to rule through Toussaint, but he was persuaded that Toussaint would be an impediment to his American empire and ordered a force of 16,000 French soldiers to Saint Domingue. Having lost the support of most of his followers, including former slaves, Toussaint lost the war, was captured, sent to France, and thrown into a dungeon at Fort de Jeux in the Jura mountains. In this freezing environment, Toussaint soon became ill and died on April 7, 1803.

"The Memoirs of Toussaint" is from John R. Beard, *Toussaint L'Ouverture: A Biography and Autobiography* (Boston, 1863), pp. 295; 323; 325–326; 328.

Meanwhile, French troops methodically razed Saint Domingue and initiated a war of extermination. Barbarous atrocities were committed on both sides as the countryside was despoiled and the economy ruined. Burdened by events in Europe, Napoleon gave up his vision of a French empire in America, sold Louisiana to the United States, and ended the fighting in Saint Domingue. He left the Blacks on the island in control of their own destiny, but devastated and impoverished. On December 31, 1803, Saint Domingue declared itself an independent republic and assumed the name of Haiti. At the end of the day, Toussaint's vision of a free, self-governing community had been realized.

The following is Toussaint's memoir written in prison in which he justified his actions and sought trial in a French court. The First Consul, Napoleon, would not concede.

Keep in Mind . . .

- According to Toussaint, how did he benefit Saint Domingue?

- What was important to Toussaint in writing this memoir? What did he request?

It is my duty to render to the French Government an exact account of my conduct. I shall relate the facts with all the simplicity and frankness of an old soldier, adding to them the reflections that naturally suggest themselves. In short, I shall tell the truth, though it be against myself.

The colony of Saint Domingue, of which I was commander, enjoyed the greatest tranquillity; agriculture and commerce flourished there. The island had attained a degree of splendor which it had never before seen. And all this—dare to say it—was my work. . . .

[Then Napoleon's aide] General Leclerc came. Why did he not inform me of his powers before landing? Why did he land without my order and in defiance of the order of the Commission? Did he not commit the first hostilities? Did he not seek to gain over the generals and other officers under my command by every possible means? . . .

If General Leclerc went to the colony to do evil, it should not be charged upon me. It is true that only one of us can be blamed; but however little one may wish to do me justice, it is clear that he is the author of all the evils which the island has suffered, since, without warning me, he entered the colony, which he found in a state of prosperity, fell upon the inhabitants, who were

at their work, contributing to the welfare of the community, and shed their blood upon their native soil. That is the true source of the evil.

I will sum up, in a few words, my conduct and the results of my administration. At the time of the evacuation of the English, there was not a penny in the public treasury; money had to be borrowed to pay the troops and the officers of the Republic. When General Leclerc arrived, he found three millions, five hundred thousand francs in the public funds. . . . Thus it is seen that I did not serve my country from interested motives; but, on the contrary, I served it with honor, fidelity, and integrity, sustained by the hope of receiving, at some future day, flattering acknowledgments from the government; all who know me will do me this justice.

I have been a slave; I am willing to own it; but I have never received reproaches from my masters.

I have neglected nothing at Saint Domingue for the welfare of the island; I have robbed myself of rest to contribute to it; I have sacrificed everything for it. I have made it my duty and pleasure to develop the resources of this beautiful colony. Zeal, activity, courage—I have employed them all.

The island was invaded by the enemies of the Republic; I had then but a thousand men, armed with pikes. I sent them back to labor in the field, and organized several regiments. . . .

If I were to record the various services which I have rendered the Government, I should need many volumes, and even then should not finish them; and, as a reward for all these services, I have been arbitrarily arrested in Saint Domingue, bound, and put on board ship like a criminal, without regard for my rank, without the least consideration. Is this the recompense due my labors? Should my conduct lead me to expect such treatment?

I was once rich. At the time of the revolution, I was worth six hundred and forty-eight thousand francs. I spent it in the service of my country. I purchased but one small estate upon which to establish my wife and family. Today, notwithstanding my disinterestedness, they seek to cover me with opprobrium and infamy; I am made the most unhappy of men; my liberty is taken from me; I am separated from all that I hold dearest in the world—from a venerable father, a hundred and five years old, who needs my assistance, from a dearly-loved wife, who, I fear, separated from me, cannot endure the afflictions which overwhelm her, and from a cherished family, who made the happiness of my life.

On my arrival in France I wrote to the First Consul [Napoleon Bonaparte] and to the Minister of Marine, giving them an account of my situation, and asking their assistance for my family and myself. Undoubtedly, they felt the justice of my request, and gave orders that what I asked should be furnished me. But, instead of this, I have received the old, half-worn dress of a soldier, and shoes in the same condition. Did I need this humiliation added to my misfortune?

When I left the ship, I was put into a carriage. I hoped then that I was to be taken before a tribunal to give an account of my conduct, and to be judged. Far from it; without a moment's rest I was taken to a fort on the frontiers of the Republic, and confined in a frightful dungeon.

It is from the depths of this dreary prison that I appeal to the justice and magnanimity of the First Consul. He is too noble and too good a general to turn away from an old soldier, covered with wounds in the service of his country, without giving him the opportunity to justify himself, and to have judgment pronounced upon him.

I ask, then, to be brought before a tribunal or council of war, before which also General Leclerc may appear, and that we may both be judged after we have both been heard; equity, reason, law, all assure me that this justice cannot be refused me. . . .

First Consul, father of all soldiers, upright judge, defender of innocence, pronounce my destiny. My wounds are deep; apply to them the healing remedy which will prevent them from opening anew; you are the physician; I rely entirely upon your justice and wisdom!

Consider This:

- What was the purpose of this memoir? Toussaint promised to "tell the truth, though it be against myself." Did he?

- Did Toussaint benefit from his revolution? Do you find any contradictions in what he says?

- Was Toussaint simply an "old soldier" who served France as he noted, or was he more? Why did Napoleon have him arrested and deported?

- Over the centuries, Toussaint L'Ouverture has become all things to all people. He has been called the "Black Savage," the "Gilded African," and the "greatest Black man in history." He influenced abolitionists in the United States and inspired poets in Europe and America. Indeed, he was a complex individual who invites stereotype just as he defies it. He was a slave, a leader and soldier of ability, who was confronted with unique choices and decisions in the context of his time. Who was Toussaint L'Ouverture? the Savage? or the Republican Martyr?

THE LIBERATOR: SIMÓN BOLÍVAR

Life and death, union and separation, follow hard upon one another. Nothing is steadfast but the will, nothing endures but one's achievements.

—*Yoshida Shōin*

The liberation of South America from Spanish control during the years 1810 to 1824 owed its success to many individuals. Noteworthy were the efforts of José de San Martín (1778–1850), whose military leadership resulted in the liberation of the southern portion of the continent. His armies marched from Argentina to Chile and finally to Peru, where he assumed the title of Protector of Peru. San Martín believed that monarchies had to be established in order to maintain control of the new political landscape. But perhaps the most important figure in the liberation and political legacy of Latin America was Simón Bolívar. His military efforts and political leadership in the northern region of New Granada, which included Venezuela, Ecuador, and Colombia, proved decisive in the establishment of republican government.

Simón Bolívar (1783–1830) was born in Caracas, Venezuela, to a wealthy, aristocratic family. Although orphaned at the age of 9, his uncle provided for him and entrusted his education to tutors who schooled the young Bolívar in the concepts and principles of Enlightenment thought. The precepts of Locke, Montesquieu, and especially Rousseau had a pivotal impact on Bolívar's future actions. As a young man from 1802 to 1807, he traveled extensively throughout Europe and the United States, severely criticizing Napoleon, whom he thought had become a dishonored tyrant in his betrayal of the principles of French republicanism. When Napoleon invaded Spain in 1808 and installed a puppet king, Bolívar and other Creole elites deposed the colonial governor in Caracas and actively sought the expulsion of all Spanish authorities. Bolívar quickly rose to the rank of colonel in the militia and felt free to act on the oath he had made to himself in 1805: "I swear by the God of my fathers, . . . upon my honor, and by my homeland that I shall not let my arm rest, nor my soul repose, until I have broken the chains laid upon us by our Spanish oppressors." These bold words guided his actions as he fought to liberate the northern regions of South America.

The "Moral Force" of Bolívar

Simón Bolívar was an inveterate writer, and his correspondence, as well as his political tracts, provide historians with a detailed record of his ideas and achievements. Nevertheless, he remains a rather enigmatic figure. He gave away much of his wealth and died practically a pauper. He yearned for glory and public acclamation just as he decried adulation. That Bolívar was a military leader of great courage and ability who was willing to risk much against great odds is undeniable. But his passion for life and his vision of hemispheric solidarity, a single community of united Americans, bespeaks a dreamy idealism. Historian Harold Bierck has noted that Bolívar's political thinking "serves dictator and democrat alike in contemporary Latin America" and that Bolívar has no parallel among leaders in the history of the United States. He combined Washington's military prowess, Jefferson's political views, and the humanity of Lincoln.

It is this "moral force" that permeates discussions of Bolívar's legacy. Though he was a man of inconsistencies and even resorted to dictatorial powers late in his governing career, Bolívar continues to provide an inspirational example of commitment to republican ideals and public service. Indeed, he wished to be remembered for the liberty and freedom he symbolized. "History will say," he mused, "that Bolívar took command in order to free his fellow citizens, and when they were free, he permitted them to govern themselves by laws, and not by his will."

This section focuses on the actions and political ideas of the "Liberator." The first selection is a proclamation to the people of Venezuela in 1813. With it, Bolívar began the "War to the Death," a savage and bloody campaign against the Spanish for control of the region. Bolívar has been both praised and condemned by historians for his actions during this time.

"Fear Not the Sword That Comes to Avenge You" (June 15, 1813)

SIMÓN BOLÍVAR

Keep in Mind . . .

- Who does Bolívar identify as enemies and what did they do?

- What was Bolívar's cause?

Simón Bolívar, Liberator of Venezuela, Brigadier of the Union, General in Chief of the Northern Army

To his fellow-countrymen:

Venezuelans: An army of your brothers, sent by the Sovereign Congress of New Granada, has come to liberate you. Having expelled the oppressors from the provinces of Merida and Trujillo, it is now among you.

We are sent to destroy the Spaniards, to protect the Americans, and to reestablish the republican governments that once formed the Confederation of Venezuela. The states defended by our arms are again governed by their former constitutions and tribunals, in full enjoyment of their liberty and independence, for our mission is designed only to break the chains of servitude which still shackle some of our towns, and not to impose laws or exercise acts of dominion to which the rules of war might entitle us.

Moved by your misfortunes, we have been unable to observe with indifference the afflictions you were forced to experience by the barbarous

Spaniards, who have ravished you, plundered you, and brought you death and destruction. They have violated the sacred rights of nations. They have broken the most solemn agreements and treaties. In fact, they have committed every manner of crime, reducing the Republic of Venezuela to the most frightful desolation. Justice therefore demands vengeance, and necessity compels us to exact it. Let the monsters who infest Colombian soil, who have drenched it in blood, be cast out forever; may their punishment be equal to the enormity of their perfidy, so that we may eradicate the stain of our ignominy and demonstrate to the nations of the world that the sons of America cannot be offended with impunity.

Despite our just resentment toward the iniquitous Spaniards, our magnanimous heart still commands us to open to them for the last time a path to reconciliation and friendship; they are invited to live peacefully among us, if they will abjure their crimes, honestly change their ways, and cooperate with us in destroying the intruding Spanish government and in the reestablishment of the Republic of Venezuela.

Any Spaniard who does not, by every active and effective means, work against tyranny in behalf of this just cause, will be considered an enemy and punished; as a traitor to the nation, he will inevitably be shot by a firing squad. On the other hand, a general and absolute amnesty is granted to those who come over to our army with or without their arms, as well as to those who render aid to the good citizens who are endeavoring to throw off the yoke of tyranny. Army officers and civil magistrates who proclaim the government of Venezuela and join with us shall retain their posts and positions; in a word, those Spaniards who render outstanding service to the State shall be regarded and treated as Americans.

And you Americans who, by error or treachery, have been lured from the paths of justice, are informed that your brothers, deeply regretting the error of your ways, have pardoned you as we are profoundly convinced that you cannot be truly to blame, for only the blindness and ignorance in which you have been kept up to now by those responsible for your crimes could have induced you to commit them. Fear not the sword that comes to avenge you and to sever the ignoble ties with which your executioners have bound you to their own fate. You are hereby assured, with absolute impunity, of your honor, lives, and property. The single title, "Americans," shall be your safeguard and guarantee. Our arms have come to protect you, and they shall never be raised against a single one of you, our brothers.

This amnesty is extended even to the very traitors who most recently have committed felonious acts, and it shall be so religiously applied that no reason, cause, or pretext will be sufficient to oblige us to violate our offer, however extraordinary and extreme the occasion you may give to provoke our wrath.

Spaniards and Canary Islanders, you will die, though you be neutral, unless you actively espouse the cause of America's liberation. Americans, you will live, even if you have trespassed.

Consider This:

- What was Bolívar's message to the Spanish government and its supporters in Venezuela?

- How did Bolívar seek to destroy the unity of his enemies before the fighting in this province ever began? What does this speech say about Bolívar as a political leader?

The Jamaica Letter (September 6, 1815)

SIMÓN BOLÍVAR

During the course of the long struggle to expel the Spanish from Latin America, Simón Bolívar often had to balance victory with defeat. Several times from 1810 to 1824, he had to retreat from the battlefront and even flee from Venezuela to fight another day. In 1815, Bolívar took refuge on the Caribbean island of Jamaica. While he was there, a local inhabitant asked him to comment on the current state of affairs in Latin America. Bolívar's "Jamaica Letter" remains the most significant of his early writings on political and international affairs.

Keep in Mind . . .

- What did Bolívar expect from European nations?

- In order to expel the Spanish, what did Latin Americans have to do?

Kingston, Jamaica, September 6, 1815

My Dear Sir,

I hasten to reply to the letter of the 29th [last] which you had the honor of sending me and which I received with the greatest satisfaction. . . .

With respect to heroic and hapless Venezuela, events there have moved so rapidly and the devastation has been such that it is reduced to frightful desolation and almost absolute indigence, although it was once among the fairest regions that are the pride of America. Its tyrants govern a desert, and they oppress only those unfortunate survivors who, having escaped death, lead a precarious existence. A few women, children, and old men are all that remain. Most of

"The Jamaica Letter" is from Vincente Lecuna and Harold A. Bierck, Jr., eds., *Selected Writings of Bolívar*, 2nd edition, Volume I (New York: The Colonial Press, 1951), pp. 103; 106–107; 115; 121–122. Copyright © 1951 by Bank of Venezuela. Reprinted by permission.

these have perished rather than be slaves; those who survive continue to fight furiously on the fields and in the inland towns, until they expire or hurl into the sea those who, insatiable in their thirst for blood and crimes, rival those first monsters who wiped out America's primitive race. Nearly a million persons formerly dwelt in Venezuela, and it is no exaggeration to say that one out of four has succumbed either to the land, sword, hunger, plague, flight, or privation, all consequences of the war. . . .

Americans [must] either defend their rights or suffer repression at the hands of Spain, which, although once the world's greatest empire, is now too weak, with what little is left her, to rule the new hemisphere or even to maintain herself in the old. And shall Europe, the civilized, the merchant, the lover of liberty allow an aged serpent, bent only on satisfying its venomous rage, to devour the fairest part of our globe? What! Is Europe deaf to the clamor of her own interests? Has she no eyes to see justice? Has she grown so hardened as to become insensible? The more I ponder these questions, the more I am confused. I am led to think that [Latin] America's disappearance is desired; but this is impossible because all Europe is not Spain. What madness for our enemy to hope to reconquer America when she has no navy, no funds, and almost no soldiers! Those troops which she has are scarcely adequate to keep her own people in a state of forced obedience and to defend herself from her neighbors. . . .

It is harder, Montesquieu has written, to release a nation from servitude than to enslave a free nation. This truth is proven by the annals of all times, which reveal that most free nations have been put under the yoke, but very few enslaved nations have recovered their liberty. Despite the convictions of history, South Americans have made efforts to obtain liberal, even perfect, institutions, doubtless out of that instinct to aspire to the greatest possible happiness, which, common to all men, is bound to follow in civil societies founded on the principles of justice, liberty, and equality. But are we capable of maintaining in proper balance the difficult charge of a republic? Is it conceivable that a newly emancipated people can soar to the heights of liberty, and, unlike Icarus, neither have its wings melt nor fall into an abyss? Such a marvel is inconceivable and without precedent. There is no reasonable probability to bolster our hopes.

More than anyone, I desire to see America fashioned into the greatest nation in the world, greatest not so much by virtue of her area and wealth as by her freedom and glory. Although I seek perfection for the government of my country, I cannot persuade myself that the New World can, at the moment, be organized as a great republic. Since it is impossible, I dare not desire it; yet much less do I desire to have all

Simón Bolívar was the liberator of much of Latin America. He inclined toward a policy of political liberalism. *(Hulton/Corbis-Bettmann)*

America a monarchy because this plan is not only impracticable but also impossible. Wrongs now existing could not be righted, and our emancipation would be fruitless. The American states need the care of paternal governments to heal the sores and wounds of despotism and war. . . .

I shall tell you with what we must provide ourselves in order to expel the Spaniards and to found a free government. It is *union*, obviously; but such union will come about through sensible planning and well-directed actions rather than by divine magic. America stands together because it is abandoned by all other nations. It is isolated in the center of the world. It has no diplomatic relations, nor does it receive any military assistance; instead, America is attacked by Spain, which has more military supplies than any we can possibly acquire through furtive means.

When success is not assured, when the state is weak, and when results are distantly seen, all men hesitate; opinion is divided, passions rage, and the enemy fans these passions in order to win an easy victory because of them. As soon as we are strong and under the guidance of a liberal nation which will lend us her protection, we will achieve accord in cultivating the virtues and talents that lead to glory. Then, will we march majestically toward that great prosperity for which South America is destined. Then will those sciences and arts which, born in the East, have enlightened Europe, wing their way to a free Colombia, which will cordially bid them welcome.

Consider This:

- Do you agree with Montesquieu that it is harder "to release a nation from servitude than to enslave a free nation?" Why or why not? What did Bolívar think?

- In Bolívar's mind, why was it "not only impractical, but also impossible" for a monarchy to unify Latin America? Why was he pessimistic that a republic could be established? How would paternalistic governments help the new nations of Latin America? How might they hinder democracy in other ways?

A Constitution for Venezuela (February 15, 1819)

SIMÓN BOLÍVAR

In 1816, with help from the young republic of Haiti, Bolívar launched a new invasion of Venezuela. He captured Bogotá and used it as a base for attacking Venezuela. By February, 1819, he had made sufficient progress to inaugurate the Second National Congress of Venezuela. Prior to this, Bolívar had assumed the "fearful and dangerous post of Dictator and Supreme Chief of the Republic." He had been compelled to assume this position, as he said, by the "force of necessity," feeling that he was "but a mere plaything in the hurricane of revolution that tossed me about like as much straw." But now at the Congress, he resigned this title and as "just a plain citizen" addressed the assembly with suggestions for a new constitution. This new constitution, he argued, should not be based on an earlier draft in the image of the United States, but should reflect the nature and character of "Latin" Americans as a people. This bold conception borrows from Enlightenment thought, but presents a new structure for republican government.

"A Constitution for Venezuela" is from Vincente Lecuna and Harold A. Bierck, Jr., eds., *Selected Writings of Bolívar*, 2nd edition, Volume I (New York: The Colonial Press, 1951), pp. 175-177; 179; 181; 185-186. Copyright © 1951 by Bank of Venezuela. Reprinted by permission.

Keep in Mind . . .

• Note Bolívar's emphasis on ignorance as a primary ingredient of Spanish tyranny.

Let us review the past to discover the base upon which the Republic of Venezuela is founded. . . .

We are not Europeans; we are not Indians; we are but a mixed species of aborigines and Spaniard. Americans by birth and Europeans by law, we find ourselves engaged in a dual conflict: we are disputing with the natives for titles of ownership, and at the same time we are struggling to maintain ourselves in the country that gave us birth against the opposition of the invaders. Thus our position is most extraordinary and complicated. But there is more. As our role has always been strictly passive and our political existence nil, we find that our quest for liberty is now even more difficult of accomplishment; for we, having been placed in a state lower than slavery, had been robbed not only of our freedom but also of the right to exercise an active domestic tyranny. . . . [Latin] America . . . received everything from Spain, who, in effect, deprived her of the experience that she would have gained from the exercise of an active tyranny by not allowing her to take part in her own domestic affairs and administration. This exclusion made it impossible for us to acquaint ourselves with the management of public affairs; nor did we enjoy that personal consideration, of such great value in major revolutions, that the brilliance of power inspires in the eyes of the multitude. In brief, Gentlemen, we were deliberately kept in ignorance and cut off from the world in all matters relating to the science of government.

Subject to the threefold yoke of ignorance, tyranny, and vice, the American people have been unable to acquire knowledge, power, or [civic] virtue. The lessons we received and the models we studied, as pupils of such pernicious teachers, were most destructive. We have been ruled more by deceit than by force, and we have been degraded more by vice than by superstition. Slavery is the daughter of Darkness: an ignorant people is a blind instrument of its own destruction. Ambition and intrigue abuse the credulity and experience of men lacking all political, economic, and civic knowledge; they adopt pure illusion as reality; they take license for liberty, treachery for patriotism, and vengeance for justice. This situation is similar to that of the robust blind man who, beguiled by his strength, strides forward with all the assurance of one who can see, but, upon hitting every variety of obstacle, finds himself unable to retrace his steps.

If a people, perverted by their training, succeed in achieving their liberty, they will soon lose it, for it would be of no avail to endeavor to explain to them that happiness consists in the practice of virtue; that the rule of law is more powerful than the rule of tyrants, because, as the laws are more inflexible, everyone should submit to their beneficent austerity; that proper morals, and not force, are the bases of law; and that to practice justice is to practice liberty. Therefore, Legislators, your work is so much the more arduous, inasmuch as you have to reeducate men who have been corrupted by erroneous illusions and false incentives. Liberty, says Rousseau, is a succulent morsel, but one difficult to digest. Our weak fellow-citizens will have to strengthen their spirit greatly before they can digest the wholesome nutriment of freedom. Their limbs benumbed by chains, their sight dimmed by the darkness of dungeons, and their strength sapped by the pestilence of servitude, are they capable of marching toward the August temple of Liberty without faltering? Can they come near enough to bask in its brilliant rays and to breathe freely the pure air which reigns therein? . . .

I am convinced of the impossibility of [the application of a federal constitution] to our state. And, to my way of thinking, it is a marvel that its prototype in North America endures so successfully and has not been overthrown at the first sign of adversity or danger. Although the people of North America are a singular model of political virtue and moral rectitude; although that nation was cradled in liberty, reared on freedom, and maintained by liberty alone; and—I must reveal everything—although those people, so lacking in many respects, are unique in the history of mankind, it is a marvel, I repeat, that so weak and complicated a government as the federal system has managed to govern them in the difficult and trying circumstances of their past. But, regardless of the effectiveness of this form of government with respect to North America, I must say that it has never for a moment entered my mind to compare the position and character of two states as dissimilar as the English-American and the Spanish-American. Would it not be most difficult to apply to Spain the English system of political, civil, and religious liberty? Hence, it would be even more difficult to adapt to Venezuela the laws of North America. . . .

But no matter how tempting this magnificent federative system [of the United States] might have appeared [to the first Venezuelan Congress], and regardless of its possible effect, the Venezuelans were not prepared to enjoy it immediately upon casting off their chains. We were not prepared for such good, for good, like evil, results in death when it is sudden and excessive. Our moral fiber did not then possess the stability necessary to derive benefits from a wholly representative government; a government so sublime, in fact, that it might more nearly befit a republic of saints. . . .

Like the North Americans, we have divided national representation into two chambers: that of Representatives and the Senate. The first is very wisely constituted. It enjoys all its proper functions, and it requires no essential revision, because the Constitution, in creating it, gave it the form and powers which the people deemed necessary in order that they might be legally and properly represented. If the Senate were hereditary rather than elective, it would, in my opinion, be the basis, the tie, the very soul of our republic. In political storms this body would arrest the thunderbolts of the government and would repel any violent popular reaction. Devoted to the government because of a natural interest in its own preservation, a hereditary senate would always oppose any attempt on the part of the people to infringe upon the jurisdiction and authority of their magistrates. . . . It is necessary, therefore, that in all governments there be a neutral body to protect the injured and disarm the offender. To be neutral, this body must not owe its origin to appointment by the government or to election by the people, if it is to enjoy a full measure of independence which neither fears nor expects anything from these two sources of authority. The hereditary senate, as a part of the people, shares its interests, its sentiments, and its spirit. For this reason it should not be presumed that a hereditary senate would ignore the interests of the people or forget its legislative duties. . . .

At the outset, these senators should be elected by Congress. The successors to this Senate must command the initial attention of the government, which should educate them in a [school] designed especially to train these guardians and future legislators of the nation. They ought to learn the arts, sciences, and letters that enrich the mind of a public figure. From childhood they should understand the career of which they have been destined by Providence, and from earliest youth they should prepare their minds for the dignity that awaits them.

The creation of a hereditary senate would in no way be a violation of political equality. I do not solicit the establishment of a nobility, for, as a celebrated republican has said, that would simultaneously destroy equality and liberty. What I propose is an office for which the candidates must prepare themselves, an office that demands great knowledge and the ability to acquire such knowledge. All should not be left to chance and the outcome of election. The people are more easily deceived than is Nature perfected by art; and, although these senators, it is true, would not be bred in an environment that is all virtue, it is equally true that they would be raised in an atmosphere of enlightened education. Furthermore, the liberators of Venezuela are entitled to occupy forever a high rank in the Republic that they have brought into existence. I believe that posterity would view with regret the effacement of the illustrious names of its first benefactors. I say, moreover, that it is a matter of public interest and national honor, of gratitude on Venezuela's part, to honor gloriously, until the end of time, a race of virtuous, prudent, and persevering men who, overcoming every obstacle, have founded the Republic at the price of the most heroic sacrifices. And if the people of Venezuela do not applaud the elevation of their benefactors, then they are unworthy to be free, and they will never be free.

Consider This:

- According to Bolívar, what is the relationship between law, justice, and liberty?

- Why does Bolívar think that the Constitution of the United States cannot provide a model for a Venezuelan constitution? What changes does Bolívar suggest?

- What do you think about Bolívar's recommendation of a hereditary senate? Why did he endorse this concept?

- Bolívar suggested that senators should be groomed from birth for their responsibilities, much as the Guardians in Plato's *Republic* would rule Athens. Why might a hereditary institution be a dangerous idea in a free republic? Is this kind of paternalism necessary in a fledgling democracy, or does it retard the progress of an electorate? Was the United States initially a paternalistic republic?

The Image of Bolívar

The "Great Man" theory of history argues that a leader, inspired by and reacting to contemporary circumstances, engages the "spirit" of his time and molds new realities for society and history. This is a particularly simplistic and romantic conception that does not take into account the primacy of other social and economic factors. Still, in the political affairs of early nineteenth century Latin America, the influence of strongmen like José de San Martín, Bernardo O'Higgins, and Simón Bolívar was decisive. The Spanish had controlled Latin American society for three hundred years after the invasion of the conquistadors. They had established an "economy of extraction" and had pacified Indians through terror and paternalistic relationships. It is ironic that the Creole elite, a minority group of propertied white men born in Latin America, moved to substitute Spanish royal control for their own. Republican or not, the new rulers of Latin America after 1824 were drawn from this minority.

This is important because local landowners simply replaced Spanish colonial officials as the dominant governors of the region. Although slavery disappeared from the former Spanish empire by the 1850s (1888 in Brazil), the caste systems were informally maintained and the new strongmen or Caudillos *kept peasants locked in a social dependency that supported the established order. The political legacy of this arrangement was to promote the singular and absolute leadership of a military dictator, over the decisions of a democratically elected assembly. Modern Latin American republics have maintained a tenuous balance with dictatorship always looming as a threat.*

Political image remains a crucial aspect of leadership. The founders of a nation are often accorded divine status in hopes of providing examples of right conduct for later generations. The images of George Washington, John Adams, Thomas Jefferson, and Benjamin Franklin linger in our minds as demi-gods, "Founding Fathers," rather than as human beings. The image of Simón Bolívar demands the scrutiny of history. In the following letters to the Marquis de Lafayette, who had so actively supported the American Revolution, Bolívar compares himself with his contemporaries, Napoleon Bonaparte and George Washington. Must every nation have a Great Man who ascends into the realm of myth?

"I Am Not, Nor Do I Care to Be a Napoleon"

SIMÓN BOLÍVAR

Keep in Mind . . .

- Compare Bolívar's opinion of Napoleon with that of Washington and Lafayette.

March 6, 1826

My dear General and friend:

I have received your very important letter of October 1 last, brought to me by Guzmán, whom I have met and heard with some surprise, for his mission is truly an extraordinary one. You tell me that Colombia is in a position similar to that of France when Napoleon was in Egypt, and that I, like him, should exclaim: "The plotters are wrecking the country; we must fly to her rescue." To be sure, virtually the whole of your letter is penned with the sharp point of truth, but the truth is not enough to make a plan effective. It seems to me that you have not judged the men and the events with sufficient impartiality. Colombia is not France, nor am I Napoleon. In France they think deeply, and their wisdom is deeper still. The population is homogeneous, and war had brought her to the brink of the precipice. No republic was as great as France, which throughout history had always been a kingdom. The republican government, discredited, had become the object of nearly universal execration. The monsters who ruled France were both cruel and incompetent. Napoleon was great and unique but highly ambitious. Here we have note of this. I am not, nor do I care to be a Napoleon. I regard these examples as unworthy of the glory that I have achieved. The title of Liberator is superior to any that human pride has ever sought. It can-

not, therefore, be degraded. Moreover, our people have nothing, nothing whatever, in common with the French. Our Republic has raised the country to heights of glory and prosperity, endowing it with laws and freedom. No Colombian leader is a Robespierre or a Marat. The danger was over when hope began to appear; accordingly, nothing justifies the course that you propose. Republics surround Colombia on all sides, and Colombia has never been a kingdom. By its elevation as by its splendor, a throne would inspire terror. Equality would end, and the men of color would lose their rights to a new aristocracy. . . .

I should most gladly employ my sword and my authority in sustaining and defending the sovereign will of the people. This assurance I give you with the same sincerity with which I remain your constant friend.

Simón Bolívar

George Washington: "The New World's Foremost Son"

SIMÓN BOLÍVAR

March 20, 1826

Dear General Lafayette:

From the public papers I have learned, with inexpressible pleasure, that Your Excellency has been so kind as to honor me with a treasure from Mount Vernon: the image of Washington, some of his mementos, and one of the monuments of his glory are to be bestowed upon me by Your Excellency in memory of that great man, the New World's foremost son. Words cannot express how greatly my heart cherishes so glorious an assembly of thoughts and objects. Washington's family honors me in a manner far exceeding my remotest hopes, as a reward from

Washington, given by the hand of Lafayette, is the ultimate in human compensations. He was the outstanding architect of political reform, even as Your Excellency is the outstanding *citizen-hero*, the champion of freedom, who on the one hand has served America and on the other the Old World of Europe. What mortal then is deserving of the high honors which Your Excellency and Mount Vernon propose to confer upon me? My embarrassment is equaled only by the infinite sense of gratitude with which I tender Your Excellency the respect and veneration due the Nestor of human freedom.

I am, Your Excellency, with the highest regard, your respectful admirer.

Simón Bolívar

Compare and Contrast:

- After reading these letters, would you agree that Bolívar was an earnest republican?

- Compare Bolívar's ideas on power presented in these letters and elsewhere in this chapter with those of Napoleon on pp. 72, 73. What is the difference in their conceptions of glory, duty, and personal responsibility?

- Read the selection subtitled "The Role of Great Men in History" by G.W.F. Hegel on p. 80. Do you think that Simón Bolívar embodies Hegel's "Hero" who possesses the inner "Spirit" of his time? To what extent can the individual change history?

Consider This:

- Why is it important for a nation to enshrine its founders with a semi-divine status? Is this a temporary or permanent status? Note the changing images of V.I. Lenin in Russia and Mao Zedong in China.

Theme: Propaganda/Women in History

The Historical Intersection

ARGENTINA: 1951

"Yes, I Am Fanatically Peronista!"

EVA PERÓN

Eva Duarte was born, the illegitimate daughter of a prosperous landowner, outside Buenos Aires in 1919. After an early career as an actress, she positioned herself among influential men who could bring her to the attention of even more prominent military commanders and political leaders. Beautiful and strong-willed, she possessed a desire for power and a need to be loved by an adoring public. In 1944, she met Colonel Juan Perón, himself an ambitious commander, who appreciated her style and determination. Their marriage was a symbiotic linking of image and power. She needed his political access and he needed her link with the descamisados, *or "unshirted" masses from whom she had originated. This popular following among the workers of the state allowed Perón to dominate Argentinean politics from 1946 to 1956.*

In the following excerpt from her book, My Mission in Life *(written in 1951 when she was ill with cancer), "Evita" links the purpose of women to the devotion of the men who are the State. It is this dedication to the Cause, the blind devotion to the image of the Leader, that characterized dictatorships in the twentieth century.*

Keep in Mind . . .

- What was Evita's cause? What is a "Peronista"?

In the same manner that a woman attains eternity and her glory, and saves herself from loneliness and from death by giving herself for love of a man, I think that perhaps no woman's movement will be glorious and lasting in the world if it does not give itself to the cause of a man.

(contd)

What is important is that the cause and the man be worthy of such a total surrender.

I believe that Perón and his cause are sufficiently great and worthy to receive the total offering of the woman's movement of my country. And, further, all the women of the world may support his justice; for with it, surrendering themselves for love of a cause which is that of humanity, they will increase in womanliness.

And if it is true that the cause itself will grow in glory by receiving them, it is not less true that they will be exalted by the surrender. That is why I am and shall be Peronista until my dying day: because Perón's cause exalts me, and because its productiveness will continue forever after I am gone. . . .

At this juncture, perhaps it might be convenient for those who think a "political marriage" took place between me and Perón to turn over a page. Those who believe this happened will find here only propaganda.

Evita Perón at a political rally: "What is important is that the cause and the man be worthy of total surrender." (Picture in Eva Perón, *My Mission in Life*, p. 34)

(*contd*)

We got married because we loved one another, and we loved one another because we both loved the same thing. In different ways we had both wanted to do the same thing: he with intelligence, I with the heart; he prepared for the fray; I ready for everything without knowing anything; he cultured and I simple; he great and I small; he master and I pupil. He the figure and I the shadow. He sure of himself, and I sure only of him!

That is why we married, even before the decisive battle for the liberty of our people, with the absolute certainty that neither triumph nor defeat, neither glory nor failure, could destroy the unity of our hearts.

Yes, I was sure of him! I knew that power would not dazzle him nor change him. That he would continue to be as he was: sober, smooth, an early riser, insatiable in his thirst for justice, simple and humble; that he would never be otherwise than as I knew him—giving his large, warm hand generously and frankly to the men of my people. . . .

It is the path which all we women take when we love a man with a cause. First, the cause is "his cause." Then we begin to call it "my cause." And when love reaches its greatest perfection, the feeling of admiration that made us say "his cause," and the selfish feeling that made us say "my cause," are superseded by a feeling of complete unity, and we say "our cause.". . .

That is why I say now: "Yes, I am Peronista, fanatically Peronista!" But I would not be able to say which I love most, Perón or his cause, for to me it is all one and the same thing, it is all one love; and when I say in my speeches and in my conversation that Perón is the nation and is the people, I do no more than prove that everything in my life is sealed by one single love.

Consider This:

- According to Evita, how does a woman attain glory and eternity? What was her relationship with Juan Perón?
- In this excerpt, how does Evita become the effective mediator between the leader and the masses? By melding "love of Perón" with "love of the Cause," by making Perón's policies synonymous with the freedom of the masses, how did Evita blur the boundaries between liberty and dictatorship?
- Why has it been especially important for Latin American leaders to establish a paternalistic relationship and a common cause with the people who are governed by the state? What lessons can be learned from the experiences of Toussaint L'Ouverture and Simón Bolívar?

"Yes, I Am Fanatically Peronista!" is from *Eva Perón, My Mission in Life,* translated by Ethel Cherry (New York: Vantage Press, 1953), pp. 42-45. Copyright © 1953 by Señor Don Juan Domingo Perón. Reprinted by permission.

4

"A World to Win!": The Industrial Revolution

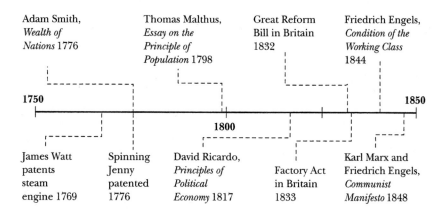

Adam Smith,
Wealth of Nations 1776

Thomas Malthus,
Essay on the Principle of Population 1798

Great Reform
Bill in Britain
1832

Friedrich Engels,
Condition of the Working Class 1844

1750

1800

1850

James Watt
patents
steam
engine 1769

Spinning
Jenny
patented
1776

David Ricardo,
Principles of Political Economy 1817

Factory Act
in Britain
1833

Karl Marx and
Friedrich Engels,
Communist Manifesto 1848

Two nations between whom there is no intercourse and no sympathy; who are as ignorant of each other's habits, thoughts and feelings as if they were . . . inhabitants of different planets; who are formed by a different breeding, are fed by a different food, are ordered by different manners, and are not governed by the same laws—the rich and the poor.

—*Benjamin Disraeli*

The inherent vice of capitalism is the unequal sharing of blessings; the inherent virtue of socialism is the equal sharing of miseries.

—*Winston Churchill*

The worth of a State, in the long run, is the worth of the individuals composing it.

—*John Stuart Mill*

Man is born free and everywhere he is in chains.

—*Jean-Jacques Rousseau*

CHAPTER THEMES

- *Revolution:* What defines an economic or social revolution as opposed to a political revolution? Does one generally cause the other, or do all revolutions depend on a complex relationship between various elements? Can we define the Industrial Revolution as primarily technological in nature?

- *Women in History:* How did the Industrial Revolution change the social relationships within the family and alter the nature of the workforce? Was this a progressive period for women?

- *Beliefs and Spirituality:* How would you define Marxism? Why did it become a popular social and economic policy in the nineteenth century? Although Marx repudiated religion, he became a spiritual leader for thousands of people. Can you explain this phenomenon?

- *Historical Change and Transition:* How did the Industrial Revolution forever change the history of humankind? What were its social and economic consequences, and how are they still felt today? Have the transistor and microchip created a second Industrial Revolution with similar social and economic impact?

- *The Big Picture:* In order for civilization to progress, to move forward technologically, must there always be a price to pay in human suffering and abuse? Is it worth it?

The word "revolution" implies drastic change, most often of a political nature, that results in a new form of government. There are other types of revolution as well. From the late eighteenth century to the late nineteenth century, Europe underwent a social and economic revolution that was the result of technological progress inspired by inventive minds. No longer would humans be harnessed to the land, completely dependent on the vicissitudes of nature for their livelihood; a new world was dawning, based in the city and filled with the prospect of employment and new lives. But this was not a move toward economic independence, for humans would soon be harnessed to an even more exacting master than the land—the machine.

Historically, the process of industrialization was a gradual one. The first stage of the Industrial Revolution began slowly, about 1760, and was made possible by several factors. First, Europe had reaped the benefits of an age of discovery during the sixteenth and seventeenth centuries. This fostered a commercial revolution that resulted in substantial economic growth. Indeed, the economic benefits of exploration were evident as nations sought to organize and compete on a grand scale. In addition, the English and French political revolutions of the seventeenth and eighteenth centuries began the ascendency of the middle class, which furnished the investment capital and expansive leadership necessary for the inception of the Industrial Revolution. At the same time, the population of Europe was growing dramatically, so much so that a rural-based economy simply could not support the growing tax requirements of governments and employ all who sought jobs.

These conditions were especially evident in England, where rural unemployment had been exacerbated by a conscious decision on the part of the wealthy landowners and the government itself to "enclose" farmland, release the tenantry from the security of farm labor, and use the land as pasture for sheep. Great profits were to be made in the textile trade, but the resulting displacement of the yeoman farmer added to the rural dilemma.

Yet England in the mid-eighteenth century was generally prosperous since it had developed a solid colonial foundation that provided ready markets for its goods. These markets were served by a maritime commercial and military fleet without peer and were supported by growing domestic production. This increase in the productive capacity of domestic industry resulted in large part from English ingenuity. The development of the flying shuttle, spinning jenny, and power loom in the mid-eighteenth century bespoke English technical superiority and advancement. The English had other natural advantages as well. Blessed with the existence of large quantities of coal and iron in close proximity, the English developed techniques for reducing the impurities in iron, thereby stimulating production; this eventually led to the development of the railroad in the mid-nineteenth century.

These new technologies were harnessed and organized in the factory. Men, women, and children were employed to keep the machines running, and the factory system was established to provide the greatest efficiency of material and labor, at the least expensive cost.

To many, industrialization became synonymous with progress. Increased production of goods meant greater potential for export, and this in turn created greater profit for the individual and government alike. The cultivation of new markets inspired competition among nations, exploration of new lands, and efficient management of time and labor. Yet industrialization, for all its glorification of the genius of the human mind, was never without its critics. It solved certain problems, but created others. What, for instance, was to be done with those people who moved to the city in search of factory employment and found themselves among the "technologically unemployed," looking for jobs that simply did not exist? And what of those who were fortunate enough to find work in the mills or the mines? The dull monotony and danger of their occupations, not to mention their subsistence living conditions, made life depressing. Factory workers dreaded unemployment, yet could do little to change their condition. As long as competition, efficiency, and profit were the primary catalysts of the Industrial Revolution, the laborer would have to be sacrificed.

The conflicts raised by industrialization were all the more bewildering because they were unprecedented. How, for example, was government to respond to the complex problems created by industrial progress? This question was of primary importance for Britain, the first industrial area and the subject of this chapter. British industrialization was stimulated in the nineteenth century by the needs of national defense in view of the threat imposed by Napoleon. Criticism by reformers was not tolerated by the government, which viewed such acts as unpatriotic and incendiary. By the 1820s, however, tentative reforms were made that led to a rather prolonged debate resulting in the Reform Bill of 1832. This ensured that most middle-class British subjects would receive parliamentary representation and opened the franchise to some of the new industrial towns whose populations had never before been represented. In the following years, further reforms were legislated, such as the Factory Act of 1833, which limited the working hours of women and children in the textile mills and provided government inspection of the workplace. Still, reform was not won without struggle. In the 1830s and 1840s, writers and literary figures such as Charles Dickens and historian Thomas Carlyle and political organizations such as the Chartists advocated constitutional and social change. Liberalism was born as a political philosophy, and intellectuals such as John

Stuart Mill (1806–1873) advocated workers' cooperatives, unions, and even women's suffrage.

Change was advocated from other directions as well. It was during this time that Karl Marx and Friedrich Engels observed the conditions of the working class in England and composed one of the most influential documents of the modern world—*The Communist Manifesto* (1848). According to Marx, the true revolutionary force in society was the workers (proletarians) who were dominated and abused by capitalists interested in profit at the workers' expense. As Marx wrote: "Let the ruling classes tremble at a Communist revolution. The proletarians have nothing to lose but their chains. They have a world to win." Other socialists less radical than Marx preached the need and inevitability of change to a more balanced society, based less on privilege and more on equality of opportunity.

The Industrial Revolution can thus be viewed in two ways: as a force for progress, an example of human ability to mold the environment, and as a demonstration of man's abuse of man, for the Industrial Revolution intensified class animosities and provided the catalyst for social change. The questions that emerge from this chapter are thus philosophical in nature yet practical in application. In order for civilization to progress, to move forward technologically, must there always be a price to pay in human suffering or abuse? And if that is the case, is it worth it? What indeed constitutes "progress"? The twentieth century has experienced some of the greatest technological change, from the invention of the automobile to the exploration of space. Have we too paid a price?

THE URBAN LANDSCAPE

Sybil (1845)

BENJAMIN DISRAELI

One of the most ardent reformers who criticized working conditions was Benjamin Disraeli. A novelist and politician, he served as prime minister of Britain from 1867 to 1868 and from 1874 to 1880. His most famous novel, Sybil, or the Two Nations, *vividly describes working and living conditions in factory towns. Disraeli hoped to gain working-class support for a group of reforming aristocrats in his Tory party. The following selection from this novel demonstrates the power of his prose.*

They come forth: the mine delivers its gang and the pit its bondsmen, the forge is silent and the engine is still. The plain is covered with the swarming multitude: bands of stalwart men, broad-chested and muscular, wet with the toil, and black as the children of the tropics; troops of youth, alas! of both sexes, though neither their raiment nor their language indicates the difference; all are clad in male attire; and oaths that men might shudder at issue from lips born to breathe words of sweetness. Yet these are to be, some are, the mothers of England! But can we wonder at the hideous coarseness of their language, when we remember the savage

"Sybil" is from Benjamin Disraeli, *Sybil, or the Two Nations* (New York: M. Walter Dunne, 1904), pp. 199–200.

rudeness of their lives? Naked to the waist, an iron chain fastened to a belt of leather runs between their legs clad in canvas trousers, while on hands and feet an English girl, for twelve, sometimes for sixteen hours a day, hauls and hurries tubs of coals up subterranean roads, dark, precipitous, and plashy; circumstances that seem to have escaped the notice of the Society for the Abolition of Negro Slavery. Those worthy gentlemen, too, appear to have been singularly unconscious of the sufferings of the little trappers, which was remarkable, as many of them were in their own employ.

See, too, these emerge from the bowels of the earth! Infants of four and five years of age, many of them girls, pretty and still soft and timid; entrusted with the fulfillment of responsible du-ties, the very nature of which entails on them the necessity of being the earliest to enter the mine and the latest to leave it. Their labour indeed is not severe, for that would be impossible, but it is passed in darkness and in solitude. They endure that punishment which philosophical philanthropy has invented for the direst criminals, and which those criminals deem more terrible than the death for which it is substituted. Hour after hour elapses, and all that reminds the infant trappers of the world they have quitted, and that which they have joined, is the passage of the coal-wagons for which they open the air-doors of the galleries, and on keeping which doors constantly closed, except at this moment of passage, the safety of the mine and the lives of the persons employed in it entirely depend.

Testimony before the Sadler Committee (1832)

In 1831 and 1832, the British government was under popular pressure to regulate factories and protect men, women, and children from abusive working conditions. The Sadler Committee was established and heard testimony from both workers and factory owners. The following selection clearly describes working conditions in a flax mill.

What age are you?—Twenty-three.

Where do you live?—At Leeds.

What time did you begin to work at a factory?—When I was six years old.

At whose factory did you work?—At Mr. Busk's.

What kind of mill is it?—Flax-mill.

What was your business in that mill?—I was a little doffer.

What were your hours of labour in that mill?—From 5 in the morning till 9 at night, when they were thronged.

For how long a time together have you worked that excessive length of time?—For about half a year.

What were your usual hours of labour when you were not so thronged?—From 6 in the morning till 7 at night.

What time was allowed for your meals?—Forty minutes at noon.

Had you any time to get your breakfast or drinking?—No, we got it as we could.

And when your work was bad, you hardly had anytime to eat at all?—No; we were obliged to leave it or take it home, and when we did not take it, the overlooker took it, and gave it to his pigs.

Do you consider doffing a laborious employment?—Yes.

Explain what it is you had to do?—When the frames are full, they have to stop the frames, and take the flyers off, and take the full bobbins off, and carry them to the roller; and then put empty ones on, and set the frame going again.

"Testimony before the Sadler Committee" is from *Parliamentary Papers, Reports from Committees, XV, "Labour of Children in Factories 1831–1832"* (London, 1932).

Does that keep you constantly on your feet?—Yes, there are so many frames, and they run so quick.

Your labour is very excessive?—Yes; you have not time for anything.

Suppose you flagged a little, or were too late, what would they do?—Strap us.

Are they in the habit of strapping those who are last in doffing?—Yes.

Constantly?—Yes.

Have you ever been strapped?—Yes.

Severely?—Yes.

Is the strap used so as to hurt you excessively?—Yes, it is.

Were you strapped if you were too much fatigued to keep up with the machinery?—Yes; the overlooker I was under was a very severe man, and when we have been fatigued and worn out, and had not baskets to put the bobbins in, we used to put them in the window bottoms, and that broke the panes sometimes, and I broke one one time, and the overlooker strapped me on the arm, and it rose a blister, and I ran home to my mother.

How long did you work at Mr. Busk's?—Three or four years.

Where did you go to then?—Benyon's factory.

That was when you were about 10 years?—Yes.

What were you then?—A weigher in the card-room.

How long did you work there?—From half-past 5 till 8 at night.

Was that the ordinary time?—Till 9 when they were thronged.

What time was allowed for meals at that mill?—Forty minutes at noon.

Any time at breakfast or drinking?—Yes, for the card-rooms, but not for the spinning-rooms, a quarter of an hour to get their breakfast.

And the same for their drinking?—Yes.

So that the spinners in that room worked from half-past 5 till 9 at night?—Yes.

Having only forty minutes' rest?—Yes.

The carding-room is more oppressive than the spinning department?—Yes, it is so dusty they cannot see each other for dust.

It is on that account they are allowed a relaxation of those few minutes?—Yes; the cards get so soon filled up with waste and dirt, they are obliged to stop them, or they would take fire.

There is a convenience in that stoppage?—Yes, it is as much for their benefit as for the working people.

When it was not necessary no such indulgence was allowed?—No.

Never?—No.

Were the children beat up to their labour there?—Yes.

With what?—A strap; I have seen the overlooker go to the top end of the room, where the little girls hug the can to the backminders; he has taken a strap, and a whistle in his mouth, and sometimes he has got a chain and chained them, and strapped them all down the room.

All the children?—No, only those hugging the cans.

What was his reason for that?—He was angry.

Had the children committed any fault?—They were too slow.

Were the children excessively fatigued at that time?—Yes, it was in the afternoon.

Were the girls so struck as to leave marks upon their skin?—Yes, they have had black marks many times, and their parents dare not come to him about it, they were afraid of losing their work.

If the parents were to complain of this excessive ill-usage, the probable consequence would be the loss of the situation of the child?—Yes.

In what part of the mill did you work?—In the card-room.

It was exceedingly dusty?—Yes.

Did it affect your health?—Yes; it was so dusty, the dust got upon my lungs, and the work was so hard; I was middling strong when I went there, but the work was so bad; I got so bad in health, that when I pulled the baskets down, I pulled my bones out of their places.

You dragged the baskets?—Yes; down the rooms to where they are worked.

Conditions in the mines were dismal and dangerous. Children were often used to "hurry coal" through low shafts, as shown in this drawing of 1842. *(New York Public Library Picture Collection)*

And as you had been weakened by excessive labour, you could not stand that labour?—No.

It has had the effect of pulling your shoulders out?—Yes; it was a great basket that stood higher than this table a good deal.

How heavy was it?—I cannot say; it was a very large one, that was full of weights up-heaped, and pulling the basket pulled my shoulders out of its place, and my ribs have grown over it.

You continued at that work?—Yes.

You think that work is too much for children?—Yes.

It is woman's work, not fit for children?—Yes.

Is that work generally done by women?—Yes.

How came you to do it?—There was no spinning for me.

Did they give you women's wages?—They gave me 5s. and the women had 6s. 6d.

What wages did you get as a spinner?—Six shillings.

Did you perceive that many other girls were made ill by that long labour?—Yes, a good many of them.

So that you were constantly receiving fresh hands to supply the places of those that could no longer bear their work?—Yes, there were fresh hands every week; they could not keep their hands.

Did they all go away on account of illness?—They were sick and ill with the dust.

Do you know whether any of them died in consequence of it?—No, I cannot speak to that.

You do not know what became of them?—No, we did not know that.

If a person was to take an account of a mill, and the hands in it that were ill, they would know very little of those who had suffered from their labour; they would be elsewhere?—Yes.

But you are sure of this, that they were constantly leaving on account of the excessive labour they had to endure?—Yes.

And the unhealthy nature of their employment?—Yes.

Did you take any means to obviate the bad effects of this dust?—No.

Did it make you very thirsty?—Yes, we drank a deal of water in the room.

Were you heated with your employment at the same time?—No, it was not so very hot as in the summer time; in the winter time they were obliged to have the windows open, it made no matter what the weather was, and sometimes we got very severe colds in frost and snow.

You were constantly exposed to colds, and were made ill by that cause also?—Yes.

You are considerably deformed in your person in consequence of this labour?—Yes, I am.

At what time did it come on?—I was about 13 years old when it began coming, and it has got worse since. . . .

Do you know of any body that has been similarly injured in their health?—Yes, in their health, but not many deformed as I am.

You are deformed in the shoulders?—Yes.

It is very common to have weak ankles and crooked knees?—Yes, very common indeed.

That is brought on by stopping the spindle?—Yes.

Do you know anything of wet-spinning?—Yes, it is very uncomfortable; I have stood before the frame till I have been wet through to my skin; and in winter time, when we have gone home, our clothes have been frozen, and we have nearly caught our death of cold.

A Defense of the Factory System (1835)

ANDREW URE

The factory system was not without its advocates. One of the most influential was Andrew Ure, a professor of applied science at the University of Glasgow. He was supportive of the efficiency and productive capabilities of mechanized manufacturing. Note how the major criticisms of the reformers (child labor, degrading and unhealthy work conditions, etc.) are methodically countered. Ure argued that the owners of the mills and mines were not devils, but were actually abused themselves by the demands of the workers.

Proud of the power of malefaction, many of the cotton-spinners, though better paid, as we have shown, than any similar set of artisans in the world, organized the machinery of strikes through all the gradations of their people, terrifying or cajoling the timid or the passive among them to join their vindictive union. They boasted of possessing a dark tribunal, by the mandates of which they could paralyze every mill whose master did not comply with their wishes, and so bring ruin on the man who had given them profitable employment for many a year. By flattery or intimidation, they levied contributions from their associates in the privileged mills, which they suffered to proceed, in order to furnish spare funds for the maintenance of the idle during the decreed suspension of labour. In this extraordinary state of things, when the inventive head and the sustaining heart of trade were held in bondage by the unruly lower members, a destructive spirit began to display itself among some partisans of the union. Acts of singular atrocity were committed, sometimes with weapons fit only for demons to wield, such as the corrosive oil of vitriol, dashed in the faces of most meritorious individuals, with the effect of disfiguring their persons, and burning their eyes out of the sockets with dreadful agony.

The true spirit of turn-outs [strikes] among the spinners is well described in the following statement made on oath to the Factory Commission, by Mr. George Royle Chappel, a manufacturer of Manchester, who employs 274 hands, and two steam-engines of sixty-four horse power.

"I have had several turn-outs, and have heard of many more, but never heard of a turn-out for short time. I will relate the circumstances of the last turn-out, which took place on the 16th October, 1830, and continued till the 17th January, 1831. The whole of our spinners, whose average (weekly) wages were 2£. 13s. 5d., turned out at the instigation, as they told us at the time, of the delegates of the union. They said they had no fault to find with their wages, their work, or their masters, but the union obliged them to turn out. The same week three delegates from the spinners' union waited upon us at our mill, and dictated certain advances in wages, and other regulations, to which, if we would not adhere, they said neither our own spinners nor any other should work for us again! Of course we declined, believing our wages to be ample, and our regulations such as were necessary for the proper conducting of the establishment. The consequences were, they set watches on every avenue to the mill, night and day, to prevent any

"A Defense of the Factory System" is from Andrew Ure, *The Philosophy of Manufactures* (London: Charles Knight, 1835), pp. 282–284, 290, 300–301, 309–311, 398–399.

fresh hands coming into the mill, an object which they effectually attained, by intimidating some, and promising support to others (whom I got into the mill in a caravan), if they would leave their work. Under these circumstances, I could not work the mill, and advertised it for sale, without any applications, and I also tried in vain to let it. At the end of twenty-three weeks the hands requested to be taken to the mill again on the terms that they had left it, declaring, as they had done at first, that the union alone had forced them to turn out. . . ."

Nothing shows in a clearer point of view the credulity of mankind in general, and of the people of these islands in particular, than the ready faith which was given to the tales of cruelty exercised by proprietors of cotton-mills towards young children. The systems of calumny somewhat resembles that brought by the Pagans against the primitive Christians, of enticing children into their meetings in order to murder and devour them. . . .

No master would wish to have any wayward children to work within the walls of his factory, who do not mind their business without beating, and he therefore usually fines or turns away any spinners who are known to maltreat their assistants. Hence, ill-usage of any kind is a very rare occurrence. I have visited many factories, both in Manchester and in the surrounding districts, during a period of several months, entering the spinning rooms, unexpectedly, and often alone, at different times of the day, and I never saw a single instance of corporal chastisement inflicted on a child, nor indeed did I ever see children in ill-humour. They seemed to be always cheerful and alert, taking pleasure in the light play of their muscles, enjoying the mobility natural to their age. The scene of industry, so far from exciting sad emotions in my mind, was always exhilarating. It was delightful to observe the nimbleness with which they pieced the broken ends, as the mule-carriage began to recede from the fixed roller-beam, and to see them at leisure, after a few seconds' exercise of their tiny fingers, to amuse themselves in any attitude they chose, till the stretch and winding-on were once

more completed. The work of these lively elves seemed to resemble a sport, in which habit gave them a pleasing dexterity. Conscious of their skill, they were delighted to show it off to any stranger. As to exhaustion by the day's work, they evinced no trace of it on emerging from the mill in the evening; for they immediately began to skip about any neighbouring playground, and to commence their little amusements with the same alacrity as boys issuing from a school. It is moreover my firm conviction, that if children are not ill-used by bad parents or guardians, but receive in food and raiment the full benefit of what they earn, they would thrive better when employed in our modern factories, than if left at home in apartments too often ill-aired, damp, and cold. . . .

Of all the common prejudices that exist with regard to factory labour, there is none more unfounded than that which ascribes to it excessive tedium and irksomeness above other occupations, owing to its being carried on in conjunction with the "unceasing motion of the steam-engine." In an establishment for spinning or weaving cotton, all the hard work is performed by the steam-engine, which leaves for the attendant no hard labour at all, and literally nothing to do in general; but at intervals to perform some delicate operation, such as joining the threads that break, taking the cops off the spindle, &c. And it is so far from being true that the work in a factory is incessant, because the motion of the steam-engine is incessant, that the fact is, that the labour is not incessant on that very count, because it is performed in conjunction with the steam-engine. Of all manufacturing employments, those are by far the most irksome and incessant in which steam-engines are not employed, as in lace-running and stocking-weaving; and the way to prevent an employment from being incessant, is to introduce a steam-engine into it. These remarks certainly apply more especially to the labour of children in factories. Three-fourths of the children so employed are engaged in piecing at the mules. "When the carriages of these have receded a foot and a half or two feet from the rollers," says Mr. Tufnell,

"[The children] seemed to be always cheerful and alert, taking pleasure in the light play of their muscles, enjoying the mobility natural to their age."—Andrew Ure, *The Philosophy of Manufactures* (1835). *(Bettmann)*

inaction. And though he attends two mules, he has still six hours of non-exertion. Spinners sometimes dedicate these intervals to the perusal of books. The scavengers, who, in Mr. Sadler's report, have been described as being "constantly in a state of grief, always in terror, and every moment they have to spare stretched all their length upon the floor in a state of perspiration," may be observed in cotton factories idle for four minutes at a time, or moving about in a sportive mood, utterly unconscious of the tragical scenes in which they were dramatized....

Mr. Hutton, who has been in practice as a surgeon at Stayley Bridge upwards of thirty-one years, and, of course, remembers the commencement, and has had occasion to trace the progress and effect, of the factory system, says that the health of the population has much improved since its introduction, and that they are much superior in point of comfort to what they were formerly. He also says that fever has become less common since the erection of factories, and that the persons employed in them were less attacked by the influenza in 1833, than other classes of work-people. Mr. Bott, a surgeon, who is employed by the operatives in Messrs. Lichfield's mills to attend them in all cases of sickness or accident, at the rate of one halfpenny a week (a sum which indicates pretty distinctly their small chances of ailment), says that the factory workmen are not so liable to epidemics as other persons; and that though he has had many cases of typhus fever in the surrounding district, nearly all the mill-hands have escaped, and not one was attacked by the cholera during its prevalence in the neighbourhood.

"nothing is to be done, not even attention is required from either spinner or piecer." Both of them stand idle for a time, and in fine spinning particularly, for three-quarters of a minute, or more. Consequently, if a child remains at this business twelve hours daily, he has nine hours of

The Condition of the Working Class in England (1844)

FRIEDRICH ENGELS

The living conditions of workers in urban industrial settings were a popular subject for reformers. One of the most important reformers, Friedrich Engels (1820–1895), was born to a family of German textile manufacturers. Engels was a keen observer of society and a talented,

"The Condition of the Working Class in England" is from Friedrich Engels, *The Condition of the Working Class in England in 1844* (London: Sonenschein & Co., 1892), pp. 51–53.

urbane writer. His close friendship and collaboration with Karl Marx were instrumental in the dissemination and success of communist ideology. In the first selection, Engels describes the condition of the working class in Manchester, the primary manufacturing town in England. In the second, he exposes the threat to women and the family engendered by the factory system.

Above Ducie Bridge, the left bank grows more flat and the right bank steeper, but the condition of the dwellings on both banks grows worse rather than better. He who turns to the left here from the main street, Long Millgate, is lost; he wanders from one court to another, turns countless corners, passes nothing but narrow, filthy nooks and alleys, until after a few minutes he has lost all clue, and knows not whither to turn. Everywhere half or wholly ruined buildings, some of them actually uninhabited, which means a great deal here; rarely a wooden or stone floor to be seen in the houses, almost uniformly broken, ill-fitting windows

This 1872 engraving of Gustave Doré's *Over London by Rail* shows the crowded, polluted, urban living conditions that had developed during the Industrial Revolution. Friedrich Engels noted: "Everywhere heaps of debris, refuse and offal; standing pools for gutters, and a stench which alone would make it impossible for a human being . . . to live in such a district." *(Art Resource)*

and doors, and a state of filth! Everywhere heaps of debris, refuse, and offal; standing pools for gutters, and a stench which alone would make it impossible for a human being in any degree civilised to live in such a district. The newly-built extension of the Leeds railway, which crosses the Irk here, has swept away some of these courts and lanes, laying others completely open to view. Immediately under the railway bridge there stands a court, the filth and horrors of which surpass all the others by far, just because it was hitherto so shut off, so secluded that the way to it could not be found without a good deal of trouble. I should never have discovered it myself, without the breaks made by the railway, though I thought I knew this whole region thoroughly. Passing along a rough bank, among stakes and washing-lines, one penetrates into this chaos of small one-storied, one-roomed huts, in most of which there is no artificial floor; kitchen, living and sleeping-room all in one. In such a hole, scarcely five feet long by six broad, I found two beds—and such bedsteads and beds!—which, with a staircase and chimney-place, exactly filled the room. In several others I found absolutely nothing, while the door stood open, and the inhabitants leaned against it. Everywhere before the doors refuse and offal; that any sort of pavement lay underneath could not be seen but only felt, here and there with the feet. This whole collection of cattle-sheds for human beings was surrounded on two sides by houses and a factory, and on the third by the river, and besides the narrow stair up the bank, a narrow doorway alone led out into another almost equally ill-built, ill-kept labyrinth of dwellings. . . .

Such is the Old Town of Manchester, and on re-reading my description, I am forced to admit that instead of being exaggerated, it is far from black enough to convey a true impression of the filth, ruin, and uninhabitableness, the defiance of all considerations of cleanliness, ventilation, and health which characterise the construction of this single district, containing at least twenty to thirty thousand inhabitants. And such a district exists in the heart of the second city of England, the first manufacturing city of the world. If any one wishes to see in how little space a human being can move, how little air—and such air!—he can breathe, how little civilisation he may share and yet live, it is only necessary to travel hither. True, this is the Old Town, and the people of Manchester emphasise the fact whenever any one mentions to them the frightful condition of this Hell upon Earth; but what does that prove? Everything which here arouses horror and indignation is of recent origin, belongs to the industrial epoch.

The Impact of the Factory System on Women and the Family

FRIEDRICH ENGELS

The employment of women at once breaks up the family; for when the wife spends twelve or thirteen hours every day in the mill, and the husband works the same length of time there or elsewhere, what becomes of the children? They grow up like wild weeds; they are put out to nurse for a shilling or eighteenpence a week, and how they are treated may be imagined.... That the general mortality among young children must be increased by the employment of the mothers is self-evident, and is placed beyond all doubt by notorious facts.

Women often return to the mill three or four days after confinement [for childbirth], leaving the baby, of course; in the dinner hour they must hurry home to feed the child and eat

"The Impact of the Factory System on Women and the Family" is from Friedrich Engels, *The Conditions of the Working Class in England in 1844* (London: Sonnenschein & Co., 1892).

something, and what sort of suckling that can be is also evident.

Lord Ashley repeats the testimony of several workwomen:

"M. H., twenty years old, has two children, the youngest a baby, that is tended by the other, a little older. The mother goes to the mill shortly after five o'clock in the morning, and comes home at eight at night; all day the milk pours from her breasts so that her clothing drips with it."

"H. W. has three children, goes away Monday morning at five o'clock, and comes back Saturday evening; has so much to do for the children then that she cannot get to bed before three o'clock in the morning; often wet through to the skin, and obliged to work in that state. She said: 'My breasts have given me the most frightful pain, and I have been dripping wet with milk.'"

The use of narcotics to keep the children still is fostered by this infamous system, and has reached a great extent in the factory districts. Dr. Johns, Registrar in Chief for Manchester, is of opinion that this custom is the chief source of the many deaths from convulsions. The employment of the wife dissolves the family utterly and of necessity, and this dissolution, in our present society, which is based upon the family, brings the most demoralizing consequences for parents, as well as children. . . .

Yet the working man cannot escape from the family, must live in the family, and the consequence is a perpetual succession of family troubles, domestic quarrels, most demoralizing for parents and children alike. Neglect of all domestic duties, neglect of the children, especially, is only too common among English working people, and only too vigorously fostered by the existing institutions of society. And children growing up in this savage way, amidst these demoralizing influences, are expected to turn out goody-goody and moral in the end! Verily the requirements are naive which the self-satisfied bourgeois makes upon the working man!

VISIONS OF A NEW WORLD

The Chartist Demands (1838)

Although the Factory Act of 1833 resulted in an improvement in factory working conditions and in restrictions on child labor, many critics favored more radical reform. The Chartist movement in Great Britain, which was popular in the 1840s, sought political participation and especially universal manhood suffrage as means of improving the living conditions of the working poor. The following is an excerpt from the People's Petition of 1838, which articulated Chartist demands to the British House of Commons.

We, your petitioners, dwell in a land whose merchants are noted for enterprise, whose manufacturers are very skillful, and whose workmen are proverbial for their industry.

The land itself is goodly, the soil rich, and the temperature wholesome; it is abundantly furnished with the materials of commerce and trade; it has numerous and convenient harbours; in facility of internal communication it exceeds all others. For three-and-twenty years we have enjoyed a profound peace.

Yet, with all these elements of national prosperity, and with every disposition and capacity to take advantage of them, we find ourselves overwhelmed with public and private suffering.

We are bowed down under a load of taxes; which, notwithstanding, fall greatly short of the wants of our rulers; our traders are trembling on the verge of bankruptcy; our workmen are starving; capital brings no profit, and labour no remuneration; the home of the artificer is desolate, and the warehouse of the pawnbroker is full; the workhouse is crowded, and the manufactory is deserted. . . .

It was the found expectation of the people that a remedy for the greater part, if not for the whole, of their grievances, would be found in the Reform Act of 1832.

They were taught to regard that Act as a wise means to a worthy end; as the machinery of an improved legislation, when the will of the masses would be at length potential.

They have been bitterly and basely deceived.

The fruit which looked so fair to the eye has turned to dust and ashes when gathered.

The Reform Act has effected a transfer of power from one domineering faction to another, and left the people as helpless as before. . . .

Required as we are, universally, to support and obey the laws, nature and reason entitle us to demand, that in the making of the laws, the universal voice shall be implicitly listened to.

We perform the duties of freemen; we must have the privileges of freemen.

WE DEMAND UNIVERSAL SUFFRAGE

The suffrage to be exempt from the corruption of the wealthy, and the violence of the powerful, must be secret. . . .

WE DEMAND THE BALLOT

The connection between the representatives and the people, to be beneficial must be intimate. . . . To public safety as well as public confidence, frequent elections are essential.

WE DEMAND ANNUAL PARLIAMENTS

With power to choose, and freedom in choosing, the range of our choice must be unrestricted.

We are compelled, by the existing laws, to take for our representatives, men who are incapable of appreciating our difficulties, or who have little sympathy with them; merchants who have retired from trade, and no longer feel its harassings; proprietors of land who are alike ignorant of its evils and their cure; lawyers, by whom the honours of the senate are sought after only as means of obtaining notice in the courts. . . .

"The Chartist Demands" is from *The Life and Struggles of William Lovett* (New York: Knopf, 1920), pp. 478–481.

We demand that in the future election of members of your Honourable House, the approbation of the constituency shall be the sole qualification; and that to every representative so chosen shall be assigned, out of the public taxes, a fair and adequate remuneration for the time which he is called upon to devote to the public service.

Finally, we would most earnestly impress on your Honourable House, that this petition has not been dictated by an idle love of change; that it springs out of no inconsiderate attachment to fanciful theories; but that it is the result of much and long deliberation, and of convictions, which the events of each succeeding year tend more and more to strengthen.

A Middle-Class Perspective (1859)

SAMUEL SMILES

For many members of the middle class, the Victorian Age was not characterized by the slums of Glasgow or the dirt of industry. To their thinking, perseverance and hard work resulted in a better life and were always rewarded. In his book Self-Help *(1859), Samuel Smiles emphasized this principle through a series of biographies of men who had risen to fame and fortune. The guiding idea was that "the most important results in daily life are to be obtained, not through the exercise of extraordinary powers, such as genius and intellect, but through the energetic use of simple means and ordinary qualities with which nearly all human individuals have more or less been endowed." One was responsible for one's own fate; it was up to the individual to change a bad situation if so desired.*

The object of the book briefly is, to re-inculcate these old-fashioned but wholesome lessons—which perhaps cannot be too often urged,—that youth must work in order to enjoy,—that nothing creditable can be accomplished without application and diligence,—that the student must not be daunted by difficulties, but conquer them by patience and perseverance,—and that, above all, he must seek elevation of character, without which capacity is worthless and worldly success is naught. If the author has not succeeded in illustrating these lessons, he can only say that he has failed in his object.

"Heaven helps those who help themselves" is a well-tried maxim, embodying in a small compass the results of vast human experience. The spirit of self-help is the root of all genuine growth in the individual; and, exhibited in the lives of many, it constitutes the true source of national vigour and strength. Help from without is often enfeebling in its effects, but help from within invariably invigorates. Whatever is done for men or classes, to a certain extent takes away the stimulus and necessity of doing for themselves; and where men are subjected to over-guidance and over-government, the inevitable tendency is to render them comparatively helpless.

Even the best institutions can give a man no active help. Perhaps the most they can do is, to leave him free to develop himself and improve his individual condition. But in all times men have been prone to believe that their happiness and well-being were to be secured by means of institutions rather than by their own conduct. Hence the value of legislation as an agent in human advancement has usually been much over-estimated. To constitute the millionth part of a Legislature, by voting for one or two men once in three or five years, however conscientiously this duty may be performed, can exercise but little active influence upon any man's life

"A Middle-Class Perspective" is from Samuel Smiles, *Self-Help* (London: John Murray, 1882), pp. v, 1, 4.

and character. Moreover, it is every day becoming more clearly understood, that the function of Government is negative and restrictive, rather than positive and active; being resolvable principally into protection—protection of life, liberty, and property. Laws, wisely administered, will secure men in the enjoyment of the fruits of their labour, whether of mind or body, at a comparatively small personal sacrifice; but no laws, however stringent, can make the idle industrious, the thriftless provident, or the drunken sober. Reforms can only be effected by means of individual action, economy, and self-denial; better habits, rather than by greater rights. . . .

Daily experience shows that it is energetic individualism which produces the most powerful effects upon the life and action of others, and really constitutes the best practical education. Schools, academies, and colleges give but the merest beginnings of culture in comparison with it. Far more influential is the life-education daily given in our homes, in the streets, behind coun-

ters, in workshops, at the loom and the plough, in counting-houses and manufactories, and in the busy haunts of men. This is that finishing instruction as members of society, which Schiller designated "the education of the human race," consisting in action, conduct, self-culture, self-control,—all that tends to discipline a man truly, and fit him for the proper performance of the duties and business of life,—a kind of education not to be learnt from books, or acquired by any amount of mere literary training. With his usual weight of words Bacon observes, that "Studies teach not their own use; but that is a wisdom without them, and above them, won by observation"; a remark that holds true of actual life, as well as of the cultivation of the intellect itself. For all experience serves to illustrate and enforce the lesson, that a man perfects himself by work more than by reading,—that it is life rather than literature, action rather than study, and character rather than biography, which tend perpetually to renovate mankind.

Utopian Socialism (1816)

ROBERT OWEN

One of the great personal success stories of the nineteenth century was Robert Owen. Born the son of a saddle maker, Owen left school at the age of 9 and went to work in a draper's shop. At the age of 18, he borrowed money and set up a small cotton mill in Manchester. Within ten years, he was very wealthy and was joint owner of the New Lanark mills, the largest textile operation in Scotland. But Robert Owen was possessed with a desire to improve the lot of humanity. He provided higher wages and better working conditions for his employees and established free schools for their children. The New Lanark mills also returned a handsome profit. Owen sought government intervention and regulation to change conditions in industry. He could not understand why all factories could not be run on his utopian model. He is generally accepted in England as the founder of British socialism. The following address was delivered in 1816 on the opening of an "Institution for the Formation of Character" at New Lanark. Note the emphasis on morality as an essential ingredient of change.

Every society which exists at present, as well as every society which history records, has been formed and governed on a belief in the following notions, assumed as *first principles:*

First,—That it is in the power of every individual to form his own character.

Hence the various systems called by the name of religion, codes of law, and punishments.

"Utopian Socialism" is from Robert Owen, *Address to the Workers of New Lanark* (1816).

Hence also the angry passions entertained by individuals and nations towards each other.

Second,—That the affections are at the command of the individual. Hence insincerity and degradation of character. Hence the miseries of domestic life, and more than one-half of all the crimes of mankind.

Third,—That it is necessary that a large portion of mankind should exist in ignorance and poverty, in order to secure to the remaining part such a degree of happiness as they now enjoy.

Hence a system of counteraction in the pursuits of men, a general opposition among individuals to the interests of each other, and the necessary effects of such a system,—ignorance, poverty, and vice.

Facts prove, however—

First,—That character is universally formed *for*, and not *by*, the individual.

Second,—That *any* habits and sentiments may be given to mankind.

Third,—That the affections are not under the control of the individual.

Fourth,—That every individual may be trained to produce far more than he can consume, while there is a sufficiency of soil left for him to cultivate.

Fifth,—That nature has provided means by which population may be at all times maintained in the proper state to give the greatest happiness to every individual, without one check of vice or misery.

Sixth,—That any community may be arranged, on a due combination of the foregoing principles, in such a manner, as not only to withdraw vice, poverty, and, in a great degree, misery, from the world, but also to place *every* individual under circumstances in which he shall enjoy more permanent happiness than can be given to *any* individual under the principles which have hitherto regulated society.

Seventh,—That all the assumed fundamental principles on which society has hitherto been founded are erroneous, and may be demonstrated to be contrary to fact. And—

Eighth,—That the change which would follow the abandonment of those erroneous maxims which bring misery into the world, and the adoption of principles of truth, unfolding a system which shall remove and for ever exclude that misery, may be effected without the slightest injury to any human being.

Here is the groundwork,—these are the data, on which society shall ere long be re-arranged; and for this simple reason, that it will be rendered evident that it will be for the immediate and future interest of every one to lend his most active assistance gradually to reform society on this basis. I say gradually, for in that word the most important considerations are involved. Any sudden and coercive attempt which may be made to remove even misery from men will prove injurious rather than beneficial. Their minds must be gradually prepared by an essential alteration of the circumstances which surround them, for any great and important change and amelioration in their condition. They must be first convinced of their blindness: this cannot be effected, even among the least unreasonable, or those termed the best part of mankind, in their present state, without creating some degree of irritation. This irritation, must then be tranquillized before another step ought to be attempted; and a general conviction must be established of the truth of the principles on which the projected change is to be founded. Their introduction into practice will then become easy,—difficulties will vanish as we approach them,—and, afterwards, the desire to see the whole system carried immediately into effect will exceed the means of putting it into execution.

The principles on which this practical system is founded are not new; separately, or partially united, they have been often recommended by the sages of antiquity, and by modern writers. But it is not known to me that they have ever been thus combined. Yet it can be demonstrated that it is only by their being *all brought into practice together* that they are to be rendered beneficial to mankind; and sure I am that this is the earliest period in the history of man when they could be successfully introduced into practice.

The Communist Manifesto (1848)

KARL MARX AND FRIEDRICH ENGELS

The Communist Manifesto, *written by Karl Marx (1818–1883) and Friedrich Engels in 1848, is the fundamental declaration of communist ideology. Marx was concerned with the process of change in history (dialectic). A keen observer of the industrial world around him, Marx saw the oppression of the worker (proletarian) by those who owned the means of production (bourgeoisie). Marx advocated a society that was devoid of capitalistic oppression, a society in which workers actually controlled the factories and regulated their own working conditions and environment. His call to revolution had little influence on the protests of 1848, but his ideas would serve as the foundation for the Russian Revolution in 1917 and are of great importance today.*

Bourgeoisie and Proletariat

The history of all hitherto existing society is the history of class struggles.

Freeman and slave, patrician and plebeian, lord and serf, guildmaster and journeyman, in a word, oppressor and oppressed, stood in constant opposition to one another, carried on an uninterrupted, now hidden, now open fight, a fight that each time ended, either in a revolutionary reconstitution of society at large, or in the common ruin of the contending classes.

In the earlier epochs of history, we find almost everywhere a complicated arrangement of society into various orders, a manifold graduation of social rank. In ancient Rome we have patricians, knights, plebeian, slaves; in the Middle Ages, feudal lords, vassals, guildmasters, journeymen, apprentices, serfs; in almost all of these classes, again, subordinate gradations.

The modern bourgeois society that has sprouted from the ruins of feudal society, has not done away with class antagonisms. It has but established new classes, new conditions of oppression, new forms of struggle in place of the old ones.

Our epoch, the epoch of the bourgeoisie, possesses, however, this distinctive feature: it has simplified the class antagonisms. Society as a whole is more and more splitting up into two great hostile camps, into two great classes directly facing each other: Bourgeoisie and Proletariat. . . .

Each step in the development of the bourgeoisie was accompanied by a corresponding political advance of the class. An oppressed class under the sway of the feudal nobility, an armed and self-governing association in the medieval commune, here independent urban republic (as in Italy and Germany), there taxable "third estate" of the monarchy (as in France), afterwards, in the period of manufacture proper, serving either the semifeudal or the absolute monarchy as a counterpoise against the nobility, and in fact, corner stone of the great monarchies in general, the bourgeoisie has at last, since the establishment of Modern Industry and of the world-market, conquered for itself, in the modern representative State, exclusive political sway. The executive of the modern State is but a committee for managing the common affairs of the whole bourgeoisie. . . .

The need of a constantly expanding market for its products chases the bourgeoisie over the whole surface of the globe. It must nestle everywhere, establish connections everywhere. . . .

The bourgeoisie, during its rule of scarce one hundred years, has created more massive and more colossal productive forces than have all preceding generations together. Subjection of

"The Communist Manifesto" is from Karl Marx and Friedrich Engels, *The Communist Manifesto*, trans. Samuel Moore (New York: Socialist Labor Party, 1888).

Nature's forces to man, machinery, application of chemistry to industry and agriculture, steam-navigation, railways, electric telegraphs, clearing of whole continents for cultivation, canalization of rivers, whole populations conjured out of the ground—what earlier century had even a presentiment that such productive forces slumbered in the lap of social labor? . . .

In proportion as the bourgeoisie, i.e., capital, is developed, in the same proportion is the proletariat, the modern working-class, developed, a class of laborers, who live only so long as they find work, and who find work only so long as their labor increases capital. These laborers, who must sell themselves piecemeal, are a commodity, like every other article of commerce, and are consequently exposed to all the vicissitudes of competition, to all the fluctuations of the market.

Owing to the extensive use of machinery and to division of labor, the work of the proletarians has lost all individual character, and, consequently, all charm for the workman. He becomes an appendage of the machine, and it is only the most simple, most monotonous, and most easily acquired knack that is required of him. Hence, the cost of production of a workman is restricted, almost entirely, to the means of subsistence that he requires for his maintenance, and for the propagation of his race. But the price of commodity, and also of labor, is equal to its cost of production. In proportion, therefore, as the repulsiveness of the work increases, the wage decreases. Nay more, in proportion as the use of the machinery and division of labor increases, in the same proportion the burden of toil also increases, whether by prolongation of the working hours, by increase of the work enacted in a given time, or by increased speed of the machinery, etc.

Modern industry has converted the little workshop of the patriarchal master into the great factory of the industrial capitalist. Masses of laborers, crowded into the factory, are organized like soldiers. As privates of the industrial army they are placed under the command of a perfect hierarchy of officers and sergeants. Not

only are they the slaves of the bourgeois class, and of the bourgeois State, they are daily and hourly enslaved by the machine, by the over-looker, and, above all, by the individual bourgeois manufacturer himself. The more openly despotism proclaims gain to be its end and aim, the more petty, the more hateful and the more embittering it is.

The less the skill and exertion or strength implied in manual labor, in other words, the more modern industry becomes developed, the more is the labor of men superseded by that of

The grave memorial of Karl Marx at Highgate Cemetery in London: "The proletarians have nothing to lose but their chains. They have a world to win. Workers of the world, unite!" *(Perry M. Rogers)*

women. Differences of age and sex have no longer any distinctive social validity for the working class. All are instruments of labor, more or less expensive to use, according to their age and sex.

No sooner is the exploitation of the laborer by the manufacturer, so far at an end, that he receives his wages in cash, than he is set upon by the other portions of the bourgeoisie, the landlord, the shopkeeper, the pawnbroker, etc. . . .

But with the development of industry the proletariat not only increases in number, it becomes concentrated in greater masses, its strength grows, and it feels that strength more. The various interests and conditions of life within the ranks of the proletariat are more and more equalized, in proportion as machinery obliterates all distinctions of labor, and nearly everywhere reduces wages to the same low level. The growing competition among the bourgeois, and the resulting commercial crises, make the wages of the workers ever more fluctuating. The unceasing improvement of machinery, ever more rapidly developing, makes their livelihood more and more precarious; the collisions between individual workmen and individual bourgeois take more and more the character of collisions between two classes. Thereupon the workers begin to form combinations (Trades' Unions) against the bourgeois; they club together in order to keep up the rate of wages; they found permanent associations in order to make provision beforehand for these occasional revolts. Here and there the contest breaks out into riots.

Now and then the workers are victorious, but only for a time. The real fruit of their battle lies, not in the immediate result, but in the ever expanding union of the workers. This union is helped on by the improved means of communications that are created by modern industry, and that places the workers of different localities in contact with one another. It was just this contact that was needed to centralize the numerous local struggles, all of the same character, into one national struggle between classes. But every class struggle is a political struggle. . . .

This organization of the proletarians into a class, and consequently into a political party, is continually being upset again by the competition between the workers themselves. But it ever rises up again, stronger, firmer, mightier. It compels legislative recognition of particular interests of the workers, by taking advantage of the divisions among the bourgeoisie itself. Thus the ten-hour bill in England was carried. . . .

The essential condition for the existence, and for the sway of the bourgeois class, is the formation and augmentation of capital; the condition for capital is wage-labor. Wage-labor rests exclusively on competition between the laborers. The advance of industry, whose involuntary promoter is the bourgeoisie, replaces the isolation of the laborers, due to competition, by their revolutionary combination, due to association. The development of Modern Industry, therefore, cuts from under its feet the very foundation on which the bourgeoisie produces and appropriates products. What the bourgeoisie therefore produces, above all, are its own gravediggers. Its fall and the victory of the proletariat are equally inevitable.

Proletarians and Communists

In what relation do the Communists stand to the proletarians as a whole?

The Communists do not form a separate party opposed to other working class parties.

They have no interests separate and apart from those of the proletariat as a whole.

They do not set up any sectarian principles of their own, by which to shape and mould the proletarian movement.

The Communists are distinguished from the other working class parties by this only: 1. In the national struggles of the proletarians of the different countries, they point out and bring to the front the common interests of the entire proletariat independently of all nationality. 2. In the various stages of development which the struggle of the working class against the bourgeoisie has to pass through, they always and everywhere represent the interests of the movement as a whole.

The Communists, therefore, are on the one hand, practically, the most advanced and resolute section of the working class parties of every country, that section which pushes forward all other; on the other hand, theoretically, they have over the great mass of the proletariat the advantage of clearly understanding the line of march, the conditions, and the ultimate general results of the proletarian movement.

The immediate aim of the Communists is the same as that of all the other proletarian parties: formation of the proletariat into a class, overthrow of the bourgeois supremacy, conquest of political power by the proletariat.

The theoretical conclusions of the Communists are in no way based on ideas or principles that have been invented, or discovered, by this or that would-be universal reformer.

They merely express, in general terms, actual relations springing from an existing class struggle, from a historical movement going on under our very eyes. The abolition of existing property relations is not at all a distinctive feature of Communism.

All property relations in the past have continually been subject to historical change consequent upon the change in historical conditions.

The French Revolution, for example, abolished feudal property in favor of bourgeois property.

The distinguishing feature of Communism is not the abolition of property generally, but the abolition of bourgeois property. But modern bourgeois private property is the final and most complete expression of the system of producing and appropriating products, that is based on class antagonism, on the exploitation of the many by the few.

In this sense, the theory of the Communists may be summed up in the single sentence: Abolition of private property. . . .

The Communist revolution is the most radical rupture with traditional property-relations; no wonder that its development involves the most radical rupture with traditional ideas.

But let us have done with the bourgeois objections to Communism.

We have seen above, that the first step in the revolution by the working class, is to raise the proletariat to the position of ruling class, to win the battle of democracy.

The proletariat will use its political supremacy, to wrest, by degrees, all capital from the bourgeoisie, to centralize all instruments of production in the hands of the State, i.e., of the proletariat organized as the ruling class; and to increase the total of productive forces as rapidly as possible.

Of course, in the beginning, this cannot be effected except by means of despotic inroads on the rights of property, and on the conditions of bourgeois production; by means of measures, therefore, which appear economically insufficient and untenable, but which, in the course of the movement, outstrip themselves, necessitate further inroads upon the old social order, and are unavoidable as a means of entirely revolutionizing the mode of production.

These measures will of course be different in different countries.

Nevertheless in the most advanced countries the following will be pretty generally applicable:

1. Abolition of property in land and application of all rents of land to public purposes.
2. A heavy progressive or graduated income tax.
3. Abolition of all rights of inheritance.
4. Confiscation of the property of all emigrants and rebels.
5. Centralization of credit in the hands of the state, by means of a national bank with State capital and an exclusive monopoly.
6. Centralization of the means of communication and transport in the hands of the State.
7. Extension of factories and instruments of production owned by the State; the bringing into cultivation of waste lands, and the improvement of the soil generally in accordance with a common plan.
8. Equal liability of all to labor. Establishment of industrial armies, especially for agriculture.

9. Combination of agriculture with manufacturing industries; gradual abolition of the distinction between town and country, by a more equable distribution of population over the country.
10. Free education for all children in public schools. Abolition of children's factory labor in its present form. Combination of education with industrial production, etc., etc.

When, in the course of development, class distinctions have disappeared, and all production has been concentrated in the hands of a vast association of the whole nation, the public power will lose its political character. Political power, properly so called, is merely the organized power of one class for oppressing another. If the proletariat during its contest with the bourgeoisie is compelled, by the force of circumstances, to organize itself as a class, if, by means of a revolution, it makes itself the ruling class, and, as such, sweeps away by force the old conditions of production, then it will, along with these conditions, have swept away the conditions for the existence of class antagonisms, and of class generally, and will thereby have abolished its own supremacy as a class.

In place of the old bourgeois society, with its classes and class antagonisms, we shall have an association, in which the free development of each is the condition for the free development of all. . . .

In short, the Communists everywhere support every revolutionary movement against the existing social and political order of things.

In all these movements they bring to the front, as the leading question in each, the property question, no matter what its degree of development at the time.

Finally, they labor everywhere for the union and agreement of the democratic parties of all countries.

The Communists disdain to conceal their views and aims. They openly declare that their ends can be attained only by the forcible overthrow of all existing social conditions. Let the ruling classes tremble at a Communistic revolution. The proletarians have nothing to lose but their chains. They have a world to win.

Workers of the world, unite!

CHRONOLOGY: "A World to Win!": The Industrial Revolution

1733 James Kay invents flying shuttle, which increases productive capacity of weavers.

1769 James Watt patents steam engine, which provided for the first time in history a steady and unlimited source of inanimate power.

1769 Richard Arkwright patents water frame, which permits the production of a purely cotton fabric, thus allowing large-scale textile manufacturing in factories.

1770 James Hargreaves patents spinning jenny, which allows for faster production of thread.

1776 Adam Smith publishes *The Wealth of Nations*, which develops the theory of capitalism, an economic system based on individual self-interest.

1787 Edmund Cartwright invents the power loom for machine, rather than hand, weaving.

1798 Thomas Malthus writes *Essay on the Principle of Population*, which contended that the plight of the working class could only become worse because the human population must eventually outstrip the food supply.

1817 David Ricardo's *Principles of Political Economy and Taxation* fashioned Malthus' theories into the "Iron Law of Wages."

1825   Death of Count Claude Henri de Saint-Simon, the earliest of socialist pioneers: Private wealth, property, and enterprise should be subject to regulation.

1832   Great Reform Bill passed by British Parliament eliminated "rotten boroughs" and extended franchise to a greater proportion of the middle class.

1833   Factory Act passed by British Parliament limited the working hours of women and children in the textile mills and provided government inspection of the workplace.

1844   *The Conditions of the Working Class in England in 1844* by Friedrich Engels, appears.

1848   *The Communist Manifesto*, by Karl Marx and Friedrich Engels, is published. Revolutions throughout Europe in support of liberal agendas are unsuccessful.

1858   Death of Robert Owen, a "Utopian Socialist," who believed that a proper working environment would improve human character. Through enlightened management, his New Lanark textile mills were successful and humanely operated.

1891   Pope Leo XIII issues the encyclical *Rerum Novarum*, which addresses the continuing struggle between capitalists and workers: Brotherly love was preferable to ruthless competition and exploitation.

STUDY QUESTIONS

1. What was the "factory system"? How and why did it originate? What was it intended to do?
2. Does the testimony about degrading working conditions constitute a realistic and accurate portrayal of urban life during the Industrial Revolution? Or is this portrait an exaggeration? How does Engels's description of the impact of the factory system on women and the family seem to reflect some of the concerns of our contemporary society?
3. How does Andrew Ure defend the factory system? What specific points does he address? Are his arguments persuasive? Why or why not?
4. Who were the Chartists and what were their demands for reform? Was this a political or social reform program?
5. What was the attitude of Samuel Smiles toward the plight of the working class? Why would this opinion be considered "middle class"? What do you think of the principle of "self-help"? Is it a realistic option—or the only option? What are the arguments against the contemporary welfare systems in Europe and America? Do they subsidize inactivity? What is "workfare"?
6. How would you define Utopian Socialism? How important is character to success? Why was Robert Owens's factory at New Lanark successful? Do the most successful capitalists place an emphasis on people over profit?
7. What do you consider to be the most important ideas or statements that can be found in the excerpt on *The Communist Manifesto?* Why is this considered one of the most influential documents in world civilization?
8. How do you view the Industrial Revolution? Was it a progressive time that demonstrated human creativity, or was it born of human greed and exploitation of others who were less fortunate or less conscientious and determined to succeed? Is there always a price to pay in human suffering for a civilization to progress? How can you apply your ideas to our contemporary age?

Part II

THE AGE OF IMPERIALISM
(1840–1900)

5

"Mark Them with Your Dead!": The Scramble for Global Empire

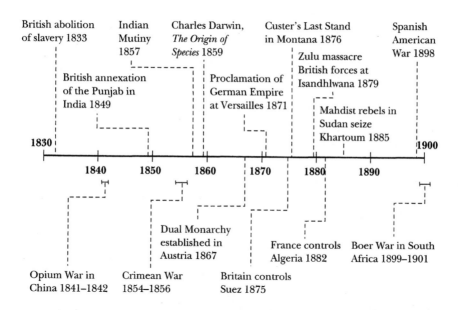

British abolition of slavery 1833

Indian Mutiny 1857

Charles Darwin, *The Origin of Species* 1859

Custer's Last Stand in Montana 1876

Spanish American War 1898

British annexation of the Punjab in India 1849

Proclamation of German Empire at Versailles 1871

Zulu massacre British forces at Isandhlwana 1879

Mahdist rebels in Sudan seize Khartoum 1885

1830

1900

1840   1850   1860   1870   1880   1890

Dual Monarchy established in Austria 1867

France controls Algeria 1882

Boer War in South Africa 1899–1901

Opium War in China 1841–1842

Crimean War 1854–1856

Britain controls Suez 1875

CHAPTER THEMES

- *Imperialism:* How did the "New Imperialism" of the late nineteenth century differ from the colonialism of the fifteenth through eighteenth centuries? What political conditions had changed that compelled European nations to establish their control abroad?

- *Church/State Relationships:* How did religious organizations encourage and support the various imperial efforts of European nations? What were the religious motives for controlling foreign populations? Was this blatantly hypocritical?

- *Beliefs and Spirituality:* How did nationalism and the fervent belief in the sanctity of one's nation and ethnic origins both contribute to the progress of a unified Europe and lead to the degeneration of personal freedom at home and abroad?

- *Propaganda:* How was propaganda used to create an image of peoples in Africa, India, and Asia that allowed European and U.S. governments to justify their imperialistic control? How was science in particular distorted to create a new ethical perspective that made such expansion not just tolerable, but socially responsible?

- *Historical Change and Transition:* Is imperialism such a part of human nature and social organization that it will always play a developmental role in world civilization?

- *The Big Picture:* Has world history always been dominated by a contentious and polarizing relationship between those who have and those who have not? To what extent is exploitation the watchword for economic and political progress? Or is justice the dominant force in the progress of world civilization?

The head of Charles "Chinese" Gordon, perhaps the most dashing and best regarded general in the British army, lay fixed on a tree in Omdurman, Sudan. Its sightless eyes were searching for the relief force that was not destined to arrive in time. Abdullah Muhammad, the Islamic visionary called the Mahdi, had warned the British garrison at Khartoum that there would be no escape from death for those who sought to control the Sudan and wage war against Allah. In February 1885, he made good his promise.

This act of resistance, at once brutal and defensible, underscores the contradictions that were inherent in the process of "civilizing" the natives of Africa, America, and Asia during the nineteenth century. The poet Rudyard Kipling spoke to "the legions of the lost ones, to the cohort of the damned," those British soldiers who sacrificed their lives for the progress of civilization, for England—it was the "white man's burden." Of course, the British were not alone in their mission and sacrifice. The road to glory and pathway to higher civilization was littered with the dead of many villages, many nations, everyone innocent and fully justified in some way.

Nationalism and imperialism were two of the most important factors that shaped the nineteenth century. These terms, however, are difficult to define and have been used so loosely as nearly to be deprived of meaning. *Nationalism* involves devotion, a patriotism that implies unity and constructive action in the service of one's country. *Imperialism* is a policy of extending a nation's authority by establishing political or economic control over another area or people. It is important to note that nationalism need not cause imperialism, but it promotes domestic unity, which is a necessity for successful expansion. The term *expansion* is basically benign, connoting progress and dedication, but *imperialism* is often pejorative in connotation and recalls economic exploitation, racial prejudice, and even war. This chapter will seek to define more clearly the origins and parameters of European and U.S. imperialism the nineteenth century.

Imperialism and nationalism were certainly not introduced in the nineteenth century. During the Renaissance and Reformation eras in the fifteenth and sixteenth centuries, countries such as Spain, France, and England, which had heretofore been decentralized feudal areas, were united under the leadership of strong monarchs. Although this unity was often achieved initially by the sword, the benefits of centralized rule soon became apparent. Unity fostered pride and cooperation among compatriots and soon provided the energy and direction that made possible an age of exploration and discovery.

In essence, the establishment of colonial empires was profitable and patriotic. But by the nineteenth century, the age of colonial empire building was at an end. Spain, Portugal, and France had lost much of their old empires, Great Britain had lost her American colonies, and Germany was too divided internally to attempt to acquire new territory. Of the continental powers, only France under Napoleon was somewhat successful in establishing overseas colonies, but realized only small gains. From 1800 to 1870, Britain acquired India, New Zealand, central Canada, and western Australia; however, these territories generally were contiguous to areas Britain already held. There was a great deal of missionary activity from Christian organizations, but little overt government support.

This period of relative disinterest did not last long. Suddenly, between 1870 and 1900, there was a general outburst of imperialistic activity among the nations of Europe and Japan. France, Belgium, Britain, and Portugal made extensive gains, especially in Africa. By 1871, both Italy and Germany had been born as nations under the aggressive political and military leadership of Camillo Cavour (1810–1861) and Giuseppe Garibaldi (1807–1882) in the case of Italy, and Otto von Bismarck (1815–1898), the first chancellor of the German Empire. Appealing to abstractions such as "fate" and "duty," politicians immediately sought new territories that would keep them economically and politically competitive with the other nations of Europe. It has been estimated that in this thirty-year period from 1870 to 1900, Europeans expanded their colonial empires by over ten million square miles and nearly one hundred fifty million people. These intense economic rivalries were often expressed as well in political alliances. In 1882, the Triple Alliance was formed among Germany, Austria-Hungary, and Italy, and in 1907, the Triple Entente among Great Britain, France, and Russia. Such organized competition resulted in a polarization of European nations that contributed to the outbreak of World War I in 1914.

This drive for colonial acquisition was not limited to European powers, however. In 1854, Japan awoke from its centuries-long isolation from the world and quickly became a competitive force as the "Rising Sun" defeated Russian forces in 1905. The United States had come of age in the mid-nineteenth century by expanding to its "natural boundaries" of Mexico and the Pacific. Impelled by the dictates of a policy called "manifest destiny," U.S. settlers moved west in quest of new lives as farmers or in pursuit of the gold of California. They were supported militarily by the U.S. government and ideologically by Christian missionaries who saw westward expansion as the fulfillment of the destiny of the United States, so ordained by God. Thus were Native Americans dehumanized and sent to reservations, and thus was Texas taken from Mexico in 1845. This expansion, however, was essentially "domestic." The United States did not become involved in foreign adventures until 1898, when the Spanish-American War resulted in the cession of the Philippines. The same arguments used by Europeans to legitimate their rule were now employed by the United States.

The imperialism of the late nineteenth century differed somewhat from the colonialism of the fifteenth to the eighteenth centuries. Earlier, nations had seized land with the intention of settling it with colonists or using it as a base from which to exploit the area economically. The "New Imperialism," as it was called, retained some of these goals, but also introduced new ones. European nations now invested capital in a "backward region" and set about building productive enterprises while also improving the area with hygienic and transportation facilities. In so doing, the colonial powers employed native labor and made cooperative arrangements with local rulers (through either enrichment or intimidation). Their main purpose was to control the region, and if such arrangements proved inadequate, the colonial power had other options, which frequently resulted in full annexation.

The twentieth century also saw its share of imperialism. Determined to secure Germany's "place in the sun," Kaiser Wilhelm II led Germany to war in 1914. Adolf Hitler resurrected a moribund German people, reminded them of their national heritage, gave them self-respect, and promised them more living space through expansion to "natural boundaries." Hitler's territorial demands could not be satisfied and became one of the primary causes of World War II. After Hitler's defeat in 1945, the Soviet Union and the United States moved from their role as allies to rivals in the scramble for territory and influence in the remains of war-ravaged Europe. In a more contemporary setting, the United States fought a war in Vietnam to maintain "principles of democracy" in a country 7500 miles from home. In 1979, the Soviet Union invaded Afghanistan and offered as justification the explanation that it was "asked in" by the Afghan people. In 1982, the Israelis invaded southern Lebanon in an attempt to eliminate dangerous Palestinian bases in the area; they ended up controlling Beirut itself. The United States in 1983 not only rescued American students from the perils of a coup d'état on the Caribbean island of Grenada, but also stayed to ensure the establishment of a democratic regime. More recently, Panama was liberated from its dictator, Manuel Noriega, by U.S. forces in 1989, as was Kuwait from Saddam Hussein in 1991, and Afghanistan from the Taliban in 2001. In the East, the communist Chinese government has controlled Tibet since 1951 and remains committed to its unification with the "renegade province" of Taiwan. The questions abound: What are the responsibilities of great powers? Impelled by their concept of rightness and geopolitical advantage, do "superpowers" constitute forces for civilization or obstructions to the principle of self-determination? Are they vanguards of freedom or proponents of narrowly defined self-interest? It is important to gain the perspective that history offers.

"SEND FORTH THE BEST YE BREED": MOTIVES FOR IMPERIALISM

No other factor in history, not even religion, has produced so many wars as has the clash of national egotisms sanctified by the name of patriotism.

—Preserved Smith

It is not to be doubted that this country [England] has been invested with wealth and power, with arts and knowledge, with the sway of distant lands, and the mastery of the restless waters, for some great and important purpose in the government of the world. Can we suppose otherwise than that it is our office to carry civilization and humanity, peace and good government, and, above all, the knowledge of the true God, to the uttermost ends of the earth?

—Reverend John Whewell

Lust for dominion inflames the heart more than any other passion.

—Tacitus

When any group sees itself as the bearer of civilization, this very belief will betray it into behaving barbarously at the first opportunity.

—Simone Weil

Racism and the Corruption of Science

Our Country (1885)

JOSIAH STRONG

In general, imperialistic nations have felt compelled to justify their actions by explaining why they have taken control of territory or populations. One of the most popular justifications has been the policy of Social Darwinism, a vulgarization of the scientific theory of Charles Darwin contained in The Origin of Species *(1859). Social Darwinists held that only the fittest peoples would survive and that "lesser breeds" would of necessity perish or be taken over. Indeed, some argued that an empire was a living organism that must either grow or die. Racism, therefore, provided a potent thrust to imperial expansion. The first selection, by American clergyman Josiah Strong (1847–1916), is typical of the racist argument. The second excerpt is from a lecture delivered in 1900 by the German scientist Karl Pearson, who presents racism as being consistent with the directives of nature.*

God, with infinite wisdom and skill, is training the Anglo-Saxon race for an hour sure to come in the world's future. Heretofore there has always been in the history of the world a comparatively unoccupied land westward, into which the crowded countries of the East have poured their surplus populations. But the widening waves of migration, which millenniums ago rolled east and west from the valley of the Euphrates meet to-day on our Pacific coast. There are no more new worlds. . . . The time is coming when the pressure of population on the means of subsistence will be felt here as it is now felt in Europe and Asia. Then will the world enter upon a new stage of its history—the final competition of races, for which the Anglo-Saxon is being schooled. Long before the thousand millions are here, the mighty centrifugal tendency, inherent in this stock and strengthened in the United States, will assert itself. Then this race of unequaled energy, with all the majesty of num- bers and the might of wealth behind it—the representative, let us hope, of the largest liberty, the purest Christianity, the highest civilization— having developed peculiarly aggressive traits calculated to impress its institutions upon mankind, will spread itself over the earth. If I read not amiss, this powerful race will move down upon Mexico, down upon Central and South America, out upon the islands of the sea, over upon Africa and beyond. And can any one doubt that the result of this competition of races will be the "survival of the fittest"?. . . Nothing can save the inferior race but a ready and pliant assimilation. Whether the feebler and more abject races are going to be regenerated and raised up, is already very much of a question. What if it should be God's plan to people the world with better and finer material? Certain it is, whatever expectations we may indulge, that there is a tremendous overbearing surge of power in the Christian nations, which, if the oth-

"Our Country" is from Josiah Strong, *Our Country* (New York: The Baker and Taylor Publishing Company, 1885), pp. 174–178.

ers are not speedily raised to some vastly higher capacity, will inevitably submerge and bury them forever. . . . To this result no war of extermination is needful; the contest is not one of arms, but of vitality and of civilization. "At the present day," says Mr. Darwin, "civilized nations are everywhere supplanting barbarous nations. . . ."

Some of the stronger races, doubtless, may be able to preserve their integrity; but, in order to compete with the Anglo-Saxon, they will probably be forced to adopt his methods and instruments, his civilization and his religion. . . . The contact of Christian with heathen nations is awakening the latter to new life. Old superstitions are loosening their grasp. The dead crust of fossil faiths is being shattered by the movements of life underneath. In Catholic countries, Catholicism is losing its influence over educated minds, and in some cases the masses have already lost all faith in it. Thus, while on this continent God is training the Anglo-Saxon race for its mission, a complemental work has been in progress in the great world beyond. God has two hands. Not only is He preparing in our civilization the die with which to stamp the nations, but . . . he is preparing mankind to receive our impress.

Is there room for reasonable doubt that this race, unless devitalized by alcohol and tobacco, is destined to dispossess many weaker races, assimilate others, and mold the remainder, until, in a very true and important sense, it has Anglo-Saxonized mankind?

The Standpoint of Science (1900)

KARL PEARSON

How many centuries, how many thousand of years, have the Kaffir or the Negro held large districts in Africa undisturbed by the white man? Yet their intertribal struggles have not yet produced a civilization in the least comparable with

"The Standpoint of Science" is from Karl Pearson, *National Life from the Standpoint of Science*, 2nd ed. (Cambridge: Cambridge University Press, 1907), pp. 21–25.

the Aryan. Educate and nurture them as you will, I do not believe that you will succeed in modifying the stock. History shows me one way, and one way only, in which a high state of civilization has been produced, namely, the struggle of race with race, and the survival of the physically and mentally fitter race. If you want to know whether the lower races of man can evolve a higher type, I fear the only course is to leave them to fight it out among themselves, and even then the struggle for existence between individual and individual, between tribe and tribe, may not be supported by that physical selection due to a particular climate on which probably so much of the Aryan's success depended.

If you bring the white man into contact with the black, you too often suspend the very process of natural selection on which the evolution of a higher type depends. You get superior and inferior races living on the same soil, and that coexistence is demoralizing for both. They naturally sink into the position of master and servant, if not admittedly or covertly into that of slave-owner and slave. Frequently they intercross, and if the bad stock be raised the good is lowered. Even in the case of Eurasians, of whom I have met mentally and physically fine specimens, I have felt how much better they would have been had they been pure Asiatics or pure Europeans. Thus it comes about that when the struggle for existence between races is suspended, the solution of great problems may be unnaturally postponed; instead of the slow, stern processes of evolution, cataclysmal solutions are prepared for the future. Such problems in suspense, it appears to me, are to be found in the Negro population of the Southern States of America, in the large admixture of Indian blood in some of the South American races, but, above all, in the Kaffir factor in South Africa.

You may possibly think that I am straying from my subject, but I want to justify natural selection to you. I want you to see selection as something which renders the inexorable law of heredity a source of progress which produces the good through suffering, an infinitely greater good which far outbalances the very obvious pain and evil. Let us suppose the alternative were possible. Let us suppose we could prevent the white man, if we liked, from going to lands of which the agricultural and mineral resources are not worked to the full; then I should say a thousand times better for him that he should not go than that he should settle down and live alongside the inferior race. The only healthy alternative is that he should go and completely drive out the inferior race. That is practically what the white man has done in North America. . . . The civilization of the white man is a civilization dependent upon free white labour, and when that element of stability is removed it will collapse like those of Greece and Rome. I venture to assert, then, that the struggle for existence between white and red man, painful and even terrible as it was in its details, has given us a good for outbalancing its immediate evil. In place of the red man, contributing practically nothing to the work and thought of the world, we have a great nation, mistress of many arts, and able, with its youthful imagination and fresh, untrammeled impulses, to contribute much to the common stock of civilized man. Against that we have only to put the romantic sympathy for the Red Indian generated by the novels of Cooper and the poems of Longfellow, and then—see how little it weighs in the balance! . . .

You will see that my view—and I think it may be called the scientific view of a nation—is that of an organized whole, kept up to a high pitch of internal efficiency by insuring that its numbers are substantially recruited from the better stocks, and kept up to a high pitch of external efficiency by contest, chiefly by way of war with inferior races, and with equal races by the struggle for trade-routes and for the sources of raw material and of food supply. This is the natural history view of mankind, and I do not think you can in its main features subvert it. Some of you may refuse to acknowledge it, but you cannot really study history and refuse to see its force. Some of you may realize it, and then despair of life; you may decline to admit any glory in a world where the superior race must either eject the inferior, or, mixing with it, or even living alongside it, degenerate itself. What beauty can there be when the battle is to the stronger, and the weaker must suffer in the struggle of nations and in the struggle of individual men? You may say: Let us cease to struggle; let us leave the lands of the world to the races that cannot profit by them to the full; let us cease to compete in the markets of the world. Well, we could do it, if we were a small nation living off the produce of our own soil, and a soil so worthless that no other race envied it and sought to appropriate it. We should cease to advance; but then we should naturally give up progress as a good which comes through suffering. I say it is impossible for a small rural community to stand apart from the world-contest and to stagnate, if no more powerful nation wants its possessions.

For God and Country

The Mandate System: Britain's Duty in Egypt (1890)

JOSEPH CHAMBERLAIN

The British in the late nineteenth century often justified their imperialism on the premise of duty. As a civilized power, it was imperative that they spread God's word and the fruits of civilization to those peoples who were not sufficiently advanced to develop them on their own. In essence, Britain held a nation "in trust" until the backward peoples could be educated and

"The Mandate System: Britain's Duty in Egypt" is from Joseph Chamberlain, *Foreign and Colonial Speeches* (London: George Routledge and Sons, 1897), pp. 41–44.

made ready to assume the responsibilities of self-government. The "mandate system," as it came to be called, is described in the following excerpt by the liberal statesman Joseph Chamberlain (1836–1914). The motive for British expansion in Egypt was not completely altruistic, however. Britain also wanted to protect the strategic Suez Canal, which controlled access to the riches of Britain's empire in India and the Far East. In 1882, Britain occupied Cairo and set about reorganizing the country. Chamberlain's address to Parliament must also be viewed in this light.

I want to say a word or two to you about the future. I am going to make a confession. I admit I was one of those—I think my views were shared by the whole Cabinet of Mr. Gladstone—who regretted the necessity for the occupation of Egypt. I thought that England had so much to do, such enormous obligations and responsibilities, that we might well escape, if we could, this addition to them; and, when the occupation was forced upon us, I looked forward with anxiety to an early, it might be even, to an immediate evacuation. The confession I have to make is that having seen what are the results of this occupation, having seen what is the nature of the task we have undertaken, and what progress we have already made towards its accomplishment, I have changed my mind. (Cheers.) I say it would be unworthy of this great nation if we did not rise to the full height of our duty, and complete our work before we left the country. (Cheers.) We have no right to abandon the duty which has been cast upon us, and the work which already shows so much promise for the advantage of the people with whose destinies we have become involved.

This great alteration is due to the influence of a mere handful of your fellow-countrymen. . . . They, by their persevering devotion, and their single-minded honesty, have wrought out this great work, and have brought Egypt from a condition which may fairly be described as one of ruin, to the promise of once more being restored to its ancient prosperity. I hear sometimes of pessimists who think the work of England is accomplished, who will tell you that we have lost the force and the capacity to govern. No; that is not true; and as long as we can spare from our abundance men like these, who,

after all, are only ordinary Englishmen—men like these, who are able and willing to carry their zeal and their intelligence wherever it may conduce to the service of humanity, and to the honour of their native land—so long as we can do that we need not despair of the future of the United Kingdom. (Cheers.) But we owe it to them, we owe it to ourselves, that their work shall not be in vain. You cannot revolutionise a country like Egypt—you cannot reform all that is wrong in her system, all that is poor and weak in the character of the people—in a few minutes, or a few years. Egypt has been submitted for centuries to arbitrary despotism. I believe there is hardly any time in her history, even if you go back to almost prehistoric ages, when she has not been in the grasp of some foreign ruler; and, under these circumstances, you cannot expect to find ready to your hands a self-governing people. They are not able—they cannot be able—to stand alone; and they do not wish to stand alone. They ask for your support and assistance, and without it, it is absolutely impossible that their welfare can be secured. If you were to abandon your responsibility, your retirement would be followed by an attempt once more to restore the old arbitrary methods and the old abuses, which in turn would no doubt be followed by anarchy and disorder; and then in time there would be again a foreign intervention, this time the intervention of some other European country. I have too much confidence in the public spirit of the country to believe that it will ever neglect a national duty. (Hear, hear.) A nation is like an individual; it has duties which it must fulfill, or else it cannot live honoured and respected as a nation. (Loud cheers.)

"The Hand of God":
American Imperialism in the Philippines (1900)
ALBERT J. BEVERIDGE

Through much of the nineteenth century, the United States was involved with establishing its own borders "from sea to shining sea," but did not try to expand internationally. In 1898, however, because of the Spanish-American War, the United States inaugurated a policy of foreign imperialism. One of the Spanish colonies ceded to the United States was the Philippine Islands. There was a strong independence movement in the islands, however, and actual warfare broke out in 1899 between Filipinos and American forces. Congress was divided about setting up a government for the newly acquired territory. One of the champions of imperialism was Albert J. Beveridge, senator from Indiana. In January 1900, he addressed Congress in support of a resolution that decreed that the United States "establish and maintain such government control throughout the archipelago as the situation may demand."

Mr. President, the times call for candor. The Philippines are ours forever, "territory belonging to the United States," as the Constitution calls them. And just beyond the Philippines are China's illimitable markets. We will not retreat from either. We will not repudiate our duty in the archipelago. We will not abandon our opportunity in the Orient. We will not renounce our part in the mission of our race, trustee under God, of the civilization of the world. And we will move forward to our work, not howling our regrets like slaves whipped to their burdens, but with gratitude for a task worthy of our strength, and thanksgiving to Almighty God that He has marked us as His chosen people, henceforth to lead in the regeneration of the world. . . .

Senators, it would be better to abandon this combined garden and Gibraltar of the Pacific, and count our blood and treasure already spent a profitable loss, than to apply any academic arrangement of self-government to these children. They are not capable of self-government. How could they be? They are not of a self-governing race. They are Orientals, Malays, instructed by Spaniards in the latter's worst estate.

They know nothing of practical government except as they have witnessed the weak, corrupt, cruel, and capricious rule of Spain. What magic will anyone employ to dissolve in their minds and characters those impressions of governors and governed which three centuries of misrule have created? What alchemy will change the Oriental quality of their blood and set the self-governing currents of the American pouring through their Malay veins? How shall they, in the twinkling of an eye, be exalted to the heights of self-governing peoples which required a thousand years for us to reach, Anglo-Saxon though we are? . . .

Mr. President, self-government and internal development have been the dominant notes of our first century; administration and the development of other lands will be the dominant notes of our second century. And administration is as high and holy a function as self-government, just as the care of a trust estate is as sacred an obligation as the management of our own concerns. . . .

The Declaration of Independence does not forbid us to do our part in the regeneration of the world. If it did, the Declaration would be wrong, just as the Articles of Confederation, drafted by the very same men who signed the Declaration, were found to be wrong. The Declaration has no application to the present situation. It was written by self-governing men for self-governing men. . . .

Mr. President, this question is deeper than any question of party politics; deeper than any question of the isolated policy of our country even; deeper even than any question of constitutional power. It is elemental. It is racial. God has not been preparing the English-speaking and

"'The Hand of God'" is from *Congressional Record*, Vol. 33 (1900), pp. 704–705, 708, 710–712.

Teutonic peoples for a thousand years for nothing but vain and idle self-contemplation and self-admiration. No! He has made us the master organizers of the world to establish system where chaos reigns. He has given the spirit of progress to overwhelm the forces of reaction throughout the earth. He has made us adept in government that we may administer government among savage and senile peoples. Were it not for such a force as this the world would relapse into barbarism and night. And of all our race He has marked the American people as His chosen nation to finally lead in the regeneration of the world. This is the divine mission of America, and it holds for us all the profit, all the glory, all the happiness possible to man. We are trustees of the world's progress, guardians of its righteous peace. The judgment of the Master is upon us: "Ye have been faithful over a few things; I will make you ruler over many things."

What shall history say of us? Shall it say that we renounced that holy trust, left the savage to his base condition, the wilderness to the reign of waste, deserted duty, abandoned glory, forgot our sordid profit even, because we feared our strength and read the charter of our powers with the doubter's eye and the quibbler's mind? Shall it say that, called by events to captain and command the proudest, ablest, purest race of

history in history's noblest work, we declined that great commission? Our fathers would not have had it so. No! They founded no paralytic government, incapable of the simplest acts of administration. They planted no sluggard people, passive while the world's work calls them. They established no reactionary nation. They unfurled no retreating flag. . . .

Blind indeed is he who sees not the hand of God in events so vast, so harmonious, so benign. Reactionary indeed is the mind that perceives not that this vital people is the strongest of the saving forces of the world; that our place, therefore, is at the head of the constructing and redeeming nations of the earth; and that to stand aside while events march on is a surrender of our interests, a betrayal of our duty as blind as it is base. Craven indeed is the heart that fears to perform a work so golden and so noble; that dares not win a glory so immortal. . . .

Mr. President and Senators, adopt the resolution offered, that peace may quickly come and that we may begin our saving, regenerating, and uplifting work. . . . Reject it, and the world, history, and the American people will know where to forever fix the awful responsibility for the consequences that will surely follow such failure to do our manifest duty. How dare we delay when our soldiers' blood is flowing?

Theme: Imperialism

The Historical Intersection

FRANCE: 1095

The Spirit of the Crusades: "It Is the Will of God!"

ROBERT THE MONK

The first expedition to free the Holy Land from the control of the Infidel Muslim was launched in 1095 at the Council of Clermont. Pope Urban II presided and in a rousing speech excited the crowd with this impassioned plea for action. Although we are not sure about the accuracy of the text (we have five contemporary versions), the following account by Robert the Monk is credible and clearly illustrates Urban's justification for the First Crusade as well as his popular appeal.

Compare and Contrast:

- Compare this justification for the initiation of the First Crusade to the Holy Land in 1095 with that of Senator Albert Beveridge for U.S. imperialism in the Philippines in 1900. How is God used in both excerpts to sanction violence and invasion?

In 1095 a great council was held in Auvergne, in the city of Clermont. Pope Urban II, accompanied by cardinals and bishops, presided over it. . . . After the council had attended to ecclesiastical matters, the pope went out into a public square, because no house was able to hold the people, and addressed them in a very persuasive speech, as follows: "O race of the Franks, O people who live beyond the mountains [the Alps], O people loved and chosen of God, as is clear from your many deeds, distinguished over all other nations by the situation of your land, your catholic faith, and your regard for the holy church, we have a

(contd)

special message and exhortation for you. For we wish you to know what a grave matter has brought us to your country. The sad news has come from Jerusalem and Constantinople that the people of Persia, an accursed and foreign race, enemies of God, a generation that set not their heart aright, and whose spirit was not steadfast with God [Ps. 78:8], have invaded the lands of those Christians and devastated them with the sword, rapine, and fire. Some of the Christians they have carried away as slaves, others they have put to death. The churches they have either destroyed or turned into mosques. They desecrate and overthrow the altars. They circumcise the Christians and pour the blood from the circumcision on the altars or in the baptismal fonts. Some they kill in a horrible way by cutting open the abdomen, taking out a part of the entrails and tying them to a stake; they then beat them and compel them to walk until all their entrails are drawn out and they fall to the ground. Some they use as targets for their arrows. They compel some to stretch out their necks and then they try to see whether they can cut off their heads with one stroke of the sword. It is better to say nothing of their horrible treatment of the women. They have taken from the Greek empire a tract of land so large that it takes more than two months to walk through it. Whose duty is it to avenge this and recover that land, if not yours? For to you more than to other nations the Lord has given the military spirit, courage, agile bodies, and the bravery to strike down those who resist you. Let your minds be stirred to bravery by the deeds of your forefathers, and by the efficiency and greatness of [Charlemagne], and of Ludwig his son, and of the other kings who have destroyed Turkish kingdoms, and established Christianity in their lands. You should be moved especially by the holy grave of our Lord and Saviour which is now held by unclean peoples, and by the holy places which are treated with dishonor and irreverently befouled with their uncleanness. . . .

The Holy Land our Savior made illustrious by his birth, beautiful with his life, and sacred with his suffering; he redeemed it with his death and glorified it with his tomb. This royal city [Jerusalem] is now held captive by her enemies, and made pagan by those who know not God. She asks and longs to be liberated and does not cease to beg you to come to her aid. She asks aid especially from you because, as I have said, God has given more of the military spirit to you than to other nations. Set out on this journey and you will obtain the remission of your sins and be sure of the incorrigible glory of the kingdom of heaven.". . .

When Pope Urban had said this and much more of the same sort, all who were present were moved to cry out with one accord, "It is the will of God, it is the will of God!" When the pope heard this he raised his eyes to heaven and gave thanks to God, and, commanding silence with a gesture of his hand, he said: "Let these words be your battle cry, because God caused you to speak them. Whenever you meet the enemy in battle, you shall all cry out, 'It is the will of God! It is the will of God!'"

(contd)

Consider This:

- Note the appeal in both this and Beveridge's speeches to past heritage, to the "deeds of your forefathers." Why is this technique often effective in focusing national will for a cause?

"The Spirit of the Crusades" is from Oliver Thatcher and Edgar McNeal, eds., *A Source Book of Medieval History* (New York: Charles Scribner's Sons, 1905), pp. 518–520.

The White Man's Burden (1899)

RUDYARD KIPLING

In commemoration of successful U.S. imperialism in the Philippines, the great British poet Rudyard Kipling wrote "The White Man's Burden" in 1899. It reflects a devotion to the demands of empire and the duty of civilized nations. In Kipling's eyes, imperialism was a nationalistic venture—a heroic necessity.

Take up the White Man's burden—
Send forth the best ye breed—
Go bind your sons to exile
To serve your captive's need;
To wait in heavy harness,
On fluttered folk and wild—
Your new-caught, sullen peoples,
Half-devil and half-child.

Take up the White Man's burden—
In patience to abide,
To veil the threat of terror
And check the show of pride;
By open speech and simple,
An hundred times made plain
To seek another's profit,
And work another's gain.

Take up the White Man's burden—
The savage wars of peace—
Fill full the mouth of Famine
And bid the sickness cease;
And when your goal is nearest

The end for others sought,
Watch sloth and heathen Folly
Bring all your hopes to nought.

Take up the White Man's burden—
No tawdry rule of kings,
But toil of serf and sweeper—

A British Officer in India, ca. 1870: "Take up the White Man's burden / And reap his old reward: / The blame of those ye better, / The hate of those ye guard."—Rudyard Kipling

"The White Man's Burden" is from Rudyard Kipling, *Collected Verse* (New York: Doubleday and Page, 1911), pp. 215–217.

The tale of common things.
The ports ye shall not enter,
The roads ye shall not tread,
Go make them with your living,
And mark them with your dead.

Take up the White Man's burden—
And reap his old reward:
The blame of those ye better,
The hate of those ye guard—
The cry of hosts ye humour
(Ah, slowly!) toward the light:—
'Why brought he us from bondage,
Our loved Egyptian night?'

Take up the White Man's burden—

Ye dare not stoop to less—
Nor call too loud on Freedom
To cloke your weariness;
By all ye cry or whisper,
By all ye leave or do,
The silent, sullen peoples
Shall weigh your gods and you.

Take up the White Man's burden—
Have done with childish days—
The lightly proferred laurel,
The easy, ungrudged praise.
Comes now, to search your manhood
Through all the thankless years,
Cold, edged with dear-bought wisdom,
The judgment of your peers!

Power and Pride

The next selections comment on another motive for imperialism. The desire for power can be justified through the pride that one has in one's nation. Nationalism and imperialism seem to be intimately connected. And the European accumulation of empire in India and Africa during the nineteenth century certainly inspired the competitive juices. If Britannia "ruled the waves" and Germany deserved its "place in the sun," then the process of global confrontation was necessary and was an opportunity to demonstrate national superiority. So thought the French prime minister, Jules Ferry, in his 1883 speech to the assembly in Paris, and so too the German Kaiser Wilhelm II, who was certainly anxious to seize the opportunity for glory as noted in the militaristic speech that follows.

"France Must Be a Great Country!" (1883)

JULES FERRY

Jules Ferry: Gentlemen, it embarrasses me to make such a prolonged demand upon the gracious attention of the Chamber, but I believe that the duty I am fulfilling upon this platform is not a useless one: it is as strenuous for me as

for you, but I believe that there is some benefit in summarizing and condensing, in the form of arguments, the principles, the motives, and the various interests by which a policy of colonial expansion may be justified. . . .

In the area of economics, I will allow myself to place before you, with the support of some figures, the considerations which justify a policy of colonial expansion from the point of view of that need, felt more and more strongly by the industrial populations of Europe and particularly those of our won rich and hard working country: the need for export markets. . . .

Gentlemen, there is a second point, a second order of ideas to which I have to give equal at-

"'France Must Be a Great Country'" is from Ralph Austen, ed., *Modern Imperialism* (Lexington, MA: D.C. Heath, 1969), pp. 70–73. Reprinted by permission of the publisher.

tention, but as quickly as possible, believe me; it is the humanitarian and civilizing side of the question. On this point the honorable Camille Pelletan [a conservative politician] has jeered in his own refined and clever manner; he jeers, he condemns, and he says "What is this civilization which you impose with cannon-ball? What is it but another form of barbarism? Don't these populations, these inferior races, have the same rights as you? Aren't they masters of their own houses? Have they called upon you? You come to them against their will, you offer them violence, but not civilization." There, gentlemen is the thesis. . . . But, I must speak from a higher and more truthful plane. It must be stated openly that, in effect, superior races have rights over inferior races.

Jules Maigne: Oh! You dare to say this in the country which has proclaimed the rights of man!

M. De Gulloutet: This is a justification of slavery and the slave trade!

Jules Ferry: If M. Maigne is right, if the declaration of the rights of man was written for the black of equatorial Africa, then by what right do you impose regular commerce upon them? They have not called upon you.

Raoul Duval: We do not want to impose anything upon them. It is you who wish to do so!

Jules Maigne: To propose and to impose are two different things!

Georges Perin: In any case, you cannot bring about commerce by force.

Jules Ferry: I repeat that superior races have a right, because they have a duty. They have the duty to civilize inferior races. . . . Gentlemen, in Europe as it is today, in this competition of so many rivals which we see growing around us, some by perfecting their military or maritime forces, others by the prodigious development of an ever growing population; in a Europe, or rather in a universe of this sort, a policy of peaceful seclusion or abstention is simply the highway to decadence! Nations are great in our times only by means of the activities which they develop; it is not simply "by the peaceful shining froth of institutions" that they are great at this hour. . . .

[The Republican Party] has shown that it is quite aware that one cannot impose upon France a political ideal conforming to that of nations like independent Belgium and the Swiss Republic; that something else is needed for France; that she cannot be merely a free country, that she must also be a great country, exercising all of her rightful influence over the destiny of Europe, that she ought to propagate this influence throughout the world and carry everywhere that she can her language, her customs, her flag, her arms, and her genius.

Germany's Place in the Sun (1901)
KAISER WILHELM II

In spite of the fact that we have no such fleet as we should have, we have conquered for ourselves a place in the sun. It will now be my task to see to it that this place in the sun shall remain our undisputed possession, in order that the sun's rays may fall fruitfully upon our activity and trade in foreign parts, that our industry and agriculture may develop within the state and our sailing sports upon the water, for our future lies upon the water. The more Germans go out upon the waters . . . whether it be in journeys across the ocean, or in the service of the battleflag, so much the better will it be for us. For when the German has once learned to direct his glance upon what is distant and great, the pettiness which surrounds him in daily life on all sides will disappear. . . .

As head of the empire I therefore rejoice over every citizen, whether from Hamburg, Bremen, or Lubeck, who goes forth with this large outlook and seeks new points where we can drive in the nail on which to hang our armor.

"Germany's Place in the Sun" is from Christian Gauss, excerpted from *The German Emperor*, pp. 181–183. Copyright © 1915 Charles Scribner's Sons. Reprinted with the permission of Charles Scribner's Sons.

Foreign Children

ROBERT LOUIS STEVENSON

The Scottish writer, Robert Louis Stevenson (1850–1894), is remembered primarily for his adventure novels, Treasure Island *and* Kidnapped. *But he was also a poet and compiled a book of children's poetry toward the end of his life. The following selection reveals the vision of superiority that justified the argument for European control of "lesser peoples." The civilizing mandate was deeply inculcated in the education of the ruling classes.*

Little Indian, Sioux or Crow,
Little frosty Eskimo,
Little Turk or Japanee,
O! don't you wish that you were me?

You have seen the scarlet trees
And the lions over seas;
You have eaten ostrich eggs,
And turned the turtles off their legs.

Such a life is very fine,
But it's not so nice as mine:

You must often, as you trod,
Have wearied *not* to be abroad.

You have curious things to eat,
I am fed on proper meat;
You must dwell beyond the foam,
But I am safe and live at home.

Little Indian, Sioux or Crow,
Little frosty Eskimo,
Little Turk or Japanee,
O! don't you wish that you were me?

"TO SEEK ANOTHER'S PROFIT AND WORK ANOTHER'S GAIN"

It is the habit of every aggressor nation to claim that it is acting on the defensive.

—Jawaharlal Nehru

The Englishman does everything on principle. He fights you on patriotic principles; he robs you on business principles; he enslaves you on imperial principles. . . . His watchword is always Duty; and he never forgets that the nation which lets its duty get on the side opposite to its interest is lost.

—Napoleon Bonaparte

The right of conquest has no foundation other than the right of the strongest.

—Jean-Jacques Rousseau

"Foreign Children" is from Robert Louis Stevenson, *Complete Poems: A Child's Garden of Verse* (New York: Scribner, 1912), p. 25.

The British Raj in India

The eyes of both Eastern and Western powers had long been attracted to the trade and wealth of India. The Mughal dynasty of Muslim rulers that had controlled India in the seventeenth century under the leadership of such visionaries as Akbar the Great (1556–1605) and Shah Jahan (1628–1658) was by the eighteenth century in danger of dissolution. The last great Mughal leader, Aurangzeb (1660–1707), predicted that his empire would break apart as local governors argued among themselves and sought their own arrangements with the competing interests of British, French, and Dutch trade. Eventually, the British took the lead in promoting agents of the East India Company, who advised and made treaty arrangements with local governors that excluded French and Dutch interests and gave Britain an unofficial dominion over the area. The British instituted a new office of Governor General in 1774 to oversee trade relations, resolve conflicts among natives, and better control the region through local Indian princes. Parliament reviewed the actions of the Governor General and eventually regularized a policy of deposing these local Indian rulers and annexing the land as part of a growing world empire.

In April 1857, a widespread but unsuccessful rebellion against British rule in India broke out among Indian troops (called sepoys*) fighting in the service of the East India Company. This revolt began in the Bengal army with the introduction of the new Enfield rifle; to load it the* sepoys *had to bite off the ends of cartridges lubricated in a mixture of pigs' and cows' lard. This oral contact with religiously forbidden substances was an insult to both Muslim and Hindu troops. When the* sepoys *refused the cartridges, they were shackled and put in jail. On May 10, their comrades shot several British officers and marched on Delhi. The rebellion spread quickly throughout northern India with massacres that provoked equally vicious British reprisals. After many desperate struggles, the British were able to suppress the revolt by July, 1858.*

To regard this mutiny as a bloody incident with a simple origin is to belie the social and economic complexities of the British presence in India. By 1820, it was evident that traditional Hindu society was being affected by the introduction of Western ideas and religious beliefs. The British Governor General, Lord Dalhousie, had introduced legislation to emancipate women and remove legal obstacles to the remarriage of Hindu widows. Christian converts were given property rights in the distribution of family estates, and it was even rumored that the British intended to end the Indian caste structure. The introduction of Western methods and educational curricula was a direct challenge to Hindu and Muslim orthodoxy. These actions threatened the traditional ruling Indian aristocracy by depriving it of its social position and administrative revenues.

The immediate result of the Indian mutiny of 1857 was a general restructuring of British administration. Great Britain abolished the East India Company in favor of direct rule by the government and rearranged the finances of India. The Indian army was also reorganized and the British instituted a policy of consultation with Indian representatives that ended insensitive, British-mandated social measures. But the failure of the mutiny confirmed British supremacy in India and opened the door to a gradual, but inevitable breakdown of traditional Indian society. In return for political and economic control, the British brought educational and public works programs, roads, railways, telegraphs, and hygienic facilities. The annexation of India in 1858 and the establishment of the British Raj, or official administration, represented a tradeoff in technological and cultural influence. When British control ended with Indian independence in 1949, the culture and political traditions of the region had been dramatically altered.

The following sources highlight the transformation of India from the early to midnineteenth century. The first selection is from the pen of Thomas Babington Macaulay, a lit-

erary figure and political liberal who argued that British rule in India was one of the highest achievements of English civilization. His vision of a proper education demonstrates the cultural insensitivity that contributed to the Indian mutiny of 1857. The second source offers the perspective of an English officer who witnessed the Indian mutiny. He describes the conditions the British faced from 1757 to 1857 in extending their control over India and in establishing the Pax Britannica *or "British peace" so vital in his mind to the progress of civilization. The last selection is the annexation decree over India by Queen Victoria that formally established the Raj and provided the "Jewel in the Crown" of Great Britain.*

Education in India: "The Intrinsic Superiority of Western Literature" (1835)

THOMAS BABINGTON MACAULAY

We now come to the gist of the matter. We have a fund to be employed as Government shall direct for the intellectual improvement of the people of this country. The simple question is, what is the most useful way of employing it?

All parties seem to be agreed on one point, that the dialects commonly spoken among the natives of this part of India contain neither literary nor scientific information, and are moreover so poor and rude that, until they are enriched from some other quarter, it will not be easy to translate any valuable work into them. It seems to be admitted on all sides, that the intellectual improvement of those classes of the people who have the means of pursuing higher studies can at present be effected only by means of some language not vernacular amongst them.

What then shall that language be? One-half of the committee maintain that it should be the English. The other half strongly recommend the Arabic and Sanscrit. The whole question seems to me to be—which language is the best worth knowing?

I have no knowledge of either Sanscrit or Arabic. But I have done what I could to form a correct estimate of their value. I have read translations of the most celebrated Arabic and Sanscrit works. I have conversed, both here and at home, with men distinguished by their proficiency in the Eastern tongues. I am quite ready to take the oriental leaning at the valuation of the orientalists themselves. I have never found one among them who could deny that a single shelf of a good European library was worth the whole native literature of India and Arabia. The intrinsic superiority of the Western literature is indeed fully admitted by those members of the committee who support the oriental plan of education.

It will hardly be disputed, I suppose, that the department of literature in which the Eastern writers stand highest is poetry. And I certainly never met with any orientalist who ventured to maintain that the Arabic and Sanscrit poetry could be compared to that of the great European nations. But when we pass from works of imagination to works in which facts are recorded and general principles investigated, the superiority of the Europeans becomes absolutely immeasurable. It is, I believe, no exaggeration to say that all the historical information which has been collected from all the books written in the Sanscrit language is less valuable than what may be found in the most paltry abridgments used at preparatory schools in England. In every branch of physical or moral philosophy, the relative position of the two nations is nearly the same. . . .

Nor is this all. In India, English is the language spoken by the ruling class. It is spoken by the higher class of natives at the seats of Government. It is likely to become the language of commerce throughout the seas of the East. It is the language of two great European communities which are rising, the one in the south of

"Education in India" is from H. Sharp, ed., *Selections from the Educational Records of the Government of India, Part I, 1781-1839* (Calcutta, 1920), pp. 110–112; 116.

Africa, the other in Australia—communities which are every year becoming more important and more closely connected with our Indian empire. Whether we look at the intrinsic value of our literature, or at the particular situation of this country, we shall see the strongest reason to think that, of all foreign tongues, the English tongue is that which would be the most useful to our native subjects. . . .

To sum up what I have said. I think it clear . . . that we are free to employ our funds as we choose, that we ought to employ them in teaching what is best worth knowing, that English is better worth knowing than Sanscrit or Arabic, that . . . it is possible to make natives of this country thoroughly good English scholars, and that to this end our efforts ought to be directed.

In one point I fully agree with the gentlemen to whose general views I am opposed. I feel with them that it is impossible for us, with our limited means, to attempt to educate the body of the people. We must at present do our best to form a class who may be interpreters between us and the millions whom we govern—a class of persons Indian in blood and color, but English in tastes, in opinions, in morals, and in intellect.

Enemies of the *Pax Britannica*

LT. GENERAL INNES

The great convulsion known as the Indian Mutiny broke out in May, 1857, consequent directly on the excitement and ill feeling engendered in the Bengal army by the well-known cartridge incident. . . . Up to the year 1856, the year before the outbreak, there had been for a whole century a continuous, aggressive advance of the British power, till it completed the ring fence of the empire by the annexation of Oude [an Indian kingdom]. During all that time it had either been engaged in actual conflict or had

"Enemies of the *Pax Britannica*" is from *Parliamentary Accounts and Papers*, Vol. 45 (East India, January 31– July 29, 1856), pp. 597–600.

been forming dominant relations with the several races of the country, and had reduced them one after another to subjection; some provinces being brought under its direct administration and others being left as feudatory or vassal states under their native rulers. At the start the old Mughal dominion had been in a war, and some of the native principalities had gladly turned for safety to the shelter of English protection and supremacy. But the great mass of the people had been brought under our rule by conquest or forcible annexation.

With ruling dynasties thus set aside, reduced, or crushed, with great races humiliated, and bitterness and misery spread broadcast by the loss of power and place and property, it would be an outrage on common sense to doubt that we had created a host of enemies. . . . The benefits of civilized rule, of the *Pax Britannica*, were felt only skin-deep, and the old fierce instincts, the outcome of centuries of strife and oppression, were still in the ascendant. The memory of injuries was still keen and vivid, the newer cases helping to recall the old ones, and to reopen sores that might otherwise have been getting healed; so that, briefly, the mood and temper which prevailed were those of a conquered people who had wrongs and humiliations to remember, and were chafing at having to endure the sway of aliens in race and creed. There existed, in fact, a mass of constant disaffection, and whole hosts of malcontents.

Of these the most powerful and dangerous were the Muslims. The entire Muhammadan population were as a body rebels at heart, and resented the Christian supremacy, if only on religious grounds and from fanatical pride; and the Mughals of the Upper Provinces had in addition a natural longing to revive their old predominance and restore their old empire.

Next may be mentioned the Mahrattas, a warlike and unscrupulous Hindu race, who, though now split up into rival States, had been most powerful as a confederacy, and felt that but for the British they would have been the masters of India.

Another extensive body of malcontents consisted of those who were actual sufferers from

British conquests or annexation, or from the action of British land policy.

And a fourth group, especially dangerous from their spirit and energy, was formed by those who fretted at the closing of those outlets for ambition, and the loss of those opportunities for aggrandizement, through political intrigue or military prowess, that had been current of old.

Such a mass of disaffection, however latent or suppressed, was obviously a standing menace to the tranquility of the country, constituting a solid basis, and providing a powerful agency for the rousing of evil passions and the promotion of seditious enterprise—a sure factor in any movement or question involving the peace or security of the state.

"The Jewel in the Crown" (1858)

QUEEN VICTORIA

Victoria, by the grace of God, of the United Kingdom of Great Britain and Ireland, and of the colonies and dependencies thereof in Europe, Asia, Africa, America, and Australia, Queen Defender of the Faith.

Whereas, for diverse weighty reasons, we have resolved, by and with the advice and consent of the Lords Spiritual and Temporal, and Commons, in Parliament assembled, to take upon ourselves the government of the territories in India heretofore administered in trust for us by the Honorable East India Company.

Now, therefore, we do by these presents notify and declare that, by the advice and consent aforesaid, we have taken upon ourselves the said government; and we hereby call upon all our subjects within the said territories to be faithful, and to bear true allegiance to us, our heirs and successors, and to submit themselves to the authority of those whom we may hereafter, from time to time, see fit to appoint to administer the government of our said territories, in our name and on our behalf. . . .

We desire no extension of our present territorial possessions; and while we will permit no aggression upon our dominions or our rights to be attempted with impunity, we shall sanction no encroachment on those of others. We shall respect the rights, dignity, and honor of native princes as our own; and we desire that they, as well as our own subjects, should enjoy that prosperity and that social advancement which can only be secured by internal peace and good government.

Firmly relying ourselves on the truth of Christianity, and acknowledging with gratitude the solace of religion, we disclaim alike the right and the desire to impose our convictions on any of our subjects. We declare it to be our royal will and pleasure that none be in any way favored, none molested or disquieted by reason of their religious faith or observances, but that all shall alike enjoy the equal and impartial protection of the law; and we do strictly charge and enjoin all those who may be in authority under us that they abstain from all interference with the religious belief of worship of any of our subjects, on pain of our highest displeasure.

And it is our further will that, so far as may be, our subjects, of whatever race or creed, be freely and impartially admitted to offices in our service, the duties of which they may be qualified, by their education, ability, and integrity duly to discharge.

We deeply lament the evils and misery which have been brought upon India by the acts of ambitious men, who have deceived their countrymen by false reports and led them into open rebellion. Our power has been shown by the suppression of that rebellion in the field; we desire to show our mercy by pardoning the offenses of those who have been thus misled, but who desire to return to the path of duty. Our clemency will be extended to all offenders, save and except those who have been or shall be convicted of having directly taken part in the murder of British subjects. With regard to such the demands of justice forbid the exercise of mercy.

To all others in arms against the government, we hereby promise unconditional pardon, amnesty, and oblivion of all offenses against ourselves, our crown and dignity, on their return to their homes and peaceful pursuits.

When, by the blessing of Providence, internal tranquility shall be restored, it is our earnest de-

"'The Jewel in the Crown'" is from *Annual Register* (1858), pp. 258–260.

sire to stimulate the peaceful industry of India, to promote works of public utility and improvement, and to administer its government for the benefit of all our subjects resident therein. In their prosperity will be our strength, in their contentment our security, and in their gratitude our best reward. And may the God of all power grant to us, and to those in authority under us, strength to carry out these our wishes for the good of our people.

The Scramble for Africa

After the political unification of Germany and Italy by 1871, a stabilized Europe embarked upon the "Great Hunt," the "scramble for empire" in Africa that provided the economic resources for industry and the image of authority so important in the vigorous competition for national prestige. Colonial enthusiasm had waned during the 1840s and 1850s when many politicians had denounced colonies as unprofitable and burdensome. But Europe's population was growing rapidly at a rate second only to the United States, while the populations of Asia and Africa were essentially static. New colonies acted as a safety valve for a domestic population often burdened and unemployed by the great push toward industrialization. The latter movement actually created the need for new markets and resources to keep the factories producing at full capacity. Added to this were the exhortations of explorers and missionaries, who fed the imperial impulse with romantic visions of adventure and the will of God.

The following selection is from a general history of the period written by Charles Seignobos, a prominent French scholar at the time. Note his disdain for the importance of African history. The quest for power and its symbols among great nations were all that mattered. European imperialism became a state of mind that subverted the relevance of indigenous peoples and denied them a past.

"The Great African Hunt"

CHARLES SEIGNOBOS

By about 1880, the political geography of Europe was fixed; the attempt of any country to acquire territory at the expense of a neighbor would have precipitated an instantaneous armed conflict. Moreover, Europe had recovered from the fatigues which had accompanied the wars for the unification of the great nations, and regained its spirit of action; but its desire for expansion could now be satisfied only outside of Europe. All the continents, however, were occupied, except Africa, until then despised. The powers threw themselves upon that continent, so long scorned, and fairly dashed into the work of partition. The rivalry and the haste of the competitors was so great that one might well speak of "the great African hunt." Within twenty years almost everything was appropriated in Africa, and when the rivals wished to extend their borders further, they could only do so at the expense of the weaker among themselves.

The annals of Africa for twenty years (1880–1900) are practically limited to the story of the partition of the continent to its very heart. Its improvement and civilization have hardly begun; it has not yet passed out of the most rudimentary industrial state; and its development, of which there can be no question, will serve as a subject for the investigation of future historians. In itself the history of native Africa offers, with some few exceptions, no events of general interest. One may say, however, that the numberless African races have been happy because they have had no history. Some of them have had a little, but it is so confused that it cannot be told. Torrents of blood, which still flow in Africa, have been caused by the exploits of slave hunters, and by internecine pillage result-

"'The Great African Hunt'" is from James Harvey Robinson and Charles A. Beard, *Readings in Modern European History*, Vol. II (Boston: Gin & Company, 1909), p. 448.

ing from the general anarchy prevailing on a large scale; but the details of these horrors are so microscopic that they must be passed by with this general mention. The real object of our study should be the partition of Africa among the civilized nations.

The Lure of Diamonds and the Colossus of Rhodes: "To Take As Much of the World As Possible"

"THE IMPERIALIST"

In 1841, the British doctor David Livingstone (1813–1873) left for southern Africa to begin a fascinating career as a missionary and explorer. His journals enthralled the world with images of exotic animals, magnificent waterfalls, tangled jungles, and strange native customs. A great humanitarian, Dr. Livingstone decried the internecine strife between rival African tribes and described the horrors of the Arab slave trade in the region. His accounts inspired a generation of adventurers such as the journalist, Henry Stanley, who explored the Congo river in the 1880s and began to penetrate the "darkness" of central Africa. These explorations attracted investors and other businessmen who sought to tap the potential wealth of Africa.

This potential had already been demonstrated when in the mid-1860s diamonds were discovered on the De Beer family farm in Kimberley, South Africa. Like the American Gold Rush of 1849, South Africa soon became a battleground between Dutch settlers called Boers, who decades earlier had established themselves as farmers in the region, and British imperial interests. Looming over the events of this period was the image of Cecil Rhodes (1853–1902), a British entrepreneur who controlled 90 percent of the world's output of diamonds by the time he was 38 years old through his ownership and management of De Beers Consolidated Mines, Ltd. He also acquired a large stake in the Transvaal gold mines and formed the Gold Fields of South Africa Company in 1887.

An ardent British nationalist, Rhodes had great dreams of controlling all of Africa for Britain by building a railway from the Cape to Cairo, reconciling the Boers under the British flag, and even recovering the American colonies for Britain. Rhodes never regarded money-making as an end in itself, but certainly used its influence in his political maneuvers as prime minister of Cape Colony in the 1890s.

The following selection by Cecil Rhodes's anonymous biographer (who called himself "The Imperialist") demonstrates the attractions of Africa to Europeans seeking wealth and competitive advantage.

Cecil Rhodes was the appointed instrument to preserve for and present to England the most permanently valuable, the most habitable portion of the last great continent that waited to be annexed; and his love of the excitement of money-making and his remarkable genius for finance were to supply the first of the two necessary instruments by which the realization of the dream of empire to the north might be made practicable—the instrument of money and the command of moneyed men. . . .

Little did his fellow-miners think as they passed the dreamy youth with impassive face gazing into vacancy, that the building of an empire, the occupation of the last unoccupied continent, was gradually assuming form under the shaping power of that youthful diamond digger's imagination. The paramount ideas in his

"The Lure of Diamonds" is from "The Imperialist" (Pseudonym), *Cecil Rhodes* (London: Chapman & Hall, Ltd., 1897), pp. 326–328.

mind—the expansion of our empire and its supremacy in South Africa—was of course developed, and gained shape and consistency under the influence of the study of history and the experience of life. An enlightened patriotism has gradually become the one paramount sentiment of the great South African's life; and putting one's self in his place and looking with his eyes upon the world, one can understand his far-reaching saying that territory is everything—that is to say, territory fit to support and breed a fine race of men. He sees with his mind's eye the vicious weaklings of our overcrowded English cities, and compares with them the magnificent race of Englishmen that might be reared on the fertile soil and in the fine air of the upland of Rhodesia, and, as he reflects, the great need for England seems to be territory. England can supply the men in ever-increasing numbers to colonize it, but suitable land for them to colonize is strictly limited, and therefore to England such

territory for her expansion is all-important. "Having read the histories of other countries," to quote Rhodes upon himself, "I saw that expansion was everything, and that the world's surface being limited, the great object of present humanity should be to take as much of the world as it possibly could."

To the judgment of the future Cecil Rhodes may appeal with the certainty that it will applaud the unrivaled achievements of his energy and estimate justly the whole patriotic purpose of his life. The expansion of which he will be the acknowledged author will then be seen to have been not only an expansion of the empire but an expansion of the race, and expansion of English ideas and English principles. Men of that time who stand on the verge of the twentieth, will wonder at the shortsighted judgment and narrow spirit that failed to recognize the greatness and the patriotism of the statesman [Cecil Rhodes]. . . .

Zulu Dawn:
The Battle At Isandhlwana (1879)

Although native resistence to the European presence in Africa was always a concern among imperial governments, it was sporadic and rarely organized on a grand scale. Perhaps the most important expression of African resistance occurred in January 1879 at the Battle of Isandhlwana in eastern South Africa.

The king of the Zulus was Cetshwayo (1826–1884), whose strong military leadership and political acumen had restored the prestige of the Zulu nation to the level established by his illustrious uncle, Shaka. Cetshwayo had assembled a disciplined force of 40,000 men armed with spears (assegai), bows, and arrows. Perceiving a threat and seeking to incorporate Zululand into the British colony of Natal, the High Commissioner, Sir Henry Bartle Frere, sent an ultimatum to Cetshwayo in December 1878 demanding the dissolution of the Zulu military system. When the demand was not met, the British invaded Zululand.

The rains in January, 1879 impeded the British expeditionary force, which failed to take normal precautions in scouting the region and posting sentries. The Zulu army attacked the central British column at Isandhlwana on January 22, 1879, killing about 1,700 men. Although the Zulus lost 3,000 to 4,000 men, they captured over 1,000 rifles with ammunition. The Zulu rear guard then advanced to the British base at Rorke's Drift, which was well-fortified but guarded by only about 120 men. In fierce fighting, the soldiers at Rorke's Drift were able to fend off the Zulu attack and this led to an eventual British victory in March. By

"Zulu Dawn" is from *The North Wales Express* [February 21, 28 and March 7, 1879: Pvt. Owen Ellis]; Francis E. Colenso and E. Durnford, *History of the Zulu War and Its Origin* (London,1880), pp. 410–413 [Uguku]; and *The Brecon County Times* [March 15, 1879: Lt. Horace Smith-Dorrian].

July 1879, Cetshwayo was decisively defeated at Ulundi and Zululand came under informal British control. It was annexed to Natal in 1887. Cetshwayo was driven from power and died in 1884. His grave, deep in the Nkandla forest, is still considered sacred land.

The following selections highlight the action at Isandhlwana and Rorke's Drift. The first excerpt comes from the diary of British Private Owen Ellis, who reveals the confidence of the British before the massacre in which he perished. It is followed by the accounts of Uguku, a Zulu warrior, and British Lieutenant, Horace Smith-Dorrien, who were both involved in the action. They testify to the price paid for freedom—and empire.

Private Owen Ellis

January 11, 1879

Since the time I sent you my last letter I have removed about ten miles inland to the border of Zululand. We are about to march from this place at an early date in order to proceed through and occupy the country of the Zulus, in as much as King Cetshwayo did not submit to the terms demanded by the British government. It is now too late for him as we have crossed the Buffalo River by means of pontoons. Rorke's Drift is the name by which the place where we crossed is known. Sooner the better we march through Cetshwayo's country, as we have about one hundred miles to travel from this locality to the place where the King resides, called the "Grand Kraals." After arriving there, the Queen's flag will be hoisted and King Cetshwayo will be made into atoms or captured by us. . . . This war will be over in two months' time and then we shall all be hurrying towards England. We are about to capture all the cattle belonging to the Zulus and also to burn their kraals; and if they dare to face us with the intention of fighting, well, woe be to them! They shall be killed as they come across us.

January 19, 1879

It is now Sunday afternoon—just after dinner—and I am sitting on a small box to write to you these few lines, hoping very much that they will meet you healthy and hearty, as I am at present; and thanks be to the Almighty God for keeping us as we are. . . . I send you this letter in order that you may understand that we are shifting from Rorke's Drift at six A.M. tomorrow morning, 20 January, for the "Grand Kraals" of King Cetshwayo and perhaps it will take us a week or

nine days to reach that place. All the regiments . . . will meet each other at the "Grand Kraals" and occupy the country and appoint English magistrates to administer the law unless Cetshwayo will submit to the terms now laid before him. Not a single word has yet been received from him, but it is said that he is willing to conform to every demand except one and that is giving up his arms. The English government will therefore do with him as was done with [other defeated tribal chiefs]. . . .

Well, I now conclude; pardon me for being so short, as I have not much time to comment, and as we are about to pack everything ready after tea. Therefore, I have only to hope that everybody at home are in good health, as all the boys are here. Dear father, perhaps I shall be for a long time after this without writing, therefore don't be uneasy about a letter. I will send one as early as possible. Good afternoon.

Uguku–Zulu Warrior

January 22, 1879

It was our intention to have rested for a day in the valley where we arrived the night before the battle, but having heard firing of the English advance guard, . . . we went up from the valley to the top of Nqutu which was between us and the camp. . . . We saw a body of horse coming up the hill towards us from the Isandhlwana side. We opened fire on them, and then the whole of our army rose and came up the hill. The enemy returned our fire. . . . We were not checked by them, but continued our march on the camp until the artillery opened upon us. . . .

As we got nearer, we saw the soldiers were beginning to fall from the effects of our fire. . . . As we rushed on, the soldiers retired on the camp, fighting all the way, and as they got into the camp [at Rorke's Drift], we were intermingled with them. . . . One party of soldiers came out from among the tents and formed up a little above the ammunition wagons. They held their ground there until their ammunition failed them, when they were nearly all speared. Those who were not killed at this place formed again in a solid square in the neck of Isandhlwana. They were completely surrounded on all sides, and stood back to back, surrounding some men who were in the center. Their ammunition was now done, except that they had some revolvers which they fired at us at close quarters. We were quite unable to break their square until we had killed a great many of them, by throwing our spears at short distances. We eventually overcame them in this way.

Lieutenant Horace Smith-Dorrien

Since I wrote the first part of my letter, a dreadful disaster has happened to us. It seems to me a pure miracle that I am alive to tell you about it. On the 21st of January an order came to me, then stationed at Rorke's Drift, to go out to advanced camp to escort a convoy of twenty-five wagons from there to Rorke's Drift and bring them back loaded with supplies. . . .

When I arrived back in camp, I found the greater part of the column gone out with the General to meet the Zulu force, so that there was really only a caretaking force left in the camp. . . . The first Zulu force appeared about six o'clock in the morning. Two companies of the 24th were sent out after them. The Zulus seemed to retire and there was firing kept up at long ranges. At about ten thirty, the Zulus were seen coming over the hills in thousands. They were in most perfect order, and seemed to be in about twenty rows of skirmishers one behind the other. They were in a semi-circle round our two flanks and in front of us and must have covered several miles of ground. Nobody knows how many there were of them, but the general idea is at least 20,000.

Well, to cut the account short, in half an hour they were right up to the camp. I was out

with the front companies of the 24th, handing them spare ammunition. Bullets were flying all over the place, but I never seemed to notice them. The Zulus nearly all had firearms of some kind and lots of ammunition. Before we knew where we were they came right into the camp, spearing everybody right and left. Everybody then who had a horse turned to fly. The enemy were going at a kind of very fast half-walk and half-run. On looking round, we saw that we were completely surrounded and the road to Rorke's Drift was cut off. The place where they seemed thinnest was where we all made for. Everybody went scattered over ground covered with huge boulders and rocks until we got to a deep gully. Lots of our men were killed there. I had lots of marvelous escapes, and was firing away at them with my revolver as I galloped along. The ground there down to the river was so broken that the Zulus went as fast as the horses, and kept killing all the way. . . .

Well, to cut it short, I struggled into Helpmakaar, about twenty miles off, at nightfall, to find a few men who had escaped, about ten or twenty. . . . We sat up all night, momentarily expecting attack. . . . We have not a single thing left. The men have no coats or anything, all being taken by the Zulus. We shall have another dreadful night of it tonight, I expect, lying on the wet ground. I have just had to drop this for a minute for one of our numerous alarms. I have no time for more now. What excitement this will cause in England, and what indignation! The troops of course were badly placed, and the arrangements for defending the camp indifferent, but there should have been enough troops; and the risk of leaving a small force to be attacked by ten or fifteen times its number should not have been allowed. As you have heard, there were no wounded, all the wounded were killed, and in a most horrible way. Every white man that was killed or wounded was ripped up and the bowels torn out, so there was no chance of anyone being left alive on the field. I saw several wounded men during the retreat all crying out for help, as they knew the terrible fate in store for them. I thank God I am alive and well, having only a few bruises. God bless you.

Theme: Imperialism

The Historical Intersection

MONTANA: 1876

Custer's Last Stand

TWO MOONS

With the end of the U.S. Civil War in 1865, settlers resumed their migrations to the frontier. The lure of the West, with its promises of land, bountiful harvest, wealth, and opportunity remained an attractive vision in the eyes of many Americans who were willing to risk the dangers that awaited. Chief among these were the Native American Indian tribes that had for centuries roamed the Great Plains, hunting, fighting, and living without restriction. Clashes with the white man had often been intense as the Indians protected their domains. In 1874, gold was discovered in the Black Hills of Dakota territory and the Sioux tribes were offered six million dollars by the government to sell the land. When the Sioux refused the offer in 1875, the army allowed prospectors to flood the region. Outraged over the intrusions of whites into their sacred Black Hills, the Sioux, joined by the Cheyenne, Blackfeet, and other tribes, left their reservations and gathered under the leadership of their primary chiefs, Sitting Bull (ca.1831–1890) and Crazy Horse (ca. 1842–1877). To force the Indians back to their reservations, the Seventh Cavalry under the command of George Armstrong Custer (1839–1876) was dispatched in the summer of 1876. Custer, who had graduated last in his class at West Point and had a spotty record at best during the Civil War, divided his command against orders as he approached the Indian encampment on the Little Bighorn River. Seeking glory, Custer chose to ignore his scouts' reports about the enormous size of the concentrated Indian forces, which numbered about fifteen thousand. Custer had about 655 men under his command and he took five companies (about 264 men) with him to attack the village. They flew headlong into a hornet's nest from which no one emerged alive.

Two Moons (1847–1917) was a Lakota Sioux warrior and chief who followed Crazy Horse into battle that day. His eyewitness account describes the ensuing disaster.

(contd)

Compare and Contrast:

- How does this account of the Native American resistence against the intrusion of United States forces compare with the accounts of Zulu resistence to British control of South Africa?

Crazy Horse said to me, "I'm glad you have come. We are going to fight the white man again." I said to Crazy Horse, "All right. I am ready to fight. . . . My people have been killed, my horses stolen; I am satisfied to fight.". . .

When I got near my lodge, I looked up the Little Big Horn towards Sitting Bull's camp. I saw a great dust rising. It looked like a whirlwind. Soon Sioux horsemen came rushing into camp shouting: "Soldiers come! Plenty of white soldiers." I ran into my lodge, and said to my brother-in-law, "Get your horses; the white man is coming. Everybody run for horses.". . .

I got on my horse, and rode out into my camp. I called out to the people all running about: "I am Two Moons, your chief. Don't run away. Stay here and fight. You must stay and fight the white soldiers. I shall stay even if I am to be killed.". . . While I was sitting on my horse, I saw flags come up over the hill. Then the soldiers rose all at once . . . and got off their horses. . . . The Sioux rode up the ridge on all sides, riding very fast. The Cheyenne went up the left way. Then the shooting was quick, quick. Pop–pop–pop, very fast. Some of the soldiers were down on their knees, some standing. Officers all in front. The smoke was like a great cloud, and everywhere the Sioux went the dust rose like smoke. We circled all around them—swirling like water round a stone. We shoot, we ride fast, we shoot again. Soldiers drop, and horses fall on them. . . . Indians keep swirling round and round, and the soldiers killed only a few. Many soldiers fell. At last all horses were killed but five. Once in a while some man would break out and run toward the river, but he would fall. At last about a hundred men and five horsemen stood on the hill all bunched together. . . . Then a chief was killed. I hear it was Long Hair [Custer]. . . . All the soldiers were now killed, and the bodies were stripped. After that no one could tell which were officers. The bodies were left where they fell. . . . Some soldiers were cut with knives, to make sure they were dead; and the war women had mangled some. Most of them were left just where they fell. . . . We came to the man with the big mustache; he lay on the hill toward the river. The Indians did not take his buckskin shirt. The Sioux said, "That is a big chief. That is Long Hair." We had no dance that night. We were sorrowful.

Consider This:

- The great Lakota Sioux Chief, Crazy Horse, was celebrated for his ferocity in battle and recognized by his own people as a visionary leader committed

(contd)

to preserving the traditions and values of the Sioux nation. In 1877, he was stabbed to death while resisting arrest by the U.S. army. On his deathbed, he gave his assessment of why he fought at the Battle of the Little Big Horn: "Long Hair came in the same way. They say we massacred him, but he would have done the same thing to us had we not defended ourselves and fought to the last. Our first impulse was to escape with our squaws and papooses, but we were so hemmed in that we had to fight." Do you believe Crazy Horse? Was the Little Bighorn a defensive battle for the Indians? Was the Battle of Isandhlwana a defensive battle for the Zulus?

"Custer's Last Stand" is from Two Moons's account as related to Hamlin Garland in *McClure's Magazine* (September, 1898).

"A Natural Inclination to Submit to a Higher Authority" (1893)

SIR FREDERICK DEALTRY LUGARD

In spite of the organized resistence of the Zulus in 1879, British tenacity and power prevailed. In his analysis of the "Scramble for Africa," Sir Frederick Lugard, British soldier and administrator of some of Britain's colonial possessions in the late nineteenth century, focused on the necessity of British action and the benefits that would naturally ensue. In 1893, fourteen years after the Zulu destruction of British forces at Isandhlwana, Lugard confidently proclaimed that Africans possessed "a natural inclination to submit to a higher authority."

The Chambers of Commerce of the United Kingdom have unanimously urged the retention of East Africa on the grounds of commercial advantage. The Presidents of the London and Liverpool chambers attended a deputation to her Majesty's Minister for Foreign Affairs to urge "the absolute necessity, for the prosperity of this country, that new avenues for commerce such as that in East Equatorial Africa should be opened up, in view of the hostile tariffs with which British manufacturers are being everywhere confronted." Manchester followed with a similar declaration; Glasgow, Birmingham, Edinburgh, and other commercial centers gave it as their opinion that "there is practically no middle course for this country, between a reversal of the free trade policy to which it is pledged, on the one hand, and a prudent but continuous territorial extension for the creation of new markets, on the other hand. . . .

The "Scramble for Africa" by the nations of Europe—an incident without parallel in the history of the world—was due to the growing commercial rivalry, which brought home to civilised nations the vital necessity of securing the only remaining fields for industrial enterprise and expansion. It is well, then, to realise that it is for our advantage—and not alone at the dictates of duty—that we have undertaken responsibilities in East Africa. It is in order to foster the growth of the trade of this country, and to find an outlet for our manufactures and our surplus energy, that our far-seeing statesmen and our commercial men advocate colonial expansion. . . .

There are some who say we have no right in Africa at all, that "it belongs to the natives." I hold

"'A Natural Inclination to Submit to a Higher Authority'" is from Sir Frederick Dealtry Lugard, *The Rise of Our East African Empire,* vol. 1 (London: William Blackwood and Sons, 1893), pp. 379–382.

that our right is the necessity that is upon us to provide for our ever-growing population—either by opening new fields for emigration, or by providing work and employment which the development of over-sea extension entails—and to stimulate trade by finding new markets, since we know what misery trade depression brings at home.

While thus serving our own interests as a nation, we may, by selecting men of the right stamp for the control of new territories, bring at the same time many advantages to Africa. Nor do we deprive the natives of their birthright of freedom, to place them under a foreign yoke. It has ever been the key-note of British colonial method to rule through and by the natives, and it is this method, in contrast to the arbitrary and uncompromising rule of Germany, France, Portugal, and Spain, which has been the secret of our success as a colonising nation, and has made us welcomed by tribes and peoples in Africa, who ever rose in revolt against the other nations named. In Africa, moreover, there is among the people a natural inclination to submit to a higher authority. That intense detestation of control which animates our Teutonic races does not exist among the tribes of Africa, and if there is any authority that we replace, it is the authority of the Slavers and Arabs, or the intolerable tyranny of the "dominant tribe."

"THE BLAME OF THOSE YE BETTER, THE HATE OF THOSE YE GUARD"

Just send in your Chief an' surrender–it's
worse if you fights or you runs:
You can go where you please, you can skid up
the trees, but you can't get away from the guns!

—*Rudyard Kipling*

For how can man die better,
Than facing fearful odds,
For the ashes of his fathers,
And the temples of his gods.

—*Thomas Macaulay*

I labored hard to avoid trouble and bloodshed. We gave up some country to the white man, thinking that then we could have peace. We were mistaken. The white men would not leave us alone.

—*Chief Joseph*

The Casualties of Power: "Your New-Caught Sullen Peoples"

"I Will Fight No More Forever"

CHIEF JOSEPH

The destruction of General Custer's forces at the Battle of the Little Bighorn on June 25, 1876, although a great Indian victory, was the beginning of the end of Native American resistence against white incursion. With the battle occurring right before the nation's centennial celebration, the mood in Washington was hostile. The effort to crush Indian resistence became a crusade to gain revenge for the death of American soldiers. Chief Joseph (ca. 1840–1904) was the leader of

"'I Will Fight No More Forever'" is from "An Indian's View of Indian Affairs," *North American Review* (1879).

the Nez Perce Indians whose ancestral lands were located in eastern Oregon, Washington, and Idaho. Defiant of the U.S. Army's attempts to restrict the Nez Perce to reservations, Chief Joseph sought to elude authorities and led his people on an arduous march of more than one thousand miles into Montana, hoping to make it to the safety of Canada. Pursued by the forces of General Oliver Howard (1830–1909), the Nez Perce, hungry and exhausted, were attacked thirty miles from the border. They surrendered and were sent to reservations in Oklahoma. The first selection is the response of Chief Joseph upon his surrender at Bear Paw Mountain in 1877.

In early 1879, Joseph was permitted to go to Washington, D.C. to make his appeal. Appearing in person before a packed chamber of legislators, cabinet officials, and diplomats, Joseph made his case and pleaded with the government to allow his people to return to their homelands. Only in 1885 were the remnants of the Nez Perce Indians transferred to reservations near their traditional homes.

Bear Paw Mountain, 1877

They tell General Howard that I know his heart. What he told me before, I have in my heart. I am tired of fighting. Our Chiefs are killed. Looking Glass is dead. Tu-hol-hil-sote is dead. The old men are all dead. It is the young men who say yes or no. He who led on the young men is dead. It is cold and we have no blankets. The little children are freezing to death. My people, some of them, have run away to the hills and have no blankets, no food; no one knows where they are—perhaps freezing to death. I want to have time to look for my children among the dead. Hear me, my chiefs. I am tired; my heart is sick and sad. From where the sun now stands, I will fight no more forever.

Washington D.C., 1879

I cannot understand why so many chiefs are allowed to talk so many different ways, and promise so many different things. I have seen the Great Father, Chief [President Hayes], . . . and many other law chiefs [Congressmen] and they all say they are my friends, and that I shall have justice, but while all their mouths talk right I do not understand why nothing is done for my people. I have heard talk and talk, but nothing is done. Good words do not last long unless they amount to something. Words do not pay for my dead people. They do not pay for my country now overrun by white men. They do not protect my father's grave. They do not pay for my horses and cattle. Good words do not give me

back my children. . . . Good words will not give my people a home where they can live in peace and take care of themselves. I am tired of talk that comes to nothing. It makes my heart sick when I remember all the good words and all the broken promises. There has been too much talking by men who had no right to talk. Too many misinterpretations have been made; too many misunderstandings have come up between the white men and the Indians. If the white man wants to live in peace with the Indian he can live in peace. There need be no trouble. Treat all men alike. Give them the same laws. Give them all an even chance to live and grow. All men were made by the same Great Spirit Chief. They are all brothers. The earth is the mother of all people, and all people should have equal rights upon it. You might as well expect all rivers to run backward as that any man who was born a free man should be contented penned up and denied liberty to go where he pleases. If you tie a horse to a stake, do you expect he will grow fat? If you pen an Indian up on a small spot of earth and compel him to stay there, he will not be contented nor will he grow and prosper. I have asked some of the Great White Chiefs where they get their authority to say to the Indian that he shall stay in one place, while he sees white men going where they please. They cannot tell me. . . .

Let me be a free man, free to travel, free to stop, free to work, free to trade where I choose, free to choose my own teachers, free to follow the religion of my fathers, free to talk, think and act for myself—and I will obey every law or submit to the penalty.

The Arab Slave Trade

DAVID LIVINGSTONE

The exploitation of Africa during the late nineteenth century was certainly not confined to European governments seeking strategic advantage and economic gain. For centuries the primary trade of Africa had been slaves. Slavery had its origins deep in the ancient world with many Eastern and Western economies and societies linked to the practice through war and commerce. But at the outset of the nineteenth century, conditions began to change. Britain abolished the transatlantic slave trade in 1807 and freed the slaves in its colonies in 1833. The United States outlawed the importation of slaves after 1807 and ended slavery at the conclusion of the Civil War in 1865. Still, the slave trade flourished in Africa as tribal rivalries and internecine war continued to provide a steady supply of slaves. In the late nineteenth century, Arabs played a primary role in the management of the slave trade by exporting to Eastern markets.

In the following excerpt, the British explorer and missionary, David Livingstone, describes the brutalities of the Arab slave trade and the massacre of women and children near the South African village of Nyangwe.

I found about three hundred slaves exposed for sale, the greater part of whom came from Lake Nyassa and the Shire River; I am so familiar with the peculiar faces and markings or tattooings, that I expect them to recognize me. Indeed, one woman said that she had heard of our passing up Lake Nyassa in a boat, but she did not see me: others came from Chipeta, south-west of the Lake. All who have grown up seem ashamed at being hawked about for sale. The teeth are examined, the cloth lifted up to examine the lower limbs, and a stick is thrown for the slave to bring, and thus exhibit his paces. Some are dragged through the crowd by the hand, and the price called out incessantly: most of the purchasers were Northern Arabs and Persians.

The Arabs are said to treat their slaves kindly, and this also may be said of native masters; the reason is, master and slave partake of the general indolence, but the lot of the slave does not improve with the general progress of civilization. While no great disparity of rank exists, his energies are little tasked; but when society advances, wants multiply; and to supply these, the slave's lot grows harder. The distance between master and man increases as the lust of gain is developed; hence we can hope for no improvement in the slave's condition, unless the master returns to or remains in barbarism. . . .

When endeavoring to give some account of the slave trade of East Africa, it is necessary to keep far within the truth, in order not to be thought guilty of exaggeration; but, in sober seriousness, the subject does not admit of exaggeration. To overdraw its evils is a simple impossibility. The sights I have seen, though common incidents of the traffic, are so nauseous that I always strive to drive them from memory. In the case of most disagreeable recollections I can succeed, in time, in consigning them to oblivion; but the slaving scenes come back unbidden, and make me start up at dead of night horrified by their vividness. To some this may appear weak and unphilosophical, since it is alleged that the whole human race has passed through the process of development. We may compare cannibalism to the stone age, and the times of slavery to the iron and bronze epochs. Slavery is as natural a step in human development as from bronze to iron. . . .

Within African tribes there are social relationships that defy explanation. There are even rankings among slaves; those who help the Arabs do their evil work obtain authority over the unfortu-

"The Arab Slave Trade" is from Horace Waller, ed., *The Last Journals of David Livingstone in Central Africa* (New York: Harper and Brothers, 1875), pp. 630–634.

nate who are newly enslaved. One of these "slave leaders" by the name of Manilla, in order to frighten and thereby impress local chieftains, organized a rifle brigade and began to destroy three villages in the vicinity of Nyangwe.

It was a hot and sultry yesterday when I arrived at the crowded market. I saw Manilla and two others with guns and felt inclined to reprove them, as one of my men did, for bringing weapons into the market, but I attributed it to their ignorance; before I had got thirty yards out of the market, the discharge of two guns in the middle of the crowd told me that the slaughter had begun: crowds dashed off from the place, and threw down their wares in confusion and ran. At the same time that the three opened fire on the mass of people near the upper end of the market-place, volleys were discharged from a party down near the creek on the panic-stricken women, who dashed at the canoes. These, some fifty or more, were jammed in the creek, and the men forgot their paddles in the terror that seized all. The canoes were not to be got out, for the creek was too small for so many: men and women, wounded by the balls, pored into them, and leaped and scrambled into the water shrieking. . . .

Shot after shot continued to be fired on the helpless and perishing. Some of the long line of heads disappeared quietly; while other poor creatures threw their arms high, as if appealing to the great Father above, and sank. . . . My friend, chief Dugumbe put people into one of the deserted vessels to save those in the water, and saved twenty-one; but one woman refused to be taken on board from thinking that she was to be made a slave of: she preferred the chance of life by swimming to the lot of a slave. The Bagenya women are expert in the water, as they are accustomed to dive for oysters and those who went down stream may have escaped; but the Arabs themselves estimated the loss of life at between three hundred and thirty and four hundred souls. The shooting-party near the canoes were so reckless they killed two of their own people. . . .

My first impulse was to pistol the murderers, but Dugumbe protested against my getting into a blood-feud, and I was thankful afterward that I took his advice. Two wretched Muslims asserted that the firing was done by the "people of the English." I asked one of them why he lied so, and he could utter no excuse; no other falsehood came to his aid as he stood abashed before me; and so telling him not to tell palpable falsehoods, I left him gaping. . . . Muhammadans are certainly famous as liars, and the falsehood of Muhammad has been transmitted to his followers in a measure unknown in other religions. . . .

As I write, I hear the loud wails on the left bank over those who are there slain, ignorant of their many friends now in the depths of Lualaba. Oh, let Thy kingdom come! No one will ever know the exact loss on this bright sultry summer morning. The massacre gave me the impression of being in hell. . . .

I counted twelve villages burning this morning. I asked the question of Dugumbe and others, 'Now, for what is all this murder?' All blamed Manilla as its cause, and in one sense he was the cause; but the wish to make an impression in the country as to the importance and greatness of the new-comers was the most potent motive; but it was terrible that the murdering of so many should be contemplated at all. It made me sick at heart. . . .

I proposed to Dugumbe to catch the murderers, and hang them up in the market-place, as our protest against the bloody deeds before the Manyuema. . . . This slaughter was particularly atrocious, inasmuch as we have always heard that women coming to or from market have never been known to be molested: even when two districts are engaged in actual hostilities, "the women," say they, "pass among us to market unmolested," nor has one ever been known to be plundered by the men. These nigger Muslims are inferior to the Manyuema in justice and right. The people under the Arab leader, Hassani, began the superwickedness of capture and pillage of all indiscriminately. . . . They remained over among the ruins, feasting on goats and fowls all night, and today continued their infamous work till twenty-seven villages were destroyed.

"Enemy of God!": Gordon's Impending Doom (1884)

ABDULLAH MUHAMMAD AL-MAHDI

Throughout much of this section, we have been focusing on the interrelationships of European, Arab, and African cultures of central and southern Africa. But Africa north of the equator also became a hotbed of contention among European powers in the nineteenth century. Islamic armies had conquered and controlled the region beginning in the seventh century, and many Muslims felt their religion and culture threatened by the growing European presence. Beginning in 1881, a Muslim mystic named Abdullah Muhammad Ahmed al-Mahdi led a rebellion against British forces in the Sudan. Al-Mahdi, a reformist religious leader who referred to himself as "the successor to the apostle of God," that is, the religious successor to the Prophet Muhammad, sought a return to the religious purity of early Islam. The expulsion of foreign oppressors was a cornerstone of the movement.

The famous British commander, General Charles Gordon, who became a national hero for his exploits in China, reached Khartoum in February 1884 and evacuated the women and children, the sick and wounded, in view of the threat posed by the Sudanese rebels. But the British government, not taking the Mahdi's threat seriously, refused Gordon's requests for aid. Gordon himself would not evacuate Khartoum, and the Mahdi issued the following ultimatum before commencing a siege in March, 1884. On January 26, 1885, the Sudanese rebels entered Khartoum and butchered the garrison. The Mahdi, with Gordon's head in tow, established his capital at Omdurman. His rule was brief—he died in June 1885, possibly of typhus. "Gordon of Khartoum" became a martyr in the eyes of the British public and the Mahdi became an important African symbol of Islamic revival. In 1898, the Mahdist army was annihilated by the British general, Lord Kitchener, who destroyed the Mahdi's tomb, exhumed the body, and sent the skull to the London College of Surgeons. In London, the slaughter was hailed as a heroic triumph.

In the name of God the Merciful, the Compassionate, Praise be to the Bountiful God, and blessings be upon our Lord Muhammad and upon his family. We, the servant of God, Abdullah Muhammad Jifarah, one of the governors of the Mahdi, on whom be peace, on the East, to Gordon, the Pasha of Khartoum:

You have paid no attention to the counsel and reasoning repeatedly sent to you, but have increased in folly; and the numerous kindly admonitions have only made you more haughty and wayward; since truth enlightens the breasts of Believers, but only increases the oppressors in their degeneration. Your letter has reached us, in which you deceived the population, saying that the British reenforcement is coming to you in three divisions, and that it will soon reach you

and give you victory; thus your letter betrays the greatness of your fear, and anxiety, and alarm, as in your deceit you have caught hold of spider-web ropes and have feared to die at our hands. Thou must inevitably die, O thou heathen!

But it is no wonder that you deny the mahdiship, for you did not believe in the apostleship of Muhammad; but the wonder is that the learned men of wickedness, who are raised to prominent positions by you, and whom God has left to go astray, and whose hearts he has closed, whose ears he has sealed, and over whose eyes he has put a veil, since they have been satisfied with you as a leader, and have taken you as a teacher, have waged war against Believers, and seek victory for those who believe in more than one God, as though they had not heard the word of God: "If

"'Enemy of God!'" is from James Harvey Robinson and Charles A. Beard, *Readings in Modern European History*, Vol. II (Boston: Gin & Company, 1909), pp. 456–458.

you wage war, war will come upon you, and if you end war, it is better for you, and if you return, God will return, and he is with the Believers." . . .

It is strange how you frighten the people, saying the English are coming, and how you think that the Allies will be affected by your false rumors. No, by God! Even though swarms of English and others should come, this would only increase the faith of the Allies, and their steadfastness would grow in the labor of the siege until God shall make you taste confusion and destruction. . . . If you are content to remain as you are, then prepare for what shall come; but if you knock at the door of repentance, perhaps it may be opened unto you.

Peace be upon those who follow after the right way.

Abdullah Muhammad

"The Judgment of Your Peers"

It would be inaccurate to characterize European imperialism in Africa and India as fully sanctioned by governments and supported by the popular will. Just as the voices of abolition were crucial in the destruction of slave economies, so too were critics who decried the arrogance and atrocities that were a part of the exploitation of these regions. The first selection is by the historian Frederick Starr, who experienced firsthand the fear and distrust that Asian and African peoples often felt for the "white man's face." His criticism is followed by that of Mark Twain, whose scathing wit and anguish at U.S. imperialism are evident in his reinterpretation of "The Battle Hymn of the Republic" (1900).

The "White Man's Face": Terror in the Congo

FREDERICK STARR

Why should we pick out the Congo Free State for our assault? Atrocities occur wherever the white man with his thirst for gold comes into contact with "a lower people." He is ever there to exploit; he believes that they were created for exploitation. If we want to find cruelty, atrocities, all kinds of frightful maltreatment, we may find them in almost every part of Negro Africa. They exist in the French Congo, in German Africa, in Nigeria, even in Uganda. If we insist on finding them, we may find cruelty, dispossession, destruction of life and property, in all these areas. . . . Wherever British trade finds native custom standing in its way, we shall find cruelty. . . .

To me the real wonder is that there are any of the Congo peoples left. Think of the constant drain due to the foreign slave trade, continued from an early date until after the middle of the

nineteenth century. Think of the continuous losses due to the barbarism of native chiefs and demands of native customs—to wars, cannibalism, execution, and ordeal. Think of the multitudes who have died from the diseases of the country and from pestilence introduced by the newcomers. . . .

Returned from the Congo country and a year and more of contact with the dark natives, I find that a curious and most disagreeable sensation has taken possession of me. I had read often and heard that other peoples find the faces of white men terrifying and cruel. The Chinese, the Japanese, and other peoples of Asia tell the same story. The white man's face is fierce and terrible. His great and prominent nose suggests the beak of some bird of prey. His fierce face causes babes to cry, children to run in terror, grown folk to tremble. I had been always inclined to think that this feeling was individual and trifling; that it was solely due to strangeness and lack of contact. Today I know better. Contrasted with the other faces of the world, the face of the fair white is terrible, fierce, and cruel. No doubt our intensity of purpose, or firmness and dislike of interference, our manner in walk and action and in speech all

"The 'White Man's Face'" is from Frederick Starr, *The Truth About the Congo* (Chicago: Forbes & Co., 1907), pp. 105–106.

add to the effect. However that may be, both in Europe and our own land, after my visit to the blacks I see the cruelty and fierceness of the white man's face as I never would have believed was possible. For the first time I can appreciate fully the feelings of the natives. The white man's face is a dreadful prediction; where the white man goes, he devastates, destroys, depopulates. Witness America, Australia, and Africa.

The Battle Hymn of the Republic (Brought Down to Date)

MARK TWAIN

Mine eyes have seen the orgy of the
   launching of the Sword;
He is searching out the hoardings where
   the stranger's wealth is stored;
He hath loosed his fateful lightnings, and
   with woe and death has scored;
HIS LUST IS MARCHING ON.

"The Battle Hymn of the Republic" is from Mark Twain, *The Complete Works of Mark Twain*, vol. 20 (New York: Harper Brothers, 1917), p. 465.

I have seen him in the watch-fires of a
   hundred circling camps,
They have builded him an altar in the
   Eastern dews and damps;
I have read his doomful mission by the
   dim and flaring lamps—
HIS NIGHT IS MARCHING ON.

I have read his bandit gospel writ in
   burnished rows of steel:
"As ye deal with my pretensions, so with
   you my wrath shall deal;
Let the faithless son of Freedom crush the
   patriot with his heel;
LO, GREED IS MARCHING ON!"

In a sordid slime harmonious, Greed was
   born in yonder ditch,
With a longing in his bosom—and for
   others' goods an itch—
As Christ died to make men holy, let men
   die to make us rich—
OUR GOD IS MARCHING ON!

CHRONOLOGY: The Scramble for Global Empire

1807	Britain abolishes slave trade.
1841–1842	Opium War in China as Great Britain tries to control Chinese markets.
1849	British annexation of the Punjab in India.
1854–1856	Crimean War: Britain, France, and the Ottoman Empire vs. Russia. Opposition to Russian expansion in Balkans leads to an ineptly managed war that shatters the invincible image of Russia and the Concert of Europe.
1857	Indian Mutiny against British rule results in abolition of East India Company's political authority.
1859	*The Origin of Species* by Charles Darwin is published and promotes the theory of "natural selection."
1861	Victor Emmanuel II proclaimed king of Italy. Serfdom abolished in Russia by Tsar Alexander II.
1861–1867	French troops occupy Mexico and install Maximilian as emperor.
1862	Otto von Bismarck becomes prime minister of Prussia.

1867	Dual monarchy established in a compromise solution between Austria and Hungary.
1868–1874	Liberal ministry of William Gladstone in Great Britain.
1869	Suez Canal completed.
1870	France declares war on Prussia over Ems dispatch. France defeated at Sedan and Emperor Napoleon III captured. Third French Republic proclaimed.
1870	Italian state annexes Rome. Italian unification completed under King Victor Emmanuel II.
1871	Proclamation of the German Empire at Versailles. Paris Commune in existence from March to May with goal to administer Paris separately from the rest of the country. The Commune is suppressed with heavy loss of life.
1874–1880	Ministry of Benjamin Disraeli in Great Britain highlighted by social legislation such as the Public Health Act and Artisans Dwelling Act, both in 1875.
1875	Britain gains control of Suez and begins to establish Protectorate over Egypt.
1882	France controls Algeria.
1884–1885	Germany establishes Protectorate over Southwest Africa, Togoland, Cameroons, and East Africa.
1894	Captain Dreyfus accused of passing secret information to the German army and convicted on forged evidence by a military court. Dreyfus conviction set aside in 1906, but military discredited and France divided politically; Abdullah Muhammad al-Mahdi destroys British general Charles Gordon's garrison at Khartoum, Sudan.
1898	Spanish-American War: United States acquires Puerto Rico, Philippines, Guam; annexes Hawaiian Islands and establishes Protectorate over Cuba; Kitchener's victory over Mahdist rebels at Omdurman, Sudan.
1899	"Open Door Policy" in the Far East is proposed by the United States.
1899–1902	Britain crushes a rebellion by Dutch farmers in South Africa called the Boer War.

STUDY QUESTIONS

1. Explain Social Darwinism and give several specific examples from the reading selections that demonstrate its practice and use as justification for imperial expansion. What phrases and ideas are consistently used? What are some of Karl Pearson's arguments? Are they compelling? To what extent is Social Darwinism a corruption of Darwinist theories? Or is it simply a logical extension and application of the theories?

2. Discuss the "mandate system." What was it and how is it evident in the speech by Joseph Chamberlain regarding Britain's duty in Egypt? Cite specific phrases in this regard.

3. Analyze Senator Beveridge's speech on U.S. control of the Philippines. What does he advocate and what are the specific arguments he uses to justify his beliefs? Note especially how he uses the abstraction of "history." Is this a logical, if not satisfying, argument? Why would

it be appealing to many? How does Kipling's poem "The White Man's Burden" complement Beveridge's statements? How do this source and other sources in this chapter define imperialism as an agent of "progress and civilization"?

4. According to the French Prime Minister Jules Ferry, why was it important for France to be a "great" country in 1883? What actions needed to be taken in order to make this a reality? Did Ferry answer his critics effectively? Compare his vision with that of the German Kaiser Wilhelm II. What is your reaction to the Kaiser's proposal that Germany must seek "new points where we can drive in the nail on which to hang our armor"?

5. In his poem, "Foreign Children," what point was Robert Louis Stevenson trying to make? Would you call this an arrogant poem? Why was Stevenson so confident in his perspective?

6. According to Lt. Colonel Innes, why was there such animosity directed against the British by the Indian population in general and by the Muslim Mughal rulers in particular? Who were the malcontents?

7. Thomas Babington Macaulay did not mince words in his assessment of education in India. He believed in teaching the Indian population "what is best worth knowing." For Macaulay, what was worth knowing and why was Arabic and Sanscrit poetry inferior to western literature?

8. Queen Victoria's annexation decree for India in 1858 seems alternately aggressive and conciliatory. Give specific examples of the benefits the Crown was willing to provide and the limits of freedom that it imposed on the Indian population. What was the bottom line for Queen Victoria?

9. Why was Africa so attractive to competing European powers in the late nineteenth century? Who was Cecil Rhodes and what was his perspective about "the expansion of English ideas and English principles"? Was he a great patriot or a vicious exploiter?

10. How did Sir Frederick Lugard connect nationalism with the economic argument for imperialism? How did he respond to the arguments presented by critics of imperialism? How did he justify his support of imperial expansion?

11. After reading the letters and eyewitness accounts of the Battle of Isandhlwana in 1879, what are your impressions? What price did the British pay for their imperialism? Was it worth it? And what does this say about the nature of native resistence? Were Zulu warriors inferior to British forces? What did the Zulus have to lose? Finally, compare the Zulu victory at Isandhlwana with the Indian victory at Little Bighorn. Ultimately, what was the fate of both the Zulus and Native Americans? Why? What did Chief Joseph have to say about this?

12. What was David Livingstone's assessment of the Arab slave trade? Describe the slaughter in the marketplace. Why was slavery so prevalent in African society and what did Livingstone think of Muslim responsibility?

13. Note the warning that Abdullah Muhammad issued to General Charles Gordon in 1884. He made good on his promises as Gordon's British forces were destroyed. Would the Mahdi have been considered an Islamic terrorist today? Did the British consider him to be so? Must imperialist foreign elements always be eliminated by military force? Must slavery be eliminated by the same tactics? What is "moral force"? Did moral force help Chief Joseph? Does that mean it is less powerful than physical force?

14. According to Frederick Starr, why did the white man's face inspire terror throughout the world? What do you think of Mark Twain's version of "The Battle Hymn of the Republic"? What point was he trying to make? Compare Twain's poem with Rudyard Kipling's "White Man's Burden." Are they both honest and truthful?

6

Japan and China: The Rising Sun and the Falling Star

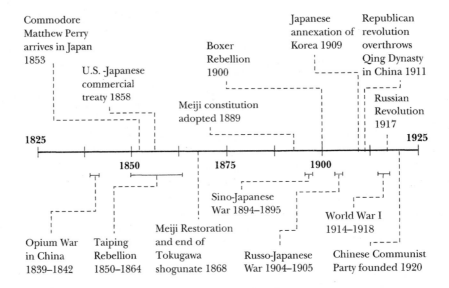

Commodore Matthew Perry arrives in Japan 1853

U.S.-Japanese commercial treaty 1858

Boxer Rebellion 1900

Meiji constitution adopted 1889

Japanese annexation of Korea 1909

Republican revolution overthrows Qing Dynasty in China 1911

Russian Revolution 1917

1825   1925

1850   1875   1900

Sino-Japanese War 1894–1895

World War I 1914–1918

Meiji Restoration and end of Tokugawa shogunate 1868

Opium War in China 1839–1842

Taiping Rebellion 1850–1864

Russo-Japanese War 1904–1905

Chinese Communist Party founded 1920

In the hot September of 1793, the British envoy Lord George Macartney, after a long procession that was most thrilling to the Chinese onlookers, presented the emperor Qianlong with gifts, examples of Western industry and expertise, all designed to awe and to initiate a trade agreement with China. There were firearms, saddles, chiming clocks, and astronomical instruments. The emperor, who had ruled for over sixty years, was not impressed. "Our ways have no resemblance to yours," he noted in a reply to King George III. "As your ambassador can see, we possess all things. I set no value on objects strange or ingenious, and have no use for your country's manufactures." The emperor, regarded by his own subjects as the Son of Heaven, wished to remain secluded from the West. As ruler of the Middle Kingdom—the center of the world—the emperor believed that China was the true font of civilization and that foreigners were "barbarians" or "devils" who could produce no more than the tribute of an inferior people.

But times were changing, and although the emperor could not see the future, it augured ill for the fortunes of the Middle Kingdom. By the close of the next century, the Qing dynasty would be swept away by the winds of change. China would bend, but eventually break in response to the coming of the West.

From the early nineteenth century on, the Western powers in Europe, and eventually the United States, expanded their influence throughout the world in search of natural resources to feed the insatiable appetites of their industrialized economies and for markets that would support their growing affluence. Missionaries, impelled by the word of God, justified this imperialism by claiming divine sanction in the conversion of heathen tribes in Africa. Others found compelling "scientific" evidence of Western racial superiority that made the desecration of foreign gods and the destruction of tribal communities consistent with the natural order of human evolution.

Western imperialism, however, was certainly not confined to Africa. In India and East Asia, the West would encounter some of the oldest and most sophisticated civilizations in the world, confident that the wisdom of their philosophy, the beauty of their art, and the sophistication of their poetry were the standards by which any civilization must be measured. But the superiority of Western technology and armament forced the Chinese and Japanese to reassess these standards, because, by about 1850, they were faced with a choice: Either modernize through the practical application of technology and become competitive with the West or face political and cultural extinction.

This was a traumatic experience for both China and Japan. Western powers insisted on an advantageous trading environment obtained through "unequal treaties." China, in particular, fell prey to the devastating opium trade that poisoned its people and provided the cornerstone of British profit for decades. Faced with such an overwhelming threat to their cultural traditions, economies, and security, both China and Japan began to modernize in imitation of the West. Both were determined to preserve their social and political institutions and to "confine Western learning to the area of utility." During the next four decades from the 1860s through the turn of the century, China's efforts to industrialize and modernize her society met with defeat, while Japan's met with resounding success. Japan reorganized its army and beat both the Chinese (1895) and the Russians (1905) on the battlefield. Japan had moved beyond the political confines of the Tokugawa shogunate by 1868 and had restored the emperor to a greater political role with a new constitution. China, on the other hand, after battling the destructive Taiping rebellions of the 1850s, initiated a "self-strengthening" program that ultimately failed to preserve the political integrity of the Qing dynasty. Faced with a rising republican movement headed by Sun Yat-sen, the last emperor abdicated in 1912, and China degenerated into the political mire of warlord rule.

In this chapter we will analyze the impact of Western imperialism on the great civilizations of China and Japan. Both nations were changed by their contact with the West and would go on to play pivotal roles in the history of the twentieth century.

THE MODERNIZATION OF JAPAN (1853–1912)

"Revere the Emperor, Repel the Barbarian!": The Opening of Japan to the West

By the beginning of the seventeenth century, the disruptions of the "Warring States" period in Japan had ended and chaos was replaced by the stable rule of the Tokugawa bakufu. *From 1600 to 1868, the Tokugawa shogunate transformed Japanese culture by regularizing the laws, and controlling the aristocracy* (daimyo) *through a "hostage system" requiring the great lords of the land to reside permanently within the shōgun's palace at Edo. Like the policy of Louis XIV at Versailles, this act transformed the independent, ambitious, and disruptive aristocracy into benign courtiers who depended on the shōgun for their position and could thus be manipulated.*

But perhaps the most important change brought by the Tokugawa shogunate was to close Japan off from the world. This national policy of seclusion, implemented in the 1630s, did not prevent cultural imports from China and Korea, but except for small trading operations at Nagasaki for the Dutch and Chinese, no foreigners were permitted to enter Japan. No ocean-going ships could be built. Nor were the Japanese allowed to go abroad, on pain of death. Aided by the natural isolation of its islands, Japan simply became its own world. This policy preserved the political stability of Tokugawa rule and allowed Japanese culture and society to develop a unique depth.

Seclusion from the world was not necessarily an easy proposition. By 1739, Russian ships were seen in Japanese waters with increasing frequency, and in 1808, a British ship actually forced its way into the Japanese port of Nagasaki. The world wanted to trade with the Japanese. There had been ongoing turmoil within the shogunate for years over this issue when Commodore Matthew Perry's U.S. ships arrived in 1853, "suggesting" that Japan sign a Treaty of Friendship to forestall more assertive measures that would force Japan to open its markets.

The Tokugawa shogunate began to split apart under the increasing agitation between those who wanted to "revere the Emperor and repel the barbarian" and a more conciliatory group that advocated a policy of strengthening the nation politically and militarily by adopting Western science and technology, while preserving the ethical and social traditions of Japan.

The first selection is from a work called the New Proposals *by Aizawa Seishisai (1782–1863) and represents the creed of the conservatives who called for national unity by maintaining Japanese seclusion. It is followed by excerpts from a book entitled* Reflections on My Errors *by Sakuma Shōzan (1811–1864). A bold advocate of Western military methods, Sakuma was thrown into jail by the Tokugawa shogunate for violating the seclusion laws in 1854 by stowing away on one of Perry's ships. He wrote this "apology," which is actually a vigorous defense of his ideas. Sakuma was assassinated in 1864 by his political opposition.*

"The Inflammatory Teaching of the Barbarians" (1825)

AIZAWA SEISHISAI

Keep in Mind . . .

* What were the specific concerns of Aizawa about Western influence? How did he describe foreigners and what were their intentions?

In the past, those who have attracted popular attention and confused the thinking of the populace with their improper teaching have only been people of our own realm. But now we must cope with the foreigners of the West, where every country upholds the law of Jesus and attempts therewith to subdue other countries. Everywhere they go they set fire to shrines and temples, deceive and delude the people, and then invade and seize the country. Their purpose is not realized until the ruler of the land is made a subject and the people of the land subservient. As they have gained momentum, they have attempted to foist themselves on our Divine Land. . . . The damaging effects of their heresies go far beyond anything done by those who attack from within our own land. Fortunately, our rulers were wise and our ministries alert, and thus were able to perceive their evil designs. The barbarians were killed and exterminated, and there has been no recurrence of this threat. Thus, for two hundred years, the designing and obstinate fellows have been prevented from sowing their seeds in our soil. That the people have been free from the inflammatory teaching of the barbarians has been due to the great virtue of our government. . . .

Recently, there has appeared what is known as Dutch Studies, which had its inception among our official interpreters [at Nagasaki]. It has been concerned primarily with the reading and writing of Dutch, and there is nothing

harmful about it. However, these students, who make a living by passing on whatever they hear, have been taken in by the vaunted theories of the Western foreigners. They enthusiastically extol these theories, some going so far as to publish books about them in the hope of transforming our civilized way of life into that of the barbarians. And the weakness of some for novel gadgets and rare medicines, which delight the eye and enthrall the heart, have led many to admire foreign ways. If someday the treacherous foreigner should take advantage of this situation and lure ignorant people to his ways, our people will adopt such practices as eating dogs and sheep and wearing woollen clothing. And no one will be able to stop it. We must not permit the frost to turn to hard ice. We must become fully aware of its harmful and weakening effects and make an effort to check it. Now the Western foreigners, spurred by the desire to wreak havoc upon us, are daily prying into our territorial waters. And within our own domain evil teachings flourish in a hundred subtle ways. It is like nurturing barbarians within our own country.

Consider This:

* Why was Aizawa so afraid of change? Note the language. Why did foreigners want to "wreak havoc" on Japan and "lure the Japanese" with their "evil" teachings? What did foreigners hope to accomplish?

Mastering the Barbarian (1854)

SAKUMA SHŌZAN

Keep in Mind . . .

* What are the "five pleasures" of a gentleman?

* According to Sakuma, what was the primary role of national defense?

From *Sources of Japanese Tradition* by de Bary, William Theodore, et al., eds., copyright © 1958 Columbia University Press, pp. 600–601. Reprinted with the permission of the publisher.

From *Sources of Japanese Tradition* by de Bary, William Theodore, et al., eds., copyright © 1958 Columbia University Press, pp. 610–611, 614–615. Reprinted with the permission of the publisher.

1. The gentleman has five pleasures, but wealth and rank are not among them. That his house understands decorum and righteousness and remains free from family rifts—this is one pleasure. That exercising care in giving to and taking from others, he provides for himself honestly, free, internally, from shame before his wife and children, and externally, from disgrace before the public—this is the second pleasure. That he expounds and glorifies the learning of the sages, knows in his heart the great Way, and in all situations contents himself with his duty, in adversity as well as in prosperity—this is the third pleasure. That he is born after the opening of the vistas of science by the Westerners, and can therefore understand principles not known to the sages and wise men of old—this is the fourth pleasure. That he employs the ethics of the East and the scientific technique of the West, neglecting neither the spiritual nor material aspects of life, combining subjective and objective, and thus bringing benefit to the people and serving the nation—this is the fifth pleasure.

2. The principal requisite of national defense is that it prevents the foreign barbarians from holding us in contempt. The existing coastal defense installations all lack method; the pieces of artillery that have been set up in array are improperly made; and the officials who negotiate with the foreigners are mediocrities who have no understanding of warfare. The situation being such, even though we wish to avoid incurring the scorn of the barbarians, how, in fact, can we do so? . . .

3. Of the men who now hold posts as commanders of the army, those who are not dukes or princes or men of noble rank, are members of wealthy families. As such, they find their daily pleasure in drinking wine, singing, and dancing; and they are ignorant of military strategy and discipline. Should a national emergency arise, there is no one who could command the respect of the warriors and halt the enemy's attack. This is the great sorrow of our times. For this reason, I have wished to follow in substance the Western principles of armament, and, by banding together loyal, valorous, strong men of old, established families not in the military class—men of whom one would be equal to ten ordinary men—to form a voluntary group which would be made to have as its sole aim that of guarding the nation and protecting the people. Anyone wishing to join the society would be tested and his merits examined; and, if he did not shirk hardship, he would then be permitted to join. Men of talent in military strategy, planning, and administration would be advanced to positions of leadership, and then, if the day should come when the country must be defended, this group could be gathered together and organized into an army to await official commands. It is to be hoped that they would drive the enemy away and perform greater service than those who do not form the military class. . . .

4. Mathematics is the basis for all learning. In the Western world after this science was discovered, military tactics advanced greatly, far outstripping that of former times. This development accords with the statement that "one advanced from basic studies to higher learning." In the *Art of War* of Sun Zi, the statement about "estimation, determination of quantity, calculation, judgment, and victory" has reference to mathematics. However, since Sun Zi's time neither we nor the Chinese have ceased to read, study, and memorize his teachings, and our art of war remains exactly as it was then. It consequently cannot be compared with that of the West. There is no reason for this other than that we have not devoted ourselves to basic studies. At the present time, if we wish really to complete our military preparations, we must develop this branch of study. . . .

5. In order to master the barbarians, there is nothing so effective as to ascertain in the beginning conditions among them. To do this, there is no better first step than to be familiar with barbarian tongues. Thus, learning a barbarian language is not only a step toward knowing the barbarians, but also the groundwork for mastering them. . . .

6. Last summer [1853], the American barbarians arrived in the Bay of Uraga with four warships, bearing their president's message. Their deportment and manner of expression were exceedingly arrogant, and the resulting insult to our national dignity was not small. Those who heard could but gnash their teeth. A certain person on guard in Uraga suffered this insult in silence, and, having been ultimately unable to do anything about it, after the barbarians had retired, he drew his knife and slashed to bits a portrait of their leader, which they had left as a gift. Thus he gave vent to his rage. In former times, Zao Wei of Song, having been demoted, was serving as an official in Shensi [province], and when he heard of the character of Chao Yuanhao, he had a person skillful in drawing paint Chao's image. Zao looked at this portrait and knew from its manly appearance that Chao would doubtless make trouble on the border in the future. Therefore, Wei wished to take steps toward preparing the border in advance, and toward collecting together and examining men of ability. Afterwards, everything turned out as he

had predicted. Thus, by looking at the portrait of his enemy, he could see his enemy's abilities and thereby aid himself with his own preparations. It can only be regretted that the Japanese guard did not think of this. Instead of using the portrait, he tore it up. In both cases there was a barbarian; in both cases there was a portrait. But one man, lacking the portrait, sought to obtain it, while the other, having it, destroyed it. Their depth of knowledge and farsightedness in planning were vastly different.

Consider This:

- According to Sakuma, what were the flaws in Japanese defense? What did Japan have to do to defend itself properly?

- Note that Sakuma advocates "employing the ethics of the East and the scientific technique of the West." How would this help the Japanese "master the barbarian?" What is the significance of Sakuma's story about the portrait of one's enemy?

In 1853, the American representative, Commodore Matthew Perry, proposed that the Tokugawa shogunate end its centuries-long seclusion and open trade with the West. The changes initiated by this venture spelled the end of Tokugawa rule and the beginning of a movement to restore the emperor to political authority with a constitution for Japan. *(Historical Pictures Collection/Stock Montage, Inc.)*

The Meiji Restoration (1868-1912)

The seclusion of Japan from the outside world had been an essential component of Tokugawa political control. With Commodore Perry's arrival in Japan in 1853 and the signing of a commercial treaty with the United States in 1858, the Tokugawa shogunate broke down amidst the criticism and infighting of dissident lords who found their influence and positions placed in jeopardy. Younger samurai, who had been frustrated by their lack of influence in the Tokugawa government, began a movement to "honor the emperor" and restore him to a position of political leadership. Although many of these young samurai were imprisoned or executed in the purges that followed, the movement gathered momentum and resulted in the destruction of the Tokugawa shogunate. On January 3, 1868, the emperor Meiji (meaning "enlightened or illustrious rule") announced his restoration as the font of political authority. By May, Tokugawa forces had been defeated and the shōgun's castle at Edo became the new Imperial palace. Edo itself was renamed Tokyo (the "eastern capital").

The Meiji period from 1868 to 1912 was one of dynamic change in Japanese history. The first task of the Meiji leaders was to centralize power in the position of emperor and establish a constitution for the new state. To do this, Meiji advisors left Japan for a year to study in the West and were exposed to the political world of Jean-Jacques Rousseau and the French Revolution, the economic world of Adam Smith and capitalism, to British liberalism, American democracy, and Prussian military theory with its vision of unity through discipline and dominant will.

Fukuzawa Yukichi (1834–1901) was an educator and journalist who perhaps best displayed the energy and dynamism of the Meiji leaders who went abroad to learn about the West. In debating ideas garnered through his travels, Fukuzawa argued that Japan required a complete "renovation" through the adoption of a new system of education based on Western civilization and science. Then Japan could truly achieve "independence and self-respect" as an active participant in the world community. In the following excerpt from his autobiography, Fukuzawa talks about his first visits to the United States and Great Britain.

Travels in the West

FUKUZAWA YUKICHI

Keep in Mind . . .

- What matters were most astonishing to Fukuzawa during his travels in the United States and Great Britain?

- What episode convinced Fukuzawa that "foreigners were not all 'devils'"?

From *Sources of Japanese Tradition* by de Bary, William Theodore, et al., eds., copyright © 1958 Columbia University Press, pp. 625–628. Reprinted with the permission of the publisher.

I am willing to admit my pride in this accomplishment for Japan. The facts are these: It was not until 1853 that a steamship was seen for the first time; it was only in 1855 that we began to study navigation from the Dutch in Nagasaki; by 1860 the science was sufficiently understood to enable us to sail a ship across the Pacific. This means that about seven years after the first sight of a steamship, after only about five years of practice, the Japanese people made a trans-Pacific crossing without help from foreign experts. I think we can without undue pride boast before the world of this courage and skill. As I have shown, the Japanese officers were to receive no aid from

Captain Brooke throughout the voyage. Even in taking observations, our officers and the Americans made them independently of each other. Sometimes they compared their results, but we were never in the least dependent on the Americans. . . .

On our part, there were many confusing and embarrassing moments [while traveling in America], for we were quite ignorant of the customs and habits of American life. . . . Things social, political, and economic proved most inexplicable. One day, on a sudden thought, I asked a gentleman where the descendants of George Washington might be. He replied, "I think there is a woman who is directly descended from Washington. I don't know where she is now, but I think I have heard she is married." His answer was so very casual that it shocked me.

Of course, I knew that America was a republic with a new president every four years, but I could not help feeling that the family of Washington should be regarded as apart from all other families. My reasoning was based on the reverence in Japan for the founders of the great line of rulers—like that for Ieyasu of the Tokugawa family of shōguns; [they are] really deified in the popular mind. So I remember the intense astonishment I felt at receiving this indifferent answer about the Washington family. As for scientific inventions and industrial machinery, there was no great novelty in them for me. It was more in matters of life and conventions of social custom and ways of thinking that I found myself at a loss in America. . . .

While we were in London, a certain member of the Parliament sent us a copy of a bill, which he said he had proposed in the House under the name of the party to which he belonged. The bill was a protest against the arrogant attitude of the British minister to Japan, Alcock, who had at times acted as if Japan were a country conquered by military force. One of the instances mentioned in the bill was that of Alcock's riding his horse into the sacred temple grounds of Shiba, an unpardonable insult to the Japanese.

On reading the copy of this bill, I felt as if "a load had been lifted from my chest." After all, the foreigners were not all "devils." I had felt that Japan was enduring some pointed affronts on the part of the foreign ministers who presumed on the ignorance of our government. But now that I had actually come to the minister's native land, I found that there were among them some truly impartial and warm-hearted human beings. So after this I grew even more determined in my doctrine of free intercourse with the rest of the world. . . .

When I asked a gentleman what the "election law" was and what kind of an institution the Parliament really was, he simply replied with a smile, meaning I suppose that no intelligent person was expected to ask such a question. But these were the things most difficult of all for me to understand. In this connection, I learned that there were different political parties—the Liberal and the Conservative—who were always "fighting" against each other in the government.

For some time it was beyond my comprehension to understand what they were "fighting" for, and what was meant, anyway, by "fighting" in peace time. "This man and that man are 'enemies' in the House," they would tell me. But these "enemies" were to be seen at the same table, eating and drinking with each other. I felt as if I could not make much out of this. It took me a long time, with some tedious thinking, before I could gather a general notion of these separate mysterious facts. In some of the more complicated matters, I might achieve an understanding five or ten days after they were explained to me. But all in all, I learned much from this initial tour of Europe.

Consider This:

- How did travel expand the perspectives of Fukuzawa and other Meiji leaders? How was this important in the construction and success of the Meiji state?

"The Status of a Civilized Nation":
The Responsibilities of Japanese Citizenship (1899)
ITŌ HIROBUMI

During this period of dazzling change, the slogan of the Meiji leadership was to "enrich the nation and strengthen its arms." Young Meiji leaders like Ōkubo Toshimichi (1830–1878), Itō Hirobumi (1841–1909), and Yamagata Aritomo (1838–1922), fashioned a constitution, established a formidable army and navy, and transformed the nation into a modern state while maintaining traditional Japanese values. Ultimately, the Japanese modeled their new constitution of 1889 on that of Germany. The emperor was sovereign and his person "sacred and inviolable." He was given direct command of the armed forces and could name the prime minister and appoint a Cabinet. There existed a representative assembly or Diet, but it was conceived to be part of a constitutional system and not fully representative of the Japanese people. In essence, the constitution of 1889 was designed to support a ruling oligarchy rather than a representative democracy. It followed a pattern already well-established in Japan.

The primary architect of this constitution was Itō Hirobumi. The next selection is a speech that Itō delivered in his native town of Hagi a decade later in 1899. Note his emphasis on balance between tradition and innovation that was so important for success in the Meiji period.

Keep in Mind . . .

- What "freedoms" did the Japanese gain through the "open door" principle?

- According to Itō, what was the "aim of the nation"?

When our enlightened emperor decided to accept the open-door principle as an imperial policy . . . it became a matter of urgent necessity to develop the intellectual faculties of our people and to increase their business activities. This led to the abolition of the feudal system and made it possible for the Japanese people to live in a new political environment and to have diverse freedoms. . . . The first of these freedoms was the freedom of movement, followed by the freedom to pursue an occupation of one's own choosing. Moreover, the freedom to study at any place of one's choosing was given to all. There was also granted freedom of speech in political affairs. Thus, the Japanese today enjoy freedom, each according to his own desires, within the limits of the law. These rights belong to people who live in a civilized government. If these rights are withheld and their enjoyment refused, a people cannot develop. And if the people cannot develop, the nation's wealth and the nation's strength cannot develop. . . . But the fact is that because of the imperial policy of the open-door, we have established a government which is civilized. And as we have advanced to such a position, it has become necessary to establish a fixed definition of the fundamental laws. This, in short, is the reason for the establishment of constitutional government. . . .

According to the Constitution, the people have the right to participate in government, but this right is at once an important obligation as well as a right. Government is a prerogative of the emperor. As you will be participating in government—which is the emperor's prerogative—you must regard this right as the responsibility of the people, the honor of the people, and the glory of the people. It is therefore a matter of the greatest importance. . . .

In the next place we must know the aims and the policies of our country. Political parties may have their arguments, and others may have their views about the government, but they must be kept within the bounds of the aims and policies of the government. What then is the aim of the nation? It is the imperial aim decided upon at the time of the Restoration of imperial rule. . . . The aim of our country has been from the very beginning, to attain among the nations of the world the status of a civilized nation and to become a member of the community of European and American nations which occupy the position of civilized countries. To join this community of nations means to become one of them, but in this connection, we must consider the rights and duties attendant upon membership. Among fellow men of civilized nations, there is a thing called common justice. To become a member of this community of nations it is necessary to respect this common justice. Generally speaking, all Oriental countries—China and Japan included—have the habit of holding foreign countries in contempt and of holding their own country in esteem. But in carrying on relations according to civilized standards of common justice, it is done according to a procedure of mutual equality without contempt for the other and esteem for oneself, or vice versa. . . .

Thus, every member of the nation—be he a farmer, craftsman, or merchant—must become familiar beforehand with the merits and demerits of questions of government. Not only on questions of government, but also on matters concerning his own occupation, the citizen must give due thought and become prosperous. When every man becomes wealthy, the village, the county, and the prefecture in turn become wealthy, and the accumulated total of that wealth becomes the wealth of Japan. The expansion of military strength and the promotion of national prestige depend upon the power of the individual members of the country. . . .

[Therefore], the people have an obligation to understand the nation's aims. They must regard the nation as their own, meet the military obligation to defend it and to pay for the cost of defending it.

Consider This:

- Itō mentioned that "government is the prerogative of the emperor." What did he mean? According to Itō, what were the responsibilities of Japanese citizenship?

- Why was it so important for Japan to attain national prestige in becoming a part of the "community of nations"?

"Never Bring Dishonor on Your Name": The Principles of Japanese Militarism (1882)

YAMAGATA ARITOMO

Another of the great reformers of the Meiji period was Yamagata Aritomo. Known in his youth as "The Wild One," and writing under the pen name, "Pure Madness," Yamagata was one of the young samurai who had launched the reform movement during the Tokugawa shogunate. Some saw him, however, as a reactionary politician because he fashioned the Japanese army into a disciplined fighting force. In any event, he possessed the political virtues of moderation and conciliation that allowed him to balance the competing demands of state. He too went abroad to study the military organization of the most advanced Western powers and returned with ideas for a new conscription system in 1872. He, more than anyone else,

From *Sources of Japanese Tradition* by de Bary, William Theodore, et al., eds., copyright © 1958 Columbia University Press, pp. 706–707. Reprinted with the permission of the publisher.

realized that a warrior class of samurai could no longer compete on a modern battlefield. Still, in this 1882 directive to the soldiers and sailors of the new conscripted military, Yamagata emphasized the virtues of self-control and disciplined loyalty that were such a part of samurai lore. These values remained a part of Japanese military tradition during the first half of the twentieth century.

Keep in Mind . . .

• According to Yamagata, what were the responsibilities of soldiers and sailors? How did he define valor?

Whether We are able to guard the Empire, and so prove Ourself worthy of Heaven's blessings and repay the benevolence of Our Ancestors, depends upon the faithful discharge of your duties as soldiers and sailors. If the majesty and power of Our Empire be impaired, do you share with Us the sorrow; if the glory of Our arms shine resplendent, We will share with you the honor. If you all do your duty, and being one with Us in spirit do your utmost for the protection of the state, Our people will long enjoy the blessings of peace, and the might and dignity of Our Empire will shine in the world. As We thus expect much of you, Soldiers and Sailors, We give you the following precepts:

1. No soldier or sailor, especially, can be considered efficient unless this spirit be strong within him. A soldier or a sailor in whom this spirit is not strong, however skilled in art or proficient in science, is a mere puppet; and a body of soldiers or sailors wanting in loyalty, however well ordered and disciplined it may be, is in an emergency no better than a rabble. Remember that, as the protection of the state and the maintenance of its power depend upon the strength of its arms, the growth or decline of this strength must affect the nation's destiny for good or for evil; . . . Never by failing in moral principle fall into disgrace and bring dishonor upon your name. . . .

3. The soldier and the sailor should esteem valor. . . . Never to despise an inferior enemy or fear a superior, but to do one's duty as soldier or sailor—this is true valor. Those who thus ap-

preciate true valor should in their daily intercourse set gentleness first and aim to win the love and esteem of others. If you affect valor and act with violence, the world will in the end detest you and look upon you as wild beasts. Of this you should take heed.

4. The soldier and the sailor should highly value faithfulness and righteousness. . . . Faithfulness implies the keeping of one's word, and righteousness the fulfilment of one's duty. . . . Ever since ancient times there have been repeated instances of great men and heroes who, overwhelmed by misfortune, have perished and left a tarnished name to posterity, simply because in their effort to be faithful in small matters they failed to discern right and wrong with reference to fundamental principles, or because, losing sight of the true path of public duty, they kept faith in private relations. You should, then, take serious warning by these examples.

5. The soldier and sailor should make simplicity their aim. If you do not make simplicity your aim, you will become effeminate and frivolous and acquire fondness for luxurious and extravagant ways; you will finally grow selfish and sordid and sink to the last degree of baseness, so that neither loyalty nor valor will avail to save you from the contempt of the world.

These articles should not be disregarded even for a moment by soldiers and sailors. Now for putting them into practice, the all important thing is sincerity. These articles are the soul of Our soldiers and sailors, and sincerity is the soul of these articles. If the heart be not sincere, words and deeds, however good, are all mere outward show and can avail nothing. If only the heart be sincere, anything can be accomplished. . . . If you, Soldiers and Sailors, in obedience to Our instruction, will observe and practice these principles and fulfil your duty of grateful service to the country, it will be a source of joy, not to Ourself alone, but to all the people of Japan.

Consider This:

- Note how Yamagata connected valor with love and esteem and not with violence. Why?

- Why did Yamagata emphasize simplicity? What role does sincerity play?

- Throughout the document, why is the first person plural capitalized? What does this mean?

THE DISINTEGRATION OF IMPERIAL CHINA (1839–1912)

The Opening of China to the West

At the time of the British envoy's visit to China in 1793, the Qing dynasty was at its zenith. It had been nearly 150 years since the Manchus, foreigners from Manchuria, had swept down from their mountain homeland north of China to oust the last Ming emperor in 1644. The new rulers absorbed the culture and religious traditions of China and set about conquering Burma, Vietnam, Korea, and Nepal. Manchu rule, organized as the Qing dynasty, was also stable politically and prosperous domestically during the seventeenth and eighteenth centuries. Silks, porcelain, and most importantly, tea were readily exported to Europe. But the West found trading with China difficult, since foreign merchants were restricted to the peninsula at Macao and the port of Canton (modern Guangzhou). Here they were kept at arm's length and barred from any direct contact with Chinese officials.

These restrictions were felt most dramatically by the East India Company of British traders. Over the years, it had built up a triangle trade by shipping British textiles to India, Indian

The superiority of British technology was evident in the destruction of this Chinese junk during the Opium War of 1839-1842. China hoped to strengthen itself by using the "instruments of the barbarians to repel the barbarians." *(Corbis-Bettmann)*

cotton to China, and Chinese silk, tea, and porcelain to Britain. Yet the Chinese demanded payment in silver (their common currency) and never really purchased enough cotton to impress the profit-minded executives of the East India Company. What commodity could be forced into the Chinese market that would demand a constant supply and produce a growing profit? The answer was opium.

The Chinese had long been opposed to the opium trade. The drug had been introduced into China by Dutch traders during the seventeenth century. As early as 1729, there were imperial decrees forbidding the sale and smoking of this "destructive and ensnaring vice." In 1796, Jiaqing, the new emperor, placed a complete ban on its importation, but he was a weak administrator and soon pirates and opium merchants were bribing officials to look the other way. By 1816, the East India Company had imported 3,000 chests of opium from its poppy fields in the north Indian state of Punjab. By 1820, this had risen to 5,000 and by 1825 to almost 10,000.

As more and more Chinese became addicts, and silver flowed out of the economy to British coffers, the Chinese government moved toward confrontation. The emperor Daoguang, who came to the throne in 1821 was a reformer, and, supported by his advisor Lin Zexu (1785–1850), the emperor banned opium in 1836 and ordered the decapitation of "foreign barbarians" who concealed and traded the drug. The following selection is a letter by Lin Zexu to Queen Victoria in 1839, exhorting her to suppress the opium trade.

"Where Is Your Conscience?": The Curse of Opium (1839)

LIN ZEXU

Keep in Mind . . .

- What were the restrictions and penalties imposed by the Chinese government on those who imported, grew, or smoked opium?

A communication: magnificently our great emperor soothes and pacifies China and the foreign countries, regarding all with the same kindness. If there is profit, then he shares it with the peoples of the world; if there is harm, then he removes it on behalf of the world. This is because he takes the mind of Heaven and earth as his mind.

The kings of your honorable country by a tradition handed down from generation to generation have always been noted for their politeness and submissiveness. We have read your successive

Reprinted by permission of the publisher from *China's Response to the West: A Documentary Survey*, 1839–1923, by Ssu-yu Teng and John King Fairbank, pp. 24–27, Cambridge, Mass.: Havard University Press, Copyright © 1954, 1979 by the President and Fellows of Harvard College, Copyright renewed 1982 by Ssu-yu Teng and John King Fairbank.

tributary memorials saying: "In general our countrymen who go to trade in China have always received His Majesty the Emperor's gracious treatment and equal justice," and so on. Privately we are delighted with the way in which the honorable rulers of your country deeply understand the grand principles and are grateful for the Celestial grace. For this reason the Celestial Court in soothing those from afar has redoubled its polite and kind treatment. The profit from trade has been enjoyed by them continuously for two hundred years. This is the source from which your country has become known for its wealth.

But after a long period of commercial intercourse, there appear among the crowd of barbarians both good persons and bad, unevenly. Consequently there are those who smuggle opium to seduce the Chinese people and so cause the spread of the poison to all provinces. Such persons who only care to profit themselves, and disregard their harm to others, are not tolerated by the laws of Heaven and are unanimously hated by human beings. His Majesty the Emperor, upon hearing of this, is in a towering rage. . . .

We find that your country is [several thousand miles] from China. Yet there are barbarian ships that strive to come here for trade for the purpose of making a great profit. The wealth of China is used to profit the barbarians. That is to say, the great profit made by barbarians is all taken from the rightful share of China. By what right do they then in return use the poisonous drug to injure the Chinese people? Even though the barbarians may not necessarily intend to do us harm, yet in coveting profit to an extreme, they have no regard for injuring others. Let us ask, where is your conscience? I have heard that the smoking of opium is very strictly forbidden by your country; that is because the harm caused by opium is clearly understood. Since it is not permitted to do harm to your own country, then even less should you let it be passed on to the harm of other countries—how much less to China! . . .

Suppose there were people from another country who carried opium for sale to England and seduced your people into buying and smoking it; certainly your honorable ruler would deeply hate it and be bitterly aroused. We have heard heretofore that your honorable ruler is kind and benevolent. Naturally you would not wish to give unto others what you yourself do not want. . . .

Only in several places of India under your control . . . has opium been planted from hill to hill, and ponds have been opened for its manufacture. For months and years work is continued in order to accumulate the poison. The obnoxious odor ascends, irritating Heaven and frightening the spirits. Indeed you, O King, can eradicate the opium plant in these places. . . .

Now we have set up regulations governing the Chinese people. He who sells opium shall receive the death penalty and he who smokes it also the death penalty. Now Keep in Mind… if the barbarians do not bring opium, then how can the Chinese people resell it, and how can they smoke it? The fact is that the wicked barbarians beguile the Chinese people into a death trap. How then can we grant life only to these barbarians? He who takes the life of even one person still has to atone for it with his own life; yet is the harm done by opium limited to the taking of one life only? Therefore, in the new regulations, in regard to those barbarians who bring opium to China, the penalty is fixed at decapitation or strangulation. This is what is called getting rid of a harmful thing on behalf of mankind.

[However] all those who within the period of the coming one year (from England) or six months (from India) bring opium to China by mistake, but who voluntarily confess and completely surrender their opium, shall be exempt from their punishment. After this limit of time, if there are still those who bring opium to China then they will plainly have committed a willful violation and shall at once be executed according to law, with absolutely no clemency or pardon. This may be called the height of kindness and the perfection of justice.

Consider This:

- What were Lin Zexu's concerns over the importation of British opium to China? Do you find his argument compelling and responsible? Why didn't the British comply respectfully?

"Use the Barbarians to Fight the Barbarians" (1842)

WEI YUAN

As the British continued to pressure the Chinese government for free trade and protection for the legal rights of their citizens in treaty ports, Chinese officials saw beyond the "fairness" argument and accused the British of pushing opium. In 1830, Chinese officials destroyed 20,000 chests of British opium, and war broke out. From 1839 to 1842, the British

From *Sources of Chinese Tradition* by de Bary, William Theodore, et al., eds., © 1958 Columbia University Press, pp. 675–677. Reprinted with the permission of the publsiher.

demonstrated their superiority in arms by sieging forts and seizing cities, soundly defeating Chinese troops equipped with their antiquated weapons. The Opium War ended in August 1842 with the Treaty of Nanjing, the first of a series of "unequal treaties" that expanded foreign access to Chinese markets. Britain got control of Hong Kong, a huge indemnity, and access to five new ports. France and the United States also made similar treaties and the Russians were active on the northern border with China.

The first selection is by Wei Yuan (1794–1856), a scholar and author of the Illustrated Gazetteer of the Maritime Countries. *This was the first systematic attempt to provide educated individuals with a view of the outside world. Wei Yuan's argument can be put succinctly: Western barbarians in their vicious pursuit of power and profit have exercised their technologies to threaten the virtuous Chinese society; China must awaken to the threat by applying its superior moral strength to finding practical solutions. That China had difficulty in "catching up" to the West technologically and defending itself against foreign domination is demonstrated in the succeeding source by You Zan, an economic scholar, who was still complaining about the opium poison in 1894.*

Keep in Mind . . .

- What did Wei Yuan mean when he said "use the barbarians to fight the barbarians?"

- What were the economic drawbacks of the opium trade for China?

What is the purpose of the present work? Its purpose is to show how to use barbarians to fight barbarians, how to make the barbarians pacify one another [to our advantage], and how to employ the techniques of the barbarians in order to bring the barbarians under control. . . .

Yet, the steady poisoning of our people by the barbarians with their opium represents a crime ten thousand times worse than [any in the past]. However, our present emperor, His Majesty, is so benevolent and diligent. His virtue matches that of His ancestors. The operations of Heaven in time and of man through his own efforts are conjoined for our advantage. Why should we fear that the time is not ripe for extermination of the barbarians; why should we fear that there may be no chance to show our might? Thus all of our courageous people must show their eagerness for the achievement of such a task, and anyone who has not lost his senses must devise some means for its accomplishment. Away with hypocrisy! Away with all window dressing! Away with the nurturing of in-

ternal evils and the tolerating of private gain at the expense of the public interest! Then the minds of men will be aroused from their ignorant lethargy.

First of all, through practical projects we must advance practical effort; and through practical effort advance practical projects. . . . Our nets must be made ready before we can go fishing in the lake. . . .

Secondly, once rid of our ignorant lethargy, the sun will shine more brightly in the sky; once the dearth of men with practical abilities is remedied, government orders will be carried out with the speed of wind and lightning. . . .

The Opium Poison (1894)

YOU ZAN

The Westerners' most effective weapon in butchering our financial well-being has been and still is opium, the poison of which permeates into every corner of the nation. We exchange precious silver for harmful drugs, and the total amount of silver that has flowed out of the country during the past fifty years is so large that we have ceased to count. The more we ban the opium traffic, the more the people violate the ban. Meanwhile the Westerners, sitting there comfortably and radiating a self-satisfied smile, collect their profit. They will not be satisfied until every Chinese looks like a skeleton and every Chinese penny goes into their pockets. They will not be happy until China, as a nation, has degenerated to such an extent that no recovery is remotely possible. Their strategy is clear: to prevent China from becoming strong, they have to keep her permanently poor. . . .

Consider This:

- Wei Yuan's argument against the "barbarians" seems to be a call for Chinese unity. What did he mean when he said "away with hypocrisy" and "away with window dressing"?

- Do you agree with You Zan that Western strategy was to prevent China from becoming strong by keeping her permanently poor? Was China dominated economically because it was inferior militarily?

The Self-Strengthening Movement (1864–1894)

In the People's Republic of China, the modern history of the nation begins with the Opium War of 1839–1842, a humiliating defeat by the Western imperialistic capitalist forces that nevertheless began the long struggle toward independence that culminated in the 1949 Communist triumph in China. Although this perspective can be readily disputed, it is true that China had been brought to its knees by Western technological superiority and commitment to the dictates of profit.

By 1860, the rulers of China had wasted twenty years by refusing to recognize and respond to the problems presented by the changing dynamics of the Western presence. But it was difficult for the Chinese to focus on relations with foreigners when they were faced with overwhelming domestic disruption.

The most immediate threat to Manchu rule was the Taiping, Nien, and Muslim rebellions between 1850 and 1873. Motivated by a desire for moral reform, a devotion to religious fervor, and the dream of an egalitarian society, the Taipings were especially threatening to Manchu rule. This was a bloody period of suffering and natural calamity where China's population dropped by sixty million people. Such catastrophic turmoil certainly hindered China's ability to respond to the Western threat.

By the summer of 1864, when Nanjing was recaptured from the Taiping rebels, most of the energy from these disturbances had been reinvested in the hope that China could develop new institutions that would help it regain economic and political authority. A foreign policy declaration by the emperor in 1861 likened China to a diseased patient on the road to recovery: "Therefore, we should suppress the Taiping and Nien bandits first, get the Russians under control next, and attend to the British last." With this intent, the Chinese set about a "self-strengthening" movement from about 1864 to 1894 to adopt Western knowledge and beat the West at their own game, thus preserving the cultural heritage and political institutions of China.

The leaders of the self-strengthening movement, Zeng Guofan (1811–1872) and Li Hongzhang (1823–1901) worked diligently to reconstruct China after the rebellions and to reform the economy by creating new industries and companies to compete with the West.

This section focuses on some of these efforts. The first selection is by Feng Guifen (1809–1874), a teacher and official who hoped to awaken China from its complacency. In this struggle, some Chinese even admired the Japanese ability to respond quickly to the Western threat. The second selection is an 1865 assessment of the practical creation of new factories in Shanghai by the reformer Li Hongzhang himself.

"Why Are Western Nations Small and Yet Strong?"

FENG GUIFEN

Keep in Mind . . .

- What elements does Feng Guifen think were important in the self-strengthening movement? What must the Chinese learn from the Western barbarians?

Why are the Western nations small and yet strong? Why are we large and yet weak? We must search for the means to become their equal, and that depends solely upon human effort. . . . We have only one thing to learn from the barbarians, and that is strong ships and effective guns.... Funds should be allotted to establish a shipyard and arsenal in each trading port. A few barbarians should be employed, and Chinese who are good in using their minds should be selected to receive instruction so that in turn they may teach many craftsmen. . . .

Our nation's emphasis on civil service examinations has sunk deep into people's minds for a long time. Intelligent and brilliant scholars have exhausted their time and energy in such useless things as the stereo-typed examination essays, examination papers, and formal calligraphy. . . . We should now order one-half of them to apply themselves to the manufacturing of instruments and weapons and to the promotion of physical studies. . . . The intelligence and ingenuity of the Chinese are certainly superior to those of the various barbarians; it is only that hitherto we have not made use of them. . . . There ought to be some people of extraordinary intelligence who can have new ideas and improve on Western methods. At first they may take the foreigners as their teachers and models; then they may come to the same level and be their equals; finally they may move ahead and surpass them. Herein lies the way to self-strengthening. . . .

From *Sources of Japanese Tradition* by de Bary, William Theodore, et al., eds., copyright © 1958 Columbia University Press, pp. 708–709. Reprinted with the permission of the publisher.

When we speak of repelling the barbarians, we must have the actual means to repel them, and not just empty bravado. If we live in the present day and speak of repelling the barbarians, we should ask with what instruments we are to repel them? . . . [The answer is that] we should use the instruments of the barbarians, but not adopt the ways of the barbarians. We should use them so that we can repel them.

Compare and Contrast:

- Compare the concerns of Feng Guifen with those of the Japanese writers, Aizawa Seishisai and Sakuma Shōzan on pp. 173–175. Why were the Chinese and Japanese so afraid of Western contamination of their cultural heritage? Why weren't the Chinese able to "master the barbarian" as did the Japanese?

New Factories in Shanghai (1865)

LI HONGZHANG

Keep in Mind . . .

- According to Liu Hongzhang, why was Western machinery both "amazing" and "easy to understand"?

As for the importance of the machine industry to the self-strengthening movement in general and national defense in particular, the Office of General Management has elaborated it in detail in a memorial submitted to Your Majesty for review. Your Majesty must be thoroughly familiar with it. Your humble servant wishes to add that Western machines are essential not only to the manufacture of modern weaponry, but also to the making of a variety of other items useful and beneficial to people's economic life, including items used on the farms, in the textile industry, in the printing of books, and in the porcelain and pottery industry. The secret of these items

"New Factories in Shanghai" is from Li, Dun J., *Modern China*, 1978, pp. 66–67.

lies in the substitution of manual labor by natural movement of any one of which will make all others move. The amazing phenomenon is clear for all to see, and the principle behind it is also easy to understand.

Since China had been isolated from the West for a long time, even our most skillful engineers, until recently, had no knowledge of how Western machines worked. However, as this knowledge becomes more widespread with the passage of time, our people will not only acquire, but also improve upon it, since basically there is no difference in intelligence between Westerners and Chinese. Your humble servant believes that in a few decades the wealthy farmers and merchants in China will use machines for their work in order to increase their production and profit, regardless of the government's regulation in this matter. Nevertheless, the manufacturing of firearms and coinage must remain a governmental monopoly, and those who are skillful in making guns and ammunition must be in the employ of the government.

However ingenious or miraculous it may look in appearance, a mechanical device comes about as a result of applying the easily understandable natural law. It will not work and certainly will not work for long if it is not based upon reason and facts. Chen Tingqing is correct when he states in a memorial to Your Majesty that even a most complicated piece of Western machinery is built upon the same principle upon which a Chinese watch or clock is made. Though our social structure and political institutions are not only different from, but superior to their Western counterparts and must therefore be maintained and strengthened, it has

been nevertheless suggested that to transform China from a weak to a strong country in order to assure her safety, we must imitate the West in technical matter, especially in the manufacturing of machinery. . . .

For several years your humble servant has paid close attention to the manufacturing of machines and firearms according to Western methods. During the past months, [we have] spent much time in locating and purchasing Western equipment. Finally, we have the opportunity of establishing this iron and machine factory. Your humble servant will do his utmost to make it succeed and prosper, though he does not expect spectacular achievement in the immediate future. Only through trial and error over a long period of time can we hope that it will bear good fruits and yield concrete results.

Compare and Contrast:

- Li Hongzhang insisted that complex Western machinery was built on "the same principle upon which a Chinese watch or clock is made." If China was, as he argued, superior in social structure and political institutions, why were the Chinese so inferior in technological application?

- Western nations like Great Britain often believed that their technological superiority reflected their moral and cultural superiority. Note Thomas Babington Macaulay's vision of British cultural superiority in Chapter 5 on pp. 149–150. Is there always a price to pay in human suffering for cultural or technological superiority? How can you apply your ideas to our contemporary age?

The Last Emperor

In the year 1894, the Chinese government, expecting an easy victory, went to war with Japan over control of Korea. China was shocked when the Japanese dominated the battlefield with their disciplined army and creative tactics. This loss in 1895 to a country of "dwarfish bandits" that the Chinese had considered inferior, demonstrated that China, in the words of the reformer, Kang Youwei, was "soundly asleep atop a pile of kindling." Although the emperor launched a new effort in 1898 called the "one hundred days of reform" with edicts to revamp

China's laws, schools, and military structure, the effort bogged down amidst court intrigue and political haggling. Sensing weakness, the Western powers began in earnest to "carve up the melon" by defining their spheres of interest. The United States, which had less presence in China, pushed for an "open-door" policy of equal commercial opportunities and the preservation of China's territorial integrity.

Domestic rebellions broke out once again, headed this time by the Boxers, a religious society that promoted nationalism and resistence to the encroachment of foreign powers. The Boxer Rebellion of 1900 was crushed by an international force and the authority and prestige of the Chinese court, corrupt and uninspired, continued to decline.

Change was on the horizon. Sun Yat-sen (1866–1925) had been born a peasant and became a Christian in Hawaii. He studied medicine in Canton and Hong Kong and in 1905 organized the Revolutionary Alliance. He was a nationalist who wanted to free China from foreign domination, but despaired, especially after the Chinese defeat in 1895. In his view, reform movements were doomed to failure because the autocratic government of the emperor had outlived its usefulness and lacked commitment to anything but its own benefit. Only a democratic republic that truly served the needs of the people and not those of the privileged classes could break China free from foreign domination and domestic hardship. "Only by taking urgent measurers," wrote Sun, "will we and our descendants not become slaves." With a price on his head as a "notorious bandit," Sun had to work outside of China. In 1906, he proposed the following program of change.

"The Righteousness of Our Cause" (1906)

SUN YAT-SEN

Keep In Mind . . .

- According to Sun Yat-sen, what was the difference between the revolution he advocated and the revolutions of his ancestors?

Since the beginning of China as a nation, we Chinese have governed our own country despite occasional interruptions. When China was occasionally occupied by a foreign race, our ancestors could always in the end drive these foreigners out, restore the fatherland, and preserve China for future generations of Chinese. Today when we raise the righteous standard of revolt in order to expel an alien race that has been occupying China [the Manchus], we are doing no

more than our ancestors have done or expected us to do. Justice is so much on our side that all Chinese, once familiarizing themselves with our stand, will have no doubt about the righteousness of our cause.

There is a difference, however, between our revolution and the revolutions of our ancestors. The purpose of past revolutions, such as those conducted by the Mings and the Taipings, was to restore China to the Chinese, and nothing else. We, on the other hand, strive not only to expel the ruling aliens and thus restore China to the Chinese, but also to change basically the political and economic structure of our country. While we cannot describe in detail this new political and economic structure since so much is involved, the basic principle behind it is liberty, equality and fraternity. The revolutions of yesterday were revolutions by and for the heroes; our revolution, on the other hand, is a revolution by and for the people. . . .

At this juncture we wish to express candidly and fully how to make our revolution today and how to govern our country tomorrow.

"The Righteousness of Our Cause" is from Li, Dun J., *Modern China*, 1978, pp. 137–140.

1. ***Expulsion of the Manchus from China:*** The Manchus of today were known as the Eastern Barbarians during bygone years. Toward the end of the Ming dynasty they repeatedly invaded our border areas and caused great difficulties. Then, taking advantage of the chaotic situation in China, they marched southward and forcibly occupied our country. They compelled all Chinese to become their slaves, and those who did not wish to subjugate themselves were slaughtered, numbering millions. In fact, we Chinese have not had a country for the past two hundred and sixty years. Now that the day has finally arrived when the brutal and evil rule by the Manchus must come to an end, we do not expect much resistance when our righteous army begins to move. We shall quickly overthrow the Manchu government so as to restore the sovereignty of China to the Chinese. All the soldiers on the Manchu side, whether they are Manchus or Chinese, will be pardoned despite their past crimes if they express repentance and surrender. If they choose to resist the people's army, they will be killed without mercy. The same can be also said about the Chinese who have collaborated with the Manchu government as traitors.

2. ***Restoration of China to the Chinese:*** China belongs to the Chinese who have the right to govern themselves. After the Manchus are expelled from China, we will have a national government of our own.

3. ***Establishment of a Republic:*** Since one of the principles of our revolution is equality, we intend to establish a republic when we succeed in overthrowing the Manchu regime. In a republic all citizens will have the right to participate in the government, the president of the republic will be elected by the people, and the parliament will have deputies elected by and responsible to their respective constituents. A constitution of the Chinese Republic will then be formulated, to be observed by all Chinese. Anyone who entertains the thought of becoming an emperor will be crushed without mercy.

4. ***Equalization of Landownership:*** The social and economic structure of China must be so reconstructed that the fruits of labor will be shared by all Chinese on an equal basis. Every tract of land in China much be assessed to determine its fair value in monetary terms, and this value belongs, of course, to the landowner. Any added value, which results from social progress after the revolution, will, however, belong to the nation as a whole and must be shared by all Chinese. The ultimate goal of a responsible society is the guarantee of a satisfactory livelihood for all of its members. . . .

To attain the four goals as outlined above, we propose a procedure of three stages . . . : During the first stage the Military Government, in cooperation with the people, will eradicate all the abuses of the past; with the arrival of the second stage, the Military Government will hand over local administration to the people while reserving for itself the right of jurisdiction over all matters that concern the nation as a whole; during the third or final stage, the Military Government will cease to exist and all governmental power will be invested in organs as prescribed in a national constitution. This orderly procedure is necessary because our people need time to acquaint themselves with the idea of liberty and equality. Liberty and equality are the basis on which the Republic of China rests.

Compare and Contrast:

- What were the four goals of Sun Yat-sen? Why did he insist on a republican form of government?

- What were the three stages whereby the goals of the revolution would be attained? Compare this process with the purposes of the Communist revolution as advocated by Karl Marx in Chapter 4 on pp. 125–129. How were they similar and different? Was Sun Yat-sen a Marxist?

The Abdication Decree (1912)

LONG YU

In the first decade of the twentieth century, Sun's greatest opposition came from those who were committed to reform, but thought that this could be attained without a change of government. By 1911, however, even these reformers knew that the Manchus had to go. An uprising in October paved the way for the establishment of a republic. The formal abdication notice, signed by the empress dowager, Long Yu, on behalf of the 6-year-old emperor, Pu Yi (1906–1967), came on February 12, 1912. Sun's new Nationalist Party (Guomintang) won the elections in 1913, but the republic faced decades of turmoil as rival warlord armies continued to tear China apart. When Sun died in 1925, his successor as head of the Guomindang, Jiang Jieshi (Chiang Kai-shek), would have to face a new rival: Mao Zedong and his Communist faction.

It is clear that the minds of the majority of the people are favorable to the establishment of a republican form of government. . . . The universal desire clearly expresses the will of Heaven, and it is not for us to oppose the desire and incur the disapproval of the millions of the People merely for the sake of the privileges and powers of a single House. It is right that this general situation should be considered and due deference given to the opinion of the People. I, the Empress Dowager, therefore, together with the Emperor, hereby hand over the sovereignty to be the possession of the whole people, and declare that the constitution shall henceforth be Republican, in order to satisfy the demands of those within the confines of the nation, hating disorder and desiring peace, and anxious to follow the teaching of the sages, according to which the country is the possession of the People.

Consider This:

- Why did the last emperor, Pu Yi, abdicate? Why was it essential that the Qing dynasty come to an end?

"The Abdication Decree" is from Harley Farnsworth MacNair, *Modern Chinese History: Selected Readings* (Shanghai: The Commercial Press, 1927), p. 722.

Part III

THE AGE OF ANXIETY
(1900–1945)

7

Democracy and Dictatorship: The Western World in Crisis (1914-1939)

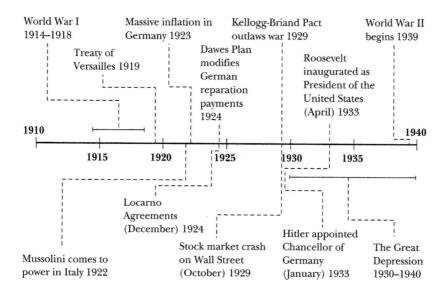

World War I 1914–1918

Treaty of Versailles 1919

Massive inflation in Germany 1923

Dawes Plan modifies German reparation payments 1924

Kellogg-Briand Pact outlaws war 1929

Roosevelt inaugurated as President of the United States (April) 1933

World War II begins 1939

1910   1915   1920   1925   1930   1935   1940

Locarno Agreements (December) 1924

Mussolini comes to power in Italy 1922

Stock market crash on Wall Street (October) 1929

Hitler appointed Chancellor of Germany (January) 1933

The Great Depression 1930–1940

CHAPTER THEMES

- *Systems of Government:* What is fascism, and why was it so popular in the 1920s and 1930s? Why did democracy fail in Germany and Italy? Why does fascism seem to strike a responsive chord in human nature? What is totalitarianism, and how did Hitler's control over Germany differ from Stalin's control over the Soviet Union? Is freedom most importantly a thing of the mind? If the institutions of government are controlled, yet appear to be free, and if you feel that you are free, are you free?

- *Revolution:* Is it legitimate to speak of a fascist revolution in Italy and Germany? Mussolini and Hitler came to power legally. How did their revolutions differ from Napoleon's revolution in France, Lenin's revolution in Russia, or even Roosevelt's New Deal in the United States?

- *Propaganda:* What propaganda techniques and themes were used by European governments to establish a martial spirit among soldiers during World War I? Did soldiers and diplomats actually believe that this was the "war to end all wars"? How were the Nazis aided in their rise to power by creating belief in their cause? What elements of their propaganda appealed to most Germans?

- *Beliefs and Spirituality:* The twentieth century has been described as a "century of holocaust" wherein the state has dominated the individual and produced an ethical vacuum. Some have asserted that technology has created an impersonal world devoid of spiritual commitment. Do you agree? Is God dead?

- *Historical Change and Transition:* What impact did new military technology such as the machine gun, tank, airplane, and poisonous gas have on the Great War? Did World War I, World War II, and the Cold War encompass a transitional period between an "old world" where personal valor and courage were esteemed and a "new world" of impersonal, abstract war where the stakes were higher and the destruction of humanity a distinct possibility? Do technological advancements make war more destructive or more antiseptic, and therefore more acceptable?

- *The Big Picture:* Why has World War I been viewed as the central event in the birth of the modern era? Why did Europe lose an entire generation of men during the Great War? What did they die for? Did the peace settlements at the end of World War I make World War II inevitable? In what ways had society, literature, and politics been altered by the Great War and the Russian Revolution? Were Hitler, Mussolini, and Stalin created by the post-war chaos, or did they create the conditions of their own success?

SECTION I: THE BIRTH OF THE MODERN ERA

After the defeat of Napoleon at the Battle of Waterloo in 1815, it was decided by the victors at the Congress of Vienna that Europe had to be governed by a policy of deterrence that resisted dominance by any one country. Nations required comparable strength in order to maintain the balance of power and thus preserve the peace. Great Britain led the way and applied this policy successfully throughout the nineteenth century. During this time, however, Europe was changing. The Industrial Revolution had increased the demand for trade, and various countries sought markets in Africa and the East, establishing hegemony over a region by military force. Imperialism and competition abroad affected the sense of security and the balance of power that were crucial to the preservation of peace at home. In addition, new factors were being introduced that further threatened to disrupt the balance.

The first serious threat to the *Pax Britannica* of the nineteenth century came from the expansion of industry and the accompanying scientific progress. In the first decade of the twentieth century, new weapons were being developed, as were more rapid forms of communication and transportation, including the telegraph, the automobile, the railway, and the steamship. These technological advancements presented new possibilities for highly mobilized warfare that could be better coordinated and managed.

The second serious threat to the balance of European power in the late nineteenth century was Germany. By 1870, the Prussians had unified north and west Germany through a policy of "blood and iron." The various regions of Germany had always been disunited, defying such masters as the Romans, Charlemagne, the Holy Roman Emperors, and Napoleon. But Kaiser Wilhelm I of Prussia (1797–1888), together with his master statesman Otto von Bismarck (1815–1898) and his general Count Helmut von Moltke, made highly effective use of the military capabilities of a thoroughly disciplined and well-supported army. To achieve unification, Prussia had beaten and humiliated the French in 1870 and succeeded in forging a unified German Reich. The balance of power had been upset and the lesson was clear: No nation in Europe could feel secure without training all of its young men for war, establishing a system of reserves, and creating a general staff that would prepare plans for potential wars and oversee a scheme for mobilization.

The concept of mobilization is very important in understanding why Europe and the world went to war. By 1914, every continental power had a complex plan and timetable for mobilizing against the most likely opponent or combination of enemies. When a country mobilized for war, its reserve troops were called to active duty, placed in the field, and supported with necessary rations, equipment, and armament. Timing was essential. Full mobilization took weeks, and it was important to get the process started before your enemy was ready to commit to such a policy. Hence the beginning of hostilities came when the various chiefs of state were convinced that military "necessity" required a mobilization order and that further delay would spell defeat by allowing the opponent to gain a military advantage that could not be overcome. Since mobilization involved a radical shift of the economy to maximum production and since troop movements could be detected by other nations within hours, the mobilization order could not be rescinded without the prospect of diplomatic and economic disaster. William H. McNeill, in *The Rise of the West*, notes that "the first weeks of World War I presented the amazing spectacle of vast human machines operating in a truly inhuman fashion and moving at least approximately according to predetermined and irreversible plans. The millions of persons composing the rival machines behaved almost as though they had lost individual will and intelligence." The "predetermined and irreversible" plans were centered on a military theory by Karl von Clausewitz that was accepted by all the general staffs of Europe: A swift and decisive battle that led to the initial destruction of the enemy's forces would achieve ultimate success. None planned for a long war—three or four months at most.

Thus, the nations of Europe were powderkegs waiting to go off when in June 1914 the heir to the Austro-Hungarian Empire, the Archduke Franz Ferdinand, was assassinated at Sarajevo. The diplomats talked and then the armies mobilized one by one. The "guns of August" soon enveloped Europe in a war that was to last not four months but four years. Over 8.5 million people were killed, with a total casualty count of over 37.5 million.

This section seeks to evaluate the impact and legacy that World War I has had on the twentieth century. This was war on a world scale, involving hostilities in Africa and the Balkans, as well as an American presence. And it was war on some of the cruelest terms. Rules were changing. There were no longer strict orders to exempt the civilian population from harm. Nor were there moral constraints on the use of submarines, machine guns, and poisonous gas; all became permanent fixtures. The Great War stands unequaled in terms of blood sacrificed for miserable accomplishment. To die for a "victory" of a hundred yards of land needed justification, which was rarely forthcoming. The questions are disturbing and perhaps unanswerable: Why did commanders send their men repeatedly "over the top" of the trenches, across "no man's land," and into the bloody rain of machine gun fire? Why was this slaughter of human life condoned by the diplomats and even the soldiers themselves? Why did Europe lose an entire generation of men?

As we look back on the twentieth century, our perspective is clearly focused at the midpoint, when the threat of fascism and all the attendant horrors of World War II seemed to be the defining moments of an age of anxiety. And yet, many historians believe that our modern world was fashioned at the outset of the century in the trenches of Europe, at the confluence of nineteenth century arrogance and twentieth century technology.

Europe in 1914 was on the brink of "becoming." In a sense, the transition had been foreshadowed in one of the great cultural moments of the period. In 1913, the young Russian composer Igor Stravinsky premiered his new ballet to elite society in Paris. The "Rite of Spring" was a story of primal ritual, of sacrifice to the earth and the ceremonial renewal of life. The irregular rhythms, dissonant harmonies, and blatant sexuality shocked the crowd, which rioted in response.

The ritual of primal sacrifice would be played out during the next four years as the great European empires devoured each other and the earth claimed so many human lives. When the war ended in 1918, the world of the nineteenth century had been forever altered. The thin veneer of civilization had been shattered and the forsaken populace had difficulty defining what had happened and why. Europe would be led out of this abyss of disillusionment and despair by those promising order and respect: Benito Mussolini and Adolf Hitler.

"They Shall Not Pass": The Great War (1914–1918)

The next dreadful thing to a battle lost is a battle won.

—*Arthur Wellesley, Duke of Wellington*

Only a general who was a barbarian would send his men to certain death against the concentrated power of my new gun.

—*Hiram Maxim (inventor of the machine gun)*

Diplomats are just as essential to starting a war as soldiers are for finishing it. . . . You take diplomacy out of war and the whole thing would fall flat in a week.

—*Will Rogers*

The rain drives on, the stinking mud becomes evilly yellow, the shell holes fill up with green-white water, the roads and tracks are covered in inches of slime, the black, dying trees ooze and sweat and the shells never cease. They alone plunge overhead tearing away the rotting tree stumps. . . . It is unspeakable, Godless, hopeless.

—*Paul Walsh*

What's the use of worrying, it never was worthwhile/So, pack up your troubles in your old kit bag and smile, smile, smile. . . .

—*World War I song*

For decades prior to 1914, Europe had been diplomatically divided into two rival camps. The Triple Alliance was formed in 1882 among Germany, Italy, and Austria-Hungary. In 1907, the Triple Entente was established among Great Britain, France, and Russia. Both organizations were pledged by treaty to support their respective allies militarily should their mutual interests or existence be threatened. Thus, the European world was shocked by the assassination of the Austrian Archduke Franz Ferdinand. Poised on the brink of crisis, each nation took stock of its diplomatic commitments, its military arsenal, and its long-range goals. Such a slap in the face of the powerful Austro-Hungarian empire by Serbian terrorists had wide-ranging implications. Response had to be quick in order to preserve the honor and integrity of the throne and to assure that such action would not invite further insolence, which could lead to outright revolt. There were other factors to consider as well. How would Russia react to a severe stand against the Serbs? Russia, after all, was a Slavic nation and was promoting a policy that advocated the independence and cultural integrity of Balkan Slavs.

The Austrians sought German support in their plans to punish Serbia for the assassination of the Austrian heir. Germany would be an important ally in countering the potential hostility of Russia. On July 6, 1914, the German kaiser, Wilhelm II, sent a "blank check" telegram that guaranteed German support for whatever punishment Austria decided to inflict upon Serbia. Austria thereupon declared war and started mobilizing her military forces. One by one, the European powers declared war on each other, constrained by the dictates of their alliance systems and by the necessity to obtain an advantage in mobilizing their military forces as quickly as possible.

The light of reason gave way to military timetables, national pride, and the celebration of war. Certain of their military superiority, the Germans expected a short conflict and looked forward to being home "before the leaves fall." As Kaiser Wilhelm drew his sword, European confidence, even arrogance, was about to meet the full fury of modern, mechanized warfare. A door had closed and the modern era was born amid the tragedy of the Great War.

The Horror of Battle

The German strategy in August 1914 had been planned long in advance by Count Alfred von Schlieffen, German chief of staff until 1905. The essence of the strategy was to sweep through Belgium and overwhelm French defenses in one swift onslaught; about 90 percent of the German army would be used for that purpose, while the remaining fraction, together with the Austrians, would hold off Russia. Once France was defeated, Germany and Austria-Hungary could concentrate their forces against the Russian army. Quite unexpectedly, however, the Belgians put up a gallant resistance, and the German attack was stalled long enough to upset the timetable. The British were able to land troops in Europe, and the war degenerated into a struggle for position that was characterized by trench warfare. New weapons such as the machine gun, the tank, and barbed wire eliminated thousands of men as attacks failed and comrades were left to die in the region between the trenches called "no man's land."

The following accounts of soldiers testify to the horrors of ceaseless shelling and destruction. The Battle of Verdun in 1916 raged for ten months, resulting in a combined total of about one million casualties. The Battle of the Somme lasted five months, with well over one million killed or wounded. Very little ground or tactical advantage was gained. Battle cries such as the French "They Shall Not Pass" were indicative of the stalemated defensive war.

This landscape of devastation in Belgium gives testimony to the mindless destruction that was such a part of the Great War. *(Imperial War Museum, London)*

The Battle of the Somme (July–November 1916)

The German Command was not thinking much about the human suffering of its troops. It was thinking, necessarily, of the next defensive line upon which they would have to fall back if the pressure of the British offensive could be maintained. . . . It was getting nervous. Owing to the enormous efforts made in the Verdun offensive the supplies of ammunition were not adequate to the enormous demand.

The German gunners were trying to compete with the British in continuity of bombardments and the shells were running short. Guns were wearing out under this incessant strain, and it was difficult to replace them. General von Gallwitz received reports of "an alarmingly large number of bursts in the bore, particularly in the field guns."

"The Battle of the Somme" is from Charles F. Horne, ed., *Source Records of the Great War*, vol. 4 (Indianapolis, IN: The American Legion, 1931), pp. 248–251. Reprinted by permission of The American Legion.

In all the letters written during those weeks of fighting and captured by us from dead or living men there is one great cry of agony and horror.

"I stood on the brink of the most terrible days of my life," wrote one of them. "They were those of the battle of the Somme. It began with a night attack on August 13th–14th. The attack lasted till the evening of the 18th, when the English wrote on our bodies in letters of blood: 'It is all over with you.' A handful of the half-mad, wretched creatures, worn out in body and mind, were all that was left of a whole battalion. We were that handful."

In many letters this phrase was used. The Somme was called the "Bath of Blood" by the German troops who waded across its shell-craters,

The French soldier defending the stronghold of Verdun, where the German high command tried "to bleed the French army white" during ten months of fighting. *(Imperial War Museum, London)*

and in the ditches which were heaped with their dead. But what I have described is only the beginning of the battle, and the bath was to be filled deeper in the months that followed.

It was in no cheerful mood that men went away to the Somme battlefields. Those battalions of gray-clad men entrained without any of the old enthusiasm with which they had gone to earlier battles. Their gloom was noticed by the officers.

"Sing, you sheep's heads, sing!" they shouted.

They were compelled to sing, by order.

"In the afternoon," wrote a man of the 18th Reserve Division, "we had to go out again: we were to learn to sing. The greater part did not join in, and the song went feebly. Then we had to march round in a circle, and sing, and that went no better."

"After that we had an hour off, and on the way back to billets we were to sing 'Deutschland über Alles,' but this broke down completely. One never hears songs of the Fatherland any more."

They were silent, grave-eyed men who marched through the streets of French and Belgian towns to be entrained for the Somme front, for they had forebodings of the fate before them. Yet none of their forebodings were equal in intensity of fear to the frightful reality into which they were flung.

A German War Letter: "One Blood-Soaked, Corpse-Strewn Field"

RICHARD SCHMIEDER, Student of Philosophy, Leipzig
Born January 24th, 1888.
Killed July 14th, 1916, near Bethenville.
In the Trenches near Vaudesincourt, March 13th, 1915

Anybody who, like myself, has been through the awful days near Penthy since the 6th of February, will agree with me that a more appalling

"A German War Letter" is from *German Students' War Letters,* translated and arranged from the original edition of Dr. Philipp Witkop by A. F. Wedd (New York: E. P. Dutton, 1929), pp. 208–209. Reprinted by permission of Methuen and Company.

struggle could not be imagined. It has been a case of soldier against soldier, equally matched and both mad with hate and anger, fighting for days on end over a single square of ground, till the whole tract of country is one blood-soaked, corpse-strewn field. . . .

On February 27th, tired out and utterly exhausted in body and mind, we were suddenly called up to reinforce the VIIIth Reserve Corps, had to reoccupy our old position at Ripont, and were immediately attacked by the French with extraordinary strength and violence. It was a gigantic murder, by means of bullets, shells, axes, and bombs, and there was such a thundering, crashing, bellowing and screaming as might have heralded the Day of Judgment.

In three days, on a front of about 200 yards, we lost 909 men, and the enemy casualties must have amounted to thousands. The blue French cloth mingled with the German grey upon the ground, and in some places the bodies were piled so high that one could take cover from shell-fire behind them. The noise was so terrific that orders had to be shouted by each man into the ear of the next. And whenever there was a momentary lull in the tumult of battle and the groans of the wounded, one heard, high up in the blue sky, the joyful song of birds! Birds singing just as they do at home in spring-time! It was enough to tear the heart out of one's body!

Don't ask about the fate of the wounded! Anybody who was incapable of walking to the doctor had to die a miserable death; some lingered in agony for hours, some for days, and even for a week. And the combatants stormed regardlessly to and fro over them: "I can't give you a hand,— You're for the Promised Land,—My Comrade good and true." A dog, dying in the poorest hovel at home, is enviable in comparison.

There are moments when even the bravest soldier is so utterly sick of the whole thing that he could cry like a child. When I heard the birds singing at Ripont, I could have crushed the whole world to death in my wrath and fury. If only those gentlemen—Grey, Asquith, and Poincaré—could be transported to this spot, instead of the war lasting ten years, there would be peace tomorrow!

Dulce et Decorum Est

WILFRED OWEN

Wilfred Owen, a poet and soldier who was killed a week before the war ended, wrote that the "Lie" of the conflict lay in the belief that it was honorable and proper to give your life for the benefit of your country (Dulce et decorum est pro patria mori). Indeed, the war seemed to many people an absurd and tragic event. Why were they fighting? Why did old men send young men off to die "for their country"? How could poisonous gas, which burned out the lungs and led to a painfully slow death, be justified—or submarines, which destroyed under cover, thus eliminating a "fair fight"? The rules of war had changed. Disillusionment was evident in mutinies and in the poetry written in the trenches and in the letters sent home. It was not enough to be complimented by your general for victory in battle.

Bent double, like old beggars under
    sacks,
Knocked-kneed, coughing like hags, we
    cursed through sludge,
Till on the haunting flares we turned our
    backs
And towards our distant rest began to
    trudge.
Men marched asleep. Many had lost their
    boots
But limped on, blood-shod. All went lame;
    all blind;
Drunk with fatigue; deaf even to the
    hoots
Of tired, outstripped Five-Nines that
    dropped behind.
Gas! Gas! Quick Boys!—An ecstasy of
    fumbling,
Fitting the clumsy helmets just in time;
But someone still was yelling out and
    stumbling
And flound'ring like a man in fire or
    lime. . . .
Dim, through the misty panes and thick
    green light,

As under a green sea, I saw him
    drowning.
In all my dreams, before my helpless
    sight,
He plunges at me, guttering, choking,
    drowning.
If in some smothering dreams you too
    could pace
Behind the wagon that we flung him in,
And watch the white eyes writhing in his
    face,
His hanging face, like a devil's sick of
    sin;
If you could hear, at every jolt, the blood
Come gargling from the froth-corrupted
    lungs,
Obscene as cancer, bitter as the cud
Of vile, incurable sores on innocent
    tongues,—
My friend, you would not tell with such
    high zest
To children ardent for some desperate
    glory,
The old Lie: Dulce et decorum est
Pro patria mori.

"This Is the Way the World Ends": The Aftermath of War

On November 9, 1918, the German kaiser abdicated his throne and fled the country. The armistice, which ended the war, was signed on November 11. The European world of 1914 had been shattered, people were changed, and the foremost question was, how to begin again?

The first selection is from the diary of Anna Eisenmenger, an Austrian whose son returned home after the armistice a changed man. The second piece is an excerpt from a poem by T. S. Eliot. Where is the bluster and confidence that gave rise to the Great War?

A German Soldier Returns Home: "A Complete Stranger"

ANNA EISENMENGER

Karl looked very ill. He had no underlinen or socks. His uniform was dirty and in rags. "Mother, I am famished!" he said, and walking straight into the kitchen without waiting for me to bring him something he began to devour our rations of bread and jam. "Forgive me, Mother, but we have got into the habit of taking what we can find." He only greeted us very casually and did not notice until much later that Erni, who had come in to welcome him on Liesbeth's arm, was wounded. "Hullo! So it's caught you too!" and then, still hurriedly chewing and swallowing: "Well, just wait! We'll pay them out yet, the war profiteers and parasites. We've grown wiser out there in the trenches, far wiser than we were. Everything must be changed, utterly changed."

I got ready the bath and clean underlinen. After his bath Karl went straight to bed, but he was too excited to sleep, although it was almost 11 o'clock at night. He telephoned to Edith, and then he made us all come to his bedside, for he wanted to tell us about himself. He told us that . . . the Italians had gone on attacking in spite of the Armistice. For another whole day they had fired on our retreating columns in the Fellathal and had captured several divisions. That, however, was the only victory they had won. It was contemptible, but war made every one base and contemptible. He had become so too. . . . After the proclamation of the Armistice all military discipline went to pieces. Everyone was intent only on getting home and made for home by the way that

seemed to him quickest and surest. The men trampled down whatever stood in their way, even if the obstacle were their own officers. Woe to the officers who were unpopular with their men. . . . In the next war there would be no one foolish enough to risk his life, they would see to that. . . . Karl was evidently in a nervous, over-excited state, but he went on talking, and only after I had entreated him several times did he consent to try to get to sleep.

"We are all tired, Karl, and it is already past midnight. . . ."

"Do you know, Mother, how I feel here? In a clean bed, washed and fed? As if I were in heaven. . . . Oh no, there is no heaven so beautiful. . . . As if I were in a beautiful dream . . . and in that dream I shall try to find sleep."

We left Karl's room in order to go to bed ourselves. As I was helping Erni undress, he said: "Mother, Karl seems to me like a complete stranger."

Although I was nervously and physically exhausted, sleep refused to close my eyelids. For a long, long time I lay awake, agitated by the horrors of the War. I found myself marvelling that civilised human beings could live through all the brutalities which war entailed for themselves and others without going utterly to pieces. . . .

The Hollow Men (1925)

A Penny for the Old Guy

T. S. ELIOT

We are the hollow men
We are the stuffed men
Leaning together

Headpiece filled with straw. Alas!
Our dried voices, when
We whisper together
Are quiet and meaningless
As wind in dry grass
Or rats' feet over broken glass
In our dry cellar
Shape without form, shade without colour,
Paralysed force, gesture without motion;
Those who have crossed
With direct eyes, to death's other
   Kingdom
Remember us—if at all—not as lost

Violent souls, but only
As the hollow men
The stuffed men.

●●●

For Thine is
Life is
For Thine is the
This is the way the world ends
This is the way the world ends
This is the way the world ends
Not with a bang but a whimper.

THE RUSSIAN REVOLUTION

The essence of Bolshevism, the essence of Soviet power, lies in exposing the fraud and hypocrisy of bourgeois democracy, in abolishing the private ownership of the land, the factories, and in concentrating all political power in the hands of the toilers and the exploited masses.

—*V. I. Lenin*

"This is the way the world ends / Not with a bang but a whimper."—T. S. Eliot. *(Library of Congress)*

Even if for every hundred correct things we did, we committed ten thousand mistakes, our revolution would still be—and it will be in the judgment of history—great and invincible; for this is the first time that the working people are themselves building a new life.

—*V. I. Lenin*

The Russian dictatorship of the proletariat has made a farce of the whole Marxist vision: developing a powerful, privileged ruling class to prepare for a classless society, setting up the most despotic state in history so that the state may wither away, establishing by force a colonial empire to combat imperialism and unite the workers of the world.

—*Herbert J. Muller*

A proletarian revolution is never proletarian.

—*Will Durant*

The Bolshevik Seizure of Power (November–December 1917)

World War I proved especially disastrous for Russia. The army suffered tremendous losses against a German onslaught of superior force and preparation. Misery, famine, and disease descended on the Russian people, and thousands were dislocated and wandered aimlessly as refugees. Tsar Nicholas II feared a general uprising and finally decided to abdicate his throne in March 1917.

A temporary body called the Provisional Government was installed to maintain stability in the country until a representative Constituent Assembly could be elected by the Russian people. The Petrograd Soviet, an elected council of workers and soldiers, immediately threatened the authority of the Provisional Government. The Marxist revolutionary, Vladimir Ulyanov, better known as Lenin (1870–1924), arrived from Switzerland to reassert his leadership of the Bolshevik party and in November 1917, persuaded his faction that the time was ripe for a coup. The first selection is Lenin's speech after his successful storming of the tsar's Winter Palace in Petrograd. Note the critical editorial from the newspaper Izvestia *on November 8. It was the last before the Bolsheviks censored the press. Lenin's seizure of power also included the establishment of a secret police (*Cheka*), an institution that had been used (in another form) by the autocratic tsar to eliminate opposition.*

Speech after the Overthrow of the Provisional Government

V. I. LENIN

Comrades, the workmen's and peasant's revolution, the need of which the Bolsheviks have emphasized many times, has come to pass.

"Speech after the Overthrow of the Provisional Government" is from Frank A. Golder, ed., *Documents of Russian History (1914–1917)*, trans. Emanuel Aronsberg (New York: The Century Company, 1927), pp. 618–619.

What is the significance of this revolution? Its significance is, in the first place, that we shall have a soviet government, without the participation of bourgeoisie of any kind. The oppressed masses will of themselves form a government. The old state machinery will be smashed into bits and in its place will be created a new machinery of government by the soviet organizations. From now on there is a new page in the history of Russia, and the present, third Russian revolution shall in its final result lead to the victory of Socialism.

One of our immediate tasks is to put an end to the war at once. But in order to end the war, which is closely bound up with the present capitalistic system, it is necessary to overthrow capitalism itself. In this work we shall have the aid of the world labor movement, which has already begun to develop in Italy, England, and Germany.

A just and immediate offer of peace by us to the international democracy will find everywhere a warm response among the international proletariat masses. In order to secure the confidence of the proletariat, it is necessary to publish at once all secret treaties.

In the interior of Russia a very large part of the peasantry has said: Enough playing with the capitalists; we will go with the workers. We shall secure the confidence of the peasants by one decree, which will wipe out the private property of the landowners. The peasants will understand that their only salvation is in union with the workers.

We will establish a real labor control on production.

We have now learned to work together in a friendly manner, as is evident from this revolution. We have the force of mass organization which has conquered all and which will lead the proletariat to world revolution.

We should now occupy ourselves in Russia in building up a proletarian socialist state.

Long live the world-wide socialistic revolution!

"Little Good Is to Be Expected" (November 8, 1917)

IZVESTIA

Yesterday we said that the Bolshevik uprising is a made adventure and today, when their attempt is crowned with success, we are of the same mind. We repeat: that which is before us is not a transfer of power to the Soviets, but a seizure of power by one party—the Bolsheviks. Yesterday we said that a successful attempt meant the breaking up of the greatest of the revolution—the Constituent Assembly. Today we add that it means, also, the breaking up of the Congress of Soviets, and perhaps the whole soviet organization. They can call themselves what they please; the fact remains that the Bolsheviks alone took part in the uprising. All the other socialistic and democratic parties protest against it.

How the situation may develop we do not know, but little good is to be expected. We are quite confident that the Bolsheviks cannot organize a state government. As yesterday, so today, we repeat that what is happening will react worst of all on the question of peace.

Censorship of the Press (November 9, 1917)

V. I. LENIN

In the trying critical period of the revolution and the days that immediately followed it the Provisional Revolutionary Committee was compelled to take a number of measures against the counter-revolutionary press of different shades.

Immediately outcries were heard from all sides that the new, socialist power had violated a fundamental principle of its programme by encroaching upon the freedom of the press.

The Workers' and Peasants' Government calls the attention of the population to the fact that what this liberal facade actually conceals is freedom for the propertied classes, having taken hold of the lion's share of the entire press, to poison, unhindered, the minds and obscure the consciousness of the masses.

"'Little Good Is to Be Expected'" is from Frank A. Golder, ed., *Documents of Russian History (1914–1917)*, trans. Emanuel Aronsberg (New York: The Century Company, 1927), p. 619.

"Censorship of the Press" is from Martin McCauley, ed., *The Russian Revolution and the Soviet State* (New York: Barnes & Noble, 1975), pp. 190–191. Permission granted by Barnes & Noble Books, Totowa, New Jersey.

Every one knows that the bourgeois press is one of the most powerful weapons of the bourgeoisie. Especially at the crucial moment when the new power, the power of workers and peasants, is only affirming itself, it was impossible to leave this weapon wholly in the hands of the enemy, for in such moments it is no less dangerous than bombs and machine-guns. That is why temporary extraordinary measures were taken to stem the torrent of filth and slander in which the yellow and green press would be only too glad to drown the recent victory of the people.

As soon as the new order becomes consolidated, all administrative pressure on the press will be terminated and it will be granted complete freedom within the bounds of legal responsibility, in keeping with a law that will be broadest and most progressive in this respect.

However, being aware that a restriction of the press, even at critical moments, is permissible only within the limits of what is absolutely necessary, the Council of People's Commissars resolves:

General Provisions on the Press

1. Only those publications can be suppressed which (1) call for open resistance or insubordination to the Workers' and Peasants' Government; (2) sow sedition through demonstrably slanderous distortion of facts; (3) instigate actions of an obviously criminal, i.e. criminally punishable, nature.
2. Publications can be proscribed, temporarily or permanently, only by decision of the Council of People's Commissars.
3. The present ordinance is of a temporary nature and will be repealed by a special decree as soon as normal conditions of social life set in.

Chairman of the Council of People's Commissars, VLADIMIR ULYANOV (LENIN)

Establishment of the Secret Police (December 20, 1917)

V. I. LENIN

The Commission is to be called the All-Russian Extraordinary Commission for the Struggle with Counter-Revolution and Sabotage and is to be attached to the Council of People's Commissars.

The duties of the Commission are to be as follows:

1. To investigate and nullify all acts of counter-revolution and sabotage throughout Russia, irrespective of origin.
2. To bring before the Revolutionary Tribunal all counter-revolutionaries and saboteurs and to work out measures to combat them.
3. The Commission is to conduct the preliminary investigation only, sufficient to suppress (the counter-revolutionary act). The Commission is to be divided into sections: (1) the information (section) (2) the organization section (in charge of organizing the struggle with counter-revolution throughout Russia) with branches, and (3) the fighting section.

The Commission shall be set up finally tomorrow. Then the fighting section of the All-Russian Commission shall start its activities. The Commission shall keep an eye on the press, saboteurs, right Socialist Revolutionaries and strikers. Measures to be taken are confiscation, imprisonment, confiscation of cards, publication of the names of the enemies of the people, etc.

Chairman of the Council of People's Commissars
V. ULYANOV (LENIN)

"Establishment of the Secret Police" is from Martin McCauley, ed., *The Russian Revolution and the Soviet State* (New York: Barnes & Noble, 1975), pp. 181–182. Permission granted by Barnes & Noble Books, Totowa, New Jersey.

The Development of the Totalitarian State (1930–1940)

The Bolsheviks were thrust into a difficult situation on achieving power. Lenin was true to his slogan "Peace, Bread, and Land," and took Russia out of the war, negotiating a peace with Germany (Brest-Litovsk) that conceded much Russian territory. Lenin then applied his energies to quelling a civil war that pitted his Red Army (led by Leon Trotsky) against the "White" forces, which consisted of supporters of the tsar or of other anti-Bolshevik elements. The tsar's execution in 1918 removed a possible impediment to the progress of the revolution. The civil war ended in 1921, and Lenin spent the next three years until his death consolidating his gains and preparing for Russia's transition from a capitalist to a communist state.

In 1922, when Lenin's stroke removed him from active leadership of the Communist party, a struggle broke out among Lenin's chief lieutenants for control of the party. Leon Trotsky appeared to be the most logical choice, for he had been, together with Lenin, the primary ideological force behind the Russian Revolution and had proved his organizational ability during the Civil War of 1918 by managing the Red Army. He was outmaneuvered, however, by Joseph Stalin, who in his capacity as general secretary of the Communist party was in a position to control the delegates to the party congress. Stalin's control over the administrative levers of the party allowed him to eliminate all rivals. Trotsky was dismissed from the party, exiled to Siberia in 1928, and deported to Turkey a year later. He was eventually murdered in Mexico at the hands of Stalin's assassins in 1940.

After establishing his dictatorship over the Communist party, Stalin moved to consolidate his control over all aspects of Soviet society. Stalin's practical mind was in direct contrast to the ideologue Trotsky. Stalin rejected Trotsky's emphasis on immediate world revolution and embarked on the rapid, large-scale industrialization of the Soviet Union. He sought to create "socialism in one country" and understood that Lenin's revolution had taken place in at best an imperfectly industrialized country, one that would have difficulty competing with the productive capacity of Western capitalism. In the mid-1920s, Stalin decided to continue the New Economic Policy (NEP) that Lenin had developed to establish rudimentary capitalism and increase production among shop workers and peasants. But by 1928, he had taken steps to replace this with an economy planned and directed by the state. In 1928, the first Five-Year Plan was introduced for "expansion of the national economy." The plan prioritized heavy industry and the construction of steel mills, dams for the production of hydraulic electricity, and plants for the production of automobiles and chemicals.

The goals of this "command economy" were impressive: Steel production was to go from 4.2 million tons to 10 million tons; coal from 35 million to 150 million tons, electric power from 5 million to 22 million kilowatt-hours. In the following speech, Stalin explains the importance of industrialization.

Industrialization: "Either Perish or Overtake Capitalistic Countries" (1931)

JOSEPH STALIN

Science, technical experience, knowledge, are all things that can be acquired. We may not have them today, but tomorrow we will. The main

"Industrialization: 'Either Perish or Overtake Capitalistic Countries'" is from Joseph Stalin, *Problems of Leninism* (Moscow: Foreign Languages Publishing House, 1953), pp. 455–456.

thing is to have the passionate Bolshevik desire to master technique, to master the science of production. Everything can be achieved, everything can be overcome, if there is a passionate desire to do so.

It is sometimes asked whether it is not possible to slow down the tempo somewhat, to put a check on the movement. No, comrades, it is not possible! The tempo must not be reduced! On the contrary, we must increase it as much as is within our powers and possibilities. This is dictated to us by our obligations to the workers and peasants of the USSR. This is dictated to us by our obligations to the working class of the whole world. . . . To slacken the tempo would mean falling behind. And those who fall behind get beaten. But we do not want to be beaten. No, we refuse to be beaten! . . .

In the past we had no fatherland, nor could we have one. But now that we have overthrown capitalism and power is in our hands, in the hands of the people, we have a fatherland, and we will defend its independence. Do you want our socialist fatherland to be beaten and to lose its independence? If you do not want this you must put an end to its backwardness in the shortest possible time and develop genuine Bolshevik tempo in building up its socialist system of economy. There is no other way. That is why Lenin said on the eve of the October Revolution: "Either perish, or overtake and outstrip the advanced capitalist countries." We are fifty or a hundred years behind the advanced countries. We must make good this distance in ten years. Either we do it, or we shall be crushed.

Collectivization and the Liquidation of the Kulaks (1929)

JOSEPH STALIN

Collectivized agriculture, wherein all land was owned by the proletariat and worked in common for the benefit of the whole community, had always been considered an integral aspect of communism. Although Karl Marx had little to say about its organization, this was a preeminent problem for Lenin and later Stalin. Lenin had conceived of the peasantry as a rural proletariat of agricultural workers who also belonged to the "working class." All income after expenses and taxes from the collective farm were to be shared based on the total number of workdays performed by each member of the collective. The farmers were also permitted a "private plot" of not more than one acre for use as a garden, and a cow, pigs, and chickens. In the 1920s the government offered special subsidies and favorable tax treatments to join the collective farms, but by 1928 only one peasant in sixty had joined. The first Five-Year Plan called for 17.5 percent of the cultivated land to be organized as collective farms. But there was great resistance, especially from a class of prosperous, middle-class farmers called Kulaks. They had prospered because of their efficiency and expected to reap the benefits of their dedicated labor. Stalin decided to force the issue and declared the Kulaks to be class enemies, as the following account confirms. Communist squads from the cities were sent into the countryside to seize the grain and livestock of the Kulaks. In response, the Kulaks often burned their property in defiance. They were executed by the thousands.

Can Soviet power and the work of socialist construction rest for any length of time on two different foundations: on the most large-scale and concentrated socialist industry, and the most scattered and backward, small-commodity peasant farming? No, they cannot. Sooner or later this would be bound to end in the complete collapse of the whole national economy.

What, then, is the solution? The solution lies in enlarging the agricultural units, in making agriculture capable of accumulation, of expanded reproduction, and in thus transforming the agricultural bases of our national economy. But how are the agricultural units to be enlarged? There are two ways of doing this. There is the *capitalist* way, which is to enlarge the agricultural units by

"Collectivization and the Liquidation of the Kulaks" is from Joseph Stalin, *Problems of Leninism* (Moscow: Foreign Languages Publishing House, 1953), pp. 392–393, 409, 411–412.

introducing capitalism in agriculture—a way which leads to the impoverishment of the peasantry and to the development of capitalist enterprises in agriculture. We reject this way as incompatible with the Soviet economic system.

There is a second way: the *socialist* way, which is to enlarge the agricultural units to introduce collective farms and state farms in agriculture, the way which leads to the amalgamation of the small-peasant farms into large collective farms, employing machinery and scientific methods of farming, and capable of developing further, for such agricultural enterprises can achieve expanded reproduction.

And so, the question stands as follows: either one way or the other, either *back*—to capitalism, or *forward*—to socialism. There is no third way, nor can there be. . . .

What does this mean? It means that we have passed from the policy of *restricting* the exploiting proclivities of the Kulaks to the policy of *eliminating* the Kulaks as a class. This means that we have made, and are still making, one of the decisive turns in our whole policy. . . .

Could we have undertaken such an offensive against the Kulaks five years or three years ago? Could we then have counted on success in such an offensive? No, we could not. That would have been the most dangerous adventurism. . . . Why?

Because we still lacked a wide network of state and collective farms in the rural districts which could be used as strongholds in a determined offensive against the Kulaks. Because at that time we were not yet able to *substitute* for the capitalist production of the Kulaks the socialist production of the collective farms and state farms. . . .

Now we are able to carry on a determined offensive against the Kulaks, to break their resistance, to eliminate them as a class and substitute for their output the output of the collective farms and state farms. No, the Kulaks are being expropriated by the masses of poor and middle peasants themselves, by the masses who are putting solid collectivization into practice. Now, the expropriation of the Kulaks in the regions of solid collectivization is no longer just an administrative measure. Now, the expropriation of the Kulaks is an integral part of the formation and development of the collective farms. Consequently it is now ridiculous and foolish to discourse on the expropriation of the Kulaks. You do not lament the loss of the hair of one who has been beheaded.

There is another question which seems no less ridiculous: whether the Kulaks should be permitted to join the collective farms. Of course not, for they are sworn enemies of the collective-farm movement.

The Purge Trials: "Traitors Must Be Shot Like Dirty Dogs!" (1938)
ANDREI VYSHINSKY

During the First Five-Year Plan, overall living standards in the Soviet Union diminished 35 percent, especially in the countryside. But by pouring nearly 35 percent of the gross national product into new production, the goals of the first plan were more or less accomplished. The Second and Third Five-Year Plans followed, but the Soviet people saw little benefit from their labor and the standard of living remained essentially unchanged. Criticism of Stalin's programs increased, especially among his supporters. The result was to purge or eliminate any opposition in political circles, the military, and the artistic community. Lenin had established the Cheka, or "secret police," to combat "counterrevolution," but Stalin honed this organization into a formidable intelligence unit that specialized in foreign espionage and domestic

"The Purge Trials: 'Traitors Must Be Shot Like Dirty Dogs!'" is from *Report of Court Proceedings: The Case of the Anti-Soviet Bloc of Rights and Trotskyites* (Moscow: People's Commissariat of Justice of the USSR, 1938), English edition, pp. 696–697.

surveillance. Stalin made his secret police the primary instrument of his ruthless purges. They conducted interrogations, tortures, and trials, and expedited the incarceration of dissidents in the Siberian labor camps known as the Gulag.

The climax of the purge trials came in 1938 when several former revolutionaries who had planned the Russian Revolution with Lenin were condemned and executed. These included "Trotskyites" and "Bukharinites," whose opposition was especially troubling. Stalin's victims even included heads of the secret police, who simply vanished one day and were quickly replaced. Stalin thus used terror effectively and maintained his preeminent authority by making sure that there were no entrenched or safe positions in the state. The estimated numbers of his purge victims including Kulaks range from ten to twenty million. Even when compared with Adolf Hitler's imposition of the Holocaust, Stalin was perhaps history's greatest mass murderer.

The following accounts of the purge trials and the Gulag give evidence of the nature of Stalin's dominance.

The Trotskyites and Bukharinites, . . . the leading lights of which are now in the prisoners' dock, is not a political party, nor a political tendency, but a band of felonious criminals, and not simply felonious criminals, but of criminals who have sold themselves to enemy intelligence services, criminals whom even ordinary felons treat as the basest, the lowest, the most contemptible, the most depraved of the depraved. . . .

The investigation established, and I deem it necessary to remind you of this here in its full scope, Comrades Judges, that in 1918, immediately following the October Revolution, . . . Bukharin and his group of so-called "Left Communists," and Trotsky with his group . . . organized a conspiracy against Lenin as the head of the Soviet government.

Bukharin and the other conspirators, as can be seen from the materials of the investigation, aimed at . . . overthrowing the Soviet government, arresting and killing Lenin, Stalin, and Sverdlov [Secretary of the Party from 1917 to 1919], and forming a new government made up of Bukharinites. . . .

It has been proved that this bloc consisted of agents of the intelligence services of several foreign states, it has been proved that the [Trotskyites] regularly engaged in espionage on behalf of these states and supplied their intelligence services with most important state secret material. . . .

It has been proved that the bloc had organized, but fortunately for us had not succeeded

in effecting, a number of terrorist acts against the leaders of our Party and government. . . .

Our whole country, from young to old, is awaiting and demanding one thing: the traitors and spies who were selling our country to the enemy must be shot like dirty dogs! Our people are demanding one thing: crush the accursed reptile!

Time will pass. The graves of the hateful traitors will grow over with weeds and thistle, they will be covered with eternal contempt of honest Soviet citizens, of the entire Soviet people. But over us, over our happy country, our sun will shine with its luminous rays as bright and as joyous as before. Over the road cleared of the last scum and filth of the past, we, our people, with our beloved leader and teacher, the great Stalin, at our head, will march as before onwards and onwards, towards communism!

The Gulag: "Stalin's Sadistic Nature Thirsted for Blood!" (1938)

Certain Trotskyists, including Vladimir Ivanov, Kossior, and Trotsky's son, Sergei Sedov, a modest and likeable youth, who had imprudently refused to follow his parents into exile in 1928,

"The Gulag: 'Stalin's Sadistic Nature Thirsted for Blood!'" is from "Trotskyists at Vorkuta: An Eyewitness Report," *International Socialist Review*, vol. 24, no. 3 (Summer 1963), p. 97.

were taken in a special convoy to Moscow. We can only believe that Stalin was not satisfied simply to hurl them into the tundra; his sadistic nature thirsted not only for blood; he wished first to immeasurably humiliate them and torture them, coercing them into false self-accusations. Ivanov and Kossior disappeared without trace behind the walls of the Lubyanka prison. As for Sergei Sedov, after a "treatment" at the Lubyanka he was "tried" at Sverdlovsk, where he had worked as an engineer at the electric station; according to the newspaper stories, "he recalled having devoted himself to acts of sabotage" and other "crimes," for which he was condemned to be shot. . . .

The whole winter of 1937–38 some prisoners, encamped in barracks at the brickyard, starved and waited for a decision regarding their fate. Finally, in March, three NKVD [Secret Police] officers, with Kashketin at their head, arrived by plane at Vorkuta, coming from Moscow. They came to the brickyard to interrogate the prisoners. Thirty to forty were called each day, superficially questioned five to ten minutes each, rudely insulted, forced to listen to vile name-calling and obscenities. Some were greeted with punches in the face; Lt. Kashketin himself several times beat up one of them, the Old Bolshevik Virap Virapov, a former member of the Central Committee of Armenia. . . .

Two days later, there was a new call, this time of forty names. Once more there was a ration of bread. Some, out of exhaustion, could no longer move; they were promised a ride in a cart. Holding their breath, the prisoners remaining in the barracks heard the grating of the snow under the feet of the departing convoy. For a long time there was no sound; but all on the watch still listened. Nearly an hour passed in this way. Then, again, shots resounded in the tundra; this time, they came from much further away, in the direction of the narrow railway which passed three kilometers from the brickyard. The second "convoy" definitely convinced those remaining behind that they had been irremediably condemned.

The executions in the tundra lasted the whole month of April and part of May. Usually one day out of two, or one day out of three, thirty to forty prisoners were called. It is characteristic to note that each time, some common criminals, repeaters, were included. In order to terrorize the prisoners, the officials, from time to time, made publicly known by means of local radio, the list of those shot. Usually broadcasts began as follows: "For counter-revolutionary agitation, sabotage, brigandage in the camps, refusal to work, attempts to escape, the following have been shot . . . " followed by a list of names of some political prisoners mixed with a group of common criminals.

At the beginning of May, a group of women were shot. . . . At the time of execution of a male prisoner, his imprisoned wife was automatically liable to capital punishment; and when it was a question of well-known members of the Opposition, this applied equally to any of his children over the age of twelve.

SECTION II: THE DEMOCRAT AND THE DICTATOR

The Great War was a turning point in the history of world civilization. The bluster of European achievement, the creation of armed states with myopic and rigid alliance systems, mobilization timetables, and uncreative leadership led the world to the greatest mass destruction yet experienced by human beings. Political arrogance had been supported in this endeavor by the perversions of science, which had produced the mechanized destruction of machine guns and the unimaginable pain of poisonous gas. Many worried that the West was an empty shell, a carcass on the desert, guilty of hubris and worthy of decline. Over the next twenty years, Europeans battled homelessness and despair, unemployment, and economic dislocation. This was the "Lost Generation," searching for an explanation, appalled by the reflection in the mirror, and seeking new inspiration.

But the outlook in the United States was different, indeed. The nation had come of age at the end of the nineteenth century with its brash entry onto the world stage in the Spanish American War of 1898. In the first decade of the twentieth century, the United States was a world of possibility, integrating its diverse populations, and consolidating its industrial foundation. The distant thunder of European war in 1914 was of little concern in the isolationist United States. President Woodrow Wilson ran for a second term in 1916 on the platform that "he kept us out of war." Still, the Russian Revolution of 1917 alerted the U.S. government to the potential of world Communist revolution and the German policy of unrestricted submarine warfare threatened U.S. trade and international security.

The United States thus entered World War I in 1917, and this fresh infusion of American troops and material proved decisive. But U.S. interests were not vested in Europe in spite of the rhetoric that we were out to "make the world safe for democracy" in a "war to end all wars." The idealism inherent in a League of Nations envisioned by Wilson at Versailles was not shared by many of his countrymen. Such international commitments were viewed as dangerous foreign "entanglements." Instead, the U.S. Congress and people opted for isolationism, and the Republican administrations of the 1920s concentrated on furthering domestic prosperity and security. "The business of America," said President Calvin Coolidge, "is business."

Freed from the political and economic constraints of international leadership, the United States embarked on a decade of domestic "fulfillment." The names of Carnegie, Vanderbilt, Rockefeller, Ford, and Morgan had taken on a mythical aura in the popular imagination. Big Business ruled the roost as the laissez-faire government allowed these captains of industry to drive the economy. For many Americans, this was a time of orgiastic indulgence in spite of the constraints of prohibition. This was a "Jazz Age" of style and fun—the "Roaring Twenties." The stock market reflected a freedom and confidence that eventually crossed the line into arrogance. While Europe slowly rebuilt and struggled in the throws of inflation, Americans danced the "Charleston" and small investors speculated in a market that couldn't fail. The dream of good times and easy wealth proved fragile indeed as the bottom fell out of the stock market in October 1929. A pyramid of good intentions began collapsing. This was truly a world catastrophe as U.S. banks called in their loans from Europe, leaving the frail democracies in Germany and Italy to cope with new economic instability.

The Republican leadership under Herbert Hoover was not equipped to handle such an abrupt breakdown of the banking system and the accompanying social dislocation. Finally, in 1932, amidst a vicious economic depression that had seen the displacement of farmers from the land, skyrocketing unemployment, a crisis of political confidence, and deep psychological despair, the American people elected Franklin Delano Roosevelt to the Presidency. The Great Depression of the 1930s created a new field of opportunity for those world leaders who could transfigure devastation through hope and trust. Franklin Roosevelt and Adolf Hitler entered office as elected leaders of their respective countries within a few months of each other in 1933. They were each men of supreme confidence, of great oratorical ability, with an intuitive understanding of popular sentiment and personal need. And they were willing to gamble on programs and policies that embraced instability in order to fashion new realities. They were both problem solvers;

but their different political solutions had stunning consequences for the world. Men of Destiny? Heroes in History? Agents of Destruction? At the outset of the twenty-first century, we continue to judge the controversial legacies of the Democrat and the Dictator.

The American Crisis: The Great Depression and the New Deal

This has been a twelvemonth of unprecedented advance, of wonderful prosperity. . . . If there is any way of judging the future by the past, this new year may well be one of felicitation and hopefulness.

–Herbert Hoover (1928)

True individual freedom cannot exist without economic security and independence. People who are hungry and out of a job are the stuff of which dictatorships are made.

–Franklin Delano Roosevelt

We do our best that we know how at the moment, and if it doesn't turn out, we modify it.

–Franklin Delano Roosevelt

In 1918, the United States, with its enormous natural and human resources, found the economic transition from wartime production of tanks and guns to peacetime production of automobiles to be an easy one. President Warren G. Harding spoke of a "return to normalcy" and the United States entered a decade of growing prosperity. By 1929, the inflation rate was 0.0 percent and unemployment was a mere 3.2 percent. Although the prosperity certainly did not extend to everyone (farmers in particular), there was an optimism and confidence in the American system of "rugged individualism" that banished the possibility of turmoil.

People began to indulge in almost frantic consumption made all the easier by new credit purchasing on the installment plan. The advantages of credit became apparent in the stock market as speculators were able to purchase stock "on margin" while putting down only a fraction of the full value of the shares. By borrowing in this way from a broker and paying back the original debt plus interest, the purchaser could recoup a substantial profit by selling when the stock price had appreciated. This, of course, all depended on a "secure" bull market where stocks would inevitably rise in value. But this postwar boom collapsed in 1929 when the stock market crashed amid this wild speculation. Among the factors that led to the disaster were the artificial price levels created by monopoly and easy credit, an inequitable distribution of consumer purchasing power, and the overproduction of many commodities under the stimulation of installment buying.

Influential bankers and business executives such as J.P. Morgan and Thomas Lamont could not contain the panic on Wall Street. The Hoover administration, confident of the benefits of pure capitalism and wary of tinkering with the economy, was ineffective in stemming the crisis of confidence that swept through the United States as banks collapsed and the savings of the emergent American middle class evaporated. By 1932, the country was enveloped in the Great Depression. Farmers lost their mortgages and were thrust from the land. Unemployment throughout the nation crested at 30 percent and everywhere there were signs of abandonment and despair as people sold pencils on the street corners reflecting the images of a popular song lyric of the time: "Brother, can you spare a dime?"

The first selection is from a speech given by Herbert Hoover near the close of the 1928 Pres-idential campaign. It is the classic statement of optimism in the "American system" that ex-alted individualism and decried government regulation of the economy and society.

The American System: "Rugged Individualism" (October 22, 1928)

PRESIDENT HERBERT HOOVER

There has been revived in this campaign a series of proposals which, if adopted, would be a long step toward the abandonment of our American system and a surrender to the destructive operation of governmental conduct of commercial business. Because the country is faced with difficulty and doubt over certain national problems—that is, prohibition, farm relief and electrical power—our opponents propose that we must thrust government a long way into the businesses which give rise to these problems. . . .

There is, therefore, submitted to the American people a question of fundamental principle. That is: shall we depart from the principles of our American political and economic system, upon which we have advanced beyond all the rest of the world, in order to adopt methods based on principles destructive of its very foundations? . . .

I should like to state to you the effect that this projection of government in business would have upon our system of self-government and our economic system. That effect would reach to the daily life of every man and woman. It would impair the very basis of liberty and freedom not only for those left outside the fold of expanded bureaucracy but for those embraced within it. . . .

It is a false liberalism that interprets itself into the Government operation of commercial busi-ness. Every step of bureaucratizing of the business of our country poisons the very roots of liberalism—that is, political equality, free speech, free assembly, free press, and equality of opportunity. It is the road not to more liberty, but to less liberty. . . .

Liberalism is a force truly of the spirit, a force proceeding from the deep realization that economic freedom cannot be sacrificed if political freedom is to be preserved. Even if Governmental conduct of business could give us more efficiency instead of less efficiency, the fundamental objection to it would remain unaltered and unabated. It would destroy political equality. It would increase rather than decrease abuse and corruption. It would stifle initiative and invention. It would undermine the development of leadership. It would cramp and cripple the mental and spiritual energies of our people. It would extinguish equality and opportunity. It would dry up the spirit of liberty and progress. For these reasons primarily it must be resisted. . . .

By adherence to the principles of decentralized self-government, ordered liberty, equal opportunity, and freedom to the individual, our American experiment in human welfare has yielded a degree of well-being unparalleled in all the world. It has come nearer to the abolition of poverty, to the abolition of fear of want, than humanity has ever reached before. Progress of the past seven years is the proof of it. . . .

I again repeat that the departure from our American system by injecting principles destructive to it which our opponents propose will jeopardize the very liberty and freedom of our people, will destroy equality of opportunity, not alone to ourselves but to our children.

"The American System" is from the Ray Lyman Wilbur, ed., *The New Day: Campaign Speeches of Herbert Hoover* (Stanford, CA: Stanford University Press, 1928), pp. 153–156; 163; 169.

"The Only Thing We Have to Fear Is Fear Itself"(March 4, 1933)
PRESIDENT FRANKLIN D. ROOSEVELT

Franklin Delano Roosevelt was elected President in 1932 by an American public in shock. The Great Depression had taken a mighty toll on the productive capacity and especially on the morale of a nation that had entered the twentieth century with such optimistic possibilities, now torn asunder.

Facing such overwhelming despair and social dislocation, it was clear that Roosevelt had to act quickly. Perhaps his most fundamental decision was whether to maintain a capitalist economy that had failed miserably. Roosevelt, however, did not propose to overthrow capitalism, but to regulate it for the common benefit. He explained to the American people early on that the situation "did not call for any complicated economic panaceas or fancy plans. We were faced with a condition, not a theory." He then set about resolving the banking crisis by closing the institutions and then only reopening those that could demonstrate their solvency.

But there remained many intractable problems in 1933 that he and his "Brain Trust" had to solve: unemployment, personal debt, poverty, relief for farmers, and the stability of the dollar. The country, he said, was "dying by inches" and the economy had been out of kilter for years because of poor planning and "a complete failure to understand the danger signals that have been flying since the close of the World War." Roosevelt promised swift action under a plan he called the New Deal.

The New Deal has been described by some historians as simply an extension of the Progressive reform movement earlier in the century. But it was much more. In fact, the New Deal changed the entire foundation of American life by injecting government into the lives of common people as a partner and positive force. Government had a responsibility, Roosevelt believed, to stabilize and enrich the lives of its citizens. This was indeed a radical proposition, but Roosevelt himself was careful, even conservative, in his conception. This was no revolution in his mind, but a practical application of common sense. Nothing infuriated Roosevelt more than being called an abstract theorist. When businessmen asked him when the government's budget was going to be balanced, Roosevelt responded: "A balanced budget isn't putting people to work. I will balance the budget as soon as I take care of the unemployed." The New Deal never had a guiding principle beyond trying to bring divergent ideas together to solve the problems of the moment. Roosevelt acknowledged that his administration was going to make mistakes, but promised to try something new in the face of disappointment.

In this spirit, the "New Dealers," together with an active Congress that was generally willing to give the President a lot of latitude, set out to create solutions to the disastrous situation. In the first hundred days of the New Deal, legislation came with bewildering speed. A variety of laws were passed to regulate and plan the use of natural resources. The Agricultural Adjustment Act (AAA), National Recovery Administration (NRA), the Securities and Exchange Commission (SEC), and the Tennessee Valley Authority (TVA), which brought electrification to thousands of rural citizens, were measures designed to reform previous practices or aid in the recovery of the economy. In addition to reform and recovery, the Roosevelt administration sought relief for the urban unemployed and for the depressed farmers. The Works Progress Administration of 1935 (WPA), the Farm Credit Administration (FCA), and the Civilian Conservation Corps (CCC) were created to offer employment to those in serious distress while at the same time helping to re-

---

"'The Only Thing We Have to Fear Is Fear Itself'" is from Samuel Rosenman, ed., *The Public Papers and Addresses of Franklin D. Roosevelt*, Volume II (New York: Random House, Inc., 1938), pp. 11–16.

build the infrastructure of the country. There were programs to promote art, theater, and music in the United States, and perhaps more importantly, to promote the concept of lifetime security with the old-age pension and unemployment insurance of the Social Security Act.

Many critics charged that Roosevelt was not trying to reform capitalism, but to fashion his own dictatorship with "un-American" and "radical socialistic" programs. And it is true that Roosevelt used aggressive and controversial tactics against his political opposition in Congress. In such a dynamic environment, it was hard to remain moderate. One either regarded Roosevelt as a god, or as "that man," Satan incarnate.

But in spite of confusion, waste, and the occasional failure resulting from improvised legislation, Roosevelt was returned to office in 1936, 1940, and 1944. No other President had supported so many humanitarian measures or regulated business and finance on so large a scale. By 1939, as Europe was going to war, the New Deal had by no means solved the domestic problems of unemployment, monopoly, or social insecurity. But much had been accomplished. When World War II came for the United States in 1941, the focus turned to world politics, and the fascist threat produced a disciplined, united, and engaged America.

The following selection is an excerpt from Roosevelt's powerful speech to a dispirited nation when he took office for the first time on March 4, 1933. In it he sketched the vision of an active federal government, soothed the fears, and rekindled the hopes of the American people.

I am certain that my fellow Americans expect that on my induction into the Presidency I will address them with a candor and a decision which the present situation of our Nation impels. This is preeminently the time to speak the truth, the whole truth, frankly and boldly. Nor need we shrink from honestly facing conditions in our country today. This great Nation will endure as it has endured, will revive and will prosper. So, first of all, let me assert my firm belief that the only thing we have to fear is fear itself, nameless, unreasoning, unjustified terror which paralyzes needed efforts to convert retreat into advance. In every dark hour of our national life a leadership of frankness and vigor has met with that understanding and support of the people themselves which is essential to victory. I am convinced that you will again give that support to leadership in these critical days.

In such a spirit on my part and on yours we face our common difficulties. They concern, thank God, only material things. Values have shrunken to fantastic levels; taxes have risen; our ability to pay has fallen; government of all kinds is faced by serious curtailment of income; the means of exchange are frozen in the currents of trade; the withered leaves of industrial enterprise lie on every side; farmers find no markets for their produce; the savings of many years in thousands of families are gone.

More important, a host of unemployed citizens face the grim problem of existence, and an equally great number toil with little return. Only a foolish optimist can deny the dark realities of the moment.

Yet our distress comes from no failure of substance. We are stricken by no plague of locusts. Compared with the perils which our forefathers conquered because they believed and were not afraid, we have still much to be thankful for. Nature still offers her bounty and human efforts have multiplied it. Plenty is at our doorstep, but a generous use of it languishes in the very sight of the supply. Primarily this is because the rulers of the exchange of mankind's goods have failed, through their own stubbornness and their own incompetence, have admitted their failure, and abdicated. Practices of the unscrupulous money changers stand indicted in the court of public opinion, rejected by the hearts and minds of men.

True they have tried, but their efforts have been cast in the pattern of an outworn tradition. Faced by failure of credit they have proposed only the lending of more money. Tripped of the lure of profit by which to induce our people to follow their false leadership, they have resorted to exhortations, pleading tearfully for restored confidence. They know only the rules of a generation of self-seekers. They have no vision, and when there is no vision the people perish.

The money changers have fled from their high seats in the temple of our civilization. We may not restore that temple to the ancient truths. The measure of the restoration lies in the extent to which we apply social values more noble than mere monetary profit. . . .

Our greatest primary task is to put people to work. This is no unsolvable problem if we face it wisely and courageously. It can be accomplished in part by direct recruiting by the Government itself, treating the task as we would treat the emergency of a war, but at the same time, through this employment, accomplishing greatly needed projects to stimulate and reorganize the use of our natural resources.

Hand in hand with this we must frankly recognize the overbalance of population in our industrial centers and, by engaging on a national scale in a redistribution, endeavor to provide a better use of the land for those best fitted for the land. The task can be helped . . . by preventing realistically the tragedy of the growing loss through foreclosure of our small homes and our farms. . . . It can be helped by the unifying of relief activities which today are often scattered, uneconomical, and unequal. It can be helped by national planning for and supervision of all forms of transportation and of communications and other utilities which have a definitely public character. There are many ways in which it can be helped, but it can never be helped merely by talking about it. We must act and act quickly.

Finally, in our progress toward a resumption of work we require two safeguards against a return of the evils of the old order; there must be a strict supervision of all banking and credits and investments; there must be an end to speculation with other people's money, and there must be provision of an adequate but sound currency. . . .

In the field of world policy, I would dedicate this Nation to the policy of the good neighbor, the neighbor who resolutely respects himself and, because he does so, respects the rights of others, the neighbor who respects his obligations and respects the sanctity of his agreements in and with a world of neighbors.

If I read the temper of our people correctly, we now realize as we have never realized before our interdependence on each other, that we cannot merely take but we must give as well; that if we are to go forward, we must move as a trained and loyal army willing to sacrifice for the good of a common discipline, because without such discipline no progress is made, no leadership becomes effective. We are, I know, ready and willing to submit our lives and property to such discipline, because it makes possible a leadership which aims at a larger good. This I propose to offer, pledging that the larger purposes will bind upon us all as a sacred obligation with a unity of duty hitherto evoked only in time of armed strife.

With this pledge taken, I assume unhesitatingly the leadership of this great army of our people dedicated to a disciplined attack upon our common problems.

Action in this image and to this end is feasible under the form of government which we have inherited from our ancestors. Our Constitution is so simple and practical that it is possible always to meet extraordinary needs by changes in emphasis and arrangement without loss of essential form. That is why our constitutional system has proved itself the most superbly enduring political mechanism the modern world has produced. It has met every stress of vast expansion of territory, of foreign wars, of bitter internal strife, of world relations. . . .

I am prepared under my constitutional duty to recommend the measures that a stricken nation in the midst of a stricken world may require. These measures, or such other measures as the Congress may build out of its experience and wisdom, I shall seek, within my constitutional authority, to bring to speedy adoption. . . .

We face the arduous days that lie before us in the warm courage of the national unity; with the clear consciousness of seeking old and precious moral values; with the clean satisfaction that comes from the stern performance of duty by old and young alike. We aim at the assurance of a rounded and permanent national life.

We do not distrust the future of essential democracy. The people of the United States have not failed. In their need they have regis- tered a mandate that they want direct, vigorous action. They have asked for discipline and direc- tion under leadership. They have made me the present instrument of their wishes. In the spirit of the gift I take it. . . .

Fireside Chat: Outlining the New Deal (May 7, 1933)

PRESIDENT FRANKLIN D. ROOSEVELT

Franklin Roosevelt sought a more intimate link with the American people than he could ob- tain through formal speeches in isolated locations. If the country were to pull together, he needed to address the issues in a national forum. On March 12, 1933, the President had his first direct "conversation" with the people over the radio in what he described as a "fireside chat." Two months later in May, Roosevelt outlined his vision of the New Deal in another chat with his American "family."

On a Sunday night a week after my Inaugura- tion, I used the radio to tell you about the bank- ing crisis and the measures we were taking to meet it. I think that in that way I made clear to the country various facts that might otherwise have been misunderstood and in general pro- vided a means of understanding which did much to restore confidence.

Tonight, eight weeks later, I come for the sec- ond time to give you my report—in the same spirit and by the same means to tell you about what we have been doing and what we are plan- ning to do.

Two months ago we were facing serious prob- lems. The country was dying by inches. It was dying because trade and commerce had de- clined to dangerously low levels; prices for basic commodities were such as to destroy the value of the assets of national institutions such as banks, savings banks, insurance companies, and others. These institutions, because of their great needs, were foreclosing mortgages, calling loans, refusing credit. . . . That situation in that crisis did not call for any complicated considera- tion of economic panaceas or fancy plans. We were faced by a condition and not a theory. . . .

A prompt program applied as quickly as possi- ble seemed to me not only justified but impera- tive to our national security. The Congress, and when I say Congress I mean the members of both political parties, fully understood this and gave me generous and intelligent support. The mem- bers of Congress realized that the methods of normal times had to be replaced in the emer- gency by measures which were suited to the seri- ous and pressing requirements of the moment. There was no actual surrender of power, Con- gress still retained its constitutional authority and no one has the slightest desire to change the bal- ance of these powers. The function of Congress is to decide what has to be done and to select the ap- propriate agency to carry out its will. This policy it has strictly adhered to. The only thing that has been happening has been to designate the Presi- dent as the agency to carry out certain of the pur- poses of the Congress. This was constitutional and in keeping with the past American tradition.

The legislation which has been passed or in the process of enactment can properly be consid- ered as part of a well-grounded plan. First, we are giving opportunity of employment to one-quarter of a million of the unemployed, especially the

"Fireside Chat" is from Samuel Rosenman, ed., *The Public Papers and Addresses of Franklin D. Roosevelt*, Volume II (New York: Random House, Inc., 1938), pp. 160–168.

young men who have dependents, to go into the forestry and flood prevention work. This is a big task because it means feeding, clothing and caring for nearly twice as many men as we have in the regular army itself. In creating this civilian conservation corps, we are killing two birds with one stone. We are clearly enhancing the value of our natural resources and second, we are relieving an appreciable amount of actual distress. This great group of men have entered upon their work on a purely voluntary basis, no military training is involved and we are conserving not only our natural resources but our human resources. One of the great values to this work is the fact that it is direct and requires the intervention of very little machinery.

Second, I have requested the Congress and have secured action upon a proposal . . . for the improvement of a vast area in the Tennessee Valley. It will add to the comfort and happiness of hundreds of thousands of people and the incident benefits will reach the entire nation.

Next, the Congress is about to pass legislation that will greatly ease the mortgage distress among the farmers and the home owners of the nation, by providing for the easing of the burden of debt now bearing so heavily upon millions of our people.

Our next step in seeking immediate relief is a grant of half a billion dollars to help the states, counties and municipalities in their duty to care for those who need direct and immediate relief. . . .

We are planning to ask the Congress for legislation to enable the Government to undertake public works, thus stimulating directly and indirectly the employment of many others in well-considered projects.

Further legislation has been taken up which goes much more fundamentally into our economic problems. The Farm Relief Bill seeks by the use of several methods, alone or together, to bring about an increased return to farmers for their major farm products, seeking at the same time to prevent in the days to come disastrous over-production which so often in the past has kept farm commodity prices far below a reasonable return. This measure provides wide powers for emergencies. The extent of its use will depend entirely upon what the future has in store.

Well-considered and conservative measures will likewise be proposed which will attempt to give to the industrial workers of the country a more fair wage return, prevent cut-throat competition and unduly long hours for labor, and at the same time to encourage each industry to prevent over-production. . . .

Today we have reason to believe that things are a little better than they were two months ago. Industry has picked up, railroads are carrying more freight, farm prices are better, but I am not going to indulge in issuing proclamations of overenthusiastic assurance. We cannot ballyhoo ourselves back to prosperity. I am going to be honest at all times with the people of the country. . . .

We are working toward a definite goal, which is to prevent the return of conditions which came very close to destroying what we call modern civilization. The actual accomplishment of our purpose cannot be attained in a day. Our policies are wholly within purposes for which our American Constitutional Government was established 150 years ago. . . .

Hand in hand with the domestic situation which, of course, is our first concern, is the world situation, and I want to emphasize to you that the domestic situation is inevitably and deeply tied in with the conditions in all of the other nations of the world. In other words, we can get, in all probability, a fair measure of prosperity return in the United States, but it will not be permanent unless we get a return to prosperity all over the world.

To you, the people of this country, all of us, the Members of the Congress and the members of this Administration owe a profound debt of gratitude. Throughout the depression you have been patient. You have granted us wide powers, you have encouraged us with a wide-spread approval of our purposes. Every ounce of strength and every resource at our command we have devoted to the end of justifying your confidence. We are encouraged to believe that a wise and sensible beginning has been made. In the present spirit of mutual confidence and mutual encouragement we go forward.

FASCISM: THE EUROPEAN LEGACY OF WORLD WAR I

Order is the mother of civilization and liberty; chaos is the midwife of dictatorship.

—*Will Durant*

It is too difficult to think nobly when one only thinks to get a living.

—*Jean-Jacques Rousseau*

With the end of the war in 1918, Europe entered a new age of change and development. Democratic governments had won the "war to make the world safe for democracy" and the aggressive German monarchy had been abolished. Indeed, most other European nations adopted or maintained democratic institutions. The dominant theme, however, in the political history of Europe from 1919 to 1939 is the decline of these democratic governments. By the beginning of World War II in 1939, authoritarian regimes had been established in Italy, Germany, Spain, and throughout most of central and eastern Europe. The world was introduced to two of the most intriguing and destructive individuals of the twentieth century: Benito Mussolini and Adolf Hitler.

In order to understand the success of Hitler and the Nazis in particular, we must first look at the doctrine of fascism to which Hitler and many other twentieth century dictators have subscribed. Fascism varies in its particular details of application, but in the simplest of terms, it is a doctrine that sanctifies the interests of the state and minimizes the rights of the individual. Fascism promotes as its great benefit the stability and security of the state.

Nearly all fascist governments have certain features in common. For example, fascism was born in direct opposition to liberal democracy and as such regards personal freedom as dangerous to the stability of the state. Democracy, according to fascist doctrine, promotes individual expression and self-aggrandizement, which in turn results in disagreement and class conflict. Fascists also oppose socialism and communism since they promote the welfare of the masses over the good of the state. Communism, in fact, with its Leninist emphasis on the immediacy of world revolution, has dangerous potential for destabilization by its very insistence on class warfare. Fascism also depends on extreme nationalism. This goes far beyond the patriotic love of one's nation, but is based on pride in the allegedly unique characteristics and achievements of a "special" people. Therefore, fascist national pride is exclusive and implies a hostility toward other countries that are considered inferior in their outlook, governmental organization, or national heritage. This hostility is a unifying factor and is often vented against particular minority groups within the state itself. Thus, Hitler promoted hatred of the Jews as a rallying point for his support. This fascist national pride often expresses itself through imperialism, since military and economic expansion actually strengthens the state. Because stability and security of the state are the watchwords of fascism, it is important to implement a strong, highly centralized, and efficient government that only dictatorial rule can provide. One man with total control over the affairs of state ensures coordination and consistency of rule. Such a dictatorship is achieved and maintained through control of the national army, but most practically through paramilitary organizations like secret police, private armies, and bodyguards, which do not hesitate to use violence.

Fascism traditionally derives its support from the "right-wing" or conservative forces of society. The military represents, by its very nature, order and discipline. Big industrialists want to enjoy the lucrative profits that state stability affords; in a fascist society, general workers' strikes, which can often cripple an economy and interrupt production, are forbidden. Socially, fascism derives its mass support from the lower middle class. In general, these are people who have worked hard within the confines of society to attain some measure of self-respect. Sociologically, they are individuals of commitment and pride who harbor dreams of social mobility, have faith in traditional values, and love their country; they have much to lose from instability and chaos. The fascist, totalitarian regime is intended to eliminate class conflict by concentrating the energy of all its members in the service of the state.

Fascism is often born of the frustration and discontent of people who have been in some way humiliated or robbed of their dignity either as individuals or collectively as a nation. According to the philosopher Eric Hoffer in his book, The True Believer, *people who are most susceptible to mass movements are filled with the burden of their present existence and seek inspiration from those who have a vision of a proud and stable future. This vision was first articulated and defined in Italy by Benito Mussolini.*

The Rise of Benito Mussolini

Benito Mussolini (1883–1945) was perhaps fascism's most articulate spokesman. He was born the son of a blacksmith and worked as a school teacher and day laborer before becoming editor of a Socialist newspaper prior to World War I. He supported Italy's entry into the war and was wounded in the conflict. In 1919, he was one of many small-time candidates trying to make a mark in Italian politics. An amazing orator and opportunist, Mussolini presented a message of order and action that won him the support of working and middle-class Italians who had been hit hard by the inflation that plagued Europe after the war. Mussolini even organized terrorist squads to contribute to the very instability that drew him adherents.

By 1922, the fascists controlled local governments in many cities in northern Italy. Mussolini initiated a march on Rome that met with no resistance from King Victor Emmanuel III. Concerned with violence and his personal safety, the king asked Mussolini to become prime minister and form a government. Although Mussolini had achieved power legally, his Italian National Fascist party ("Blackshirts") did not enjoy even a near majority in the Chamber of Deputies. He immediately disrupted the parliamentary government with threats and physical acts of violence against its elected members. Mussolini was then given temporary dictatorial powers by the king to stabilize the political situation; he soon turned these into a permanent and personal dominance.

Mussolini's vision of a "corporate state," in which each individual worked for the welfare of the entire nation, guaranteed employment and satisfactory wages for labor but did not permit strikes. He favored industrialists by allowing lucrative profits and gave respect to Italy by closely identifying his regime with the glorious heritage of the ancient Roman Empire. Mussolini succeeded in giving Italy direction and dignity, but he accomplished this through suppression of civil rights and individual liberties. He was, indeed, the quintessential fascist.

The following selection is perhaps the defining statement of fascism. Mussolini believed that the twentieth century was a new historical epoch that required a different political premise based on popular loyalty to the state and supported by violent force.

The Doctrine of Fascism: "This Will Be the Century of the State"

BENITO MUSSOLINI

Fascism was not the nursling of a doctrine worked out beforehand with detailed elaboration; it was born of the need for action and it was itself from the beginning practical rather than theoretical; it was not merely another political party but, even in the first two years, in opposition to all political parties as such. . . . If one were to re-read . . . the report of the meeting in which the *Fasci Italiani di Combáttimento* [Italian Bands of Combat] were constituted, one would there find no ordered expression of doctrine, but a series of aphorisms, anticipations, and aspirations which, when refined by time from the original ore, were destined after some years to develop into an ordered series of doctrinal concepts, forming the Fascists' political doctrine—different from all others either of the past or of the present day. . . .

We want to accustom the working-class to real and effectual leadership, and also to convince them that it is no easy thing to direct an industry or a commercial enterprise successfully. . . . We shall combat every retrograde idea, technical or spiritual. . . . When the succession to the seat of government is open, we must not be unwilling to fight for it. We must make haste; when the present regime breaks down, we must be ready at once to take its place. It is we who have the right to the succession, because it was we who forced the country into the War, and led her to victory. . . .

The years which preceded the March to Rome were years of great difficulty, during which the necessity for action did not permit research of any complete elaboration of doctrine. The battle had to be fought in the towns and villages. There was much discussion, but—what was more important and more sacred—men

died. They knew how to die. Doctrine, beautifully defined and carefully elucidated, with headlines and paragraphs, might be lacking; but there was to take its place something more decisive—Faith. . . . But, since there was inevitably some lack of system, the adversaries of Fascism have disingenuously denied that it had any capacity to produce a doctrine of its own, though that doctrine was growing and taking shape under their very eyes . . . in the laws and institutions of the regime as enacted successively in the years 1926, 1927 and 1928. . . .

Above all, Fascism, the more it considers and observes the future and the development of humanity quite apart from political considerations of the moment, believes neither in the possibility nor the utility of perpetual peace. It thus repudiates the doctrine of Pacifism—born of a renunciation of the struggle and an act of cowardice in the face of sacrifice. War alone brings up to its highest tension all human energy and puts the stamp of nobility upon the peoples who have the courage to meet it. All other trials are substitutes, which never really put men into the position where they have to make the great decision—the alternative of life or death. Thus a doctrine which is founded upon this harmful postulate of peace is hostile to Fascism. . . . This anti-pacifist spirit is carried by Fascism even in the life of the individual. . . . The Fascist accepts life and loves it, knowing nothing of and despising suicide; he rather conceives of life as duty and struggle and conquest, life which would be high and full, lived for oneself, but above all for others—those who are at hand and those who are far distant contemporaries, and those who will come after. . . .

Such a conception of life makes Fascism the complete opposite of that doctrine, the base of the so-called scientific and Marxian Socialism, the materialist conception of history; according to which the history of human civilization can be explained simply through the conflict of interests among the various social groups and by the change and development in the means and instruments of production. That the changes in the economic field . . . have their importance no one

Reprinted by permission of the publisher from "The Political and Social Doctrine of Fascism," Benito Mussolini, *International Conciliation*. Washington, DC: Carnegie Endowment for International Peace, January 1935, pp. 5–17.

can deny; but that these factors are sufficient to explain the history of humanity excluding all others is an absurd delusion. Fascism now and always, believes in holiness and in heroism; that is to say, in actions influenced by no economic motive, direct or indirect. . . . And above all Fascism denies that class war can be the preponderant force in the transformation of society. . . .

After Socialism, Fascism combats the whole complex system of democratic ideology; and repudiates it, whether in its theoretical premises or in its practical application. Fascism denies that the majority, by the simple fact that it is a majority, can direct human society; it denies that numbers alone can govern by means of a periodical consultation, and it affirms the immutable, beneficial, and fruitful inequality of mankind, which can never be permanently leveled through the mere operation of a mechanical process such as universal suffrage. The democratic regime may be defined as from time to time giving the people the illusion of sovereignty, while the real effective sovereignty lies in the hands of other concealed and irresponsible forces. Democracy is a regime nominally without a king, but it is ruled by many kings—more absolute, tyrannical, and ruinous than one sole king, even though a tyrant. . . .

Political doctrines pass, but humanity remains; and it may rather be expected that this will be a century of Fascism. For if the nineteenth century was the century of individualism (Liberalism always signifying individualism) it may be expected that this will be the century of collectivism, and hence the century of the State. . . .

The foundation of Fascism is the conception of the State. Fascism conceives of the State as an absolute, in comparison with which all individuals or groups are relative, only to be conceived of in their relation to the State. . . .

The Fascist State has drawn into itself even the economic activities of the nation, and through the corporative social and educational institutions created by it, its influence reaches every aspect of the national life and includes, framed in their respective organizations, all the political, economic and spiritual forces of the nation. A State which reposes upon the support of millions of individuals who recognize its authority, are continually conscious of its power and are ready at once to serve it, is not the old tyrannical State of the medieval lord nor has it anything in common with the absolute governments either before or after 1789. The individual in the Fascist State is not annulled but rather multiplied, just in the same way that a soldier in a regiment is not diminished but rather increased by the number of his comrades. The Fascist State organizes the nation, but leaves a sufficient margin of liberty to the individual; the latter is deprived of all useless and possibly harmful freedom, but retains what is essential. . . .

The Fascist State is an embodied will to power and government; the Roman tradition is here an ideal of force in action. According to Fascism, government is not so much a thing to be expressed in territorial or military terms as in terms of morality and the spirit. It must be thought of as an empire—that is to say, a nation which directly or indirectly rules other nations, without the need for conquering a single square yard of territory. For Fascism, the growth of empire, that is to say the expansion of the nation, is an essential manifestation of vitality, and its opposite a sign of decadence. Peoples which are rising, or rising again after a period of decadence, are always imperialist: any renunciation is a sign of decay and of death.

Fascism is the doctrine best adapted to represent the tendencies and the aspirations of a people, like the people of Italy, who are rising again after many centuries of abasement and foreign servitude. But empire demands discipline, the coordination of all forces and a deeply felt sense of duty and sacrifice; . . . for never before has the nation [Italy] stood more in need of authority, of direction, and of order. If every age has its own characteristic doctrine, there are a thousand signs which point to Fascism as the characteristic doctrine of our time. For if a doctrine must be a living thing, this is proved by the fact that Fascism has created a living faith; and that this faith is very powerful in the minds of men, is demonstrated by those who have suffered and died for it.

Theme: Propaganda/Systems of Government

The Historical Intersection

MADRID: 1940

The Fascist Image of Francisco Franco

Fascism and communism, the ideologies that were dividing Europe, formally came into conflict during the Spanish Civil War from 1936–1939. Madrid's Republican government was a diverse and weak coalition of left-wing groups that struggled to suppress a revolt led by army commanders in Spanish Morocco. These rebels were soon supported for many different reasons by the Catholic church, the middle class, and a small fascist party led by General Francisco Franco called the Falangists.

None of Europe's democratic governments responded to Republican pleas for support, although both Benito Mussolini and Adolf Hitler furnished Franco with ammunition, troops, and the latest in fighter aircraft. In this way, Hitler hoped to test his new weapons and air force. The Republican forces were bolstered by over 40,000 multinationals who were enlisted in the International Brigades by the Communists. The Soviet Union also sent aid.

This was a brutal war that dragged on with over one million Spanish killed and many atrocities like the tragic Nazi bombing of unarmed civilians in the Basque city of Guernica in 1937. Eventually, Franco's better-disciplined and equipped forces cut through the Republican lines. This post-war mural portrays Franco as a medieval knight, a crusader for peace and justice who united both church and state for the benefit of the Spanish people. In contrast to both Mussolini and Hitler, whose fascist regimes ended with their defeat in World War II, Spain remained neutral and Franco's rigid fascist control over Spain lasted until his death in 1975. Propaganda and the cultivation of image as "El Caudillo" was an important part of his longevity.

(contd)

Mural of Francisco Franco as a Crusader *(Photo Oronoz, Madrid; Archivo Histórico Militar).*

Compare and Contrast:

- Why was propaganda like this mural essential in Franco's consolidation of power after the Spanish Civil War? What makes it effective propaganda?
- In the end, does it matter whether the "leader" is a fascist or a democrat? Isn't the image essentially the same? Why?

THE NAZI RISE TO POWER

Power is given only to him who dares to stoop and seize it. There is only one thing that matters, just one thing: you have to dare!

—*Fyodor Dostoevsky*

Tyranny consists in the desire of universal power beyond its scope; it is the wish to have in one way what can only be had in another.

—*Blaise Pascal*

There is nothing more terrible than ignorance in action.

—*Johann von Goethe*

Perhaps the most important and influential of the authoritarian regimes in the post-war history of Europe was established legally in Germany by Adolf Hitler and the National Socialist party.

After the abolition of the aggressive German monarchy in 1918, the Weimar Republic was established amidst lofty ideals. Yet it labored under the burden of antirepublican pressures from the army, judiciary, bureaucracy, and even monarchists who wanted to reinstate the kaiser. Germany had never had a strong democratic tradition and had been united under a central monarch for only about fifty years. The German republic was also weakened because it had been created during a time of national defeat and humiliation. Critics used the Republic as a scapegoat for Germany's ills and accused its democratic leaders of betraying the German armies by making an unacceptable peace. Faced with the threat of communist revolution in Germany and economic dislocation, which was prompted by incredible price inflation and devaluation of currency, the Weimar Republic struggled through the early 1920s. Even during a period of relative economic stability after 1924, the leaders of the Republic were unable to foster a coherent program because of the conflicting demands of coalition government.

In the summer of 1929, Germany felt the first effects of the worldwide depression. By the winter of 1929–1930, three million Germans were unemployed, a figure that increased to six million by 1933. The deepening depression made it increasingly difficult for the various parties in the coalition government to work together. In the elections of 1930, the moderate and prorepublican parties suffered a significant defeat; the greatest gains were made by the National Socialist party, headed by Adolf Hitler. The Nazis, as its members were called, had been a small, violent group on the fringes of antirepublican politics during the early 1920s. But by 1930, their membership had increased greatly and they were the most dynamic of the antidemocratic parties. Their success and popularity lay in providing, or at least promising, something for everyone. The Nazis promised a renegotiation of peace treaties and reestablishment of German honor and power to those who saw Germany's greatness shattered by the defeat in 1918 and the Treaty of Versailles in 1919. They promised efficient authoritarianism to those who were frustrated by the inadequacy of republican politics. The Nazis promised a strong economy to those (especially in the middle class) whose savings were threatened by the depression. Hitler also promised protection to the industrialists whose profits and very existence were jeopardized by the communist movement.

The central doctrine, however, of the National Socialist party was anti-Semitism. In his autobiography, Mein Kampf (My Struggle), *and in speeches and party announcements, Hitler blamed the Jews for the economic crises of the 1920s. The inflation and depression, he argued, had been caused by Jewish international financiers. The Nazis also believed that the Jews controlled the international communist movement. Jews had to be excluded from German life, they concluded. In the unstable and violent years after 1929, more and more Germans seemed willing to accept this explanation for their difficult times.*

As Hitler's influence grew, his followers advocated a violent seizure of power. Although he sanctioned violent political disruption and intimidation, Hitler insisted on attaining power legally. On January 30, 1933, after much political maneuvering, Hitler was appointed chancellor of the Weimar Republic. By July 1934, Hitler had legally altered the Weimar constitution, changed the nature of the Republic, removed all Jews and "politically unreliable" people from the bureaucracy, dissolved all opposition political parties, and purged the army. On August 2, 1934, President von Hindenburg died, and Hitler combined the offices of president and chancellor. The army formally supported these developments by swearing "unconditional obedience to the Führer of the German Reich and People, Adolf Hitler." Hitler then began fashioning his own dictatorship.

In this section, we will look carefully at the political, social, and economic conditions that existed in Germany during the 1920s and early 1930s in an effort to understand why the Nazis were able to gain power. Themes that will emerge from the material include the use of racism and propaganda in the pursuit of power, as well as the role of the individual in history. Could Hitler have risen to lead Germany had he not been presented with the devastating social and economic conditions of the time? To what extent did Hitler change the course of history? In essence, why did Germany follow the leadership of Adolf Hitler? The complicated political maneuverings are not at issue here. Rather, it is important to try to understand people in crisis.

Germany's Unstable Democracy: The Best and Worst of Times

Loyalty to the Weimar Republic

LILO LINKE

The Weimar Republic, burdened by the specter of defeat and shame, was impotent to meet the economic and political problems of the 1920s. Although there was much opposition to democratic beliefs from the National Socialist (Nazi) party, among others, many Germans were still loyal to the Republic, as the following selection from a young student reveals.

A procession was formed, headed by the military band with triangles and drums and clarinets and followed by the members of the movement, two abreast, holding their torches in their upraised hands. We marched through the town, our ghostly magnified shadows moving restlessly over the fronts of the houses.

Never before had I followed the flag of the Republic, which was now waving thirty yards in front of me, spreading its colours overhead, the black melting in one with the night, the red glowing in the light of the torches, and the gold overshining

them like a dancing sun. It was not just a torchlight march for me, it was a political confession. I had decided to take part in the struggle for German democracy. I wanted to fight for it although I knew that this meant a challenge to my parents and my whole family, who all lived with their eyes turned towards the past and thought it disloyal and shameful to help the Socialists.

We marched out of the town to the cemetery, where the first President of the Republic, Fritz Ebert, has been buried. Silently we assembled round the grave. Wilhelm Wismar, national leader of the Young Democrats and youngest member of the Reichstag, stepped forward and spoke slowly the oath.

"We vow to stand for the Republic with all our abilities and strength."

"We vow to work for the fulfillment of the promises given to the German people in the Weimar Constitution."

"We vow to shield and defend democracy against all its enemies and attackers whoever they might be."

And out of the night in a rolling echo two thousand citizens of tomorrow answered, repeating solemnly word for word:

"We vow to stand for the Republic with all our abilities and strength."

"We vow to work for the fulfillment of the promises given to the German people in the Weimar Constitution."

"We vow to shield and defend democracy against all its enemies and attackers whoever they might be."

Inflation: "The Boiling Kettle of a Wicked Witch"

LILO LINKE

Inflation, or the decline in the value of currency with the attendant rise in prices, engulfed Germany in the early 1920s, reaching a peak in 1923. The following accounts reflect some of the difficulties and frustrations felt by people of the time. The middle classes were especially affected, and their hard-earned savings became worthless. Both Lilo Linke and Konrad Heiden witnessed the hardship of these days. Heiden was particularly active against the Nazis in street confrontations as a student at the University of Munich in 1923.

The time for my first excursions into life was badly chosen. Rapidly Germany was precipitated into the inflation, thousands, millions, milliards of marks whirled about, making heads swim in confusion. War, revolution, and the wild years after had deprived everyone of old standards and the possibility of planning a normal life. Again and again fate hurled the helpless individual into the boiling kettle of a wicked witch. Now the inflation came and destroyed the last vestige of steadiness. Hurriedly one had to make use of the moment and could not consider the following day.

The whole population had suddenly turned into maniacs. Everyone was buying, selling, speculating, bargaining, and dollar, dollar, dollar was the magic word which dominated every conversation, every newspaper, every poster in Germany. Nobody understood what was happening. There seemed to be no sense, no rules in the

mad game, but one had to take part in it if one did not want to be trampled underfoot at once. Only a few people were able to carry through to the end and gain by the inflation. The majority lost everything and broke down, impoverished and bewildered.

The middle class was hurt more than any other, the savings of a lifetime and their small fortunes melted into a few coppers. They had to sell their most precious belongings for ten milliard inflated marks to buy a bit of food or an absolutely necessary coat, and their pride and dignity were bleeding out of many wounds. Bitterness remained for ever in their hearts. Full of hatred, they accused the international financiers, the Jews and Socialists—their old enemies—of having exploited their distress. They never forgot and never forgave and were the first to lend a willing ear to Hitler's fervent preaching.

In the shop, notices announced that we should receive our salaries in weekly parts; after a while we queued up at the cashier's desk every evening, and before long we were paid twice daily and ran out during the lunch hour to buy a few things, because as soon as the new rate of exchange became known in the early afternoon our money had again lost half its value.

In the beginning I did not concern myself much with these happenings. They merely added to the excitement of my new life, which was all that mattered to me. Living in the east of Berlin and in hard times, I was long accustomed to seeing people around me in hunger, distress, and poverty. My mother was always lamenting that it was impossible for her to make both ends meet, my father—whenever he was at home—always asking what the deuce she had done with all the money he had given her yesterday. A few tears, a few outbreaks more did not make a difference great enough to impress me deeply.

Yet, in the long run, the evil influence of the inflation, financially as well as morally, penetrated even to me. Berlin had become the centre of international profiteers and noisy new rich. For a few dollars they could buy the whole town, drinks and women, horses and houses, virtue and vice, and they made free use of these possibilities.

Hitler's Response to Germany's Problems

The National Socialist party produced a program in 1920 that formed the basis of Hitler's campaign against the Weimar Republic. The succeeding selections of speeches and rally announcements not only reveal Nazi ideology but also testify to the dynamism of Nazi propaganda.

The Nazi Program (1920)

The program is the political foundation of the NSDAP [Nazi Party] and accordingly the primary political law of the State. It has been made brief and clear intentionally.

All legal precepts must be applied in the spirit of the party program.

Since the taking over of control, the Fuehrer has succeeded in the realization of essential portions of the Party program from the fundamentals to the detail.

The Party Program of the NSDAP was proclaimed on the 24 February 1920 by Adolf Hitler at the first large Party gathering in Munich and

"The Nazi Program" is from "National Socialist Yearbook, 1941," Office of the U.S. Chief Counsel for Prosecution of Axis Criminality, *Nazi Conspiracy and Aggression* (Washington, DC: Government Printing Office, 1946), vol. 4, pp. 208–211.

since that day has remained unaltered. Within, the national socialist philosophy is summarized in 25 points:

1. We demand the unification of all Germans in the Greater Germany on the basis of the right of self-determination of peoples.
2. We demand equality of rights for the German people in respect to the other nations; abrogation of the peace treaties of Versailles and St. Germain.
3. We demand land and territory [colonies] for the sustenance of our people, and colonization for our surplus population.
4. Only a member of the race can be a citizen. A member of the race can only be one who is of German blood, without consideration of creed. Consequently no Jew can be a member of the race.
5. Whoever has no citizenship is to be able to live in Germany only as a guest, and must be

under the authority of legislation for foreigners.

6. The right to determine matters concerning administration and law belongs only to the citizen. Therefore we demand that every public office, of any sort whatsoever, whether in the Reich, the county or municipality, be filled only by citizens. . . .

7. We demand that the state be charged first with providing the opportunity for a livelihood and way of life for citizens. If it is impossible to sustain the total population of the State, then the members of foreign nations (non-citizens) are to be expelled from the Reich.

8. Any further immigration of non-citizens is to be prevented. We demand that all non-Germans, who have immigrated to Germany since the 2 August 1914, be forced immediately to leave the Reich.

9. All citizens must have equal rights and obligations.

10. The first obligation of every citizen must be to work both spiritually and physically. . . .

13. We demand the nationalization of all [previous] associated industries [trusts].

14. We demand a division of profits of all heavy industries.

15. We demand an expansion on a large scale of old age welfare.

16. We demand the creation of a healthy middle class and its conservation. . . .

18. We demand struggle without consideration against those whose activity is injurious to the general interest. Common national criminals, usurers . . . and so forth are to be punished with death, without consideration of confession or race.

20. The state is to be responsible for a fundamental reconstruction of our whole national education program, to enable every capable and industrious German to obtain higher education and subsequently introduction into leading positions. . . .

21. The State is to care for the elevating of national health by protecting the mother and child, by outlawing child-labor, by the encouragement of physical fitness, by means of the legal establishment of a gymnastic and sport obligation, by the utmost support of all organizations concerned with the physical instruction of the young. . . .

23. We demand legal opposition to known lies and their promulgation through the press. In order to enable the provision of a German press, we demand, that: (a) All writers and employees of the newspapers appearing in the German language be members of the race: (b) Non-German newspapers be required to have the express permission of the State to be published. They may not be printed in the German language: (c) Non-Germans are forbidden by law any financial interest in German publications, or any influence on them, and as punishment for violations the closing of such a publication as well as the immediate expulsion from the Reich of the non-German concerned. Publications which are counter to the general good are to be forbidden. We demand legal prosecution of artistic and literary forms which exert a destructive influence on our national life, and the closure of organizations opposing the above made demands.

24. We demand freedom of religion for all religious denominations within the state so long as they do not endanger its existence or oppose the moral senses of the Germanic race. The Party as such advocates the standpoint of a positive Christianity without binding itself confessionally to any one denomination. It combats the Jewish-materialistic spirit within and around us, and is convinced that a lasting recovery of our nation can only succeed from within on the framework: common utility precedes individual utility.

25. For the execution of all of this we demand the formation of a strong central power in the Reich. Unlimited authority of the central parliament over the whole Reich and its

organizations in general. The forming of state and profession chambers for the execution of the laws made by the Reich within the various states of the confederation. The leaders of the Party promise, if necessary by sacrificing their own lives, to support the execution of the points set forth above without consideration.

Speech on the Treaty of Versailles (April 17, 1923)

ADOLF HITLER

With the armistice begins the humiliation of Germany. If the Republic on the day of its foundation had appealed to the country: "Germans, stand together! Up and resist the foe! The Fatherland, the Republic expects of you that you fight to your last breath," then millions who are now enemies of the Republic would be fanatical Republicans. Today they are the foes of the Republic not because it is a Republic but because this Republic was founded at the moment when Germany was humiliated, because it so discredited the new flag that men's eyes must turn regretfully towards the old flag.

So long as this Treaty stands there can be no resurrection of the German people; no social reform of any kind is possible! The Treaty was made in order to bring 20 million Germans to their deaths and to ruin the German nation. But those who made the Treaty cannot set it aside. As its foundation our Movement formulated three demands:

1. Setting aside of the Peace Treaty.
2. Unification of all Germans.

Baynes, Normal H., trans. & ed., *The Speeches of Adolf Hitler, April 1922–1939, Vol. I* (London: Oxford University Press for the Royal Institute of International Affairs, 1942), pp. 56–57. Reprinted by permission of the Royal Institute of International Affairs.

This photograph of Benito Mussolini and Adolf Hitler expresses the image of discipline and vision that was so much a part of fascist propaganda. They both rose to power amidst the political and economic dislocation of the 1920s and 1930s. "Order is the mother of civilization and liberty; chaos is the midwife of dictatorship."—Will Durant. *(UPI/Bettman)*

3. Land and soil [*Grund und Boden*] to feed our nation.

Our movement could formulate these demands, since it was not our Movement which caused the War, it has not made the Republic, it did not sign the Peace Treaty.

There is thus one thing which is the first task of this Movement: it desires to make the German once more National, that his Fatherland shall stand for him above everything else. It desires to teach our people to understand afresh the truth of the old saying: He who will not be a hammer must be an anvil. An anvil are we today, and that anvil will be beaten until out of the anvil we fashion once more a hammer, a German sword!

Nazi Political Rally Announcement (February 1921)

NATIONAL SOCIALIST GERMAN WORKERS' PARTY

Fellow Citizens!

A year ago we called you to the Zirkus Krone. For the first time we invited you to a giant protest against making Germany defenseless by disarmament. We declared that this making her defenseless would be the prelude for the loss of Upper Silesia.

For the second time we invite you to resist against the Paris Dictate. We called it the permanent enslavement of Germany....

Poverty no longer begins to appear, it is here. And though one does not feel it in the armchairs of the parliaments and in the soft cushions of our people's leaders it is felt all the more by the millions who have been cheated, by the masses of the people who do not live by cheating, profiteering and usury, but by the sweat of their honest work. But we are not only a poor people, we are also a miserable people.

We have forgotten the millions of our fellow citizens who once, during a long four and a half years, bled for Germany's existence on innumerable battlefields, and of whom our fatherland has been robbed by a cruel fate.

We have forgotten the millions of those Germans who longingly await the day which brings them home to a country that even as the poorest would still present the happiness of being their fatherland. We have forgotten the Rhineland and Upper Silesia, forgotten German-Austria and the millions of our brothers in Czechoslovakia, forgotten Alsace-Lorraine and the Palatinate, and while our beloved Germany thus lies dismembered, powerless and torn, disgracefully robbed, a colony of the international world criminals, there—we dance.

We invite you to come Thursday, February 2, 1921, to a GIANT DEMONSTRATION for a coming GREATER GERMANY to the Zirkus Krone, Engineer Rudolf JUNG, Deputy of the Prague Parliament, and Party Member Adolf HITLER will speak about:

"GERMANY IN HER DEEPEST HUMILIATION"

Beginning 8 p.m., end 10 p.m. Jews not admitted To cover expenses of the hall and posters, admission M.I. War invalids free.
Fellow citizens, white collar and manual workers, Germans from all countries of our fatherland, come in masses!
[The meeting was attended by more than seven thousand persons.]

Elections to the German Reichstag (1924–1932)

The statistical table on the following page reveals the increasing popularity of the National Socialist party from 1924, when the Nazis first appeared on a ballot, to 1932, the last free election before Hitler's accession to power. Note the direct relationship of Nazi popularity to the unemployment figures.

	May 4, 1924	December 7, 1924	May 20, 1928	September 14, 1930	July 31, 1932	November 6, 1932
Number of eligible voters (in millions)	38.4	39.0	41.2	43.0	44.2	44.2
Votes cast (in millions)	29.7	30.7	31.2	35.2	37.2	35.7
National Socialist German Workers' party (Nazi)	1,918,000 6.6%	908,000 3%	810,000 2.6%	6,407,000 18.3%	13,779,000 37.3%	11,737,000 33.1%
German Nationalist People's party (Conservative)	5,696,000 19.5%	6,209,000 20.5%	4,382,000 14.2%	2,458,000 7%	2,187,000 5.9%	3,131,000 8.8%
Center party (Catholic)	3,914,000 13.4%	4,121,000 13.6%	3,712,000 12.1%	4,127,000 11.8%	4,589,000 12.4%	14,230,000 11.9%
Democratic party (The German State Party)	1,655,000 5.7%	1,921,000 6.3%	1,506,000 4.9%	1,322,000 3.8%	373,000 1%	339,000 1%
Social Democratic party	6,009,000 20.5%	7,886,000 26%	9,153,000 29.8%	8,575,000 24.5%	7,960,000 21.6%	7,251,000 20.4%
Communist party	3,693,000 12.6%	2,712,000 9%	3,265,000 10.6%	4,590,000 13.1%	5,370,000 14.3%	5,980,000 16.9%

Unemployment in Germany (1924–1932)*

1924	1928	1930	July 31, 1932	October 31, 1932
978,000	1,368,000	3,076,000	5,392,000	5,109,000

*The figures are those of annual average unemployment, except for 1932, where some precise end-of-the-month figures are available, and the two dates that coincide with the Reichstag elections are given.

Nazi Conversion and Resistance

By 1932, the Nazis had emerged as Germany's strongest single party. Hitler demanded the chancellorship of the Weimar Republic. The president, Paul von Hindenburg, disliked Hitler and resisted entrusting all governmental authority to a single party that "held to such a one-sided attitude toward people with convictions different from theirs." But on January 30, 1933, Hindenburg gave in to political pressure and popular demand and appointed Hitler chancellor. The Nazis were confirmed in power and immediately began to dismantle the Weimar Constitution. The famous Enabling Act allowed Hitler and his Reich Cabinet to issue laws that could deviate from the established constitution, yet could not practically be challenged by representatives of the Parliament or Reichstag. Its overwhelming passage (444 to 94) gave the destruction of parliamentary democracy an appearance of legality; from then on, the Reichstag became a rubber stamp of approval for Hitler's decrees.

The people of Germany were generally enthusiastic about Hitler, his image of a strong, successful fatherland, and his promises of prosperity. Membership in the National Socialist party rose steadily. Some people found that joining the Nazis was even more than a political experience; for them it was almost a religious conversion. The following section presents the experience of two such converts.

"Now I Know Which Road to Take"

JOSEPH GOEBBELS

Someone was standing up and had begun to talk, hesitatingly and shyly at first. . . . Then suddenly the speech gathered momentum. I was caught, I was listening. . . . The crowd began to stir. The haggard grey faces were reflecting hope. . . . Two seats to my left, an old officer was crying like a child. I felt alternately hot and cold. . . . It was as though guns were thundering. . . . I was beside myself. I was shouting hurrah. Nobody seemed surprised. The man up there looked at me for a moment. His blue eyes met my glance like a flame. This was a command. At that moment I was reborn. . . . Now I know which road to take.

[Goebbels became member No. 8,762.]

"Now I Know Which Road to Take" is from *Joseph Goebbels* by Riess, Curt, 1948, Doubleday, p. 14.

"I Had Given Him My Heart"

KURT LUDECKE

Hitler's words were like a scourge. When he spoke of the disgrace of Germany, I felt ready to spring on any enemy . . . glancing around, I saw that his magnetism was holding these thousands as one. . . . I was a man of 32, weary of disgust and disillusionment, a wanderer seeking a cause . . . a yearner after the heroic without a hero. The intense will of the man, the passion of his sincerity, seemed to flow from him into me. I experienced a feeling that could be likened only to a religious conversion. . . . I felt sure that no-one who heard Hitler that night could doubt he was the man of destiny. . . . I had given him my heart.

"I Had Given Him My Heart" is from *Joseph Goebbels*, by Reiss, Curt, 1948, Doubleday, p. 14.

Hitler Youth: "Tough as Leather, Hard as Krupp Steel"

ADOLF HITLER

Any political or religious movement that seeks stability and longevity must ultimately cultivate the loyalty of those who will inherit the future. Hitler established several youth organizations for boys and girls that sought to inculcate the values and ideals that would maintain his authority in the future. Ten-year-olds were taught to "serve the Führer" by stressing the virtues of duty, obedience, and strength. The following speech at a Nuremburg party rally demonstrates how earnestly the Nazis looked to the future.

Each year at the gatherings of youth at the Parteitage (Nuremberg Party Day celebrations) I note the difference: in each year I see the same development which we can discern today in all the other spheres of German life. Our people grows continuously more disciplined, more taut, more sturdy, and youth begins to do the same. . . .

What we wish from our German youth is different from what past generations asked. In our eyes the German youth of the future must be slim and slender, swift as the greyhound, tough as leather, and hard as Krupp steel. We must educate a new type of manhood so that our people does not go to ruin amongst all the degeneracy of our day. We do not talk, we act. We have undertaken to educate this people in a new school, to give it an education which begins in youth and shall never come to an end. . . .

"Hitler Youth" is from Norman H. Baynes, trans. and ed., *The Speeches of Adolf Hitler, April 1922–1939*, vol. 1 (London: Oxford University Press, 1942), pp. 542–545. Reprinted by permission of the publisher.

Nazi propaganda poster: "Youth Serve the Führer. All ten-year-olds in Hitler Youth." *(Bundesarchiva)*

Everyone is bound to serve his people, everyone is bound to arm himself for that service, to steel his body, to prepare and fortify his mind.

And the sooner these preparations begin, the better. . . .

Nothing is possible if there is not a single will which issues its commands and which the others must always obey, beginning from above and ending only at the lowest point. And that is alongside of the training and hardening of the body the second great task. We are a "following," and that means that it is our duty to "follow," to obey. We must educate our whole people so that wherever one is appointed to command the others recognize their duty to obey him, because perhaps an hour later they in their turn will be called upon to command and can only do so precisely as others render to them obedience. That is the expression of an authoritarian State, not of a weak chattering democracy; and in the authoritarian State everyone is proud to owe obedience because he knows: I shall in just the same way find obedience when I have to give a command. . . .

If the others fail to understand us, that need not trouble us. . . . We are no bullies. If the rest of the world misconceives us in our discipline, we cannot help it. From this discipline of ours there will come fewer brawls for the world than from the parliamentary democratic chaos of today. We go our own way: we do not wish to cross the way of another. Would that the others would let us pursue our way in peace!. . . But never do we wish to forget that only the strong deserves friendship, only the strong keeps friendship. And so our will is to make ourselves strong: that is our solution!

Leaflets of "The White Rose" (1942)

HANS AND SOPHIE SCHOLL

The degree to which the German people resisted the Nazi regime has been an ongoing and important topic of research among historians. Resistance was not simply confined to intellectuals, and many dissident Germans were incarcerated in concentration camps along with Jews, Gypsies, and homosexuals. One of the more courageous acts of defiance came from a group of university students and young professionals who called themselves "the White Rose."

In the summer of 1942, leaflets of the White Rose were nailed on poster boards, handed out to the public, and distributed through the mail. They contained attacks on the cultural and political policies of the National Socialist regime. In particular, members of the White Rose accused the Nazis of atrocities against the Jews. Their goal was to resist and obstruct the government through passive resistance. Hans and Sophie Scholl were leaders of the movement. Hans attended medical school and had served in the German army with the rank of sergeant. His sister Sophie first worked as a kindergarten teacher and then attended the University of Munich as a science and philosophy student. They were apprehended in February 1942, accused of treason, and executed that same month after a perfunctory trial. The following is an excerpt from the second leaflet they distributed.

It is impossible to engage in intellectual discourse with National Socialism because it is not an intellectually defensible program. It is false to speak of a National Socialist philosophy, for if there were such an entity, one would have to try by means of analysis and discussion either to prove its validity or to combat it. In actuality, however, we face a totally different situation. At its very inception this movement depended on the deception and betrayal of one's fellow man; even at that time it was inwardly corrupt and could support itself only by constant lies. After all, Hitler states in an early edition of "his" book (a book written in the worst German I have ever read, in spite of the fact that it has been elevated to the position of the Bible in this nation of poets and thinkers): "It is unbelievable to what extent one must betray a people in order to rule it." If at the start this cancerous growth in the nation was not particularly noticeable, it was only because there were still enough forces at work that operated for the good, so that it was kept under control. As it grew larger, however, and finally in an ultimate spurt of growth attained ruling power, the tumor broke open, as it were, and infected the whole body. The greater part of its former opponents went into hiding. The German intellectuals fled to their cellars, there, like plants struggling in the dark, away from light and sun, gradually to choke to death. Now the end is at hand. Now it is our task to find one another again, to spread information from person to person, to keep a steady purpose, and to allow ourselves no rest until the last man is persuaded of the urgent need of his struggle against this system. When thus a wave of unrest goes through the land, when "it is in the air," when many join the cause, then in a great final effort this system can be shaken off. After all, an end in terror is preferable to terror without end. . . .

Since the conquest of Poland [1939], three hundred thousand Jews have been murdered in this country in the most bestial way. Here we see the most frightful crime against human dignity, a crime that is unparalleled in the whole of history. For Jews, too, are human beings—no matter what position we take with respect to the Jewish question—and a crime of this dimension has been perpetrated against human beings. Someone may say that the Jews deserved their fate. This assertion would be a monstrous impertinence. . . .

Why do the German people behave so apathetically in the face of all these abominable crimes, crimes so unworthy of the human race? Hardly anyone thinks about that. It is accepted as fact and put out of mind. The German people slumber on in their dull, stupid sleep and encourage these fascist criminals; they give them the opportunity to carry on their depredations; and of course they do so. Is this a sign that the Germans are brutalized in their simplest human feelings, that no chord within them cries out at the sight of such deeds, that they have sunk into a fatal consciencelessness from which they will never, never awake? It seems to be so, and will certainly be so, if the German does not at last start up out of his stupor, if he does not protest wherever and whenever he can against this clique of criminals, if he show no sympathy for these hundreds of thousands of victims. He must evidence not only sympathy; no, much more: a sense of complicity in guilt. For through his apathetic behavior he gives these evil men the opportunity to act as they do; he tolerates this "government" which has taken upon itself such an infinitely great burden of guilt; indeed, he himself is to blame for the fact that it came about at all! Each man wants to be exonerated of a guilt of this kind, each one continues on his way with the most placid, the calmest conscience. But he cannot be exonerated; he is guilty, guilty, guilty!

Up until the outbreak of the war the larger part of the German people was blinded; the Nazis did not show themselves in their true aspect. But now, now that we have recognized them for what they are, it must be the sole and first duty, the holiest duty of every German to destroy these beasts!

CHRONOLOGY: Democracy and Dictatorship (1914–1939)

June 28, 1914	Assassination of Archduke Franz Ferdinand, heir to the Austro-Hungarian Empire.
July 28, 1914	Austria-Hungary declares war on Serbia after receiving "blank check" of support from Germany.
August 1914	Germany declares war on Russia (Aug. 1) and France (Aug. 3); Germany invades Belgium, followed immediately by Britain's declaration of war on Germany (Aug. 4).
September 5–9, 1914	Battle of the Marne: French and British are able to stop the German advance in the west. Thereafter, the nature of the war in the west changed completely and became one of position instead of movement.
April 22, 1915	Germans employ poisonous gas for the first time at the Second Battle of Ypres.
April 25, 1915	British land at Gallipoli, start of Dardanelles campaign.
May 7, 1915	German submarine sinks the American ship, Lusitania. Among 1200 drowned were 118 Americans.
February–December 1916	Battle of Verdun results in 550,000 French and 450,000 German casualties.
July–November 1916	Battle of the Somme fails to achieve major breakthrough for Allied forces; British use tanks for the first time.
March 1917	Revolution in Russia leads to abdication of Tsar Nicholas II.
April 6, 1917	United States declares war on Germany.
November 8, 1917	Bolsheviks seize power in Petrograd. Russia pulls out of the war.
January 8, 1918	President Woodrow Wilson issues the "Fourteen Points" framework for peace.
March 3, 1918	Bolsheviks accept German peace terms at Brest Litovsk.
November 9, 1918	Kaiser Wilhelm II abdicates German throne and flees to Holland. Armistice concluded on western front.

June 28, 1919	Treaty of Versailles signed between Germany and the Allies. Germany ceded territory and all her colonies to the Allies, returned Alsace-Lorraine to France, promised to pay large reparations, and had its armed forces restricted. The Rhineland was demilitarized and occupied, and the League of Nations was created. Germany admitted "war guilt."
August 1919	Constitution of the Weimar Republic promulgated.
1920	Women receive full franchise in the United States.
October–November 1922	After Fascist takeovers in Bologna and Milan, Mussolini marches on Rome where an intimidated King Victor Emmanuel asks him to form a government. Mussolini is granted temporary dictatorial powers to institute reforms.
January 11, 1923	German nonpayment of reparations leads to French and Belgian troops occupying the industrial Ruhr; Germany adopts passive resistance to the occupation. France leaves in 1925.
September–November 1923	Massive inflation in Germany. Interest rates raised to 90 percent, but by October German mark trading at 10,000 million to the English pound.
November 8–9, 1923	Unsuccessful "Beer Hall" putsch in Munich led by Hitler and Ludendorff. Hitler spends eight months in jail, where he writes *Mein Kampf.*
April 9, 1924	Dawes Plan provides a modified settlement of the reparations issue.
December 1, 1924	Locarno Agreements signed that guarantee Franco-German and Belgian-German frontiers and demilitarization of the Rhineland.
December 24, 1925	Mussolini's dictatorial powers increased in Italy. Press censorship tightened, secret nonfascist organizations banned, and widespread arrests.
1927	Charles Lindbergh flies monoplane Spirit of St. Louis nonstop from New York to Paris (33.5 hours).
1929	Women receive full franchise in Great Britain.
February 6, 1929	Germany accepts Kellogg-Briand Pact, outlawing war and providing for the pacific settlements of disputes.
October 29, 1929	Wall Street crash and cessation of American loans to Europe.
September 14, 1930	In Reichstag elections, Hitler and the National Socialists (Nazis) emerge as a major party with 107 seats, second only to the Social Democrats with 143 seats.
July 1931	Worsening economic crisis in Germany. Unemployment reaches over 4 million.

July 31, 1932	In Reichstag elections, Nazis win 230 seats and become largest party.
November, 1932	Franklin Delano Roosevelt elected President of the United States.
January 30, 1933	President von Hindenburg accepts a cabinet with Hitler as chancellor.
February 27, 1933	Reichstag fire blamed on Communists and made pretext for suspension of civil liberties and freedom of the press.
March 4, 1933	Roosevelt inaugurated President of the United States: "The only thing we have to fear is fear itself."
March 23, 1933	Hitler obtains Enabling Law, granting him dictatorial powers for four years.
May, 1933	Roosevelt lays out plans for the New Deal to provide relief for citizens, to aid recovery through government programs, to reform the capitalist economic system, and to preserve democracy.
July 14, 1933	All parties, other than the Nazis, suppressed. The National Socialist party is formally declared the only political party in Germany.
August 2, 1934	Death of President von Hindenburg. Hitler assumes presidency, but retains title *Der Führer*. Army swears oath of allegiance.

STUDY QUESTIONS

SECTION I: THE BIRTH OF THE MODERN ERA

1. What are your most vivid impressions from the personal accounts of combat under the section "The Horrors of Battle"? Granted that all wars are horrible, what made this war unique?

2. Evaluate the statement "It is sweet and proper to die for one's country." Is it an "Old Lie" as Wilfred Owen said? Was this war a game started by the old, fought by the young, and suffered by the innocent? What about patriotism and honor? Were they hollow concepts in this war? How about in World War II or in Vietnam, or more recently in the Persian Gulf War or the War against terrorism?

3. What measures did Lenin take to protect the position of the Bolsheviks once they had achieved power? How does Lenin justify censorship of the press? Do fallacies or inconsistencies exist in his argument? Note especially the vocabulary. For example, how is the phrase "workmen's and peasants' revolution" used? How was the *Izvestia* newspaper editorial dangerous to the Bolshevik revolution?

4. What are the duties of the secret police? What elements of society was this organization directed against? The tsar also had an active secret police that protected against "enemies of the monarchy." What is the difference between "enemies of the monarchy" and "enemies of the people"? Is a secret police therefore a necessary instrument for maintaining power, regardless of political philosophy?

5. The 1936 Constitution of the Soviet Union guaranteed citizens freedom of speech, press, and assembly. In view of this, how do you account for Stalin's liquidation of the Kulaks, the purge trials, and the establishment of the Gulag?

SECTION II: THE DEMOCRAT AND THE DICTATOR

6. How did Herbert Hoover define the "American System" in his "Rugged Individualism" speech of 1928? What values did he applaud and why was it so important for the government to remain aloof from commercial affairs? How did Hoover define the term, "liberalism"? How did his conception differ from that of Franklin Roosevelt?

7. Analyze Franklin Roosevelt's First Inaugural Address of March 1933. What were the most important images that Roosevelt wanted to convey? What pressures did the country and the President face at this point? Why was this a successful speech?

8. According to the excerpt from Roosevelt's Fireside Chat of May 1933, what were the primary tenets of the New Deal? Why was he so concerned about acting within the boundaries of the Constitution? Although FDR was a member of America's elite aristocracy, what did he do in this speech to identify himself with the common citizen? How did the policies he outlined in this conversation change the foundation of the U.S. economy and society? How is the New Deal with us today?

9. According to Benito Mussolini, what are the primary tenets of fascist doctrine? Why was he especially critical of socialism (Marxism) and democracy? Do you find his arguments compelling or flawed? Why is war such an important requirement for the fascist state? What did Mussolini mean by "[the individual] is deprived of all useless and possibly harmful freedom, but retains what is essential"? What is "harmful freedom" as opposed to "essential freedom"? In what ways was Hitler's concept of fascism (as expressed in the various documents) consistent or inconsistent with Mussolini's concept?

10. Why was the National Socialist party able to rise to power? What were the main political, social, and economic problems of the 1920s and early 1930s, and what were the solutions offered by the Nazis? Why was the Weimar Republic unable to cope with the major problems facing Germany? Was its destruction inevitable?

11. Statistics often reveal much after close analysis. What statements about the comparative strength of political parties can you make based on these data? Which party lost the most support from 1924 to 1932? How successful was the Communist party? What relationships do you see between political election and unemployment?

12. Carefully read the conversion accounts of Joseph Goebbels and Kurt Ludecke. Why did they join the Nazi party? The philosopher Eric Hoffer, in his book *The True Believer*, described such converts as "permanent misfits." He noted that no achievement can give them a sense of fulfillment; they pursue goals passionately, but never arrive: "The permanent misfits can find salvation only in a complete separation from the self; and they usually find it by losing themselves in the compact collectivity of a mass movement. By renouncing individual will, judgment, and ambition, and dedicating all their powers to the service of an eternal cause, they are at last lifted off the endless treadmill which can never lead them to fulfillment. A rising mass movement attracts and holds a following not by its doctrine or promises, but by the refuge it offers from the anxieties [and] barrenness of an individual existence." Do you agree? Why do people give their fanatical devotion to a cause? How might

you apply Hoffer's ideas to our contemporary world? Are terrorists permanent misfits "in the service of an eternal cause"?

13. Analyze the selection on Hitler Youth. How were German children propagandized? What impression was Hitler trying to convey in the poster on Hitler Youth?

14. Analyze the Nazi resistance leaflet distributed by Hans and Sophie Scholl ("The White Rose"). The Scholls ask the question "Why do the German people behave so apathetically in the face of all these abominable crimes? . . . Is this a sign that the Germans are brutalized in their simplest human feelings?" How would you answer these questions? Why didn't more Germans join in the resistance?

15. Was the victory of National Socialism in Germany dependent on Adolf Hitler? How important was he to the Nazi movement? To what extent can the individual mold the events of history? What conditions in a state present the greatest opportunity for individual assertion of will and power? Were these same conditions present in the United States during the Great Depression?

16. Konrad Heiden, in his book *Der Fuehrer* (New York: Houghton Mifflin, 1944, p. v), stated that "Hitler was able to enslave his own people because he gave them something that even the traditional religions could no longer provide; the belief in a meaning to existence beyond the narrowest self-interest." How do you see this statement reflected in the various sources? In what ways did Franklin Roosevelt expand the narrow self-interest of the American people?

17. Compare the accomplishments of Hitler and Roosevelt. They acceded to power in Germany and in the United States within a few months of each other and were faced with the same dire economic and national morale problems. In what ways were their solutions similar? How did their attitudes to the constraints of their national constitutions differ? Is it a fair evaluation to term Roosevelt the "Democrat" and Hitler the "Dictator"? Weren't they both "freeing" their people? Some have viewed Roosevelt's New Deal as an enslavement of U.S. capitalism through the dictates of an imperious government. Do you agree? What is the role of a leader in a crisis?

18. During the 1930s and 1940s, Hitler and Germany led the world to war, with all its attendant suffering and destruction. Some historians argue that the victory of Adolf Hitler and the National Socialist party was consistent with the racism, militarism, and blind obedience to authority that mark the German national character. Can you describe French, Italian, British, Russian, or American character? Is there even such a thing as "national character," and is it legitimate to explain historical events on the basis of such a characterization?

8

"The Abyss Also Looks into You": War and Holocaust

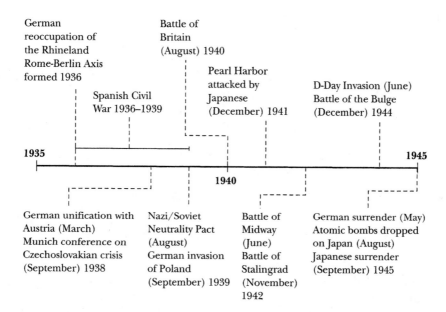

German reoccupation of the Rhineland Rome-Berlin Axis formed 1936

Spanish Civil War 1936–1939

Battle of Britain (August) 1940

Pearl Harbor attacked by Japanese (December) 1941

D-Day Invasion (June) Battle of the Bulge (December) 1944

1935

1940

1945

German unification with Austria (March) Munich conference on Czechoslovakian crisis (September) 1938

Nazi/Soviet Neutrality Pact (August) German invasion of Poland (September) 1939

Battle of Midway (June) Battle of Stalingrad (November) 1942

German surrender (May) Atomic bombs dropped on Japan (August) Japanese surrender (September) 1945

War will never be avoided until babies come into the world with larger cerebrums and smaller adrenal glands.

—*H. L. Mencken*

War is an ugly thing, but not the ugliest of things; the decayed and degraded state of moral and patriotic feeling which thinks nothing worth a war, is worse.... A war to protect other human beings against tyrannical injustice; a war to give victory to their own ideas of right and good, and which is their own war, carried on for an honest purpose by their own free choice—is often the means of their regeneration.

—*John Stuart Mill*

> This is no war for domination or imperial aggrandizement or material gain. . . . It is a war . . . to establish on impregnable rocks, the rights of the individual and it is a war to establish and revive the stature of man.
>
> —*Winston Churchill*

> There was never a good war or a bad peace.
>
> —*Benjamin Franklin*

> The real trouble with war is that it gives no one a chance to kill the right people.
>
> —*Ezra Pound*

CHAPTER THEMES

- *Imperialism:*   Was the German and Japanese desire to expand and acquire more territory the primary cause of World War II? Was the same kind of imperialism the root cause of World War I?

- *Propaganda:*   Why has World War II been termed the "Good War" in the United States and the "Great Patriotic War" in Russia? Was there a distinct clash of ideologies and values that provided the primary motivation for Allied victory? Why was World War II never billed as the "war to end all wars"? Had Europeans and Americans grown less naïve and more cynical?

- *Women in History:*   How essential were the contributions of women to the prosecution of World War II? What were the different expectations of German, British, and American women in particular? How did their efforts affect their social and political status in the postwar years?

- *Beliefs and Spirituality:*   After the massive destruction of World War I, how were soldiers motivated a scant twenty years later to engage once again in war? Was there something spiritual, almost sacred, in the image of "Mother Russia" that motivated twelve million Russian soldiers to sacrifice their lives?

- *Historical Change and Transition:*   Could the Holocaust happen again, and would contemporary technology make genocide a reality? Can the "ethnic cleansing" by Serbian soldiers in Bosnia and Kosovo be likened to the Final Solution of the Nazis? What is the value of studying history?

- *The Big Picture:*   Was World War II merely a continuation of World War I? Or had political and social conditions changed so much that World War II was set apart by new ideologies and technologies? Was World War II inevitable?

At the conclusion of the Great War in November 1918, the peoples of Europe paused amidst their ruined cities, twisted landscapes, and shattered lives to consider the remnants of Western Civilization. They understood that an era had truly ended. They had passed from the structured formalism of polite Victorian company, from an era of effete monarchs, to a world of disillusioned reality. An entire generation of men had been sacrificed to aggressive monarchs, shortsighted politicians, incompetent generals, and the ruinous effects of modern military technology. Everywhere people sought to justify the many lives that had been lost—some might say wasted—on the battlefields of Europe. This had been "the war to make the world safe for democracy," the "war to end all wars." It was termed the "Great War" because no one could envision another of such magnitude and destructive capacity. And yet, as we now view the twentieth century, we refer to it as the First World War, to be followed twenty years later by another that was truly global in scope and far more destructive, consuming the lives and property of over thirty million people.

Some historians have viewed the First and Second World Wars as one conflict with an intervening period of "festering peace," as the Greek historian Thucydides might have termed it. There is no doubt that the origins of the Second World War certainly sprang in part from the harsh peace that had been imposed on the Germans in the Treaty of Versailles in 1919. Adolf Hitler had used the restrictions, reparations, and guilt imposed on the struggling German Weimar Republic in the 1920s to remind the German populace of a distant past of dignity and glorious culture that could once again be gained by following a regimen of discipline and devotion to the nation and to the Führer. After coming to power in 1933 and gaining success in solving some of the employment and monetary problems engendered by the depression, Hitler obtained the confidence and mass support of a majority of Germans. He worked carefully to persuade through propaganda and punish through terror. By 1936, the Nazi state had consolidated its domestic situation and was eager to be recognized by the international community as an equal, no longer burdened by reparations or military and territorial restriction. Feeling buoyed by his domestic success, Hitler invited the world to the 1936 Olympics in Berlin as a way of showcasing German discipline and talent.

But his vision was focused on a broader agenda to be gained, if possible, by subtlety and, if not, by intimidation and force. Hitler sought to incorporate territory into the German Reich to which Germany had historical or racial connections. This need for *Lebensraum,* or "living space," was essential, Hitler argued, for the development of the German nation. In 1936, Hitler reoccupied the Rhineland, a region between Germany and France, in defiance of the Treaty of Versailles. To his surprise, he encountered little reaction from Great Britain and France, which were charged with guaranteeing the provisions of Versailles. Hitler's next step in obtaining more territory for the Reich was the *Anschluss,* or unification with Austria, in March 1938. This was achieved when Germany invaded Austria the day before a plebiscite on unification was to be held because Hitler feared defiance and a defeat at the polls. His assertive policy of incorporation reached its apex in September 1938 as Hitler demanded the Sudentenland of Czechoslovakia, where ethnic Germans resided and were (as he claimed) abused. As a result of the Munich agreements, Hitler gained access to this territory.

At each step, Hitler was confronted and pacified by the figure of British Prime Minister Neville Chamberlain, who believed that Hitler could be satisfied and war averted by conceding territory and respect to Germany. This policy of "appeasement," as it came to be called, depended on the assumption that Germany's demands were legitimate and limited. It is to Hitler's credit that he understood the domestic divisions within Britain and France and was able to take bold risks at crucial times. As the concessions mounted and Hitler realized his visions of greater "living space" for the German *Volk* and the consolidation of a greater

German Reich that would last a thousand years, he moved into areas that could no longer be viewed as having special significance to German history and culture. Hitler's desire to link the Reich with East Prussia by a corridor through Poland was the final straw in Chamberlain's appeasement concessions, and the line was drawn. War broke out on September 3, 1939, after Hitler had invaded Poland two days earlier.

World War II, however, is not simply the story of Hitler and Chamberlain. The world was enrolled as the Axis alliance joined together the other fascist powers of Italy and Japan. The influence and independence of Benito Mussolini soon faded amidst the dominance and military power of Germany. Japan had pursued its own policy of imperialism in the Far East by grabbing valuable mineral-rich areas like Manchuria from China and by imposing its presence in Indochina and Malaya in pursuit of oil and tin. Japanese relations with the United States were tenuous at best. The fascist Japanese government under the leadership of General Hideki Tojo received sanction from Emperor Hirohito to cripple the U.S. fleet at Pearl Harbor to prevent any restriction of an aggressive Japanese policy. The "Rising Sun" of Japan would not be restrained.

The war itself gave new meaning to the definition of destruction. The world now fell to the unleashed might of mechanized warfare supported by the full commitment of national will. Societies were transformed as men went to war and women moved to the factories. Civilian populations felt the pain of war as never before. Cities were bombed and refugees were rarely spared—this was total war, war with no restriction and no innocents. Ultimately, the developing technologies of war blurred the boundaries of civilization as nuclear weapons were finally detonated over the Japanese cities of Hiroshima and Nagasaki.

World War II truly causes a pause in the consideration of civilization. In the eyes of the Western powers this became "the Good War," the struggle against the evil of Hitler, Mussolini, and Tojo. There was purpose and justification for our destruction. And yet at the conclusion of hostilities in 1945, the world had not been "made safe for democracy." The Soviet Union had indeed made a "strange bedfellow" in the war against fascism, but the Cold War against Soviet authoritarianism would continue for an additional forty years. With the looming specter of the "Red Menace" and the subsequent undeclared wars in Korea and Vietnam, the claim was never made that the "Good War" was the "war to end all wars."

TOTAL WAR

It takes twenty years of peace or more to make a man; it takes only twenty seconds of war to destroy him.

—*Baudouin I, King of Belgium*

What war has always been is a puberty ceremony. It's a rough one, but you went away a boy and came back a man, maybe with an eye missing or whatever but godammit you were a man and people had to call you a man thereafter.

—*Kurt Vonnegut*

Europe on the Eve of World War II. Germany's secret neutrality pact with the Soviet Union allowed Hitler to invade Poland on September 1, 1939. Britain had guaranteed Poland's independence and declared war on Germany two days later. *(From The War in Maps: An Atlas of the New York Times Maps, 4/e, by Francis Brown and Lucas Manditch. Copyright © 1942, 1943, 1946, 1973 by Oxford University Press, Inc., renewed 1973 by Francis Brown. Reprinted by permission of the publisher.)*

"At Dawn We Crossed into Poland"
(September 1, 1939)

LIEUTENANT BARON TASSLIO VON BOGENHARDT

The German invasion of Poland on September 1, 1939 not only drove Europe into another world conflict, but it instituted a new form of warfare called blitzkrieg, *or "lightning war." The emphasis was on speed and focused aggression through massed armored columns of tanks supported by airpower. The Germans quickly overwhelmed Polish defenses, as the following account by a German officer indicates.*

The ordering of general mobilization came almost on top of Britain's and France's guarantee of Poland; reservists were called up, vehicles and troops mobilized and ammunition distributed. We loaded our tanks and trucks onto the train and travelled for three days to Paprad in Slovakia, where we waited about ten miles from the Polish border. Several of us went up to the frontier to reconnoitre, and after the third day we got orders to move up during the night. At dawn we crossed into Poland.

The whole thing was so like an occupation of a manoeuvre that we could hardly believe this was really war; it all seemed too well-ordered and familiar. There was virtually no resistance, and for days on end we advanced towards the Polish Ukraine. There were rumors of sharp-shooters and partisans, but I never saw or heard anything of them, except for the occasional sound of a shot in the distance. There was a certain amount of sporadic fighting when we got to the river barriers, but the Luftwaffe [Air Force] had already cleared the way for us. Their Stuka dive-bombers were deadly accurate, and as there was no opposition they had it all their own way. The roads and fields were swarming with unhappy peasants who had fled in panic from their villages when the bombing began, and we passed hundreds and hundreds of Polish troops walking dejectedly towards Slovakia. The Poles seemed to be completely apathetic, and there were so many prisoners that nobody bothered to guard them or even tell them where to go.

The Invasion of France: "We Were Through the Maginot Line!"
(May 15, 1940)

GENERAL ERWIN ROMMEL

The German invasion of Poland was so successful that the Russians moved quickly to claim their division of Poland and the Baltic countries of Estonia, Latvia, and Lithuania. After this, events slowed dramatically into a sitzkrieg, *or "phony war," as Germany consolidated its gains and prepared for the next phase of war. In April, Hitler invaded Denmark and Norway and followed this with attacks on Belgium and the Netherlands. France had relied for its defense on the renowned Maginot Line, a series of artillery fortifications built after World War I to repel an attack. But the new German mobilized warfare, together with the fact that the fortifications were never completed through Belgium to the sea, allowed the Germans to maneuver around and through the Maginot Line. The French army, poorly led by generals who could not fathom the changes in mechanized warfare since 1918, collapsed. Hitler defeated France in five weeks.*

General Erwin Rommel was one of the most able of all German commanders. A specialist in tank warfare, he wrote the following account of the invasion of France that reveals a sense of wonder at the ease of the Nazi victory.

The way to the west was now open. The moon was up and for the time being we could expect no real darkness. I had already given orders in the plan for the break-through, for the leading tanks to scatter the road and converge with machine and anti-tank gunfire at intervals during the drive to Avesnes, which I hoped would prevent the enemy from laying mines. . . .

The tanks now rolled in a long column through the line of fortifications and on towards the first houses, which had been set alight by our fire. . . . Our artillery was dropping heavy harassing fire on villages and the road far ahead of the regiment. Gradually the speed increased. Before long we were five hundred—a thousand—two thousand—three thousand yards into the fortified zone. Engines roared, tank tracks clanked and clattered. Whether or not the enemy was firing was impossible to tell in the ear-splitting noise. . . .

Civilians and French troops, their faces distorted with terror, lay huddled in the ditches, alongside hedges and in every hollow beside the road. We passed refugee columns, the carts abandoned by their owners, who had fled in panic into the fields. On we went, at a steady speed, towards our objective. . . . Every so often [I took] a look out of the hatch to assure myself that there was still no resistance and that contact was being maintained to the rear. The flat countryside lay spread out around us under the cold light of the moon. We were through the Maginot Line! It was hardly conceivable. Twenty-two years before we had stood for four and a half long years before this self-same enemy [the French] and had won victory after victory and yet finally lost the war. And now we had broken through the renowned Maginot Line and were driving deep into enemy territory. It was not just a beautiful dream. It was reality.

The Japanese Attack on Pearl Harbor: "I Saw My Maker on Sunday"
PRIVATE NICHOLAS GAYNOS

Although U.S. support of the British through lend-lease arrangements might have justified a German declaration of war against the United States, Hitler knew that his chances for victory in Europe were greater without the involvement of the "sleeping giant." In fact, the United States may not have overcome its isolationist caution and entered the European conflict had not war been thrust on it in the Pacific.

Since the early 1930s, Japan had been forging a policy of conquest in Asia. Japan had conquered the mineral-rich Chinese region of Manchuria in 1931 and renamed it Manchukuo. After allying itself with Germany and Italy and signing a neutrality pact with the Soviet Union, Japan exploited the weakness of Britain and France abroad. In July 1941, the Japanese occupied Indochina. In response, the United States and Britain froze Japanese assets and cut off oil supplies. Without control over the Indonesian oil fields and the supplies of rubber and tin in Malaya, Japanese plans for expansion would fail. The solution, imposed by a war faction in the Japanese government led by General Hideki Tojo, was to end the constraint of the United States.

On Sunday morning, December 7, 1941, while Japanese representatives were still negotiating in Washington, Japan launched a surprise air attack on the U.S. naval base at Pearl Harbor, Hawaii. Its aim was to severely cripple America's ability to respond to Japanese aggression in the Pacific and allow Japan to consolidate its gains before the United States could rebuild its fleet. Eyewitness accounts of the disaster follow, and the section ends with President Roosevelt's famous request in Congress for a declaration of war against Japan.

December 9, 1941

Dear Folks,

Well, I'm okay and feeling fine. We sure had a hot time here for a while and I thought that my end had come—God, was it hell. I'll give you an eyewitness account of the Japanese air raid on Pearl Harbor and Hickam Field on Sunday, 7 December 1941. This ought to make a good news copy for the *Bridgeport Post*.

Well, Sunday as usual, all of the men were sleeping late because we had no work to do. I was sound asleep, having gone to bed at 4:30 A.M. after being relieved of duty. It was exactly 7:55 when I was almost tossed out of bed by a terrific roar and the ensuing concussion. Most of the fellows also got up and, on looking out the window, we could see flames about five hundred feet high and huge clouds of smoke coming from Pearl Harbor.

No one thought it was war until we looked out of our eastern windows and saw some of our hangars in flames. Somebody yelled, "They are Japanese planes," but nobody believed it. We all ran out of the barracks and looked skyward. It was plain to see them. They were only from fifty to one hundred feet off the ground, and the huge red circle under their wings proved their identity. Some of them had huge torpedoes under the fuselage almost as long as the ship itself.

The thunder of bombs and the staccato of machine guns made such a deafening roar you had to yell to be heard a few feet away. The splintering of wood as fifty-caliber bullets ripped through the wooden barracks was mixed with screams of men as they ran from one shelter to another. We soon collected our senses and the full realization that war was here.

Some men cried, some laughed, others were terrified, some just couldn't seem to understand what it was all about. I soon had my senses under control and jumped in a car headed for my post. With a hail of bullets and with the planes roaring right over our heads, we raced down the street. I arrived at my transmitters and dove into a hole caused by an exploded bomb. One young fellow was dead, and his legs stuck out of the hole. It reminded me of a book I once read back home. I stayed here until things had quieted down and then scurried for safety in my flimsy office. We all knew they would be back soon so we hurriedly made preparations for their return. It was at 10:20 when the second attack came.

I was busy removing a radio truck to safety. Three men and I kept working as they dived into the big barracks and dropped load after load of bombs. The very ground shook, and my ears were ringing. By this time they spotted my equipment and headed straight for my men and me. I was lying in a small hole about ten feet to the right of my trucks. As the planes dove down at us, I could peek out under the brim of my tin helmet and see them spitting fire at us. The ground in front of me was spraying up and I could see the bombs leave the planes and head straight down at us. One of them was a one-thousand-pound bomb

"A date which will live in infamy." The Japanese attack on the American naval base at Pearl Harbor, Hawaii, on December 7, 1941, brought the United States into World War II. This picture shows the destruction of the battleships Arizona, Tennessee, and West Virginia. *(National Archives)*

and landed fifty feet on my right. Three kids with a machine gun were shooting at the plane and the bomb landed almost on them. It blew them sky-high—gun and all.

The dirt and stones fell all over us and I ached all over. I emptied my forty-five pistol time after time into the planes, but it was futile. I thumbed my nose as they roared right over my head. We all swore like hell.

The planes were still roaring around strafing us unmercifully as those of us that were alive got into cars and started to pick up the dead and wounded. One of the kids who was blown up with the machine gun was lying about fifty feet away. I tried to pick him up and he fell apart in my arms. He was covered with dirt and smiling. We rushed as many as we could to the hospital and gave first aid to those lying near us. Things were now getting quiet and then ambulances, nurses, and trucks came to pick up the men. Some of the things were so ghastly I cannot write of them. All I can say is that my baptism under fire sure was hell on earth and I saw my Maker on Sunday, December 7, 1941.

The U.S.S. *Arizona*: "Some Sort of Hellish Nightmare!"

SEAMAN JOHN RAMPLEY

On 7 December, a beautiful, clear, typical island day dawned. Being Sunday, the entire ship would be on "holiday routine." Sunrise over the harbor on Sunday was in itself a religious experience. With the stillness and quietness which surrounded the water, it was as if every Sunday was an Easter sunrise service. Certainly, this Sunday was to be no exception. . . .

Within moments, general quarters were sounded. "This is no drill. I repeat, this is no drill," echoed down the steel corridors of the ship. The words sent a cold, shuttering chill down my spine. At our battle stations on the fourteen-inch guns, there was little to do but pray. In the space of a few seconds, some men made up for twenty and more years of tardy

Travers, Paul Joseph, *Eyewitness to Infamy: An Oral History of Pearl Harbor.* Copyright © 1991 by Madison Books Inc. Reprinted with permission.

prayers. Inside the turret, there was an eerie silence. Everyone seemed afraid to breathe, much less speak, as if that would somehow give away our position to the enemy or attract the attention of one of the bombs. We waited anxiously for some word from topside. Even though we were protected by the heavy plating of the turret, we felt helpless and defenseless, not being able to take any kind of action to defend ourselves and our fellow sailors. We could hear the thunder and feel the ship shudder as the bombs fell upon her. At one point in time, we felt a tremendous jolt, as if the ship had been lifted up in the air and slammed back down. Little did we realize that this was the fatal blow for the Arizona. Rivets popped from the steel walls and flew about the place. . . .

After what seemed like an eternity, the order came over the speakers, "All hands abandon ship." I looked around for some comfort, but all my shipmates seemed to have the same awareness as myself. Our life together aboard the old Arizona was over. I climbed down the ladder on the outside of the turret. Everywhere I touched or grabbed onto the ship, I felt the effects of the fires and explosions. The ship had become a piece of molten steel, a kind of giant tea kettle, where heat was being transferred to all metal and steel parts. . . . Finally being outside the turret, it looked as if the rest of the ship was a blazing inferno, encircled by a wall of fire which was quickly closing in. I remember looking around the deck and seeing my shipmates from the deck division with their bodies burned black or lying on the deck bleeding from open wounds. Some men were screaming and jumping over the side of the ship. Others were spread about the deck in various positions, crying and moaning in agony. Charred and mutilated bodies were scattered everywhere in the wreckage of the ship. They lay crumpled like broken dolls who had been picked up in the air by some giant hand and slammed against the structures of the ship. With all the smoke and fire on the decks, it seemed difficult to catch one's breath. . . . All around, the air was filled with the smell of burning oil and burning flesh. It was a smell which lingered in the air like a heavy fog, saturating one's clothes and body.

I walked, then crawled, very calmly and carefully to the side of the ship and looked down into the water. The water was partially covered with oil, most of which was burning. . . . From where I stood, all I could see forward was a crumbling mass of twisted metal that had only minutes before been the proud superstructure. The command to abandon ship was being repeated over and over again. Enemy planes were still strafing the ship when I made the decision to jump. The warm water was certainly a refresher. When I came to the surface, I was hoping that the whole thing was a bad dream, some sort of hellish nightmare. . . . I began swimming toward Ford Island. The swim wasn't far, but it was very exhausting swimming an obstacle course filled with oil, debris, and bodies. I reached the island in relatively good shape, considering the ordeal which I had been through. After a short rest and a couple of mouthfuls of water, I got my second wind and was ready to help wherever needed.

It wasn't until many hours later that I learned so many of my shipmates were dead. Of the fifteen from my boot platoon that I went aboard with, I was the only one who survived.

"A Date Which Will Live in Infamy"
PRESIDENT FRANKLIN DELANO ROOSEVELT

Yesterday, December 7, 1941—a date which will live in infamy—the United States of America was suddenly and deliberately attacked by naval and air forces of the Empire of Japan.

The United States was at peace with that nation and, at the solicitation of Japan, was still in conversation with its Government and its Emperor looking toward the maintenance of peace in the Pacific. . . .

It will be recorded that the distance of Hawaii from Japan makes it obvious that the attack was deliberately planned many days or even weeks ago. During the intervening time the Japanese Government has deliberately sought to deceive

"A Date Which Will Live in Infamy" is from Department of State, *Bulletin*, December 13, 1941, p. 474.

the United States by false statements and expressions of hope for continued peace.

The attack yesterday on the Hawaiian Islands has caused severe damage to American naval and military forces. Very many American lives have been lost. In addition American ships have been reported torpedoed on the high seas between San Francisco and Honolulu. . . .

As Commander-in-Chief of the Army and Navy I have directed that all measures be taken for our defense. Always will we remember the character of the onslaught against us. No matter how long it may take us to overcome this premeditated invasion, the American people in their righteous might will win through to absolute victory. . . .

With confidence in our armed forces—with the unbounded determination of our people—we will gain the inevitable triumph—so help us God.

I ask that the Congress declare that since the unprovoked and dastardly attack by Japan on Sunday, December seventh, a state of war has existed between the United States and the Japanese Empire.

Women in the Factories: "My Hands Are as Smooth as the Steel I Worked on" (August 1943)

ELIZABETH HAWES

Perhaps the most amazing feat of logistical supply in history occurred after the disaster at Pearl Harbor when American industry was transformed to produce the implements of war. Much more than the economy was altered, however. An entire society was transformed as men went to war and women went into the factories.

"Rosie the Riveter" became an endearing image of women who decided to leave their jobs as homemakers, teachers, and sales clerks to become crane operators and machinists. At proving grounds, women loaded and tested machine guns and antiaircraft weapons. Women became guards at plants, foundry workers, hydraulic press operators, and miners. In January 1942, 4,000 women were employed as war workers. Within a year the number had swollen to 43,000.

The standard workweek was forty-eight hours (six days of eight hours each) with only Sundays off, and many women routinely worked overtime. Many doubted that women could handle the long hours and grind of grueling, repetitive work. But most women truly felt that their contributions were essential to victory and proved to themselves and to the country that they could compete in traditional male occupations. The following account explains the demands and benefits of wartime factory work for women.

A few months ago, when everybody was talking about the production crisis—can women do it?—will women do it?—how are you going to make women do it?—I began to murmur that I guessed I'd go into a factory and find out how the wheels went round. . . .

Now that I've worked a few months in a plant—on the graveyard shift too—the only wonder to me is that all the women in the USA aren't storming the factory gates. I'm convinced that any healthy woman can work in a factory—and like it. My biggest regret is that I had to leave because I'd agreed to do some writing. My biggest ambition is to get back.

Sure, I caught a bad cold. My hands aren't soft any more but they're as smooth as the steel I worked on. . . . So what! All the other women had to do cleaning and laundry as well as cooking and shopping. I was spared that. . . .

"'My Hands Are as Smooth as the Steel I Worked On'" is from Elizabeth Hawes, "My Life on the Midnight Shift," *Woman's Home Companion* (August 1943), pp. 24, 47.

The plant itself was exciting. It's one of the Wright aeronautical plants in northern New Jersey—I believe the biggest airplane engine plant in the country. You feel you're in a small town, only the streets are lined with machines. Electric trucks honk at you constantly and people on bicycles flip past as you wend your way from the locker room to your machine a mile or so distant. There are no windows. Air conditioning and thousands of long blue lights take the place of the breezes and the sun. . . .

It was a great pleasure to me that nobody gave a darn who anyone was or whether you'd ever had your picture in the paper or shaken hands with the Duchess of Windsor or Gertie Lawrence. . . . Of course there are little discords. The foremen and subforemen are honestly scared to death of us women. When first you arrive they look at you out of the corner of their eyes. . . . Every woman machinist has to endure sheer torture from her fellow male employees at one point in her career. You discover that you can't work without tools and that the company doesn't provide all of them. First you borrow from your lead man or somebody near by who owns a toolbox. Ultimately you buy your own toolbox and quite a few dollars' worth of wrenches, hammers, micrometers and such.

The men see that now you think you're a mechanic. Some honestly don't believe the Lord ever intended women to be mechanics. Others are infuriated by your presumption that you can do their work. . . .

Thank heaven, none of the women in the plant had ever been told by "authoritative sources," as I had, that the women of the USA are unpatriotic—that they're just working for money.

They are working for money—money to feed their kids, money to keep their homes together—so their sons and husbands can fight. They never speak of being useful because it might sound boastful. It might sound as if you were taking credit for losing sleep, for tending sick children at home, for not having time to shop carefully and for still turning up at work.

But mostly I want to go back to Wright's new plant because I think the women who work in war plants, and the men who first help them and then work with them are the luckiest people in the world. There's an equality developing there unlike any I've ever seen. Joe was an Italian—Nel, a Negro—Suzy, Irish—there were Germans, Poles, Hungarians, Gentiles, Jews. Slowly you could see there was no difference between any two of us. Gradually everybody was beginning to work as one unit. When you see something like that happening you feel you're not just doing a job to help win the war. You also have the profound pleasure of seeing the future peace being worked out before your eyes.

HOLOCAUST: THE FINAL SOLUTION (1941–1945)

I mean the clearing out of the Jews, the extermination of the Jewish race. . . . Most of you must know what it means when 100 corpses are lying side by side, or 500, or 1,000. To have stuck it out and at the same time . . . to have remained decent fellows, that is what has made us hard. This is a page of glory in our history which has never been written and is never to be written. . . .

—*Heinrich Himmler to his S.S. Officers*

In spite of everything, I still believe that people are really good at heart.

—*Anne Frank*

Whoever fights monsters should see to it that in the process he does not become a monster; and when you look long into an abyss, the abyss also looks into you.

—*Friedrich Nietzsche*

Despair is no solution. I know that. What is the solution? Hitler had one. And he tried it while a civilized world kept silent. I remember. And I am afraid.

—*Elie Wiesel*

The name Adolf Hitler has become synonymous with evil. Much of this reputation has been derived from his attempt to commit genocide, to exterminate an entire race of people. One of the more distinctive differences between Italian fascism under Benito Mussolini (1883–1945) and the Nazi movement was Hitler's use of anti-Semitism. Hitler demanded that Germany be composed of racially pure Aryan stock. The blond, blue-eyed German, untainted by inferior blood, became Hitler's ideal and the image he tried to cultivate in his propaganda. Hitler saw the Jews as the source of all of Germany's trouble. According to Hitler, Jews were cowards who did not support the fatherland in the Great War. They had deep communist sympathies, controlled international finance, and dominated the most important offices in government. Jews also controlled the purse strings of the nation and thus prevented worthier and more talented individuals from holding jobs and contributing to German culture. Indeed, Hitler had once been a frustrated artist in Vienna who blamed his failure on such Jewish influence. Hitler understood that hatred often unifies a nation more readily than does love. In troubled times, people want a simple explanation for their pain and insecurity. For Hitler, and consequently for Germany, that explanation was the Jew.

Anti-Semitism certainly did not originate with Hitler. Jews had been persecuted since the Middle Ages and even blamed for such things as outbreaks of bubonic plague. Still, never before was there such a systematic, methodical attempt to exterminate an entire race.

Although Hitler had exhibited his racism from the early 1920s in speeches and writings, and had incorporated it into the philosophy of National Socialism, nothing could be implemented until the Nazis came into power. By 1935, Jews were excluded from citizenship by law in order to preserve German blood and honor. Germany was saturated with propaganda that presented the Jew as an immoral pervert whose presence was a threat to the health and morality of the German community. Nazi policy slowly evolved toward deportation and then toward isolation of the Jews in city ghettos. The "Final Solution" to the Jewish problem actually began in June 1941. As Hitler's armies drove into Russia, special mobile killing units (Einsatzgruppen) were set up and followed just behind the front lines. For eighteen months, the Einsatzgruppen operated and killed over 1.3 million Jews. The Nazis also built several concentration camps generally designed to house workers and remove Jews from society. The treatment of prisoners was cruel, and hundreds of thousands died of exhaustion, starvation, and disease. The Nazi commitment to Jewish extermination even exceeded the bounds of practicality. Although there was a widespread shortage of labor throughout German-controlled Europe during the war, the Nazis continued to wipe out valuable workers. The camps, run by Hitler's private army called the S.S. (Schutzstaffel), often served as holding pens until the inmates were sent by train to six death camps located in Poland. Created solely for the task of killing, the camps at Auschwitz and Treblinka have become infamous—over 2.7 million Jews were eliminated, 1 million in Auschwitz alone. Thousands of other undesirable people such as Gypsies, Slavs, and even dissident Germans were also killed.

Many questions arise out of the Holocaust that make this a particularly important and relevant historical problem. How could such a violation against humanity have happened? Could it happen again? Can one view the Jewish Holocaust as a precedent that legitimized the dropping of the atomic bomb on Hiroshima and Nagasaki? Can one say, "War is Hell," and let it go at that? How deep and penetrating is the racial argument? Do we all have prejudices, that, if exploited properly, can lead to such results? The urgency of these questions is intensified when we consider other issues such as the policy of "ethnic cleansing" by the Serbs in Bosnia or the influence of the Ku Klux Klan; the millions who were murdered by Stalin during Soviet collectivization, industrialization, and the Great Purges of the 1930s; the butchery in Rwanda; the ruthlessness of the Cambodian dictator Pol Pot; or the maniacal ranting of Muammar Gaddafi or Saddam Hussein.

Not forgetting is the responsibility of the living.

Nazi Racial Policy and Propaganda

In 1936, Germany hosted the Olympic Games, and Hitler ordered the temporary removal of anti-Jewish placards in order to appease foreign opinion. Still, anti-Semitic propaganda continued to flow, especially from Der Stürmer, *a sensationalistic journal published by Julius Streicher. The following excerpt is from a book for older children called* Der Giftpilz (The Poisonous Mushroom), *which presented the Jew as an evil deviate who preyed on the innocence of children.*

"I Got You at Last, You Little German Girl"

ERNST HIEMER

"It is almost noon," he said, "now we want to summarize what we have learned in this lesson. What did we discuss?"

All the children raise their hands. The teacher calls on Karl Scholz, a little boy on the first bench. "We talked about how to recognize a Jew."

"Good! Now tell us about it!"

Little Karl takes the pointer, goes to the blackboard and points to the sketches.

"One usually recognizes a Jew by his nose. The Jewish nose is crooked at the end. It looks like the figure 6. Therefore it is called the 'Jewish Six.' Many non-Jews have crooked noses, too. But their noses are bent, not at the end but further up. Such a nose is called a hook nose or eagle's beak. It has nothing to do with a Jewish nose."

"Right!" says the teacher. "But the Jew is recognized not only by his nose. . . ." The boy continues. "The Jew is also recognized by his lips. His lips are usually thick. Often the lower lip hangs down. This is called 'sloppy.' And the Jew is also recognized by his eyes. His eyelids are usually thicker and more fleshy than ours. The look of the Jew is lurking and sharp."

Then the teacher goes to the desk and turns over the blackboard, on its back is a verse. The children recite it in chorus:

From a Jew's countenance—the evil devil talks to us,
The devil, who in every land—is known as evil plague.
If we shall be free of the Jew—and again will be happy and glad,
Then the youth must struggle with us—to subdue the Jew devil.

Inge sits in the reception room of the Jew doctor. She has to wait a long time. She looks through the journals which are on the table. But she is almost too nervous to read even a few sentences. Again and again she remembers the talk with her mother. And again and again her mind reflects on the warnings of her leader of the BDM [League of German Girls]: "A German must not consult a Jew doctor! And particularly not a German girl! Many a girl that went to a Jew doctor to be cured, found disease and disgrace!"

When Inge had entered the waiting room, she experienced an extraordinary incident. From the doctor's consulting room she could hear the sound of crying. She heard the voice of a young girl: "Doctor, doctor leave me alone!"

"'I Got You at Last'" is from the Office of the U.S. Chief of Counsel for the Prosecution of Axis Criminality, *Nazi Conspiracy and Aggression* (Washington, DC: Government Printing Office, 1947), vol. 4, pp. 358–359 (PS-1778).

Then she heard the scornful laughing of a man. And then all of a sudden it became absolutely silent. Inge had listened breathlessly.

"What may be the meaning of all this?" she asked herself and her heart was pounding. And again she thought of the warning of her leader in the BDM.

Inge was already waiting for an hour. Again she takes the journals in an endeavor to read. Then the door opens. Inge looks up. The Jew appears. She screams. In terror she drops the paper. Frightened she jumps up. Her eyes stare into the face of the Jewish doctor. And this face is the face of the devil. In the middle of this devil's face is a huge crooked nose. Behind the spectacles two criminal eyes. And the thick lips are grinning. A grinning that expresses: "Now I got you at last, you little German girl!"

And then the Jew approaches her. His fleshy fingers stretch out after her. But now Inge has her wits. Before the Jew can grab hold of her, she hits the fat face of the Jew doctor with her hand. Then one jump to the door. Breathlessly she escapes the Jew house.

Decree of the Reich Marshal
(July 31, 1941)

HERMANN GOERING

By 1940, the Nazis had embarked on a policy that was designed to "cleanse" the German homeland of Jews by confining them to ghettos in cities, especially in Poland. There the Nazis could control them and, upon demand, export them to concentration camps where they would be put to work or die. But in July 1941, preparations were made for a secretive "Final Solution" to the Jewish problem. It was discussed in more detail at the Wansee Conference in January 1942, as the following excerpts indicate.

To: The Chief of the Security Police and the Security Service; SS-Gruppenfuehrer Heydrich

Complementing the task that was assigned to you on 24 January 1939, which dealt with the carrying out of emigration and evacuation, a solution of the Jewish problem, as advantageous as possible, I hereby charge you with making all necessary preparations in regard to organizational and financial matters for bringing out a complete solution of the Jewish question in the German sphere of influence in Europe.

Wherever other governmental agencies are involved, these are to cooperate with you. I charge you furthermore to send me, before long, an overall plan concerning the organizational, factual and material measures necessary for the accomplishment of the desired solution of the Jewish question.

Wansee Conference
(January 20, 1942)

II. At the beginning of the meeting the Chief of the Security Police and the SD, SS Lieutenant General Heydrich, reported his appointment by the Reich Marshal to service as Commissioner for the Preparation of the Final Solution of the

"Wansee Conference" is from the Nuremberg Military Tribunals, *Trials of War Criminals* (Washington, DC: Government Printing Office, 1947–1949), vol. 13, pp. 211–213.

"Decree of the Reich Marshal" is from the Office of the U.S. Chief Counsel for Prosecution of Axis Criminality, *Nazi Conspiracy and Aggression* (Washington, DC: Government Printing Office, 1947), vol. 3, pp. 525–526 (PS-710).

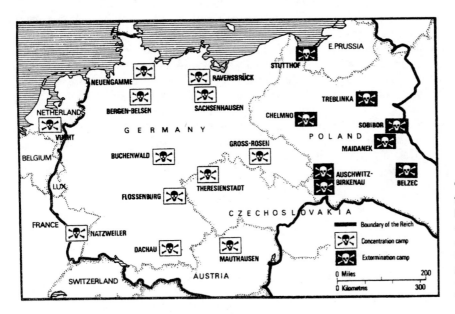

"Sites of Nazi Concentration Camps" is from Louis L. Snyder, *Encyclopedia of the Third Reich*. (New York: McGraw-Hill Book Company, 1976, p. 57. Reprinted by permission of the publisher.)

• • •

European Jewish Problem, and pointed out that the officials had been invited to this conference in order to clear up the fundamental problems. The Reich Marshal's request to have a draft submitted to him on the organizational, factual, and material requirements with respect to the Final Solution of the European Jewish Problem, necessitated this previous general consultation by all the central offices directly concerned, in order that there should be coordination in the policy.

The primary responsibility for the administrative handling of the Final Solution of the Jewish Problem will rest centrally with the Reich Leader SS and the Chief of the German Police (Chief of the Security Police and the SD)—regardless of geographic boundaries.

The Chief of the Security Police and the SD thereafter gave a brief review of the battle conducted up to now against these enemies. The most important are—

1. Forcing the Jews out of the various fields of the community life of the German people.
2. Forcing the Jews out of the living space [*Lebensraum*] of the German people.

Meanwhile, in view of the dangers of emigration during the war and in view of the possibilities in the East, the Reich Leader SS and Chief of the German Police had forbidden the emigrating of the Jews.

III. The emigration program has now been replaced by the evacuation of the Jews to the East as a further solution possibility, in accordance with previous authorization by the Fuehrer.

These actions are of course to be regarded only as a temporary substitute; nonetheless, here already, the coming Final Solution of the Jewish Question is of great importance. In the course of this Final Solution of the European Jewish Problem, approximately 11 million Jews are involved.

Under proper direction the Jews should now in the course of the Final Solution be brought to the East in a suitable way for use as labor. In big labor gangs, with separation of the sexes, the Jews capable of work are brought to these areas and employed in road building, in which task undoubtedly a great part will fall out through natural diminution.

The remnant that finally is able to survive all this—since this is undoubtedly the part with the strongest resistance—must be treated accordingly since these people, representing a natural selection, are to be regarded as the germ cell of a new Jewish development. (See the experience of history.)

In the program of the practical execution of the Final Solution, Europe is combed through from the West to the East.

The evacuated Jews are brought first group by group into the so-called transit ghettos, in order to be transported from these farther to the East.

The Death Camps

The "Final Solution" ordered the implementation of a policy of genocide. Hitler wanted to rid the world of a people whom he found responsible for most of humanity's ills. The following selections present the system of extermination from the trip to the death camp by train through the selection process and the gas chambers. Much of the testimony in this section comes from the Nuremberg trial proceedings in 1946. Hermann Gräbe ("The Pit") was a German construction engineer working in the Ukraine in 1942. Kurt Gerstein ("Gas") was the S.S. head of Disinfection Services in early 1942. The gassing of Jews did not take place at concentration or death camps alone, as is noted by the selection entitled "Mobile Killing." This is a top secret dispatch concerning the Einsatzgruppen *that often followed advancing troops. Excerpts from the autobiography and Nuremberg testimony of Rudolf Hoess are also included. He was commandant of the notorious Auschwitz death camp and was himself executed there in 1947 after being judged guilty of crimes against humanity.*

Train Stop near Jassy: "German S.S. guards surrounded the human cargo, shouting, 'All the dead are to be thrown out! All the dead are to be thrown out!'"— Elie Wiesel. *(Yad Vashem, Jerusalem)*

Genocide

RUDOLF HOESS

I, Rudolf Franz Ferdinand Hoess, being first duly sworn, depose and say as follows:

1. I am forty-six years old, and have been a member of the NSDAP since 1922; a member of the SS since 1934; a member of the Waffen-SS since 1939. I was a member from 1 December 1934 of the SS Guard Unit, the so-called Deaths-head Formation [*Totenkopf Verband*].

2. I have been constantly associated with the administration of concentration camps since 1934, serving at Dachau until 1938; then as Adjutant in Sachenhausen from 1938 to May 1, 1940, when I was appointed Commandant of Auschwitz. I commanded Auschwitz until 1 December 1943, and estimate that at least 2,500,000 victims were executed and exterminated there by gassing and burning, and at least another half million succumbed to starvation and disease making a total dead of about 3,000,000. This figure represents about 70% or 80% of all persons sent to Auschwitz as prisoners, the remainder having been selected and used for slave labor in the concentration camp industries. Included among the executed and burnt were approximately 20,000 Russian prisoners of war (previously screened out of Prisoner of War cages by the Gestapo) who were delivered at Auschwitz in Wehrmacht transports operated by regular Wehrmacht officers, 100,000 German Jews, and great numbers of citizens, mostly Jewish from Holland, France, Belgium, Poland, Hungary, Czechoslovakia, Greece, or other countries. We executed about 400,000 Hungarian Jews alone at Auschwitz in the summer of 1944. . . .

4. Mass executions by gassing commenced during the summer of 1941 and continued until fall 1944. I personally supervised executions at

"Genocide" is from the Office of the U.S. Chief of Counsel for the Prosecution of Axis Criminality, *Nazi Conspiracy and Aggression* (Washington, DC: Government Printing Office, 1947), vol. 6, pp. 787–790 (PS-3868).

Auschwitz until the first of December 1943 and know by reason of my continued duties . . . that these mass executions continued as stated above. All mass executions by gassing took place under the direct orders, supervisions, and responsibility of RSHA [Reich Security Main Office]. I received all orders for carrying out these mass executions directly from RSHA. . . .

6. The "final solution" of the Jewish question meant the complete extermination of all Jews in Europe. I was ordered to establish extermination facilities at Auschwitz in June 1941. At that time, there were already in the general government three other extermination camps; Belzek, Treblinka, and Wolzek. These camps were under the Einsatzkommando of the Security Police and SD. I visited Treblinka to find out how they carried out their extermination. The Camp Commandant at Treblinka told me that he had liquidated 80,000 in the course of one-half year. He was principally concerned with liquidating all the Jews from the Warsaw ghetto. He used monoxide gas and I did not think that his methods were very efficient. So when I set up the extermination building at Auschwitz, I used Cyclon B, which was a crystallized prussic acid which we dropped into the death chamber from a small opening. It took from 3 to 15 minutes to kill the people in the death chamber depending upon climatic conditions. We knew when the people were dead because their screaming stopped. We usually waited about one-half hour before we opened the doors and removed the bodies. After the bodies were removed our special commandos took off the rings and extracted the gold from the teeth of the corpses.

7. Another improvement we made over Treblinka was that we built our gas chambers to accommodate 2,000 people at one time, whereas at Treblinka their 10 gas chambers only accommodated 200 people each. The way we selected our victims was as follows: we had two SS doctors on duty at Auschwitz to examine the incoming transports of prisoners. The prisoners would be marched by one of the doctors who would make spot decisions as they walked by. Those who were fit for work were sent into the Camp.

Others were sent immediately to the extermination plants. Children of tender years were invariably exterminated since by reason of their youth they were unable to work. Still another improvement we made over Treblinka was that at Treblinka the victims almost always knew that they were to be exterminated and at Auschwitz we endeavored to fool the victims into thinking that they were to go through a delousing process. Of course, frequently they realized our true intentions and we sometimes had riots and difficulties due to that fact. Very frequently women would hide their children under their clothes but of course when we found them we would send the children in to be exterminated. We were required to carry out these exterminations in secrecy but of course the foul and nauseating stench from the continuous burning of bodies permeated the entire area and all of the people living in the surrounding communities knew that exterminations were going on at Auschwitz.

8. We received from time to time special prisoners from the local Gestapo office. The SS doctors killed such prisoners by injections of benzine. Doctors had orders to write ordinary death certificates and could put down any reason at all for the cause of death.

9. From time to time we conducted medical experiments on women inmates, including sterilization and experiments relating to cancer. Most of the people who died under these experiments had been already condemned to death by the Gestapo. . . .

I understand English as it is written above. The above statements are true; this declaration is made by me voluntarily and without compulsion; after reading over the statements, I have signed and executed the same at Nuremberg, Germany, on the fifth day of April 1946.

Rudolf Franz Ferdinand Hoess

Subscribed and sworn to before me this 5th day of April 1946, at Nuremberg, Germany
Smith W. Brookhart Jr., Lt. Colonel, IGD

"I remember and I am afraid."—Elie Wiesel. *(Yad Vashem, Jerusalem)*

Theme: Imperialism

The Historical Intersection

CHINA: 1937

The Rape of Nanjing

On December 13, 1937, Nanjing, the capital city of Nationalist China, fell to the on-slaught of the invading Japanese army. For the Chinese forces of Jiang Jieshi, which had fought to defend the Yangtze Valley, this was a bitter defeat. The ancient walled city of Nanjing lay open to the fury of the Japanese who, for the next six weeks, pillaged and burned the town, executed tens of thousands of Chinese soldiers, slaughtered civilian men, and raped the women and children. This was no temporary lapse of military discipline in the Japanese ranks, but a methodical and horrific act of terror that resulted in the death of nearly 300,000 Chinese. The Rape of Nanjing, as it was immediately called, was not pub-licized after the war and has been termed by some historians, the "forgotten Holocaust." But its lingering memory has poisoned Chinese-Japanese relations for over sixty years. The following transcript of the 1947 sentencing of a convicted Japanese war criminal testifies to the savagery and tragedy of the Rape of Nanjing.

Compare and Contrast:

- Compare this account of the atrocities in Nanjing with those described in the Nazi death camps. What motivated the Japanese and German sol-diers to commit such acts?

File Number: *Shen 1, 1947*

Defendant: Tani Hsiao, male, age 66, native of Japan; a former lieutenant gen-eral and division commander of the Japanese army. The above defendant was accused by the public prosecutor of this Tribunal as a war criminal. The trial has been duly conducted. The decision is as follows:

(contd)

Decision: During the period of war, Tani Hsiao, the defendant, condoned and encouraged the soldiers under his command to commit mass murder against prisoners of war as well as civilians, in addition to rape, looting, and deliberate destruction of properties. The defendant is hereby sentenced to death.

Facts: The defendant is regarded as one of the most ferocious and ablest generals among the Japanese militarists. He joined the Japanese army as early as the Russo-Japanese War [1905] and distinguished himself repeatedly on the battlefield. He was the commander of the Japanese Sixth Division when the Sino-Japanese War began in 1937; in August of that year, he came to China with his command and participated in the war of aggression. . . . Since Nanjing was the capital of our country and the center of resistance against the Japanese aggression, the Japanese militarists mobilized their best and most ferocious military units, including the Sixth Division headed by the defendant . . . to launch an all-out attack under the overall supervision of General Matsu Iwane. Because of the fact that the defenders of the city had continued to resist and refused to surrender, the Japanese army, after capturing the city, conducted a systematic campaign of murder to show its revenge, hatred, and frustration.

On the afternoon of December 12, the invaders, led by the Sixth Division under the command of the defendant, captured the Zhonghua Gate. Massacre began the moment they roped over the city wall and descended upon the civilians. . . . The massacre was followed by looting, rape, and arson. The worst slaughter occurred between December 12 and 21, the time when the defendant's troops were stationed inside the city. . . . The total number of captured soldiers and civilians who were collectively machine-gunned and then burned into ashes amounted to more than 190,000. The total number of victims who were murdered on an individual basis and whose bodies were later buried by philanthropic organizations were more than 150,000. Thus, the grand total of civilians and prisoners of war who fell victim to this campaign of mass murder was well beyond 300,000. Dead bodies were piled from one street corner to another, and no words, however eloquent, were adequate enough to describe this atrocity of unprecedented scale. . . .

On December 12, Mrs. Wang of Xu, a peasant woman, was beheaded on the harbor outside of the Zhonghua Gate. . . . On December 14, Yao Qialong, a native of Nanjing, was ordered to watch the performance when Japanese soldiers took turns raping his wife. When his eight-year-old son and three-year-old daughter pleaded for mercy on behalf of their mother, the rapists picked them up with their bayonets and roasted them to death over a camp fire. . . . In another case, two Japanese officers entered a murder contest; later, the one who had killed 106 persons was declared the winner over the other who had killed 105. On December 19, Xie Shanzhen, a peasant woman more than sixty years old, was cut into pieces after a Japanese soldier had pierced her vagina with a bamboo stick. In each and every case, the atrocities committed by the Japanese

(contd)

army were brutal to the greatest extreme. From December 12 to 21, the total number of atrocity cases that can be documented amounts to 886.

Consider This:

- Until recently, why did the Japanese brutality in Nanjing go relatively unnoticed? Why has Nanjing been called the "forgotten Holocaust"?

- The poet W. H. Auden reflected on the holocausts of World War II: "And maps can really point to places/Where life is evil now: Nanjing; Dachau." What do you think? Can evil be defined by the atrocities conducted on these sites? Or is evil such a relative concept that it defies definition? Was Hitler evil?

"The Rape of Nanjing" is from Military Tribunal for the Trial of War Criminals (March 10, 1947), contained in Dun J. Li, *The Road to Communism* (New York: Van Nostrand Reinhold Company, 1969), pp. 207–208. Copyright © 1969 by Litton Educational Publishing, Inc. Reprinted by permission.

The Pit

HERMANN GRÄBE

On October 5, 1942, when I visited the building office at Dubno, my foreman told me that in the vicinity of the site, Jews from Dubno had been shot in three large pits, each about 30 metres long and 3 metres deep. About 1,500 persons had been killed daily. All the 5,000 Jews who had still been living in Dubno before the pogrom were to be liquidated. As the shooting had taken place in his presence, he was still much upset.

Thereupon, I drove to the site accompanied by my foreman and saw near it great mounds of earth, about 30 metres long and 2 metres high. Several trucks stood in front of the mounds. Armed Ukrainian militia drove the people off the trucks under the supervision of an S.S. man. The militiamen acted as guards on the trucks and drove them to and from the pit. All these people had the regulation yellow patches on the

front and back of their clothes, and thus could be recognized as Jews.

My foreman and I went directly to the pits. Nobody bothered us. Now I heard rifle shots in quick succession from behind one of the earth mounds. The people who had got off the trucks—men, women and children of all ages—had to undress upon the orders of an S.S. man, who carried a riding or dog whip. They had to put down their clothes in fixed places, sorted according to shoes, top clothing and underclothing. I saw a heap of shoes of about 800 to 1,000 pairs, great piles of underlinen and clothing.

Without screaming or weeping, these people undressed, stood around in family groups, kissed each other, said farewells, and waited for a sign from another S.S. man, who stood near the pit, also with a whip in his hand. During the fifteen minutes that I stood near I heard no complaint or plea for mercy. I watched a family of about eight persons, a man and a woman both about fifty with their children of about one, eight and ten, and two grown-up daughters of about twenty to twenty-nine. An old woman with snow-white hair was holding the one-year-old child in her arms and singing to it and tickling it. The child was cooing with delight. The couple were looking on with tears in their eyes. The father was holding the hand of a boy about ten years old and speaking to him softly; the boy was fighting his tears. The father pointed to the sky, stroked his head, and seemed to explain something to him.

At that moment the S.S. man at the pit shouted something to his comrade. The latter counted off about twenty persons and instructed them to go behind the earth mound. Among them was the family which I have mentioned. I well remember a girl, slim and with black hair, who, as she passed close to me pointed to herself and said "23." I walked around the mound and found myself confronted by a tremendous grave. People were closely wedged together and lying on top of each other so that only their heads were visible. Nearly all had blood running over their shoulders from their heads. Some of the people shot were still moving. Some were lifting their arms and turning their heads to show that they were still alive. The pit was already two-thirds full. I estimated that it already contained about 1,000 people.

Gas

KURT GERSTEIN

In January, 1942, I was named chief of the Waffen SS technical disinfection services, including a section for extremely toxic gases. . . . SS Gruppenführer Globocnik was waiting for us at Lublin. He told us, "This is one of the most secret matters there are, even the most secret. Anybody who talks about it will be shot immediately." He explained to us that there were three installations:

1. Belzec, on the Lublin-Lwow road. A maximum of 15,000 people per day.
2. Sobibor (I don't know exactly where it is), 20,000 people a day.

Reprinted by permission of the American Jewish Committee from Leon Poliakov's *Harvest of Hate,* 1954.

3. Treblinka, 120 kilometers NNE of Warsaw.
4. Maidanek, near Lublin (under construction).

Globocnik said: "You will have to disinfect large piles of clothing coming from Jews, Poles, Czechs, etc. Your other duty will be to improve the workings of our gas chambers, which operate on the exhaust from a Diesel engine. We need a more toxic and faster working gas, something like prussic acid. . . ."

The following morning, a little before seven there was an announcement: "The first train will arrive in ten minutes!" A few minutes later a train arrived from Lemberg: 45 cars with more than 6,000 people. Two hundred Ukrainians assigned to this work flung open the doors and drove the Jews out of the cars with leather whips. A loud speaker gave instructions: "Strip, even artificial limbs and glasses. Hand all money and valuables in at the 'valuables window.' Women and young girls are to have their hair cut in the 'barber's hut.'"

Then the march began. Barbed wire on both sides, in the rear two dozen Ukrainians with rifles. They drew near. Wirth and I found ourselves in front of the death chambers. Stark naked men, women, children, and cripples passed by. A tall S.S. man in the corner called to the unfortunates in a loud minister's voice: "Nothing is going to hurt you! Just breathe deep and it will strengthen your lungs. It's a way to prevent contagious diseases. It's a good disinfectant!" They asked him what was going to happen and he answered: "The men will have to work, build houses and streets. The women won't have to do that, they will be busy with the housework and the kitchen." This was the last hope for some of these poor people, enough to make them march toward the death chambers without resistance. The majority knew everything; the smell betrayed it! They climbed a little wooden stairs and entered the death chambers, most of them silently, pushed by those behind them. A Jewess of about forty with eyes like fire cursed the murderers; she disappeared into the gas chambers after being struck several times by Captain Wirth's whip. . . .

All were dead after thirty-two minutes! Jewish workers on the other side opened the wooden doors. They had been promised their lives in return for doing this horrible work, plus a small percentage of the money and valuables collected. The men still standing, like columns of stone, with no room to fall or lean. Even in death you could tell the families, all holding hands. It was difficult to separate them while emptying the rooms for the next batch. The bodies were tossed out, blue, wet with sweat and urine, the legs smeared with excrement and menstrual blood. Two dozen workers were busy checking mouths which they opened with iron hooks. "Gold to the left, no gold to the right." Others checked anus and genitals, looking for money, diamonds, gold, etc. Dentists knocked out gold teeth, bridges and crowns, with hammers. . . .

Then the bodies were thrown into big ditches near the gas chambers, about 100 by 20 by 12 meters. After a few days the bodies swelled and the whole mass rose up 2–3 yards because of the gas in the bodies. When the swelling went down several days later, the bodies matted down again. They told me later they poured Diesel oil over the bodies and burned them on railroad ties to make them disappear.

Mobile Killing

Kiev, 16 May 1942

Field Post Office
No 32704
B Nr 40/42

TOP SECRET

To: SS-Obersturmbannfuehrer Rauff
Berlin, Prinz-Albrecht-Str. 8

pers.

R/29/5 Pradel n.R

b/R

Sinkkel [?] b.R., p 16/6

"Mobile Killing" is from the Office of the U.S. Chief Counsel for Prosecution of Axis Criminality, *Nazi Conspiracy and Aggression* (Washington, DC: Government Printing Office, 1946), vol. 3, pp. 418–419 (PS-501).

The overhauling of vans by groups D and C is finished. . . .

I ordered the vans of group D to be camouflaged as house trailers by putting one set of window shutters on each side of the small van and two on each side of the larger vans, such as one often sees on farm-houses in the country. The vans became so well-known, that not only the authorities, but also the civilian population called the van "death van," as soon as one of these vehicles appeared. It is my opinion, the van cannot be kept secret for any length of time, not even camouflaged. . . .

I ordered that during application of gas all the men were to be kept as far away from the vans as possible, so they should not suffer damage to their health by the gas which eventually would escape. I should like to take this opportunity to bring the following to your attention: several commands have had the unloading after the application of gas done by their own men. I brought to the attention of the commanders of the Sonder-Kommando [special unit] concerning the immense psychological injuries and damages to their health which that work can have for those men, even if not immediately, at least later on. The men complained to me about headaches which appeared after each unloading. Nevertheless prisoners called for that work, could use an opportune moment to flee. To protect the men from these damages, I request orders be issued accordingly.

The application of gas usually is not undertaken correctly. In order to come to an end as fast as possible, the driver presses the accelerator to the fullest extent. By doing that the persons to be executed suffer death from suffocation and not death by dozing off as was planned. My directions now have proved that by correct adjustment of the levers death comes faster and the prisoners fall asleep peacefully. Distorted faces and excretions, such as could be seen before, are no longer noticed.

Today I shall continue my journey to group B, where I can be reached with further news.

Signed: D. Becker

SS Untersturmfuehrer

Warsaw Jews on the way to the Treblinka death camp. *(Wide World)*

Commandant of Auschwitz

RUDOLF HOESS

I must emphasise here that I have never personally hated the Jews. It is true that I looked upon them as the enemies of our people. But just because of this I saw no difference between them and the other prisoners, and I treated them all in the same way. I never drew any distinctions. In any event the emotion of hatred is foreign to my nature. But I know what hate is, and what it looks like. I have seen it and I have suffered it myself.

When the Reichsfuhrer SS modified his original Extermination Order of 1941, by which all Jews without exception were to be destroyed, and ordered instead that those capable of work were to be separated from the rest and employed in the armaments industry, Auschwitz became a Jewish camp. It was a collecting place for Jews, exceeding in scale anything previously known.

Hoess, Rudolf, *Commandant of Auschwitz: The Autobiography of Rudolf Hoess,* trans. Constantine Ritzgibbon. Copyright © 1959 by Weidentfeld & Nicolson. Reprinted with permission.

Whereas the Jews who had been imprisoned in former years were able to count on being released one day and were thus far less affected psychologically by the hardships of captivity, the Jews in Auschwitz no longer had any such hope. They knew, without exception, that they were condemned to death, that they would live only so long as they could work.

Nor did the majority have any hope of a change in their sad lot. They were fatalists. Patiently and apathetically, they submitted to all the misery and distress and terror. The hopelessness with which they accepted their impending fate made them psychologically quite indifferent to their surroundings. This mental collapse accelerated its physical equivalent. They no longer had the will to live, everything had become a matter of indifference to them, and they would succumb to the slightest physical shock. Sooner or later, death was inevitable. I firmly maintain from what I have seen that the high mortality among the Jews was due not only to the hard work, to which most of them were unaccustomed, and to the insufficient food, the overcrowded quarters and all the severities and abuses of camp life, but principally and decisively to their psychological state. . . .

What I have just written applies to the bulk, the mass of the Jewish prisoners. The more intelligent ones, psychologically stronger and with a keener desire for life, that is to say in most cases those from the western countries, reacted differently.

These people, especially if they were doctors, had no illusions concerning their fate. But they continued to hope, reckoning on a change of fortune that somehow or other would save their lives. They also reckoned on the collapse of Germany, for it was not difficult for them to listen to enemy propaganda.

For them the most important thing was to obtain a position which would lift them out of the mass and give them special privileges, a job that would protect them to a certain extent from accidental and mortal hazards, and improve the physical conditions in which they lived.

They employed all their ability and all their will to obtain what can truly be described as a "living" of this sort. The safer the position the more eagerly and fiercely it was fought for. No quarter was shown, for this was a struggle in which everything was at stake. They flinched from nothing, no matter how desperate, in their efforts to make such safe jobs fall vacant and then to acquire them for themselves. Victory usually went to the most unscrupulous man or woman. Time and again I heard of these struggles to oust a rival and win his job. . . .

So it can be seen that even in a small prison the governor is unable to prevent such behavior; how much more difficult was it in a concentration camp the size of Auschwitz! I was certainly severe and strict. Often perhaps, when I look at it now, too severe and too strict.

In my disgust at the errors and abuses that I discovered, I may have spoken many hard words that I should have kept to myself. But I was never cruel, and I have never maltreated anyone, even in a fit of temper. A great deal happened in Auschwitz which was done ostensibly in my name, under my authority and on my orders, which I neither knew about nor sanctioned. But all these things happened in Auschwitz and so I am responsible. For the camp regulations say: the camp commandant is fully responsible for everything that happens in his sphere.

GÖTTERDÄMMERUNG:
THE FINAL DESTRUCTION (1944–1945)

War alone brings up to their highest tension all human energies and imposes the stamp of nobility upon the peoples who have the courage to make it.

—*Benito Mussolini*

When you lose a friend, you have an overpowering desire to go back home and yell in everybody's ear, "This guy was killed fighting for you. Don't forget him—ever." Keep him in your mind when you wake up in the morning and when you go to bed at night. Think of him as a guy who wanted to live every bit as much as you do.

—*Bill Mauldin*

The D-Day Invasions (June 6, 1944)

By 1944, with Allied victories in Northern Africa, Italy, and Russia beginning to turn the tide of battle, the Allied High Command, led by General Dwight Eisenhower, had developed plans for the invasion of Europe. The Germans were aware that an invasion was imminent and had constructed formidable defenses along the French coast under the direction of Field

Marshal Erwin Rommel. But the Germans could not defend the entire coast with equal troop strength and focused more of their attention on the area surrounding Calais, which marked the shortest invasion route across the English Channel. Because British intelligence had secretly broken German codes and could better estimate the strength of enemy defenses, the decision was made to invade along the Normandy beaches.

An amphibious assault is a delicate operation, and even the most meticulous plans are vulnerable to changes of wind and weather. The operation was a high-risk gamble that cost thousands of lives but resulted in the establishment of a "second front" against the Germans. The next drive was to Berlin itself.

The following personal accounts of "The Longest Day" capture the confusion and heroism displayed by soldiers in the greatest amphibious operation in history. The fiftieth anniversary commemorative speech by President Clinton on June 6, 1994, offers perspective on the cost and importance of this day.

The Paratrooper: "He Was Blown Away"

KEN RUSSELL

I was just a boy, seventeen—I should have been in high school rather than in a strange country. I should have been going to school. I think my class was graduating that night. Sainte-Mere-Eglise was the area that we had to take, and as we came in, there was a building on fire. The fire gave light for miles around, and we came in and when we saw the fire, we jumped. I knew we were in trouble, and it was so horrifying, because most of our stick were killed.

They didn't even hit the ground. They hit the telephone poles—Lieutenant Cadish, H. T. Bryant, and Laddie Tlapa landed on telephone poles down the street, and it was like they were crucified there. Coming down, one fellow had a Gammon grenade on his hip, and I looked to my right, and I saw the guy, and instantaneously, I looked around and there was just an empty parachute coming down. He was blown away.

I got hit in the hand—just a kind of a valley up through my hand. To be honest, I was trying to hide behind my reserve chute, because you could hear the shells hitting. We were all sitting ducks coming down. The heat drew the nylon chutes toward the fire, and the air to feed the fire was actually drawing us into it, and I saw one trooper land in the fire. I heard him scream one time before he was engulfed, and he didn't scream any more.

When I came down, I knew that we were going to hit in the town, but I didn't know exactly where. I finally hit the roof of the church first and a couple of my suspension lines went around the church steeple and I slid off the roof. I was hanging on the edge of the roof, and when Steele had come down, his chute covered the steeple.

While I was there, a buck sergeant who was in our unit who had jumped from our plane by the name of John Ray came down. I was on the right side of the church, and Steele was hung up on the steeple, and Sergeant Ray came down and missed the edge of the church, but he hit in front of it. A Nazi soldier, billeted on the next street behind the church, came around from behind the church. He was a red-haired German soldier, and he came to shoot Steele and myself, who were still hanging there. As he came around, he shot Ray in the stomach. Ray being a sergeant, had been armed with a .45 pistol, and while he was dying in agony, got his .45 out and when this German soldier started turning around to us, Ray shot him in the back of the head and killed him.

American troops land on Normandy beach during the D-day assault, June 6, 1944: "I waded through the waist-deep water, watching many of my buddies fall alongside of me. The water was being shot up all around, and many a bullet ricocheted off the water."—Harold Baumgarten *(Bettmann)*

The Assault on Omaha Beach: "I'm Hit! I'm Hit!"

HAROLD BAUMGARTEN

At 7:00 A.M. I saw the beach with its huge seawall at the foot of a massive 150-foot bluff. We'd made it. And then an 88-millimeter shell landed right in the middle of the LCA [landing craft] on the side of us, and splinters of the boat, equipment, and bodies were thrown into the air. Lieutenant Donaldson cautioned us to get down. Bullets were passing through the thin wooden sides of our vessel. The ramp was lowered and the inner door was opened. In a British LCA, we could only get out one at a time, and a German machine gun trained on the opening took a heavy toll of lives. Many of my thirty buddies went down as they left the LCA.

"The Assault on Omaha Beach" is from Ronald J. Drez, *Voices of D-Day* (Baton Rouge: Louisiana State University Press, 1994), pp. 215–217. Copyright © 1994 by Louisiana State University Press. Reprinted by permission of the publisher.

I got a bullet through the top of my helmet first, and then as I waded through the deep water, a bullet aimed at my heart hit the receiver of my M-1 rifle as I carried it at port arms, embedding itself in my ammunition. I waded through the waist-deep water, watching many of my buddies fall alongside of me. The water was being shot up all around, and many a bullet ricocheted off the water. Clarius Riggs, who left the assault boat in front of me, went under, shot to death, and eight or ten feet to my right, just as we hit the beach, I heard a hollow thud and I saw Private Robert Ditmar hold his chest and yell, "I'm hit! I'm hit!" I hit the ground and watched him as he continued to go forward ten more yards and then trip over a tank obstacle. As he fell, his body made a complete turn and he lay sprawled on the damp sand with his head facing the German, his face looking skyward. He seemed to be suffering from shock, and was yelling, "Mother, Mom . . ." as he kept rolling around on the sand.

There were three or four others wounded and dying right near him. Sergeant Barnes got shot down right in front of me, and Lieutenant

Donaldson, and another sergeant had a gaping wound in the upper right corner of his forehead. He was walking crazily in the water, without his helmet, and then he got down on his knees and started praying with his rosary beads, and at that moment the Germans cut him in half with their deadly cross fire. The fire came from a pillbox [machine gun emplacement] built into the mountain on the right flank of the beach. We had snipers firing at us from the vantage points in front of us and from dugouts and pillboxes. I saw the reflection from the helmet of one of the snipers, and took aim, and later on found out I got a bull's-eye. It was the only shot that rifle fired, because the rifle broke in half and I had to throw it away. The shot that had hit my rifle must have shattered the wood. . . .

Finally, I came to dry sand, and there was another hundred yards to go, and I started across the sand, crawling very fast. When I reached the stone wall without further injury, I looked back on the beach I had crossed and saw two of our battalion's twelve special tanks knocked out in the water, a dead man hanging out of the turret of one of them. The other one fired his 75-millimeter gun shells right into the pillbox on the right flank and could not knock them out.

At the wall, I met a fellow from Company B from my boat team named Dominick Surrow, a boy from Georgia about my age, a rugged fellow, who looked at my face and said, "Stay here, I'm going to run down the beach and get help." He got killed.

I watched him being washed around by the incoming water, and I saw the bodies of my buddies who had tried in vain to clear the beach. It looked like the beach was littered with the refuse of a wrecked ship that were the dead bodies of what once were the proud, tough, and the well-trained combat infantrymen of the 1st Battalion of the 116th Infantry.

I saw Sergeant Draper and Vargos and all of Company A dying in the water to my left. . . . There was no medical aid available at this time, and many had bled to death and many drowned. I ran down the wall to the left a hundred yards or so, giving a hand to many of the wounded who were trying to pull themselves against the wall. . . .

Lying in the sand in front of the Vierville draw was our boat's walkie-talkie radio man and my best buddy, PFC Robert Garbed of Newport News, Virginia. He was facedown with his back to the enemy, probably spun around by the force of a bullet. . . .

Sergeant Cecil Bredan dressed my face wound. I had received five individual wounds that day in Normandy.

Fiftieth Anniversary of D-Day: "When They Were Young, These Men Saved the World"
PRESIDENT BILL CLINTON

In these last days of ceremonies, we have heard wonderful words of tribute. Now we come to this hallowed place that speaks, more than anything else, in silence. Here on this quiet plateau, on this small piece of American soil, we honor those who gave their lives for us fifty crowded years ago. Today, the beaches of Normandy are calm. If you walk these shores on a summer's day, all you might hear is the laughter of children playing on the sand, or the cry of seagulls overhead, or perhaps the ringing of a distant church bell—the simple sounds of freedom barely breaking the silence.

But June 6th, 1944 was the least ordinary day of the 20th century. On that chilled dawn, these beaches echoed with the sounds of staccato gunfire, the roar of aircraft, the thunder of bombardment. And through the wind and the waves came the soldiers, out of their landing craft and into the water, away from their youth and toward a savage place many of them would sadly never leave.

"Fiftieth Anniversary of D-Day" is from President Bill Clinton, speech delivered at the United States National Cemetery above Omaha Beach, Colleville-sur-Mer, France, on June 6, 1994. Contained in *Vital Speeches of the Day*, July 1, 1994, pp. 546–547.

They had come to free a continent—the Americans, the British, the Canadians, the Poles, the French Resistance, the Norwegians and the others—they had all come to stop one of the greatest forces of evil the world has ever known.

As news of the invasion broke back home in America, people held their breath. In Boston, commuters stood reading the news on the electric sign at South Station. In New York, the Statue of Liberty, its torch blacked out since Pearl Harbor, was lit at sunset for 15 minutes. . . .

During those first hours on bloody Omaha nothing seemed to go right. Landing craft were ripped apart by mines and shells. Tanks sent to protect them had sunk, drowning their crews. Enemy fire raked the invaders as they stepped into chest-high water and waded past the floating bodies of their comrades. And as the stunned survivors of the first wave huddled behind a seawall, it seemed the invasion might fail.

Hitler and his followers had bet on it. They were sure the Allied soldiers were soft, weakened by liberty and leisure, by the mingling of races and religion. They were sure their totalitarian youth had more discipline and zeal.

But then, something happened. Although many of the American troops found themselves without officers on unfamiliar ground, next to soldiers they didn't know, one by one, they got up. They inched forward and together in groups of threes and fives and tens, the sons of democracy improvised and mounted their own attacks. At that exact moment on these beaches, the forces of freedom turned the tide of the 20th century. . . .

Today, many of them are here among us. Oh, they may walk with a little less spring in their step and their ranks are growing thinner, but let us never forget—when they were young, these men saved the world. . . .

Millions of our GIs did return home from that war to build up our nations and enjoy life's sweet pleasures. But on this field, there are 9,386 who did not. . . . They were the fathers we never knew, the uncles we never met, the friends who never returned, the heroes we can never repay. They gave us our world. And those simple sounds of freedom we hear today are their voices speaking to us across the years. . . .

Fifty years ago, the first Allied soldiers to land here in Normandy came not from the sea, but from the sky. They were called Pathfinders, the first paratroopers to make the jump. Deep in the darkness they descended upon these fields to light beacons for the airborne assaults that would soon follow. Now, near the dawn of a new century, the job of lighting those beacons falls to our hands.

To you who brought us here, I promise, we will be the new pathfinders, for we are the children of your sacrifice.

Theme: Systems of Government

The Historical Intersection

ATHENS: 430 B.C.E.

"Freedom Depends on Being Courageous": The Funeral Oration of Pericles (430 B.C.E.)

THUCYDIDES

The leader of the Athenian democracy in the middle of the fifth century B.C.E. was the great orator Pericles. After the first year of the Peloponnesian War (430 B.C.E.), Pericles spoke to the wives and parents of those who had died in the fighting in an attempt to justify their loss. This Funeral Oration that follows was recorded by the Athenian historian Thucydides; it is the quintessential expression of the structure and values of the Athenian democracy.

Compare and Contrast:

- Paying tribute to soldiers who have sacrificed their lives during war is an important obligation of the political head of a state. Compare this speech of Pericles during the Peloponnesian War in 430 B.C.E. with President Bill Clinton's commemoration of the fiftieth anniversary of the D-Day invasion of Europe. What did the soldiers die for?

"This, then, is the kind of city for which these men, who could not bear the thought of losing her, nobly fought and nobly died. It is only natural that every one of us who survive them should be willing to undergo hardships in her service. And it was for this reason that I have spoken at such length about our city, because I wanted to make it clear that for us there is more at stake than there is for others who lack our advantages; also I wanted my words of praise for the dead to be set in the bright light of evidence. And now the most important of

(contd)

these words has been spoken. I have sung the praises of our city; but it was the courage and gallantry of these men, and of people like them, which made her splendid. Now would you find it true in the case of many of the Greeks, as it is true of them, that no words can do more than justice to their deeds. . . .

"So and such they were, these men—worthy of their city. We who remain behind may hope to be spared their fate, but must resolve to keep the same daring spirit against the foe. It is not simply a question of estimating the advantages in theory. I could tell you a long story (and you know it as well as I do) about what is to be gained by beating the enemy back. What I would prefer is that you should fix your eyes every day on the greatness of Athens as she really is, and should fall in love with her. When you realize her greatness, then reflect that what made her great was men with a spirit of adventure, men who knew their duty, men who were ashamed to fall below a certain standard. If they ever failed in an enterprise, they made up their minds that at any rate the city should not find their courage lacking to her, and they gave to her the best contribution they could. They gave her their lives, to her and to all of us, and for their own selves they won praises that never grow old, the most splendid of sepulchres— not the sepulchre in which their bodies are laid, but where their glory remains eternal in men's minds, always there on the right occasion to stir others to speech or to action. For famous men have the whole earth as their memorial: it is not only the inscriptions on their graves in their own country that mark them out; no, in foreign lands also, not in any visible form but in people's hearts, their memory abides and grows. It is for you to try to be like them. Make up your minds that happiness depends on being free, and freedom depends on being courageous. Let there be no relaxation in face of the perils of the war. The people who have most excuse for despising death are not the wretched and unfortunate, who have no hope of doing well for themselves, but those who run the risk of a complete reversal in their lives, and who would feel the difference most intensely, if things went wrong for them. Any intelligent man would find a humiliation caused by his own slackness more painful to bear than death, when death comes to him unperceived, in battle, and in the confidence of his patriotism."

Consider This:

- What are the most impressive phrases from each speech? What emotions do they evoke from the audience? Is this kind of speech the privilege of the victors? Why did Spartan or German soldiers die? For the same reasons? For the same causes? Why did U.S. soldiers die in Vietnam? Why did they never receive such a verbal testimonial?

The Peloponnesian War by Thucydides, translated by Rex Warner (Penguin Classics, 1954) copyright Rex Warner, 1954. Reproduced by permission of Penguin Books Ltd.

The Divine Wind: Kamikaze!

In 1943, U.S. forces began a campaign of "island hopping" in hopes of capturing several strategic islands that would provide important bases for an eventual assault on Japan. By March 1945, the islands of Iwo Jima and Okinawa had fallen despite determined Japanese resistance. The Japanese High Command realized the gravity of the moment and focused their resistance with suicide attacks on U.S. ships and aircraft carriers by Japanese planes filled with explosives. These planes, called kamikazes, *were named after the "Divine Wind" that had saved Japan from Mongolian invasion in the thirteenth century. The following diary account is from a kamikaze pilot who was about to sacrifice his life with honor and dignity.*

"Death and I Are Waiting"

ENSIGN HEIICHI OKABE

22 February 1945

I am actually a member at last of the Kamikaze Special Attack Corps. My life will be rounded out in the next thirty days. My chance will come! Death and I are waiting. The training and practice have been rigorous, but it is worthwhile if we can die beautifully and for a cause.

I shall die watching the pathetic struggle of our nation. My life will gallop in the next few weeks as my youth and life draw to a close. . . .

The sortie has been scheduled for the next ten days. I am a human being and hope to be neither saint nor scoundrel, hero nor fool—just a human being. As one who has spent his life in wistful longing and searching, I die resignedly in the hope that my life will serve as a "human document."

The world in which I lived was too full of discord. As a community of rational human beings it should be better composed. Lacking a single

great conductor, everyone lets loose with his own sound, creating dissonance where there should be melody and harmony.

We shall serve the nation gladly in its present painful struggle. We shall plunge into enemy ships cherishing the conviction that Japan has been and will be a place where only lovely homes, brave women, and beautiful friendships are allowed to exist.

What is the duty today? It is to fight.

What is the duty tomorrow? It is to win.

What is the daily duty? It is to die.

We die in battle without complaint. I wonder if others, like scientists, who pursue the war effort on their own fronts, would die as we do without complaint. Only then will the unity of Japan be such that she can have any prospect of winning the war.

If, by some strange chance, Japan should suddenly win this war it would be a fatal misfortune for the future of the nation. It will be better for our nation and people if they are tempered through real ordeals which will serve to strengthen.

Like cherry blossoms
In the spring,
Let us fall
Clean and radiant.

Rikihei Inoguchi and Tadashi Nakajima, *The Divine Wind.* Copyright © 1958 by the U.S. Naval Institute. Reprinted with permission.

THE AFTERMATH OF WAR

The Destruction of Hiroshima (August 6, 1945)

HARRY S. TRUMAN

On August 6, 1945, the world entered the nuclear age with the detonation of the atomic bomb over the city of Hiroshima, Japan. Persuaded by the argument that such use would ultimately save Allied lives, President Truman ordered another bomb dropped on Nagasaki two days later.

The Japanese surrendered, and World War II finally came to an end. The United States respon-
sibly attempted to control the destructive power it had unleashed, but the race was on to match
America's technological achievement. The escalation of nuclear arms became a focal point for the
Cold War competition between the United States and the Soviet Union for the next forty years.

Sixteen hours ago an American airplane dropped one bomb on Hiroshima, an important Japanese Army base. That bomb had more power than 20,000 tons of T.N.T. It had more than two thousand times the blast power of the British "Grand Slam" which is the largest bomb ever yet used in the history of warfare.

The Japanese began the war from the air at Pearl Harbor. They have been repaid many fold. And the end is not yet in sight. With this bomb we have now added a new and revolutionary increase in destruction to supplement the growing power of our armed forces. In their present form these bombs are now in production and even more powerful forms are in development. It is an atomic bomb. It is a harnessing of the basic power of the universe. The force from which the sun draws its power has been loosed against those who brought war to the Far East.

Before 1939, it was the accepted belief of scientists that it was theoretically possible to release atomic energy. But no one knew any practical method of doing it. By 1942, however, we knew that the Germans were working feverishly to find a way to add atomic energy to the other engines of war with which they hoped to enslave the world. But they failed. We may be grateful to Providence that the Germans got the V-1's and V-2's late and in limited quantities and even more grateful that they did not get the atomic bomb at all. . . .

We are now prepared to obliterate more rapidly and completely every productive enterprise the Japanese have above ground in any city. We shall destroy their docks, their factories, and their communications. Let there be no mistake; we shall completely destroy Japan's power to make war. . . .

I shall recommend that the Congress of the United States consider promptly the establishment of an appropriate commission to control the production and use of atomic power within the United States. I shall give further consideration and make further recommendations to the Congress as to how atomic power can become a powerful and forceful influence towards the maintenance of world peace.

The Crimes of the Nazi Regime

JUSTICE ROBERT H. JACKSON

In the spring of 1945, Allied troops fought their way into the heart of Nazi Germany. Infa-
mous concentration camps such as Dachau and Buchenwald were liberated by soldiers; the
German inhabitants of the area were forced to view the horrors perpetrated by their "neigh-
bors." Judgment was demanded, and an international court was established in Nuremberg.
Its responsibility was to pass sentence on the various Nazi leaders after first examining docu-
mentary evidence and transcripts of oral testimony. No court has ever attained such univer-
sal recognition. Transcripts and documents of the proceedings fill forty-two large volumes.
The following selection is from the summation of Justice Robert H. Jackson, the chief Ameri-
can prosecutor.

"The Destruction of Hiroshima" is from *Public Papers of the President*, Harry S. Truman, 1947 (Washington, DC: Government Printing Office, 1963), pp. 197–200.

"The Crimes of the Nazi Regime" is from Office of the U.S. Chief of Counsel for the Prosecution of Axis Criminality, *Nazi Conspiracy and Aggression* (Washington, DC: Government Printing Office, 1947), Supplement A, pp. 15–16, 44.

The Nazi movement will be an evil memory in history because of its persecution of the Jews, the most far-flung and terrible racial persecution of all time. Although the Nazi party neither invented nor monopolized anti-Semitism, its leaders from the very beginning embraced it, and exploited it. They used it as "the psychological spark that ignites the mob." After the seizure of power, it became an official state policy. The persecution began in a series of discriminatory laws eliminating the Jews from the civil service, the professions, and economic life. As it became more intense it included segregation of Jews in ghettos, and exile. Riots were organized by party leaders to loot Jewish business places and to burn synagogues. Jewish property was confiscated and a collective fine of a billion marks was imposed upon German Jewry. The program progressed in fury and irresponsibility to the "final solution." This consisted of sending all Jews who were fit to work to concentration camps as slave laborers, and all who were not fit, which included children under 12 and people over 50, as well as any others judged unfit by an SS doctor, to concentration camps for extermination. . . .

The chief instrumentality for persecution and extermination was the concentration camp, sired by defendant Goering and nurtured under the overall authority of defendants Frick and Kaltenbrunner.

The horrors of these iniquitous places have been vividly disclosed by documents and testified to by witnesses. The Tribunal must be satiated with ghastly verbal and pictorial portrayals. From your records it is clear that the concentration camps were the first and worst weapons of oppression used by the National Socialist State, and that they were the primary means utilized for the persecution of the Christian Church and the extermination of the Jewish race. This has been admitted to you by some of the defendants from the witness stand. In the words of defendant Frank: "A thousand years will pass and this guilt of Germany will still not be erased.". . .

It is against such a background that these defendants now ask this Tribunal to say that they are not guilty of planning, executing, or conspiring to commit this long list of crimes and wrongs. They stand before the record of this trial. . . . If you were to say of these men that they are not guilty, it would be as true to say there has been no war, there are no slain, there has been no crime.

The Destruction of the European Jews

RAUL HILBERG

At the close of World War II, humanity paused, much as it had at the end of the Great War in 1918, stunned by the prolonged destruction that shook the very foundations of world civilization. But in 1945, there was a clear winner and a clear loser. This time there was joy, a celebration that evil had been vanquished and the world made safe from the horrors of fascism. Still, Europe was in ruins, over thirty million people lay dead or wounded, and the new threat, the Soviet Union, with its totalitarian government and "creeping Communism," was the next obstacle to freedom. The post-war world would again pick up the pieces of its destruction and rearrange its alliances in order to reflect the new realities. The century had begun with devastation, followed at midpoint by even greater annihilation—and the looming potential to destroy the human race. Such events demand reflection. Raul Hilberg, one of the world's foremost authorities on the Holocaust, and existentialist philosopher Jean-Paul Sartre comment on the carnage and lend perspective to the age of anxiety. The responsibility for war, life, and death, according to Sartre, was a burden that could not be shirked and was not easily borne. The alienation of the individual from society was an axiom for the intellectual crisis that followed World War II.

Hilberg, Raul, *The Destruction of the European Jews*, revised and definitive edition, 3 vols. Copyright © 1985 by Yale University Press, pp. 1187, 1193–1194. Reprinted by permission.

The destruction of the European Jews between 1933 and 1945 appears to us now as an unprecedented event in history. Indeed, in its dimensions and total configuration, nothing like it had ever happened before. Five million people were killed as a result of an organized undertaking in the short space of a few years. The operation was over before anyone could grasp its enormity, let alone its implications for the future.

Yet if we analyze that singularly massive upheaval, we discover that most of what happened in those twelve years had already happened before. The Nazi destruction process did not come out of a void; it was the culmination of a cyclical trend. We have observed the trend in the three successive goals of anti-Jewish administrators. The missionaries of Christianity had said in effect: You have no right to live among us as Jews. The secular rulers who followed had proclaimed: You have no right to live among us. The German Nazis at last decreed: You have no right to live. . . .

As time passes, the destruction of the European Jews will recede into the background. Its most immediate consequences are almost over, and whatever developments may henceforth be traced to the catastrophe will be consequences of consequences, more and more remote. Already the Nazi outburst has become historical. But this is a strange page in history. Few events of modern times were so filled with unpredicted action and suspected death. A primordial impulse had suddenly surfaced among the Western nations; it had been unfettered through their machines. From this moment, fundamental assumptions about our civilization have no longer stood unchallenged, for while the occurrence is past, the phenomenon remains.

Before the emergence of the 20th century and its technology, a destructive mind could not play in fantasy with the thoughts that the Nazis were to translate into action. The administrator of earlier centuries did not have the tools. He did not possess the network of communications; he did not dispose over rapid small arms fire and quick-working poison gasses. The bureaucrat of tomorrow would not have these problems; already, he is better equipped than the German Nazis were. Killing is not as difficult as it used to be. The modern administrative apparatus has facilities for rapid, concerted movements and for efficient massive killings. These devices not only trap a larger number of victims; they also require a greater degree of specialization, and with that division of labor the moral burden too is fragmented among the participants. The perpetrator can now kill his victims without touching them. He may feel sure of his success and safe from its repercussions. This ever-growing capacity for destruction cannot be arrested anywhere. . . .

Since the end of the Jewish catastrophe, basic decisions have been made about the future. In the Christian world the remaining alternatives are gradually moving toward polar ends. After two thousand years there is no defensible middle ground. The ancient compromise, with all its contradictions, is weakening day by day. To the Jewish community that growing dichotomy conveys unique opportunities and unprecedented vulnerabilities. Jewry is faced with ultimate weapons. It has no deterrent. The Jews can live more freely now. They can also die more quickly. The summit is within sight. An abyss has opened below.

The Responsibility of the Individual (1956)

JEAN-PAUL SARTRE

Existentialism has been an important philosophical movement in the twentieth century. Its premier spokesman, Jean-Paul Sartre, in his book Being and Nothingness, *contends that human beings are condemned to be free and that with freedom comes responsibility for one's*

The Responsibility of the Individual from Sartre, Jean-Paul, *Existentialism and Human Emotions,* 1957, Philosophical Library, Inc., pp. 52–54, 56–57.

choices and actions. Such responsibility for war, life, and death is a burden that cannot be shirked and is not easily borne. The alienation of the individual from society was an axiom for the intellectual crisis that followed World War II.

The essential consequence of our earlier remarks is that man, being condemned to be free, carries the weight of the whole world on his shoulders; he is responsible for the world and for himself as a way of being. . . . Thus there are no *accidents* in a life. . . . If I am mobilized in a war, this war is *my* war; it is in my image and I deserve it. I deserve it first because I could always get out of it by suicide or by desperation; these ultimate possibilities are those which must always be present for us when there is a question of envisaging a situation. For lack of getting out of it, I have *chosen* it. This can be due to inertia, to cowardice in the face of public opinion, or because I prefer certain other values to the value of the refusal to join in the war (the good opinion of my relatives, the honor of my family, etc.). Any way you look at it, it is a matter of a choice. This choice will be repeated later on again and again without a break until the end of the war. . . . Thus, totally free, undistinguishable from the period for which I have chosen to be the meaning, as profoundly responsible for the war as if I had myself declared it, unable to live without integrating it in my situation, engaging myself in it wholly and stamping it with my seal, *I must be without remorse or regrets as I am without excuse; for from the instant of my upsurge into being, I carry the weight of the world by myself alone without anything or any person being able to lighten it.*

CHRONOLOGY: The "Good War": World War II (1939–1945)

September 1931	Seeking to fuel its growing war machine, Japan invades the mineral-rich area of Manchuria in China.
January 1933	National Socialist (Nazi) party victorious in general elections. Hitler becomes chancellor of Germany.
October 1933	Germany withdraws from the League of Nations.
March 1935	Hitler renounces disarmament as required by the Treaty of Versailles, starts an air force, and begins conscription into the army.
October 1935	Mussolini attacks Ethiopia and achieves glorious victory over opponents armed with spears.
March 1936	Germany reoccupies and remilitarizes Rhineland in defiance of Versailles and Locarno agreements.
July 1936–1939	Spanish Civil War. Fascist forces victorious with armaments supplied by Germany and Italy. Francisco Franco in power until his death in 1975.
October 1936	Formation of the Rome-Berlin Axis. Japan joins Axis in the Anti-Comintern Pact.
December 1937	Japanese soldiers enter Nanjing, China, and begin six-week devastation of the city known as the Rape of Nanjing. Nearly 300,000 Chinese soldiers and civilians are slaughtered.
March 1938	German *Anschluss* (unification) with Austria after Nazi invasion halted Austrian plebiscite.

September 1938	Munich conference between Hitler and British Prime Minister Neville Chamberlain. Policy of appeasement results in partition of Czechoslovakia: "Peace for our time."
November 9–10, 1938	Anti-Jewish pogrom, the *Kristallnacht* (Crystal Night).
March 1939	Hitler occupies Prague. Great Britain and France decide to guarantee Polish independence.
August 1939	Nazi-Soviet neutrality pact established. Poland secretly divided between Soviet Union and Germany; Stalin allowed to occupy Baltic States and Bessarabia in Romania in return for neutrality.
September 1, 1939	Germany invades Poland.
September 3, 1939	Britain and France declare war on Germany.
September 21, 1939	Polish Jews ordered into ghettos.
October 12, 1939	Austrian Jews deported to east.
October 1939–March 1940	*Sitzkrieg,* or "phony war." Hitler consolidates Poland and equips military in preparation for coming attacks against Europe.
April–May 1940	*Blitzkrieg,* or "lightning war," as German invades Denmark, Norway, the Netherlands, Luxembourg, and France. France falls by June.
August 1940	Battle of Britain begins as Hitler bombs Britain in preparation for invasion across English Channel. Britain saved by Royal Air Force: "So much owed by so many to so few."
June 1941	Germany opens eastern front by invading Soviet Union.
July 1941	Japan takes over Indochina in search of sources of petroleum.
July 31, 1941	Reich Marshall Hermann Goering gives SS Lt. Colonel Reinhard Heydrich a written order to achieve a "general solution to the Jewish problem in areas of Jewish influence in Europe."
August 1941	FDR and Churchill meet and agree to Atlantic Charter, a broad set of peace principles in the spirit of Wilson's Fourteen Points.
December 7, 1941	Japan attacks American Pacific fleet at Pearl Harbor, Hawaii: "A day which will live in infamy." United States enters war against Axis powers (December 9).
January 20, 1942	Heydrich proposes Final Solution to the "Jewish problem" at Wansee Conference.
June 1942	Battle of Midway. Japan defeated by United States, thus halting Japanese advance in the Pacific and preventing another attack on Hawaii.
July 1942	Liquidation of Jewish ghetto in Warsaw begins.

November 1942	Battle of Stalingrad begins. After months of fighting and tremendous losses, the Soviet army defeats the Germans and assumes the offensive.
July–August	Led by Generals Montgomery and Patton, Allies take Sicily 1943 and invade Italy.
June 6, 1944	"D-day." Allies land in Normandy in the greatest amphibious invasion in history. Begin move toward Berlin.
December 1944	Battle of the Bulge. Germans launch a counterattack in Belgium through the Ardennes forest. "Last gasp" of German strength in the West as Allies cross Rhine River in March 1945.
February 1945	Allied firebombing of Dresden. Yalta conference held with "Big Three" in attendance (FDR, Churchill, and Stalin) to plan postwar arrangements.
March 1945	American firebombing of Tokyo kills more than eighty thousand Japanese. Battle of Iwo Jima ends after a vicious struggle, leaving six thousand Americans dead. Allies continue move toward Japan. Okinawa falls to Allies in April.
April 12, 1945	Death of Franklin Roosevelt. Harry S. Truman succeeds. Liberation of the concentration camp at Dachau by British forces.
May 1945	Germany surrenders. Hitler and associates commit suicide in Berlin bunker.
July 1945	Potsdam conference (Truman, Atlee, and Stalin) to discuss postwar arrangements.
August 1945	Atomic bombs dropped on Hiroshima and Nagasaki.
September 2, 1945	Surrender of Japanese forces.

STUDY QUESTIONS

1. After reading the documents and firsthand accounts of the Japanese attack on Pearl Harbor, what images stand out in your mind? Was the attack well planned? How did the Japanese miscalculate?

2. What roles did women play during World War II? How important were their contributions to the war effort? Answer this question with specific reference to the selections by and about women.

3. What solutions to the Jewish problem were presented at the Wansee Conference? On the basis of this evidence and on the directive of Hermann Goering, how would you define the "Final Solution"? What did it entail? Why was there no specific talk of extermination in these documents?

4. After reading through the accounts concerning the death camps, what are your feelings? What statements by the Commandant of Auschwitz, Rudolf Hoess, in his autobiography stand out in your mind? Why? How does he free himself from guilt while still accepting it?

5. Why did the Japanese resort to suicide attacks on U.S. aircraft carriers during 1944 and 1945? What general impression do you receive from the letter written by the kamikaze pilot? Was the Japanese government asking a greater sacrifice from these suicide pilots than the British and American governments asked of their pilots and soldiers during the D-day invasions? How do you interpret the phrase of Ensign Heiiche Okabe that should Japan suddenly win the war "it would be a fatal misfortune for the future of the nation"? What did he mean?

6. Do you think that President Truman was justified in his use of the atomic bomb on Hiroshima and Nagasaki? Does "total war" have limits? Is there an acceptable versus unacceptable degree of destruction, and where is the line of demarcation?

7. The first and only time nuclear weapons have been directed against human beings occurred in 1945. For those born after this date, can the terror of that long-ago event maintain our allegiance toward arms control, or must we have an example of an atomic explosion every generation or so in order to promote the seriousness of negotiation? Will people forget the horrors of Hiroshima the further they are removed by time from the experience?

8. In your opinion, was justice served and the dead avenged by the Nuremberg trials and execution of Nazi leaders? After reading the selection by Raul Hilberg, "The Destruction of the European Jews," do you think such a thing as the Holocaust could happen again?

9. In a way, was the Holocaust the inevitable outcome of the racist and Social Darwinist ideas that were discussed in Chapter 5 on "The Scramble for Global Empire"? Was the Holocaust "conditioned" by the expendability of life that was so characteristic of battles during World War I? Was the Holocaust itself a precedent for the U.S. bombing of Hiroshima? As you look at the world today, give some examples of attitudes, specific organizations, or individuals that might threaten reoccurrence of genocide. What can be done?

10. According to Jean-Paul Sartre, why are there no "accidents" in life? Why has existentialism often been called a "depressing philosophy"? If being "free" is usually considered an advantageous human condition, why does the existentialist believe that he is "condemned to be free"? Do you think that Albert Einstein was correct in his assessment that "As long as there will be man, there will be wars"?

Part IV

New Departures and the Emerging World of the Twenty-First Century (1945–2000)

9

The Era of the Superpowers: Confrontation and the Dynamics of Change

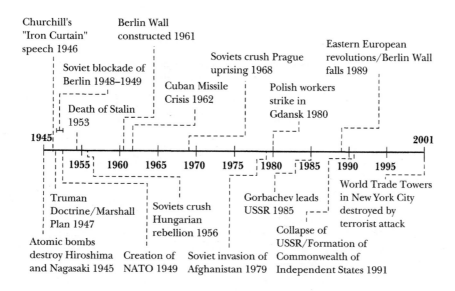

History teaches us that enmities between nations do not last forever. However fixed our likes and dislikes, the tide of time and events will often bring surprising changes in the relations between nations and neighbors.

—*John F. Kennedy*

In the end we beat them with Levi 501 jeans. Seventy-two years of Communist indoctrination and propaganda was drowned out by a three-ounce Sony Walkman. A huge totalitarian system . . . has been brought to its knees because nobody wants to wear Bulgarian shoes. Now they're lunch, and we're number one on the planet.

—*P. J. O'Rourke*

The autopsy of history is that all great nations commit suicide.

—*Arnold Toynbee*

CHAPTER THEMES

- *Systems of Government:* Was the Cold War an ideological struggle between two different systems of government, or did it have very little to do with government at all? What was the root cause of the Cold War?

- *Imperialism:* Was the Cold War just another term for "ideological imperialism"? Was the Cold War really about the accumulation of territory or about the winning of "hearts and minds"? How does this differ from nineteenth-century imperialism?

- *Propaganda:* Just how does one spot a communist? Were the fear and distrust during the Cold War real or were they manufactured by governments seeking justification for authority?

- *Beliefs and Spirituality:* How did the Cold War transform the concepts of freedom and tyranny, of democracy and totalitarianism into a spiritual realm where abstractions obscured reality? Was nuclear destruction such a threat that each side deified its leaders and transformed its ideologies into pure truth, to be supported without equivocation?

- *The Big Picture:* How should we measure progress in civilization? Is it a quantifiable commodity linked to advances in technology? Or is the ethical development of humanity the only real determinant of whether a society has evolved and progressed? Is human nature basically good or evil? Is this the fundamental question that must be answered before political systems can be developed or social programs instituted? Where are we headed in this new century, and what is the value of studying history?

The use of atomic weapons by U.S. forces on the Japanese cities of Hiroshima and Nagasaki in August 1945 presaged not only the end of World War II but also the end of an era. The world entered the nuclear age when modern science joined with military necessity to produce an astonishing desolation. The horrors of trench warfare, poisonous gas, dislocated refugees, and the deprivation and starvation that had plagued the victims of two world wars could not compare with the new possibilities: Human beings had finally discovered a way to destroy themselves and their world. The power unleashed by the splitting of the atom had created a completely new distribution of power. Those countries that had access to the necessary materials and technologies were in a position to dominate and impose their will on less developed regions. As the people of Europe and the East struggled to find food and shelter, to repair their lives and mourn their dead, another game was being played with the ultimate

The erection of the Berlin Wall in August 1961 separated East and West Berlin but also symbolized the Cold War rivalry that had developed between the United States and the Soviet Union. *(UPI/Bettmann)*

risk at stake. This was a contest between good and evil, between dominance and survival—between the United States and the Soviet Union.

The uneasy relationship between the United States and the Soviet Union was not created at the end of World War II. Its roots were deep and primarily philosophical. The United States had been founded on the principles of the eighteenth-century Enlightenment. There existed "natural rights" that were the birthright of each individual: life, liberty, and property. The government was to exist in balance with its citizens, protecting the rights of the individual while seeing to the general welfare of its population. Capitalism, with its inherent emphasis on private enterprise and the reward of individual ability, hard work, and perseverance, blended nicely with the ideals of the democratic political system. As it was applied in the United States, capitalism was not always successful and not always fair. It was regulated by the federal government at various intervals in order to protect the general welfare of the citizenry. But the U.S. commitment to personal liberty was never in question. The fear of communism as a threat to the "American way" was inculcated in the public consciousness in the first decades of the twentieth century.

The Soviet Union was founded on a different philosophical premise. It was created in 1917 when the Bolshevik party seized power from a Provisional Government that had opposed the absolutism of the Russian tsar and was both democratic and capitalistic. The Bolsheviks were led by Vladimir Lenin, a disciple of the German philosopher Karl Marx. Marx had developed the economic theory of communism, which decried the exploitation of workers by middle-class entrepreneurs who sought a profit at all costs. Marx's complex philosophy argued that the conflict engendered by competing capitalistic forces would eventually lead to a communist society where the state would "wither away" and all people would live in harmony, giving what labor they could to the community and taking just what they needed to live a life of mutual respect and tolerance. Communism theoretically looks to the best in human nature—that people are basically good and that they will share the necessities of life with others. Thus, Marx expected "world revolution" that would free people from the class exploitation of capitalism: "The proletarians have nothing to lose but their chains. They have a world to win. Workers of the world unite!"

Communism, it should be noted, is an economic theory, not a political system. If anything, the state is supposed to remove itself from the life of its citizens. Marx believed that the world would naturally evolve toward communism, but he left no practical plans for the application of his ideas. Lenin based the Russian Revolution of 1917 on Marx's philosophy but found himself having to make adjustments in Marx's theory. Americans felt threatened by the coming "world revolution," which sought the overthrow of their cherished principles of individualism and capitalism. The United States even sent troops to fight against the communists in 1918 when Lenin had not yet consolidated control of the government.

Communism therefore became a great evil in the American mind. When Lenin died in 1924 and Joseph Stalin struggled for control of the new Soviet state, there were further modifications in Marx's philosophy that confirmed U.S. fears. Instead of the Soviet state "withering away," Stalin increased its authority and actually "redefined" Marxism to justify his reorganization of agriculture and industry in order to protect the Soviet state from hostile Western democracies. From about 1928 to 1940, Stalin imprisoned and eliminated millions of Russians who resisted his authority. Secret police and a Siberian prison system known as the "Gulag" sought to maintain total control over the population. The term "totalitarian" has been coined to describe this complete imprisonment of society to the dictatorship of the state.

It was therefore with great delicacy that the Western Allies in 1940 decided to "sleep with the enemy" and join Stalin in the crusade against Hitler and Nazism during World War II. This was from the first an expedient relationship—Hitler, the Great Evil, had to be vanquished, and Stalin became a tolerable, lesser evil.

But with the victory over Hitler assured in 1945, Europe became the battleground once again for a new war—the Cold War. As European governments licked their wounds and looked to the immediate needs of their citizens, they retreated from the empires that they had established and depended on for decades. Britain removed itself from controlling interests in Africa, India, and the Middle East, while France loosened its control over countries in Africa and Southeast Asia. Into this power vacuum flowed the interests of the new emerging "superpowers," each trying to compete for the "hearts and minds" as well as the territory of the remnants. Even though the Soviet Union had suffered the greatest losses (nearly eighteen million military and civilian dead) of all combatants in World War II, the need to maintain and expand its position in the face of perceived Western encroachment became Stalin's obsession. By 1946, Winston Churchill spoke of an "Iron Curtain" that had descended over eastern Europe, trapping Hungary, Czechoslovakia, Bulgaria, Romania, Poland, and East Germany. The United States sought to reinforce Western democracies by providing financial aid through the Marshall Plan in 1947. The United States also moved to halt Soviet expansionism in 1947 by proclaiming the Truman Doctrine, which justified intervention against communist movements. Containment of communist "world revolution" became the watchword of American foreign policy throughout the 1950s and 1960s.

The Cold War between the United States and the Soviet Union lasted from about 1945 to 1990. This was a bipolar arrangement in which the world in a sense was held hostage by two nations, philosophically opposed to one another, paranoid about losing face and territory to the unspeakable evil of the other. New alliance systems like NATO and the Warsaw Pact were developed to achieve a balance of power. Military competition was intense as both countries expended billions in order to develop new weapons systems and accumulate more tanks, more missiles, more bombers. The world became a dangerous place in the 1960s as the arms race was on, fueled by military theories that demanded "parity" with the enemy. Mutually Assured Destruction (MAD) was presented as a security measure—if each side could destroy the other many times over, then it would be too dangerous to start a war with a "first strike." The balance of power was thus maintained and peace assured by building ever more sophisticated weaponry, the mere threat of which was enough to keep the peace.

This is not to say that there weren't outbreaks of "hot war." The Korean "police action" (1950–1953), the Cuban "missile crisis" (1962), and the Vietnam "conflict" (1960–1975) were euphemistic struggles in which the two superpowers "fought," often through surrogates without formally declaring war, in order to achieve geopolitical position and influence over strategic regions of the world.

There was a price to pay for the tension of the Cold War, even if the world was spared a nuclear holocaust. Weapon systems developed during the 1980s such as the B-1 bomber, the M-1 tank, stealth fighter aircraft, and the laser-based Strategic Defense Initiative (SDI, or "Star Wars") cost hundreds of billions of dollars and drove defense expenditures to nearly one-quarter of the national budget.

In the Soviet Union, the expense of competing in the arms race proved fatal. The Soviets could put cosmonauts in space and sophisticated MIG fighters in the air but could not put bread on the table or refrigerators in the houses of Soviet citizens. The managed economy of a Soviet state that was supposed to have "withered away" proved disastrous as the workforce became apathetic and inefficient. The Soviets were never able to solve the many ethnic problems that plagued the unity of their political system, and, more importantly, the government was never able to cultivate the trust and commitment of its people that are essential to success and stability. By the time that Mikhail Gorbachev came on the scene in 1985 with his policies of *glasnost* ("openness") and *perestroika* ("political restructuring"), social and economic problems were spinning out of control. The ossified political leadership that had survived Stalin by committing itself to his policies, methods, and priorities for so long could not prepare the Soviet Union for the future.

By 1991, the Soviet Union had collapsed, with its empire of dependent countries broken apart and left to fend for themselves. The United States had won the Cold War and rejoiced in its "victory," the triumph of Capitalism over Communism, of Right over Wrong, of Good over Evil. But it is up to each of us to assess the damage wrought by fifty years of distrust and destructive competition.

The world in the year 2000 was very different than it was in 1945 when the evil of Hitler could be defined and destroyed. After the Cold War from 1991 to 2001, when there is no longer an evil to be vanquished, the United States as the sole remaining superpower seemed adrift in foreign affairs. Which road to take? What did we stand for and what were we willing to fight and die for? These questions were answered on September 11, 2001 when the twin towers of the World Trade Center in New York City collapsed after two hijacked commercial jetliners, missiles really, slammed into them thus destroying the lives of thousands, jeopardizing the nation's economy, and shaking the confidence and security of the American people. Subsequent attacks on the Pentagon and the anthrax contamination of the mail produced a defensive reaction as the United States prepared for a new war, a war on terrorism with the great evil redefined as Osama bin Laden, the wealthy Saudi exile and mastermind of the al-Qaida terrorist network. As the United States provided leadership in this ongoing struggle, old enemies like Russia were themselves given new opportunities to refashion their images and redefine their loyalties. President John Kennedy was correct when he noted: "History teaches us that enmities between nations do not last forever. . . . The tide of time and events will often bring surprising changes in the relations between nations and neighbors." We are witnessing the transition to a new paradigm where nations that have enjoyed a dominant military or economic status must confront their vulnerabilities or perhaps lose their "superpower" designation. New threats to old power relationships create new expediencies, alliances, and opportunities for a greater alienation or integration of the world community. The twenty-first century unfolds.

THE COLD WAR (1945–1990)

The "Superpower" Rivalry

Whether you like it or not, history is on our side. We will bury you.

—*Nikita Khrushchev*

The Soviet Victory: Capitalism versus Communism (February 1946)

JOSEPH STALIN

The term "Cold War" describes the era of uneasy relations between the Western Allies and the Soviet Union after World War II. Each was competing for influence in Europe through propaganda and troop placement. In the first excerpt, the Soviet leader Joseph Stalin offered a glimpse of the ideological combat that was to be waged in the future. A month later, Winston Churchill, who had largely directed the British war effort, warned the West of the deceptive Soviet Union in his famous "Iron Curtain" speech.

It would be wrong to believe that the Second World War broke out accidentally or as a result of the mistakes of some or other statesmen, though mistakes certainly were made. In reality, the war broke out as an inevitable result of the development of world economic and political forces on the basis of modern monopoly capitalism.

"The Soviet Victory" is from Embassy of the U.S.S.R., speech delivered by J. V. Stalin at a Meeting of Voters of the Stalin Electoral Area of Moscow (Washington, DC: Government Printing Office, 1946).

Marxists have stated more than once that the capitalist system of world economy conceals in itself the elements of general crisis and military clashes, that in view of this in our time the development of world capitalism takes place not as a smooth and even advance but through crises and war catastrophes.

The reason is that the unevenness of the development of capitalist countries usually results, as time passes, in an abrupt disruption of the equilibrium within the world system of capitalism, and that a group of capitalist countries which believes itself to be less supplied with raw materials and markets usually attempts to alter the situation and re-divide the "spheres of influence" in its own favour by means of armed force. . . .

This results in the splitting of the capitalist world into two hostile camps and in war between them. Perhaps the catastrophes of war could be avoided if there existed the possibility of re-distributing periodically raw materials and markets among the countries in accordance with their economic weight—by means of adopting coordinated and peaceful decisions. This, however, cannot be accomplished under present capitalist conditions of the development of world economy. . . .

As to our country, for her the war was the severest and hardest of all the wars our Motherland has ever experienced in her history. But the war was not only a curse. It was at the same time a great school in which all the forces of the people were tried and tested. The war laid bare all the facts and events in the rear and at the front, it mercilessly tore off all the veils and covers which had concealed the true faces of States, governments, and parties, and placed them on the stage without masks, without embellishments, with all their shortcomings and virtues.

• • •

And so, what are the results of the war? . . .

Our victory means, in the first place, that our Soviet social system has won, that the Soviet so-

cial system successfully withstood the trial in the flames of war and proved its perfect viability. It is well known that the foreign press more than once asserted that the Soviet social system is a "risky experiment" doomed to failure, that the Soviet system is a "house of cards," without any roots in life, imposed upon the people by the organs of the "Cheka" [secret police], that a slight push from outside would be enough to blow this "house of cards" to smithereens.

Now we can say that the war swept away all these assertions of the foreign press as groundless. The war has shown that the Soviet social system is a truly popular system, which has grown from the people and enjoys its powerful support, that the Soviet social system is a perfectly viable and stable form of organisation of society.

More than that, the point is now not whether the Soviet social system is viable or not, since after the objective lessons of the war no single skeptic now ventures to come out with doubts concerning the viability of the Soviet social system. The point now is that the Soviet social system has proved more viable and stable than a non-Soviet social system, that the Soviet social system is a better form of organisation of society than any non-Soviet social system.

"An Iron Curtain Has Descended Across the Continent" (March 1946)
SIR WINSTON CHURCHILL

I now come to the . . . danger which threatens the cottage home and ordinary people, namely tyranny. We cannot be blind to the fact that the liberties enjoyed by individual citizens throughout the United States and British Empire are not valid in a considerable number of countries, some of which are very powerful. In these states control is forced upon the common people by

---

"'An Iron Curtain Has Descended Across the Continent'" is from *Congressional Record*, 79th Congress, 2nd session, pp. A1145–A1147.

various kinds of all-embracing police governments, to a degree which is overwhelming and contrary to every principle of democracy. The power of the state is exercised without restraint, either by dictators or by compact oligarchies operating through a privileged party and a political police. It is not our duty at this time, when difficulties are so numerous, to interfere forcibly in the internal affairs of countries whom we have not conquered in war, but we must never cease to proclaim in fearless tones the great principles of freedom and the rights of man, which are the joint inheritance of the English-speaking world and which, through Magna Carta, the Bill of Rights, the habeas corpus, trial by jury, and the English common law find their famous expression in the Declaration of Independence. . . .

A shadow has fallen upon the scenes so lately lighted by the Allied victory. Nobody knows what Soviet Russia and its Communist international organization intends to do in the immediate future, or what are the limits, if any, to their expansive and proselytizing tendencies. . . . From Stettin in the Baltic to Trieste in the Adriatic, an iron curtain has descended across the continent. Behind that line lie all the capitals of the ancient states of central and eastern Europe. Warsaw, Berlin, Prague, Vienna, Budapest, Belgrade, Bucharest, and Sofia, all these famous cities and the populations around them lie in the Soviet sphere and all are subject, in one form or another, not only to Soviet influence but to a very high and increasing measure of control from Moscow. Athens alone, with its immortal glories, is free to decide its future at an election under British, American, and French observation.

In a great number of countries, far from the Russian frontiers and throughout the world, Communist fifth columns are established and work in complete unity and absolute obedience to the directions they receive from the Communist center. Except in the British Commonwealth, and in the United States, where communism is in its infancy, the Communist parties and fifth columns constitute a growing challenge and peril to Christian civilization. These are somber facts for anyone to have to recite on the morrow of a victory gained by so much splendid comradeship in arms and in the cause of freedom and democracy, and we should be most unwise not to face them squarely while time remains. . . .

On the other hand, I repulse the idea that a new war is inevitable, still more that it is imminent. It is because I am so sure that our fortunes are in our own hands and that we hold the power to save the future, that I feel the duty to speak out now that I have occasion to do so. I do not believe that Soviet Russia desires war. What they desire is the fruits of war and the indefinite expansion of their power and doctrines. But what we have to consider here today while time remains, is the permanent prevention of war and the establishment of conditions of freedom and democracy as rapidly as possible in all countries.

Our difficulties and dangers will not be removed by closing our eyes to them; they will not be removed by mere waiting to see what happens; nor will they be relieved by a policy of appeasement. What is needed is a settlement, and the longer this is delayed, the more difficult it will be and the greater our dangers will become. From what I have seen of our Russian friends and allies during the war, I am convinced that there is nothing they admire so much as strength, and there is nothing for which they have less respect than for military weakness. For that reason the old doctrine of a balance of power is unsound. We cannot afford, if we can help it, to work on narrow margins, offering temptations to a trial of strength. If the western democracies stand together in strict adherence to the principles of the United Nations Charter, their influence for furthering these principles will be immense and no one is likely to molest them. If, however, they become divided or falter in their duty, and if these all-important years are allowed to slip away, then indeed catastrophe may overwhelm us all.

The Truman Doctrine (March 1947)

HARRY S. TRUMAN

In the first months of 1946, President Truman received urgent requests from the Greek government for economic assistance, which, it was hoped, would put an end to the chaos and strife hindering its recovery from the war. Hoping to forestall Communist dissidents who were threatening the stability of the government, Truman appealed to Congress to appropriate such financial assistance. He also asked for military as well as economic aid to Turkey. The controversial Truman Doctrine, as it came to be called, committed the United States to an active policy of promoting ideological divisions between it and the Soviet Union and further escalated Cold War tensions. The Marshall Plan of 1947, which advocated the rebuilding of West Germany after the war, is an example of this policy of Soviet containment.

One of the primary objectives of the foreign policy of the United States is the creation of conditions in which we and other nations will be able to work out a way of life free from coercion. This was a fundamental issue in the war with Germany and Japan. Our victory was won over countries which sought to impose their will, and their way of life, upon other nations.

To ensure the peaceful development of nations, free from coercion, the United States has taken a leading part in establishing the United Nations. The United Nations is designed to make possible lasting freedom and independence for all its members. We shall not realize our objectives, however, unless we are willing to help free peoples to maintain their free institutions and their national integrity against aggressive movements that seek to impose upon them totalitarian regimes. This is no more than a frank recognition that totalitarian regimes imposed upon free peoples, by direct or indirect aggression, undermine the foundations of international peace and hence the security of the United States.

The peoples of a number of countries of the world have recently had totalitarian regimes forced upon them against their will. The Government of the United States has made frequent protests against coercion and intimidation, in violation of the Yalta agreement, in Poland, Ru-

mania, and Bulgaria. I must also state that in a number of other countries there have been similar developments.

At the present moment in world history nearly every nation must choose between alternative ways of life. The choice is too often not a free one.

One way of life is based upon the will of the majority, and is distinguished by free institutions, representative government, free elections, guarantees of individual liberty, freedom of speech and religion, and freedom from political oppression.

The second way of life is based upon the will of a minority forcibly imposed upon the majority. It relies upon terror and oppression, a controlled press and radio, fixed elections, and the suppression of personal freedoms.

I believe that it must be the policy of the United States to support free peoples who are resisting attempted subjugation by armed minorities or by outside pressures. I believe that we must assist free peoples to work out their own destinies in their own way. I believe that our help should be primarily through economic and financial aid which is essential to economic stability and orderly political processes.

The world is not static, and the status quo is not sacred. But we cannot allow changes in the status quo in violation of the Charter of United

"The Truman Doctrine" is from *Public Papers of the President*, Harry S. Truman, 1947 (Washington, DC: Government Printing Office, 1963), pp. 177–180.

Nations by such methods as coercion, or by such subterfuges as political infiltration. In helping free and independent nations to maintain their freedom, the United States will be giving effect to the principles of the Charter of the United Nations. . . .

The seeds of totalitarian regimes are nurtured by misery and want. They spread and grow in the evil soil of poverty and strife. They reach their full growth when the hope of a people for a better life has died. We must keep that hope alive. The free peoples of the world look to us for support in maintaining their freedoms.

If we falter in our leadership, we may endanger the peace of the world—and we shall surely endanger the welfare of this Nation. Great responsibilities have been placed upon us by the swift movement of events. I am confident that the Congress will face these responsibilities squarely.

The Marshall Plan (June 1947)

GEORGE C. MARSHALL

The truth of the matter is that Europe's requirements for the next three or four years of foreign food and other essential products—principally from America—are so much greater than her present ability to pay that she must have substantial additional help or face economic, social, and political deterioration of a very grave character.

The remedy lies in breaking the vicious circle and restoring the confidence of the European people in the economic future of their own countries and of Europe as a whole. The manufacturer and the farmer throughout wide areas must be able and willing to exchange their products for currencies the continuing value of which is not open to question.

Aside from the demoralizing effect on the world at large and the possibilities of distur-

bances arising as a result of the desperation of the people concerned, the consequences to the economy of the United States should be apparent to all. It is logical that the United States should do whatever it is able to do to assist in the return of normal economic health in the world, without which there can be no political stability and no assured peace. Our policy is directed not against any country or doctrine but against hunger, poverty, desperation, and chaos. Its purpose should be the revival of a working economy in the world so as to permit the emergence of political and social conditions in which free institutions can exist. Such assistance, I am convinced, must not be on a piecemeal basis as various crises develop. Any assistance that this Government may render in the future should provide a cure rather than a mere palliative. Any government that is willing to assist in the task of recovery will find full cooperation, I am sure, on the part of the United States Government. Any government which maneuvers to block the recovery of other countries cannot expect help from us. Furthermore, governments, political parties, or groups which seek to perpetuate human misery in order to profit therefrom politically or otherwise will encounter the opposition of the United States.

It is already evident that, before the United States Government can proceed much further in its efforts to alleviate the situation and help start the European world on its way to recovery, there must be some agreement among the countries of Europe as to the requirements of the situation and the part those countries themselves will take in order to give proper effect to whatever action might be undertaken by this Government. It would be neither fitting nor efficacious for this Government to undertake to draw up unilaterally a program designed to place Europe on its feet economically. This is the business of the Europeans. The initiative, I think, must come from Europe. The role of this country should consist of friendly aid in the drafting of a European program and of later support of such a program so far as it may be practical for us to do so. The program should be

---

"The Marshall Plan" is from *Department of State Bulletin* (June 15, 1947), pp. 1159–1160.

a joint one, agreed to by a number, if not all, European nations.

An essential part of any successful action on the part of the United States is an understanding on the part of the people of America of the character of the problem and the remedies to be applied. Political passion and prejudice should have no part. With foresight, and a willingness on the part of our people to face up to the vast responsibility which history has clearly placed upon our country, the difficulties I have outlined can and will be overcome.

How to Spot a Communist (1955)

As the United States actively countered the Soviet threat to the stability of Europe with the Truman Doctrine and the Marshall Plan, a campaign of fear was launched domestically in the early 1950s when Senator Joseph McCarthy and his Select Committeee on Un-American Activities tried through false accusation and intimidation to identify Communists in the halls of Congress and in the studios of Hollywood. The following article was issued by the U.S. First Army Headquarters for public dissemination and reveals the Cold War paranoia that was so much a part of the decade of the 1950s.

Events of recent years have made it obvious that there is no fool-proof way of detecting a Communist. The Communist individual is no longer a "type" exemplified by the bearded and coarse revolutionary with time bomb in briefcase. U.S. Communists come from all walks in life, profess all faiths, and exercise all trades and professions. In addition, the Communist Party, USA, has made concerted efforts to go underground for the purpose of infiltration.

If there is no fool-proof system in spotting a Communist, there are, fortunately, indications that may give him away. These indications are often subtle but always present, for the Communist, by reason of his "faith" must act and talk along certain lines.

While a certain heaviness of style and preference for long sentences is common to most Communist writing, a distinct vocabulary provides the . . . more easily recognized feature of the "Communist Language."

Even a superficial reading of an article written by a Communist or a conversation with one will probably reveal the use of some of the following expressions: integrative thinking, vanguard, comrade, hootenanny, chauvinism, book-burning, syncretistic faith, bourgeois-nationalism, jingoism, colonialism, hooliganism, ruling class, progressive, demagogy, dialectical, witch-hunt, reactionary, exploitation, oppressive, materialist.

This list, selected at random, could be extended almost indefinitely. While all of the above expressions are part of the English language, their use by Communists is infinitely more frequent than by the general public. . . .

The tell-tale signs of the "Communist Religion" are not easy to detect. There is, above all, a rigidity in views insofar as they pertain to the Communist doctrine. This is not to say that the Communist lacks persuasiveness or variety of expression. It does mean, however, that he will stubbornly cling to the "line" even when proven wrong in debate. The Communist has implicit faith in Marxist philosophy and in the truth of the "line" as transmitted from Moscow. Because of this faith, he cannot and will not give ground

---

"How to Spot a Communist" was first issued by First Army Headquarters in a pamphlet entitled *How to Spot a Communist.* It was reprinted by *U.S.A., An American Magazine of Fact and Opinion,* in a special supplement on June 22, 1955. Copyright © 1955 by U.S.A. Contained in Anthony Bouscaren, ed., *A Guide to Anti-Communist Action* (Chicago: Henry Regnery Company, 1958), pp. 174–185.

when challenged on basic Marxist issues or political pronouncements made by his leaders. The possibility of compromising on these issues is utterly beyond his comprehension. . . .

His "religion," then, can give away the Communist. His naive and unquestioning acceptance of the "line," his refusal to accept criticism are excellent indications. Last but not least, the Communist feels a strong compulsion to speak his "faith" and can frequently be spotted by his never-ceasing attempts at conversion of others.

The "Communist Logic" . . . is diametrically opposed to our own. Thus, the Communist refers to the iron curtain police states as "democracies," and any defensive move on the part of the Western powers is condemned as "aggression." The Communist thus builds for himself a topsy-turvy world with a completely distorted set of values. For this reason, it is practically impossible to win an argument with a hard-core Communist. . . . The Communist mind cannot and will not engage in a detached examination of ideas. Talking to a Communist about his own ideas, then, is like listening to a phonograph record. His answers will invariably follow a definite pattern because he can never admit, even hypothetically, that the basis for his ideas may not be sound. This attitude is typical not only for the individual but also on a national scale. . . . The answer is final and no arguments are permitted so far as the Communists are concerned. The Communist, then, is not really "logical." The finality of his arguments and the completeness of his condemnation marks him clearly, whether as a speaker, a writer or a conversation partner.

In addition to these very general principles common to Communist tactics, a number of specific issues have been part of the Communist arsenal for a long period of time. These issues are raised not only by Communist appeals to the public, but also by the individual Party member or sympathizer who is a product of his Communist environment. They include: "McCarthyism," violation of civil rights, racial or religious discrimination, immigration laws, anti-subversive legislation, any legislation concerning labor unions, the military budget, "peace."

While showing standard opposition to certain standard issues, the U.S. Communist has traditionally identified himself with certain activities in the hope of furthering his ultimate purposes. Such hobbies as "folk dancing" and "folk music" have been traditionally allied with the Communist movement in the United States. . . . The reason for their choice [of hobbies] is not altogether an attempt to hide political activities. The Communist's fondness for everything that comes from "the people" is not an entirely theoretical preference and has found expression in his everyday life. Most Communists are likely to show preference for group activities rather than such bourgeois forms of recreation as ballroom dancing. . . .

A study such as this can lead to only one certain conclusion: There is no sure-fire way of spotting a Communist. . . . The principle difficulty involved is the distinction between the person who merely dissents in the good old American tradition and the one who condemns for the purpose of abolishing that tradition.

In attempting to find the answer to the question: "Is this man a Communist?" a checklist such as this can prove helpful, although in itself it cannot provide the answer:

Does the individual use unusual language? ("Communist Language")
Does he stubbornly cling to Marxist ideals without being willing to question them?
Does he condemn our American institutions and praise those of Communist countries?
Does he pick on any event, even the most insignificant occurrences in this country for his criticism?
Is he secretive about certain of his contacts?
Does he belong to groups exploiting controversial subjects?

Above all, the approach to the problem of discovering Communists must be detached and completely free from prejudice. Using some of the clues mentioned in this study in connection with a factual approach provides the best system at present of spotting a Communist.

"The Victory of Communism Is Inevitable!":
Speech to the 22nd Communist Party Congress (1962)

NIKITA KHRUSHCHEV

After Stalin's death in 1953, the power vacuum was eventually filled by Sergeyevich (Nikita) Khrushchev. At the 20th Communist Party Congress, Khrushchev quite unexpectedly attacked Stalin and his legacy of fear. The Soviets were looking for a new beginning. Although there may have been hope that the fears of the Cold War would be reduced, the decade from 1955 to 1966 was especially intense in its rhetoric and ideological conflict. As Khrushchev menacingly said of capitalist states in 1956, "Whether you like it or not, history is on our side. We will bury you!" This was the era of Senator Joseph McCarthy, who played on the fears of Americans with his deceitful rantings that communists had infiltrated the highest echelons of government. It was during this time (1961) that the Berlin Wall was built, sealing off the city into communist and democratic sectors—a symbolic as well as practical measure. And finally, in 1962, the two superpowers nearly went to nuclear war as President Kennedy demanded the removal of Soviet missiles from Cuba. The following excerpt is from Khrushchev's speech to the 22nd Congress of the Communist party. Note the argument carefully.

The most rabid imperialists, acting on the principle of "after us the deluge," openly voice their desire to undertake a new war venture. The ideologists of imperialism, intimidating the peoples, try to instill a kind of philosophy of hopelessness and desperation. Hysterically they cry: "Better death under capitalism than life under communism." They do not like free peoples to flourish, you see. They fear that the peoples in their countries too will take the path of socialism. Blinded by class hatred, our enemies are ready to doom all mankind to the catastrophe of war. The imperialists' opportunities to carry out their aggressive designs, however, are becoming smaller and smaller. They behave like a feeble and greedy old man whose powers have been exhausted, whose physical capacity has weakened, but whose avid desires remain. . . .

As long as the imperialist aggressors exist, we must be on guard, keep our powder dry, improve the defense of the socialist countries, their armed forces and the state security agencies. If, in the face of common sense, the imperialists dare attack the socialist countries and plunge mankind into the abyss of a world war of annihilation, this mad act of theirs would be their last, it would be the end of the whole system of capitalism. (*Applause.*)

Our party clearly understands its tasks, its responsibility, and will do everything in its power to see to it that the world socialist system continues to grow stronger, gathers fresh strength and develops. We believe that in the competition with capitalism socialism will win. (*Prolonged applause.*) We believe that this victory will be won in peaceful competition and not by way of unleashing a war. We have stood, we stand and we will stand by the positions of peaceful competition of states with different social systems; we will do everything to strengthen world peace. (*Prolonged applause.*)

The most important component of our party's foreign policy activities is *the struggle for general and complete disarmament.* The Soviet Union has been waging this struggle for many years now, and doing so firmly and perseveringly. We have always been resolutely opposed to the arms race, since rivalry in this sphere in the past not only saddled the peoples with a terrible burden but inevitably led to world wars. We are even more resolutely opposed to the arms race now that there has been a colossal technical revolution in the art of war and the use of today's weapons would inevitably entail the deaths of hundreds of millions of people.

The stockpiling of these weapons, proceeding as it is in a setting of cold war and war hysteria, is fraught with disastrous consequences. All that has to happen is for the nerves of some fellow in uniform to crack while he is on duty at a "push-button" somewhere in the West, and things may happen that will bring more than a little misfortune upon the peoples of the whole world.

Naturally, when we put forward a program of general and complete disarmament, we are talking not about the unilateral disarmament of socialism in the face of imperialism or vice versa, but about universal renunciation of arms as a means of solving problems at issue among states. . . .

The example of the Soviet Union inspires all progressive mankind. Never has the great vital force of Marxist-Leninist teaching been so clearly evident as in our days, now that socialism has triumphed fully and finally in the Soviet Union, the cause of socialism is winning new victories in the countries of the world socialist commonwealth, and the international Communist and workers' movement and the national liberation struggle of peoples are growing and expanding tempestuously.

The revolution awakened the great energy of peoples, which is transforming the world on the principles of socialism and communism. Colossal changes are taking place and will take place throughout the world under the influence of the successes of communism.

The victory of communism is inevitable! (*Stormy applause.*)

The great army of Communists and of Marxist-Leninists acts as the vanguard of the peoples in the struggle for peace, for social progress and for communism, the bright future of mankind. New and ever newer millions of people will assemble and rally under the great banner of communism. The cause of progress, the cause of communism will triumph! (*Stormy applause.*)

Long live the great and heroic Soviet people, the builders of communism! (*Stormy applause.*)

Long live the indestructible unity and fraternal friendship of the peoples of the world socialist camp! (*Stormy applause.*)

Long live the heroic party of the Communists of the Soviet Union, created and tempered in struggle by the great Lenin! (*Stormy applause.*)

Long live the indestructible unity of the international Communist and workers' movement and the fraternal solidarity of the proletarians of all countries! (*Stormy applause.*)

Long live peace the world over! (*Stormy applause.*)

Under the all-conquering banner of Marxism-Leninism, under the leadership of the Communist Party, forward to the victory of communism! (*Stormy, prolonged applause, turning into an ovation. All rise.*)

"A World Turned Upside Down!": The Gorbachev Era and Beyond

There is nothing more difficult to take in hand, more perilous to conduct, or more uncertain in its success than to take the lead in a new order of things.

—*Niccolò Machiavelli*

Much of what accumulated in the stifling and repressive atmosphere of Stalinism and stagnation, and is now surfacing, is far from pleasant and constructive. But this has to be tolerated. This is what a revolution is all about. Its primary function is always to give people freedom. And *perestroika* with its democratization and *glasnost* has already fulfilled its primary task.

—*Mikhail Gorbachev*

Many people feel empty, a world that seemed so strong just collapsed. Forty years have been wasted on stupid strife for the sake of an unsuccessful experiment.

—*George Konrad*

Russia is doomed to be governed by fools; she knows no other way.

—*Alexander Solzhenitsyn*

During the early 1970s, the Soviet Union and United States, under the leadership, respectively, of Leonid Brezhnev and Richard Nixon, demonstrated cooperation through cultural exchanges and even negotiated a Strategic Arms Limitation Treaty (SALT) in 1972. This policy of détente, as it was called, was a hopeful sign that the world was becoming a safer place. But internally, the Soviet Union continued to stifle dissent in an effort to preserve the integrity of its image as a united and stable state, proof of the success and superiority of the communist philosophy.

During the presidency of Jimmy Carter, the Soviet Union invaded the sovereign state of Afghanistan (December 1979), an act that drew international criticism and contributed to the Carter Doctrine of January 1980: Any threat upon U.S. oil interests in the Persian Gulf would be considered provocative and tantamount to war. In 1981, Ronald Reagan was inaugurated as president, having won the election in part on a "get-tough" stance toward the U.S.S.R. His verbal attacks characterized the Soviet Union as "the evil Empire" and "the focus of evil in the world." Such rhetoric did little to encourage cooperation between the two nations.

A new era in international relations dawned on the death of the old-guard Soviet leader Constantine Chernenko in 1985. His government had been transitional, a geriatric accommodation to the demands of a new-style Soviet leadership waiting in the wings. Mikhail Gorbachev was 48 years old when he secured entry to the Politburo in 1979 and only 54 when he assumed the position of general secretary of the Communist party in 1985. A career bureaucrat with primary assignments in agricultural administration, Gorbachev was nevertheless ready to embark on a radical departure from established Soviet policies. He sought to define and implement the new concepts of perestroika *("restructuring") and* glasnost *("openness") through which he hoped to liberalize the political, economic, and cultural bases of Soviet society. Change was imminent, but no one could predict its full impact on travel restrictions and emigration, censorship, state control of artistic expression, and ultimately political organization itself through democratization and self-determination of ethnic nationalities.*

Gorbachev's initial declarations in 1985 were met with international and domestic astonishment. Gorbachev was hailed in the West as the "man of the century," personally responsible for overcoming the legacy of Stalinism, for eliminating an authoritarian mindset, for offering flexible positions on arms reduction in pursuit of a safer world. The "Evil Empire" was fast losing its threatening aura as each of the eastern European "satellite" nations broke away from Soviet control in popular revolutions throughout 1989. This time there was no military attempt to maintain Soviet control as in Hungary (1956) and in Czechoslovakia (1968). The symbolic culmination of this process occurred on November 10, 1989, with the destruction of the Berlin Wall by the people of East and West Germany.

But Mikhail Gorbachev also faced severe opposition at home, both from the political right, which feared chaos and a loss of influence, and from the political left, led by Boris Yeltsin, who argued that perestroika was not being instituted fast enough, nor with a deep democratic conviction. Also in the late 1980s, the various ethnic minorities in the Soviet republics of Armenia, Azerbaijan, and Georgia began testing the limits of Gorbachev's commitment to democracy and self-determination of peoples. So too did the Baltic States of Estonia, Latvia, and Lithuania seek to break away from the Soviet "Union" and once again run their own affairs independent of Moscow.

Add to this turmoil a tense domestic background of deprivation as evidenced by food shortages and a heritage of consumer neglect, and Gorbachev was pressed at every turn. However, he was a maneuverer, a political tactician, an orchestrator of change. In an effort to maintain the union of the Soviet republics, Gorbachev tried to run a center position against the divergent agendas of the reformists and conservatives. He promised the former continued democratization and progress toward a market economy, and he reassured the latter that he was a loyal Communist party man, who would respect them and protect their traditional interests. In late 1990, Gorbachev felt the need to conciliate the right wing of the party, which was increasingly concerned about demonstrations of independence in the republics. Gorbachev regarded this placation as necessary for the maintenance of his authority; however, it drove away some of the most talented and avid reformers in the Gorbachev orbit. Eduard Shevardnadze resigned as foreign minister and warned of dictatorship.

On August 19, 1991, Shevardnadze's fears threatened to become reality as hard-line members of Gorbachev's advisory cabinet tried to institute a coup d'état. Gorbachev was confined in the Crimea for three days while an "emergency committee" of eight coup leaders explained that he was "ill" and needed a long rest. The incompetency of the conspirators, the refusal of the army and KGB security forces to fire on the Russian people, and most importantly the defiance of the Soviet citizenry and their commitment to the tenets of popular sovereignty resulted in the swift collapse of the coup. But the Soviet state emerged from this drama a changed entity. Boris Yeltsin, the popularly elected president of the Republic of Russia, now seemed to hold the keys to the future. By August 24, Gorbachev's cabinet had been reappointed with reformers scrutinized by Yeltsin; the Communist party newspaper, Pravda, had been shut down; and Gorbachev had resigned from his position as general secretary of the Communist party. Indeed, the Communist party was in complete disarray after having ruled the country for nearly seventy-five years. Each of the Baltic states as well as the Ukraine and other Soviet republics had declared independence, a foreshadowing of the dissolution of the Soviet empire. Some scholars have hailed this as the "Second Russian Revolution." That revolution left Gorbachev behind. He had styled himself a reforming communist and a convinced socialist, an image essential to the initial phases of reform. Paradoxically, this close identification with the Communist party afforded him the path to success, but it also sowed the seeds of failure. Gorbachev faced the great challenge of transition, of creating revolution and controlling it at the same time. As Lenin, Napoleon, Robespierre, and the Roman emperor Augustus understood in earlier ages, it is difficult to hold onto a world turned upside down.

The following selections address the transitional dilemmas facing the Russian people as they continue to cope with political instability, social chaos, economic dislocation, and ethnic rebellion.

Perestroika and the Socialist Renewal of Society (September 11, 1989)

MIKHAIL GORBACHEV

Good evening, comrades, I am here to talk to you about our current affairs. The situation in the country is not simple. We all know and feel this. Everything has become entangled in a tight knot: scarcity on the consumer goods market, conflicts in ethnic relations, and difficult and sometimes painful processes in the public consciousness, resulting from the overcoming of distortions and from the renewal of socialism. People are trying to understand where we have found ourselves at the moment, evaluating the pluses and minuses of the path we have covered during the last four-plus years, the development of democracy and the pace of the economic and political reforms.

It is only natural that people want to know the real causes of our weaknesses and failures in carrying out specific programs for *perestroika* and in tackling urgent problems and to find out why the situation in some areas has deteriorated rather than improved.

In short, political life today is characterized by intense debate. But the main thing I want to emphasize is that the mass of people have become involved in this movement and they play an every growing role in discussing and accomplishing social, economic, and political tasks.

Comrades, this is a fact of fundamental importance because it gives *perestroika* the elements of constructive and businesslike effort and helps overcome people's alienation from power. Yet one cannot fail to see a different trend. Against the background of heated debate and a rapid succession of events, things are happening that must not be ignored or left unaccounted for. Ef-

forts are being made to discredit *perestroika* from conservative, leftist and sometimes unmistakably anti-socialist positions. One can hear in this discordant choir voices predicting an imminent chaos and speculation about the threat of a coup and even civil war. It is a fact that some people would like to create an atmosphere of anxiety, despair and uncertainty in society. . . .

In effect, the conservative forces are trying to impose on us such evaluations of the situation that would provoke resistance to *perestroika* and mold in people's mind the view that the process of change begun in society should be halted or at least slowed down; these forces demand that the old command methods of government should be restored. Otherwise, they say, chaos will set in. Meanwhile, the leftist elements suggest tackling extremely difficult problems in one go, without taking into account our actual possibilities or the interests of society. Such demands are presented as concern for the people and its well-being.

Recommendations have also been made lately from which one can assume that our only "salvation" is renouncing the values of socialism and conducting *perestroika* in the capitalist manner. Such views do exist. Needless to say, such ideas go against the grain of *perestroika*, which implies socialist renewal of society. . . .

True, *perestroika* is meeting with many difficulties. But it is radical change, a revolution in the economy and in policy, in the ways of thinking and in people's consciousness, in the entire pattern of our life. Besides, we have not been able to avoid mistakes in our practical actions in the course of *perestroika*.

But *perestroika* has opened up realistic opportunities for society's renewal, for giving society a new quality and for creating truly humane and democratic socialism. It has returned to the great nation a sense of dignity and given the Soviet people a sense of freedom. It is a powerful source of social, spiritual, and, I should say, patriotic energy for decades to come.

That is why we must do everything to continue *perestroika* on the basis of the ideas and principles

"Perestroika and the Socialist Renewal of Society" is from Mikhail Gorbachev, speech delivered to the people of the U.S.S.R., September 11, 1989. Contained in *Vital Speeches of the Day*, October 15, 1989, pp. 5–7.

proclaimed by the party. And we must not stop. We must continue along the way of changes we have embarked upon. . . . The community is casting off its illusions. It no longer believes that there are simple solutions to be brought ready-made from above for all our problems. . . .

I think it very important that the community is coming to better understand the primary link between *perestroika* and labor—dedicated, creative, efficient work fully implementing every worker's knowledge and abilities. This is essential because until recently, we concentrated not so much on labor as on the distribution of benefits. One could think that redistribution of fictitious wealth was all *perestroika* was about. We have at last begun to shed this delusion. . . .

The Government of the U.S.S.R. is elaborating a program of extraordinary measures to improve the economy and, above all, to normalize the consumer market. The program is to be submitted to the Congress of People's Deputies. We believe that this program will give clear answers to the questions of how and when the most urgent social and economic problems will be solved. I think society will not accept it if the program does not determine clear and concrete measures, stages, and time limits as well as the responsibility of the republic and local bodies and labor collectives. I presume that this package may include unpopular, probably tough and even painful measures. This will be justified, however, only if they are prompted by the need to get out of the present situation.

Shortages, which arouse the sharpest criticisms and discontent of the people, are a special issue. The government is to give an explanation on this urgent social problem and come up with practical measures shortly. . . .

Of major political importance will be the laws on republic and regional cost-accounting and self-government. They are an important step toward realistically strengthening the sovereignty of the republics and expanding the rights of the local *Soviets* [councils].

The party, which is society's consolidating and vanguard force, has a unique role to play in this process. Those who strive to use the difficul-

ties of the transition period for certain unseemly purposes and try to undermine the influence of the party should know that they will not succeed. We are sure that with all the critical sentiments concerning the activities of some or other party committee or communists, the working people realize perfectly well the importance of the party of Lenin for the fate of socialism, which today is inseparable from the success of *perestroika*. On the other hand, it is clear that the new tasks call for a deep renewal of the party.

By restructuring itself, getting rid of all that hinders its activities, overcoming dogmatism and conservatism, mastering a new style and new methods of work, renewing its personnel, and working side by side with the working people, the Communist Party of the Soviet Union will be able to fulfill its role of the political vanguard of society. The party will firmly pursue the policy of *perestroika*, heading the revolutionary transformation of society. We should realistically assess all processes and phenomena of the present-day situation, show restraint, see clearly where we are and not become confused. On this basis we should draw conclusions for our action at the given moment and in the future. We must act responsibly and prudently, without deviating from the course of *perestroika* in society.

Dear comrades, I wish you success in work, determination and firm spirit.

Gorbachev's Resignation: "The Old System Fell Apart Before the New System Began to Work" (December 25, 1991)

MIKHAIL GORBACHEV

Dear fellow countrymen, compatriots. Due to the situation which has evolved as a result of the formation of the Commonwealth of Independent States, I hereby discontinue my activities at

"Gorbachev's Resignation" is from Mikhail Gorbachev, speech delivered over Russian television on December 25, 1991. Contained in *Vital Speeches of the Day*, January 15, 1992, pp. 194–195.

the post of President of the Union of Soviet Socialist Republics.

I am making this decision on considerations of principle. I firmly came out in favor of the independence of nations and sovereignty for the republics. At the same time, I support the preservation of the union state and the integrity of this country. The developments took a different course. The policy prevailed of dismembering this country and disuniting the state, which is something I cannot subscribe to. . . .

This being my last opportunity to address you as President of the U.S.S.R., I find it necessary to inform you of what I think of the road that has been trodden by us since 1985. I find it important because there have been a lot of controversial, superficial, and biased judgments made on this score. Destiny so ruled that when I found myself at the helm of this state it already was clear that something was wrong in this country.

We had a lot of everything—land, oil and gas, other natural resources—and there was intellect and talent in abundance. However, we were living much worse than people in the industrialized countries were living and we were increasingly lagging behind them. The reason was obvious even then. This country was suffocating in the shackles of the bureaucratic command system. Doomed to cater to ideology, and suffer and carry the onerous burden of the arms race, it found itself at the breaking point.

All the half-hearted reforms—and there have been a lot of them—fell through, one after another. This country was going nowhere and we couldn't possibly live the way we did. We had to change everything radically. It is for this reason that I have never had any regrets—never had any regrets—that I did not use the capacity of General Secretary just to rein in this country for several years. I would have considered it an irresponsible and immoral decision. I was also aware that to embark on reform of this caliber and in a society like ours was an extremely difficult and even risky undertaking. But even now, I am convinced that the democratic reform that we launched in the spring of 1985 was historically correct.

The process of renovating this country and bringing about drastic change in the international community has proven to be much more complicated than anyone could imagine. However, let us give its due to what has been done so far. This society has acquired freedom. It has been freed politically and spiritually, and this is the most important achievement that we have yet fully come to grips with. And we haven't, because we haven't learned to use freedom yet. However, an effort of historical importance has been carried out. The totalitarian system has been eliminated, which prevented this country from becoming a prosperous and well-to-do country a long time ago. A breakthrough has been effected on the road of democratic change.

Free elections have become a reality. Free press, freedom of worship, representative legislatures and a multi-party system have all become reality. Human rights are being treated as the supreme principle and top priority. Movement has been started toward a multi-tier economy and the equality of all forms of ownership is being established. . . .

We're now living in a new world. An end has been put to the Cold War and to the arms race, as well as to the mad militarization of the country, which has crippled our economy, public attitudes and morals. The threat of nuclear war has been removed. Once again, I would like to stress that during this transitional period, I did everything that needed to be done to ensure that there was reliable control of nuclear weapons. We opened up ourselves to the rest of the world, abandoned the practices of interfering in others' internal affairs and using troops outside this country, and we were reciprocated with trust, solidarity, and respect. . . .

All this change had taken a lot of strain, and took place in the context of fierce struggle against the background of increasing resistance by the reactionary forces, both the party and state structures, and the economic elite, as well as our habits, ideological bias, the sponging attitudes. The change ran up against our intolerance, a low level of political culture and fear of change. That is why we have wasted so much time. The old system fell apart even before the new system began to work. Crisis of society as a result aggravated even further.

I'm aware that there is popular resentment as a result of today's grave situation. I note that authority at all levels, and myself are being subject to harsh criticisms. I would like to stress once again, though, that the cardinal change in so vast a country, given its heritage, could not have been carried out without difficulties, shock and pain.

The August [1991] coup brought the overall crisis to the limit. The most dangerous thing about this crisis is the collapse of statehood. I am concerned about the fact that the people in this country are ceasing to become citizens of a great power and the consequences may be very difficult for all of us to deal with. I consider it vitally important to preserve the democratic achievements which have been attained in the last few years. We have paid with all our history

and tragic experience for these democratic achievements, and they are not to be abandoned, whatever the circumstances, and whatever the pretexts. Otherwise, all our hopes for the best will be buried. I am telling you all this honestly and straightforwardly because this is my moral duty. . . .

I am very much concerned as I am leaving this post. However, I also have a feeling of hope and faith in you, your wisdom and force of spirit. We are heirs of a great civilization and it now depends on all and everyone whether or not this civilization will make a comeback to a new and decent living today. . . . Of course, there were mistakes made that could have been avoided, and many of the things that we did could not have been done better. But I am positive that sooner or later, some day our common efforts will bear fruit and our nations will live in a prosperous, democratic society.

Communism: "Far Away from the Main Stream of Civilization" (December 31, 1999)

VLADIMIR PUTIN

On December 31, 1999, Boris Yeltsin resigned as President of the Russian Federation and was replaced by his foreign minister, Vladimir Putin, who became the newly elected president in June 2000. Putin was a former KGB officer who brought with him a relentless determination to institute changes in the government that would increase economic production and promote efficiency in the campaign to eliminate organized crime and redefine Russia's international image. In the following speech given as Yeltsin stepped down, Putin sketched the problems facing Russia and some of his proposed solutions.

Russia is completing the first transition stage of economic and political reforms. Despite problems and mistakes, it has entered the highway by which the whole of humanity is traveling. Only this way offers the possibility of dynamic economic growth and higher living standards, as the world experience convincingly shows. There is no alternative to it.

The question for Russia now is what to do next. How can we make the new, market mecha-

nisms work to full capacity? How can we overcome the still deep ideological and political split in society? What strategic goals can consolidate Russian society? What place can Russia occupy in the international community in the 21st century? What economic, social and cultural frontiers do we want to attain in 10–15 years? What are our strong and weak points? And what material and spiritual resources do we have now?

"Communism: 'Far Away from the Mainstream of Civilization'" is from Vladimir Putin, speech delivered to the Russian People, The Kremlin, Moscow, Russia, on December 31, 1999. Contained in *Vital Speeches of the Day*, February 1, 2000, pp. 232–236.

These are the questions put forward by life itself. Unless we find clear answers to them that would be understandable to all the people, we will be unable to move forward at the pace and to the goals that are worthy of our great country.

The Lessons Russia HAS to Learn

The answers to these questions and our very future depend on what lessons we will learn from our past and present. This is a work for society as a whole and for more than one year, but some of these lessons are already clear:

For almost three-fourths of the outgoing century, Russia lived under the sign of the implementation of the communist doctrine. It would be a mistake not to see and, even more so, to deny the unquestionable achievements of those times. But it would be an even bigger mistake not to realize the outrageous price our country and its people had to pay for that Bolshevik experiment.

What is more, it would be a mistake not to understand its historic futility. Communism and the power of the Soviets did not make Russia a prosperous country with a dynamically developing society and free people. Communism vividly demonstrated in inaptitude for sound self-development, dooming our country to a steady lag behind economically advanced countries. It was a road to a blind alley, which is far away from the mainstream of civilization. . . .

Every country, Russia included, has to search for its own way of renewal. We have not been very successful in this respect thus far. Only in the past year or the past two years have we started groping for our road and our model of transformation. We can pin hopes for a worthy future only if we prove capable of combining the universal principles of a market economy and democracy with Russian realities. . . .

A Chance for a Worthy Future

Strong State: We are at a stage where even the most correct economic and social policy starts misfiring while being realized due to the weakness of the state power, of the managerial bod-

ies. A key to Russia's recovery and growth is in the state-policy sphere today.

Russia needs a strong state power and must have it. I am not calling for totalitarianism. History proves all dictatorships, all authoritarian forms of government are transient. Only democratic systems are intransient. Whatever the shortcomings, mankind has not devised anything superior. A strong state power in Russia is a democratic, law-based, workable federative state. . . .

Efficient Economy: Another important lesson from the 1990s is the conclusion that Russia needs to form a wholesome system of state regulation of the economy and social sphere. I do not mean to return to a system of planning and managing the economy by fiat, where the all-pervasive state was regulating all aspects of any factory's work from top to bottom. I mean to make the Russian state an efficient coordinator of the country's economic and social forces that balances out their interests, optimizes the aims and parameters of social development and creates conditions and mechanisms of their attainment.

The above naturally exceeds the commonplace formula which limits the state's role in the economy to devising rules of the game and controlling their observance. With time, we are likely to evolve to this formula. But today's situation necessitates deeper state involvement in the social and economic processes. While setting the scale and planning mechanisms for the system of state regulation, we must be guided by the principle: The state must be where it is needed; freedom must be where it is required. . . .

Russia is in the midst of one of the most difficult periods in its history. For the first time in the past 200–300 years, it is facing a real threat of sliding to the second, and possibly even the third, echelon of world states. We are running OUT OF TIME for removing this threat. We must strain all intellectual, physical and moral forces of the nation. We need coordinated creative work. Nobody will do it for us. Everything depends on us, and on us alone—on our ability to see the size of the threat, to pool forces, and set our minds to hard and lengthy work.

THE FUTURE OF THE WEST

Few years have seen such fundamental political, social, and economic changes as occurred throughout eastern Europe in 1989. Poland, Hungary, Czechoslovakia, and East Germany all peacefully established new governments with democratic overtones after more than four decades of Marxist rule. The Soviet Union, continuing to pursue its own liberalization, gave most of its former satellites wide latitude in carrying out reforms in contrast to its earlier suppression of popular movements in Hungary (1956) and Czechoslovakia (1968). Only in Romania was the transition violent, as a swift but bloody revolution toppled the regime of hard-line Communist dictator Nicolai Ceausescu in December 1989. He and his wife were charged with genocide and executed.

Perhaps the most symbolic act of freedom occurred on November 9, 1989, when East Germany opened all its borders and allowed its citizens to travel and emigrate freely. The notorious Berlin Wall, constructed in 1961 at the height of the Cold War, was subsequently torn down, and thousands made their way to the West in search of new lives. This act would have serious consequences for the future of Germany.

Germany has occupied a central position in the history of the late nineteenth and twentieth centuries. After nearly forty-five years of division, the events of 1989 presented opportunities for reunification. But the new realities posed new problems for Europe: Would Germany once again threaten its neighbors militarily? Would the financial costs of reunification stall the process? Who would bear the economic burden? Would the new Germany be politically neutral or maintain its central position in the NATO alliance? In 1990, German Chancellor Helmut Kohl addressed several of these questions in his speech to the American Council on Germany in New York City.

A United Germany in a United Europe (June 5, 1990)

HELMUT KOHL

We Germans are not oblivious of the fact that here and in other countries we are being asked questions as we head for unity:

What kind of Germany will emerge?
What will German unity mean for peace and security in the heart of Europe?
Will this Germany revert to old patterns of behaviour, or has it learned the lessons of history?

I shall attempt to provide answers here for the future, bearing in mind that we Germans can

"A United Germany in a United Europe" is from Helmut Kohl, speech delivered to the American Council on Germany, New York City, New York, on June 5, 1990. Contained in *Vital Speeches of the Day,* July 1, 1990, pp. 546–548.

build on proven foundations as we move towards unity. Moreover, we Germans are determined, as we prove by our actions, to heed the lessons of our and of European history.

My first answer is this: A future united Germany will remain linked to the United States in close friendship and responsible partnership. . . . We shall remain together! This responsible partnership entails a future united Germany being a full member of the North Atlantic defense alliance.

We are thus drawing the first and most important conclusion from history: Peace, stability and security in Europe were ensured whenever Germany, the country in the heart of Europe, maintained firm ties, a fair balance of interests and mutually beneficial interchange with all its neighbours. On the other hand, when the Germans chose to go it alone or follow a separate nationalistic path, whether out of blind arrogance or criminal hubris, or when they were forced into isolation after a lost war, this resulted in discord, instability and insecurity for the whole of Europe.

A future Germany cannot and will not, therefore, drift back and forth between two camps. We do not seek neutrality or demilitarization, and we reject a non-aligned status. We Germans want to exercise our sovereign right, as enshrined in the Charter of the United Nations. . . . We want to be a member of . . . the North Atlantic defense alliance. Our immediate neighbours in the East—the Poles, Czechs and Hungarians support this position.

Our commitment to the Western Alliance—and this is my second answer—implies above all our commitment to the Western community of shared values. A future Germany will be a free and democratic state based on social justice and the rule of law, on respect for human dignity and human rights. Right- or left-wing extremism does not, as more than forty years of domestic stability prove, stand a chance in our country in the future either.

A future Germany will also remain a federal state. . . . There is no better a means of preventing tyranny and totalitarianism than a constitution which not only provides for checks and balances, but also envisages a federal system. We in the Federal Republic of Germany have such a constitution: Our Basic Law has in more than forty years proved to be the most liberal constitution in German history. . . .

My third answer is this: A united Germany will be an economically sound and socially stable country. The unanimous opinion of international economic organizations is that German unification will significantly boost world economic growth. The pent-up demand in the GDR [formerly East Germany] and in the reformist countries of Central, Eastern and South-Eastern Europe affords substantial market opportunities for everyone. . . .

The Federal Republic of Germany will strongly support this new economic and social start in the GDR. We are well prepared for this. For eight years our economy has been expanding. Business earnings, investments and employ-

ment are at a high level. We want to pave the way for private enterprise and the influx of private capital into the GDR. . . . I would like to repeat my invitation to American business: Become actively involved in the GDR to the mutual benefit. We Germans do not seek a monopoly; on the contrary, we seek competition and the common advantages of the international division of labour.

A future Germany—and this is my fourth answer—will from the very beginning be a member of the European Community. A united Germany will take part in 1992 when the large single market with 336 million people is completed. A united Germany will, together with France, be a driving force behind European unification. Before the end of this year two parallel intergovernmental conferences will be started to lay the

The Berlin Wall begins to fall on the night of November 9–10, 1989, near Bernauer Strasse. *(Wolfgang Kohler/Action Press)*

contractual foundation not only for economic and monetary union, but also for political union.

Finally, our commitment to federalism does not end at our borders. Federalism is our real goal for Europe as a whole. A united Germany will therefore also espouse the ambitious goal of laying the groundwork for a United States of Europe before the end of this century. We are thus drawing a further conclusion from our history: German unity has a future only if it is achieved in harmony with our neighbours, and not through confrontation with them. . . .

A future Germany, firmly anchored in the West, will—and this is my fifth answer—in the future, too, live up to its share of responsibility for ensuring peaceful and stable reforms in the neighbouring Eastern and South-Eastern countries. In following our path to national unity, we Germans do not call borders into question. On the contrary, we want to make them more permeable. We are willing to achieve lasting understanding and comprehensive, forward-looking cooperation. Our goal is international reconciliation. In particular we are willing to take account of the legitimate security interests of all our neighbours, not the least the Soviet Union.

We are convinced that this recognition will soon prevail in the whole of Europe: A future united Germany as a member of the Western defense alliance will increase the security of everyone concerned and thus become a cornerstone of a stable, peaceful order in Europe.

The Reconciliation of France and Germany
(September 24, 1990)
FRANÇOIS MITTERRAND

As Europe moved away from the wasteland of World War II and the intellectual confines of the Cold War, toward a new era of intranational economic cooperation, many variables exist that may radically alter its face. A tunnel under the English Channel was constructed (dubbed "the Chunnel"), that not only physically links Great Britain and France but "threatens" to meld the cultures as well. Britain has lost the island status that protected it and offered a unique identity for centuries, in exchange for a more intimate link with the economic destiny of continental Europe. So too will the great enemies of the first half of the twentieth century, France and Germany, lie down together and reconcile past offenses for future gains. With the reunification of Germany and the reintroduction of the Czech Republic, Slovakia, Hungary, and Poland into the heart of Europe, there are great financial opportunities and the very real potential for domestic strife. With the introduction of the Euro in January 2002, most of the European continent set a new course as trading partners with a common currency and mission to link fortunes in world economic competition. The following speeches by European leaders of the late twentieth century testify to the changing nature of Europe.

Think of the events that have shaken up Europe and the World in 1939, the popular movements that have emerged from the depths which, like the French revolution of two hundred years ago, have triumphed over structures and systems, set ways of thinking and acting, powers and fears, because of the simple, irresistible need to live differently, in accordance with the requirements of the mind. When the walls separating peoples came down, walls built on the foolish assumption that the order they were protecting would never be untouched by the great winds of space,

"The Reconciliation of France and Germany" is from François Mitterrand, speech delivered to the 45th Session of the United Nations General Assembly, New York, New York, on September 24, 1990. Contained in *Vital Speeches of the Day*, October 15, 1990, pp. 5, 7–8.

dreams and ideas, I remember saying to my compatriots in France ... that the end of one order did not necessarily mean that another order would be born immediately thereafter, and that it would be a very difficult process. And I would ask you this: what are we to do with this era we are entering, so promising, so perilous? What shall we make of it? ...

I think that an era of hope is opening up for mankind, if the peoples of the world accept to overcome what they take to be the fatality of history, and of their own interest. Believe me, such a goal is within our reach. After destroying each other in three wars in less than a century, France and Germany have sealed their reconciliation, a rare occurrence indeed: They belong to the same community, they meet together, they are forging a genuine friendship. While I speak, on the eve of German unity, instead of harping on the tragic events they experienced in the past because of each other, our two peoples are turned toward the same future. And so it is that here in New York, I can send the best wishes of France to the Germans, who are preparing to celebrate a great moment of their history. The deep understanding between France and Germany is a reality. As you know, it makes itself felt in the twelve-nation European Community. Can you imagine the trouble and strife, the conflicts of age-old ambitions that were overcome forty years ago by a bold, almost unbelievable undertaking engaged in first by six, nine, then ten, now twelve countries of Europe? ...

We Europeans are looking beyond the Community, to the horizon of the continent of Europe, the Europe of geography and history. ... Where would our old continent be now if audacity had not managed to overthrow well-established patterns of thought? And if peoples and their leaders had not accepted to build a future different from the past? In this Europe these are countries which yesterday were known as Eastern bloc countries and which belonged to a rival system. Now they control their own destiny, but with what means at their disposal? ... We must think of them, they are our brethren and we will be by their side, until as I said in France, a more fixed relationship will bring together all the countries of Europe, those of the East, those of the Community, those of the Free Trade Area, those who are part of no system, in what I have called a Confederation. ... Europe has been the first field of application thereof and a very real one. ...

At the beginning of this century and at the end of the previous one, our forebears expressed their dreams of peace with these three words: disarmament, arbitration, collective security. Theirs came to be an era of unrest, dictatorship and war. Let us act in such a way, I beseech you, that through the United Nations, law, solidarity and peace may finally rule over a new era.

Ethnic Strife in Eastern Europe
(April 15, 1994)

HELMUT TUERK

One of the most tragic consequences of the collapse of the Soviet Union was the political, social, and economic chaos that accompanied the liberation of eastern Europe. For nations whose political freedoms and ethnic identities were so long suppressed, the disintegration of Soviet control meant a search for order and equity. This posed new problems that have strained domestic relations at a crucial time when stability was most necessary. In the following selection, then Austrian ambassador to the United States, Helmut Tuerk, provided some perspective.

"Ethnic Strife in Eastern Europe" is from Helmut Tuerk, speech delivered at the Town Hall of California, Los Angeles, California, on April 15, 1994. Contained in *Vital Speeches of the Day,* June 15, 1994, pp. 517–518, 521.

When talking about ethnic strife in Central and Eastern Europe, it must, first of all, be recalled that the continent of Europe has traditionally been a mosaic of peoples with different cultures, languages, traditions, and religions. This diversity has, in the past and present, often been a source of conflict. The tragic events we are witnessing today in parts of the former Yugoslavia are a case in point for the continuing explosiveness of unresolved issues stemming from this diversity.

This very diversity, however, constitutes, at the same time, through a cross-fertilization process, a powerful source of richness of European culture and civilization. If preserved and allowed to flourish everywhere on our continent under conditions of respect for human rights, democracy and the rule of law, this diversity can be a tremendous asset instead of being a source of chaos.

It is obvious that the living together of different ethnic, linguistic and/or religious groups as a rule presupposes that one group forms a majority while one or more other groups constitute minorities. The existence of such minorities is an undeniable feature of almost every European country. With dozens of distinct ethnic groups in Europe alone, the ideas of a separate state for each one of these groups would be totally unrealistic if not altogether absurd. Very often ethnic groups forming a minority in one country are the dominant nationality in another country. On the other hand there are groups which only constitute minorities in a single country or in several countries. . . .

Totalitarian States—as until quite recently was the case in most of Central and all of Eastern Europe—often try to resolve the problem by either denying the very existence of such minorities or by theoretically granting them certain rights which in practice, however, remain largely on paper. When such systems of government collapse, the minorities' aspiration to safeguard and develop their identity may take on a violent form. The comparison has often been made to lifting a lid from a boiling pot. The collapse of communism in Central and Eastern Europe has thus been accompanied by a resurgence of nationalism among peoples and ethnic groups seeking to right the wrongs to which they had been subjected. . . .

Let me now refer to some regions of Europe, formerly under communist domination, where the coexistence of different ethnic groups has either already led to strife, even armed conflict, or is of serious concern for the future. Let me begin with . . . the case of the former Yugoslavia, where conflicting aspirations of various ethnic groups did not only lead to the disintegration of the confederation, but to continuing bloodshed and atrocities of a kind Europe has not experienced since World War II. . . .

The former Soviet Union poses even greater problems. Let me only point to the fact that on the territory of the former Soviet Union there are over 100 different ethnic groups, speaking 130 different languages. The largest groups include Russians, Ukrainians, Uzbeks, Byelorussians, and Azeris.

Tsarist politics aimed at strengthening the empire and at transforming its multi-ethnic character into that of a Russian national State. Under communist rule, the various nationalities at first enjoyed relative autonomy within the Federation and saw their culture and languages promoted. Stalin's policies, however, aimed at putting an end to the various cultural traditions and to forcibly achieve russification of the Soviet Union.

Gorbachev's *perestroika* finally brought about liberation of the various ethnic groups, however, the Soviet Union fell apart. This development was in no small measure the consequence of decades of oppression. The process of the assertion of rights by certain ethnic groups is still continuing and is threatening peace and stability in some areas of the former Soviet Union.

The problems the former Soviet Republics are facing also stem from the fact that many members of ethnic groups live outside the boundaries of the State where they form the majority, i.e., that State boundaries do not correspond to ethnic boundaries; e.g., out of 145 million Russians, 25 million live outside the Russian Federation; only one fourth of the 6.5

million Tartars live in Tartastan. In the Russian Federation itself, 19 percent of the population is non-Russian. . . .

Looking at today's Europe with its multitude of ethnic groups and the actual and potential conflicts stemming therefrom, the urgency of codifying the rights of these groups on an international level, coupled with an international control mechanism, becomes obvious. Important steps in this direction have already been taken with Austria being at the forefront of these endeavors. We firmly believe that the future of the European continent in no small measure depends on a satisfactory resolution of these issues, the alternative being unending confrontation, strife and even armed conflict.

Ethnic groups should serve as bridges between nations and as an element promoting greater understanding between peoples. This presupposes a democratic political framework based on the rule of law, with a functioning independent judiciary. Such a framework must guarantee full respect for human rights and fundamental freedoms, equal rights and status for all citizens, the free expression of all their legitimate interests and aspirations, political pluralism, social tolerance and the implementation of legal rules that place effective restraints on the abuse of governmental power.

Respect for and promotion of rights of ethnic groups cannot aim at establishing separate states for each and every ethnic group. What we should rather aim for, is to speed up the process of European integration and extend that process as far as possible to Central and Eastern Europe. The importance of the national State will diminish due to the existence of supranational institutions on the one hand and the increasing role of regions on the other hand. Thus, issues relating to ethnic groups should become less burning, as every individual, no matter to which group he or she belongs, will enjoy the advantage of living in a broader European framework. . . .

In view of the fundamental political changes in Central and Eastern Europe in favor of democracy, the rule of law and a system of market economy there is every reason to believe that the process of European integration can in due course be extended to the east of Vienna. This would be the best guarantee that ethnic strife can be resolved by peaceful means and a new European order will emerge out of ethnic chaos. Austria as a traditional bridge between East and West on the European continent will be happy to make its contribution and will be even more in a position to do so as member of the European Union.

"We Are Witnesses to a Process of Death in the Balkans" (January 12, 1994)

POPE JOHN PAUL II

The nation of Yugoslavia was created shortly after World War I by the provisions of the Treaty of Versailles in 1919. The Balkan region, which includes the areas of Romania, Bulgaria, and Yugoslavia, had been a "powder keg" of ethnic strife and violence for centuries as Serbs, Slovenes, Croats, Bosnians, and other Slavs who lived in the region sought freedom from foreign control and fought among themselves over disputed boundaries. The spark that set off World War I was lit by a Serb nationalist who resented Austrian presence in the area. After World War II, as eastern Europe succumbed to the onslaught of Soviet troops, Yugoslavia, although communist, resisted Soviet domination under the strong leadership of

"We Are Witnesses to a Process of Death in the Balkans" is from a general audience of Pope John Paul II on January 12, 1994, contained in *The Pope Speaks*, vol. 39 (1994), pp. 180–182.

Marshal Josip Broz Tito. Tito, who had been a military commander of Slavic partisans during World War II, argued that the different Slavic peoples who had been artificially thrust together in the nation of Yugoslavia could remain independent of Soviet control only if they exchanged their individual ethnic demands in return for the stability of his leadership. But when Tito died in 1980, Yugoslavian unity began to break apart. Upon the collapse of the Soviet Union in 1991, there was no longer the fear of a foreign threat to curb domestic bickering. Yugoslavia broke apart quickly in the face of Serbian aggression to capture and control territory where Bosnians and Croats had formed ethnic majorities. Thousands have died thus far, including Muslims who form minorities throughout the region. The Serbs justified their aggression on the basis of a need for more "living space," echoing Hitler's demands just before World War II. In addition, the Serbs embarked on a program of "ethnic cleansing," which had all the earmarks of another holocaust. Since the United Nations was ineffective in limiting the violence and working out acceptable boundaries, the United States, late in 1995, took the lead in negotiating the Dayton Peace Accords, which required the presence of NATO troops in Bosnia. In 1999, NATO forces were once again active in trying to protect Kosovar Albanians from hostile Serbian forces. In the following selection, Pope John Paul II offered perspective and a solution.

We are witnesses to a process of death precisely in the Balkans, and, unfortunately, powerless witnesses at that.... The overwhelming majority of the victims in the war in the Balkans are innocent people. Even among the soldiers themselves there are relatively few who bear full responsibility for the present warfare....

But is it really possible to say that the people and the circles responsible for the tragic events of the former Yugoslavia do not know what they are doing? In fact, they cannot possibly fail to know. Perhaps the truth is that they are trying to find some justification for their actions. Unfortunately our century has provided us with more than one example of this sort. Totalitarian systems, whether of a nationalistic or a collectivistic character, have been very widespread in the recent past, and all have been based on obedience to ideologies of "salvation" promising heaven on earth for individuals and for all society. In this context, it could be said that everything presently taking place in the Balkans, if viewed against the backdrop of recent European history, is nothing new. Tragically, we are already familiar with demands for "living space" (*lebensraum*), as well as the idea of a chosen nation, or of a privileged race or class.

At the end of the Second World War, at a time when consciences were reawakening, humanity realized how contrary all this was to the good of man and of nations. The first response to the atrocities of that terrible conflict was the Universal Declaration of Human Rights. And now, in the Balkans it seems that in a certain sense we have gone right back to the beginning. Human rights are being violated in a frightening and tragic way and those responsible go so far as to justify their actions by the principle of obedience to orders and to particular ideologies.... Those responsible for the terrible crimes of the Second World War were brought to judgment and in the West the trial was concluded in a relatively short time. In Eastern Europe, however, it was necessary for the most part to wait until 1989, and not everyone guilty of repeated and documented violations of human rights has yet received a just condemnation....

The Apostolic See, for its part, does not cease to recall the principle of humanitarian intervention. Not in the first place a military intervention, but rather every kind of action which aims at "disarming" the aggressor. This is a principle which has a specific application in the troubling events taking place in the Balkans. In the Church's moral teaching all military aggression is judged to be morally evil; legitimate defense on the other hand is considered admissible and even at times a duty. The history of our century has provided many confirmations of this teaching.

The most powerful humanitarian intervention is always prayer. Prayer represents an enormous spiritual power, especially when accompanied by sacrifice and suffering. How many sacrifices and how much suffering are faced by the people and nations of the war-torn region of the Balkans! Even if it is not apparent to a superficial glance and many people do not acknowledge it, prayer joined to sacrifice constitutes the most powerful force in human history.

"We Wage a War to Save Civilization Itself" (2001)

GEORGE W. BUSH

On the morning of September 11, 2001, the United States was stunned when two hijacked commercial jetliners slammed into the twin towers of the World Trade Center in New York City. As the towers burned, another airplane was flown into the Pentagon in Washington, D.C. and still another missed its potential target when the passengers forced a crash landing in the rural fields of Pennsylvania. Thousands of people were killed in the eventual collapse of the towers and in the rescue efforts that ensued. Never before, not even in the Japanese surprise attack on Pearl Harbor, had the United States suffered so aggressive a threat to its citizens and its values as a nation.

The perpetrators of the horror belonged to the al-Qaida terrorist network masterminded by Osama bin Laden, a Saudi exile who was also implicated in attacks against American embassies in Tanzania and Kenya, and in the 2000 bombing of the U.S.S. Cole in Yemen.

In subsequent action, President George W. Bush declared war against terrorism throughout the world with specific orders to hunt down bin Laden and dismantle his terrorist network. Congress passed an anti-terrorist law that tightened immigration controls, granted greater latitude to law enforcement officials, and confirmed executive authority to detain foreign nationals, try and even execute them, if judged guilty of terrorist acts in military tribunals. These controversial measures held precedents during the wartime administrations of Abraham Lincoln and Franklin Roosevelt, but engendered debate over the potential restriction of civil liberties among U.S. citizens.

Basking in the faint glow of Cold War victory and somewhat adrift in foreign affairs during the 1990s, the United States, its image as a bastion of security and freedom now tarnished, had entered a new era. No longer the invulnerable "superpower," the United States once again was given purpose and direction—an evil to confront. The war against terrorism provided a new forum for the confirmation of its values as a nation and for its leadership in the Western world as these excerpts from President Bush's speeches following the disaster indicate.

"'We Wage a War to Save Civilization Itself'" is from George W. Bush, speeches delivered to the people of the United States and to the General Assembly of the United Nations on September 11, November 8 and 10, 2001. Contained in *Vital Speeches of the Day*, October 1, 2001, p. 738 and December 1, 2001, pp. 98–99; 103–104.

**Address Delivered to the Nation
(September 11, 2001)**

Today, our fellow citizens, our way of life, our very freedom came under attack in a series of deliberate and deadly terrorist acts. The victims were in airplanes, or in their offices; secretaries, businessmen and women, military and federal workers; moms and dads, friends and neighbors. Thousands of lives were suddenly ended by evil, despicable acts of terror. The pictures of airplanes flying into buildings, fires burning, huge structures collapsing, have filled us with disbelief, terrible sadness and a quiet, unyielding anger. These acts of mass murder were intended to frighten our nation into chaos and retreat. But they have failed; our country is strong.

A great people has been moved to defend a great nation. Terrorist attacks can shake the foundations of our biggest buildings, but they cannot touch the foundation of America. These acts shattered steel, but they cannot dent the steel of American resolve. American was targeted for attack because we're the brightest beacon for freedom and opportunity in the world. And no one will keep that light from shining. . . .

Address to the Nation (November 8, 2001)

We are a different country than we were on September the 10th—sadder and less innocent; stronger and more united; and in the face of ongoing threats, determined and courageous. Our nation faces a threat to our freedoms, and the stakes could not be higher. We are the target of enemies who boast they want to kill—kill all Americans, kill all Jews, and kill all Christians. We've seen that type of hate before—and the only possible response is to confront it, and to defeat it.

This new enemy seeks to destroy our freedom and impose its views. We value life; the terrorists ruthlessly destroy it. We value education; the terrorists do not believe women should be educated or should have health care, or should leave their homes. We value the right to speak

our minds; for the terrorists, free expression can be grounds for execution. We respect people of all faiths and welcome the free practice of religion; our enemy wants to dictate how to think and how to worship even to their fellow Muslims.

The enemy tries to hide behind a peaceful faith. But those who celebrate the murder of innocent men, women, and children have no religion, have no conscience, and have no mercy. We wage war to save civilization, itself. We did not seek it, but we must fight it—and we will prevail.

This is a different war from any our nation has ever faced, a war on many fronts, against terrorists who operate in more than 60 different countries. And this is a war that must be fought not only overseas, but also here at home. . . .

**Address to the United Nations General Assembly
(November 10, 2001)**

We're asking for a comprehensive commitment to this fight. We must unite in opposing all terrorists, not just some of them. In this world there are good causes and bad causes, and we may disagree on where the line is drawn. Yet, there is no such thing as good terrorist. No national aspiration, no remembered wrong can ever justify the deliberate murder of the innocent. Any government that rejects this principle, trying to pick and choose its terrorist friends, will know the consequences.

We must speak the truth about terror. Let us never tolerate outrageous conspiracy theories concerning the attacks of September the 11th; malicious lies that attempt to shift the blame away from the terrorists, themselves, away from the guilty. To inflame ethnic hatred is to advance the cause of terror.

The war against terror must not serve as an excuse to persecute ethnic and religious minorities in any country. Innocent people must be allowed to live their own lives, by their own customs, under their own religion. And every nation must have avenues for the peaceful expression of opinion and dissent. When these avenues are closed, the temptation to speak through violence grows. . . .

As I've told the American people, freedom and fear are at war. We face enemies that hate not our policies, but our existence; the tolerance of openness and creative culture that defines us. But the outcome of this conflict is certain: There is a current in history and it runs toward freedom. Our enemies resent it and dismiss it, but the dreams of mankind are defined by liberty—the natural right to create and build and worship and live in dignity. When men and women are released from oppression and isolation, they find fulfillment and hope, and they leave poverty by the millions. These aspirations are lifting up the peoples of Europe, Asia, Africa, and the Americas, and they can lift up all of the Islamic world. We stand for the permanent hopes of humanity, and those hopes will not be denied. We're confident, too, that history has an author who fills time and eternity with His purpose. We know that evil is real, but good will prevail against it. This is the teaching of many faiths, and in that assurance we gain strength for a long journey. . . .

We did not ask for this mission, yet there is honor in history's call. We have a chance to write the story of our times, a story of courage defeating cruelty and light overcoming darkness. This calling is worthy of any life, and worthy of every nation. So let us go forward, confident, determined, and unafraid.

CHRONOLOGY: The Era of the Superpowers

August 6–9, 1945	The United States drops atomic bombs on Hiroshima and Nagasaki in an attempt to bring a speedy conclusion to World War II.
March 6, 1946	Churchill makes "Iron Curtain" speech at Fulton, Missouri: "From Stettin in the Baltic to Trieste in the Adriatic, an Iron Curtain has descended upon the Continent."
1947	Bell Laboratories scientists invent the transistor.
March 1947	In a message to Congress, President Truman outlines the Truman Doctrine, which effectively commits the United States to intervene against Communist or Communist-backed movements in Europe and elsewhere.
June 1947	George Marshall, U.S. Secretary of State, calls for a European recovery program (Marshall Plan) supported by U.S. aid.
1948–1949	Soviets impose a complete blockade of traffic into Berlin. Successful airlift of supplies into Berlin continues for nearly one year until blockade is lifted.
April 1949	Creation of NATO (North Atlantic Treaty Organization), a defensive alliance, which pledges mutual military assistance.
September 1951	First Soviet atomic bomb exploded.
1952	First hydrogen bomb exploded by United States at Eniwetok Atoll.
1953	U.S.S.R. explodes hydrogen bomb.
March 1953	Death of Stalin. Khrushchev confirmed as first secretary of the Communist party (September).

1954   Dr. Jonas Salk, developer of antipolio serum, starts inoculating schoolchildren.

1956   Oral vaccine developed by Albert Sabin against polio.

February 1956   Khrushchev attacks the abuses of the Stalin era at the Communist 20th Party Congress.

October–November 1956   General strike and street demonstrations in Budapest. Soviets intervene, depose Nagy, and crush the uprising.

1957   U.S.S.R. launches Sputnik I and Sputnik II, first earth satellites.

1958   NASA established to administer scientific exploration of space.

1961   Yuri Gagarin (U.S.S.R.) orbits the earth in a six-ton satellite.

August 1961   Berlin Wall constructed to prevent flight from East to West Berlin.

1962   John Glenn orbits earth.

October 1962   Cuban missile crisis after Soviet Union attempts to construct ballistic missile bases in Cuba. Imposition of naval "quarantine" by the United States forces the Soviet Union to back down in the face of the threat of nuclear war.

October 1964   Leonid Brezhnev replaces Khrushchev as general secretary of the Communist party.

1966   U.S. and U.S.S.R. spacecraft make separate landings on the moon.

1967   People's Republic of China explodes its first hydrogen bomb. Dr. Christiaan Barnard performs the world's first human heart transplant operation.

August 1968   The Soviet Union and other Warsaw Pact forces invade Czechoslovakia and end the "Prague Spring" liberation movement. Czech leaders are forced to agree to reimposition of censorship, centralized Communist control, military occupation, and abandonment of closer links with the West.

1969   Apollo 11 lands lunar module on moon's surface. Neil Armstrong first man to step on moon.

1977   U.S. space shuttle Enterprise makes its first manned flight. United States confirms testing of neutron bomb, which kills with massive radiation, leaving most buildings intact.

1978   First "test-tube baby" born in England.

December 1979   Soviet invasion of Afghanistan. United States imposes a grain embargo on Soviet Union.

January 1980   Andrei Sakharov sentenced to internal exile in Gorky.

July–September 1980   Widespread strikes among Polish workers led by Lech Walesa at Gdansk result in published demands for free trade unions. New Solidarity unions recognized and reforms on wages and working hours agreed upon.

1981   Scientists identify acquired immune deficiency syndrome (AIDS). IBM launches its "home" or personal computer (PC).

1983   The world's first artificially made chromosome created at Harvard University. Compact disk is introduced.

1985   Mikhail Gorbachev becomes General Secretary of the Communist party of the Soviet Union.

1988   Development of Gorbachev's concepts of *perestroika* and *glasnost.* New constitution adopted in Soviet Union, which permits openly contested elections. Soviet withdrawal from Afghanistan. European Economic Community agrees to work toward free trade zone by 1992.

1989   Revolutionary movements throughout eastern Europe result in fall of Communist regimes in Hungary, Czechoslovakia, Romania, Bulgaria, and East Germany. Berlin Wall opened in November and thousands of East Berliners cross into the West.

1990   Gorbachev calls for the end of the Communist party's monopoly on political power in the Soviet Union. Reunification of Germany.

June 1991   Boris Yeltsin elected president of Russian Republic in general election. Open competition with Gorbachev for future political direction of Soviet Union.

August 1991   Gorbachev survives an abortive coup attempt by conservative members of his advisory cabinet. Boris Yeltsin's prestige grows as a result of his defiant public stand during the uprising. Gorbachev resigns as general secretary of Communist party with his authority in question and the party in disarray. Future of the U.S.S.R. as a political entity is in doubt as several republics declare their intention to secede from the union.

December 1991   Ukraine's independence declaration makes Soviet dissolution certain. On December 25, 1991, the Soviet Union ceased to exist, Gorbachev left office, and the Commonwealth of Independent States came into being.

1992   Croatian and Serbian forces fight over division of Bosnia. Sarajevo bombarded by Serbs, who begin policy of "ethnic cleansing."

September 1993   Boris Yeltsin emerges as the strongest leader within the new Commonwealth. Popularity high in 1992, but opposition to economic and political policies forms in Russian Parliament. Yeltsin suspends Parliament in September.

October 1993	After pro-Parliament rioters rampaged through Moscow, Yeltsin orders tanks to attack the Parliament building, crushing the revolt. In December, Russians vote for a new Parliament and approve a new constitution limiting parliamentary authority and investing the president with strong emergency powers.
1994–1996	United Nations tries unsuccessfully to mediate the Bosnian conflict and imposes sanctions to little effect. NATO airstrikes on Serbian military positions temporarily force Serbs to withdraw from Sarajevo. Dayton Peace Accords separate warring factions and establish NATO military presence in Bosnia.
1998–2000	Tensions increase in the Balkans as Serbs eradicate ethnic-Albanian population of Kosovo in an attempt to stifle nationalist liberation movement. NATO airstrikes against Serb forces begin in response. Serb leader, Slobodan Milosevik, loses election and with hesitation surrenders power (2000).
September 11, 2001	World Trade Center in New York City destroyed by terrorists linked to Osama bin Laden. United States leads international efforts to combat worldwide terrorism.

STUDY QUESTIONS

1. What did Stalin mean in his speech of February 1946 by the phrase "Soviet victory"? What policy was Churchill advocating in his "Iron Curtain" speech? Was he pessimistic or optimistic about the possibility of war?

2. In his book *Why War?* (Paris, 1933), the great physicist Albert Einstein wrote, "Mankind can only gain protection against the danger of unimaginable destruction and wanton annihilation if a supranational organization has alone the authority to produce or possess [nuclear] weapons . . . and the legal right and duty to solve all the conflicts which in the past have led to war." What is your reaction to this opinion? To what extent are organizations like the United Nations and Amnesty International useful and effective? Would it make a difference if they did not exist?

3. Analyze the document entitled "How to Spot a Communist." Select what you consider the most effective and most ridiculous arguments from this source. How do vocabulary, logic, and religion easily give away the communist? Do you find any hypocrisy in this document?

4. According to Theodore White, why was communism successful and what were its weaknesses? What are the main points about capitalism and communism that Khrushchev stressed in his speech to the 22nd Communist Party Congress? After analysis of this document, do you agree or disagree with White's assessment of communism?

5. How did Mikhail Gorbachev define the concept of *perestroika*? In 1989, Gorbachev described the Communist party as "society's consolidating and vanguard force." Why did the Communist party fail? What was Gorbachev's explanation in his resignation speech? What had Russians gained from his leadership? Will Gorbachev be viewed by history as a great leader who, as John Le Carré said, "had the nerve to mount the rostrum and declare he had no clothes"?

6. According to Vladimir Putin in his address to the Russian people at the outset of 2000, what were some of Russia's most immediate problems and what did Putin propose as necessary solutions? In this speech, Putin was careful to decry the past mistakes of Communist economy and totalitarian rule. Yet, he was adamant about the need for a strong and directive government.

7. How did Chancellor Helmut Kohl view the impact of a "new" reunited Germany on Europe? What "lessons of history" has Germany learned? What did Kohl mean when noting that "federalism is our real goal for Europe as a whole"? Do you think Kohl was realistic in his assumptions?

8. In 1990, François Mitterrand of France offered a philosophical perspective on the unity and the progress of Europe. He appeared optimistic. What was the foundation of his optimism? What perspective had been gained over time that Mitterrand could say that "an era of hope is opening up for mankind"?

9. Helmut Tuerk saw the problems of dealing with ethnic minorities throughout eastern Europe as one of the most pressing issues facing Europe in the late twentieth century. Why? What solutions did he propose?

10. What are the main problems in the Balkan region that have resulted in war between the Serbs, Croats, and Bosnians? How does this continuing conflict threaten the stability of Europe and the Western alliance? Why did the United Nations had such difficulty resolving the issues? Why did NATO step in? What fundamental solution did the pope propose? Given the history of this situation, can this problem be resolved? What must happen?

10

"Cry Freedom!":
Independence Movements in India, Africa, and the Middle East

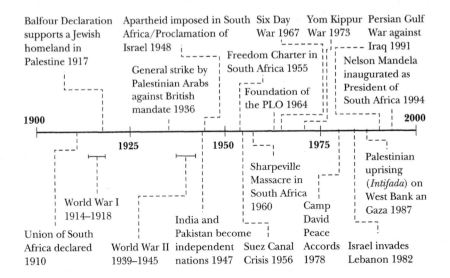

Balfour Declaration supports a Jewish homeland in Palestine 1917

Apartheid imposed in South Africa/Proclamation of Israel 1948

General strike by Palestinian Arabs against British mandate 1936

Freedom Charter in South Africa 1955

Foundation of the PLO 1964

Six Day War 1967

Yom Kippur War 1973

Persian Gulf War against Iraq 1991

Nelson Mandela inaugurated as President of South Africa 1994

1900

1925

1950

1975

2000

World War I 1914–1918

Union of South Africa declared 1910

World War II 1939–1945

India and Pakistan become independent nations 1947

Suez Canal Crisis 1956

Sharpeville Massacre in South Africa 1960

Camp David Peace Accords 1978

Palestinian uprising (*Intifada*) on West Bank an Gaza 1987

Israel invades Lebanon 1982

At the conclusion of World War II in 1945, amidst the rubble of Europe, thousands of people wandered the landscape, homeless, hungry, victims of the horrors of war. The Allied victory over the dark forces of fascism was celebrated with relief and pride, but also tinged with a sense of apprehension and foreboding. The great European powers of the nineteenth and early twentieth centuries had failed to live up to their claims of superiority, both racial and cultural, that had emboldened them to seize territory, dominate markets, erect new altars, and justify these acts as the progressive force of civilization.

The thin veneer of this superiority had collapsed, and Europeans, exhausted and disillusioned, retreated from control of the colonial holdings that had provided the foundation of their imperial vision since the seventeenth century. In Africa, southwest and central Asia, south and southeast Asia, and Latin America, the process of "decolonization" accelerated so that within two decades, the last significant colonial holdings had been dismantled and given independence. In the postwar superpower competition, Britain no longer "ruled the waves," and France could not afford to maintain its former empire in Africa and Indo-China. New emerging nations like India, Pakistan, most Arab states, and Latin American countries still depended on relationships with their former imperial masters, but did so with an increasing thirst for autonomy. In the late twentieth century, post-colonial tensions often remained linked to ill-defined interdependencies over trade restrictions, oil reserves, or the restructuring of interest debt.

And yet, at the outset of the twenty-first century, amidst global problems of overpopulation, environmental degradation, and public health, the positive political vision of civil society and participatory government that was confirmed in the Allied victory of 1945 has gained ground throughout the world. The fall of the Soviet Union in 1990, the economic developments in China after Mao Zedong's death in 1976, the collapse of dictatorships in central and eastern Europe, Latin America, and Indonesia, the overtures of goodwill in North Korea, and the new vision of racial equality in South Africa provide foundations of opportunity for international cooperation and progress in the future.

This chapter recounts some of the most extraordinary developments in the establishment of new postwar societies in India, South Africa, and the Middle East. In each of these areas, the year 1947/1948 proved to be a watershed, the culmination of years of tension and complex negotiations, the beginning of a new chapter in the struggle for human dignity and justice. While the superpowers hunkered down for a Cold War of ideas, the policy of apartheid in South Africa was confirmed and fully institutionalized; modern India and Pakistan were born from the womb of a Britain in retreat from the world stage; and the modern state of Israel was proclaimed under the aegis of the United Nations, the established vehicle for international cooperation and justice. But these events created new political paradigms that exacerbated deep-seated religious and cultural animosities. Hindu India and Muslim Pakistan today pose nuclear threats to each other and to the world. And the conflict between Israel's "right to exist" with secure borders and the Palestinian search for national identity and a homeland remains the most intransigent of political puzzles. This constancy of strife points out the difficulties in finding solutions to ancient enmities and in establishing stable, interdependent, and just societies. This is the story of both success and failure, unrealized opportunity and terrorist rage, progress and retrenchment. The experience of these nations reflects perhaps the greatest challenge of the twenty-first century: whether the variety of cultural and religious traditions will become a creative or divisive force in the world.

TWILIGHT OF THE RAJ: THE TRANSITION TO POLITICAL INDEPENDENCE IN INDIA

Human dignity is best preserved not by developing the capacity to deal destruction, but by refusing to retaliate. If it is possible to train millions in the black art of violence, which is the art of the beast, it is more possible to train them in the white art of nonviolence, which is the law of regenerate man.

—Mahatma Gandhi

India is prepared to take risks and face dangers. We do not want the so-called protection of the British Army and Navy. We will shift for ourselves.

—Jawaharlal Nehru (1944)

Long years ago we made a tryst with destiny, and now the time comes when we shall redeem our pledge, not wholly or in full measure, but very substantially. At the stroke of the midnight hour, while the world sleeps, India will awake.

—Jawaharlal Nehru (1947)

The Vision of Modern India

On April 13, 1919, in the northern Indian province of Punjab, a crowd of more than 10,000 people gathered together in an open space called the Jallianwala Bagh, which was enclosed by high walls in the city of Amritsar. Many had come from out of town to attend the annual horse fair and others were there for a political meeting. As the crowd filed into the square, few knew that the assembly was illegal. Amritsar had recently been the scene of violent demonstrations against the British, who had reneged on a promise that India would be self-governing at the end of World War I. Instead, in March 1919, the British Parliament had passed laws to suppress nationalist agitators. In fact, the violent demonstrations in Amritsar had occurred in response to the arrest of several leaders who had previously organized a peaceful protest.

Without warning, the British General, Reginald Dyer, positioned his troops at the entrance to the Jallianwala Bagh and ordered them to fire on the unarmed crowd. In just ten minutes, the soldiers expended 1,650 rounds of ammunition with deadly accuracy. According to official reports, 379 people were killed and 1,208 wounded. The bodies and blood that filled the Jallianwala Bagh that day confirmed the arrogance of imperial rule and augured the end of British political hegemony. The sun was setting on the British empire—the twilight was palpable.

"The Jewel in the Crown"

Britain had had a closer relationship with India than with any other part of its empire. India had been called the "Jewel in the Crown" ever since the formal establishment of the British Raj or government in 1858. British interests in India dated back even further to the early seventeenth century as the first merchants and settlers arrived, lured by the prospects of wealth and the geographical proximity of India to the riches of the East. But trust and good-will played as much a part in the administration of India as did military force. Many army officers and administrative officials had family links with India for generations and Indians themselves had traveled to Britain for university study. This interwoven relationship could perhaps best be demonstrated by the several hundred Indian princes who were allowed to rule their states under British patronage.

But if there were distinct ties, the British had also remained aloof from the Indian popula-tion, refusing to learn native languages or understand local culture. In fact, many of the British were handicapped by their own prejudices and confirmed in the superiority of their own culture. So while the British constructed roads, bridges, and hygienic facilities through-out the country, they also constructed country clubs and playing fields for cricket and polo, all designed to isolate themselves from Indians, who became second-class citizens in their own land. One particular cause of resentment was Britain's economic exploitation. Pure Indian cotton was purchased cheaply, sent back to Britain for the production of textiles, which were then sold at great profit to the Indian population. In such a manner, natural resources and money were methodically extracted from India, resulting in the maintenance of an underclass, poor and hungry, tied to their Hindu social castes, and vulnerable to the slightest changes in British economic policy.

The Indian Independence Movement

Many of the early leaders of the Indian independence movement were drawn from the small middle class of professionals—teachers, lawyers, journalists, and businessmen—who were often educated in Britain and filled the lower ranks of the Indian civil service. They spoke English, had access to Western political philosophy, and harbored visions of self-rule. In 1885, the British allowed the creation of the Indian National Congress, an assembly that had no effective power, but served as a forum for debate on Indian national issues. Year by year, the Congress grew more radical. By 1906, the Congress became a Hindu organization when its Muslim representatives formed the All-India Muslim League to promote their own political interests.

By 1919, the British were still not prepared to bestow self-government on their subject peo-ple and the Indian nationalists were demanding it as an inalienable right. The massacre at Amritsar simply swelled the ranks of nationalists and strengthened their resolve. And in the following year, a leader emerged who so possessed the will, charisma, and intuitive under-standing of the pain of India that he would extend the movement for independence to the masses.

Mohandas K. Gandhi was born in 1869 to a Hindu family in western India, where his father served as chief minister of a small Indian state. He was raised as a pacifist and left for London at age 18 to study law. When he returned to India in 1891, he was unsuccessful in his law practice and left to try South Africa, which was also under British administration. He remained there for twenty-two years as he developed the personal philosophy of ahimsa or non-violent action. For Gandhi, the prime objective of life was the pursuit of truth through self-discipline and nonviolence. His faith in the moral power of passive resistence never wavered and his protests resulted in the repeal of many repressive South African laws. In 1915, Gandhi returned to India with a new commitment to change in his homeland and a new title of respect—Mahatma, or "Great Soul," in recognition of his work and teaching.

The first selection is from an essay on swaraj, *or "self-rule, independence," that Gandhi wrote while in South Africa in 1908. He revised it for publication in 1921 in the form of a dialogue between the editor of a newspaper and his readers. In this way, Gandhi shaped the arguments about Indian independence and also introduced the idea of "soul-force" (satyagraha). The second excerpt provides the essence of Gandhi's philosophy of nonviolence.*

"How Can India Become Free?" (1921)

MOHANDAS GANDHI

Keep in Mind . . .

- How is *swaraj* or "self-rule" defined differently by the Reader and the Editor?

- What is the difference between "soul-force" and "body-force?"

What Is *Swaraj?*

Editor: It is quite possible that we do not attach the same meaning to the term. You and I and all Indians are impatient to obtain *swaraj*, but we are certainly not decided as to what it is. To drive the English out of India is a thought heard from many mouths, but it does not seem that many have properly considered why it should be so. I must ask you a question. Do you think that it is necessary to drive away the English, if we get all we want? . . .

Reader: That question cannot be answered at this stage. The state after withdrawal will depend largely upon the manner of it. If, as you assume, they retire, it seems to me we shall still keep their constitution and shall carry on the Government. If they simply retire for the asking, we should have an army, etc., ready at hand. We should, therefore, have no difficulty in carrying on the Government.

Editor: You may think so; I do not. But I will not discuss the matter just now. . . . Why do you want to drive away the English?

Reader: Because India has become impoverished by their Government. They take away our

Gandhi, Mohandas K., *Hindi Swaraj or Indian Home Rule.* Copyright © 1938 by The Navajivan Trust. Reprinted with permission.

money from year to year. The most important posts are reserved for themselves. We are kept in a state of slavery. They behave insolently towards us and disregard our feelings.

Editor: If they do not take our money away, become gentle, and give us responsible posts, would you still consider their presence to be harmful?

Reader: That question is useless. It is similar to the question whether there is any harm in associating with a tiger if he changes his nature. Such a question is sheer waste of time. When a tiger changes his nature, Englishmen will change theirs. This is not possible, and to believe it to be possible is contrary to human experience.

Editor: Supposing we get Self-Government similar to what the Canadians and the South Africans have, will it be good enough?

Reader: That question also is useless. We may get it when we have the same powers; we shall then hoist our own flag. As is Japan, so must India be. We must own our navy, our army, and we must have our own splendor, and then will India's voice ring through the world.

Editor: You have drawn the picture well. In effect it means this: that we want English rule without the Englishman. You want the tiger's nature, but not the tiger; that is to say, you would make India English. And when it becomes English, it will be called not Hindustan, but *Englistan*. This is not the *swaraj* that I want. . . .

How Can India Become Free?

Reader: What, then, holding the views you do, would you suggest for freeing India?

Editor: I do not expect my views to be accepted all of a sudden. My duty is to place them before readers like yourself. Time can be trusted to do the rest. We have already examined the conditions for freeing India, but we have done so in-directly; we will now do so directly. It is a world-known maxim that the removal of the cause of a disease results in the removal of the disease it-self. Similarly if the cause of India's slavery be removed, India can become free.

Reader: If Indian civilization is, as you say, the best of all, how do you account for India's slavery?

Editor: This civilization is unquestionably the best, but it is to be observed that all civiliza-tions have been on their trial. That civilization which is permanent outlives it. Because the sons of India were found wanting, its civiliza-tion has been placed in jeopardy. But its strength is to be seen in its ability to survive the shock. Moreover, the whole of India is not touched. Those alone who have been affected by Western civilization have become enslaved. We measure the universe by our own miserable foot-rule. When we are slaves, we think that the whole universe is enslaved. Because we are in an abject condition, we think that the whole of India is in that condition. As a matter of fact, it is not so, yet it is as well to impute our slavery to the whole of India. But if we bear in mind the above fact, we can see that if we become free, India is free. And in this thought you have a definition of *swaraj*. It is *swaraj* when we learn to rule ourselves. It is, therefore, in the palm of our hands. Do not consider this *swaraj* to be like a dream. There is no idea of sitting still. The *swaraj* that I wish to picture is such that, after we have once realized it, we shall en-deavor to the end of our life-time to persuade others to do likewise. But such *swaraj* has to be experienced, by each one for himself. One drowning man will never save another. Slaves ourselves, it would be a mere pretension to think of freeing others. Now you will have seen that it is not necessary for us to have as our goal the expulsion of the English. If the Eng-lish become Indianized, we can accommodate them. If they wish to remain in India along with their civilization, there is no room for them. It lies with us to bring about such a state of things.

Reader: It is impossible that Englishmen should ever become Indianized.

Editor: To say that is equivalent to saying that the English have no humanity in them. And it is really beside the point whether they become so or not. If we keep our own house in order, only those who are fit to live in it will remain. Others will leave of their own accord. Such things occur within the experience of all of us. . . .

Reader: I cannot follow this. There seems little doubt that we shall have to expel the English by force of arms. So long as they are in the country we cannot rest. One of our poets says that slaves cannot even dream of happiness. We are day by day becoming weakened owing to the presence of the English. Our greatness is gone; our peo-ple look like terrified men. The English are in the country like a blight which we must remove by every means.

Editor: In your excitement, you have forgotten all we have been considering. We brought the English, and we keep them. Why do you forget that our adoption of their civilization makes their presence in India at all possible? Your ha-tred against them ought to be transformed to their civilization. . . .

Passive Resistance

Reader: Is there any historical evidence as to the success of what you have called soul-force or truth-force? No instance seems to have happened of any nation having risen through soul-force. I still think that the evil-doers will not cease doing evil without physical punishment. . . .

Editor: Passive resistance is a method of secur-ing rights by personal suffering; it is the reverse of resistance by arms. When I refuse to do a thing that is repugnant to my conscience, I use soul-force. For instance, the Government of the day has passed a law which is applicable to me. I do not like it. If by using violence, I force the Government to repeal the law, I am employing what may be termed body-force. If I do not obey the law and accept the penalty for its breach, I use "soul-force." It involves sacrifice of self.

Everybody admits that sacrifice of self is infinitely superior to sacrifice of others. Moreover, if this kind of force is used in a cause that is unjust, only the person using it suffers. He does not make others suffer for his mistakes. Men have before now done many things which were subsequently found to have been wrong. No man can claim that he is absolutely in the right or that a particular thing is wrong because he thinks so, but it is wrong for him so long as that is his deliberate judgment. It is therefore true that he should not do that which he knows to be wrong, and suffer the consequence whatever it may be. This is the key to the use of "soul-force."

Consider This:

- According to Gandhi, how could India become free? Why was he less afraid of the English than of English culture?

- "If we keep our own house in order, only those who are fit to live in it will remain." What did Gandhi mean by this statement?

- According to Gandhi, what was the key to "soul-force" and why was it so powerful?

The Doctrine of the Sword
MOHANDAS GANDHI

Keep in Mind . . .

- Why is nonviolence infinitely superior to violence?

- Is violence always to be avoided?

I do believe that, where there is only a choice between cowardice and violence, I would advise violence. Thus when my eldest son asked me

"The Doctrine of the Sword" is from Ronald Duncan, ed., *Selected Writings of Mahatma Gandhi* (London: Faber & Faber, Ltd., 1951), pp. 53–54; 56; 58; 60; 66;. Copyright © 1951 by The Navajivan Trust. Reprinted by permission.

what he should have done, had he been present when I was almost fatally assaulted in 1908, whether he should have run away and seen me killed or whether he should have used his physical force which he could and wanted to use, and defended me, I told him that it was his duty to defend me even by using violence. Hence it was that I took part in the Boer War, the so-called Zulu Rebellion and the late war [World War I]. Hence also do I advocate training in arms for those who believe in the method of violence. I would rather have India resort to arms in order to defend her honor than that she should, in a cowardly manner, become or remain a helpless witness to her own dishonor.

But I believe that nonviolence is infinitely superior to violence, forgiveness is more manly than punishment. Forgiveness adorns a soldier. But abstinence is forgiveness only when there is the power to punish; it is meaningless when it pretends to proceed from a helpless creature. . . . But I do not believe India to be helpless. I do not believe myself to be a helpless creature. Only I want to use India's and my strength for a better purpose.

Let me not be misunderstood. Strength does not come from physical capacity. It comes from an indomitable will. . . . I am not a visionary. I claim to be a practical idealist. The religion of nonviolence is not meant merely for the *rishis* [holy men] and saints. It is meant for the common people as well. *Nonviolence* is the law of our species as violence is the law of the brute. The spirit lies dormant in the brute, and he knows no law but that of physical might. The dignity of man requires obedience to a higher law—to the strength of the spirit.

I have therefore ventured to place before India the ancient law of self-sacrifice. . . . The *rishis*, who discovered the law of nonviolence in the midst of violence, were greater geniuses than Newton. They were themselves greater warriors than Wellington. Having themselves known the use of arms, they realized their uselessness, and taught a wary world that its salvation lay not through violence but through nonviolence.

Nonviolence in its dynamic condition means conscious suffering. It does not mean meek submission to the will of the evil-doer, but it means the pitting of one's whole soul against the will of the tyrant. Working under this law of our being it is possible for a single individual to defy the whole might of an unjust empire to save his honor, his religion, his soul, and lay the foundation for that empire's fall or its regeneration. . . .

The next point, that of *ahimsa* [nonviolence], is more abstruse. My conception of *ahimsa* impels me always to dissociate myself from almost every one of the activities I am engaged in. My soul refuses to be satisfied so long as it is a helpless witness of a single wrong or a single misery. But it is not possible for me—a weak, frail, miserable being—to mend every wrong or to hold myself free of blame for all the wrong I see. The spirit in me pulls one way, the flesh in me pulls in the opposite direction. There is freedom from the action of these two forces, but that freedom is attainable only by slow and painful stages. I can attain freedom not by a mechanical refusal to act, but only by intelligent action in a detached manner. This struggle resolves itself into an incessant crucifixion of the flesh so that the spirit may become entirely free. . . .

I have not the capacity for preaching universal nonviolence to the country. I preach, therefore, nonviolence restricted strictly to the purpose of winning our freedom [India's freedom from British rule] and therefore perhaps for preaching the regulation of international relations by nonviolent means. But my incapacity must not be mistaken for that of the doctrine of nonviolence. I see it with my intellect in all its effulgence. My heart grasps it. But I have not yet the attainments of preaching universal nonviolence with effect. I am not advanced enough for the great task. I have yet anger within me, I have yet a duality in me. I can regulate my passions, I keep them under subjection, but before I can preach universal nonviolence with effect, I must be wholly free from passions. I must be wholly incapable of sin. Let the revolutionary pray with and for me that I may soon become that. But meanwhile, let him take with me the one step to it which I see as clearly as daylight, i.e. to win India's freedom with strictly nonviolent means. And then you and I shall have a disciplined, in-

telligent educated police force that would keep order within and fight raiders from without, if by that time I or someone else does not show a better way of dealing with either. . . .

Not to believe in the possibility of permanent peace is to disbelieve in godliness of human nature. Methods hitherto adopted have failed because rock-bottom sincerity on the part of those who have striven has been lacking. Not that they have realized this lack. Peace is unattainable by partial performance of conditions, even as chemical combination is impossible without complete fulfilment of conditions of attainment thereof. If recognized leaders of mankind who have control over engines of destruction were wholly to renounce their use with full knowledge of implications, permanent peace can be obtained. This is clearly impossible without the great powers of the earth renouncing their imperialistic designs. This again seems impossible without these great nations ceasing to believe in soul-destroying competition and to desire to multiply wants and therefore increase their material possessions. It is my conviction that the root of the evil is want of a living faith in a living God. It is a first-class human tragedy that peoples of the earth who claim to believe in the message of Jesus, whom they describe as the Prince of Peace, show little of that belief in actual practice. It is painful to see sincere Christians . . . limiting the scope of Jesus's message to select individuals. I have been taught from my childhood, and I have tested the truth by experience, that primary virtues of mankind are possible of cultivation by the meanest of the human species. It is this undoubted universal possibility that distinguishes the human from the rest of God's creation. If even one great nation were unconditionally to perform the supreme act of renunciation, many of us would see in our lifetime visible peace established on earth.

Consider This:

- What did Gandhi mean when he said, "I am a practical idealist"?

- How is nonviolence (*ahimsa*) related to "soul-force" (*satyagraha*)?

- If one must struggle to obtain a nonviolent attitude, does this mean that violence is a dominant characteristic of human nature? What is the key to the "root of evil"?

Gandhi and Nehru: "Two Utterly Different Standpoints"

JAWAHARLAL NEHRU

One of the most influential members of the Indian National Congress was the sophisticated and urbane Jawaharlal Nehru, a graduate of Cambridge University. He met Gandhi in 1916 and was impressed by his commitment to active civil disobedience. Nehru realized in 1919 "how brutal and immoral imperialism was and how it had eaten into the souls of the British upper classes." Although Nehru admired Gandhi's self-control and supported his emphasis on nonviolence, Nehru was no ascetic, but rather a practical politician with his own personal vision for India. In the following excerpt from his autobiography, Nehru discusses the differences between himself and Gandhi. Ultimately, their combined wisdom negotiated the path toward Indian independence.

Keep in Mind . . .

- How did Nehru differ from Gandhi in his personal vision of life and in the future of India?

I imagine that Gandhiji is not so vague about the objective as he sometimes appears to be. He is passionately desirous of going in a certain direction, but this is wholly at variance with modern ideas and conditions, and he has so far been unable to fit the two, or to chalk out all the intermediate steps leading to his goal. Hence the appearance of vagueness and avoidance of clarity. . . .

"India's salvation consists," he wrote in 1909, "in unlearning what she has learned during the last fifty years. The railways, telegraphs, hospitals, lawyers, doctors, and suchlike have all to go; and the so-called upper classes have to learn consciously, religiously, and deliberately the simple peasant life, knowing it to be a life giving true happiness." And again: "Every time I get into a railway car or use a motor bus, I know that I am doing violence to my sense of what is right"; "to attempt to reform the world by means of highly artificial and speedy locomotion is to attempt the impossible."

All this seems to me utterly wrong and harmful doctrine, and impossible of achievement. Behind it lies Gandhiji's love and praise of poverty and suffering and the ascetic life. For him, progress and civilization consist not in the multiplication of wants, of higher standards of living, "but in the deliberate and voluntary restriction of wants, which promotes real happiness and contentment, and increases the capacity for service."

Personally, I dislike the praise of poverty and suffering. I do not think they are at all desirable, and they ought to be abolished. Nor do I appreciate the ascetic life as a social ideal, though it may suit individuals. I understand and appreciate simplicity, equality, self-control; but not the mortification of the flesh. . . . To be in good moral condition requires at least as much training as to be in good physical condition. But that certainly does not mean asceticism or self-mortification.

Nor do I appreciate in the least the idealization of the "simple peasant life." I have almost a horror of it, and instead of submitting to it my-

"Gandhi and Nehru" is from Jawaharlal Nehru, *The Autobiography of Jawaharlal Nehru* (New York: John Day Company, 1942), pp. 185–186.

self, I want to drag out even the peasantry from it, not to urbanization, but to the spread of urban cultural facilities to rural areas. Far from this life's giving me true happiness, it would be almost as bad as imprisonment for me. . . .

Present-day civilization is full of evils, but also full of good; and it has the capacity in it to rid itself of those evils. To destroy it root and branch is to remove that capacity from it and revert to a dull, sunless, and miserable existence. But even if that were desirable, it is an impossible undertaking. We cannot stop the river of change or cut ourselves adrift from it, and psychologically we who have eaten of the apple of Eden cannot forget that taste and go back to primitiveness.

It is difficult to argue this, for the two standpoints are utterly different. Gandhiji is always thinking in terms of personal salvation and of sin, while most of us have society's welfare uppermost in our minds. I find it difficult to grasp the idea of sin, and perhaps it is because of this that I cannot appreciate Gandhiji's general outlook.

Consider This:

• How was Nehru's approach to the future very practical in contrast to Gandhi's idealism? Did the eventual independence of India depend on both approaches?

Progress and Independence

Both Gandhi and Nehru were at first prepared to cooperate with the British in negotiating Indian independence, but in light of the massacre at Amritsar in 1919, they decided to oppose the Raj. Their immediate objectives were to cement an alliance between the Congress

Jawaharlal Nehru and Mahatma Gandhi were charismatic leaders in the nationalist movements that saw the end of the British Raj and the creation of the independent states of India and Pakistan. *(Hulton-Getty).*

and the Muslims. Then they wanted to launch a new policy of passive resistence to British rule. The masses would be schooled in Gandhi's doctrine of "soul-force" and in nonviolent tactics. The Muslim leader, Muhammad Ali Jinnah, was suspicious of Gandhi's reliance on "inexperienced youths and the ignorant and illiterate," but eventually supported the stance.

The response to the policy of noncooperation was enthusiastic and widespread. People refused to pay taxes and participated in illegal political assemblies. There were many arrests, including Gandhi himself, who was sentenced to six years in prison for sedition. But by 1924, the Hindu–Muslim coalition was breaking down. Worse, there were many instances of violence and hundreds of deaths. Disappointed, Gandhi worked to strengthen the will and commitment of his followers to nonviolent protest by deliberately fasting, a strategy he later employed almost to the point of death.

In 1930, Gandhi began a new campaign of civil disobedience with a grand gesture. He would march two hundred miles to the sea in order to make salt. This act was in defiance of the British monopoly on the manufacture and sale of salt. As Gandhi marched through India, people lined the roads to greet him as he passed. When he arrived at the sea, Gandhi picked up some salt that had dried on the sand when the tide went out, held it above his head, and declared that he had manufactured salt. This was the signal for nationwide demonstrations to begin. Throughout the next sixteen years, the process of defiance continued with violence, fasting, concessions, jail time, overtures, nonviolent protest, and negotiation.

During World War II, the Congress continued to demand progress in the negotiations even as the Indian army fought with Britain against the Japanese in Burma. The war drained Britain of the will and the economic resources to hold on to India and negotiations began in earnest. In 1946, a compromise between Muslims and the Congress about the administration of regions in the new India seemed to have satisfied both parties, but fell apart. The Muslim leader, Jinnah, was looking to a new Muslim state apart from India. Amidst violent confrontations between Hindus and Muslims in the streets of Calcutta in which six thousand were killed, Jinnah remarked, "We shall have India divided, or we shall have India destroyed." In the face of civil war, Nehru conceded the creation of a homeland for Muslims to be called Pakistan. Only the 77-year-old Gandhi clung to the dream of a united India. On August 15, 1947, Britain handed over power to two countries, India and Pakistan. Nehru became the first president of an independent India and although disputes between India and Pakistan continued to dull the celebration, the British Raj had come to an end and a new era had begun.

On January 30, 1948, as Mahatma Gandhi made his way through a crowd toward his daily prayer meeting, he was shot in the chest at point-blank range. His assassin was a young Hindu, who believed that Gandhi's dedication to nonviolence and toleration of Muslims had undermined both Hinduism and India. Gandhi died as he wished, with the name of God on his lips, but without his vision of a united India. India was free, but the price paid was the separation of Pakistan. The irony of Gandhi's death, the violent murder of a man of peace, would not be lost on the world. The scene would be replayed in 1968 with the assassination of Martin Luther King Jr., a disciple of Gandhi's nonviolent vision.

The following sources examine the process of independence in India through the perspectives of British government ministers in 1930 and 1946, and through Nehru's contrasting analysis of British rule.

The British Contribution to Indian Progress (1930)

Keep in Mind . . .

- How did the British contribute to India's progress as a civilization?

- What is necessary for Indian success in achieving self-rule?

In writing this Report, we have made no allusion to the events of the last few months in India. In fact, the whole of our principal recommendations were arrived at and unanimously agreed upon before these events occurred. We have not altered a line of our Report on that account, for it is necessary to look beyond particular incidents and to take a longer view. . . .

No one of either race ought to be so foolish as to deny the greatness of the contribution which Britain has made to Indian progress. It is not racial prejudice, nor imperialistic ambition, nor commercial interest, which makes us say so plainly. It is a tremendous achievement to have brought to the Indian subcontinent and to have applied in practice the conceptions of impartial justice of the rule of law, of respect for equal civic rights without reference to class or creed, and of a disinterested and incorruptible civil service. These are essential elements in any state which is advancing towards well-ordered self-government. In his heart, even the bitterest critic of British administration in India knows that India has owed these things mainly to Britain. But, when all this is said, it still leaves out of account the condition essential to the peaceful advance of India, and Indian statesmanship has now a great part to play. Success can only be achieved by sustained goodwill and cooperation, both between the great religious communities of India which have so constantly been in conflict, and be-

tween India and Britain. For the future of India depends on the collaboration of East and West, and each has much to learn from the other.

We have grown to understand something of the ideals which are inspiring the Indian national movement, and no man who has taken part in working the representative institutions of Britain can fail to sympathise with the desire of others to secure for their own land a similar development. But a constitution is something more than a generalisation: it has to present a constructive scheme. We submit our Report in the hope that it may furnish materials and suggest a plan by means of which Indian constitutional reconstruction may be peacefully and surely promoted.

British Rule in India (1946)
JAWAHARLAL NEHRU

Keep in Mind . . .

- How did India contribute to the imperial success of the British Empire?

- How was India forced to pay for its own enslavement by the British?

Then there was the Indian Army, consisting of British and Indian troops, but officered entirely by Englishmen. This was reorganized repeatedly, especially after the Mutiny of 1857, and ultimately became organizationally linked up with the British Army. This was so arranged as to balance its different elements and keep the British troops in key positions. . . . The primary function of these forces was to serve as an army of occupation—"internal Security Troops" they were called, and a majority of these were British. The Frontier Province served as a training ground for the British Army at India's expense. The

"The British Contribution to Indian Progress" is from *Report of Indian Statutory Commission* (The Simon Commission), 1930, Cmd. 3568–3569, pp. 315-316.

"British Rule in India" is from Jawaharlal Nehru, *The Discovery of India* (New York: John Day Company, 1946), pp. 304–306.

field army (chiefly Indian) was meant for service abroad and it took part in numerous British imperial wars and expeditions, India always bearing the cost. Steps were taken to segregate Indian troops from the rest of the population.

Thus India had to bear the cost of her own conquest, and then of her transfer (or sale) from the East India Company to the British crown and for the extension of the British empire to Burma and elsewhere, and expeditions to Africa, Persia, etc., and for her defense against Indians themselves. She was not only used as a base for imperial purposes, without any reimbursement for this, but she had further to pay for the training of part of the British Army in England—"capitation" charges these were called. Indeed, India was charged for all manner of other expenses incurred by Britain, such as the maintenance of British diplomatic and consular establishments in China and Persia, the entire cost of the telegraph line from England to India, part of the expenses of the British Mediterranean fleet, and even the receptions given to the sultan of Turkey in London.

The buildings of railways in India, undoubtedly desirable and necessary, was done in an enormously wasteful way. The government of India guaranteed five percent interest on all capital invested, and there was no need to check or estimate what was necessary. All purchases were made in England.

The civil establishment of government was also run on a lavish and extravagant scale, all the highly paid positions being reserved for Europeans. The process of Indianization of the administrative machine was very slow and only became noticeable in the twentieth century. This process, far from transferring any power to Indian hands, proved yet another method of strengthening British rule. The really key positions remained in British hands, and Indians in the administration could only function as the agents of British rule.

To all these methods must be added the deliberate policy, pursued throughout the period of British rule, of creating divisions among Indians, of encouraging one group at the cost of the other. This policy was openly admitted in the early days of their rule, and indeed it was a natural one for an imperial power. With the growth of the nationalist movement, that policy took subtler and more dangerous forms, and though denied, functioned more intensively than ever.

Nearly all our major problems today have grown up during British rule and as a direct result of British policy: the princes; the minority problem; various vested interests, foreign and Indian; the lack of industry and the neglect of agriculture; the extreme backwardness in the social services; and, above all, the tragic poverty of the people. This attitude to education has been significant in Kaye's *Life of Metcalfe*, it is stated that . . . "it was our policy . . . to keep the natives of India in the profoundest state of barbarism and darkness, and every attempt to diffuse the light of knowledge among the people, either of our own or of the independent states, was vehemently opposed and resented."

Imperialism must function in this way or else it ceases to be imperialism. The modern type of finance imperialism added new kinds of economic exploitation which were unknown in earlier ages. The record of British rule in India during the nineteenth century must necessarily depress and anger an Indian, and yet it illustrates the superiority of the British in may fields, not least in their capacity to profit by our disunity and weaknesses. A people who are weak and who are left behind in the march of time invite trouble and ultimately have only themselves to blame. If British imperialism with all its consequences was, in the circumstances, to be expected in the natural order of events, so also was the growth of opposition to it inevitable, and the final crisis between the two.

Consider This:

- What specific modern problems did Nehru attribute to British policy in India? Why were the British able to rule India for so many years?

The British Exit India (1946)

Keep in Mind . . .

• What was the British mission in India just before independence in 1947?

On the 15th March last, just before the dispatch of the Cabinet Mission to India, Mr. Attlee, the British Prime Minister, used these words:

"My colleagues are going to India with the intention of using their utmost endeavours to help her to attain her freedom as speedily and fully as possible. What form of Government is to replace the present regime is for India to decide; but our desire is to help her to set up forthwith the machinery for making that decision. . . .

"I hope that the Indian people may elect to remain within the British Commonwealth. I am certain that she will find great advantages in doing so. . . . But if she does so elect, it must be by her own free will. The British Commonwealth and Empire is not bound together by chains of external compulsion. It is a free association of free peoples. If, on the other hand, she elects for independence, in our view she has a right to do so. It will be for us to help to make the transition as smooth and easy as possible. . . .

"Whatever that choice may be, we look forward with you to your ever-increasing prosperity among the greatest nations of the world and to a future even more glorious than your past."

Consider This:

• This official statement maintained in 1946 that "the British Commonwealth and Empire is not bound together by chains of external compulsion. It is an association of free peoples." If that was true, why was there such a struggle for independence in India?

• How did this statement demonstrate progress by the British in the assessment of their imperial relationship with India? Compare this with the British assessment of their role in 1930.

"The British Exit India" is from *India (Cabinet Mission): Statement by the Cabinet Mission and His Excellency the Viceroy,* Cmd. 6821 (London: H.M.S.O., 1946), pp. 2–3; 9.

SOUTH AFRICA AND THE END OF APARTHEID

To overthrow oppression is the highest aspiration of every free man.

—*Nelson Mandela*

Of course, apartheid cannot be reformed. It must be dismantled. You don't reform a Frankenstein—you destroy it!

—*Archbishop Desmond Tutu*

It is a struggle of the African people, inspired by their own suffering and their own experience. It is a struggle for the right to live. . . . I have cherished the ideal of a democratic and free society to live for and to achieve. But if needs be, it is an ideal for which I am prepared to die.

—*Nelson Mandela (1963)*

The Policy of Apartheid

On February 11, 1990, the political landscape of South Africa was radically altered when Nelson Mandela, the 72-year-old leader of the African National Congress, was released from prison. For twenty-seven years, he had been isolated, often starved, beaten, and tortured, kept from public view. In this way, the government hoped to silence its most severe critic of the system of apartheid, the legal and enforced separation between the races in South Africa. This was a fatal miscalculation. Mandela became the most visible symbol, especially in prison, of the injustice of apartheid. The release of Mandela marked a boldness on the part of the South African government to replace the indignities of the past with the vision of a fully integrated society where political control would be invested in the vote of the majority, represented most dramatically by a native population of Black and mixed blood.

The system of apartheid began in 1948 and within one generation had woven itself into all aspects of life in South Africa. But apartheid was merely the formal extension of a system of segregation that had evolved over many decades through attitudes, institutions, and laws dating from the late nineteenth and early twentieth centuries. In fact, the origins of apartheid might be traced as far back as 1652, when the Dutch East India Company established a fort at Table Bay. The initial clashes between the native population and Dutch merchants and farmers known as Boers began a difficult history of colonial conquest as the White settlers expanded beyond the Cape to the interior of South Africa. The Dutch established control of conquered Africans through a pass-carrying system that restricted them to certain areas at certain times and forced them to live in particular regions.

In the eighteenth century, the British entered the Cape region, viewing it as an important link to their developing empire in India. By 1806, after supporting a local native rebellion against the Boers, the British were able to establish permanent control over the Cape. The Boers then began "The Great Trek" to the north and west from 1835 to 1840 in order to escape the political and economic constraints of the British. The Boer Trekkers established two republics in the interior called the Transvaal and the Orange Free State. The Boers had especially disagreed with the British opposition to slavery and insistence that freed slaves be placed on an equal social footing with Christians. This was an ideological divide that the Trekkers regarded as contrary to the laws of God and the natural distinction of race and color.

During the second half of the nineteenth century, the European "scramble for empire" in Africa, impelled by the dictates of Social Darwinism, missionary zeal, economic expansion, and political competition, forced each European state to address the issues of race. With the discovery of diamonds in South Africa in 1867, the rivalry between the British and Boers for control became even more intense. Fighting broke out in 1881, and again from 1899 to 1901 in what was called the Boer War. This resulted in British victory, but only after severe devastation and loss of life. The Africans had played a major role in the Boer defeat by relaying messages and acting as look-outs and guides for the British. But the Africans were repaid poorly for this loyalty. After 1905, the British began to reorganize African land and labor in order to reap the benefits of the diamond and gold mines and to effect a more permanent reconciliation with the Boers. The Union of South Africa was formally declared in 1910. In order to preserve White unity between the British and Dutch populations in the new political construction, the Africans paid the price in terms of political rights, land tenancy, and social restriction.

In 1913, the Native Lands Act restricted rural Africans to certain areas known as "reserves" apart from the White farming communities. In 1923, the Native Urban Areas Act carried segregation a step further by allowing Blacks in South African cities only "for so long as their presence is demanded by the wants of the white population." Shantytowns grew up outside cities as slum life became the norm for native families. The "Black Peril" echoed a major theme of the White government in the 1930s and 1940s as the road to formal apartheid was paved methodically and linked to White nationalism. The best way to preserve the stability of the South African state was to preserve the integrity of the White race.

But African churches and Black nationalist leaders in the 1920s—such as Wellington Butelezi and John Dube—emphasized the principle "Africa for the Africans" and organized their own political opposition in the African National Congress (ANC) and the Zulu Inkatha Party.

Finally, in 1948, the White National Party, which had been formed in 1934 through the support of Afrikaner (Dutch) paramilitary groups under the leadership of D. F. Malan, narrowly defeated the more moderate United Party. The new government quickly set about separating all South Africans by race. People were officially classified into four distinct groups: White, Colored (mixed race), Asiatic (Indian), and Native (African). Mixed marriages were prohibited and the 1950 Immorality Act prohibited all sexual contact between races. The Bantu Education Act of 1953 removed missionary funding for native schools in an effort to limit the access of Africans to Western thought. The National Party from 1948 to 1994 imposed the system of apartheid with a methodical ruthlessness that created terrible bitterness and strife for over forty years.

The first selection reveals the general principles of apartheid as laid down by the National Party in 1948. It is followed by the Freedom Charter of 1955, written by a committee of Blacks in protest, that would become the foundation of ANC policy and inspiration during the struggle for African civil liberties.

Protection of the White Race (1948)

Keep in Mind . . .

- What were the two policy directions affecting the non-European community that were open for consideration by the South African government? Which direction did the government choose?

There are two sections of thought in South Africa in regard to the policy affecting the non-European community. On the one hand, there is the policy of equality, which advocates equal rights within the same political structure for all civilized and educated persons, irrespective of race or color, and the gradual granting of the franchise to non-Europeans as they become qualified to make use of democratic rights.

"Protection of the White Race" is from United Nations, General Assembly, *Official Records: Eighth Session*, Supplement No. 16 (A/205 and A/2505/Add.1), "Report of the United Nations Commission on the Racial Situation in the Union of South Africa," Annex V (New York, 1952), pp. 139–140.

On the other hand, there is the policy of separation (*apartheid*) which has grown from the experience of the established European population of the country, and which is based on the Christian principles of justice and reasonableness.

We can act in only one of two directions. Either we must follow the course of equality, which must eventually mean national suicide for the White race, or we must take the course of separation (*apartheid*) through which the character and the future of every race will be protected and safeguarded with full opportunities for development and self-maintenance in their own ideas, without the interests of one clashing with the interests of the other, and without one regarding the development of the other as undermining or a threat to himself.

The party therefore undertakes to protect the White race properly and effectively against any policy, doctrine or attack which might undermine or threaten its continued existence. At the same time the party rejects any policy of oppression and exploitation of the non-Europeans by the Europeans as being in conflict with the

Christian basis of our national life and irreconcilable with our policy.

The party believes that a definite policy of separation (*apartheid*) between the White races and the non-White racial groups, and the application of the policy of separation also in the case of the non-White racial groups, is the only basis on which the character and future of each race can be protected and safeguarded and on which each race can be guided so as to develop its own national character, aptitude, and calling.

All marriages between Europeans and non-Europeans will be prohibited.

In their areas, the non-European racial groups will have full opportunities for development in every sphere and will be able to develop their own institutions and social services whereby the forces of the progressive non-Europeans can be harnessed for their own national development (*volkeepbou*). The policy of the country must be so planned that it will eventually promote the ideal of complete separation (*algehele apartheid*) in a national way. . . .

The State will exercise complete supervision over the moulding of the youth. The party will not tolerate interference from without or destructive propaganda from the outside world in regard to the racial problems of South Africa.

The party wishes all non-Europeans to be strongly encouraged to make the Christian religion the basis of their lives and will assist churches in this task in every possible way. Churches and societies which undermine the policy of *apartheid* and propagate doctrines foreign to the nation will be checked.

The Coloured community takes a middle position between the European and the Natives. A policy of separation between the Europeans and Coloureds and between Natives and Coloureds will be applied in the social, residential, industrial, and political spheres. The Coloureds will be protected against unfair competition from the Natives in so far as where they are already established. . . .

The present unhealthy system, which allows Coloureds in the Cape to be registered on the same voters' roll as Europeans and to vote for the same candidate as Europeans, will be abolished and the Coloureds will be represented in the House of Assembly by three European representatives. . . .

Attention will be given to the provision of social, medical and welfare services in which the efforts of the Coloured themselves can be harnessed, and in which they will be taught as far as possible to be self-supporting.

Consider This:

- Why did the White South African government choose the policy of apartheid over the alternative of equal rights for all races? How could apartheid be "based on the Christian principles of justice and reasonableness"?

- Note that the White National Party rejected "any policy of oppression and exploitation of the non-Europeans by the Europeans." Compare this policy with the U.S. Supreme Court decision *Plessy v. Ferguson* in 1896, which also advocated "separate but equal" status between races in the United States. Is separate ever equal?

The Freedom Charter (1955)

Keep in Mind . . .

- What are the specific civil rights and liberties demanded in this document?

- What do these demands tell you about the lives of non-Whites in South Africa?

We, the people of South Africa, declare for all our country and the world to know:

That South Africa belongs to all who live in it, black and white, and that no government can justly claim authority unless it is based on the will of the people; That our people have been robbed of their birthright to land, liberty, and peace by a form of government founded on injustice and

"The Freedom Charter" is from Public Affairs Office, South African Embassy, Washington D.C.

inequality; That our country will never be prosperous or free until all our people live in brotherhood, enjoying equal rights and opportunities; That only a democratic state, based on the will of the people, can secure to all their birthright without distinction of colour, race, sex, or belief;

And therefore, we, the people of South Africa, black and white, together—equals, countrymen, and brothers—adopt this Freedom Charter. And we pledge ourselves to strive together, sparing nothing of our strength and courage, until the democratic changes here set out have been won.

THE PEOPLE SHALL GOVERN!

Every man and woman shall have the right to vote for and stand as a candidate for all bodies which make laws. All the people shall be entitled to take part in the administration of the country. The rights of the people shall be the same regardless of race, colour, or sex. All bodies of minority rule, advisory boards, councils, and authorities shall be replaced by democratic organs of self-government.

ALL NATIONAL GROUPS SHALL HAVE EQUAL RIGHTS!

There shall be equal status in the bodies of state, in the courts, and in the schools for all national groups and races; All national groups shall be protected by law against insults to their race and national pride; All people shall have equal rights to use their own language and to develop their own folk culture and customs; The preaching and practice of national, race, or colour discrimination and contempt shall be a punishable crime; All apartheid laws and practices shall be set aside. . . .

THE LAND SHALL BE SHARED AMONG THOSE WHO WORK IT!

Restriction of land ownership on a racial basis shall be ended, and all the land redivided amongst those who work it, to banish famine and land hunger; Freedom of movement shall be guaranteed to all who work on the land; All shall have the right to occupy land wherever they choose; People shall not be robbed of their cattle, and forced labour and farm prisons shall be abolished.

ALL SHALL BE EQUAL BEFORE THE LAW!

No one shall be condemned by the order of any government official; The courts shall be representative of all the people; Imprisonment shall be only for serious crimes against the people and shall aim at reeducation, not vengeance; The police force and army shall be open to all on an equal basis and shall be the helpers and protectors of the people; All laws which discriminate on grounds of race, colour, or belief shall be repealed.

ALL SHALL ENJOY EQUAL HUMAN RIGHTS!

The law shall guarantee to all their right to speak, to organise, to meet together, to publish, to preach, to worship, and to educate their children; The primacy of the house from police raids shall be protected by law; All shall be free to travel without restriction from countryside to town, from province to province, and from South Africa abroad; Pass laws, permits, and all other laws restricting these freedoms shall be abolished. . . .

THE DOORS OF LEARNING AND OF CULTURE SHALL BE OPENED!

The government shall discover, develop, and encourage national talent for the enhancement of our cultural life; All the cultural treasures of mankind shall be open to all, by free exchange of books, ideas, and contact with other lands; The aim of education shall be to teach the youth to love their people and their culture, to honour human brotherhood, liberty, and peace; Education shall be free, compulsory, universal, and equal for all children; Higher education and technical training shall be opened to all by means of state allowances and scholarships awarded on the basis of merit; Adult illiteracy shall be ended by a mass state education plan;

Teachers shall have all the rights of other citizens; The colour bar in cultural life, in sport, and in education shall be abolished.

THERE SHALL BE HOUSES, SECURITY AND COMFORT!

All people shall have the right to live where they choose, to be decently housed, and to bring up their families in comfort and security; . . . Free medical care and hospitalisation shall be provided for all, with special care for mothers and young children; Slums shall be demolished, and new suburbs built where all have transport, roads, lighting, playing fields . . . and social centres; . . . Fenced locations and ghettos shall be abolished, and laws which break up families shall be repealed.

THERE SHALL BE PEACE AND FRIENDSHIP!

South Africa shall be a fully independent state, which respects the rights and sovereignty of all nations; South Africa shall strive to maintain world peace and the settlement of all international disputes by negotiation—not war; Peace and friendship among all our people shall be secured by upholding the equal rights, opportunities, and status for all; The right of all the peoples of Africa to independence and self-government shall be recognised and shall be the basis of close cooperation.

Let all who love their people and their country now say, as we say here: "THESE FREEDOMS WE WILL FIGHT FOR, SIDE BY SIDE, THROUGHOUT OUR LIVES, UNTIL WE HAVE WON OUR LIBERTY."

Compare and Contrast:

• Compare this Freedom Charter with the French Declaration of the Rights of Man (1789) on pages 64–66. To what extent was this Charter affected by European Enlightenment thought?

• Compare this Charter with the declaration of White rule in South Africa entitled "Protection of the White Race." What was the National Party's argument against the progressive principle of equality?

"The Struggle Is My Life" (1961)

NELSON MANDELA

The 1950s was a difficult decade for the African National Congress. The South African government was consolidating the system of apartheid with new laws and trigger reflexes, an aggressive policy against civil protest, a disposition for violence and quick imprisonment. In March 1960, as demonstrators marched toward a police station to protest pass laws, the police panicked at the size of the crowds and opened fire: sixty-nine were killed and 180 wounded. The "Sharpeville Massacre," as it was called, focused international criticism on the Nationalist government. Uncomfortable under the spotlight, South Africa withdrew from the British Commonwealth and declared itself a republic; this began a twenty-year retreat from the international community as South Africa staggered into a self-imposed isolation. Within the country, the Nationalist government began a forced relocation of Africans into their "homelands" where dispossessed Blacks could be removed from the sight of White citizens, restricted, and better controlled.

It was in this environment that the protests of Oliver Tambo (1917–1993), Walter Sisulu (1912–), and Nelson Mandela (1918–) exacerbated the situation and focused the senti-

---

"The Struggle Is My Life" is from *Freedom, Justice and Dignity for All South Africa: Statements and Articles by Mr. Nelson Mandela* (New York: Centre Against Apartheid, United Nations Department of Political and security Council Affairs, 1978), pp. 6–8.

ment of many Africans. All three men had been active in organizing the ANC during the 1950s. In response to the Sharpeville Massacre, the ANC went underground and decided that peaceful protest and nonviolent action had not been effective against the violent tactics of the government. The time had arrived, in their minds, for active confrontation.

In many ways, Nelson Mandela's life encapsulates the setbacks and successes of Black nationalist politics in South Africa. The son of a minor tribal chief, Mandela was raised by his Christian mother before being taken into the household of a Thembu chief for education. Expelled from school for organizing resistence, Mandela trained as a lawyer in 1941 and became part of Oliver Tambo's legal practice. Encouraged by older and experienced protesters like his friend, Walter Sisulu, Mandela became an important and articulate advocate for the pain and alienation of native sentiment. In 1961, Mandela moved through the country in disguise, a renegade from South African law.

The first selection is from one of Mandela's underground letters dictated on June 26, 1961, where he made clear his decision to oppose the government. On August 5, 1962, Mandela was arrested in Natal and brought to trial in Pretoria from October 15 to November 7. Mandela was accused on two counts of inciting people to strike illegally and of leaving the country without a valid passport. The second excerpt from the trial transcript reveals much about Mandela's character and purpose. He conducted his own defense.

Keep in Mind . . .

- Why did Mandela want to launch a campaign of noncollaboration and militant action against the Nationalist government?

NONCOLLABORATION IS OUR WEAPON

A full-scale and country-wide campaign of non-cooperation with the Government will be launched immediately. The precise form of the contemplated actions, its scope and dimensions and duration, will be announced to you at the appropriate time.

At the present moment, it is sufficient to say that we plan to make government impossible. Those who are voteless cannot be expected to continue paying taxes to a Government which is not responsible to them. People who live in poverty and starvation cannot be expected to pay exorbitant house rents to the government and industry. We produce the work of the gold mines, the diamonds, and the coal, of the farms and industry, in return for miserable wages.

Why should we continue enriching those who steal the products of our sweat and blood?

Those who side with the Government when we stage peaceful demonstrations to assert our claims and aspirations? . . . Which African does not burn with indignation when thousands of our people are sent to jail every month under cruel pass laws? Why should we continue carrying badges of slavery?

Noncollaboration is a dynamic weapon. We must refuse. We must use this weapon to send this Government to the grave. It must be used vigorously and without delay. The entire resources of the black people must be mobilized to withdraw all cooperation with the Nationalist Government.

Various forms of industrial and economic action will be employed to undermine the already tottering economy of the country. We will call upon the international bodies to expel South Africa and upon nations of the world to sever economic and diplomatic relations with the country.

THE STRUGGLE IS MY LIFE

I am informed that a warrant for my arrest has been issued, and that the police are looking for me. The National Action Council has given full and serious consideration to this question, and has sought advice of many trusted friends and bodies, and they have advised me not to surrender myself. I have accepted this advice and will not give myself up to a Government I do not recognize. Any serious politician will realize that, under the present-day conditions in this country to seek for cheap martyrdom by handing myself to the police is naive and criminal. We have an important program before us and it is important to carry it out very seriously and without delay.

I have chosen this latter course which is more difficult and which entails more risk and hardship than sitting in jail. I have had to separate myself from my dear wife and children, from my mother and sisters, to live as an outlaw in my own land. I have had to close my business, to abandon my profession, and to live in poverty and misery, as many of my people are doing. I will continue to act as the spokesman of the National Action Council during the phase that is unfolding and in the tough struggles that lie ahead.

I shall fight the Government side by side with you, inch by inch, and mile by mile, until victory is won.

What are you going to do? Will you come along with us, or are you going to cooperate with the Government in its efforts to suppress the claims and aspirations of your own people? Or are you going to remain silent and neutral in a matter of life and death to my people, to our people?

For my part, I have made the choice, I will not leave South Africa, nor will I surrender. Only through hardship, sacrifice and militant action can freedom be won. The struggle is my life.

I will continue fighting for freedom until the end of my days.

Consider This:

- In this underground letter from Mandela, is his call for noncollaboration a plea for nonviolent protest? How do you interpret the phrase, "Only through hardship, sacrifice, and militant action can freedom be won"?

- Compare Mandela's methods of resistance with those of Mohandas Gandhi in the selection entitled the "Doctrine of the Sword." Did these men share the same spirit of protest?

Black Man in a White Court (1962)

Keep in Mind . . .

- Why did Mandela want the Court to recuse itself from his case?

Mandela: Your Worship, before I plead to the charge, there are one or two points I would like to raise. . . . I want to apply for Your Worship's recusal from this case. I challenge the right of this Court to hear my case on two grounds:

Firstly, I challenge it because I fear that I will not be given a fair and proper trial. Secondly, I consider myself neither legally nor morally bound to obey laws made by a Parliament in which I have no representation.

In a political trial such as this one, which involves a clash of the aspirations of the African people and those of whites, the country's courts, as presently constituted, cannot be impartial and fair. . . .

The Universal Declaration of Human Rights provides that all men are equal before the law, and are entitled without any discrimination to equal protection of the law. . . . It is true that an African who is charged in a court of law enjoys, on the surface the same rights and privileges as an accused who is white in so far as the conduct of this trial is concerned. He is governed by the same rules of procedure and evidence as apply to a white accused. But it would be grossly inaccurate to conclude from this fact that an African consequently enjoys equality before the law.

In its proper meaning equality before the law means the right to participate in the making of the laws by which one is governed, a constitution which guarantees democratic rights to all sections of the population, the right to approach the court for protection or relief in the case of the violation of rights guaranteed in the constitution, and the right to take part in the administration of justice as judges, magistrates, attorneys-general, law advisers and similar positions.

In the absence of these safeguards the phrase "equality before the law," in so far as it is intended to apply to us, is meaningless and misleading. All the rights and privileges to which I have referred are monopolized by whites, and we enjoy none of them.

The white man makes all the laws, he drags us before his courts and accuses us, and he sits in judgment over us.

It is fit and proper to raise the question sharply, what is this rigid colour-bar in the administration of justice? Why is it that in this courtroom, I face a white magistrate, am confronted by a white prosecutor, and escorted into the dock by a white orderly? Can anyone honestly and seriously suggest that in this type of atmosphere, the scales of justice are evenly balanced?

Why is it that no African in the history of this country has ever had the honour of being tried by his own kith and kin, by his own flesh and blood?

I will tell Your Worship why: the real purpose of this rigid colour-bar is to ensure that the justice dispensed by the courts should conform to the policy of the country, however much that policy might be in conflict with the norms of justice accepted in judiciaries throughout the civilized world.

I feel oppressed by the atmosphere of white domination that lurks all around in this courtroom. Somehow this atmosphere calls to mind the inhuman injustices caused to my people outside this courtroom by this same white domination.

It reminds me that I am voteless because there is a Parliament in this country that is white-controlled. I am without land because the white minority has taken a lion's share of my country and forced me to occupy poverty-stricken Reserves, over-populated and over-stocked. We are ravaged by starvation and disease. . . .

Magistrate: What has that got to do with the case, Mr. Mandela?

Mandela: Your Worship, this to me is an extremely important ground which the Court must consider.

Magistrate: I fully realise your position, Mr. Mandela, but you must confine yourself to the application and not go beyond it. I don't want to know about starvation. That in my view has got nothing to do with the case or the present moment.

Mandela: Well, Your Worship has already raised the point that here in the country there is only a white Court. What is the point of all this? Now if I can demonstrate to Your Worship that outside this Courtroom race discrimination has been used in such a way as to deprive me of my rights, not to treat me fairly, certainly this is a relevant fact from which to infer that wherever race discrimination is practised, this will be the same result, and this is the only reason why I am using this point.

Magistrate: I am afraid that I will have to interrupt you, and you will have to confine yourself to the reasons, the real reasons for asking me to recuse myself. . . .

Consider This:

- What was Mandela's primary argument before the Court? Why didn't an African "enjoy equality before the law"?

- In the decree entitled "Protection of the White Race," the National Party characterized apartheid as a policy "based on Christian principles of justice and reasonableness." How did Mandela's argument in Court disprove this point?

- Would you agree that in the eyes of the White government and Court, the concept of equal rights was not a principle of "justice and reasonableness"?

Themes: Revolution/Historical Transition

The Historical Intersection

ALABAMA: 1963

Letter from Birmingham Jail

MARTIN LUTHER KING, JR.

In April 1963, Martin Luther King, Jr. and other U.S. civil rights leaders began a campaign to desegregate Birmingham, Alabama, generally regarded as the nation's most segregated city. A supporter of Mohandas Gandhi's ideals, King believed that the moral force of nonviolence was overwhelming and that each person had "a moral responsibility to disobey unjust laws." Tired of the unfulfilled promises of gradual change, King proposed direct, nonviolent action in the form of demonstrations and marches. A few days into the Birmingham campaign, he and hundreds of other demonstrators were arrested. From a Birmingham jail, King began writing his most famous essay on the margins of a newspaper and published it in his 1963 book, Why We Can't Wait. *The American Civil Rights movement flowed from King's vision and was waged in the pulpits, at lunch counters, on the buses, and in the streets of cities throughout the United States.*

Keep in Mind . . .

- According to King, what constituted direct nonviolent action? Why was this approach criticized by many civil rights leaders who advocated negotiation with political authority?

- What constitutes an unjust law?

We know through painful experience that freedom is never voluntarily given by the oppressor; it must be demanded by the oppressed. Frankly, I have yet to engage in a direct-action campaign that was "well timed" in the view of those who have not suffered unduly from the disease of segregation. For years now I have

(contd)

heard the word "Wait!" It rings in the ear of every Negro with piercing familiarity. This "Wait" has almost always meant "Never." We must come to see, with one of our distinguished jurists, that "justice too long delayed is justice denied."

We have waited for more than 340 years for our constitutional and God-given rights. The nations of Asia and Africa are moving with jet-like speed toward gaining political independence, but we still creep at horse-and-buggy pace toward gaining a cup of coffee at a lunch counter. Perhaps it is easy for those who have never felt the stinging darts of segregation to say, "Wait." But when you have seen vicious mobs lynch your mothers and fathers at will and drown your sisters and brothers at whim; when you have seen hate-filled policemen curse, kick, and even kill your black brothers and sisters; when you see the vast majority of your twenty million Negro brothers smothering in an airtight cage of poverty in the midst of an affluent society; . . . when you take a cross-country drive and find it necessary to sleep night after night in the uncomfortable corners of your automobile because no motel will accept you; when you are humiliated day in and day out by nagging signs reading "white" and "colored"; when your first name becomes "nigger," you middle name becomes "boy" (however old you are) and your last name becomes "John," and your wife and mother are never given the respected title "Mrs."; when you are harried by day and haunted by night by the fact that you are a Negro, living constantly at tiptoe stance, never quite knowing what to expect next, and are plagued with inner fears and outer resentments; when you are forever fighting a degenerating sense of "nobodiness"—then you will understand why we find it difficult to wait. There comes a time when the cup of endurance runs over, and men are no longer willing to be plunged into the abyss of despair. I hope, sirs, you can understand our legitimate and unavoidable impatience.

You express a great deal of anxiety over our willingness to break laws. This is certainly a legitimate concern. . . . One may well ask: "How can you advocate breaking some laws and obeying others?" The answer lies in the fact that there are two types of laws: just and unjust. I would be the first to advocate obeying just laws. One has not only a legal, but a moral responsibility to obey just laws. Conversely, one has a moral responsibility to disobey unjust laws. I would agree with St. Augustine that "an unjust law is no law at all."

Now, what is the difference between the two? How does one determine whether a law is just or unjust? A just law is a man-made code that squares with the moral law or the law of God. An unjust law is a code that is out of harmony with the moral law. To put it in the terms of St. Thomas Aquinas: An unjust law is a human law that is not rooted in eternal law and natural law. Any law that uplifts human personality is just. Any law that degrades human personality is unjust. All segregation statutes are unjust because segregation distorts the soul and damages the personality. It gives the segregator a false sense of superiority and the segregated a false sense of inferiority. . . .

(contd)

One who breaks an unjust law must do so openly, lovingly, and with a willingness to accept the penalty. I submit that an individual who breaks a law that conscience tells him is unjust, and who willingly accepts the penalty of imprisonment in order to arouse the conscience of the community over its injustice, is in reality expressing the highest respect for law.

Consider This:

- How do Martin Luther King's ideals compare to Mohandas Gandhi's conception of nonviolent will and moral strength in "The Doctrine of the Sword"?

- Compare King's thoughts to Nelson Mandela's arguments concerning justice in "The Struggle Is My Life" and "Black Man in a White Court." Were they both in favor of direct nonviolent action?

- How did King and Mandela each seek to arouse the "conscience of the community" over injustice? Does this approach constitute, as King argued, the "highest respect for law"?

- In the writings of Gandhi, Mandela, and King, there is a common focus: "Why we can no longer wait." Why was time of the essence in achieving independence from the constraints of authority?

The End of Apartheid

Although Nelson Mandela had been sentenced to five years in prison at the end of his trial in November 1962, African resistence continued from Mandela's underground guerilla army called "Spear of the Nation." Organized acts of sabotage plagued the White Nationalist government and led to Mandela's celebrated Rivonia trial in 1963. During the trial, Mandela stated that a democratic free society was an ideal "for which I am prepared to die." He was convicted of sabotage along with seven others and sentenced to life imprisonment.

Many were willing to pick up the mantle of resistance into the 1970s and 1980s, including Steve Biko, who died in prison while under torture in 1977. Amidst the growing pressure of international scrutiny and boycott, which was fostered by churches and prominent South African writers such as Alan Paton (Cry the Beloved Country), *the South African government made attempts to improve sanitary conditions and unemployment in the native "reserves." Black leaders were not impressed.*

One of the most outspoken critics of apartheid in South Africa was Archbishop Desmond Tutu (1931–). In the first excerpt from 1983, he discussed the South African policy of "pop-

ulation removal." At that time, the Black majority was barred from living in the affluent cities and was forced into "homelands" or townships where they provided an inexpensive labor force to be exploited by the White minority. Tutu's commitment to the inevitability of political and racial accommodation earned him the Nobel Peace Prize in 1984 and sustained the movement in the face of the abuses of Anglo-Boer rule.

On August 14, 1989, South African President P. W. Botha resigned and was succeeded by Frederik de Klerk (1936–). De Klerk's commitment to liberalization and an integrated nation is revealed in his speech to the South African Parliament. Note its visionary, yet cautious tone. De Klerk had to walk a political tightrope in order to keep the process of racial accommodation truly viable. One of the most important acts in this process was the release of Nelson Mandela after twenty-seven years in prison. Mandela's speech to his followers was given just nine days after de Klerk's address. On May 10, 1994, Nelson Mandela was inaugurated as President of South Africa. The last selection is from the 1996 Bill of Rights for the new democracy. The move away from apartheid and toward full integration has not been easy, and South Africa has had to confront its past and begin to heal its wounds through the work of the Truth and Reconciliation Commission headed by Archbishop Tutu. At the turn of the century, South Africa still has much to do in working toward the shared vision of unity that will transcend years of racial indoctrination and thirst for revenge and transform the violent past into a peaceful future.

"Blacks Will Be Free Whatever You Do or Don't Do" (1983)

ARCHBISHOP DESMOND TUTU

Keep in Mind . . .

- What was the purpose of "resettlement camps"?

- What did Tutu see as the short-term and long-term solutions to save the people of South Africa?

1948 and After

When the [South African] Nationalists came to power in 1948, they resurrected their ideal of the Boer republics of the late nineteenth century and early twentieth century. They developed discriminatory legislation that was to

hand, and initiated their own amazing creativity—the Race Classification, the Job Reservation, Mixed Marriages, Immorality and other racist laws. . . . Basically, the South African crisis is one that hinges on political power, for it is this, if you have it, which commands access to other kinds of power—economic well-being, social amenities and facilities. That is why it is such a charade to talk about improving the quality of life of Blacks in their own areas, in talking about the so-called changes which have been wrought in the matter of sport, the creation of international hotels and restaurants, in the removal of discriminatory signs. It is a charade because no matter how wonderful the improvements in the Black person's lot may be (and I don't doubt that there will be very significant improvements), these will always be mere concessions that are always at risk, and vulnerable because they depend on the whim of those who have political power. When they deem it convenient for themselves, they will withhold these privileges and when they think otherwise, they will dole them out lavishly, or not, from their bounty.

Basically it is a question of how you can maintain political power in the hands of a White Oligarchy. Perhaps there is a preliminary stage—how do you, as a White minority outnumbered five to one, survive in a continent that has on the whole shown itself hostile to White presence? And the answer which the imperialistic Europeans decided upon with almost uncanny unanimity was to subjugate the native peoples and to retain most power in White hands. And so Africa in particular, but much of the so-called Third World in general, found itself ruled by these White foreigners. In time most of this colonial empire came to throw off the yoke of oppression. Southern Africa has been tardy in joining the liberation movement, but the waves of freedom have now washed away most White minority rule even in this sub-continent, the latest to fall being that in Zimbabwe, where we had famous last words from Mr. Ian Smith [former Prime Minister of Rhodesia (Zimbabwe)], such as that it would not happen during his lifetime or only over his dead body and not in a thousand years.

During our period, it has been quite clear that the Whites were determined to keep political power in their hands exclusively. It did not strike them as at all odd (at least, the majority of them) that the way they were going about things was totally at variance with the accepted meaning of that democracy whose virtues they extolled so much, as they vilified Communism and Marxism.

On accession to power, the Nationalist Party made no bones about their determination to maintain White domination with policies that were nakedly racist. They had stepped into the corridors of political power on the waves of White apprehension of the so-called Black period ... and they did not conceal this from anybody. . . .

And the Total Strategy is a developing one. Some very specially blessed Blacks (urban Blacks) will also be part of this "gravy train." Their quality of life will be significantly enhanced, their children are likely to go to good White schools, they will get very good salaries, etc., etc., and they will be coopted into the sys-

tem as a Black middle class to be a buffer between the *have*-Whites and the *have-not*-Blacks, and being so greatly privileged they will be supporters of the status quo such as you cannot ever hope to find anywhere. That is the new strategy of the nationalist government. The bitter pill is very significantly coated with sugar. Those who will belong to this core economy and society will be numerically insignificant, and will pose hardly any threat to the power-wielding White group. But what of the rest—the hapless *hoi polloi*? They will be, and are being, relegated to the outer darkness, the limbo of the forgotten. They must get out. . . . Nobody repudiated Mr. Mulder when he pointed out in Parliament that the logical conclusion of apartheid was that there would be no Black South Africans.

And to get to that conclusion, they have with very little compunction moved nearly two million Blacks. They have moved them often from places where they had reasonably adequate housing, where they were able to work—some in the informal sector, as casual labourers, within walking or reasonable distance of their places of work. They have moved them, dumped them as if they were potatoes, in largely inhospitable areas, often with no alternative accommodation. . . .

People are starving in most of these resettlement camps. I know for I have seen it. They are starving because of deliberate Government policy made in the name of White Christian civilization. They are starving; a little girl can tell you that when they can't borrow food, they drink water to fill their stomachs. This is the solution the Nationalists have decided upon. Many can't work, not because they won't work, but because there is no work available. So they sit listlessly while we reap the benefits of a soaring gold price and ore boom, which makes us want to import skilled labour from overseas. They are there as a reservoir, deliberately created, of cheap labour. When Black labour is needed, the laws forced Blacks into town when they were often well-to-do farmers. They had to become wage earners in order to pay the taxes levied on them. Now they are not really wanted, so they are endorsed out. There are probably two million Blacks unemployed and another million likely to lose their jobs, but they are out of sight and so are out of mind. . . .

The Cost

The cost in terms of human suffering is incalculable. Undernourishment, starvation and malnutrition have serious consequences in growing children. They may suffer irreversible brain damage. . . . But how do we compute the cost in the legacy of bitterness, anger, frustration, and indeed hatred which we are leaving behind for our children? In the body of this paper, I have described many things that have happened to us Blacks in this country during the several decades of our oppression and exploitation and deprivation. It is, I believe, a miracle of God's grace that Blacks still talk to Whites, to any Whites. It is a miracle of God's grace that Blacks still say that we want a nonracial South Africa for all of us, Black and White together. It is a miracle of God's grace that Blacks can still say they are committed to a ministry of justice and reconciliation and that they want to avert the bloodbath which seems more and more inevitable as we see little bending and give on the crucial issue of power-sharing. We are told that the Afrikaners [White, South African minority of Dutch extraction] have found it very difficult to forgive, certainly difficult to forget what the British did to them in the concentration camps. I want to say that Blacks are going to find it difficult, very difficult, to forgive, certainly difficult to forget what Whites have done and are doing to us in this mater of population removals.

All Blacks live in a constant state of uncertainty. Even I, a bishop in the Church of God and General Secretary of the South African Council of Churches, have no security. The township manager could in his wisdom decide that my continued presence in Soweto [impoverished black suburb of Johannesburg] was detrimental to its good ordering and peace, and by the stroke of his pen would withdraw my permission to reside there, just like that. We each have such a sword of Damocles hanging over our heads. I don't suppose many Whites know this or, if they do, care too much about it. . . .

What the Church Can Do

The solutions are both long-term and short-term. The short-term strategy is to oppose all removals. We suggest that representations are made to the authorities to persuade them to desist forthwith. If we know about any removals likely to happen, then let us do all we can to oppose them. If all our efforts to dissuade the authorities fail, then we should be there, physically present as the witnessing and caring Church. We must use all nonviolent methods to hinder the act of demolition.

We should support those in resettlement camps, providing them with as much relief that they will need as possible—food, blankets, etc. And the Church should help to rehabilitate these shocked persons by being a serving Church, helping to develop a community spirit and helping the people help themselves. . . .

In the long term, the solution must be political. There are not two ways about it. Either there is going to be power-sharing or there is not. If not, then we must give up hope of a peaceful settlement in South Africa. If the Government is determined to go ahead with its Balkanization of South African on ethnic lines, and depriving Blacks of their South African citizenship, then we have had it, the ghastly alternative will be upon us. Population removals must stop immediately if we are to be able to work for a new kind of South Africa, and the Church should be in the forefront to prepare all of us for this new South Africa.

There is still a chance, but if we let it slip then it will be gone forever. Neither the most sophisticated arsenal nor the best army or police force will give White South Africa true security, for that will come and come automatically when all of us, Black and White, know we count as of equal worth in the land of our birth, which we love with a passionate love. Please God, we pray you, let them hear us, let them hear us before it is too late.

White South Africa, please know that you are deluding yourselves, or you are allowing yourselves to be deluded, if you think that the present ordering of our society can continue. Blacks will be free whatever you do or don't do. That is not in question. Don't let the *when* and the *how* be in doubt. Don't delay our freedom, which is your freedom as well, for freedom is indivisible. Let it be now, and let it be reasonably peaceful. . . .

Consider This:

- According to Archbishop Tutu in 1983, what was the "strategy" of the White Nationalist government toward Blacks in South Africa?

- How did Tutu use religion as a basis of appeal?

"Walk Through the Open Door" (1990)

F. W. DE KLERK

Keep in Mind . . .

- What are some of de Klerk's specific solutions for the future?

Mr. Speaker, Members of Parliament. The general election on September the 6th, placed our country irrevocably on the road of drastic change. Underlying this is the growing realisation by an increasing number of South Africans

"Walk Through the Open Door" is from F. W. de Klerk, speech delivered to the Second Session of the Ninth Parliament of the Republic of South Africa, Capetown, February 2, 1990. Contained in *Vital Speeches of the Day* (March 1, 1990), pp. 290–295.

that only a negotiated understanding among the representative leaders of the entire population is able to ensure lasting peace.

The alternative is growing violence, tension and conflict. That is unacceptable and in nobody's interest. The well-being of all in this country is linked inextricably to the ability of the leaders to come to terms with one another on a new dispensation. No one can escape this simple truth.

On its part, the Government will accord the process of negotiation the highest priority. The aim is a totally new and just constitutional dispensation in which every inhabitant will enjoy equal rights, treatment and opportunity in every sphere of endeavour—constitutional, social and economic. . . .

The government accepts the principle of the recognition and protection of the fundamental individual rights which form the constitutional basis of most Western democracies. We acknowledge, too, that the most practical way of protecting those rights is vested in a declaration of rights justifiable by an independent judiciary. However, it is clear that a system for the protection of the rights of individuals, minorities and national entities has to form a well-rounded and balanced whole. South Africa has its own national composition and our constitutional dispensation has to take this into account. The formal recognition of individual rights does not mean that the problems of a heterogeneous population will simply disappear. Any new constitution which disregards this reality will be inappropriate and even harmful.

Naturally, the protection of collective, minority and national rights may not bring about an imbalance in respect of individual rights. It is neither the Government's policy nor its intention that any group—in whichever way it may be defined—shall be favoured above or in relation to any of the others. . . .

Practically every leader agrees that negotiation is the key to reconciliation, peace, and a new and just dispensation. However, numerous excuses for refusing to take part, are advanced.

Some of the reasons being advanced are valid. Others are merely part of a political chess game. And while the game of chess proceeds, valuable time is being lost. . . .

I wish to urge every political and community leader, in and outside Parliament, to approach the new opportunities which are being created, constructively. There is no time left for advancing all manner of new conditions that will delay the negotiating process.

The steps that have been decided are the following:

—The prohibition of the African National Congress, the Pan Africanist Congress, the South African Communist Party and a number of subsidiary organisations is being rescinded.

—People serving prison sentences merely because they were members of one of these organisations or because they committed another offence which was merely an offence because a prohibition on one of the organisations was in force, will be identified and released. Prisoners who have been sentenced for other offenses such as murder, terrorism, or arson are not affected by this.

—The media emergency regulations as well as the education emergency regulations are being abolished in their entirety. . . .

These decisions by the Cabinet are in accordance with the Government's declared intention to normalise the political process in South Africa without jeopardising the maintenance of the good order. They were preceded by thorough and unanimous advice by a group of officials which included members of the security community. Implementation will be immediate. . . .

Therefore, I repeat my invitation with greater conviction than ever: Walk through the open door, take your place at the negotiating table together with the Government and other leaders who have important power bases inside and outside Parliament.

Henceforth everybody's political points of view will be tested against their realism, their workability, and their fairness. The time of negotiation has arrived.

"Apartheid Has No Future" (1990)
NELSON MANDELA

Keep in Mind . . .

* What was Mandela's agenda in 1990 for the future of South Africa?

My friends, comrades and fellow South Africans, I greet you all in the name of peace, democracy and freedom for all. . . . Your tireless and heroic sacrifices have made it possible for me to be here today. I therefore place the remaining years of my life in your hands. On this day of my release, I extend my sincere and warmest gratitude to the millions of my compatriots and those in every corner of the globe who have campaigned tirelessly for my release. . . .

Today the majority of South Africans, black and white, recognize that apartheid has no future. It has to be ended by our own decisive mass actions in order to build peace and security. The mass campaigns of defiance and other actions of our organizations and people can only culminate in the establishment of democracy.

The apartheid destruction on our subcontinent is incalculable. The fabric of family life of millions of my people has been shattered. Millions are homeless and unemployed. . . . The factors which necessitated the armed struggle still exist today. We have no option but to continue. We express the hope that a climate conducive to a negotiated settlement would be created soon so that there may no longer be the need for the armed struggle.

Today, I wish to report to you that my talks with the Government have been aimed at normalizing the political situation in the country. We have not as yet begun discussing the basic

"Apartheid Has No Future" is from Nelson Mandela, speech delivered to the public, Cape Town, South Africa, February 11, 1990. Contained in *Vital Speeches of the Day* (March 1, 1990), pp. 295-297.

demands of the struggle. I wish to stress that I myself had at no time entered into negotiations about the future of our country, except to insist on a meeting between the A.N.C. [African National Congress] and the government. Mr. de Klerk has gone further than any other nationalist president in taking real steps to normalize the situation. . . .

I reiterate our call for *inter alia* the immediate ending of the state of emergency and the freeing of all, and not only some, political prisoners. . . . Negotiations cannot take place above the heads or behind the backs of our people. It is our belief that the future of our country can only be determined by a body which is democratically elected on a nonracial basis.

Negotiations on the dismantling of apartheid will have to address the overwhelming demand of our people for a democratic nonracial and unitary South Africa. There must be an end to white monopoly on political power. And a fundamental restructuring of our political and economic systems to insure that the inequalities of apartheid are addressed and our society thoroughly democratized.

It must be added that Mr. de Klerk himself is a man of integrity who is acutely aware of the dangers of a public figure not honoring his undertakings. But as an organization, we base our policy and strategy on the harsh reality we are faced with, and this reality is that we are still suffering under the policies of the nationalist Government.

Our struggle has reached a decisive moment. We call on our people to seize this moment so that the process toward democracy is rapid and uninterrupted. We have waited too long for our freedom. We can no longer wait. Now is the time to intensify the struggle on all fronts. To relax our efforts now would be a mistake which generations to come will not be able to forgive. The sight of freedom looming on the horizon should encourage us to redouble our efforts. It is only through disciplined mass action that our victory can be assured. . . .

In conclusion, I wish to go to my own words during the trial in 1964. They are as true today

as they were then. I wrote: "I have fought against white domination, and I have fought against black domination. I have cherished the idea of a democratic and free society in which all persons live together in harmony and with equal opportunities. It is an ideal which I hope to live for and to achieve. But if needs be, it is an ideal for which I am prepared to die." My friends, I have no words of eloquence to offer today except to say that the remaining days of my life are in your hands.

I hope you will disperse with discipline. And not a single one of you should do anything which will make other people say that we can't control our own people.

A new era in South African history began on May 10, 1994 when Nelson Mandela was inaugurated as President of the Republic of South Africa. Mandela and former President F. W. de Klerk worked to dismantle the system of apartheid that had dominated society since 1948. *(Bettmann/Reuters)*.

Consider This:

- What role did de Klerk play in the Nationalist government's abandonment of apartheid as an official policy? Would you regard him as a courageous figure?

- Are human beings inherently racist, or is racism an aberration that must be taught and cultivated through education and societal reaffirmation? To what extent has the United States progressed in its race relations?

Bill of Rights for the Republic of South Africa (1996)

Keep in Mind . . .

- How does this document define the concept of equality in the state?

RIGHTS

7.1 This Bill of Rights is a cornerstone of democracy in South Africa. It enshrines the rights of all people in our country and affirms the democratic values of human dignity, equality and freedom.

7.2 The state must respect, protect, promote, and fulfill the rights in the Bill of Rights. . . .

EQUALITY

9.1 Everyone is equal before the law and has the right to equal protection and benefit of the law.

9.2 Equality includes the full and equal enjoyment of all rights and freedoms. To promote the achievement of equality, legislative and other measures designed to protect or advance persons, or categories of persons, disadvantaged by unfair discrimination may be taken.

"Bill of Rights for the Republic of South Africa" is from Public Affairs Office, South African Embassy, Washington D.C.

9.3 The state may not unfairly discriminate directly or indirectly against anyone on one or more grounds, including race, gender, sex, pregnancy, marital status, ethnic or social origin, colour, sexual orientation, age, disability, religion, conscience, belief, culture, language, and birth. . . .

HUMAN DIGNITY

10 Everyone has inherent dignity and the right to have their dignity respected and protected.

LIFE

11 Everyone has the right to life.

FREEDOM AND SECURITY OF THE PERSON

12.1 Everyone has the right to freedom and security of the person, which includes the right (a) not to be deprived of freedom arbitrarily or without just cause; (b) not to be detained without trial; (c) to be free from all forms of violence from both public and private sources; (d) not to be tortured in any way; and (e) not to be treated or punished in a cruel, inhuman or degrading way.

12.2 Everyone has the right to bodily and psychological integrity, which includes the right (a) to make decisions concerning reproduction; (b) to security in and control over their body; and (c) not to be subjected to medical or scientific experiments without their informed consent. . . .

FREEDOM OF EXPRESSION

16.1 Everyone has the right to freedom of expression, which includes (a) freedom of the press and other media; (b) freedom to receive and impart information and ideas; (c) freedom of artistic creativity; and (d) academic freedom and freedom of scientific research.

16.2 The right in subsection (1) does not extend to (a) propaganda for war; (b) incitement of imminent violence; or (c) advocacy of hatred that is based on race, ethnicity, gender or religion, and that constitutes incitement to cause harm. . . .

HOUSING

26.1 Everyone has the right to have access to adequate housing.

26.2 The state must take reasonable legislative and other measures, within its available resources, to achieve the progressive realisation of this right.

26.3 No one may be evicted from their home, or have their home demolished, without an order of court made after considering all the relevant circumstances. No legislation may permit arbitrary evictions.

HEALTH CARE, FOOD, WATER, AND SOCIAL SECURITY

27.1 Everyone has the right to have access to (a) health care services, including reproductive health care; (b) sufficient food and water; and (c) social security, including, if they are unable to support themselves and their dependants, appropriate social assistance.

27.2 The state must take reasonable legislative and other measures, within its available resources, to achieve the progressive realisation of each of these rights.

27.3 No one may be refused emergency medical treatment.

EDUCATION

29.1 Everyone has the right (a) to a basic education, including adult basic education; and (b) to further education, which the state must take reasonable measures to make progressively available and accessible.

29.2 Everyone has the right to receive education in the official language or languages of their choice in public educational institutions where that education is reasonably practicable. . . .

ARRESTED, DETAINED, AND ACCUSED PERSONS

35.2 Everyone who is detained, including every sentenced prisoner, has the right . . . (e) to conditions of detention that are consistent with human dignity, including at least exercise and the provision, at state expense, of adequate accommodation, nutrition, reading material, and medical treatment; and (f) to communicate with, and be visited by, that person's (i) spouse or partner; (ii) next of kin; (iii) chosen religious counsellor; and (iv) chosen medical practitioner.

Compare and Contrast:

• Compare this Bill of Rights in 1996 with the Freedom Charter of 1955. Would you say that Africans achieved their demands for political, economic, and social equality over the course of forty years?

• Does this document insure freedom and equal civil rights for all in South Africa? What else must be done in order to maintain peace between the races in the future?

ARAB AND JEW: THE SEARCH FOR A HOMELAND

Palestine is the cement that holds the Arab world together, or it is the explosive that blows it apart.

—Yasser Arafat

Strength means to excel in the Profession of Death.

—Sami Shawkat

Whoever thinks of stopping the uprising [*intifada*] before it achieves its goals, I will give him ten bullets in the chest.

—Yasser Arafat (1989)

My generation swore on the Altar of God that whoever proclaims the intent of destroying the Jewish state or the Jewish people, seals his fate.

—Menachem Begin

We have always said that in our war with the Arabs, we had a secret weapon—no alternative.

—Golda Meir

The tormenting dilemma of the Middle East is this: either we have one people too many, or one state too few.

—Afif Safieh

The Zionist Movement and the Creation of Israel

The Middle East has always been an important region in world history. It lies at the cross-roads of Africa, Asia, and Europe, a location that has facilitated the exchange of ideas and commercial goods for thousands of years. Its strategic geopolitical position has also invited conflict over control of land and water rights, over access to sacred religious shrines, and perhaps most importantly, over the very survival of the many peoples who claim title to a part of the region as a homeland.

The struggle to establish Jewish and Arab states in the area of Palestine has bedeviled Middle Eastern politics and international diplomacy for most of the twentieth century and remains one of the most intransigent conflicts filtering into the twenty-first. This is truly an enduring struggle as both Jews and Palestinian Arabs claim the region as a homeland through ancient descent. According to the Bible, God led the Hebrew tribes out of bondage in Egypt to safety in Palestine, which was called "the land of Israel." The Palestinians claim descent through the Canaanites, Philistines, and other tribes who were the ancient inhabitants of this land known in Arabic as "Filastin." For centuries, Jews and Palestinians had lived together on the land, controlled variously by Persians, Macedonians, Romans, Christians, and after the Arab conquest in 637 C.E., Muslims.

The contest for statehood in Palestine began in earnest in the late nineteenth century, as Jews and Arabs were caught in the tide of nationalism sweeping Europe at the time. Arabs sought independence from the degenerating control of the Ottoman Turkish empire. And many Jews, who over the centuries had generally been displaced from the region in a series of dispersions (or diaspora), longed to return to Zion, a Biblical name for Jerusalem, and found a state of their own.

Theodor Herzl (1860–1904), a Jewish journalist living in Austria, founded the Zionist movement in response to the virulent anti-Semitism in Europe. Zionism as a doctrine and movement advocated and justified the creation of a Jewish state in Palestine. In a short pamphlet entitled, The Jewish State *(1896), Herzl posed the question whether Jews should continue to work for assimilation into European society or emigrate to Zion and a new state in "the promised land." The first excerpt details his plan. Many Jews who had suffered from persecution especially in Russia during the 1880s greeted Herzl's ideas with enthusiasm. But Jewish philanthropists and religious leaders were more hesitant. Undeterred, Herzl founded a Zionist newspaper (*Die Welt*) and transformed his ideas into an international political movement. The "Basel Program" of 1897 gave direction and continuity to the Zionist cause.*

The Jewish State (1896)

THEODOR HERZL

Keep in Mind . . .

- How would you define Zionism and what are its goals?

- How specifically would Jewish settlement in Palestine take place?

The entire plan is in its essence perfectly simple, as it must be if it is to become comprehensible to all.

Let sovereignty be granted us over a portion of the earth's surface that is sufficient for our rightful national requirements; we shall take care of everything else ourselves.

The creation of a new sovereign state is neither ludicrous nor impossible. After all, we have seen it happen in our own day—among nations which are not largely middle-class, as we are, but poorer, uneducated, and therefore weaker than ourselves. The governments of the countries scourged by anti-Semitism will be keenly interested in securing a sovereign status for us. . . .

As has already been stated, the departure of the Jews must not be imagined as a sudden one. It

will be gradual, taking decades. The poorest will go first and make the land arable. In accordance with a predetermined plan, they will build roads, bridges, and railways, set up telegraphy installations; regulate rivers and provide themselves with homesteads. Their labor will bring trade, trade will create markets and markets will attract new settlers—for everyone will come voluntarily, at his own expense and his own risk. The labor that we put into the soil will enhance the value of the land. The Jews will soon realize that a new and permanent field has opened up for their spirit of enterprise which has heretofore been met with hatred and contempt. . . .

The emigrants standing lowest in the economic scale will gradually be followed by those of the next grade. Those who are now in desperate straits will go first. They will be led by the average intellects whom we overproduce and who are persecuted everywhere. . . . Let anyone who does not want to go along stay behind. The opposition of individuals is immaterial. Let all those who wish to join us line up behind our banner and fight for it with word, pen, and deed. . . .

[We] will negotiate with the present authorities of the country—under the protectorate of the European Powers, if the matter makes sense to them. We shall be able to offer the present authorities enormous advantages—assume part of their national debt, build new thoroughfares (which we should require ourselves), and do

Herzl, Theodor, *The Jewish State (Der Judenstaat)*, trans. Harry Zohn, 1970, pp. 49–52.

many other things. But the very creation of the Jewish State will be beneficial to the neighboring countries, because the cultivation of an area enhances the value of its surroundings, on a large as on a small scale. . . .

Palestine is our unforgettable historic homeland. The very name would be a powerfully moving rallying cry for our people. If His Majesty the Sultan were to give us Palestine, we could in return pledge ourselves to regulate the entire finances of Turkey. For Europe we could constitute part of the wall of defense against Asia; we would serve as an outpost of civilization against barbarism. As a neutral state we would remain in contact with all Europe, which would have to guarantee our existence. Some form of extraterritoriality under international law could be found for the Holy Places of Christendom. We would form a guard of honor around the Holy Places, answering for the fulfilment of this duty with our existence. This guard of honor would be the symbol of the solution of the Jewish Question after what were for us eighteen centuries of affliction.

The Basel Program (1897)

The aim of Zionism is to create for the Jewish people a home in Palestine secured by public

"The Basel Program" is from *The Jewish Chronicle* (September 3, 1897), p. 13.

law. The Congress contemplates the following means to the attainment of this end:

1. The promotion, on suitable lines, of the colonization of Palestine by Jewish agricultural and industrial workers.
2. The organization and binding together of the whole of Jewry by means of appropriate institutions, local and international, in accordance with the laws of each country.
3. The strengthening and fostering of Jewish national sentiment and consciousness.
4. Preparatory steps towards obtaining government consent, where necessary, to the attainment of the aim of Zionism.

Consider This:

- According to Herzl, how would the creation of a Jewish state benefit the European powers? Why was Herzl concerned with pleasing them?

- Herzl expected that the new Jewish State would be neutral and that Europe would have to "guarantee our existence." In return, the Jews would "form a guard of honor around the Holy Places" of Christendom. What about the holy places of Islam? Is the absence of any mention of Arab peoples at this early juncture significant?

The Balfour Declaration (1917)

The Zionists summed up their dream by the phrase, "a land without a people, for a people without a land." But the land in Palestine had certainly been inhabited for centuries by Arabs and Jews alike in the Ottoman Empire. By 1914, 85,000 Jews, many recently emigrated from Russia, lived in Palestine alongside some 600,000 Arabs, both Muslim and Christian. During World War I, Great Britain hoped to undermine Ottoman control of the region by sparking independence movements among both Jews and Arabs. The British Foreign Secretary David Balfour, in his famous declaration of 1917, endorsed the Zionist desire for a homeland, but did not promise to transform Palestine into a Jewish state. Arab leaders were justifiably concerned, for Balfour's letter seemed to disparage assurances given by the British government in 1916 for the establishment of an Arab state or states within the same area. The Balfour Declaration was, in fact, a masterpiece of equivocation. The British were

"The Balfour Declaration" is from Harold W. V. Temperley, ed., *A History of the Peace Conference of Paris*, Vol. 6 (London: Henry Frowde and Hodder & Stoughton, 1922), p. 170.

looking to realize short-term goals for victory in the war. But they tapped into ethnic and nationalist sentiment that proved far more volatile than they had anticipated. By raising expectations for future sovereignty, the British peddled hope to both sides without a realistic commitment to resolution. Satisfying the competing claims of Arab and Jew has proven impossible ever since.

Keep in Mind . . .

- Why is this document considered among the most important for an understanding of the disagreements between Arabs and Israelis?

Foreign Office

November 2, 1917

Dear Lord Rothschild,

I have much pleasure in conveying to you, on behalf of His Majesty's Government, the following declaration of sympathy with Jewish Zionist aspirations which has been submitted to, and approved by the Cabinet.

"His Majesty's Government view with favour the establishment in Palestine of a national home for the Jewish people, and will use their best endeavours to facilitate the achievement of this object, it being clearly understood that nothing shall be done which may prejudice the civil and religious rights of existing non-Jewish communities in Palestine, or the rights and political status enjoyed by Jews in any other country."

I should be grateful if you would bring this declaration to the knowledge of the Zionist Federation.

Arthur James Balfour

The Arab Nationalist Movement and the Creation of Israel

Arab nationalism as an ideology and as a primary factor in the politics of the Middle East is a comparatively recent development. It was only after World War I, in the mandated territories under British and French rule, that a comprehensive doctrine of Arab nationhood was formulated. But the roots of Arab nationalism go back to the nineteenth century, when Muslim states in North Africa and South Asia were subjugated militarily by European powers, and Islam as a system of belief and social organization was ridiculed and belittled in comparison with Western learning, philosophy, and technical expertise. A response to this attitude came from early Arab revolutionaries such as Jamal al-Din (1838–1897), commonly known as al-Afghani, who lived among Indian Muslims, was expelled from Egypt for dissident activities, and edited an underground newspaper in Paris, preaching Muslim unity and solidarity in the face of European encroachment.

After victory in World War I, Britain and France carved up the Arab portions of the defeated Ottoman Empire into zones of influence or "mandates." Although the mandates for Syria and Iraq were designed to prepare those countries for independence, the mandate for Palestine was intended to bolster Britain's strategic presence in the region while accommodating Zionist goals. The Arabs were furious that Britain had reneged on its wartime support for Arab self-determination. As more Jews emigrated into the region in the 1930s to escape Nazi persecution, Arab nationalists broke into rebellion in 1936.

The following document is a manifesto from the First Arab Students' Congress held in Brussels in December 1938. It is an expression of frustration and an attempt to define and promote Arab unity in response to the effects of European diplomacy.

The Arab Homeland:
"Compromise Is National Treason"
(1938)

Keep in Mind . . .

- How did the Arab Students' Congress define the Arab homeland, Arab nationalism, and the goals of the Arab Movement?

Our National Pact

I am an Arab, and I believe that the Arabs constitute one nation. The sacred right of this nation is to be sovereign in her own affairs. Her ardent nationalism drives her to liberate the Arab homeland, to unite all its parts, and to found political, economic, and social institutions more sound and more compatible than the existing ones. The aim of this nationalism is to raise up the standard of living and to increase the material and the spiritual good of the people; it also aspires to share in working for the good of the human collectivity; it strives to realize this by continuous work based on national organization.

I pledge myself to God, that I will strive in this path to my utmost, putting the national interest above any other consideration.

First Principles

The Arabs: All who are Arab in their language, culture, and loyalty, those are the Arabs. The Arab is the individual who belongs to the nation made up of those people.

The Arab Homeland: It is the land which has been or is, inhabited by an Arab majority, in the above sense, in Asia and Africa. As such it is a whole which cannot be divided or partitioned. It is a sacred heritage no inch of which may be tri-

fled with. Any compromise in this respect is invalid and is national treason.

Arab Nationalism: It is the feeling for the necessity of independence and unity which the inhabitants of the Arab lands share. It is based on the unity of the homeland, of language, culture, history, and a sense of the common good.

The Arab Movement: It is the new Arab renaissance which pervades the Arab nation. Its motive force is her glorious past, her remarkable vitality and the awareness of her present and future interests. This movement strives continuously and in an organized manner toward well-defined aims. These aims are to liberate and unite the Arab homeland, to found political, economic, and social organizations more sound than the existing ones, and to attempt afterward to work for the good of the human collectivity and its progress. These aims are to be realized by definite means drawn from the preparedness of the Arabs and their particular situation, as well as from the experience of the West. They will be realized without subscribing to any particular creed of the modern Western ones such as Fascism, Communism, or Democracy.

Foreign Elements in the Arab Countries

We have said that the Arab countries belong to the Arabs and that benefits therefrom must accrue to them. By Arabs we mean those whom the political report has included under this appellation. As for those elements who are not Arabized and who do not intend to be Arabized, but are, rather, intent on putting obstacles in the way of the Arab nation, they are foreign to the Arab nation. The most prominent problem of this kind is that of the Jews in Palestine.

If we looked at the Jews in Palestine from an economic angle, we would find that their economy is totally incompatible with the Arab economy. The Jews are attempting to build up a Jewish state in Palestine and to bring into this state great numbers of their kind from all over the world. Palestine is a small country, and they will therefore have to industrialize it so that this large number of inhabitants can find subsistence. And in order to make their industry a success, they will have to find markets for their products. For this they depend on the Arab market; their products will therefore flood the Arab countries and compete with Arab industries. This is very harmful to the Arabs.

Moreover, Palestine, placed as it is between the Arab countries in Asia and Africa, occupies an important position in land, sea, and air communications. A foreign state in Palestine will impede these communications and have a harmful effect on commerce. And even if the Jews in Palestine presented no danger other than the economic, this would be enough for us to oppose them and to put an end to their intrigues, so that we may ensure for our country a happy and glorious future.

Among the dangerous alien elements in the Arab countries are the foreign colonies such as the Italians in Troplitania, the French, and the Frenchified Jews in Tunisia, Algeria, and Morocco. The danger of these elements is akin to that of the Jews in Palestine, even though less prominent and less critical.

Consider This:

- Why were the Jews in Palestine a threat to the Arabs? Are you persuaded by the economic argument?

- If one of the goals of the Arab Movement was to work "for the good of the human collectivity and its progress," why must Arabs oppose the Jewish state?

Proclamation of the State of Israel (1948)

In order to forestall Arab hostility and maintain political stability in the Middle East during the anticipated war with Germany in 1939, the British indicated that they would end the mandate over Palestine within ten years if possible and restricted Jewish immigration to the region. At this point, the Jews felt betrayed and Britain wanted out of the quicksand altogether.

At the end of the war in 1945, Britain announced its intention to leave Palestine and transferred the problem to the newly created United Nations. The UN passed a resolution to partition Palestine into independent Jewish and Arab states with Jerusalem becoming an international zone administered by the UN in permanent trusteeship. The Arabs were bitter that the new Jewish state would be given more than half the territory of Palestine, though the Jews constituted only a third of the population. The Arabs rejected the plan and fighting broke out. Israel declared itself a sovereign state on May 14, 1948 in the following proclamation. The next day, Arab armies from Syria, Egypt, Lebanon, Transjordan, and Iraq attacked Israel. With their backs to the wall, the Israelis took advantage of their united command, forcing the Arab armies back and extending their control to 78 percent of the territory, more than it would have received under the UN plan. By mid-1949, Israel had concluded armistices with the demoralized Arab nations. This was a tenuous peace, since no Arab state conceded Israel's right to exist.

Keep in Mind . . .

- On what bases does this Proclamation justify the creation of the state of Israel?

The land of Israel was the birthplace of the Jewish people. Here their spiritual, religious and national identity was formed. Here they achieved independence and created a culture of national and universal significance. Here they wrote and gave the Bible to the world.

Exiled from Palestine, the Jewish people remained faithful to it in all the countries of their dispersion, never ceasing to pray and hope for

"Proclamation of the State of Israel" is from *Foreign Relations of the United States, 1948. Volume V: The Near East, South Asia and Africa, Part 2* (Washington DC: U.S. Government Printing Office, 1976), pp. 976–978.

their return and the restoration of their national freedom.

Impelled by this historic association, Jews strove throughout the centuries to go back to the land of their fathers and regain their statehood. In recent decades they returned in masses. They reclaimed the wilderness, revived their language, built cities and villages, and established a vigorous and ever-growing community, with its own economic and cultural life. They sought peace yet were prepared to defend themselves. They brought the blessing of progress to all inhabitants of the country.

In the year 1897, the First Zionist Congress, inspired by Theodor Herzl's vision of the Jewish State, proclaimed the right of the Jewish people to national revival in their own country.

This right was acknowledged by the Balfour Declaration of November 2, 1917, and reaffirmed by the Mandate of the League of Nations, which gave explicit international recognition to the historic connection of the Jewish people with Palestine and their right to reconstitute their National Home.

The Nazi holocaust, which engulfed millions of Jews in Europe, proved anew the urgency of the reestablishment of the Jewish State, which would solve the problem of Jewish homelessness by opening the gates to all Jews and lifting the Jewish people to equality in the family of nations.

The survivors of the European catastrophe, as well as Jews from other lands, proclaiming their right to a life of dignity, freedom and labor, and undeterred by hazards, hardships and obstacles, have tried unceasingly to enter Palestine.

In the Second World War, the Jewish people in Palestine made a full contribution in the struggle of the freedom-loving nations against the Nazi evil. The sacrifices of their soldiers and the efforts of their workers gained them title to rank with the peoples who founded the United Nations.

On November 29, 1947, the General Assembly of the United Nations adopted a Resolution for the establishment of an independent Jewish State in Palestine, and called upon the inhabitants of the country to take such steps as may be necessary on their part to put the plan into effect.

This recognition by the United Nations of the right of the Jewish people to establish their independent State may not be revoked. It is, moreover, the self-evident right of the Jewish people to be a nation, as all other nations, in its own sovereign State.

ACCORDINGLY, WE, the members of the National council, representing the Jewish people in Palestine and the Zionist movement of the world, . . . by virtue of the natural and historic right of the Jewish people and of the Resolution of the General Assembly of the United Nations,

HEREBY PROCLAIM the establishment of the Jewish State in Palestine, to be called ISRAEL . . .

We offer peace and unity to all the neighboring states and their peoples, and invite them to cooperate with the independent Jewish nation for the common good of all.

Our call goes out to the Jewish people all over the world to rally to our side in the task of immigration and development and to stand by us in the great struggle for the fulfillment of the dream of generations—the redemption of Israel.

Consider This:

- This proclamation advocated the "reestablishment" of the Jewish State as if Jews had once had a political homeland and had lost it. What is this passage referring to?

- Is this proclamation the realization of Herzl's dream for the establishment of a Jewish state? Is Zionism a positive or negative movement?

- This proclamation argued that it was the "self-evident right of the Jewish people to be a nation." In what way is this right "self-evident"? Why didn't the Palestinians have a "self-evident" right?

Life in the Refugee Camps: "A Two-Bit Palestinian"

FAWAZ TURKI

The war from 1948 to 1949 that followed Israel's declaration of sovereignty resulted in major population shifts. About 133,000 Arabs remained in the new state of Israel and became citizens, while an estimated 600,000 to 750,000 fled the area. Most of these entered the West Bank territory that was under the control of Jordan and the rest went south to the Gaza Strip, occupied by Egypt in 1949, and to other Arab states, especially Syria and Lebanon. These Palestinians, with their political aspirations dashed, wandered the landscape as refugees, often trying to establish their lives in states that, although Arab, were not always receptive to a new population competing for jobs and economic relief. The Palestinian exodus was paralleled by an influx of 500,000 Jews into Israel from Arab states and war-torn Europe. Many Palestinians ended up in refugee camps run by the United Nations where, in their poverty and unemployment, they kept alive a sense of national identity that would later find expression in political associations like the Palestine Liberation Organization (PLO).

The trauma and burden of dislocation felt by so many Palestinians in the diaspora after 1948 is reflected in the following account of Fawaz Turki, a Palestinian intellectual who struggled in the refugee camps as a boy with hardships that fueled his later association with PLO guerillas. Turki's autobiography presents the human drama that is often forgotten amidst the impersonal declarations, treaties, and violence of the Arab–Israeli struggle.

Keep in Mind . . .

- What trials and challenges did the Palestinians face in their plight as refugees after 1948?

A breeze began to blow as we moved slowly along the coast road, heading to the Lebanese border— my mother and father, my two sisters, my brother and I. Behind us lay the city of Haifa, long the scene of bombing, sniper fire, ambushes, raids, and bitter fighting between Palestinians and Zionists. Before us lay the city of Sidon and indefinite exile. Around us the waters of the Mediterranean sparkled in the sun. Above us eternity moved on unconcerned, as if God in his heavens watched the agonies of men, as they walked on crutches, and smiled. And our world had burst, like a bubble, a bubble that had engulfed us within its warmth. From then on, I would know only crazy sorrow and watch the glazed eyes of my fellow Palestinians burdened by loss and devastated by pain. April 1948. And so it was the cruelest month of the year; but there were crueler months, then years. . . .

After a few months in Sidon, we moved again, a Palestinian family of six heading to a refugee camp in Beirut, impotent with hunger, frustration, and incomprehension. But there we encountered other families equally helpless, equally baffled, who like us never had enough to eat, never enough to offer books and education to their children, never enough to face an imminent winter. In later years, when we left the camp and found better housing and a better life outside and grew up into our early teens, we would complain about not having this or that and would be told by our mothers: "You are well off, boy! Think of those still living there in the camps. Just think of them and stop making demands." We would look out the window and see the rain falling and hear the thunder. And we would remember. We would understand. We would relent as we thought "of those still living there."

Man adapts. We adapted, the first few months, to life in a refugee camp. In the adaptation, we were also reduced as men, as women, as children, as human beings. At times, we dreamed. Reduced dreams. Distorted ambitions. . . .

The days stretched into months and those into a year and yet another. Kids would play in the mud of the winters and the dust of the summers, while "our problem" was debated at the UN and moths died around the kerosene lamps. A job had been found for me in a factory not far from the camp, where I worked for six months. I felt pride in the fact that I was a bread earner and was thus eligible to throw my weight around the house, legitimately demand an extra spoonful of sugar in my tea, and have my own money to spend on comic books and an occasional orange on the side. I had even started saving to buy my own bed, but I was fired soon after that.

A kid at work had called me a two-bit Palestinian and a fist fight ensued. The supervisor . . . decided I had started it all, slapped me hard twice, deducted three lira from my wages for causing trouble (I earned seven lira a week), paid me the rest, called me a two-bit Palestinian, and, pointing to my blond hair, suggested I had a whore mother and shoved me out the door.

I went to the river and sat on the grass to eat my lunch. I was shaken more by the two-bit Palestinian epithet than by the plight of being unemployed. At home and around the camp, we had unconsciously learned to be proud of where we came from and to continue remembering that we were Palestinians. If this was stigmatic outside, there it was an identity to be known, perpetuated, embraced. My father, reproaching us for an ignoble offense of some kind, would say: "You are a Palestinian." He would mean: as a Palestinian one is not expected to stoop that low and betray his

tradition. If we came home affecting a Lebanese accent, our mother would say: "Hey, what's wrong with your own accent? You're too good for your own people or something? You want to sound like a foreigner when we return to Haifa? What's wrong with you, hey?" . . .

Our Palestinian consciousness, instead of dissipating, was enhanced and acquired a subtle nuance and a new dimension. It was buoyed by two concepts: the preservation of our memory of Palestine and our acquisition of education. We persisted in refusing the houses and monetary compensation offered by the UN to settle us in our host countries. We wanted nothing short of returning to our homeland. And from Syria, Lebanon, and Jordan, we would see, a few miles, a few yards, across the border, a land where we had been born, where we had lived, and where we felt the earth. "This is my land," we would shout, or cry, or sing, or plead, or reason. And to that land a people had come, a foreign community of colonizers, aided by a Western world in a hurry to rid itself of guilt and shame, demanding independence from history, from heaven, and from us.

Consider This:

- Why did it bother the author so much to be called a "two-bit Palestinian?"

- Fawaz Turki stated that a "foreign community of colonizers, aided by a Western world" had taken Palestinian land. Compare this idea with the Zionist argument that the Jews had been deprived of their homeland. Are both arguments valid? Is this the problem?

"Those Who Attack Egypt Will Never Leave Egypt Alive": The Suez Canal Incident (1956)

GAMAL ABDUL NASSER

Perhaps the most demonstrative advocate of Arab nationalism was Gamal Abdul Nasser (1918–1970). The son of a postal clerk, Nasser was active in student demonstrations against British control of Egypt in 1935. He led the 1952 Egyptian revolution that ousted the corrupt

"Those Who Attack Egypt" is from *The Suez Canal Problem, 26 July-22 September 1956, U.S. Department of State Publication No 6392* (Washington, DC: U. S. Government Printing Office, 1956), pp. 345–351.

King Farouk and became President of Egypt in 1954. But he did not become a popular and charismatic leader in the international arena until the Suez Crisis of 1956, when he defied Britain and France by nationalizing the Suez Canal and defending it against counterattack. This event was of seminal importance in the world's eyes because it revealed weaknesses in the exhausted European imperial powers and underscored the possibilities of Arab nationalism. In fact, Nasser saw himself as the international spokesman for Arab liberation and envisioned a united Arab state. But domestic difficulties and his aggressive confrontation with Israel in 1967 constrained his potential. The following speech on the Suez Canal incident and his vision of Arab unity testify to his dominant will and influence on Arab nationalism.

Keep in Mind . . .

- According to Nasser, in order to be independent, what must the Arabs do?

In these decisive days in the history of mankind, these days in which truth struggles to have itself recognized in international chaos where powers of evil domination and imperialism have prevailed, Egypt stands firmly to preserve her sovereignty. Your country stands solidly and stanchly to preserve her dignity against imperialistic schemes of a number of nations who have uncovered their desires for domination and supremacy.

In these days and in such circumstances Egypt has resolved to show the world that when small nations decide to preserve their sovereignty, they will do that all right and that when these small nations are fully determined to defend their rights and maintain their dignity, they will undoubtedly succeed in achieving their ends. . . .

Those who attack Egypt will never leave Egypt alive. We shall fight a regular war, a total war, a guerrilla war. Those who attack Egypt will soon realize they brought disaster upon themselves. He who attacks Egypt attacks the whole Arab world. They say in their papers the whole thing will be over in forty-eight hours. They do not know how strong we really are.

We believe in international law. But we will never submit. We shall show the world how a small country can stand in the face of great powers threatening with armed might. Egypt might be a small power, but she is great inasmuch as she has faith in her power and convictions. I feel quite certain every Egyptian share the same convictions as I do and believes in everything I am stressing now.

We shall defend our freedom and independence to the last drop of our blood. This is the stanch feeling of every Egyptian. The whole Arab nation will stand by us in our common fight against aggression and domination. Free peoples, too, people who are really free will stand by us and support us against the forces of tyranny.

The Arab Revolution (1958)

GAMAL ABDUL NASSER

This, my dear brethren, was the great conspiracy carried out by imperialism at the outbreak of World War I. The forces of imperialism allied themselves then with the Arab people in order to have them stage a revolution, and when the Arab revolution broke out during the First World War, it called for the liberation of the Arab peoples and allied itself with imperialism and with Britain. But has Britain been true to the promises it made to the Arab peoples? Have the Arab people been able to achieve their liberty and independence? . . . Britain did not fulfill its promises. Furthermore, the whole region was divided between Britain and France. Britain failed its allies and carried out the Balfour Declaration by giving Palestine to the Zionists thus establishing the national home they craved. Having reached this stage in their experience with the imperialist powers, the Arab people became convinced, that if they really wanted free-

"The Arab Revolution" is from *President Gamal Abdul Nasser's Speeches and Press-Interviews*, March 9, 1958 (Cairo: United Arab Republic Information Department, 1958), pp. 95–98.

dom, they should depend only on themselves and their own strength and not on any alliance with imperialism or with Britain. . . . The fact is, imperialism does not want us to be strong or to be united. If we really want freedom and independence, we must depend on ourselves alone. We must learn our lessons from the past and know that any alliance with imperialism results in weakness, despotism, and occupation. . . .

The revolution in Egypt was launched in 1952, and we all proclaimed that it had a vital scope that included the whole Arab area. . . . This, my dear brethren, is the true Arab revolution which depends solely on the Arab peoples in every Arab country. This is the revolution which believed in you—you, the Arab peoples in every Arab country as well as elsewhere. This is the revolution which refused to join any foreign or imperialist alliances to achieve its freedom, for freedom stands in open contradiction to imperialism which can only imply slavery. This is the revolution which depended first on God and then on the Arab peoples everywhere. It rose to fight Zionism, to fight imperialism and its agents.

This is the revolution we can pride ourselves on and say that it grew up in our soil, from our blood and from our hearts, the revolution that expressed Arab feelings and aspirations. This is the revolution which has suffered no contamination because it firmly believed in God, and in the Arab people everywhere. These beliefs it considered were the power which could defeat the navies and land forces of the Big Powers. You remember, my brethren, how at Port-Said, when we were besieged by the Big Powers, you rose from Syria, Lebanon and practically every Arab country to support your brethren in Egypt. Out unity of heart succeeded in defeating their naval forces, in destroying the Big Powers, and causing them to slide down to rank among second-class

powers. God willing, our unity will never suffer any weakness. No power in the world can drive us apart. They may succeed in raising artificial partitions or boundaries, they may succeed in winning over some agents in the area, but they cannot reach those hearts who firmly believed in their right to freedom and independence, those hearts that believed that their unity was the only way to strength. They may succeed in having agents in the Arab fatherland, but they will never succeed in suppressing the feelings of the Arab peoples.

Consider This:

- Nasser states that the Arab Revolution rose "to fight Zionism, to fight imperialism and its agents." Is Zionism an imperialistic philosophy? Who are the "agents" Nasser mentions? Who are the "Big Powers"?

- Compare Nasser's speech on the Arab Revolution with Gandhi's arguments in "How Can India Become Free" or with Nehru's "British Rule In India" or Mandela's "The Struggle Is My Life" earlier in this chapter. Are the arguments justifying independence movements from "unjust authority" essentially the same? Was Nasser a nationalist leader on the same level as Gandhi, Nehru, and Mandela?

- Since Nasser's death, several politicians from the Middle East have tried to assume leadership of a pan-Arab movement, among them Anwar Sadat of Egypt and Sadaam Hussein of Iraq. Why is it so difficult to lay claim to Arab leadership? Was such political leadership a goal of Osama bin Laden's terrorist attacks against the United States in 2001? Or was his focus limited to the cultivation of Islamic religious unity?

Visions of the Promised Land

The impetus to create a greater international awareness for the Palestinian cause grew out of the Arab nationalist movement and the experiences of Palestinians in the refugee camps after 1949. The Palestine Liberation Organization (PLO) remains an umbrella organization for various Palestinian factions. It was organized in 1964 in order to better articulate the issues affecting Palestinian refugees, exiles, and prisoners. The predominant group within the PLO at its inception was Fatah, organized by Yasser Arafat in 1959. Arafat (1929–) criticized the pan-Arabism of Nasser for failing to unify Arab states against Israel. He urged aggressive action and, gaining support from Syria, won credibility for leading daring guerrilla raids into Israeli territory. Under Arafat, the PLO became a focused terrorist vehicle for publicizing the Palestinian cause. The move toward organized violence became more pronounced after the defeat of Arab forces during the Six-Day War with Israel in 1967. Under attack, Israel delivered a humiliating blow to the Egyptian, Jordanian, and Syrian armies while acquiring the West Bank (including East Jerusalem) from Jordan and the Gaza Strip and Sinai from Egypt (though the latter was returned in 1982). Through successful violent confrontation, Arafat hoped to boost Palestinian morale and present a profile to the international community of a neglected people with a just cause, who were now willing to fight for their promised homeland.

As Chairman of the PLO, Arafat established terrorist bases in Jordan, Syria, Lebanon, and Libya, training guerillas in explosives, hostage taking, and subversive activities. Arafat's legendary ability to mediate between competing factions allowed the PLO to draw recruits from a new generation of Palestinians who had grown up in the refugee camps with a hatred for Israel and a determination to regain their homeland.

In October 1973, Egypt and Syria launched a surprise attack on Israel during the observance of Yom Kippur. Again, with their imminent survival in doubt, the Israelis, supported by a massive airlift of U.S. arms, prevailed. But Arab armies had performed credibly and the 1973 oil embargo by the Arab-led Organization of Petroleum Exporting Countries (OPEC) punished the United States for its involvement and restored Arab morale. In 1974, the PLO was designated by the Arab League as "the sole representative of the Palestinian people," although terrorist bombings of airplanes and high profile executions of diplomats and Olympic athletes had drawn international condemnation after 1972.

In 1978, Egyptian President Anwar Sadat (1918–1981) and Israeli Prime Minister Menachem Begin (1913–1992) met to work out differences at the request of President Jimmy Carter. Carter was able to broker a peace treaty called the Camp David Accords whereby Egypt recognized Israel's right to exist in return for a restoration of the Sinai to Egypt and peace between the two nations. Although Sadat and Begin shared the Nobel Peace prize for this achievement, Sadat's Egypt was isolated by other Arab states and he was assassinated in 1981 by soldiers of his own army who resented his peace overtures as humiliating.

With their southern flank stabilized, the Israelis moved against the PLO, invading Lebanon in 1978 and 1982, eventually controlling Beirut itself and forcing the PLO out of the country. Faced with a divided and disintegrating PLO, Arafat forced a confrontation within the organization. Convinced that he could obtain more concessions through legitimate discussion than through terrorism, Arafat moderated his image, renounced terrorism, and presented himself as an international diplomat. The PLO was to become a positive force in the restoration of Palestinian rights. Hard-liners in the PLO, such as the violent Abu Nidal, broke away and other Islamic fundamentalist organizations such as Hamas and Hizballah took up the crusade against Israel with terrorist attacks and suicide bombings.

In December 1987, spontaneous demonstrations broke out in Gaza and the West Bank and quickly mushroomed into a general rebellion called the Intifada. *At first the objective was to improve the conditions of Israeli occupation. But soon, the primary demand was for a Palestinian state. In December 1988, the Palestine National Council (PNC), regarded as the PLO's government in exile, in a symbolic act declared the existence of a Palestinian state on the West Bank and Gaza. The PNC also accepted UN Security Council resolutions 242 and 338 that officially recognized Israel and renounced terrorism. In May 1989, Arafat referred to the PLO charter, which says that "armed struggle is the only way to liberate Palestine," as having "lapsed."*

By 1994, most of the Arab states had followed Egypt's lead and signed peace treaties with Israel. But in 1995, Israeli Prime Minister Yitzhak Rabin (1922–1995), who had reluctantly negotiated with Arafat, was assassinated by a disgruntled Israeli citizen. The peace process then slowed as the two dominant political parties in Israel, Likud and Labor, could not formulate a consistent policy that would trade land (the West Bank and Gaza) for peace. The Israeli settlements in the West Bank, the independence of Palestinian authority in Gaza, and the administration of Jerusalem, remain intransigent obstacles to progress in the Arab-Israeli search for a homeland.

The following sources take us from the creation of the PLO in 1964 and its symbolic declaration of a Palestinian state in 1988, to the policy guidelines of the Likud government of Benjamin Netanyahu (1949–) in 1996. This conservative Israeli stand on the retention of the Golan Heights, the prevention of a Palestinian state on the West Bank and Gaza Strip, and the extension of Israeli settlements throughout the Occupied Territories, demonstrates the difficulty of providing Israel with national security, while providing the Palestinians with a national homeland.

Creation of the Palestine Liberation Organization (1964)

Keep in Mind . . .

- Was terrorism an important strategy in uniting Palestinian factions and did it contribute to the legitimacy of the PLO?

- How do you interpret the phrase: "Judaism being a religion is not a separate nationality"?

Article 1: Palestine is the homeland of the Palestinian Arab people. . . .

Article 3: The Palestinian Arab people alone have legitimate rights to their homeland, and shall exercise the right of self-determination after the liberation of their homeland, in keeping with their wishes and entirely of their own accord.

Article 4: Neither the Zionist occupation, nor the dispersal of the Palestinian Arab people . . . can erase this Palestinian identity. . . .

Article 6: Jews who were normally resident in Palestine up to the beginning of the Zionist invasion are Palestinians. . . .

Article 9: Armed struggle is the only way of liberating Palestine. . . .

Article 13: Arab unity and the liberation of Palestine are two complementary objectives. . . . Arab unity will lead to the liberation of Palestine and the liberation of Palestine will lead to Arab unity. . . .

Article 19: The partition of Palestine in 1947, and the establishment of Israel, are fundamentally invalid, however long they last, for they are contrary to the will of the people of Palestine and their natural right to their homeland and contradict the principles of the United Nations Charter, especially the right of self-determination.

Article 20: The Balfour Declaration, the Mandate for Palestine, and all their consequences, are hereby declared null and void. . . . Judaism, being a religion, is not a separate nationality. . . .

"Creation of the Palestine Liberation Organization" is the official translation from the Palestine Liberation Organization United Nations Observer Office, New York.

Declaration of the Palestinian State (1988)

Despite the historical injustice inflicted on the Palestinian arab people resulting in their dispersion and depriving them of their right to self-determination, following upon U.N. General Assembly Resolution 181 (1947), which partitioned Palestine into two states, one Arab, one Jewish, yet it is this resolution what still provides those conditions of international legitimacy that ensure the right of the Palestinian Arab people to sovereignty. . . .

The massive national uprising, the *intifada* . . . has elevated awareness of the Palestinian truth and right. . . . The *intifada* has set siege to the mind of official Israel, which has for too long . . . denied Palestinian existence altogether. . . .

In pursuance of resolutions adopted by Arab Summit conferences and relying on the authority . . . [of] the Resolutions of the United Nations Organizations since 1947, . . . the Palestine National council . . . hereby proclaims the establishment of the State of Palestine on our Palestinian territory with its capital Jerusalem.

The State of Palestine is the state of Palestinians wherever they may be. . . . In it will be safeguarded their political and religious convictions and their human dignity by means of a parliamentary democratic system of governance. . . .

The state of Palestine herewith declares that it believes in the settlement of regional and international disputes by peaceful means, in accordance with the U.N. charter and resolutions. Without prejudice to its natural right to defend its territorial integrity and independence, it therefore rejects the threat or use of force, violence and terrorism against its territorial integrity or political independence, as it also rejects their use against the territorial integrity of other states.

"Declaration of the Palestinian State" is the official translation from the Palestine National Council, Palestine Liberation Organization.

Compare and Contrast:

- Note the use of specific phrases: "Zionist occupation," "right of self-determination," "Zionist invasion," "Palestinian truth and right," "International legitimacy." What does the vocabulary tell you about the Arab-Israeli conflict? Is it about land? Or dignity?

- Compare the "Creation of the PLO" (1964) with "The Arab Homeland" (1938). In what important ways are the two documents consistent in argument?

- How important was the Intifada of 1987 to Palestinian identity and unity?

- Both Arabs and Jews talk of legitimacy, of homeland, of human dignity, of justice and independence. Where does truth lie? What is the solution?

Guidelines for the Government of Israel (1996)

Keep in Mind . . .

- What were the most important goals of the Israelis in 1996?

- What was the Israeli stance on Jerusalem?

The Government presented to the Knesset [parliament] will act on the premise that the right of the Jewish people to the Land of Israel is eternal and indisputable, that the State of Israel is the State of the Jewish people. . . .

GOALS

The government will work to achieve the following goals:

1. Achieving peace with all our neighbors, while safeguarding national and personal security.

"Guidelines of the Government of Israel" is from Report on Israeli Settlement in the Occupied Territories (Washington, DC: Foundation for Middle East Peace), Volume 6 (July, 1996), p. 6.

Current State of the Peace Talks

"Strength means to excel in the Profession of Death"—Sami Shawkat *(Danziger © 1997 The Christian Science Monitor: "Current State of the Peace Talks").*

2. Reinforcing the status of Jerusalem as the eternal capital of the Jewish people.
3. Increasing immigration to Israel, and integrating new immigrants in all walks of life.
4. Creating conditions for a free, thriving economy and social welfare.
5. Strengthening, broadening and developing settlement in Israel. . . .

PEACE, SECURITY, AND FOREIGN RELATIONS

2. The Government of Israel will propose to the Palestinians an arrangement whereby they will be able to conduct their lives freely within the framework of self-government. The Government will oppose the establishment of a Palestinian state or any foreign sovereignty west of the Jordan River, and will oppose "the right of return" of Arab populations to any part of the Land of Israel west of the Jordan river. . . .
8. In any political arrangement, Israel shall insist on ensuring the existence and security

of Jewish settlements and their affinity with the State of Israel. . . .
9. The Government views the Golan Heights as essential to the security of the state and its water resources. Retaining Israeli sovereignty over the Golan will be the basis for an arrangement with Syria.

JERUSALEM

1. Jerusalem, the capital of Israel, is one city, whole and undivided, and will remain forever under Israel's sovereignty.
2. Freedom of worship and access to the holy places will be guaranteed to members of all faiths.
3. The government . . . will prevent any action which is counter to Israel's exclusive sovereignty over the city. . . .

SETTLEMENT

1. Settlement in the Negev, the Galilee, the Golan Heights, the Jordan Valley, and in

Judea, Samaria and Gaza is of national importance to Israel's defense and an expression of Zionist fulfillment. The Government will . . . develop the settlement enterprise in these areas, and allocate the resources necessary for this.

2. The government of Israel will safeguard its vital water supplies, from water sources on the Golan Heights and in Judea and Samaria.

Consider This:

- The Israeli Government stated in 1996 that "the right of the Jewish people to the Land of Israel is eternal and indisputable." Could the Palestinians ever accept this as an established truth?

- What are the most contentious passages in these guidelines that would make progress toward a resolution of the Arab–Israeli conflict difficult, if not impossible? What must happen in order for Arabs and Jews to live together in peace?

11

The Chinese Revolution

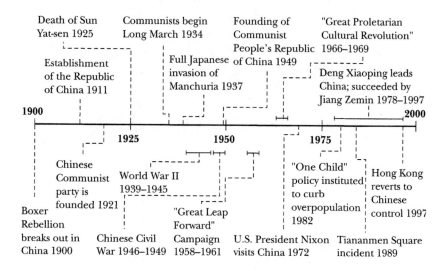

Death of Sun Yat-sen 1925

Establishment of the Republic of China 1911

Communists begin Long March 1934

Full Japanese invasion of Manchuria 1937

Founding of Communist People's Republic of China 1949

"Great Proletarian Cultural Revolution" 1966–1969

Deng Xiaoping leads China; succeeded by Jiang Zemin 1978–1997

1900

1925

1950

1975

2000

Chinese Communist party is founded 1921

World War II 1939–1945

"One Child" policy instituted to curb overpopulation 1982

Hong Kong reverts to Chinese control 1997

Boxer Rebellion breaks out in China 1900

Chinese Civil War 1946–1949

"Great Leap Forward" Campaign 1958–1961

U.S. President Nixon visits China 1972

Tiananmen Square incident 1989

The radical invents the views. When he has worn them out, the conservative adopts them.

—Mark Twain

How a minority/Preaching majority/Seizing authority/Hates a minority.

—Leonard Robbins

Every Communist must grasp the truth: political power grows out of the barrel of a gun.

—Mao Zedong

I love Chairman Mao/Chairman Mao loves me.

—Chinese Nursery Rhyme

对伟大导师毛主席心怀一个"忠"字
对伟大毛泽东思想根抓一个"用"字

This poster of Mao Zedong as the Great Helmsman, the revered leader of the Chinese people, encapsulates the Communist vision of a China united through Mao's vision of the future garnered from teachings in his "Little Red Book" *(David King Collection)*.

CHAPTER THEMES

- *Imperialism:*   How did Western imperialism during the nineteenth century inspire and define the Nationalist and Communist movements in China during the early decades of the twentieth century? To what extent was the success of the Communist victory in 1949 dependent on the Japanese invasion of China in 1937? How did the fear of foreign domination shape Chinese thought and action throughout the twentieth century?

- *Systems of Government:*   During the twentieth century, China shifted from the imperial rule of the Qing dynasty to the republican vision of Sun Yat-sen, to the regional despotism of warlord rule, to the tyrannical authority of Jiang Jieshi and the Guomindang, to Mao's totalitarian "dictatorship of the people," and to Deng Xiaoping's blend of economic freedom and political repression. Why has there been such a variety of political experience? And what kind of government will emerge in the future?

- *Revolution:*   What were the origins of the Chinese Revolution? Why did it become a Communist Revolution? In what ways did the second Chinese Revolution after 1976 differ from Mao's vision in 1949? When will the Chinese Revolution end?

- *Propaganda:*   The Communist Revolution was at base a struggle for the hearts and minds of the Chinese peasant—for the soul of China. How did Mao blend ideology with visual elements to create the image of a worker's utopia bathed in a "red sun"? How divorced from reality was the image of a "People's Revolution"? How did Mao manipulate the atheistic state to become a religious idol in the pantheon of Chinese heroes?

- *Women in History:*   How did the status of women in China change as a result of the Chinese Revolution? How were women asked to serve the Chinese state after 1949 and what roles do women play in contemporary Chinese society?

- *Historical Change and Transition:*   The Chinese have often viewed their history as a continuum of dynastic cycles. But the end of Imperial China in 1911 and the upheavals of the twentieth century have challenged the relevancy of this cyclical view of history. Has the continuity of Chinese society been forever altered by the challenges of the twentieth century? Is Mao's concept of "perpetual revolution" alive and well?

- *The Big Picture:*   What path will China take in the twenty-first century? Does the collapse of the Soviet Union and the authoritarian regimes in Central and Eastern Europe testify to the flaw of Marxism as an economic and social system of organization? Can China sustain a society precariously balanced between a growing capitalist economy and a repressive government? Is democracy even possible in a society as traditional and complex as China's?

The death of Chinese Nationalist leader Dr. Sun Yat-sen in March 1925 aroused more heartfelt grief than had been shown for any recent emperor of China. Sun had dedicated the last thirty years of his life, as he said, to the "overthrow of the Manchus, the restoration of China to the Chinese, and the establishment of a republican government." Although at the time of his death he could claim success on the first count, the second goal proved more elusive, and the third was not to be.

Since the early nineteenth century, the rule of the foreign (Manchu) Qing dynasty had been punctuated with corruption at every level of administration and proved inadequate in managing the nation. The rapid growth of the Chinese population strained agricultural production, and with the oppressive burden of exorbitant land rents paid to the landlord gentry, the peasantry was often just one step ahead of famine and destitution. By mid-century, rebellions had spread throughout the countryside. These internal crises coincided with the dominance of foreign imperialists—the British, the French, the Russians—who sought to reduce China, perhaps the world's most enduring civilization, to colonial status. Through "unequal treaties," signed by China under threat of force, these colonial powers established nearly one hundred "treaty ports" where they could reside, conduct business, and live exempt from Chinese jurisdiction. Sun Yat-sen bitterly complained that China had become "not the colony of one nation, but of all."

Although these treaty ports were an affront to Chinese national pride, they also provided the catalyst for the establishment of modern industrial and financial institutions on Western models. But China was running out of time. In 1895, Japan's revamped military inflicted a harsh defeat on Chinese forces and continued to pursue its designs on the vast lands and resources of northern China. Thinking the time ripe for revolution, Sun launched the first of ten unsuccessful revolts against the Manchus. For the next sixteen years, he traveled the world as a political exile, advocating the cause of Chinese nationalism. In 1905, he founded the Revolutionary Alliance, forerunner of what was to become the Guomindang party and organized it loosely around his "Three People's Principles"—nationalism, democracy, and "people's livelihood."

Sun was abroad when the Qing dynasty fell in 1911 after a revolutionary uprising; he nevertheless was elected provisional president of the new Chinese Republic. But Sun received no foreign support and within forty-seven days, he had resigned his post in favor of Yuan Shikai (1859–1916), the former war minister of the Qing dynasty. Yuan was no democrat and quickly set himself up as a military dictator with visions of crowning himself emperor. As the hopes of the new republic faded, China disintegrated into a patchwork of regional rulers, or warlords, who controlled local forces and fought among themselves for military and political supremacy.

After Yuan's death in 1916, Sun cajoled rival warlords, cut deals with potential backers, and even sought to enlist the support of the United States, Great Britain, and France in the cause of national unification. But at each turn he was rebuffed by all but the Soviet Union. Close on the heels of its own 1917 Communist revolution, Russia was anxious to spread its Marxist ideals to China. The Chinese Communist Party (CCP) was founded in 1921 and collaborated with Sun's nationalist Guomindang party. The Soviets sent military aid and helped restructure the Guomindang along centralized party lines. Although Sun was uncomfortable with Soviet influence, he believed that the Communist element could be controlled. On Sun's death in 1925, the new leaders of China, Communist and Nationalist, began the struggle for political supremacy. Sun's successor as leader of the Guomindang was a 37-year-old military leader named Jiang Jieshi, better known in the West as Chiang Kai-shek (1887–1975). His Communist rivals included a cast of formidable intellects and talented organizers like Zhou Enlai (1898–1976), the elegant, cultivated political commissar, who had recently returned from Paris; in addition, Lin Biao (1907–1969), Deng Xiaoping (1904–1997), and Li Shaoqi (1989–1969) were all committed to a China free from the clutches of Western imperialists. But they were dwarfed by the momentum of a 31-year-old member of the Guomindang's Central Committee—Mao Zedong (1893–1976).

Born in the village of Shaoshan, Hunan province, Mao was the eldest son of a poor peasant, who became modestly prosperous as a farmer and grain dealer. In 1918, Mao graduated from the Hunan Fourth Provincial Normal School and was encouraged to attend university in Beijing. By 1920, he had become deeply immersed in Marxist philosophy and political thought. Mao soon moved from the world of theory to a leadership position in the newly formed Communist Party and began a long commitment as an active organizer of the Chinese peasantry. These impoverished masses, Mao argued, were the key to China's revolutionary success.

Throughout the 1930s and 1940s, as the Chinese Communists struggled against the Nationalist forces of Jiang Jieshi, Mao was adamant in the rightness of Marxist theory and in the determination that all foreign influence was a threat to the purity of his vision. The Communist triumph in the Chinese civil war from 1946 to 1949, and consequent expulsion of the Nationalists to Taiwan, led to Mao's establishment of the People's Republic of China on October 1, 1949. The pathway was now open for the reconstruction and redirection of China in accordance with the Marxist vision of a worker's utopia. But it was a difficult march to paradise as millions died from famine and disease, the victims of mismanagement and misdirection.

In 1976, as the United States celebrated two hundred years of existence as a nation "conceived in liberty," the Chinese were mourning the death of Mao Zedong. It has always been difficult to be neutral about Mao. To millions in the People's Republic of China at the time, he was the "Great Helmsman," who, as "champion of all oppressed people and nations" led China to victory against the imperialist forces of capitalism. To others, both within and outside China, he was a brutal psychopath whose excuse of "proletarian dictatorship" masked his own ambition and lust for power. The purges that accompanied programs like the "Great Leap Forward" from 1958 to 1961 and the "Great Proletarian Cultural Revolution" from 1966 to 1969, eliminated so many people as to qualify Mao, along with Hitler and Stalin, among the elite of the world's mass murderers.

But it has now been nearly thirty years since Mao's death and a new China has emerged under the leadership of Deng Xiaoping and Jiang Zemin. China is a world power again with a vast territory that extends to the Himalayas in the southwest, the Gobi wastes of the north, and to the edge of arable land in the west. But to unlock the potential of its resources and people, the Chinese leadership has been confronted with substantial problems that threaten political stability and national security. Population control and famine, industrialization and pollution, land mismanagement, political repression, and economic freedom—these are the issues that demand creative solutions for a secure future.

Problems are nothing new for China. In its long history, the Chinese have seen political chaos, social instability, and corruption. They have faced the Mongol hoards, fallen to plague and famine, endured foreign occupation and the evils of opium addiction. But they have also built the infrastructure of civil empire, scaled the heights of artistic brilliance, and demonstrated a continuity of civilization without peer in the world. Confucian historians of China had long ago identified patterns of rule that they called the "dynastic cycle." It explained the stages of historical development that saw chaos blend into stability through political consolidation, public works, aggressive military expansion, and then fade to overextension, moral decadence, political intrigue, and decline. In the last stage, social rebellions lead to a collapse of the ruling dynasty, only to have the cycle begin again.

Some historians have seen the same dynamic in operation today. During the Tiananmen Square uprisings of June 4, 1989, an informal coalition of merchants, entrepreneurs, urban workers, students, and intellectuals joined in revolt against the Communist government. In the ensuing confrontation, the army remained loyal to the government and the disturbance was quelled. The lessons that China's leaders learned from Tiananmen Square could be found in China's history. They knew that in the past, many rebels were more concerned about economic conditions than about political freedom. They also knew that anarchy, from the Ming rebellions to Mao's Cultural Revolution, cost millions of lives. And for China's leaders, chaos and political instability have never been abstractions. Deng Xiaoping, who led China from 1978 to 1997, had himself been thrice purged and "rehabilitated," living with the memories of public humiliation and personal tragedy during the Cultural Revolution.

In order to contain popular discontent after Tiananmen Square, the Communist party "readopted" a Confucian pragmatism. China is currently undergoing a tremendous economic expansion fostered by urban growth, foreign investment, minimal environmental restrictions, and access to the sophisticated commercial models in newly restored Hong Kong. This, of course, carries with it the seeds of social and political change.

At the outset of the twenty-first century, after a two-hundred-year hiatus, China has returned to the world stage as a great power. Although this may be normal for the Chinese when viewed through the long-range perspective of their "dynastic cycles," it is not usual for the West. The Chinese Revolution that was initiated by Sun Yat-sen in 1905, revised by Mao Zedong in 1949, and again by Deng Xiaoping in 1978, will significantly affect world politics in the twenty-first century. This chapter affords us the opportunity to gain a perspective on the Chinese past in order to better understand our contemporary world.

THE COMMUNIST REVOLUTION (1920-1976)

Revolution is not a dinner party, nor an essay, nor a painting, nor a piece of embroidery; it cannot be advanced softly, gradually, carefully, considerately, respectfully, politely, plainly and modestly. A revolution is an insurrection, an act of violence by which one class overthrows another.

—*Mao Zedong*

Years of Struggle (1920–1940)

After helping to form the Chinese Communist Party in 1921, Mao Zedong was assigned in 1925 to organize the peasants in his native Hunan province. He became convinced that the Communist Revolution must be based among the peasants, whom he insisted would form the core of an active resistance against local landlords and officials. In the following report, prepared in 1927, Mao argued that terror tactics employed by the peasants were the key to revolution. Although extremism ran counter to Chinese traditions of balance and harmony, Mao's commitment to the political instincts and methods of the peasants defined his systematic program of class warfare. This following report therefore is a seminal document in the development of the Chinese Revolution.

The Peasant Revolution: "It Is Necessary to Bring about a Brief Reign of Terror" (1927)

MAO ZEDONG

During my recent visit to Hunan, I conducted an investigation on the spot into the conditions in five counties. . . . In the thirty-two days from January 4 to February 5, in villages and in county towns, I called together for fact-finding conferences experienced peasants and comrades working for the peasant movement, listened attentively to their reports, and collected a lot of material. Many of the hows and whys of the peasant movement were quite the reverse of what I had heard from the gentry in Hangzhou and Changsha. And many strange things there were that I had never seen or heard before. I think these conditions exist in many other places.

"The Peasant Revolution" is from *Selected Works of Mao Zedong* (Beijing: Foreign Languages Press, 1977), Vol. 1, pp. 21–22; 25–27; 32.

All kinds of arguments against the peasant movement must be speedily set right. The erroneous measures taken by the revolutionary authorities concerning the peasant movement must be speedily changed. Only thus can any good be done for the future of the revolution. For the rise of the present peasant movement is a colossal event. In a very short time, in China's central, southern, and northern provinces, several hundred million peasants will rise like a tornado or tempest, a force so extraordinarily swift and violent that no power, however great, will be able to suppress it. They will break all trammels that now bind them and rush forward along the road to liberation. They will send all imperialists, warlords, corrupt officials, local bullies, and bad gentry to their graves. All revolutionary parties and all revolutionary comrades will stand before them to be tested, and to be accepted or rejected as they decide.

To march at their head and lead them? Or to follow at their rear, gesticulating at them and criticizing them? Or to face them as opponents? Every Chinese is free to choose among the three alternatives, but circumstances demand that a quick choice be made. . . .

But the fact is, as stated above, that the broad peasant masses have risen to fulfill their historic mission, that the democratic forces in the rural areas have risen to overthrow the rural feudal power. The patriarchal-feudal class of local bullies, bad gentry, and lawless landlords has formed the basis of autocratic government for thousands of years, the cornerstone of imperialism, warlordism and corrupt officialdom. To overthrow this feudal power is the real objective of the national revolution. What Dr. Sun Yat-sen wanted to do in the forty years he devoted to the national revolution but failed to accomplish, the peasants have accomplished in a few months. This is a marvelous feat which has never been achieved in the last forty or even thousands of years. It is very good, indeed. It is not "a mess" at all. It is anything but "an awful mess."

There is another section of people who say: "Although the peasant association ought to be formed, it has gone rather too far in its present actions." This is the opinion of the middle-of-the-roaders. But how do matters stand in reality? True, the peasants do in some ways "act unreasonably in the countryside." The peasant association, supreme in authority, does not allow the landlords to have their say and makes a clean sweep of all their prestige. This is tantamount to trampling the landlords underfoot after knocking them down. . . .

[But], a revolution is not the same as inviting people to dinner, or writing an essay, or painting a picture, or doing fancy needlework; it cannot be anything so refined, so calm and gentle, or so mild, kind, courteous, restrained, and magnanimous. A revolution is an uprising, an act of violence whereby one class overthrows another. A rural revolution is a revolution by which the peasantry overthrows the authority of the feudal landlord class. If the peasants do not use the maximum of their strength, they can never overthrow the authority of the landlords which has been deeply rooted for thousands of years. In the rural areas, there must be a great fervent revolutionary upsurge, which alone can arouse hundreds and thousands of the people

to form a great force. All the actions mentioned as "going too far," are caused by the power of the peasants, generated by a great, fervent, revolutionary upsurge in the countryside. Such actions were quite necessary in the second period of the peasant movement (the period of revolutionary action). In this period, it was necessary to establish the absolute authority of the peasants. It was necessary to stop malicious criticisms against the peasant associations. It was necessary to overthrow all the authority of the gentry, to knock them down and even trample them underfoot. All actions labeled as "going too far" had a revolutionary significance in the second period. To put it bluntly, it was necessary to bring about a brief reign of terror in every rural area; otherwise one could never suppress the activities of the counter-revolutionaries in the countryside or overthrow the authority of the gentry. To right a wrong, it is necessary to exceed the proper limits, and the wrong cannot be righted without the proper limits being exceeded.

The main force in the countryside which has always put up the bitterest fight is the poor peasants. Throughout both the period of underground organization and that of open organization, the poor peasants have fought militantly all along. They accept most willingly the leadership of the Communist Party. They are the deadliest enemies of the local bullies and bad gentry and attack their strongholds without the slightest hesitation.

Without the poor peasants (the "riffraff" as the gentry call them), it would never have been possible to bring about in the countryside the present state of revolution, to overthrow the local bullies and bad gentry, or to complete the democratic revolution. Being the most revolutionary, the poor peasants have won the leadership in the peasant association. . . . This leadership of the poor peasants is absolutely necessary. Without the poor peasants there can be no revolution. To reject them is to reject the revolution. To attack them is to attack the revolution. Their general direction of the revolution has never been wrong.

"How to Be a Good Communist" (1939)

LI SHAOQI

Just before his death in 1925, Sun Yat-sen had appointed the young military officer, Jiang Jieshi, to succeed him as leader of the Guomindang party and head of the National Revolutionary Army. It became Jiang's responsibility to organize a Northern Expedition to "crush the warlords and unify the country." The Guomindang party at that time was composed of a coalition of Nationalists and Communists, united in their opposition to the warlords and Western influence. But the Communist faction also viewed the campaign primarily as an anti-imperialist and anti-feudal struggle whereas the Nationalists were looking to end the interference of the West through negotiation. The Nationalists sought the support of Western powers while the Communists, true to their Marxist roots, wanted a domestic revolution and establishment of a workers' and peasants' state. By 1930, the Nationalist campaigns against warlord control had evolved into anti-Communist forays.

Mao's success in organizing peasants, promoting strikes against landlords, and eventually redistributing land to the needy peasants demonstrated his dangerous organizational genius. Jiang launched four military campaigns against Mao's new Chinese Soviet Republic from 1930 to 1932; all four proved unsuccessful. The Communist Red Army, though poorly trained and equipped, was incredibly motivated and able to resist these assaults. But by 1934, an effective economic blockade and a fifth Nationalist offensive proved too much for the Communists. Rather than risk total annihilation, Mao broke through Jiang's encirclement and began a retreat to the hills called the "Long March" on October 16, 1934. Attacked and harried by Nationalist forces during a 6,000 mile trek, the Red Army was decimated and but a skeleton force when the march ended a year later. As Mao recalled in 1971: "The Red Army had had 300,000 men prior to the Long March, but it was reduced to 25,000 men when it arrived in Shensi province." As Jiang's forces moved in for the kill, the Communists were rescued, most ironically, by a Japanese invasion of Manchuria in northern China. Encouraged by the Chinese civil war, the Japanese had seized the opportunity to attack, forcing Jiang to deflect his attention.

The Soviet Union's leader, Joseph Stalin, encouraged both Mao and Jiang to end their civil war, and China entered World War II against Japan in 1937. This reprieve of the Communists was a crucial turning point in the Chinese Revolution. For while Jiang directed the Chinese resistance against Japan, Mao reorganized his political movement. At the end of World War II in 1945, Mao stood ready to meet Jiang once again in a fight to the death.

The following selection is an indoctrination tract by Li Shaoqi (1898–1969), one of Mao's closest advisors and theoreticians. This was part of the Communist strengthening movement that focused Party discipline and revived Communist fortunes. Such instructive tracts gave inspiration to the peasants movement and Red Army in their duel with the Nationalists.

Comrades! What is the most fundamental and common duty of us Communist Party members? As everybody knows, it is to establish Communism, to transform the present world into a Communist world. Is a Communist world good or not? We all know that it is very good. In such a world there will be no exploiters, oppressors, landlords, capitalists, imperialists, or fascists.

"How to Be a Good Communist" is from Li Shaoqi, *How to Be a Good Communist* (New York: New Century Press, 1952), pp. 15–16; 24; 29–32.

There will be no oppressed and exploited people, no darkness, ignorance, backwardness, etc. In such a society all human beings will become unselfish and intelligent Communists with a high level of culture and technique. The spirit of mutual assistance and mutual love will prevail among mankind. There will be no such irrational things as mutual deception, mutual antagonism, mutual slaughter and war, etc. Such a society will, of course, be the best, the most beautiful, and the most advanced society in the history of mankind. Who will say that such a society is not good? Here the question arises: Can Communist society be brought about? Our answer is "yes." About this the whole theory of Marxism-Leninism offers a scientific explanation that leaves no room for doubt. It further explains that as the ultimate result of the class struggle of mankind, such a society will inevitably be brought about. The victory of Socialism in the U.S.S.R. has also given us factual proof. Our duty is, therefore, to bring about at an early date this Communist society, the realization of which is inevitable in the history of mankind. . . .

Comrades! If you only possess great and lofty ideals but . . . do not carry on genuinely practical work, you are not a good Communist Party member. You can only be a dreamer, a prattler, or a pendant. If on the contrary, you only do practical work, but do not possess the great and lofty ideals of Communism, you are not a good Communist, but a common careerist. A good Communist Party member is one who combines the great and lofty ideals of Communism with practical work and the spirit of searching for the truth from concrete facts.

The Communist ideal is beautiful while the existing capitalist world is ugly. It is precisely because of its ugliness that the overwhelming majority of the people want to change it and cannot but change it. . . .

At all times and on all questions, a Communist Party member should take into account the interests of the Party as a whole, and place the Party's interests above his personal problems and interests. It is the highest principle of our Party members that the Party's interests are supreme. . . .

A Communist Party member should possess all the greatest and noblest virtues of mankind. . . . Such ethics are not built upon the backward basis of safeguarding the interests of individuals or a small number of exploiters. They are built, on the contrary, upon the progressive basis of the interests of the proletariat, of the ultimate emancipation of mankind as a whole, of saving the world from destruction, and of building a happy and beautiful Communist world.

The New Communist State (1940-1950)

Jiang Jieshi's decision, as leader of the Guomindang's Nationalist forces, to resist the Japanese invasion of Manchuria in summer 1937 was hailed by most Chinese as a valiant and proper decision in the face of foreign aggression. The Communist Chinese led by Mao Zedong were perhaps most elated, for they had been on the brink of annihilation by the Guomindang when the threat instantly disappeared. With the Japanese now viewed as the primary threat to China, the Communists entered a rather unnatural collaboration with the Guomindang from 1937 to 1941. They both pledged cooperation, but the distrust and even hatred of these rival factions immediately produced tension that exhausted their energies and made effective resistance to Japan an impossibility. Although the United States sent military advisors and diplomats, the gulf between the Nationalists and the Communists could not be breached.

After the surrender of Japan in 1945, the Nationalist forces of Jiang enjoyed tremendous prestige and even signed a treaty of friendship with the Soviet Union, which promised to recognize and support Jiang's government. As Mao emerged from the Yenan caves where he and his Communist supporters had directed their operations against the Nationalists, it was not clear whether he would concede authority to Jiang or renew the civil war. By 1947, despite the diplomatic efforts of American General George Marshall, it was evident that China was about to embark on a path of destruction even more brutal than had just been experienced in World War II. Millions of Chinese, Communist and Nationalist, were killed in the ensuing civil war. Finally, the Nationalist forces of the Guomindang were defeated and pushed to the coast where they fled to the island of Taiwan.

It is difficult to assess the reasons for the Guomindang's defeat; they are varied and complex. Ultimately, this was a struggle not only for China's sovereignty and national independence, as it had been since the beginning of the century, but for China's soul. The Communists won most importantly because they were committed and outstanding organizers of a new political force in Chinese history: the peasant masses. Mao knew quite early in the history of Chinese Communism that the social and economic welfare of the peasantry was the key to its mobilization as a revolutionary force. The vision of a peasant rarely extended past his village, but he understood exorbitant rents and landlord villains; he advocated land confiscations and redistribution, and he desired dignity as an individual. These had never been priorities in China's modern history and Mao directed his organizational genius to the hearts and minds of an underclass that had never known opportunity. The peasants rewarded the Communists with their loyalty as the backbone of the Red Army, and with their inspiration as the keystone of a new nation independent of foreign control. Under Mao's direction, the Chinese people envisioned a future of possibility.

As the year 1949 opened, the Nationalist forces were in disarray and the Red Army was marching toward Nanjing, the Nationalist capital. Mao demanded unconditional surrender and the punishment of war criminals; foremost among them was Jiang Jieshi, as noted in the first selection. It is followed by an assessment of the situation by U.S. Secretary of State, Dean Acheson.

"Jiang Jieshi Is China's Number One War Criminal" (January 1949)

MAO ZEDONG

Two and a half years have gone by since July, 1946, when the reactionary Nanjing Guomindang government, with the aid of the U.S. imperialists, violated the will of the people, tore up the truce agreement and the resolutions of the Political Consultative Conference, and launched the countrywide counter-revolutionary civil war. In these two and a half years of war, the reactionary Nanjing Guomindang government has, in violation of the will of the people, convened a bogus National Assembly, promulgated a bogus constitution, elected a bogus president, and issued a bogus decree on the so-called "mobilization for putting down the rebellion"; sold out the national interest wholesale to the U.S. government and received loans amounting to thousands of millions of U.S. dollars; invited the U.S. navy and air force to occupy China's territory and territorial sea and air; signed a large batch of treasonable treaties with the U.S. government and accepted the U.S. Military Advisory Group's participation in China's civil war; and obtained from the U.S. government huge quantities of aircraft, tanks, light and heavy artillery, machine-guns, rifles, shells, bullets

"Jiang Jieshi Is China's Number One War Criminal" is from *Selected Works of Mao Zedong* (Beijing: Foreign Languages Press, 1967), Vol. 4, pp. 315–319.

and other war material for slaughtering the Chinese people.

And it was on the basis of these reactionary and traitorous basic policies, domestic and foreign, that the reactionary Nanjing Guomindang government ordered millions of troops to launch ruthless attacks on the Chinese People's Liberated Areas and the Chinese People's Liberation Army. . . . Wherever they went, they massacred and raped, burned and looted, and stopped at nothing.

In the areas under its rule, the reactionary Nanjing Guomindang government sucks the lifeblood of the broad masses of the people—the workers, peasants, soldiers, intellectuals, and businessmen—by exacting grain levies, taxes, and forced labor for "putting down the rebellion and suppressing the bandits." The reactionary Nanjing Guomindang government deprives the people of all their freedoms denying them their legal status; it suppresses the righteous movement of the students against civil war, hunger, and persecution and against U.S. interference in China's internal affairs. . . . In short, the reactionary Nanjing Guomindang government has plunged the whole nation into dire suffering by waging a civil war based on its reactionary and traitorous basic policies, domestic and foreign; it absolutely cannot escape full responsibility.

In contrast to the Guomindang, the Communist Party of China did all it could after Japan's surrender to press the Guomindang government to prevent and stop the civil war and realize domestic peace. Basing itself on this policy, the Communist Party of China struggled steadfastly and, with the support of the people of the whole country. . . . But it is regrettable that the reactionary Guomindang government showed no respect for any of the actions we took in defense of internal peace and the democratic rights of the people. On the contrary, they thought that the people could be bullied. . . . Therefore, the reactionary Guomindang government had the audacity to violate the will of the people of the

whole country and to unleash the counter-revolutionary war.

Under the circumstances, the Communist Party of China had no choice but to rise resolutely against the Guomindang government's reactionary policies and to fight to safeguard the county's independence and the people's democratic rights. Since July, 1946, the Communist Party of China has led the heroic People's Liberation Army to repulse the attacks of . . . the reactionary Guomindang government and then to go over to the counter-offensive, recover all the lost territories of the Liberated Areas and liberate many large cities. . . . The People's Liberation Army has overcome unparalleled difficulties, grown in strength, and equipped itself with huge quantities of arms given to the Guomindang government by the U.S. government. In two and a half years, it has wiped out the main military forces of the reactionary Guomindang government and all its crack divisions. Today the People's Liberation Army is superior to the remnant military forces of the reactionary Guomindang government in numbers, morale, and equipment. It is only now that the Chinese people can begin to breathe freely. The Guomindang regime will crumble and perish if the People's Liberation Army launches a few more powerful attacks against its remnant forces.

Having pursued a policy of civil war, the reactionary Guomindang government is now reaping what it has sown: the masses are in rebellion, its close followers are deserting, and it can no longer maintain itself. . . . Jiang Jieshi, chieftain of the Guomindang bandit gang and bogus president of the Nanjing government, is China's number one war criminal.

Comrade Commanders and fighters of the People's Liberation Army, attention! You should not slacken your fighting efforts in the slightest until the reactionary Nanjing Guomindang government has accepted a genuine democratic peace and carried it out. Any reactionaries who dare to resist must be resolutely, thoroughly, wholly and completely annihilated.

The Failure of the Nationalist Government: The American Assessment (1949)

DEAN ACHESON

The reasons for the failure of the Chinese National Government appear in some detail in the attached record. They do not stem from any inadequacy of American aid. Our military observers on the spot have reported that the Nationalist armies did not lose a single battle during the crucial year of 1948 through lack of arms or ammunition. The fact was that the decay which our observers had detected ... early in the war had fatally sapped the powers of resistance of the Guomindang. Its leaders had proved incapable of meeting the crisis confronting them, its troops had lost the will to fight, and its Government had lost popular support. The Communists, on the other hand, through a ruthless discipline and fanatical zeal, attempted to sell themselves as guardians and liberators of the people. The Nationalist armies did not have to be defeated; they disintegrated.

"The Failure of the Nationalist Government" is from U.S. Department of State, *United States Relations with China: With Special Reference to the Period 1944-1949* (China White Paper), pp. xiv–xvii.

History has proved again and again that a regime without faith in itself and an army without morale cannot survive the test of battle. . . .

It must be admitted frankly that the American policy of assisting the Chinese people in resisting domination by any foreign power or powers is now confronted with the greatest difficulties. The heart of China is in Communist hands. The Communist leaders have foresworn their Chinese heritage and have publicly announced their subservience to a foreign power, Russia. . . . The foreign domination has been masked behind the facade of a vast crusading movement which apparently has seemed to many Chinese to be wholly indigenous and national. Under these circumstances, our aid has been unavailing. . . .

And now it is abundantly clear that we must face the situation as it exists in fact. We will not help the Chinese or ourselves by basing our policy on wishful thinking. We continue to believe that, however tragic may be the immediate future of China and however ruthlessly a major portion of this great people may be exploited by a party in the interest of a foreign imperialism, ultimately the profound civilization and the democratic individualism of China will reassert themselves and she will throw off the foreign yoke.

"From the Countryside to the City" (May 1949)

MAO ZEDONG

As the Communists rolled toward victory against Nationalist Chinese forces, Mao directed his rhetoric toward the establishment of a "people's democratic dictatorship" that would extend "from the countryside to the city" and integrate rural peasants and urban workers, as the following speech of May 1949 indicates. On October 1, 1949, Mao, flush with victory, proclaimed the establishment of the People's Republic of China.

From 1927 to the present, the center of gravity of our work has been in the villages—gathering strength in the villages, using the villages in

order to surround the cities, and then taking the cities. The period for this method of work has now ended. The period of "from the city to

"From the Countryside to the City" is from *Selected Works of Mao Zedong* (Beijing: Foreign Languages Press, 1967), Vol. 4, pp. 363–365; 373–374.

the village" and of the city leading the village has now begun. The center of gravity of the party's work has shifted from the village to the city. In the south the People's Liberation Army will occupy first the cities and then the villages. Attention must be given to both city and village and it is necessary to link closely urban and rural work, workers and peasants, industry and agriculture. Under no circumstances should the village be ignored and only the city given attention; such thinking is entirely wrong. Nevertheless, the center of gravity of the work of the party and the army must be in the cities; we must do our utmost to learn how to administer and build the cities. In the cities we must learn how to wage political, economic, and cultural struggles against the imperialists, the Guomindang, and the bourgeoisie and also how to wage diplomatic struggles against the imperialists. . . .

On whom shall we rely in our struggles in the cities? Some muddle-headed comrades think we should rely not on the working class but on the masses of the poor. Some comrades who are even more muddle-headed think we should rely on the bourgeoisie. As for the direction of industrial development, some muddle-headed comrades maintain that we should chiefly help the development of private enterprise and not state enterprise, whereas others hold the opposite view, that it suffices to pay attention to state enterprise and that private enterprise is of little importance. We must criticize these muddled views. We must wholeheartedly rely on the working class, unite with the rest of the laboring masses, win over the intellectuals and win over

to our side as many as possible of the national bourgeois elements and their representatives who can cooperate with us—or neutralize them—so that we can wage a determined struggle against the imperialists, the Guomindang and the bureaucrat-capitalist class and defeat these enemies step by step. Meanwhile we shall set about our task of construction and learn, step by step, how to administer cities and restore and develop their production. . . .

Very soon we shall be victorious throughout the country. This victory will breach the eastern front of imperialism and will have great international significance. To win this victory will not require much more time and effort, but to consolidate it will. The bourgeoisie doubts our ability to construct. The imperialists reckon that eventually we will beg alms from them in order to live. With victory, certain moods may grow within the party—arrogance, the airs of a self-styled hero, inertia and unwillingness to make progress, love of pleasure and distaste for continued hard living. With victory, the people will be grateful to us and the bourgeoisie will come forward to flatter us. . . .

We must guard against such a situation. To win country-wide victory is only the first step in a long march. . . . Even if this step is worthy of pride, it is comparatively tiny; what will be more worthy of pride is yet to come. . . . We are not only good at destroying the old world, we are also good at building the new. Not only can the Chinese people live without begging alms from the imperialists, they will live a better life than that in the imperialist countries.

Consolidation and the "Great Leap Forward" (1950-1960)

As for the men in power, they are so anxious to establish the myth of infallibility that they do their utmost to ignore truth.

—*Boris Pasternak*

Who shall guard the guardians themselves?

—*Juvenal*

The creation of the People's Republic of China on October 1, 1949 was, in a sense, an award ceremony. The Communists had persevered in their ideological and military struggle with the Nationalists and against great odds had created an historic opportunity. Riding to power largely on the discontent of the Chinese peasantry, the Communists could not rest on their laurels, but had to respond quickly to the agrarian demands of the peasants. The enticements of rent reduction and the vilification of the landlord class had attracted a large popular following to the Communists during the war years. But now that they had attained absolute power, the "excesses" of an angry peasantry had to be quelled for a successful economic and political consolidation of Communist authority. The Communist Party repaid its debt to the peasantry with the Agrarian Reform Law of 1950. This law provided for land confiscation and redistribution in accordance with class status, but it also protected so-called rich or "middle peasants" and did not call for their elimination as Stalin had annihilated the Russian Kulaks as a class in the 1930s.

Another debt that needed to be settled by the new Communist regime was to the women of China. They had been important contributors to the war effort against the Nationalists through their support activities. The laws that created the land revolution and guaranteed full equality of property rights to all Chinese also attacked the traditional restrictions on women's participation in the political and economic life of the nation. It was important at this juncture to define the legal position and economic role of women in the new Communist state. The following directive from the Central Committee of the Communist Party in December 1948 called for the liberation of women from feudal restrictions and linked women's equality with the ongoing struggle for land redistribution, economic growth, and political victory.

Women and the Revolution

Women, who form half the population, have played a big role and have become an indispensable force for defeating the enemy and building a new China. . . . Ordinary village women of the liberated areas were further mobilized and organized to work in handicrafts, supplementary enterprises, and agriculture, and to contribute to the war effort with all their strength. . . . Women have become much more aware and enthusiastic, and consequently there has been a fundamental change in their political and economic position and in their position in the family and in society, opening the way to complete liberation.

But there are certain shortcomings in women's work in the liberated areas. . . . The central task in women's work is to organize women to take an active part in production. This is also a guarantee of women's special interests and the key to freeing them from the constraints on them which still survive. Some areas have even completely disregarded these decisions and so have not carried them out conscientiously or thoroughly. Moreover, in some districts conscientious care has not been given to eliminating the survivals of feudalism which hold women back or to satisfying women's special interests and demands in the course of mobilizing women for production, land reform, and work to aid the front. . . .

The whole party, all cadres engaged in women's work, and all women activists must understand that under new democratic government, all the laws of the old society which constrained or mistreated women and forced them into a humiliating position of obedience have

"Women and the Revolution" from *Woman-Work: Women and the Party in Revolutionary China* by Delia Darin (1976), pp. 201–203. Reprinted by permission of Oxford University Press.

ceased to exist. The new laws guaranteeing absolute equality of the sexes in the economy, in politics, and in society have been formulated . . . in the first period of new democratic power. The question is whether these laws can truly be realized. The attitude of valuing men and despising women handed down from the old society, all kinds of constraining feudal customs, especially the economic dependence of women on men and the handicaps of not excelling at all sorts of labor and even despising it, have obstructed the rapid realization by women of the rights already granted to them in law. So if women's rights are to be properly realized, the work must be done. . . .

In accordance with what is necessary to the development of the present revolutionary situation, a large group of party and nonparty women cadres must be boldly educated and fully utilized and pushed forward to take up posts of every sort and reinforce the cadres in women's organizations at every level. The same work should be allocated and the same training and educational opportunities given to men and women cadres of equal ability without discrimination. Moreover, taking into account the special position of women cadres, greater attention would be given to training their political, theoretical, and cultural levels and their ability at work. In order to assist with their special difficulties, day care centers and nurseries should be organized to care for children. This will not only lighten the burden of the women cadres, it will also be a start in the nursery care of children by society. . . .

From now on the whole party must recognize properly that the mobilization of ordinary women for revolutionary struggle is indispensable to the revolutionary victory in the whole country. . . .

"Let a Hundred Flowers Blossom" (1957)

MAO ZEDONG

After the death of the Soviet leader Joseph Stalin in 1953, all eyes turned to Mao Zedong as the most prominent theoretician of Communist ideology. Mao delivered the following speech at the Supreme State Conference on February 27, 1957 with the shock of the anti-Soviet Hungarian uprising of 1956 clearly in the minds of the audience. The tacit questions posed to Mao demanded answers: How was angry dissatisfaction in a seemingly well-established Communist regime like Hungary possible? How might the Chinese Communists deal with insurrection in the "People's Republic"? Mao's response was not to liberalize the state or to loosen ideological control, but to reaffirm the validity of Marxist doctrine. In this important speech, Mao promoted ideological unity by recognizing some natural "contradictions among the people" in their economic, social, and political relations. In resolving contradictions, Mao urged a tolerant attitude by letting a "hundred flowers blossom" and a "hundred schools of thought contend." Mao believed that the "unity of opposites" was a fundamental Marxist law and that balancing freedom within the "bounds of socialist discipline" was essential in achieving the Marxist utopian vision.

Yet some scholars have argued that in this speech, Mao was less interested in smelling "fragrant flowers" than in identifying "poisonous weeds." Those who stepped over the invisible line of acceptable speech and thought could not expect to be rewarded. Mao and the Party were the sole judges of ideological purity.

"Let a Hundred Flowers Blossom" is from *Selected Works of Mao Zedong* (Beijing: Foreign Languages Press, 1977), Vol. 5, pp. 384–389; 408–412.

The People's Democratic Dictatorship and the Correct Handling of Contradictions

Never has our country been as united as it is today. The victories of the bourgeois-democratic revolution and the socialist revolution, coupled with our achievements in socialist construction, have rapidly changed the face of old China. A still brighter future lies ahead for our motherland. The days of national disunity and chaos which the people detested are gone forever. Led by the working class and the Communist Party, and united as one, our 600 million people are engaged in the great work of building socialism. The unification of our country, unity of the people, and unity among our various nationalities—these are the basic guarantees for the sure triumph of our cause. However, this does not mean that contradictions no longer exist in our society. It would be naive to imagine that there are no more contradictions. . . .

Our state is a people's democratic dictatorship led by the working class and based on the worker-peasant alliance. What is this dictatorship for? Its first function is internal, namely, to suppress the reactionary classes and elements and those exploiters who resist the socialist revolution, to suppress those who try to wreck our socialist construction, or in other words, to resolve the contradictions between ourselves and the internal enemy. For instance, to arrest, try and sentence certain counter-revolutionaries, and to deprive landlords and bureaucrat-capitalists of their right to vote and their freedom of speech for a certain period of time—all this comes within the scope of our dictatorship. . . . The second function of this dictatorship is to protect our country from subversion and possible aggression by external enemies. In such contingencies, it is the task of this dictatorship to resolve the contradiction between ourselves and the external enemy. The aim of this dictatorship is to protect all our people so that they can devote themselves to peaceful labor and make China a socialist country with modern industry, modern agriculture, and modern science and culture.

Who is to exercise this dictatorship? Naturally, the working class and the entire people under its leadership. . . .

Our Constitution lays it down that citizens of the People's Republic of China enjoy freedom of speech, the press, assembly, association, procession, demonstration, religious belief, and so on. Our Constitution also provides that the organs of state must practice democratic centralism, that they must rely on the masses and that their personnel must serve the people. Our socialist democracy is the broadest kind of democracy, such as is not to be found in any bourgeois state. Our dictatorship is based on the worker-peasant alliance. That is to say, democracy operates within the ranks of the people, while the working class, uniting with all others enjoying civil rights, and in the first place with the peasantry, enforces dictatorship over the reactionary classes and elements and all those who resist socialist transformation and oppose socialist construction. By civil rights, we mean, politically, the rights of freedom and democracy. But this freedom is freedom with leadership and this democracy is democracy under centralized guidance, not anarchy. Anarchy does not accord with the interests or wishes of the people. . . .

Some people in our country . . . think that there is too little freedom under our people's democracy and that there is more freedom under Western parliamentary democracy. They ask for the adoption of the two-party system of the West, where one party is in office and the other in opposition. But this so-called two-party system is nothing but a means of maintaining the dictatorship of the bourgeoisie; it can never guarantee freedoms to the working people. As a matter of fact, freedom and democracy exist not in the abstract, but only in the concrete. . . .

Those who demand freedom and democracy in the abstract regard democracy as an end and not a means. . . . The same is true of freedom. Both democracy and freedom are relative, not absolute, and they come into being and develop under specific historical circumstances.

Within the ranks of the people, democracy stands in relation to centralism, and freedom to discipline. They are two conflicting aspects of a single entity, contradictory as well as united, and we should not one-sidedly emphasize one to the exclusion of the other. Within the ranks of the people, we cannot do without freedom, nor can we do without discipline. Our democratic centralism means the unity of democracy and centralism and the unity of freedom and discipline. Under this system, the people enjoy a wide measure of democracy and freedom, but at the same time they have to keep themselves within the bounds of socialist discipline. All this is well understood by the people.

In advocating freedom with leadership and democracy under centralized guidance, we in no way mean that coercive measures should be taken to settle ideological questions or questions involving the distinction between right and wrong among the people. All attempts to use administrative orders or coercive measures to settle ideological questions or questions of right and wrong are not only ineffective, but harmful. We cannot abolish religion by administrative order or force people not to believe in it. We cannot compel people to give up idealism, any more than we can force them to embrace Marxism. The only way to settle questions of an ideological nature or controversial issues among the people is by the democratic method, the method of discussion, criticism, persuasion, and education, and not by the methods of coercion or repression. . . .

Marxist philosophy holds that the law of the unity of opposites is a fundamental law of the universe. This law operates everywhere, in the natural world, in human society, and in man's thinking. Between the opposites in a contradiction, there is at once unity and struggle, and it is this that impels all things to move and change. Contradictions exist everywhere, but their nature differs in accordance with the different nature of different things. The unity of opposites is conditional, temporary and transitory, and hence relative, whereas struggle between opposites is absolute. . . .

"Let a Hundred Flowers Blossom"

"Let a hundred flowers blossom" and "let a hundred schools of thought contend," "long-term coexistence and mutual supervision"—how did these slogans come to be put forward?

They were put forward in the light of China's specific conditions, in recognition of the existence of various kinds of contradictions in socialist society, and in response to the country's urgent need to speed up its economic and cultural development.

The policy of letting a hundred flowers blossom and a hundred schools of thought contend is the policy for promoting progress in the arts and sciences and a flourishing socialist culture in our land. Different forms and styles in art can develop freely and different schools in science can contend freely. We think that it is harmful to the growth of art and science if administrative measures are used to impose one particular style of art or school of thought and to ban another. Questions of right and wrong in the arts and sciences should be settled through free discussions in artistic and scientific circles and in the course of practical work in the arts and sciences. They should not be settled in summary fashion. . . .

People may ask: Since Marxism is accepted by the majority of people in our country as the guiding ideology, can it be criticized? Certainly it can. Marxism is scientific truth and fears no criticism. . . . Marxists should not be afraid of criticism from any quarter. Quite the contrary, they need to steel and improve themselves and win new positions in the teeth of criticism and the storm and stress of struggle. Fighting against wrong ideas is like being vaccinated—a man develops greater immunity from disease as a result of vaccination. Plants raised in hot-houses are unlikely to be hardy. Carrying out the policy of letting a hundred flowers blossom and a hundred schools of thought contend will not weaken, but strengthen the leading position of Marxism in the ideological field.

What should our policy be toward non-Marxist ideas? As far as unmistakable counter-revolutionaries and wreckers of the socialist cause are concerned, the matter is easy; we simply deprive them of their freedom of speech. But it is quite a different matter when we are faced with incorrect ideas among the people. Will it do to ban such ideas and deny them any opportunity for expression? Certainly not. It is not only futile but very harmful to use crude methods in dealing with ideological questions among the people, with questions relating to the spiritual life of man. You may ban the expression of wrong ideas, but the ideas will still be there. On the other hand, if correct ideas are pampered in hot-houses and never exposed to the elements and immunized against disease, they will not win out against wrong ones. That is why it is only by employing methods of discussion, criticism, and reasoning that we can really foster correct ideas, overcome wrong ideas, and really settle issues. . . . We are against poisonous weeds of whatever kind, but we must carefully distinguish between what is really a poisonous weed and what is really a fragrant flower. Together with the people, we must learn to differentiate carefully between the two and use correct methods to fight the poisonous weeds. . . .

In the political life of our country, how are our people to determine what is right and what is wrong in our words and actions? Basing ourselves on the principles of our constitution, the will of the overwhelming majority of our people and the political programs jointly proclaimed on various occasions by our political parties and groups, we believe that, broadly speaking, words and actions can be judged right if they:

1. Help to unite the people of our various nationalities, and do not divide them.

2. Are beneficial, not harmful, to socialist transformation and socialist construction.

3. Help to consolidate, not undermine or weaken, the people's democratic dictatorship.

4. Help to consolidate, not undermine or weaken, democratic centralism.

5. Tend to strengthen, not to cast off or weaken, the leadership of the Communist Party.

6. Are beneficial, not harmful, to international socialist unity and the unity of the peace-loving people of the world.

Of these six criteria, the most important are the two about the socialist path and the leadership of the Party. These criteria are put forward in order to foster, and not hinder, the free discussion of various questions among the people. Those who do not approve of these criteria can still state their own views and argue their cases. When the majority of the people have clear-cut criteria to go by, criticism and self-criticism can be conducted along proper lines, and these criteria can be applied to people's words and actions to determine whether they are fragrant flowers or poisonous weeds. These are political criteria. Naturally, to judge the validity of scientific theories or assess the aesthetic value of works of art, other relevant criteria are needed. But these six political criteria are applicable to all activities in the arts or sciences. In a socialist country like ours, can there possibly be any useful scientific or artistic activity which runs counter to these political criteria?

The People's Commune (1958)

In 1949, the Communist leadership knew that land redistribution was only the first phase of achieving economic stability. In fact, poverty was the real problem and they needed a long-range program to increase agricultural and industrial production. It was imperative to establish centralized control over taxation, production, and inflation. In 1953, China launched

"The People's Commune" is from *People's Communes in China* (Beijing: Foreign Languages Press, 1958), pp. 61–65.

its first five-year plan based on "advanced Soviet practice." The Chinese created a vast bureaucracy that was organized vertically from top to bottom to regulate all aspects of the economy. Although this policy conflicted with revolutionary rhetoric to broaden the participation of the people in making decisions for the state, Mao deferred to the needs of consolidation and the fears that economic chaos would threaten the revolution. The Chinese also experimented with a variety of approaches, including mutual-aid teams and other cooperative ventures. By 1957, however, the lagging agricultural output threatened industrial projects. Mao was aware of China's backwardness. He declared: "We say that our country has such an enormous population, it has such a vast territory, abundant resources, four thousand years of history and culture. . . . We have bragged so much about this, yet we cannot compare with a country like Belgium."

In 1958, China broke sharply with the Soviet-inspired elements of the first five-year economic plan with a new slogan: "Catch up with the Great Britain in Fifteen Years." To do this, Mao called for a "Great Leap Forward," a visionary program that promoted technological innovation and emphasized decentralized local planning and mass participation. It was also a means of affirming China's national dignity and of strengthening ideology: "In making revolution," Mao insisted, "one must strike while the iron is hot—one revolution must follow another, the revolution must constantly advance."

This emphasis on "perpetual revolution" linked the peasants and workers to a confident vision of the future. They were all marching together toward inevitable social progress and economic prosperity. At the heart of this leap of faith was the new "commune system" of 1958. The system was hailed by its innovators as bold and progressive. Here was the true worker's paradise, an advanced economic and social system that was the quintessential expression of Marxist principle: "From each according to his ability, to each according to his needs." But the theory was divorced from harsh reality. Both agricultural and industrial production fell sharply after 1958 and by the early 1960s had reached disastrous proportions. Even Mao realized the depth of his mistake. In January 1962, he proposed to overtake the most advanced capitalist countries, not in fifteen years, as he had said in 1958, but by fifty or one hundred years.

The first document describes the organizational plans for the "People's Commune" in 1958. It is followed by Mao's speech of July 1959 at the Lushan Conference and his own assessment of the price paid for the "Great Leap Forward."

Article 1: The people's commune is a basic unit of society in which the working people unite of their own free will under the leadership of the Communist Party and the People's Government. Its task is to manage all industrial and agricultural production, trade, cultural and education work and political affairs within its own sphere.

Article 2: The intent and purpose of the people's commune is to consolidate the socialist system and energetically create the conditions for the gradual transition to the communist system.

To this end, we must exert our utmost effort, and press ahead consistently to achieve greater, faster, better, and more economical results in developing industry, agriculture and cultural and educational work, to carry through the technical and cultural revolution, to gradually reduce the differences between town and country and between mental and manual labor.

As the social product becomes abundant and the people have high political consciousness, so will the transition from the principle of "from each according to his ability, to each according to his work" to the principle of "from each according to his ability, to each according to his needs" be gradually effected. . . .

Article 4: When the agricultural producers' cooperatives merge into the people's commune, they must, regardless of excess or deficiency, turn over all their collectively owned property to the commune in the communist spirit of wide-scale coordination. . . .

Article 5: In changing over to the commune, the members of the cooperative must turn over to the common ownership of the commune all privately owned plots of farmland and house sites and other means of production such as livestock, tree holdings, etc., on the basis that common ownership of the means of production is essentially in effect. However, the cooperative members may keep a small number of domestic animals and fowls as private property. . . .

Article 6: To ensure a continuously expanding agricultural output, the commune must continue to build irrigation works, apply more manure, improve the soil, use good strains of seed over large areas, breed draught animals, prevent and control ploughing and careful cultivation. . . .

The commune must develop industry as rapidly as possible. The first things to be done are to set up mines, iron and steel plants and factories for manufacturing ball-bearings, farm tools, fertilizer, and building materials and for processing farm produce, repairing machinery, building hydroelectric power projects, installations for utilizing methane, and other enterprises.

Article 9: The commune should, step by step, train its members to be cultured working people with professional skill and all-around qualifications. The commune should institute a system of universal, compulsory education combined closely with labor. Primary schools and spare-time continuation schools should be set up on a wide scale so that by degrees all school-age children may attend school and all young people and the middle-aged

may reach the educational level of senior primary school. . . . Conditions permitting, colleges or universities will be set up to meet the requirements of the commune. The working hours of the members may be duly reduced and their time for study increased when production reaches a higher level. . . .

Article 10: A system of citizen soldiery shall operate throughout the commune. The age groups of young and middle-aged men as well as demobilized servicemen, should be organized into militia units that will undertake regular military training and fulfill tasks assigned by the state. The militiamen will be paid the usual wages when they undergo training and carry out tasks. . . .

Article 13: The commune shall institute a system of centralized leadership, with management organs at various levels, in order to operate a responsibility system in production. In accordance with the principle of facilitating production and leadership the commune shall organize its members into a number of production contingents which will divide up into a number of production brigades. . . . The production brigade is a basic unit for organizing labor. While ensuring the fulfilment of the general plan of the commune, the production contingent has, to a limited degree, the discretion of organizing production, undertaking capital construction, handling production expenses and distributing awards. . . .

The commune shall operate a wage system when it acquires stability of income and adequate funds and when the members are able voluntarily to consolidate labor discipline. Wages of members will be fixed by the masses through discussion, taking into account the intensity and complexity of the work, physical condition, technique and attitude towards work. Wages will be paid monthly. Technical allowances may be paid to those who have special skill. One month's wage may differ from another. In months when the commune gets more income and the members need more, the members may get more pay; in other months they may get less. In case of a serious natural calamity the commune may, according to circumstances, pay less to its members. . . .

With the introduction of the wage system, deduction from his wage should be effected when a member absents himself from work. Every member may have two days' paid leave each month and women members three days' paid leave. Women members may have a months' maternity leave during which time they will be paid half wages. Anyone injured in the course of work will be paid full wages during the period of treatment and recovery. Subsidies will be given out of the public welfare funds to anyone whose livelihood is affected by disability due to chronic disease. . . .

Article 21: The commune shall encourage cultural, recreational and sports activities among the masses so as to bring forward communist people healthy in body and in mind. Steps should be taken to ensure that each commune has its own library, theater, and film projector team; that each production contingent has its own club room, amateur theatrical troupe, choir and sports team; and that each production brigade has a small reading room and radio sets.

"We Have Paid a High Price" (1959)
MAO ZEDONG

Now that you have said so much, let me say something will you? I have taken sleeping-pills three times, but I can't get to sleep. . . .

We are under combined attack from within and outside the Party. . . . Gentlemen, all of you have ears, so listen. They all say we are in a mess. Even if it is hard to listen to it, we must listen to it and welcome it. As soon as you think in this way, it ceases to be unpleasant to the ears. Why should we let the others talk? The reason is that

China will not sink down, the sky will not fall. We have done some good things and our backbones are strong. The majority of comrades need to strengthen their backbones. Why are they not all strong? Just because for a time there were too few vegetables, no soap, a lack of balance in the economy and tension in the market, everyone became tense. . . .

People say that we have become isolated from the masses, yet the masses still support us. I think this was temporary, just for two or three months before and after the Spring Festival. I think that we and the masses are now combining well. There is a bit of petit-bourgeois fanaticism, but not all that much. . . . It's a matter of wanting to do a bit more, it's nothing else but wanting to do a bit more, a bit faster. . . . We must not pour cold water on this kind of broad mass movement. We can only use persuasion and say to them: Comrades, your hearts are in the right place. When tasks are difficult, don't be impatient. Do things step-by-step. . . .

Could the people's communes collapse? Up to now not one has collapsed. We were prepared for the collapse of half of them, and if seventy percent collapsed there would still be thirty percent left. If they must collapse, let them. If they are not well run, they are sure to collapse. The Communist Party aims to run things well, to run the communes well, to run all enterprises well, to run agriculture, industry, commerce, communications, transport, and culture and education well. . . .

Coal and iron cannot walk by themselves; they need vehicles to transport them. This I did not foresee. I and the Premier did not concern ourselves with this point. You could say that we were ignorant of it. I ought not to make excuses, but I shall too, because I am not the head of the Planning Commission. Before August of last year my main energies were concentrated on revolution. I am a complete outsider when it comes to economic construction, and I understand nothing about industrial planning. . . .

About the people's communes, I said that they were a system of collective ownership. I said that for the transition to be completed from collective ownership to communist ownership by the whole people two five-year plans was too short a period. Maybe it will take twenty-five-year plans!

If you want to talk about haste, Marx also made many mistakes. Every day he hoped that a European revolution would arrive, but it did not arrive. There were many ups and downs and it had still not arrived when he died. It only arrived in Lenin's time. . . .

Have we failed this time? All the comrades present say there have been gains; it is not a complete failure. Is it mainly a failure? No, it's only a partial failure. We have paid a high price. A lot of "communist wind" has blown past, but the people of the whole country have learned a lesson. The chaos caused was on a grand scale and I take responsibility. Comrades, you must all analyze your own responsibility. If you have to shit, shit! If you have to fart, fart! You will feel much better for it.

The Great Proletarian Cultural Revolution (1966–1969)

Power corrupts the few, while weakness corrupts the many.

—*Eric Hoffer*

You are making the socialist revolution, and yet don't know where the bourgeoisie is. It is right in the Communist Party—those in power taking the capitalist road.

—*Mao Zedong*

Are you afraid? You people! If you don't make revolution, the revolution will be directed against you!

—*Mao Zedong*

By the first months of 1959, the Communist Party's reports of the Promethean achievements of the Great Leap Forward were tempered by increasingly serious warnings of dislocation and lack of production on the farms and in the factories. The central error of the Great Leap Forward, according to Mao, was the "Communist wind" of adventurism that sought to impose full communism in the collective farms by eliminating private plots of land and privately tended animals before individuals were ready to make the transition to a full communal existence. In essence, an economic system that condemned workers to a meager existence and undercut their dreams for personal achievement was doomed.

The Great Leap Forward, indeed, turned out to be a great failure, a tragic retrograde step that had resulted in widespread famine and a breakdown in morale among the people who had formed the core of the revolution. Mao, however, continued to believe that China's peasants would eventually invest their hopes in the communes, but the Communist Party in its desire to catch up with the West could not omit stages of development that would demoralize the masses and lead to economic disaster. By restructuring the communes, investing in oil production, and moderating the transition to full communism, China began to produce steady, though not spectacular gains after 1962.

But within this improving economy lurked the specter of success that might eventually produce a new bourgeoisie of competent, ambitious farmers and industrial managers, and consequently, an unequal distribution of wealth to undermine the Marxist vision. Mao, ever concerned with ideological purity and the necessity of perpetual revolution, advocated vigilance against "budding capitalists," who deviated from the socialist norm. Following the disastrous Great Leap Forward, Mao had accumulated many critics at the highest levels of the Communist Party, among them "heroes" of the revolution like Liu Shaoqi, Zhou Enlai, and Deng Xiaoping, who had been at Mao's side during the Long March in 1934. It is difficult to assess the extent to which Mao's authority was challenged, but in June and July 1966, the stage was set for confrontation. At the Eleventh Plenum of the Communist Party in August, Mao unveiled a new campaign to reinforce revolutionary values and reassert his leadership— the Great Proletarian Cultural Revolution.

This movement sought to reinforce the cultural and ideological premises of the revolution and to target Mao's opposition within the Party who, as he put it, "are in authority and are taking the capitalist road." These deviates were to be isolated, attacked, removed from power, silenced, and "reeducated" if necessary. This purge of the Party elite and any other dissidents was to be led by the Red Guards—revolutionary youth, indoctrinated and fanatical, who spread Mao's ideology throughout the nation. Many of the "Long March Heroes," who occupied key positions in the administration and army, were subjected to public humiliation. The Red Guards descended on the cities in a wave of destruction. They broke into stores, homes, and schools, intimidating and assaulting residents in a campaign of terror. Thousands were killed in the ensuing destruction before Mao released them to the countryside. The Chairman then called upon the army to restore order. Finally, Revolutionary Committees were established to regulate local institutions, from factories and communes, to schools, hospitals, and municipal government. Mao's position as the Great Helmsman of the revolution was resecured.

New Guidelines for the Revolution (August 1966)

The following document is an official statement in August 1966 from the Central Committee of the Communist Party that provided the basic guidelines for the Cultural Revolution. The last selection is an interview done in 1984 of a woman known only as Ting, one of the original members of the Red Guards from Qinghua University Middle School. In 1984, she recalled her role in the inspiration and destruction of the Cultural Revolution.

A New Stage in the Socialist Revolution

The Great Proletarian Cultural Revolution now unfolding is a great revolution that touches people to their very souls and constitutes a new stage in the development of the socialist revolution in our country, a deeper and more extensive stage. . . .

Although the bourgeoisie has been overthrown, it is still trying to use the old ideas, culture, customs, and habits of the exploiting classes to corrupt the masses, capture their minds and endeavor to stage a comeback. The proletariat must do just the opposite: it must meet head-on every challenge of the bourgeoisie in the ideological field and use the new ideas, culture, customs, and habits of the proletariat to change the mental outlook of the whole of society. At present, our objective is to struggle against and crush those persons in authority who are taking the capitalist road, to criticize and repudiate the reactionary bourgeois academic "authorities" and the ideology of education, literature, art, and all other parts of the superstructure that do not corre-

"New Guidelines for the Revolution" is from "Decision of the Central Committee of the Chinese Communist Party Concerning the Great Proletarian Cultural Revolution" in *Peking Review* (August 12, 1966), pp. 6–11.

At a mass demonstration staged during China's Cultural Revolution, youthful Red Guards recite from the "Little Red Book," a collection of the thoughts of Chairman Mao Zedong. The Red Guards served as Mao's vanguard of "perpetual revolution" and took an active role in the intimidation and humiliation of intellectuals and other "poisonous weeds" from 1966 to 1969 *(Camera Press, London).*

spond to the socialist economic base, so as to facilitate the consolidation and development of the socialist system.

The Main Current and the Zigzags

The masses of the workers, peasants, soldiers, revolutionary intellectuals, and revolutionary cadres form the main force in this Great Cultural Revolution. Large numbers of revolutionary young people, previously unknown, have become courageous and daring pathbreakers.

They are vigorous in action and intelligent. Through the media of big character posters and great debates, they argue things out, expose and criticize thoroughly, and launch resolute attacks on the open and hidden representatives of the bourgeoisie. . . .

Since the Cultural Revolution is a revolution, it inevitably meets with resistance. This resistance comes chiefly from those in authority who have wormed their way into the party and are taking the capitalist road. It also comes from the old force of habit in society. At present, this resistance is still fairly strong and stubborn. However, the Great Proletarian Cultural Revolution is, after all, an irresistible general trend. There is abundant evidence that such resistance will crumble fast once the masses become fully aroused. . . .

Educational Reform

In the Great Proletarian Cultural Revolution, the most important task is to transform the old educational system and the old principles and methods of teaching.

In this Great Cultural Revolution, the phenomenon of our schools being dominated by bourgeois intellectuals must be completely changed.

In every kind of school we must apply thoroughly the policy advanced by Comrade Mao Zedong, of education serving proletarian politics and education being combined with productive labor, so as to enable those receiving an education to develop morally, intellectually, and physically and to become laborers with socialist consciousness and culture.

The period of schooling should be shortened. Courses should be fewer and better. The teaching material should be thoroughly transformed, in some cases beginning with simplifying complicated material. While their main task is to study, students should also learn other things. That is to say, in addition to their studies they should also learn industrial work, farming, and military affairs, and take part in the struggles of the Cultural Revolution as they occur in order to criticize the bourgeoisie.

Mao Zedong's Thought Is the Guide for Action in the Great Proletarian Cultural Revolution

In the Great Proletarian Cultural Revolution, it is imperative to hold aloft the great red banner of Mao Zedong's thought and put proletarian politics in common. The movement of the creative study and application of Chairman Mao Zedong's works should be carried forward among the masses of the workers, peasants and soldiers, the cadres and the intellectuals, and Mao Zedong's thought should be taken as the guide for action in the Cultural Revolution. . . .

Party committees at all levels must abide by the directions given by Chairman Mao over the years, namely that they should thoroughly apply the mass line of "from the masses and to the masses" and that they should be pupils before they become teachers. They should try to avoid being one-sided or narrow. They should foster materialist dialectics and oppose metaphysics and scholasticism.

The Disillusionment of the Red Guards: "An Absolute and Total Mistake" (1984)

TING

Repudiating the Cultural Revolution means more than calling it names: what we really need, especially people like me who were involved, is cool analysis and critique.

I was fifteen and in the third year of junior middle school when the Cultural Revolution

started. . . . We didn't have much idea at the time of what it was all about. . . . We were too busy preparing for the exams for entrance to senior middle school in May. But the whole thing hit the fan before classes finished.

My overall assessment of the Cultural Revolution is that it was an absolute and total mistake, not a question of some rights and some wrongs, this or that percentage. The Cultural Revolution was initiated by conflict at the Central Committee level; it was the product of parties outside the Party and factionalism within the Party. In the later stages they lost control, but what about the beginning? Actually it was meant to be the way it was, to overthrow a bunch of people. . . . It was also letting out years of pent-up bitterness. Chairman Mao was afraid of a "capitalist restoration," afraid of "the masses going through misery a second time," afraid of "bad people usurping the leadership at every level." He meant well, and it led to disaster.

Later, when he wanted to put the brakes on, it was too late, the careerists were running it. Our generation were educated for years into "infinite love, infinite faith, infinite worship," and—what's that other infinite?—"infinite loyalty." So, ablaze with righteous indignation, we were off. From our leftist standpoint, everything appeared to be to the right, and once the Red Guards had been formed, I joined in beating up landlords, beating up rightists and raiding people's homes. I thought that was the only way to be revolutionary—"revolution isn't a dinner party"—but what was it in fact? It was beating up bad people with leather belts. Then we went out on the streets, smashing road signs and neon lights; we thought they represented non-socialist ideology, so we replaced them with a red ocean of slogans and quotations. It was physically and mentally much more exhausting than school. . . .

You could probably take the period from June '66 to January '67 as the formative stage for the Red Guards. . . . The way I see it, the spontaneous "Works of Chairman Mao Study Groups," which burst on to the scene from classrooms and dormitories, were the embryonic Red Guards. . . .

Just as in earlier Chinese revolutions, it was the young intellectuals who were the vanguard and the bridges in the Cultural Revolution, and the Red Guards were originally supposed to be an organization for middle-school and university students. The sad thing is that this "revolution" wasn't like earlier ones; the Red Guards had only just started up and were still in their formative stage when their mission was completed.

We were given the task of establishing revolutionary ties, going out from Beijing to light the fires of revolution elsewhere. . . . The first time I went out "establishing ties," I was in deadly earnest about revolution. I went to Shanghai and Hangzhou to encourage others to rebel against "the reactionary line of the bourgeoisie," telling people that the Cultural Revolution was meant not only to overthrow Liu Shaoqi and Deng Xiaoping, but also to eliminate capitalist roaders in the political establishment at every level. When we came back to Beijing, we got into fights with Red Guards from the north-east.

After that we formed Pickets. They were like Red Guard military police. But they weren't much use since the Red Guards never had any unified organization. These Pickets were pretty heavy; they beat a lot of people to death. If they hadn't, they would have had no authority. . . .

After the dispute with the north-eastern Red Guards, I went off "establishing ties" again, this time for fun. I went to Guangxi, Guangdong, Zhejiang, Fujian and Hunan. For the first time I felt confused and disappointed. In Hunan, I saw a mother and her seven- or eight-year-old daughter begging. The little girl was singing for money. She had [Mao's] *Little Red Book* held tightly to her chest and she was singing revolutionary songs. The mother was next to her saying, "Please take pity on us, comrades-in-arms of the proletarian revolutionary faction." I didn't make that up. If you write about the strange and tragic events of the Cultural Revolution, the last thing you need to do is make things up.

I didn't dare, I couldn't, question the Cultural Revolution itself, but I did start questioning the factional fighting. While I was out "establishing revolutionary ties," I saw how the Red Guards had smashed things up everywhere. . . . The rifts that occurred between rival organizations weren't only to protect some people or overthrow others, they were because everyone had a different notion of what an ideal model was. They all claimed they were supporting the Central Committee and the Central Committee Cultural Revolution Group, but underneath they were all jockeying for power. Armed fighting was in the cards. . . . The armed fighting was almost like a religious war: it was fighting for beliefs. It was to establish who were the true disciples.

I broke away during the fighting. It went against my beliefs, I couldn't go on feeling so confused any more. Carrying the Cultural Revolution through to the end wasn't just the supreme command, it was also my own personal ideal. But I just couldn't keep up with things. I couldn't even understand what was going on before my very eyes. It had all gone way beyond ideals; if you'd been me you would have been confused and uncertain too. . . .

In '68, we were called on to go down to the countryside, although actually it was compulsory. Some of my classmates sincerely intended to be "integrated" and "to carry out revolution for a lifetime," but I was already turned off. Marx had enough ideas all right. It all depends on which ones you're using at the time. That's how I saw it then. Some of them really got into it, but I didn't. . . . I didn't get married until 1977 and I have a daughter now. It's hard to say, but when she grows up, maybe she'll get caught up in something confusing too—I mean, if there's something really big going on.

I'm a grade-four worker now. I lead a quiet life: nothing special, but it's okay. I read in my spare time, and I don't give a damn about night school or the television university. If they don't promote you because you haven't a graduation certificate, then so be it. You can only be yourself.

Political Culture and Art

MAO ZEDONG

In his battle against real or imagined enemies during the Cultural Revolution, Mao's greatest asset was his complete domination of the media. The Selected Works of Mao Zedong were required reading throughout the nation, and the more condensed Quotations from Chairman Mao Zedong, the distinctive "Little Red Book," was carried for easy reference while loudspeakers burned Mao's thoughts into the hearts and minds of the Chinese. Mao's image dominated public parks and squares, schools and hospitals, and even occupied a sacred position in private homes, once revered for ancestral worship. Movies and dramas eulogized the Chairman and "revolutionary" ballets served to indoctrinate the masses with the singular theme of proletarian victory over capitalist swine. Even children's books glorified the unity of cuddly forest animals in their pursuit and destruction of the capitalist wolf. Ironically, the atheistic Communist state had created a new god to revere and follow without question. Mao's image as the Great Helmsman had blended into myth. No one in Chinese history, perhaps not even the Buddha himself, had been worshiped by so many people with such fervent devotion.

The first short selections are from the Quotations from Chairman Mao Zedong and testify to the importance of literature and the arts in the amplification of Communist ideology. The second document is from the Party's official journal, the Peking Review, on the benefits of "reeducation" through physical labor. Mao distrusted intellectuals as threats to his regime and used the Cultural Revolution to humiliate and eliminate those who refused to be "ideologically young again."

In the world today, all culture, all literature and art belong to definite classes and are geared to definite political lines. There is in fact no such thing as art for art's sake, art that stands above classes, art that is detached from or independent of politics. Proletarian literature and art are part of the whole proletarian revolutionary cause; they are, as Lenin said, cogs and wheels in the whole revolutionary machine.

****

Revolutionary culture is a powerful revolutionary weapon for the broad masses of the people. It prepares that ground ideologically before the revolution comes and is an important, indeed essential, fighting front in the general revolutionary front during the revolution.

****

All our literature and art are for the masses of the people, and in the first place for the workers, peasants and soldiers; they are created for the workers, peasants and soldiers, and for their use.

****

Our purpose is to ensure that literature and art fit well into the whole revolutionary machine as a component part, that they operate as powerful weapons for uniting and educating the people and for attacking and destroying the enemy, and that they help the people fight the enemy with one heart and one mind.

****

What we demand is the unity of politics and art, the unity of content and form, the unity of revolutionary political content and the highest

"Political Culture and Art" is from Mao Zedong, *Quotations from Chairman Mao Zedong* (Beijing: Foreign Languages Press, 1966), pp. 299–303.

possible perfection of artistic form. Works of art which lack artistic quality have no force, however progressive they are politically. Therefore, we oppose both works of art with a wrong political viewpoint and the tendency towards the "poster and slogan style," which is correct in political viewpoint, but lacking in artistic power. On questions of literature and art, we must carry on a struggle on two fronts.

Reeducation:
The "Great Furnace"
of the Cultural Revolution

The intellectuals at Zonghua and Beijing Universities, having been tempered with experience during the Great Proletarian Cultural Revolution, made an urgent request that they be allowed to change their world outlook from that of the bourgeois to that of the proletarians. They made this request because, during the process of thought-struggle, they had been able to look at their own past objectively, reached their own conclusions as to what course they must follow, and learned to apply Mao Zedong's thought to the conduct of their daily lives. Last year, under the leadership of the revolutionary elements among the faculty and staff, namely, the proletarians who were employed by these two universities and the propaganda teams of

"Reeducation" is from "The Reform of Intellectuals by Physical Labor" in the *Peking Review* (May 9, 1970).

the People's Liberation Army, these intellectuals, full of revolutionary enthusiasm, went to the village of Liuzhou, on the shore of Lake Poyang, Kiangsi province, where they established an experimental farm from scratch, amid great hardship and enormous difficulties. Following Chairman Mao's May Seventh Directive, they have been marching steadily forward.

During the past year, as a result of having been reeducated by peasants, workers, and soldiers through physical labor, the intellectuals from these two universities, under the correct ideological leadership of the Chinese Communist Party, have undergone a great transformation, not only spiritually, but physically as well. Tempered and strengthened in the great furnace of Cultural Revolution, they have found mud on their bodies and calluses on their hands and knees. Spiritually, however, they have never been so clean. They have cleansed themselves of the revisionist poison and washed away all the bourgeois dirt; for the rest of their lives they are going to march, shoulder by shoulder, with peasants, workers, and soldiers on the same revolutionary road. In this experimental farm, white-haired professors work side by side with young intellectuals and revolutionary cadres; jointly and with great enthusiasm, they are following the directives of our leader Chairman Mao, as they are determined to be ideologically young again, regardless of their physical age. They fully realize that only by traveling on Chairman Mao's May Seventh road, can they expect to be ideologically reformed.

China and the World (1960–1976)

When the Communists seized power in 1949, there was immediate pressure to consolidate their gains from the threat of counterrevolution. Therefore, Mao and his advisors focused on ideological persuasion and the construction of an economic framework that would stabilize agricultural and industrial production. This domestic consolidation proved to be a rocky road at best. China also had to establish its authority in the international arena. Mao's challenge was to achieve legitimacy in the world community while maintaining China's political independence and adherence to the Marxist vision of world revolution.

In walking this tightrope, Mao cleaved to a few primary principles. First, the People's Republic of China neither had perpetual friends nor enemies; self-interest would always remain its closest ally and China would make friends or create enemies as necessity dictated, regardless of ideological considerations. Domestically, China demanded ideological purity, but expediency ruled its foreign relations. Second, in all of its policy decisions, China strove to have only one primary enemy at a time. In 1949, China either had to stay neutral or lean toward the support of the United States or the Soviet Union. Since Mao needed an enemy to struggle against in order to establish the ideological and political unity necessary for domestic consolidation, neutrality was out of the question; instead, he chose an alliance with the Soviet Union during the 1950s and identified the United States as the "running dog" capitalist threat. This is not to say that Mao ever trusted Joseph Stalin or his successors, but he needed financial support and technical advice that the Soviets, as Communists, were willing to offer. China proved its worth to the Soviets by sustaining over a million casualties during the Korean War from 1950 to 1953. Soviet aid in return was essential to Mao's early consolidation efforts.

By 1959, however, the Soviets were demanding more than China was willing to give. The Soviet leader, Nikita Khrushchev, wanted to construct submarine bases and airfields on the Chinese coast to monitor U.S. ships in the region. Mao, who had fought against the foreign domination of China since his youth, refused to concede. There were other issues as well. The long, four thousand mile border between China and the Soviet Union deepened the distrust and fear of military confrontation, as did the Russian presence in Mongolia. The Sino-Soviet split in 1959 left China rather isolated diplomatically with two powerful enemies and no influential allies. The withdrawal of Soviet aid also intensified the economic disaster of the Great Leap Forward.

But China, because of its enormous population, natural resources, and acquisition of nuclear weapons by the mid-1960s, saw itself as a player. The following two selections emphasize China's growing importance on the international stage. The first is an official criticism of China from the Communist Party of the Soviet Union (CPSU) in 1963. The second is a tract against U.S. imperialism during the Vietnam War in 1965. Its author, Lin Biao, a brilliant commander of Communist forces against the Nationalist Chinese in 1949, became Mao's primary spokesman and designated heir during the Cultural Revolution. Fearing that he and others within the high command were about to be purged, Lin Biao apparently plotted a coup that was discovered. He reportedly died, perhaps too conveniently, when his airplane crashed in 1971 as he fled to Mongolia.

The Soviet Message to China: "No One Has the Right to Play with the Destinies of Millions of People" (1963)

The Communist Party of the Soviet Union (CPSU) Central Committee considers it its duty

"The Soviet Message to China" is from "Open Letter of the Central Committee of the Communist Party of the Soviet Union to All Party Organizations, to All Communists of the Soviet Union," (July 14, 1963) contained in *The Polemic on the General Line of the International Communist Movement* (Beijing: Foreign Languages Press, 1965), pp. 540–546.

to tell the party and the people with all frankness that on the question of war and peace the Communist Party of China (CPC) leadership has cardinal, fundamental differences with us, with the world communist movement. Their essence lies in the diametrically opposite approach to such vital problems as the possibility of averting a world thermonuclear war, peaceful co-existence with different social systems, the interconnection between the struggle for peace and the development of the world revolutionary movement.

Our party, in the decisions of the 20th and 22nd Congresses . . . set before Communists, as a vital and urgent task, the struggle for peace, the struggle to avert a world thermonuclear catastrophe. We realistically appraise the balance of strength in the world and draw the conclusion that, though the nature of imperialism has not changed, and the danger of war breaking out has not been averted, in modern conditions the forces of peace, of which the mighty community of socialist states is the main bulwark, can, through their joint efforts, prevent a new world war. . . .

But what is the position of the CPC leadership? What can be the meaning of the propositions they advocate, viz., that we cannot put an end to war as long as imperialism exists; that peaceful co-existence is an illusion, and is not the general principle of the socialist countries; that the struggle for peace hinders revolutionary struggle?

These propositions mean that the Chinese comrades are acting contrary to the general policy of the world communist movement on questions of war and peace. They do not believe in the possibility of preventing a new world war, they underestimate the forces of peace and socialism and overestimate the forces of imperialism, and virtually ignore the mobilization of the masses to fight the war danger. . . .

To follow the road proposed by the Chinese comrades would be to alienate the masses from the Communist parties, which have won the sympathies of the peoples by their persevering and courageous struggle for peace. . . . The Chinese comrades obviously underestimate all the danger a thermonuclear war would present. "The atomic bomb is a paper tiger," it "is not at all terrible," they contend. The main thing, they say, is to put an end to imperialism as quickly as possible, but how and with what losses this will be achieved appears to be a secondary question. Secondary for whom, it may be asked—for the hundreds of millions of people who would be doomed to death if a thermonuclear war were unleashed? For the countries that would be wiped off the face of the earth in the very first hours of such a war?

No one, not even a big state, has the right to play with the destinies of millions of people.

Those who do not want to exert themselves to banish world war from the life of the peoples, to avert mass annihilation and destruction of the values of human civilization, deserve condemnation. . . .

The fact cannot pass unnoticed, in this connection, that instead of the class, internationalist approach expressed in the slogan "Workers of all countries, unite!" the Chinese comrades stubbornly propagate a slogan deprived of all class meaning: "The wind from the East prevails over the wind from the West." No party that has the interests of the people at heart can fail to appreciate its responsibility in the struggle to avert another world war and ensure peaceful co-existence of states with different social systems.

The People's War against U.S. Imperialism (1965)

LIN BIAO

Since World War II, U.S. imperialism has stepped into the shoes of German, Japanese, and Italian fascism and has been trying to build a great American empire by dominating and enslaving the whole world. It is actively fostering Japanese and West German militarism as its chief accomplices in unleashing a world war. Like a vicious wolf, it is bullying and enslaving various peoples, plundering their wealth, encroaching upon their countries' sovereignty and interfering in their internal affairs. It is the most rabid aggressor in human history and the most ferocious common enemy of the people of the world. Every people or country in the world that wants revolution, independence and peace cannot but direct the spearhead of its struggle against U.S. imperialism. . . .

U.S. imperialism is stronger, but also more vulnerable, than any imperialism of the past. It sets itself against the people of the whole world,

"The People's War Against U.S. Imperialism" is from Lin Biao, *Long Live the Victory of People's War!* (Beijing: Foreign Languages Press, 1966), pp. 53–58.

including the people of the United States. Its human, military, material and financial resources are far from sufficient for the realization of its ambition of dominating the whole world. U.S. imperialism has further weakened itself by occupying so many places in the world, overreaching itself, stretching its fingers wide and dispersing its strength, with its rear so far away and its supply lines so long. As comrade Mao Zedong has said, "Whenever it commits aggression, it puts a new noose around its neck. It is besieged ring upon ring by the people of the whole world."

U.S. imperialism relies solely on its nuclear weapons to intimidate people. But these weapons cannot save U.S. imperialism from its doom. Nuclear weapons cannot be used lightly. U.S. imperialism has been condemned by the people of the whole world for its towering crime of dropping two atom bombs on Japan. If it uses nuclear weapons again, it will become isolated in the extreme. Moreover, the U.S. monopoly of nuclear weapons has long been broken; U.S. imperialism has these weapons, but others have them too. If it threatens other countries with nuclear weapons, U.S. imperialism will expose its own country to the same threat. For this reason, it will meet with strong opposition not only from the people elsewhere, but also inevitably from the people in its own country. Even if U.S. imperialism brazenly used nuclear weapons, it cannot conquer the people, who are indomitable. . . .

Vietnam is the most convincing current example of a victim of aggression defeating U.S. imperialism by a people's war. The United States had made South Vietnam a testing ground for the suppression of people's war. It has carried on this experiment for many years, and everybody can now see that the U.S. aggressors are unable to find a way of coping with people's war. On the other hand, the Vietnamese people have brought the power of people's war into full play in their struggle against the U.S. aggressors. The U.S. aggressors are in danger of being swamped in the people's war in Vietnam. They are expanding the war in an attempt to save themselves from defeat. But the more they expand the war, the greater will be the chain reaction. The more they escalate the war, the heavier will be their fall and the more disastrous their defeat. The people in other parts of the world will see still more clearly that U.S. imperialism can be defeated, and that what the Vietnamese people can do, they can do too. . . . U.S. imperialism, like a mad bull dashing from place to place, will finally be burned to ashes in the blazing fires of the people's wars it has provoked by its own actions.

Theme: Propaganda

The Historical Intersection

BEIJING: 1966

"The False Doctrine of Non-Violence":
Support for the American Negro

GUO MORUO

In August 1963, when the American civil rights movement was gathering momentum under the leadership of Reverend Martin Luther King Jr., Mao Zedong issued a statement supporting the "American Negroes in their just struggle against racial discrimination by U.S. imperialism." Mao hoped to position China as the leader "of all oppressed people and nations of the world." Three years later in 1966, Mao's statement was commemorated in a staged Beijing rally of 10,000 Chinese "supporters" of Black liberation in the United States. Guo Moruo, Chairman of the China Peace Committee, addressed the rally in the Great Hall of the People and reiterated Mao's official vision on race relations.

Keep in Mind . . .

- Note how the thoughts of Mao Zedong are officially regarded as the "Gospel of Freedom" and that he has assumed the title "Champion of Liberation."

This day three years ago, our most esteemed and beloved leader Chairman Mao Zedong issued the "Statement Supporting the American Negroes in Their Just Struggle Against Racial Discrimination by U.S. Imperialism." Today, when the just struggle of the American Negro people against racial discrimination is witnessing a new upsurge, it is of great practical significance that we people of all circles in Beijing are gathered here at this rally in solemn commemoration of

(contd)

the third anniversary of the publication of Chairman Mao's statement. First of all, let us pay high tribute and express firm support and heartfelt regards to our American Negro brothers who are waging a heroic struggle against racial discrimination in defiance of U.S. imperialism's barbarous suppression and persecution.

Chairman Mao's brilliant analysis of the national struggle, which, when one gets right down to the bottom of it, is a matter of class struggle, has opened the way for the rise of the black freedom struggle to a new stage, for the beginning of a new anti-imperialist mass movement in America. . . . The American Negro people are abandoning the false doctrine of "non-violence" for slogans of "meet counter-revolutionary violence with revolutionary violence." They are increasingly identifying their fight with the Champion of Liberation, Mao Zedong and the Gospel of Freedom, Mao Zedong's thought.

Chairman Mao's statement has a far-reaching political influence and is of great historic significance. It is a great call to fight against the racial discrimination practiced by U.S. imperialism. It has immensely inspired the fighting will of the American Negroes. The entire Chinese people firmly support it! The American people and particularly the American Negroes, warmly respond to it! The people of Asia, Africa, and Latin America actively support it! And the people of the whole world fervently praise it! They say that Chairman Mao's statement has brought hope to the American Negroes so that, like a torch, it has lighted up the hearts of the Negro people! They say Chairman Mao's statement has pointed to the correct path and direction for the American Negroes and all oppressed nations and oppressed peoples to win independence, freedom, and liberation!

Consider This:

- Why did Mao position himself as the international "Champion of Liberation"? Why was he concerned with the freedom struggle for Black Americans?

- Mao argued that the "American Negro people are abandoning the false doctrine of 'non-violence' for slogans of 'meet counter-revolutionary violence with revolutionary violence.'" Why did Mao advocate violence for a movement that, under the leadership of Martin Luther King Jr., was devoted to nonviolent action? Was this wishful thinking or was Mao hoping to rally violent splinter groups such as the Black Panthers? How important was revolutionary leadership in the international arena to the continuing transformation of the Chinese revolution?

"The False Doctrine of Non-Violence" is from Guo Moruo, *Peking Review* (August 12, 1966).

The Transformation of Tibet (1975)

During the summer of 1970, as American B-52 bombers pounded targets in Vietnam, the People's Daily *in China referred to President Richard Nixon as "god of the plague," the bringer of death and disease. But by 1972, secret negotiations had permitted Nixon to go to China and sign the Shanghai Communique in which both China and the United States agreed to the principle of peaceful coexistence, scientific and cultural exchanges, and a normalization of relations. Nixon was rechristened "a progressive element among the capitalist class" and became a popular American in the People's Republic of China in spite of the domestic humiliation of the Watergate scandal. This reopening of China to the West underscored China's expedient flexibility. The Soviet threat could be countered by an overture to the United States, in spite of ideological differences and the Vietnam war that was still being fought.*

China, however, tried to hide its own imperialism from foreign eyes. The following selection from the People's Daily *in 1975 recounts the Chinese "liberation" of Tibet in 1950. This, in fact, was a brutal takeover of this mountain region as thousands were killed and the Tibetan spiritual leader, the Dalai Lama, was forced from his homeland. Since then, the Communists have settled thousands of Chinese in the area, hoping to alter the language and culture of the region as part of its political consolidation. Note how the Communist account emphasizes "peaceful liberation" and the joy Tibetans felt to "wake up and look forward to the future with hope."*

In 1950, the People's Liberation Army marched into Tibet and succeeded in driving out the imperialist forces of aggression, thus returning Tibet to the fatherland of all nationalities. After the peaceful liberation of Tibet, the Chinese Communist Party began to construct highways, factories, hospitals, and schools, in addition to the granting of loans for agricultural development. . . . They posed no burden whatsoever on the Tibetan people.

Having witnessed and experienced the sharp contrast between the old and the new Tibet, the one million serfs and slaves began to wake up and look forward to the future with hope. . . . They said, "We have had the opportunity of doing our own comparison for eight years, and we cannot tolerate for another day the feudal system of serfs and slaves. Only Chairman Mao and the Chinese Communist Party can save us." Facing this demand, the reactionary ruling class of Tibet was frightened and full of hatred; it was

more than determined to maintain its reactionary rule. In 1959, despite the patient education by chairman Mao and the CCP that had lasted for eight years, the reactionary local government of Tibet, headed by the Dalai Lama, violated and betrayed the agreement of peaceful liberation between the central and the local government. In liaison with the imperialists and the reactionaries abroad, they launched an armed rebellion.

The People's Liberation Army, under the leadership of Chairman Mao and the CCP's Central Committee and in conjunction with the one million serfs and slaves of Tibet, quickly crushed the rebellion. This was soon followed by the democratic reform conducted in a grand and enthusiastic manner. The democratic reform was a great struggle, and also a decisive battle, waged by the serfs and slaves against their slave-owning and reactionary slave owners, burned all the contracts, and divided the land among themselves. For the first time in history they enjoyed the fruit of their own labor. The feudal system of serfs and slaves, inhuman and cruel, was buried for good, and the former serfs and slaves, having freed themselves, became the new masters of Tibet. Following the democratic reform, Tibet became a region of self-government.

The history of the Tibetan revolution teaches us that we must eliminate the system of exploitation before we can solve the nationality problem. If, after the democratic reform, the system of private properties persisted, sooner or later a new exploiting class would emerge among the former serfs and slaves who had overthrown the old system of exploitation. In other words, there is no way of solving the nationality problem in a true and fundamental sense other than traveling on the socialist road.

Therefore, subsequent to the democratic reform, the CCP conducted a massive campaign of socialist education among the Tibetans.... In 1965, some areas in Tibet, where conditions were ready, began to experiment with the organization of people's communes. Soon the superiority of this new system was recognized by all

the Tibetans. During the Great Proletarian Cultural Revolution and during the campaign of criticizing Lin Biao and Confucius, the revolutionary line of Chairman Mao made an even deeper impression in Tibet, and the freed peasants and herdsmen also increasingly raised their class consciousness. Socialist reform, like a new tide, spread across Tibet, and in a period of only ten years the whole region was communized. Finally, the Tibetan people, like their brethren elsewhere in China, began to march on the broad road of socialism....

For the twenty-five years since its liberation, the history of Tibet has been a history of intensive class struggle. It is a history of how one million serfs and slaves, under the leadership of the CCP, have successfully overthrown a feudal, slave society and its reactionary rulers, who were supported by imperialists and reactionaries abroad. It is a history of how, step by step, Tibet marched toward socialism and became more and more revolutionized in the process. It is a living testimony to the validity of one of chairman Mao's sayings, namely, "The nationality struggle, fundamentally speaking, is nothing but a class struggle."

The Word from Taiwan:
"We Shall Continue to Oppose Communism" (1975)

The Shanghai Communique signed by China and the United States in 1972 acknowledged that "all Chinese on either side of the Taiwan Strait maintain there is but one China, and that Taiwan is a part of China." In spite of its verbal support of the Nationalist Chinese in Taiwan, the United States has not challenged this stance and has consistently reaffirmed a peaceful settlement of the Taiwan question by the Chinese themselves. At the turn of the twenty-first century, this position remains unchanged, though one can see in this 1975 statement from Taiwanese Premier Jiang Jinguo that Taiwan's decision to remain independent has been constant and determined.

Many things have happened during the past thirty years [since 1945]; needless to say, we have encountered many, many difficulties. But

the basic policy of this nation [Taiwan] has not changed and will not change, regardless of the change of circumstances. What is this basic

"The Word from Taiwan" is from *Central Daily News*, Taiwan (March 28, 1975) in Dun J. Li, *Modern China* (New York: Charles Scribner's Sons, 1978), pp. 455–458. Copyright © 1978 by Dun J. Li. Reprinted by permission.

policy? It is our continuous, relentless struggle against communism and the restoration of China to the free Chinese. With determination and hard work, we shall succeed.

Having waged a long struggle against the Communists, we shall maintain our basic convictions as follows:

The first conviction is that the Republic of China [Taiwan] and the 700 million people on the mainland share the same destiny and are indeed inseparable. We in Taiwan ... believe that the Republic of China will not only continue to exist but also, in some future time, recover the mainland. The second conviction is that as long as the mainland is not recovered and as long as those Communists still exist on the mainland, our task remains unfinished. The recovery of the mainland and the extermination of the Communists are a responsibility that we cannot and will not shirk. The third conviction is that Taiwan ... will not only exist, permanently and forever, but also serve as a base for the recovery of the mainland. The fourth conviction is that success depends upon our own effort, not somebody else's. The key to victory is the constancy of our unshakable determination, no matter how circumstances change. Those who dare struggle will succeed; those who are willing to make sacrifices will win victory. It is we who have to solve all the problems. . . .

We want peace, pray for peace, and do everything we can for peace. But we are not going to sacrifice our basic principle for peace. Some people ask, "Why do you not negotiate with the Communists and see what happens"? My reply is that while other countries have not had the painful experience of negotiating with these bandits, we have had too much of it to try again. We will not contact them, and certainly we will not negotiate with them. To me the Communist strategy has always been and still is: "If you are not afraid of me, I shall be afraid of you." We have learned about this Communist strategy through painful experience.

The Communist bandits recently convened a National People's Congress and proclaimed a new constitution. . . . Now let us look at this so-called constitution. It is not a constitution, really; it is a blueprint for worldwide rebellion. It says specifically that Marxism-Leninism is its highest ideological command. What is this Marxism-Leninism? It contains at least three major points. It advocates class struggle and the abolition of private properties. It promotes world revolution and the elimination of individual states. It authorizes dictatorship and the deprivation of individual freedom. If you do not believe me, ask any Communist who will tell you that I am right. If communism succeeds in China, China itself will cease to exist.

Face to face with our enemy on the mainland, we have to know his evil scheme. His evil scheme consists of infiltration, "divide and conquer," and sudden military attack. Knowing his scheme, we have taken strong measures to make sure that his agents cannot infiltrate our ranks and thus "divide and conquer." We must be united; we must strengthen our security. If the enemy ever dares to launch a military attack, he will be defeated.

Today what we need most is psychological reconstruction—the strengthening of our determination. The fact that people are satisfied with things as they are is not enough; we have to strengthen our will in order to shoulder our responsibilities. We shall never cast doubt on the righteous stand we have taken, and we shall never despair.

CHINA'S SECOND REVOLUTION (1976–2000)

The certainties of one age are the problems of the next.

—*R. H. Tawney*

The sterile radical is basically conservative. He is afraid to let go of the ideas and beliefs he picked up in his youth lest his life be seen as empty and wasted.

—*Eric Hoffer*

Loyalty to a petrified opinion never yet broke a chain or freed a human soul.

—*Mark Twain*

You can't learn too soon that the most useful thing about a principle is that it can always be sacrificed to expediency.

—*Somerset Maugham*

The New China

The watchword of any revolution is power. And in the Chinese revolution, we have seen how Mao Zedong, through some of the most trying circumstances, established the foundation of his authority in the trust of the masses and tenaciously advanced his Communist cause first against the Nationalists, then against countercurrents in his own party. With his victory in 1949, he unified mainland China for the first time since 1911 and subsequently improved the living standard for peasants, instilling in their minds a dignity and greater purpose in their sacrifice for utopia.

Although Mao raised the position of China to that of a major world power, he never succeeded in attaining that Marxist ideal of communal equality that has always been illusory. In fact, disasters like the Great Leap Forward and the Cultural Revolution proved that Mao was no miracle worker. Because of these missteps, millions of Chinese died of famine or were reeducated or purged in order to consolidate Mao's power. As long as he was alive, no matter how many competitors were arrayed against him, Mao constituted the majority. Some historians have argued that had Mao died in 1956 rather than in 1976, China might have been better served. Instead, the future of China was invested for those twenty years in the quest for a Marxist illusion, rather than in a cold calculation of reality. As Mao became increasingly feeble after 1973, the man became a myth, and the mortal a god in the pantheon of Chinese heroes.

Within the space of nine months in 1976, three of China's preeminent leaders passed away: Zhou Enlai in January, Marshal Zhu De in July, and Mao himself on September 9. Expressions of grief were palpable, but while the country mourned each death, there was another revolution afoot. The radicals, subsequently termed the "Gang of Four," were led by Mao's own wife, Jiang Qing. They had been plotting their own seizure of power during Mao's increasing debility and preceded confidently in the first months of 1976. Mao had made known his choice for premier in Hua Guofeng, who represented a compromise between the ideological radicals and the moderate pragmatists. Hua moved behind the scenes to expand his base of support among the moderates and the military leadership. Within one month after

Mao's death, the Gang of Four had been arrested and placed in solitary confinement. On October 24, an enormous rally in Tiananmen Square celebrated the new leadership of Hua Guofeng.

The opening selections demonstrate the difference in perspective that was elicited after Mao's death. The first is from the official Communist newspaper, the People's Daily; *it is followed by a Taiwanese Nationalist editorial from the* Central Daily News. *Finally, in 1978, Hua discussed the "New Look" of China and his vision for the future.*

The Death of Mao: Two Views (1976)

The *People's Daily*: "Champion of All the Oppressed People"

At 12.10 A.M., September 9, 1976, Comrade Mao Zedong, the esteemed and beloved leader of our party, armed forces and nation, the great teacher of international proletarianism, and the champion of all the oppressed people and nations, passed away, despite all meticulous medical care after he had fallen ill.

Chairman Mao Zedong was the founder and long-time leader of the Chinese Communist Party, the Chinese People's Liberation Army, and the People's Republic of China. He led our party, our armed forces, and all the Chinese people in waging a successful struggle against imperialism, feudalism, and bureaucratic capitalism. This great victory has not only liberated the Chinese people and improved the situation in the East, but also raised new hope for all the oppressed people and nations in the world that wish to be free.

The death of Chairman Mao Zedong is a great loss to our party, our armed forces, and all the people in the nation. It is a great loss to the international proletariat and all the revolutionary people in the world. The grief over his death is bound to be immensely felt by all the revolutionaries both at home and abroad.

The Central Committee of the Chinese Communist Party calls upon the Party, the armed

forces, and all the people in the nation to transform their grief into strength. It calls upon them to carry on the cause left behind by our great leader and teacher Chairman Mao Zedong. Eternal glory to our great leader and teacher Chairman Mao Zedong.

The *Central Daily News*: "A Brutal Treacherous Psychopath"

Mao Zedong, the bandit chieftain of the Chinese Communist Party, finally died early yesterday morning. A brutal, treacherous psychopath, Mao Zedong embodied the worst in human nature. His career was a career of unmitigated betrayal of his nation and immeasurable harm to his own people. His crime was a crystallization of all the crimes committed by the most wanton traitors and bandits. He was in fact the number one tyrant in history, unprecedented both here and abroad.

After the Chinese Communist Party's illegal occupation of the Chinese mainland in 1949, Mao Zedong, by invoking the excuse of a "proletarian dictatorship," conducted a systematic campaign of murdering the Chinese people. According to evidence provided by a variety of sources, the people whom he had murdered numbered no less than 60 million between 1949 and 1976. During his whole career that covered a period of fifty years, the number of people who had died because of his rebellion and violence came close to 100 million. No one, not even Hitler and Stalin, could match him in bloodthirstiness.

To maintain his tyrannical rule, he did not hesitate to declare as his enemy the five-thousand-year-old civilization of China and all the noble values that formed part of this civiliza-

"The Death of Mao" is respectively from the *People's Daily* (September 10, 1976) and *Central Daily News* (September 10, 1976) in Dun J. Li, *Modern China* (New York: Charles Scribner's Sons, 1978), pp. 347–348. Copyright © 1978 by Dun J. Li. Reprinted by permission.

tion. He opposed heavenly reason, as well as the humanity of man. What was objectively right became wrong to him, and vice versa. . . . Now that he is dead, it is most natural that all of us should rejoice.

The death of Mao Zedong marks not only the end of the darkest period in Chinese history, but also the beginning of a new era when the Republic of China will rise to restore the mainland and to save all the people therein.

The New Look of Modern China (1978)

HUA GUOFENG

In order to make China a modern, powerful socialist country by the end of the century, we must work and fight hard in the political, economic, cultural, military, and diplomatic spheres, but in the final analysis what is of decisive importance is the rapid development of our socialist economy. . . .

By the end of the century, the output per unit of major agricultural products is expected to reach or surpass advanced world level and the output of major industrial products to approach, equal, or outstrip that of the most developed capitalist countries. . . . As our social productive forces become highly developed, our socialist relations of production will be further improved and perfected, the dictatorship of the proletariat in our country consolidated, our national defense strengthened, and our people's material well-being and cultural life substantially enriched. By then, China will have a new look and stand unshakably in the East as a modern, powerful socialist country. . . .

As the economy becomes modernized, the leading role of industry, and especially that of the basic industries, becomes more and more prominent. . . . The state plans to build or

"The New Look of Modern China" is from "Unite and Strive to Build a Modern Powerful Socialist Country." Report to the Fifth National People's Congress, February 26, 1978 in *Peking Review* (March 10, 1978).

complete 120 large-scale projects, including ten iron and steel complexes, nine nonferrous metal complexes, eight coal mines, ten oil and gas fields, thirty power stations, six new trunk railways, and five key harbors. The completion of these projects added to the existing industrial foundation will provide China with fourteen fairly strong and fairly rationally located industrial bases. This will be decisive in changing the backward state of our basic industries. . . .

By 1985, in the main, eight-year schooling should be made universal in the rural areas and ten-year schooling in the cities. We should fully tap the potential of existing institutions of higher learning, actively expand the student enrollment, rapidly set up new colleges and institutes, and endeavor to run the vocational and technical schools and colleges well. . . .

The repertoires of the performing arts should be enlarged to enrich the people's cultural life. Literature and art must keep to the orientation of serving the workers, peasants, and soldiers. . . . There should be variety in the subject matter of our literature and art. Modern revolutionary themes should be dominant, particularly those reflecting the three great revolutionary movements of the socialist period, but attention should also be given to historical and other themes. Revolutionary realism combined with revolutionary romanticism should be encouraged in artistic creation. . . .

Planned control of population growth is conducive to the planned development of the national economy and to the health of mother and child. It also benefits the people where production, work, and study are concerned. We must continue to give it serious attention and strive to lower the annual rate of growth of China's population to less than one percent within three years. . . .

Giving full scope to the abilities of intellectuals is important for speeding up the development of our science, education, and other cultural undertakings and building a modern, powerful socialist country. The overwhelming majority of the intellectuals are devoted to the party and socialism and support Chairman Mao's revolutionary line.... The "Gang of Four" maligned the intellectuals as "the stinking ninth category." We must make a clean sweep of the Gang's pernicious influence of uniting with, educating, and remolding the intellectuals. We must give due weight to their work, improve their working conditions, turn their specializations to account, and commend their achievements. At the same time, we must warmly help and encourage them to make a real effort to remold their world outlook in the three great revolutionary movements, persevere in identifying themselves with the workers and peasants and advance along the "red and expert" road. ...

"Let a hundred flowers blossom, let a hundred schools of thought contend" is the basic policy for making China's socialist science and culture flourish. Its essence is to adopt a policy of "opening wide" within the ranks of the people while adhering to the six political criteria so as to constantly expand the positions of Marxism in matters of ideology and to promote science and culture. ...

To accelerate the development of socialist science and culture, we must stick to the policy of "making the past serve the present": and "making foreign things serve China." We must conscientiously study the advanced science and technology of all countries and turn them to our account. We must be critical in assimilating things from our ancient culture and from the culture of foreign countries, taking the essence, discarding the dross, and weeding through the old to bring forth the new, in order to promote a socialist culture which is national in its traits and rich in the characteristics of the age.

Problems on the Ideological Front (1981)

DENG XIAOPING

During the memorial service for Zhou Enlai on January 15, 1976, Deng Xiaoping, one of the original "Long Marchers" in 1934, stepped forward to give a stirring eulogy. A small man at four feet eleven inches, whose shoes did not touch the floor when he sat, Deng nevertheless possessed a dominant personality and was known for his tenacity, frankness, and organizational ability. During a 1957 visit to Moscow, Mao took the Soviet General Secretary Nikita Khrushchev aside and pointed out the diminutive Deng: "See that little man there? He's highly intelligent and has a great future ahead of him."

Mao would have known. They met in 1926 when Deng had returned from studying Marxist-Leninist thought in Paris and Moscow. The two became fast friends, were denounced together by pro-Russian elements in the Chinese Communist Party during the early 1930s for advocating guerrilla tactics, and suffered through the Long March together in 1934. After the revolution of 1949, Deng rose quickly in the pecking order and became one of Mao's Deputy Premiers and General Secretary of the Communist Party.

But the friendship became strained during the Great Leap Forward as Deng cautioned Mao and tried to sidetrack his policies by adopting a pragmatic stance designed to end the famine. In light of the failure of the Great Leap Forward, Mao never forgave Deng's disloyalty. In 1962, Mao attacked Deng, screaming, "You have put the screws to me for a very long time. ... Now, for once, I am going to put a scare into you!" Mao's revenge came during the Great Proletarian Cultural Revolution in 1966. By August 1967, Deng was placed on trial

"Problems on the Ideological Front" is from *Selected Works of Deng Xiaoping, 1975–1982* (Beijing: Foreign Language Press, 1983), pp. 367–371.

by the Red Guards and denounced as a "traitor," a "fascist," and a "capitalist roader." His younger brother was driven to suicide by the Red Guards and his son was hounded by radicals until he fell—or was pushed—from a fourth-storey window. His spine was fractured, leaving him a paraplegic. For his own part, Deng and his wife were kept under house arrest for two years until they were sent south to be reeducated and worked in a tractor factory.

By 1973, as the Red Guards were nearly a spent force and Mao was ailing, Deng was recalled to stabilize the country and control the military. After Mao's death, Deng worked behind the scenes to build his base of support especially among the moderates, who feared the excesses of the Gang of Four. Deng's third comeback began in 1977 and by 1979, he had outmaneuvered Hua and eased the Maoists out of power. Intent on remaking China, Deng forged ahead in the face of unmanageable foreign debt, growing inflation, and political agitation from dissidents and students that was fast approaching unacceptable levels. Deng responded to these challenges by emphasizing the principles of political stability, openness, and economic development.

In 1979, Deng revived a policy first enunciated by Zhou Enlai in 1974 called the "Four Modernizations." Its goals were the development of agriculture, industry, national defense, and science and technology. Deng also proposed an open-door policy with the West by sending Chinese students abroad and establishing special economic zones or cities that would serve as sites for direct foreign investment and adoption of foreign technology. However, Deng insisted that this and all future policies and public attitudes had to be in conformity with the "Four Cardinal Principles": to keep to the socialist road, to uphold the people's democratic dictatorship, to accept leadership by the Communist Party, and to adhere to Marxism-Leninism and Mao Zedong Thought.

Under Deng's pragmatic policies, millions of peasants were allowed to cultivate private plots of land, sell surplus crops, and invest in village factories. Within a few years, the peasantry and workers in the cities were able to build houses and fill them with televisions, refrigerators, and washing machines. In the following selections, Deng explained the ideological and economic transition to a new society. There would be limits on speech and ideas that might threaten revolutionary values and lead to "bourgeois liberalization or anarchy," but China would enter the modern world.

A short time ago, I told Comrade Hu Yaobang [Chairman of the Chinese Communist Party] that I wanted to talk with the propaganda departments about problems on the ideological front, especially those in literature and art. The Party's leadership on this front—including literature and art—has achieved noteworthy success. This should be affirmed. But certain tendencies towards a crude approach and over-simplification cannot be ignored or denied. However, a more important problem at present, I think, is laxity and weakness and a fear of criticizing wrong trends. As soon as you criticize something, you are accused of brandishing a big stick. It is very

hard nowadays for us to carry out criticism, let alone self-criticism. . . .

Prior to June, 1981, the General Political Department of the Chinese People's Liberation Army raised the question of criticizing the film script *Unrequited Love*. I have been taken aback by some other things I've read recently too. A young poet made an irresponsible speech at Beijing Normal University. Some students commented that although the Party organization had done a lot of ideological and political work among the students, that speech blew it all away. The university Party committee was aware of this matter but took no measures. . . . Some persons are not on the right track ideologically. They make statements contrary to Party principles and are neither honest nor upright. Yet there are other people who admire them and eagerly publish their articles. This is quite wrong. Some Party members don't act in accordance with Party spirit, but persist in factionalism. They must not be allowed to influence others, let alone to become leaders. . . . This is an abnormal phenomenon and we must work seriously to eradicate it. Its social and historical background can be traced mainly to the ten-year turmoil of the "Cultural Revolution;" it is also connected with corrosion by bourgeois ideology from abroad. . . . After that young poet delivered his speech at Beijing Normal University, some students said that if we allowed things to go on this way, our country would be ruined. He took a position opposite to ours. I have seen the movie *Sun and Man*, which follows the script of *Unrequited Love*. Whatever the author's motives, the movie gives the impression that the Communist Party and the socialist system are bad. It vilifies the latter to such an extent that one wonders what has happened to the author's Party spirit. Some say the movie achieves a fairly high artistic standard, but that only makes it all the more harmful. . . .

Some young people are discontented with certain social conditions today. There is nothing strange about this and it is nothing to be afraid of. But we must guide such young people or they may go astray. It is good that many young writers have emerged in recent years. They have written a number of fine works. But we must admit that among them—and among some middle-aged writers too—there are also bad tendencies that have an adverse influence on some young readers, listeners and viewers. Our veteran writers, who stick to the socialist position, have the responsibility to unite and give proper guidance to the new generation. Otherwise, it won't be able to advance along the right path. . . . In a word, we must uphold Party leadership and the socialist system. They must be improved, but that doesn't mean we can have bourgeois liberalization or anarchy. Just imagine what sort of

influence *Sun and Man* would have if shown to the public. Someone has said that not loving socialism isn't equivalent to not loving one's motherland. Is the motherland something abstract? If you don't love socialist New China led by the Communist Party, what motherland do you love? . . . If the Party can't discipline its own members, how can it lead the masses? We insist on the policy of "letting a hundred flowers bloom, a hundred schools of thought contend," and on handling contradictions among the people correctly. . . . The main way to correctly handle contradictions among the people is to start

The official portrait of Deng Xiaoping, who eventually succeeded Mao as the inspiration for the "New China" from 1978 until his death in 1997 *(Foreign Language Press, Beijing).*

from the desire for unity, carry out criticism and self-criticism and arrive at a new unity. The policy of "letting a hundred flowers bloom, a hundred schools of though contend" cannot be separated from the practice of criticism and self-criticism, for it is important in bringing along the next generation. . . . Why is it that *Unrequited Love* and the speech by the young poet have the support of some people? That is something our comrades on the ideological front should ponder. . . .

Some people are raising a banner in support of Comrade Hua Guofeng [former Party Chairman], while actually trying to overthrow you know who. Watch out! This shows how complicated the present struggle is, and how necessary it is to sharpen our vigilance.

The Four Cardinal Principles and the New Economy: "Veteran Comrades Must Emancipate Their Minds" (1984)

DENG XIAOPING

A closed-door policy prevents any country from developing. We suffered from insolation, and so did our forefathers. China remained isolated for more than three hundred years from the middle of the Ming Dynasty to the Opium War. . . . As a consequence, the country declined into poverty and ignorance. After the founding of the People's Republic [1949], during the period of the First Five-Year Plan [1953–1958], we did open our country to the outside world, but only to the Soviet Union and the East European countries. And later we closed our doors. It's true that we achieved certain things, but on the whole we did not make striking progress. Of course, that was due to many domestic and international factors, including the mistakes we

made ourselves. But the lessons of the past tell us that if we don't open to the outside, we can't make much headway.

Opening will not hurt us. Some of our comrades are always worried that if we open up, undesirable things may be brought into China. Above all, they worry that the country might go capitalist. I'm afraid some of our veteran comrades do harbor such misgivings. Since they have been devoted to socialism and communism all their lives, they are horrified by the sudden appearance of capitalism. They can't stand it. But it will have no effect on socialism. No effect. Of course, some negative elements will come in, and we must be aware of that. But it will not be difficult for us to overcome them; we'll find ways of doing so. If we isolate ourselves and close our doors again, it will be absolutely impossible for us to approach the level of the developed countries in fifty years. Even if our country remains as open as it is now, . . . no new bourgeoisie will emerge, because the basic means of production will still be state-owned or collectively owned—in other words, publicly owned. And if the country prospers and the people's material and cultural life continually improves, what's wrong with that? However much we open up in the next sixteen years until the end of the century, the publicly owned sector of the economy will remain predominant. Even in a joint venture with foreigners, half is socialist-owned. And we shall take more than half of the earnings of the joint ventures. So, don't be afraid. It is the country and the people who will benefit most from them, not the capitalists. . . .

Our experience has enabled us to answer new questions that have arisen under new circumstance. We have been stressing the need to uphold the Four Cardinal Principles: to keep to the socialist road and to uphold the people's democratic dictatorship, leadership by the Communist Party, and Marxism-Leninism and Mao Zedong Thought. That is truly upholding socialism. Otherwise, we would merely be "preferring socialist weeds to capitalist seedlings" as the Gang of Four wanted. Veteran comrades must emancipate their minds.

"The Four Cardinal Principles and the New Economy" is from *Selected Works of Deng Xiaoping, 1982–1992* (Beijing: Foreign Language Press, 1994), pp. 96–98.

Tiananmen Square and Beyond

By 1984, economic reform had been embraced by the urban Chinese so enthusiastically that Old Guard Marxists decried the "spiritual pollution" found in Shanghai's discotheques. By the late 1980s, however, the economic liberalization had spilled into the political arena. Workers and students alike yearned for the political and personal freedom that was tacitly promised by the flexibility and success of economic reform. They demonstrated regularly in such public forums as Beijing's Tiananmen Square. But Deng was no democrat and in his mind certainly no capitalist. "I have explained time and again that our modernization program is a socialist one," he insisted in 1986. And Deng could be as reactionary as the conservatives who criticized his economic reforms. His goal was always pragmatic: Make China strong and competitive with the West, but not democratic.

During the 1980s, China's sudden wealth had engendered a pandemic of corruption, crime, and soaring inflation. By spring of 1989, the hardliners were restive, worried about the occupation of Tiananmen Square by thousands of students, who were peacefully constructing a statue termed the "Goddess of Democracy," demanding open dialogue and political freedom. Early in the morning of June 4, 1989, Deng finally ordered the People's Liberation Army to storm the Square with tanks and an array of weapons, killing and wounding thousands of unarmed protesters in the melee. The arrest, trial, and sentencing of dissidents followed as China retreated into the darkness of repression. Deng's extraordinary balancing act between economic liberalization and political repression fell apart and his reputation as a sage of reform seemed damaged beyond repair. In the following excerpts, first from a speech a month before the Tiananmen Square incident, then following the catastrophe, Deng offered his political testament and an assessment of the damage.

Deng's Political Testament: "Establish a Third Generation of Leaders Worthy of the Name" (May, 1989)

DENG XIAOPING

In the history of the Communist Party, Mao Zedong, Liu Shaoqi, Zhou Enlai, and Zhu De formed the first generation of truly mature leadership. During the early period of their tenure of office, that generation of leaders was good, but during the later period the "cultural revolution" caused a catastrophe. Hua Guofeng was merely an interim leader and cannot be

"Deng's Political Testament" is from *Selected Works of Deng Xiaoping, 1982–1992* (Beijing: Foreign Language Press, 1994), pp. 290–293.

counted as representing a generation. He had no ideas of his own. We are of the second generation, now being replaced by the third.

We should establish a new third generation of leaders worthy of the name. These leaders should win the trust of the people and the Party members. People don't necessarily have to be pleased with each and every member of the leading group, but they have to be pleased with the group as a collective. By and large, the people are pleased with our collective, because we have carried out the policies of reform and opening to the outside world, put forward the line of concentrating on modernization and brought about tangible results. The third generation of leaders must likewise win the trust of the people and bring about tangible results. We must never close our doors. China can never go back to the days of isolationism. Isolationism brought about disasters like the "cultural revolution." Under those circumstances it was impossible to develop the economy, improve the people's lives, or increase the strength of the country. The world today is progressing by leaps and bounds; changes are taking place from one day to the next, especially in the realm of science and technology. It will be difficult for us to catch up.

The third generation of leaders of the Central Committee should win the trust of the people, so that they will rally around it. We should unswervingly combat bourgeois liberalization and adhere to the Four Cardinal Principles. On this point I have never made any concessions. Can China reject the Four Cardinal Principles? Can we refrain from exercising the people's democratic dictatorship? It is a matter of fundamental importance that we uphold the people's democratic dictatorship, Marxism, socialism, and leadership of the Communist Party. . . .

When it comes to promoting people, you must abandon all your personal prejudices and try to find those who the people believe will keep to the line of reform. When selecting the right person for the right job, you should forget about settling old scores and choose from among people who were once against you. . . . When considering candidates, you should be more broad-minded. This too is a kind of reform, an ideological reform, an emancipation of the mind. . . .

Once the new leading group has established its prestige, I am resolved to withdraw and not interfere in your affairs. I hope all the members will unite closely around Comrade Jiang Zemin. So long as the collective leadership is united and adheres to the policies of reform and opening to the outside world, fundamental changes will take place in China even if our country develops only at a measured pace for dozens of years. The core leader will play the key role. I should like you to convey my words to every comrade who will be working in the new leading bodies. This can be considered my political testament.

"The Sea of Blood" (June 9, 1989)
DENG XIAOPING

Comrades, you have been having a hard time! First of all, I should like to express my deep grief over the officers and men of the People's Liberation Army, the People's Armed Police Force and the Public Security Police who have died heroically in this struggle. . . . Let us stand in silent tribute to these martyrs!

This disturbance would have occurred sooner or later. It was determined by both the international environment and the domestic environment. It was bound to occur, whether one wished it or not; the only question was the time and the scale. That it has occurred now is to our advantage, especially because we have a large number of veteran comrades who are still in good health. They have experienced many disturbances and understand the possible consequences of different ways of dealing with them. They support the resolute action taken against the rebellion. Some comrades do not understand that action for the time being, but they will come to understand it and support the decision of the central authorities.

The *People's Daily* described the disturbance as turmoil. The word "turmoil" is quite appropriate. It is this word that some people object to are trying to change. But facts show that the assessment is accurate. It was also inevitable that the turmoil should grow into a counterrevolutionary rebellion. . . .

The major difficulty in handling it has been that we have never encountered a situation in which a handful of bad people were mingled with so many young students and crowds of onlookers. Since for the moment we were not able to distinguish between innocent and guilty, we could scarcely take the actions that should have been taken. . . . Some comrades did not understand its nature and thought that

"The Sea of Blood" is from *Selected Works of Deng Xiaoping, 1982–1992* (Beijing: Foreign Language Press, 1994), pp. 294–296; 299.

we were only dealing with the masses. In fact, we were dealing not only with people who merely could not distinguish between right and wrong, but also with a number of rebels and many persons who were the dregs of society. They tried to subvert our state and our Party. This is the crux of the matter. If we don't understand this fundamental question, we shall not be clear about the nature of the incident. I believe that if we work at it, we can win the support of the overwhelming majority of Party comrades, for our assessment of the nature of the incident and for the measures we have taken to cope with it.

The nature of the incident should have been obvious from the very beginning. The handful of bad people had two basic slogans: overthrow the Communist Party and demolish the socialist system. Their goal was to establish a bourgeois republic, an out-and-out vassal of the West. Naturally, we accepted the people's demand for a fight against corruption. We even had to accept as well-intentioned the so-called anti-corruption slogans of the bad individuals. Of course, these slogans were simply pretexts, and their ultimate aim was to overthrow the Communist Party and demolish the socialist system. . . .

I therefore want to express our thanks to the officers and men for their handling of the rebellion. The losses were grievous, but they helped win the people's sympathy and support and enabled those who had confused right and wrong to change their point of view. From those losses everyone could tell what the soldiers were like, whether they turned Tiananmen into a sea of blood and who it was that shed blood. Once these questions had been clarified, we were able to gain the initiative. . . .

The outbreak of this incident has given us much food for thought, impelling us to reflect soberly on the past and the future. Perhaps this bad thing will enable us to progress more steadily and even faster than before in carrying out the policies of reform and opening to the outside world, to correct our errors more quickly and give better play to our advantages. . . .

What should we do from now on? In my opinion, we should continue to follow unswervingly the basic line, principles and policies we have

Alone and unarmed, a man confronts a column of tanks before the suppression of dissidents during the demonstrations at Tiananmen Square in June, 1989. This study in courage is symbolic of the contest of wills between advocates of personal freedom and the guardians of power in the Communist state *(Associated Press).*

formulated. There should be no changes in them except for a few changes of wording, if necessary.... We should carefully review our experience, keep on doing what is right, correct what is wrong and make up for what is inadequate. In short, we should learn from the past and look to the future.

"The Chinese People Will Not Be Intimidated"

DENG XIAOPING

In the wake of the Tiananmen Square massacre, a disastrous event broadcast throughout the world, Deng demonstrated the kind of tenacity that had been his salvation through three political purges and subsequent rebirths. His commitment as a pragmatist was to economic liberalization and even bloodshed could not change his mind. The following was Deng's defensive reaction to world criticism after Tiananmen Square. Frail at age 85, Deng continued to promote Special Economic Zones and market enclaves that would serve as centers of entrepreneurial activity that would encourage the return of foreign investment in the New China.

I'm still in good health and have a clear mind and a good memory. Recently, I've begun to swim for an hour every day in the sea at Beidaihe. I don't like indoor pools; I like to swim in an expansive natural setting where you have a greater sense of freedom. I'm trying to get used to complete retirement....

I have never believed in exaggerating the role of any one individual, because that is dangerous and makes it difficult for others to carry on. The stability of a country and a party cannot be based merely on the prestige of one or two persons. That tends to create problems. It is therefore necessary to have a retirement system. I'm already eighty-five years old. For many years I have been proposing to retire. But every time I do, I meet opposition from everybody.... My chief desire is to retire completely, but if there are disturbances, I shall have to intervene.

I am certain that after the recent disturbances, China will be even more successful in its drive for modernization and in reform and opening to the outside world. They have taught us an important lesson. For many years, some of our comrades, immersing themselves in specific affairs, have shown no concern for political developments and attached no importance to ideological work. They have not been sufficiently vigilant against corruption and have not taken effective measures to stop it. The fact that corruption has become such a serious problem is related to their failure to resolutely combat bourgeois liberalization. The disturbances have sobered us all. If we had not upheld the Four Cardinal Principles, the turmoil would not have been brought to an end. And if it had not been, how could we be talking here today? If the rebels had had their way, there would have been a civil war. If there had been a civil war, we would have won, but how many people would have died, and how many more would have grieved for them? That would have been a real disaster! We had no choice but to act decisively. In our efforts to quell the rebellion, our principle was to do everything possible not to harm the people, especially students. But if we had not taken resolute measures to put it down, the consequences would have been unimaginable.

The West really wants unrest in China. It wants turmoil not only in China, but also in the Soviet Union and Eastern Europe. The United States and some other Western countries are

"The Chinese People Will Not Be Intimidated" is from *Selected Works of Deng Xiaoping, 1982–1992* (Beijing: Foreign Language Press, 1994), pp. 314–317.

trying to bring about a peaceful evolution towards capitalism in socialist countries. The United States coined an expression: waging a world war without gun smoke. We should be on guard against this. Capitalists want to defeat socialists in the long run. In the past they used weapons, atomic bombs and hydrogen bombs, but they were opposed by the peoples of the world. So now they are trying peaceful evolution. The affairs of other countries are not our business, but we have to look after our own. China will get nowhere if it does not build and uphold socialism. Without leadership by the Communist Party, without socialism and without the policies of reform and opening to the outside world, the country would be doomed. Without them, how could China have gotten where it is today? . . .

I'd like to focus on two points. First, the current situation in China is stable. . . . Second, the Chinese people will not be intimidated. We don't want to offend other people; we only want to do solid work in our own country. Anyone who tries to interfere in our affairs and bully us will fail. . . .

Our gravest failure has been in education—we did not provide enough education to young people, including students. We can curb inflation quickly, but it is much more difficult to make up for lost education. For many of those who participated in the demonstrations and hunger strikes, it will take years, not just a couple of months, of education to change their thinking. The ones who took part in the hunger strikes and demonstration and signed petitions are not to blame. Only those leaders who had ulterior motives and violated the law will be prosecuted. As for the students, including the hunger strikers, we shall deal with them chiefly through education. I hope you will tell the people you know, including those who demonstrated and signed petitions abroad, that China takes no offence at their actions and that they need not be worried.

"Let Us Work Together for a Better World" (1995)

JIANG ZEMIN

On February 19, 1997, Deng passed away. He left a mixed legacy. Deng had prepared China to break the bonds of isolation and engage the world with a new economic model and a commitment to reform. But he left a powerful authoritarian system in place, still bent on the suppression of political dissent with little regard for human rights. Titular control of the state passed to Jiang Zemin (b. 1926), who had been groomed for succession after Tiananmen Square and had been proclaimed by Deng as the "core" of the third generation of revolutionary leadership. Jiang has maintained Deng's policies by encouraging free-market economic reforms while pressing the Communist Party's monopoly on political power. Under Jiang's leadership, Hong Kong was incorporated into the Chinese nation on July 1, 1997 without incident. But overpopulation, environmental pollution, cultural transformation, and the maintenance of social stability through the equal distribution of the blessings of economic prosperity will provide the challenges for China's future. The following speech was delivered at the Special Commemorative Meeting on the Occasion of the Fiftieth Anniversary of the United Nations on October 24, 1995. In it, Jiang characterized the United States as an aggressive power, bent on world hegemony. He proposed that the principles of autonomy, mutual respect for territorial integrity, and peaceful coexistence should guide international relations.

"Let Us Work Together for a Better World" is from *The UN at 50: Statements by World Leaders* (New York: United Nations, 1996)

In a few years time, mankind will bid farewell to the twentieth century, a century full of vicissitudes, and enter the twenty-first century, a century full of promises. At this turn of millennia, it is of great significance for national leaders to come here from all corners of the world to commemorate the fiftieth anniversary of the United Nations—the widely representative and authoritative inter-governmental organization of our age. We can use this opportunity to take a look at the past and into the future from a higher plane and share our views on how to turn the lofty missions of the United Nations into reality. . . .

What the changing and evolving world tells us is that people make history and push it forward. As history surges forward like an unstoppable deluge, human society evolves toward progress with an irresistible force. Any country, if it worships force and seeks hegemony and expansion by dint of its power, is doomed to failure. Those who fabricate excuses to infringe upon other countries' sovereignty and interfere in their internal affairs will in the end eat their own bitter fruit. To deliberately ignore the colorful and diverse reality of the world and practice such hegemonic acts as imposing one's social system, mode of development and values upon others and willfully threatening them with isolation and sanctions can only begin by harming others and end by hurting whoever does this. To base one's own prosperity on the continued poverty and backwardness of others under the unjust and irrational international economic order is unpopular, and to attempt to monopolize world affairs and dominate the destiny of other nations will get nowhere. In a word, any act that is anachronistic and goes against the fundamental interests of the people of all countries will inevitably meet with resistance and opposition. . . .

China is a populous country with a time-honored history. It is home of a splendid ancient civilization and a major contributor to human progress. Starting from the mid-nineteenth century, China was gradually reduced to a semi-colonial and semi-feudal society increasingly impoverished and backward. The Chinese people waged a protracted and unyielding struggle to uphold the independence, sovereignty and unifi-cation of their country and to realize its rejuvenation, which culminated in the founding of the People's Republic of China in 1949. Right now, the Chinese people are advancing with confident strides on the road of building socialism with Chinese characteristics, concentrating their energy on economic development and improvement of their living standards. Loving peace and desiring development, the Chinese people are willing to cultivate friendly relations and cooperation with the people in the rest of the world and steadfastly pursue an independent foreign policy of peace. Even when China becomes stronger and more developed, it will not seek hegemony or pose a threat to any one. On the contrary, China, as an important force for the maintenance of world peace and stability, will make even greater contribution to mankind. If China, a country of nearly one quarter of world population, remains underdeveloped in prolonged poverty and backwardness, that will cause serious consequences to peace and stability of the Asia-Pacific region and that of the world at large.

There is only one China in the world and Taiwan is an inalienable part of Chinese territory. The Government of the People's Republic of China is China's sole legal government and its sole representative in the United Nations. The peaceful reunification of the two sides of the Taiwan Straits is the unshakable will and determination of the entire Chinese people, including the Taiwan compatriots, and an irresistible trend of history. With a proud patriotic tradition that dates back several thousand years, the Chinese people have the ability, the resourcefulness and confidence to overcome any interference and make the reunification of their motherland a reality. . . .

The political leaders of our generation have on their shoulders the historical mission of carrying forward the cause of world peace, development and progress into the future. This is no ordinary responsibility. History is both fair and unmerciful. We must not fail the ardent expectations of the people throughout the world. Looking forward to the new century, let us join hands and work together for a still better world.

CHRONOLOGY: The Chinese Revolution

1899–1901   The Boxer Rebellion, a popular uprising against the Western presence in China, erupts and is crushed by imperial forces.

October 1911 Revolution breaks out in Wuchang, signaling the end of the monarchy and the beginning of the Republic.

1911   In October, revolution breaks out in Wuchang province signaling the end of the monarchy and beginning of the Republic of China.

1912   In February, Yuan Shihkai becomes President of the Republic of China, but seeks to fashion his own monarchy; in August, Guomindang (GMD) revolutionary party formed.

1917–1918   After death of Yuan Shihkai in 1916, civil war breaks out and warlords begin claiming territory across China.

1921   Chinese Communist Party (CCP) founded.

1925   Death of Sun Yat-sen (March 12).

1926–1934   Jiang Jieshi leads Guomindang and begins "Northern Expedition" to reunify the country; he turns against the Communists (1927); under pressure from the GMD forces, the Communists begin the "Long March" in 1934 to escape GMD encirclement.

1937–1949   Japan begins full invasion of China in 1937 and CCP allies with GMD in the face of this threat. Japan surrenders in 1945 and Chinese civil war recommences.

1949   Jiang Jieshi and the Nationalist forces of the GMD lose the civil war and retreat to Taiwan; founding of the Communist-led People's Republic of China (October 1).

1950   Sino-Soviet Treaty of Friendship, Alliance, and Mutual Assistance is signed in Moscow; Chinese "volunteers" sent to Korea where war had broken out; Tibet seized by Chinese troops and proclaimed an "autonomous region."

1953–1958   China's first five-year plan for economic development; agricultural cooperatives launched as a step toward communization of the countryside.

1958–1961   "Great Leap Forward" campaign. Disappointed with results of collectivization and the first five-year plan, Mao launches a new campaign to unleash the productive potential of the nation by establishing large communes in the country and creating "instant" industries. The result was economic dislocation and a disaster for China as millions of Chinese starve to death; Soviet Union halts economic aid and withdraws technical support (1960); Sino-Soviet rift forces deployment of millions of troops along common border.

1964   China explodes its first atomic bomb.

1966–1969   "Great Proletarian Cultural Revolution." Mao reclaims his political authority after the disaster of the "Great Leap Forward" and launches a program to create a truly egalitarian culture in China. Books and Buddhist art are destroyed and emphasis is placed on transforming education and pursuing ideological indoctrination. High officials and intellectuals are purged, humiliated, and "reeducated." The state enlists the cultural arts to reflect the glory of Communism with "revolutionary ballets" and other artistic "events."

1971–1972   The People's Republic of China is admitted to the United Nations; President Richard Nixon visits China.

1976   Death of Zhou Enlai (January), Commander Zhu De (July), and Mao Zedong (September); "Gang of Four" arrested and Hua Guofeng named Chairman of the Central Committee of the CCP.

1978   Deng Xiaoping begins third comeback, outmaneuvers Maoists, and eases them out of power.

1979   The United States recognizes the People's Republic of China, thus foregoing its political recognition of Taiwan as the legitimate government of China; United States continues to trade and sell weaponry to Taiwan.

1979–1989   Full diplomatic relations established between China and the United States (1979); Government institutes "one-child" policy in order to reduce population pressure (1981–1982); universities reestablished and greater freedom allowed, but Communist government organizes campaigns against "capitalist thinking" and "bourgeoisie democracy" (1985 and 1987).

1989   Amidst greater economic freedom and relative prosperity for workers in the cities, students at Beijing University demonstrate for greater political freedom. On orders from Deng Xiaoping, the movement is crushed by tanks and troops at Tiananmen Square in Beijing (June); Jiang Zemin is elected general secretary and member of the Standing Committee of the Politburo and succeeds Deng as chairman of the Central Military Commission (November); martial law lifted (1990).

1996   Taiwan holds its first free election for president (March); China agrees to support the global ban on nuclear explosions (August).

1997   Deng Xiaoping dies (February); Hong Kong reverts to Chinese control as a special administrative zone (July).

STUDY QUESTIONS

1. According to the first selection on the Peasant Revolution, how did Mao characterize the process of revolution? Why did he have such confidence in the collective and instinctive leadership of the Chinese masses? Mao advocated a "brief reign of terror" as a necessity for a successful revolution. Compare his thoughts with those of Robespierre during the French revolution in Chapter 2. Do revolutions, by their very natures, exceed the "proper limits"? Must they have periods of terror?

2. Li Shaoqi's 1939 political tract, "How to Be a Good Communist," sought to inspire unity and focus commitment to the Communist cause. Why was such an effort so important at the time? Note especially the link between idealism and practical necessity argued by Li Shaoqi. How does one become a "good Communist"? Li notes that "Marxism-Leninism offers a scientific explanation that leaves no room for doubt" and that "such a society will

inevitably be brought about." Over sixty years later, why has this "happy and beautiful Communist world" not materialized?

3. Why did Mao Zedong regard Jiang Jieshi as "China's number one war criminal" in 1949? According to Mao, why did the civil war take place, who was to blame, and what was the Communist role? Ultimately, why did the Communists win the civil war? On this point, compare the account of American Secretary of State, Dean Acheson.

4. According to Mao in the selection, "From the Countryside to the City," why did the Communists turn their attention to the cities in order to achieve the consolidation of Communism? Who did he identify as "muddle-headed" and why? What did the Communists have to protect against in the consolidation of the new Chinese nation? What role did women play in the Communist revolution and how did their social and legal status change following the revolution?

5. In Marxist theory, revolution flows through stages. Once the masses seize control of the state from capitalist forces, they enter into a "dictatorship of the proletariat" that acts as a transition to full communism. How did Mao define the "People's Democratic Dictatorship"? What were the functions of this dictatorship and what was its ultimate goal? Did Mao adhere closely to Marxist theory?

6. Mao defined civil rights as the rights of "freedom and democracy," which were guaranteed in the Chinese constitution. But he also described this freedom as controlled under the "centralized guidance" of the Party that would prevent anarchy: "The people enjoy a wide measure of democracy and freedom, but at the same time they have to keep themselves within the bounds of socialist discipline." What did he mean? In what ways was the People's Democratic Dictatorship inherently undemocratic?

7. In the selection entitled, "Let a Hundred Flowers Blossom," what did Mao mean by this slogan? What are "poisonous weeds" and how should the Party deal with "contradictions among the people"? Although Mao denied that it was possible to coerce people by banning ideas or actions, what were the political criteria he established for judging the "rightness" of thought and action in Communist China? Was this a form of coercion?

8. The "People's Commune" was a centerpiece of the Great Leap Forward campaign. What was its intent and purpose? In what specific ways did it structure and control the lives of rural workers? How was labor organized around the production brigade and how were people to be compensated under the wage system? Why was the Great Leap Forward such a failure? In his defense of the program, Mao asserted that there were problems in the details of production rather than a misconception in the theory. Who was responsible and what did Mao advocate as remedies?

9. What was the intent and purpose of the Cultural Revolution according to the official guidelines established in August 1966? Compare these ideals with the 1984 reflections of Ting, who served in the Red Guards. Why did she become detached and disillusioned?

10. How did Mao organize public opinion and employ the arts in support of the Cultural Revolution? According to Mao, what was the purpose of art and what did he mean by the "unity of politics and art"? What is your reaction to the selection on the process of "reeducation"? Note that the article from the official *Peking Review* states that university intellectuals "made an urgent request that they be allowed to change their world outlook from that of the bourgeois to that of the proletarians." Do you buy this? Why did Mao distrust the intellectuals? What did it mean to be "ideologically young again"?

11. What was the Chinese strategy regarding foreign policy after 1949? Why was the Soviet Union so upset with China's independent policies toward nuclear weapons and international

peace? What was Lin Biao's argument regarding U.S. aggression in Vietnam? Did U.S. imperialism, as Lin Biao contended, "burn to ashes in the blazing fire of the people's wars it provoked"?

12. The official Communist account of "The Transformation of Tibet" gives the impression that this was a great democratic struggle to free the Tibetans from the feudal control of a hated ruling class. What benefits were the Communists supposed to have brought to Tibet? Why did the Communist leadership believe that such obvious propaganda would be effective information for its own people? Why have the Taiwanese resisted unification with mainland China? Why not negotiate with the Communists?

13. After reading the diametrically opposed views of Mao's death in 1976, which do you believe? Where is the truth and how would you write the obituary of Mao Zedong?

14. After reading Hua Guofeng's account of "The New Look of Modern China," to what extent does it represent a break with the policies of Mao Zedong? Analyze this with reference to education, the role of the government in the regulation of the arts, and the attitude toward intellectuals. Has the interpretation of "Let a Hundred Flowers Blossom" changed at all? Compare Hua's approach to that of Deng Xiaoping, who warned of "Problems on the Ideological Front" in 1981. Does Deng sound like a reformer? What was his approach to "bourgeois ideology" and the perspective of young writers in the "New China"? Did the New China differ much in this regard from Mao's China?

15. What were the "Four Modernizations" and what were the "Four Cardinal Principles" as advocated by Deng Xiaoping in 1984? Although Deng seemed to fear any domestic challenge to his political control, why was he so confident that opening China to the outside world and especially to the influence of capitalism would not alter the "Four Cardinal Principles"? On the one hand, Deng asks veteran comrades to "emancipate their minds," while he questions the "Party spirit" of young writers and film directors in China. Can you reconcile this contradiction? For Deng, where was the line between innovative overtures and dangerous criticism?

16. In May 1989, a month before the incident at Tiananmen Square, Deng Xiaoping was concerned with succession. What are the most important points that he made to the "third generation" of Chinese leaders? What was Deng's political testament?

17. What happened in Tiananmen Square in June 1989? Why did it happen and how did Deng justify the aggressive actions of the People's Liberation Army in suppressing the demonstrations? Deng mentioned that the incident had to happen eventually and blamed it on "bad people" who led the Chinese populace astray and into the hands of Western bourgeois capitalists. Did Deng slip off the tightrope between economic liberalization and political control? Compare Mikhail Gorbachev's struggle to control the forces of social and economic change in the Soviet Union while satisfying the conservative demands for political stability during the period 1989 to 1990. How did Deng analyze the lessons of Tiananmen Square in simplistic terms that were reminiscent of Mao's combat against Western ideas? Deng argued in 1989 that the West was trying to destroy China, not by atomic weapons, but by "peaceful evolution" without "gun smoke." What do you think of this argument? What was the real problem at Tiananmen Square?

18. Analyze the 1995 speech by Jiang Zemin. How did he view China's role on the world stage and why did Jiang maintain his critical approach to the West? Does this seem like a defensive speech or a confident exposition of the New China? What challenges does China face in the future and how will the Taiwanese issue be resolved?